Contents Overview

LAW ENFORCEMENT RESPONDER

PRINCIPLES OF EMERGENCY MEDICINE, RESCUE, AND FORCE PROTECTION

Randy G. Stair, RN, BSN, NREMT-P
Supervisory Emergency Services Specialist
United States Secret Service
US Department of Homeland Security

EMS Program Director
Carroll Community College
Carroll County Volunteer Emergency Services Associations
Westminster, Maryland, USA

Adjunct Faculty
Emergency Health Services
University of Maryland, Baltimore County
Baltimore, Maryland, USA

Dwight A. Polk, MSW, NREMT-P
Paramedic Program Director
Department of Emergency Health Services
University of Maryland, Baltimore County
Baltimore, Maryland, USA

Mobile Crisis Team Counselor
Grassroots Crisis Intervention Center
Columbia, Maryland, USA

Geoffrey L. Shapiro
Coordinator, Operational Medicine Programs
Emergency Health Services Program
Department of Emergency Medicine
The George Washington University School of Medicine & Health Sciences
Washington, DC, USA

Nelson Tang, MD, FACEP
Associate Professor of Emergency Medicine
The Johns Hopkins University School of Medicine
Baltimore, Maryland, USA

Director, Division of Special Operations
Department of Emergency Medicine
Johns Hopkins Medical Institutions

Chief Medical Officer
Center for Law Enforcement Medicine
Baltimore, Maryland, USA

Andrew N. Pollak, MD, FAAOS
AAOS Medical Editor

AAOS

JONES & BARTLETT LEARNING

JONES & BARTLETT LEARNING
World Headquarters
Jones & Bartlett Learning
5 Wall Street
Burlington, MA 01803
978-443-5000
info@jblearning.com
www.jblearning.com

Jones & Bartlett Learning books and products are available through most bookstores and online booksellers. To contact Jones & Bartlett Learning directly, call 800-832-0034, fax 978-443-8000, or visit our website, www.jblearning.com.

Substantial discounts on bulk quantities of Jones & Bartlett Learning publications are available to corporations, professional associations, and other qualified organizations. For details and specific discount information, contact the special sales department at Jones & Bartlett Learning via the above contact information or send an email to specialsales@jblearning.com.

Production Credits
Chief Executive Officer: Ty Field
President: James Homer
SVP, Editor-in-Chief: Michael Johnson
SVP, Chief Technology Officer: Dean Fossella
SVP, Chief Marketing Officer: Alison M. Pendergast
Executive Publisher: Kimberly Brophy
Executive Acquisitions Editor—EMS: Christine Emerton
Associate Managing Editor: Amanda Brandt
Associate Managing Editor: Janet Morris
Editor: Alison Lozeau
Senior Editorial Assistant: Carly Lavoie
Production Manager: Jenny L. Corriveau
Associate Production Editor: Nora Menzi
Vice President of Sales, Public Safety Group: Matthew Maniscalco
Director of Sales, Public Safety Group: Patricia Einstein
Director of Marketing: Alisha Weisman
VP, Manufacturing and Inventory Control: Therese Connell
Composition: Publishers' Design and Production Services, Inc.
Cover Design: Kristin E. Parker
Rights & Photo Research Assistant: Gina Licata
Cover Images: Courtesy of Nelson Tang and Liam Holtzman
Printing and Binding: Courier Companies
Cover Printing: Courier Companies

Library of Congress Cataloging-in-Publication Data
Law enforcement responder / American Academy of Orthopaedic Surgeons ; Randy Stair … [et al.].
p. ; cm.
ISBN-13: 978-0-7637-8149-1 (pbk.)
ISBN-10: 0-7637-8149-5 (pbk.)
I. Stair, Randy. II. American Academy of Orthopaedic Surgeons.
[DNLM: 1. Emergencies. 2. Emergency Treatment--methods. 3. Law Enforcement--methods. 4. Police--education. WB 105]
LC classification not assigned
362.18--dc23
2011032910

6048

Printed in the United States of America
26 25 24 12 11 10 9

Contents

Resources

INSTRUCTOR RESOURCES

Instructor's ToolKit

ISBN: 978-1-4496-7091-7

The disc includes:

- PowerPoint presentations
- Lecture outlines
- Teaching tips, enhancements, support materials, and preparation guidance
- Student activities and assignments
- Final exams
- Image and table bank

Acknowledgments

Dana, thank you. My family, Aidan, Emma, Garrett, and Lauren; I will never be able to make up the lost time that my careers have demanded. Thank you for your understanding. To my students and colleagues, your success provides me with the drive to do more; your struggles provide me the drive to do better. To my instructors, professors, and mentors, your message has been received and passed.

—Randy G. Stair

To my students, who always remind me to keep learning; to my EMS and law enforcement colleagues, who give so much of their lives for others; and to Simon, who has always believed in me and given me words of hope and encouragement.

—Dwight A. Polk

Thank you to my family and all the people, from all parts of my personal and professional life, who have mentored and motivated me. In particular AMW, ERS, GFB, BSR, SM, RGS, JLB, and all the "boys." I continue to learn from everyone I work with.

—Geoffrey L. Shapiro

To my parents for teaching me the value of hard work and giving me the strength to work hard. To Mollie, Samantha, and Christopher for your unending love, support, and understanding. To my friends and colleagues in the DSO and Center for your wisdom, dedication, and commitment. To all the men and women who selflessly place themselves in harm's way, ready to do the tasks that make the world a better and safer place for everyone else. You are all my inspiration.

—Nelson Tang

Special Dedication

On January 19, 2011, Mark Gray Falkenhan sacrificed his life while saving others. Mark was known to many of us on this project, and contributed to the text. Mark was the sort of person you were glad to see when you got to work. Mark was also the sort of person you hoped had your back when things went bad.

Mark, of all of the lives we have saved, we wish one could have been yours.

Peace be with you, brother.

Contributors

Nina C. Bingham, RN, BSN, FI, D-ABMDI, CMS
Program Manager
Division of Special Operations
Department of Emergency Medicine
The Johns Hopkins Medical Institutions
Baltimore, Maryland, USA

Forensic Investigator
Office of the Chief Medical Examiner
State of Maryland

Tactical Nurse
Maryland State Police

Senior Medical Officer and Faculty
Center for Law Enforcement Medicine
Baltimore, Maryland, USA

David W. Callaway, MD, MPA
Assistant Professor
Medical Director, Carolinas MED-1
Department of Emergency Medicine
Carolinas Medical Center
Charlotte, North Carolina, USA

Director
The Operational Medicine Institute
Boston, Massachusetts, USA

Robert Carter, BSN, RN, CFRN, NREMT-P
Nurse Clinician
Pediatric Intensive Care Unit
Pediatric Critical Care Transport
Johns Hopkins Children's Center
The Johns Hopkins Hospital
Baltimore, Maryland, USA

Flight Nurse
STAT MedEvac
Center for Emergency Medicine
University of Pittsburgh Medical Center
Pittsburgh, Pennsylvania, USA

Bruce Conrad, BS, NREMT-P
Emergency Services Specialist
United States Secret Service
US Department of Homeland Security

Captain (Ret.)
Baltimore County Fire Department
Baltimore County, Maryland, USA

Joy E. Crook, MD, MPH
Assistant Professor
Department of Emergency Medicine
University of New Mexico

Medical Director
Center for Disaster Medicine
University of New Mexico

EMS Consortium Physician
University of New Mexico
Albuquerque, New Mexico, USA

Deputy Medical Director (Ret.)
Bureau of Alcohol, Tobacco, Firearms and Explosives
US Department of Justice

Senior Medical Officer and Affiliate Faculty
Center for Law Enforcement Medicine
Baltimore, Maryland, USA

J. David Davis, NREMT-P
Supervisory Special Agent
Program Manager
Tactical Medical Program
Homeland Security Investigations
US Department of Homeland Security

Mark G. Falkenhan, NREMT-P
Emergency Services Specialist
United States Secret Service
US Department of Homeland Security

Firefighter/Paramedic/Chief
Middle River Volunteer Ambulance Rescue Company
Lutherville Volunteer Fire Company
Baltimore County, Maryland, USA

Firefighter/Paramedic/Instructor (Ret.)
Baltimore County Fire Department
Baltimore County, Maryland, USA

J. Michael Fayer, NREMT-P
Safety & Wellness Coordinator
Chesapeake Health Education Program, Inc.
Perry Point, Maryland, USA

Timothy J. Gabourie, BA, NREMT-I, EMT-Tactical
Special Agent
Bureau of Alcohol, Tobacco, Firearms and Explosives
US Department of Justice

Kevin B. Gerold, DO, JD, FCCM, FCCP, FCLM
Assistant Professor of Anesthesiology & Critical Care Medicine
Assistant Professor of Emergency Medicine
Division of Special Operations
The Johns Hopkins University School of Medicine
Baltimore, Maryland, USA

Medical Director
Tactical Medical Unit
Maryland State Police

Acting Program Medical Director (Ret.)
Office of Operational Medicine
Bureau of Diplomatic Security
United States Department of State
Dunn Loring, Virginia, USA

Special Deputy
United States Marshals Service
US Department of Justice

Senior Medical Officer and Faculty
Center for Law Enforcement Medicine
Baltimore, Maryland, USA

Brandon W. Graham, MPS, EMT-P
Associate Director
The George Washington University Office of Homeland Security
Washington, DC, USA

Michael J. Hite, RN, MBA, MHA, CFRN, CEN, EMT-P
Associate Professor, Department of Emergency Medicine
The George Washington University Medical Center
Washington, DC, USA

Chief Operating Officer
Chestnut Hill Health System
Philadelphia, Pennsylvania, USA

Liam C. Holtzman, DO, FACEP
Instructor, Emergency Medicine
Division of Special Operations
The Johns Hopkins University School of Medicine
Baltimore, Maryland, USA

Deputy Medical Director
Bureau of Alcohol, Tobacco, Firearms and Explosives
US Department of Justice

Auxiliary State Trooper (Ret.)
Florida Highway Patrol

Senior Medical Officer and Faculty
Center for Law Enforcement Medicine
Baltimore, Maryland, USA

Steven Kasser, NREMT-P
Emergency Services Specialist
United States Secret Service
US Department of Homeland Security

Scott C. Kimball, EMT-B/ES
Medic
Special Operations Group
Program Manager
Operational Medical Support Unit
United States Marshals Service
US Department of Justice

Joshua G. Knapp, RN, NREMT-P
Special Agent/Project Officer
Tactical Medic Program
Bureau of Alcohol, Tobacco, Firearms and Explosives
US Department of Justice

Buddy G. Kozen, MD, MPH
Emergency Physician
United States Navy

Instructor, Emergency Medicine
Division of Special Operations
The Johns Hopkins University School of Medicine
Baltimore, Maryland, USA

Deputy Medical Director (Ret.)
Bureau of Alcohol, Tobacco, Firearms and Explosives
US Department of Justice

Senior Medical Officer and Affiliate Faculty
Center for Law Enforcement Medicine
Baltimore, Maryland, USA

Dennis R. Krebs, NREMT-P
Captain (Ret.)
Baltimore County Fire Department
Baltimore County, Maryland, USA

Senior Medical Officer (Ret.)
Center for Law Enforcement Medicine
Baltimore, Maryland, USA

Frank Larkin, NREMT-P
SES Special Programs
US Department of Defense

Deputy Assistant Director (Ret.)
United States Secret Service
US Department of Homeland Security

Matthew J. Levy, DO, MSc
Assistant Professor of Emergency Medicine
Division of Special Operations
The Johns Hopkins University School of Medicine
Baltimore, Maryland, USA

Associate Medical Director
Howard County Fire & Rescue Services
Howard County, Maryland, USA

Tactical Physician
Howard County Police Department
Howard County, Maryland, USA

Tactical Physician
Maryland State Police

Deputy Medical Director
Tactical Medical Program
ICE/Homeland Security Investigations
US Department of Homeland Security

Clinical Assistant Professor & Medical Director
Department of Emergency Health Services
University of Maryland, Baltimore County
Baltimore, Maryland, USA

Deputy Unit Commander
Maryland-1 (MD-1) Disaster Medical Assistance Team
US Department of Health and Human Services

Senior Medical Officer and Faculty
Center for Law Enforcement Medicine
Baltimore, Maryland, USA

Horace K. Liang, M.D.
Assistant Professor, Emergency Medicine
The Johns Hopkins University School of Medicine
Baltimore, Maryland, USA

Affiliate Faculty
Center for Law Enforcement Medicine
Baltimore, Maryland, USA

Zhanna Livshits, MD
Medical Toxicologist
Attending Physician, Emergency Medicine
Bellevue Hospital Center
New York University School of Medicine
New York, New York, USA

John B. Marshall, MD, MBA
Clinical Assistant Professor
Department of Surgery, Division of Emergency Medicine
University of Texas Southwestern Medical Center
Dallas, Texas, USA

Reserve Officer, Narcotics Division
ATF—Dallas IV (HIDTA) Violent Crime Task Force
Dallas Police Department
Dallas, Texas, USA

Special Deputy
United States Marshals Service
US Department of Justice

Senior Medical Officer and Affiliate Faculty
Center for Law Enforcement Medicine
Baltimore, Maryland, USA

Daniel J. McGuire, FAAETS, BCETS
President
CISM Perspectives, Inc.
Rochester, New York, USA

Keith McMinn, BS, NREMT-P
First Sergeant
Aviation Command
Tactical Medical Unit
Maryland State Police

Tactical Educator
Division of Special Operations
Department of Emergency Medicine
The Johns Hopkins University School of Medicine
Baltimore, Maryland, USA

Michael R. Melia, MD
LCDR MC (FMF/UMO/PJ)
United States Navy

Fellow, Tactical Emergency Medical Services
Division of Special Operations
Department of Emergency Medicine
The Johns Hopkins University School of Medicine
Baltimore, Maryland, USA

Medical Officer and Faculty
Center for Law Enforcement Medicine
Baltimore, Maryland, USA

Lewis S. Nelson, MD
Associate Professor
Department of Emergency Medicine
New York University School of Medicine

Director
Medical Toxicology Fellowship
New York City Poison Control Center
New York, New York, USA

William Northington, MD, MPH
EMS Regional Medical Director
Navy Medicine National Capital Area

Department of Emergency Medicine
Walter Reed National Military Medical Center
Bethesda, Maryland, USA

Assistant Professor of Emergency Medicine
Division of Special Operations
The Johns Hopkins University School of Medicine
Baltimore, Maryland, USA

Senior Medical Officer and Affiliate Faculty
Center for Law Enforcement Medicine
Baltimore, Maryland, USA

Dwight A. Polk, MSW, NREMT-P
Paramedic Program Director
University of Maryland, Baltimore County
Baltimore, Maryland, USA

Mobile Crisis Team Counselor
Grassroots Crisis Intervention Center
Columbia, Maryland, USA

Ali S. Raja, MD, MBA, MPH
Assistant Professor
Harvard Medical School

Tactical Physician
Boston FBI

SWAT and Medical Director
Brewster Ambulance Service
Boston, Massachusetts, USA

Herbert J. Reynolds, NREMT-P
Emergency Services Specialist
United States Secret Service
US Department of Homeland Security

Paramedic (Ret.)
Baltimore County Fire Department
Baltimore County, Maryland, USA

Joshua J. Roberts, NREMT-P
Education Manager
Susquehanna Valley EMS

Dawn S. Ruben, DVM
Assistant Professor
Department of Molecular and Comparative Pathobiology
The Johns Hopkins University
Baltimore, Maryland, USA

William Seifarth, MS, NREMT-P
Instructor
Maryland Fire and Rescue Institute
EMS Administrator

Adjunct Faculty
Emergency Health Services
University Of Maryland, Baltimore County
Baltimore, Maryland, USA

Geoffrey L. Shapiro
Coordinator, Operational Medicine Programs
Emergency Health Services Program
Department of Emergency Medicine
The George Washington University School of Medicine & Health Sciences
Washington, DC, USA

Andrew C. Smith, BS, NREMT-P, EMT-Tactical
Operational Medical Support Unit
United States Marshals Service
US Department of Justice

Paramedic Preceptor
Bethesda-Chevy Chase Rescue Squad
Bethesda, Maryland, USA

Zachary E. Smith, MMS, PA-C
Senior Physician Assistant
Department of Emergency Medicine
Division of Special Operations
The Johns Hopkins Hospital
Baltimore, Maryland, USA

Medical Officer and Affiliate Faculty
Center for Law Enforcement Medicine
Baltimore, Maryland, USA

David R. Stair
Chief (Ret.)
Carroll County Animal Control
Carroll County, Maryland, USA

Randy G. Stair, RN, BSN, NREMT-P
Supervisory Emergency Services Specialist
United States Secret Service
US Department of Homeland Security

EMS Program Director
Carroll Community College
Carroll County Volunteer Emergency Services Associations
Westminster, Maryland, USA

Crista Lenk Stathers, MA, NREMT-P
Clinical Assistant Professor
Director, Professional and Continuing Education
Department of Emergency Health Services
University of Maryland, Baltimore County
Baltimore, Maryland, USA

Lisa A. Steiner, MMS, PA-C
Senior Physician Assistant
Department of Emergency Medicine
Division of Special Operations
The Johns Hopkins Hospital
Baltimore, Maryland, USA

Medical Officer and Faculty
Center for Law Enforcement Medicine
Baltimore, Maryland, USA

Matthew D. Sztajnkrycer, MD, PhD
Associate Professor
Department of Emergency Medicine
Mayo Clinic
Rochester, Minnesota, USA

Medical Director
RPD/OCSO Emergency Response Unit
Rochester, Minnesota, USA

Medical Director
Rochester Police Department
Rochester, Minnesota, USA

Reserve Deputy
Olmsted County Sheriff's Office
Olmsted County, Minnesota, USA

Nelson Tang, MD, FACEP
Associate Professor of Emergency Medicine
The Johns Hopkins University School of Medicine
Baltimore, Maryland, USA

Director
Division of Special Operations
Johns Hopkins Medical Institutions
Baltimore, Maryland, USA

Medical Director
United States Secret Service
US Department of Homeland Security

Medical Director
Tactical Medical Program
ICE/Homeland Security Investigations
US Department of Homeland Security

Medical Director & Special Deputy
United States Marshals Service
US Department of Justice

Medical Director
Bureau of Alcohol, Tobacco, Firearms and Explosives
US Department of Justice

Tactical Physician
Maryland State Police

Director & Chief Medical Officer
Center for Law Enforcement Medicine
Baltimore, Maryland, USA

Cathleen W. Vandenbraak, BSN, MBA/MHA, CEN, CCRN, CFRN, FP-C
Emergency Department
Paoli Hospital
Paoli, Pennsylvania, USA

RN Transport Specialist
Temple Transport Team (T3)
Philadelphia, Pennsylvania, USA

High Risk Obstetrics
Virtua Health System
Voorhees, New Jersey, USA

Bruce J. Walz, PhD
Professor and Chair
Department of Emergency Health Services
Affiliate Professor, Doctoral Program in Gerontology
University of Maryland, Baltimore County
Baltimore, Maryland, USA

Robert R. Yonas, NREMT-P
Emergency Services Specialist
United States Secret Service
US Department of Homeland Security

Chief
Norrisville Volunteer Fire Company
Harford County, Maryland, USA

Supervisory Hazardous Materials Specialist (Ret.)
Hazardous Materials Response Team
United States Capitol Police

Reviewers

Jones & Bartlett Learning, the American Academy of Orthopaedic Surgeons, and the author team would like to acknowledge the reviewers of *Law Enforcement Responder*.

Cpl. Christopher Boor, AS, NREMT-P, TCCC-I
Artesia Police Department
Artesia, New Mexico

William P. Bozeman, MD, FACEP
Department of Emergency Medicine
Wake Forest University School of Medicine
Winston Salem, North Carolina

Hugh Dick
Deputy, Delaware County Sheriff's Office
Retired Flight Medic, Grant LifeFlight/Medflight
Delaware Career Center/Adult Law Enforcement
Delaware, Ohio

Neal J. Dolan, BS, MCJ, NREMT-P
Special Agent in Charge (Ret.)
United States Secret Service
Columbia, South Carolina

Alexander L. Eastman, MD, MPH
Field Services Division (SWAT), Dallas Police Department
The University of Texas Southwestern Medical Center
Dallas, Texas

Norris F. Edwards
Paramedic, Firefighter
Seattle Fire Department
Seattle, Washington

David Ellis
Children's Healthcare of Atlanta
Atlanta, Georgia

Charles R. Epstein, JMCP, EMT, EMSI
State of Connecticut, Judicial Branch
Judicial Marshal Services Administration
Southern Connecticut State University
Hartford, Connecticut

Barry A. Frasier
Assessment & Training Solutions
Virginia Beach, Virginia

Sgt. Tim Harten
MTAPD/Training Unit
New York, New York

Sgt. Anthony Hoffmann
Mamaroneck Town Police Department
Mamaroneck, New York

Mark Hollinger, RN, MICN, EMT
Senior Instructor: Emergency Nursing, Los Angeles County College of Nursing and Allied Health
Educator and Consultant, Department of Emergency Medicine, Los Angeles County/USC Medical Center
Los Angeles, California

C. Nathan Hox, BS, LPN, NREMT
Pacific EMS Training
Honolulu, Hawaii

Eddie Ivy
Meridian Public Safety Training Facility
Meridian, Mississippi

James C. Johnson, III, MPAS, PA-C
Wake Forest Baptist Health, Department of Emergency Medicine
Winston-Salem, North Carolina

Ricky Kue, MD, MPH, FACEP
Boston EMS
Boston Police Department SWAT Team
Boston, Massachusetts

Dan Lescallett
Police Training Center, Illinois Central College
Peoria, Illinois
Law and Justice Center, Heartland College
Normal, Illinois

Fred J. McAnn, MS, CFO, NREMT-I
Assistant Fire Chief and Reserve Police Officer
Haughton Fire Department
Haughton, Louisiana

William McElhiney
Massachusetts State Police Academy
New Braintree, Massachusetts

Lawrence "Lars" Mester, NREMT-P, EMT-T
Lakes Region General Healthcare
Laconia, New Hampshire

Jeffery C. Metzger, MD, FACEP
University of Texas, Southwestern Medical Center
Dallas Police Department
Dallas, Texas

Jim Mobley, RN, BSN, CEN, CFRN, CHS, NREMT-P, FP-C, CMTE
Senior Partner, Nimshi International
Charlotte, North Carolina
Director, Regional One Air Medical Service
Spartanburg, South Carolina

Frank Pierson, BS, NREMT-P
Lieutenant (Ret.), Baltimore County Fire Department
Durham Technical Community College
Raleigh, North Carolina

Brad Pittman, EMT-P, CTM
McDuffie County Fire Service
Thomson, Georgia

Kari L. Scantlebury, MD
George Washington University
Washington, DC

Matt Schaefer
President
Tactical Defense Training, Inc.
Louisville, Ohio

Joel S. Schiller, BS, EMT-D
SpringHill Ambulance (Ret.)
Spring Valley, New York
Police Officer, City of Sunrise
Sunrise, Florida

Buzz Shaw
NH EMS District B2
Richmond, New Hampshire

Alexander M. Silverstein, JD, NREMT-P
Jacksonville, Florida

John Vickers
Moultrie Police Department
Moultrie, Georgia

Raf Vittone, EMT-P
District Chief, Polk County Fire Rescue
Polk State College EMS Program Instructor
Winter Haven, Florida

Christopher Weaver, NREMT-P
Venturing Crew 911
Lakewood, Colorado

James Wood, NREMT-P
Regional Safety Training
South Hutchinson, Kansas

Jason H. Zahn, BA, MS (Candidate)
Baltimore, Maryland

Foreword

Emergency medical care has become an integral part of public safety preparedness and response worldwide, particularly in the United States. In most locales, not only is a fire fighter crew the designated first responder for medical emergencies, but, in many venues, law enforcement and security personnel may also provide the first lifesaving interventions in critical public safety responses. In some communities, police officers are credited with facilitating some of the highest reported survival rates for out-of-hospital cardiac arrest through their very early delivery of basic defibrillation using an automated external defibrillator (AED).

More importantly, we now know that most of the lifesaving effects of modern emergency medical services (EMS) responses (eg, 911/999 dispatches) are derived not from the high-profile advanced life support (ALS) interventions delivered by paramedics, but rather from the earliest possible basic life support (BLS) actions of professional first responders and, more likely, those persons already on scene.

Two of my perennial mantras have been, "the earlier the intervention, the better the result" and "an ounce of good on-scene care can save a ton of intensive care unit care."

Indeed, studies have shown that ALS is of no relative value in resuscitative drowning incidents if BLS is not provided immediately by bystanders. However, if basic cardiopulmonary resuscitation (CPR) is implemented by bystanders, the great majority of patients survive neurologically intact, often awakening before hospital arrival.

Likewise, the actions of fellow travelers and airport employees who have no traditional duty to act can save the great majority of sudden death victims at airports. Not only do these immediate on-scene actions greatly improve the victim's chances of returning to full capacity, but the majority of patients awaken on scene, long before hospital arrival. Before the installation of AEDs for access by the public in airport terminals, the chances of long-term, neurologically intact survival was grim, and few persons even had restoration of pulse using the traditional EMS response.

In the case of severe military and civilian trauma, it has been well demonstrated that on-scene interventions such as staving off hemorrhage and tourniquet application can be lifesaving. Again, without these immediate actions, the outcome will likely be of no value if one waits for the arrival of traditional responders.

More recently, in the tactical law enforcement environment it has been demonstrated that fellow tactical responders with medical training can definitively save the lives of team members by their immediate on-scene interventions. In those cases reported, the saving of lives would not have occurred without that on-scene support by fellow team members.

Simply put, CPR, AED use, airway management, hemorrhage control, first aid techniques, and other basic actions by those on scene are definitively lifesaving, but also dramatically increase the odds of survival with return of full function.

Accordingly, there has been a growing need for law enforcement personnel to better understand basic on-scene medical care, especially with the recent evolution of tactical law enforcement operations, counter-terrorism preparedness, event and mass gathering deployments, executive security details, and the general need for security and law enforcement responses in daily 911-type incidents.

Whether the first to attend to a collapsed person in a crowded celebratory parade with impeded public safety access, or attending to a wounded partner following a resisted arrest, the police officer, security professional, or federal agent may be the single most important person in terms of saving a life. Day-to-day, that officer may the first to respond to a critical motor vehicle crash, an injured principal, or a mental health crisis. He or she may be the only responder within miles or may need to be the first to recognize a health threat, be it from natural or malicious causes.

Today, whether there is a codified duty to act or not, the law enforcement officer may be best positioned to provide medical security for the citizens we serve, those we specially protect, or our friends, neighbors, and professional colleagues who need our help.

This textbook is a long overdue compendium that has been carefully designed to enhance the chances of that law enforcement officer saving a life—perhaps even saving his own or his partner's life. I am indebted to the editors and authors for their time, dedication, and thoughtfulness in terms of putting together this labor of love and promoting the growth of law enforcement medicine worldwide.

—Paul E. Pepe, MD, MPH
Professor of Medicine, Surgery, Pediatrics, Public Health and Chair, Emergency Medicine
The University of Texas Southwestern Medical Center and the Parkland Health & Hospital System

Director
City of Dallas Medical Emergency Services for Public Safety, Public Health and Homeland Security

Medical Director
Dallas Metropolitan Medical Response System (MMRS) for
Counter-Terrorism and Disaster Mitigation and the Dallas Metropolitan Area BioTel (EMS) System
Dallas, Texas, USA

SECTION 1

Law Enforcement Responder

Section Contents

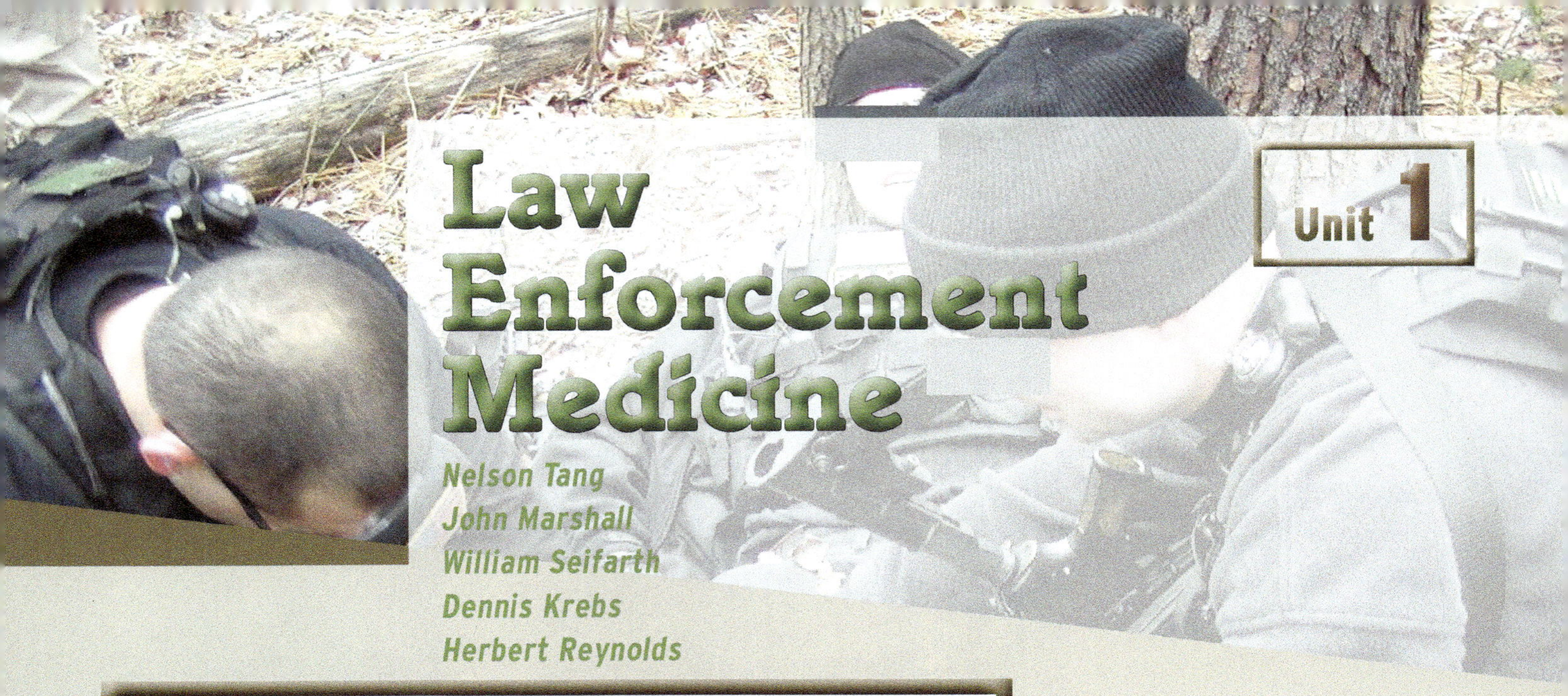

Unit 1

Law Enforcement Medicine

Nelson Tang
John Marshall
William Seifarth
Dennis Krebs
Herbert Reynolds

Law Enforcement Responder Objectives

The Law Enforcement Responder

- Describe basic therapeutic maneuvers for bleeding control. (p 4)
- Describe law enforcement responder priorities during a hostile event. (p 4)
- Identify information needed during a medical or trauma emergency involving a law enforcement responder. (pp 15–19)
- Identify steps for medical logistical support and the need for rapid evacuation to a trauma center. (pp 5–6)

EMS Systems

- Identify the elements of an EMS system. (pp 7–13)
- Describe the types of EMS systems. (pp 7–8)
- Describe the levels of EMS providers. (pp 9–10)
- Describe the roles, responsibilities, and professionalism of EMS personnel. (pp 10–12)
- Explain the role of quality improvement within EMS systems. (pp 12–13)
- Discuss the basic principles of public health in EMS systems. (p 13)

Mission Planning

- Discuss the importance of medical intelligence. (p 14)
- Identify the six planning principles to use when developing the medical plan for a law enforcement mission. (pp 14–15)
- Describe the three functions of a medical plan. (pp 14–15)
- Gather the appropriate medical intelligence to support development of a mission plan. (pp 15–19)
- Discuss the role of operational security in planning for missions. (pp 19–20)
- Discuss the similarities and differences between law enforcement and other emergency responders. (pp 3–4)

Logistics

- Discuss mission-specific logistics and how best to evaluate rescue products. (pp 20–25)

National EMS Education Standard Competencies

Preparatory

Uses simple knowledge of the emergency medical services (EMS) system, the safety and well-being of the emergency medical responder (EMR), and medical/legal issues at the scene of an emergency while awaiting a higher level of care.

EMS Systems

- EMS systems (pp 7–13)
- Roles, responsibilities, and professionalism of EMS personnel (pp 10–12)
- Quality improvement (pp 12–13)

EMS System Communication

Communication needed to

- Call for resources (pp 10–12)
- Transfer care of the patient (pp 10–12)
- Interact within the team structure (pp 10–12)

Public Health

Have an awareness of local public health resources and the role EMS personnel play in public health emergencies.

INTRODUCTION

Law enforcement responders (LERs) are frequently the point of attack at a rescue or medical incident. Frequently reaching the scene of a problem before other responders, the LER will be called to take life-saving action until additional help arrives. In the United States and many other countries, emergency medicine response has become a routine part of public safety. These systems can vary greatly from one jurisdiction to another. These systems can be governed by different regulations, laws, and levels of patient care. LERs should make an effort to determine what type of emergency medical response is available to them and how they fit into that system.

Emergency medical services (EMS) is the label applied to a system of care that is provided to acutely injured or ill individuals. Care is provided by competent personnel who have received specialized training and who are part of an EMS system, which includes 911 call centers; LERs; fire, rescue, and EMS departments; hospitals; and specialty referral centers. There are national standards for the education of responders, as well as defined skills and knowledge sets that EMS providers possess.

Roles and responsibilities, certification, and licensure of providers are established and accomplished through state EMS offices. Assurance of continued competency of EMS knowledge and skills is typically achieved at the local level through quality improvement and assurance processes that, like certification and licensure processes, are designed to protect the public by ensuring competent providers. LERs who provide emergency medical care are also an integral part of ensuring public health by enforcing seat belt usage and helmet laws, participating in car seat installations, and contributing to other processes.

Law enforcement is an often unrecognized link in the chain of survival for many trauma victims. Every investigative operation, traffic citation, domestic disturbance call, and arrival at an accident scene serves to prevent or deter potential injuries to emergency responders and the general public. Emergency medical care designed to support law enforcement is often thought of solely in the relatively narrow context of specialized tactical operations. In reality, every uniformed officer, criminal investigator, and security professional routinely faces the same, or greater, potential for violent confrontation on a daily basis. The training, preparation, and deployment in response to emergencies by law enforcement professionals collectively define the LER.

The first objective of this unit is to describe basic strategies for self-aid should the LER become wounded, as well as emergency treatment modalities for patients encountered at the scene. The second is to define logistical support during emergency situations in which the actions of LERs may directly impact the survival of a casualty.Critical lessons learned from the tactical emergency medical support (TEMS) arena are increasingly being applied and translated across all types of LER for self-aid and buddy-aid to increase survival from traumatic injuries.

The Law Enforcement Responder

On many levels, the individual patrol officer epitomizes modern law enforcement and the LER. Patrol is a starting point and training ground for most people who enter police service in city or county municipalities. It is frequently patrol work that provides the foundation for "street sense"—recognition of imminent threat or danger. This sense, paired with detailed knowledge of their area of operation, gives officers a tactical advantage that can be exploited to care for themselves or others. The patrol officer knows the addresses and locations of high-threat areas, understands traffic patterns, has an appreciation for normal activities in a given area, and, more often than not, is the first to respond to any scene.

Certain high-profile events have demonstrated that law enforcement officers must often rely only on themselves initially, as evidenced by the Bank of America shootout in North Hollywood, California, in 1997 (**Figure 1**). The dispatch records since released to the public make clear that there were multiple police officers severely injured at separate locations. The emergency communications network rapidly became overwhelmed with calls for aid by officers. Matters were further complicated when dispatchers and supervisors had difficulty locating with precision those needing assistance. The officers present at the scene used their judgment and creativity not only to arm themselves sufficiently to repel the offenders,

Figure 1 The Bank of America shootout in North Hollywood, California, is an example of a SWAT event requiring self-aid and buddy-aid.

but also to improvise a high-threat rescue through the use of an armored vehicle for cover and concealment.

The North Hollywood incident changed policies around the country and prompted a rethinking about the way in which patrol officers are armed and how self-aid may be deployed. It also served as a practical demonstration of the logistics that may be used by LERs to realize their own rescue and prompt evacuation to definitive medical care. Many patrol rifle programs are direct descendants of such incidents and policy changes, often with medical self-aid and buddy aid being taught in parallel with rifle instruction.

BASIC SELF-AID STRATEGIES

The variety of tasks and different locations in which LERs operate often limit the amount of medical equipment that may be carried and that is therefore immediately available. Nevertheless, there are many actions a LER can take in the field that may directly impact his or her own survival and well-being and that of fellow officers. At the agency or departmental level, a major first step toward addressing the potential for traumatic injuries is recognizing this risk exists and developing a proactive, realistic, and methodical plan to respond.

Bleeding Control

Injuries that may be sustained by LERs may be secondary to blunt trauma, like motor vehicle crashes or falls, and penetrating trauma such as gunshot or stab wounds. Regardless of the mechanism, when a LER encounters major ongoing bleeding (often called **exsanguinating hemorrhage**), it is imperative to stop or minimize the blood loss as quickly as possible. Significant external blood loss is generally obvious to LERs, and there are specific interventions that may be deployed to stop it (**Figure 2**). It must also be remembered, however, that internal bleeding is equally life threatening and may be more difficult to assess.

Tourniquets

Modern military combat experience has demonstrated the benefit of body armor in protecting the torso and vital internal organs of soldiers. However, fatalities to these same soldiers continued to occur through exsanguinating hemorrhage from penetrating extremity wounds. **Tourniquets**, constricting bands that reduce or stop blood flow to extremities, have re-emerged as an effective tool to deploy for these types of wounds. Small devices that require relatively little training, tourniquets can be applied quickly by LERs to limit blood loss, allowing time for rescue and evacuation from a hostile environment.

Trauma Bandages

Recent advancements in the development of military-style pressure bandages have made them more efficient and effective. Generally, these bandages include a surface meant to cover dressing materials and absorb fluids from the wound, coupled with a compression device that allows direct pressure to be applied to wounds without the need for the patient's or responder's hand to be continuously applying that pressure. These bandages are typically small and relatively inexpensive.

Hemostatic Agents

Hemostatic agents are chemical materials, usually in powder form or impregnated into a textile, that are designed to hasten the natural blood clotting process. Hemostatic agents are often mistakenly thought of as a "magic bullet" to bleeding control, but their proper use requires specific training and specific techniques. Hemostatic agents should be considered for use when the wound is in a location that is not suited for tourniquet use or when other methods of bleeding control have failed. There are multiple generations of hemostatic agents, and different hemostatic agents work in different ways, so it is imperative to adhere to local policies and physician medical direction for recommendations, training, and protocols.

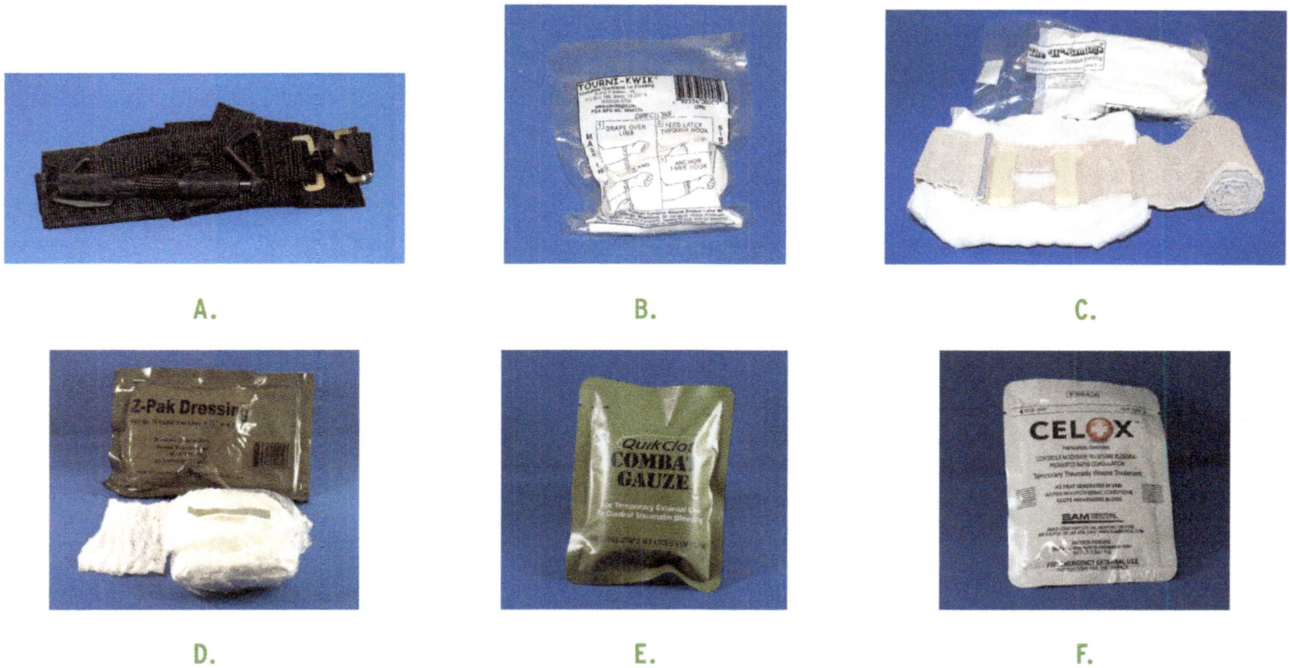

Figure 2 Examples of interventions for bleeding control. **A.** Tourniquet. **B.** Tourniquet. **C.** Trauma bandage. **D.** Trauma bandage. **E.** Trauma bandage. **F.** Hemostatic agent.

Recovery Position

When a patient is unconscious, the tongue can easily fall back into the oropharynx and become an obstruction to the ability to breathe. The LER may arrange the body and limbs of a patient in an effort to maintain the patency of that patient's airway. The recovery position relies on gravity to move the tongue away from the back of the airway and to assist in clearing the airway of obstructions (**Figure 3**). By placing the patient on his or her side, the patient's downside arm supports the head, allowing the jaw to hang open and the tongue to be pulled forward and down. The downside leg is generally straightened and the leg on top is bent 90 degrees, allowing the hips to rotate slightly forward. This allows fluids to drain from the nose and face; it also keeps the tongue from becoming an obstruction.

The recovery position is not recommended in cases where a patient has possibly sustained an injury to any level of the spine. Moving such patients may result in further insult to the spinal cord. In such instances, the LER may need to defer any positioning to emergency personnel trained in spinal immobilization.

MEDICAL LOGISTICAL SUPPORT

Communication

A basic tenet of real estate is "location, location, location." This is also true of police work. Most officers, after graduating from the police academy, will go to field training under a more experienced officer. Knowing your location at all times is

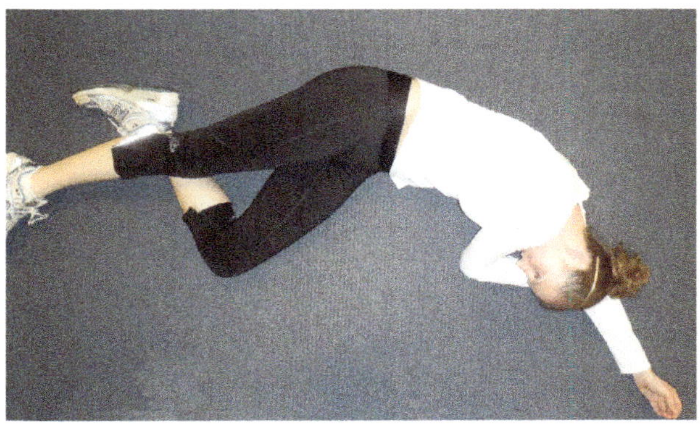

Figure 3 The recovery position.

one of the very first skills a trainee must acquire. Most police officers have been involved in a vehicular or foot pursuit where it becomes critical to call out ever-changing locations in order for cover officers to respond. Particularly in medical or rescue situations, LERs must have a constant awareness of physical addresses, block ranges, intersections, and well-known landmarks or businesses. Relaying such critical information verbally is essential for directing aid to themselves or other injured officers. Relaying the approximate location or direction of the ongoing threat is also helpful in protecting additional responding officers or emergency personnel.

Evacuation

During an incident in which an officer is wounded, it is incumbent on LERs to prevent any further injuries from occurring. This may include, but is not limited to, elimination by force of whatever threat is present before casualty injuries can be assessed and addressed. Moving despite injuries and getting to appropriate cover (most preferred) or concealment (less preferred) is of highest priority. Rapid evaluation of locations that can provide hard cover for the patient should be noted when first approaching the scene.

Egress

A consideration that may occur in parallel or conjunction with an evacuation should be the locations of the most beneficial or efficient points of entry or exit from a scene. Experienced LERs will know in great detail about locations of almost all parts of their assigned patrol areas. Some preplanning while driving through neighborhoods and districts prior to any incidents can allow a more rapid response to contingencies. A LER can also assist supervisors who have not yet arrived at the scene in directing other patrol assets to control traffic on other streets and intersections to allow emergency medical personnel to respond more quickly to a casualty.

Predictable traffic patterns are essential information when it is critical for injured persons to be transported quickly to a hospital. The locations and phone numbers of hospital emergency departments and trauma centers should be noted and widely accessible. This will allow LERs to know which route an ambulance will take when leaving the scene. If air evacuation assets become needed, knowledge of large intersections, parking lots, and open fields will aid the LER in determining patient collection points and helicopter landing zones (LZs).

SPECIAL CONSIDERATIONS

Disarming a Person

To facilitate evacuation and the safe transport of an injured officer, keep in mind that the person might still be armed. It is generally best to disarm the officer, after the threat is secured. If the officer is injured to the point where he or she loses consciousness, a subsequent resumption of consciousness may cause an officer to grasp for weapons in a defensive effort. Further, many air medical services will not accept any functioning firearms onboard the aircraft. In all instances, deference to that officer's injured status and dignity should be preserved while disarming and treating him or her.

Body Armor

The specifications for body armor issued to patrol officers are typically established at the departmental and/or unit level. Some departments specify or issue the exact make and model of armor that personnel must wear, whereas others specify National Institute of Justice (NIJ) ballistic resistance levels and allow officers to make individual purchases. These personal selections will typically be driven by price, fit, durability, reputation, and comfort. Maximizing all of these factors will ultimately impact individual compliance with wearing armor consistently. Patrol officers most typically wear concealable soft armor, invisible underneath standard issue uniforms, whereas tactical team members will typically deploy with bulkier, heavier armor offering greater degrees of body coverage.

An additional tier of protection used by some departments is the addition of hard trauma plates, typically metal or ceramic, that officers may don in specific circumstances such as active shooter scenarios (**Figure 4**). Rectangular or torso-shaped, these plates are usually held in place on the body by fabric, vest-shaped plate carriers and are worn either singly (in front of the chest) or doubly (in front and behind). The plate carriers themselves may also be constructed with embedded ballistic protection material, further enhancing the cumulative level of layered protection.

An interesting consideration in conceptualizing the emergency medical care of patients wearing body armor is the inverse relationship between the amount of armor coverage and the ability to access areas of the body for medical treatment. A full-coverage ballistic vest that includes neck and bicep protection presents a real challenge if medical responders must access areas of the torso for assessment and interven-

Figure 4 Hard trauma plates may be worn in special circumstances for extra protection.

tion. Most recently, armor of this type is being constructed with rapid release features that allow the vest to disassemble and fall away should emergency medical care be necessary.

SURVIVAL MINDSET

A key factor that is emerging as a major determinant of individual officer survival is the development and fostering of a survival mindset. Historically, most law enforcement training scenarios end with the injury (eg, gunshot wound) of an officer. Medical elements are typically deployed at these junctures and treatment and transport ensues. This is inconsistent with real world events. In actuality, officers who are violently injured must continue to engage hostile threats, return fire, initiate self-care when possible, and seek cover until medical rescue can be conducted. These steps take time, and during this time it is the determination of the individual officer to survive that enhances both the likelihood of the officer to perform lifesaving actions and the likelihood of those interventions to be successful.

PITFALLS

A common misconception is that simply issuing law enforcement personnel individual first aid kits (IFAKs) will serve the purpose of increasing medical preparedness and survival rates. This approach is highly flawed. Some degree of initial training is required for officers to become familiar with kit contents, their intended purposes, and how and when to use them. Further, regular retraining is critical to retain this knowledge and ideally to develop real understanding of how to deploy these interventions effectively under different circumstances.

Most IFAKs come from commercial sources and have variable contents ranging from simple dressings of limited utility to invasive surgical devices that are inappropriately advanced for many LERs. It is critical to seek proper medical consultation with the designated physician medical director to procure the appropriate kits for the appropriate personnel and missions.

EMS Systems

THE CURRENT EMS SYSTEM

When an emergency involving illness or injury happens, care is often provided by specially trained EMS providers. EMS providers impart lifesaving skills when a life is on the line and also provide basic care to treat those with less severe illnesses and injuries. EMS providers are part of the health care and public health systems, which incorporate prehospital (EMS providers), hospital (nurses, physicians, therapists), specialty referral centers (trauma centers, burn centers, pediatric hospitals, etc), public health facilities, and rehabilitation centers. In the prehospital environment, EMS is provided by personnel from the spectrum of the law enforcement community, fire departments, ambulance and rescue squad services, and hospital-based EMS systems (**Figure 5**).

Types of EMS Systems

LERs provide emergency medical care to persons in the communities they serve as well as to fellow officers and, in some circumstances, to themselves. In some areas of the country, LERs are highly trained EMS professionals who provide frontline EMS care as the area's primary care providers. Additionally, in select areas LERs offer medevac EMS

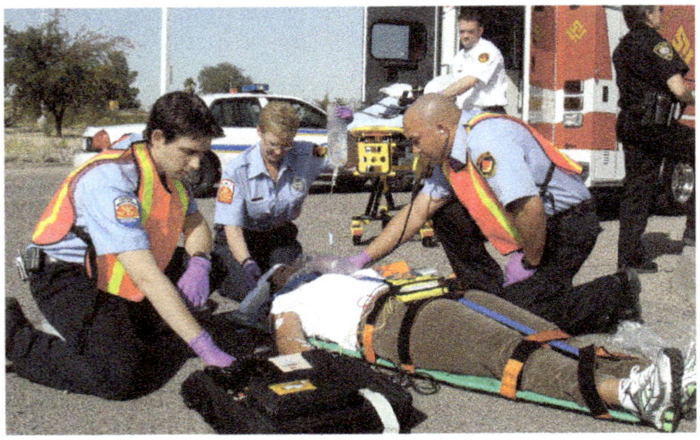

Figure 5 EMS is provided by personnel from a wide spectrum of responders, including law enforcement, fire fighters, ambulance and rescue services, and hospital-based EMS systems.

resources by treating and transporting patients from scenes of incidents to specialized hospitals, including trauma centers, via helicopter.

Fire-based EMS systems have integrated within their department an EMS division to provide trained and educated EMS providers to respond to EMS calls. With fire-based EMS systems, fire apparatus often respond to assist the EMS crews with providing care on the scene of an emergency. The personnel on the fire apparatus are trained and certified to provide prehospital emergency medical care. In some communities, fire-based EMS departments are staffed with volunteer providers who are trained to the same standards as paid providers and possess equal certifications.

In other communities, EMS is provided through a hospital-based system. EMS providers working in this type of system are based in a hospital, usually within the emergency department, and respond to emergency calls in ambulances and EMS chase/sprint units. Hospital-based EMS providers, like fire- and police-based services, employ highly trained professionals who are certified to provide both lifesaving and routine emergency medical and trauma care to the ill and injured. Often, hospital-based EMS providers care for patients in the emergency department when not responding to a call or providing prehospital care.

Third services, those not affiliated directly with a hospital, law enforcement agency, or fire department, also offer prehospital EMS services. Although they are usually not directly affiliated with other services, third services work collaboratively with fire and law enforcement departments during emergency calls. Third services are stand-alone EMS systems that typically have ambulances, rescue apparatus, chase vehicles, or medevac assets to respond to medical and trauma emergencies. They can be community based, nonprofit, or for profit, and may include volunteer EMS professionals in addition to (or instead of) paid EMS personnel.

The method by which EMS care is provided in the prehospital environment varies throughout the country, depending on the local needs and available resources. All prehospital professionals are generally trained to the same standards, tested and certified to similar standards (depending on the state), and have similar scopes of practice by level to define what care they can provide. Regardless of the type of EMS system in place, all have the same goal: to provide quality emergency medical care to the ill and injured.

The National Highway Traffic Safety Administration

EMS systems originated in the 1960s, when US citizens were dying at a higher rate from automobile crashes than armed services personnel were dying in the Vietnam War. The National Academy of Sciences and the National Research Council published a white paper in 1966 entitled *Accidental Death and Disability: The Neglected Disease of Modern Society*. The paper pointed out the variety of care that was provided in the prehospital environment and how there was a lack of standardized training, care, transportation methods, and, in many instances, medical and governmental oversight. The white paper advocated greater standardization in EMS systems and training, as well as improved medical and governmental oversight. As a result, the Highway Safety Act of 1966 charged the Department of Transportation's National Highway Traffic Safety Administration (NHTSA) with enhancing and standardizing EMS in the United States. With this charge came funding to develop national training standards for EMS providers and minimum equipment standards, and also to improve highway safety. To support these EMS standards, the American Academy of Orthopaedic Surgeons prepared and published the first EMT textbook—*Emergency Care and Transportation of the Sick and Injured*—in 1971, often called the Orange Book.

Access to EMS Services

The mission of the NHTSA Office of EMS is to "reduce death and disability by providing leadership and coordination to the EMS community in assessing, planning, developing, and promoting comprehensive, evidence-based emergency medical services and 911 systems." The gateway to EMS is through

911 centers or **public safety access points (PSAPs)**. PSAPs receive calls for police and fire service, as well as EMS. In most cases, a PSAP is more than a dispatch center. It may have supervisory personnel who help determine hospital availability or facilitate interaction among other agencies (eg, police, power companies, medevac, transportation). Other public health functions, such as epidemiologic tracking, can also be performed at more advanced PSAPs. Throughout most of the United States, persons seeking emergency police, fire, or EMS assistance dial 911.

EDUCATION OF EMS PROFESSIONALS

Since the beginning of EMS, the NHTSA has facilitated the progression of the EMS profession by updating the National Standard Curricula (NSC) and by leading the development of the *National EMS Agenda for the Future*, the *National EMS Education Agenda for the Future: A Systems Approach*, and other EMS-related resources. *The National EMS Education Agenda for the Future: A Systems Approach* addresses the scope of practice and core content, defining what prehospital professionals can and cannot do in the field, the education standards for training EMS professionals, and the accreditation and certification requirements of prehospital providers.

The *National EMS Scope of Practice Model* provides the boundaries of what prehospital professionals can and cannot do in the prehospital setting. State licensing EMS boards use this national model to set the scope of practice for licensing or certifying EMS providers in a given state. The number of EMS provider levels that a state has, as well as the scope of practice for each level, is determined based on the needs of the state. In the prehospital setting, there are typically four levels of providers delivering emergency medical care: **emergency medical responders (EMRs)**, **emergency medical technicians (EMTs)**, **advanced emergency medical technicians (AEMTs)**, and **paramedics**.

EMRs, formerly called first responders, have the necessary knowledge and skills to address basic medical and trauma life threats. EMRs usually receive around 50 hours of training that covers basic patient assessment, bleeding control, **cardiopulmonary resuscitation (CPR)** and the use of **automated external defibrillators (AEDs)**, basic airway management, oxygen therapy, auto-injector assistance, spinal stabilization, fracture stabilization, emergency moves, and so forth. EMRs typically are not involved with the transport of patients from a scene to a hospital or medical center. They do, however, work collaboratively with other EMS professionals in the field to provide emergency medical care to the ill and injured. LERs are typically trained to this level and also have specialized training, such as care under fire, to meet the specific emergency medical training needs of the law enforcement community.

The EMT is trained to provide basic life support (BLS) care to the ill and injured. The level of training offered to EMTs is typically at least 150 hours and prepares the EMT to provide all care specified under the EMR role plus additional airway and oxygen management maneuvers and skills, additional medications, more detailed splinting skills, equipment monitoring, and other skills. EMTs may transport patients from the scene of an incident to hospitals and medical facilities. EMTs within the law enforcement community may function on specialized teams and are qualified to offer emergency medical care to both fellow officers and citizens alike.

The AEMT is trained to provide both basic and advanced life support (ALS) care to the ill and injured. The training needed to become an AEMT is approximately 150 hours more than that required for an EMT. The AEMT is able to provide advanced airway maneuvers, intravenous medication and fluid administration, and the administration of medications to treat a variety of common medical emergencies and can use a variety of monitoring devices (**Figure 6**).

The paramedic receives approximately 1,100 hours of education and is qualified to perform all the skills of the EMR, EMT, and AEMT, as well as advanced airway maneuvers and

Figure 6 An AEMT is trained to provide both BLS and ALS care.

management, advanced assessment techniques (including 12-lead electrocardiograms and blood chemistry analysis), intravenous medication and fluid administration, advanced medications for a variety of medical emergencies, cardiac care, and other care.

The education that EMRs, EMTs, AEMTs, and paramedics receive is detailed within the *National EMS Education Standards*. These standards outline the objectives for EMS students to achieve while preparing to become EMS professionals. The standards are designed to ensure that no matter what EMS course a student takes (at a particular level) throughout the country, he or she will learn the same content. Upon successful completion of a state-approved EMS course (EMR, EMT, AEMT, or paramedic), the student can apply for national EMS certification and subsequent state licensure.

Authorization to Practice

The state EMS office issues a **license** or **certification** to EMS professionals upon successful completion of an approved or accredited EMS educational program and successful completion of an EMS certification or licensing examination. The purpose of EMS certification and subsequent licensure is to protect the public by ensuring that the student applying for certification or licensure is able to perform the duties of an EMS professional safely. Verification of basic competency is usually determined through a cognitive (written) and a practical examination.

The state EMS office also oversees EMS systems and determines the **scope of practice** for each level of provider. The scope of practice is the list of skills that a given provider can perform. For example, EMRs who are certified or licensed within a state may be authorized to perform splinting of injured arms or legs. EMTs may be authorized to administer certain lifesaving medications within their scope of practice. These skills are routinely defined by each state and ultimately apply to the applicable licensed EMS professionals functioning within that state.

In addition to the state certifying or licensing EMS providers, medical oversight is provided to address quality improvement, protocols, and other administrative functions. The **medical director**, as a medical expert, provides expertise to the EMS program and helps ensure that the care rendered to patients is medically appropriate, current, and in conformance with acceptable practices. The medical director interacts with the EMS system officials and helps to establish and ultimately approves **medical protocols** (standards to which EMS professionals must perform given particular emergency situations). When the **standard of care**, as defined in protocols, is not followed, the medical director, in conjunction with EMS officials, meets with the provider to remediate and retrain, as needed. The medical director is involved in the routine review of calls and EMS encounters to ensure that the highest possible level of care is provided. He or she works in conjunction with the EMS program in **credentialing** providers to function within that jurisdiction. EMS providers, once certified, are required to become acclimated to local standard operating procedures (SOPs), including radio procedures, documentation practices, transport locations, and other similar, locally determined procedures.

RESPONDER ROLES, RESPONSIBILITIES, AND PROFESSIONALISM

Roles and Responsibilities

All EMS personnel must maintain a state of readiness to ensure that they are prepared and able to respond to virtually any emergency when called. Readiness includes being mentally prepared to address a host of diverse medical, trauma, and behavioral emergencies. The provider must not only be prepared mentally but also must be prepared to competently perform a variety of medical skills. A provider who is not prepared may do more harm than good.

Another important aspect of preparedness deals with equipment. EMS professionals must routinely assess their equipment to ensure it is current and in working order (**Figure 7**). This includes taking an inventory of the equipment

Figure 7 Routinely evaluate your emergency equipment to ensure that it is current.

available, inspecting equipment to determine its continued functionality, and verifying expiration dates of equipment and supplies, when applicable. The equipment necessary is discussed in more detail later in this unit.

In addition to ensuring the readiness of providers and equipment, LERs must continually be aware of safety in all aspects of job performance. If the responder is injured during an emergency situation, not only is the responder affected, but his or her partner (or partners) and the patient are also affected. The partner, presuming he or she is not hurt, now has to care for two patients. Also, the patient who initially had two EMS professionals to care for his or her injuries now has only one. Often, LERs are called to unsafe environments to provide assistance; the safety of the responder, fellow officers, and the patients must always take priority over all other actions.

When arriving at the scene of an emergency incident, the LER must first ensure scene safety and then quickly determine the need for additional resources. Because it takes time for other officers, EMS and fire crews, medevacs, and other resources to arrive, it is important that these resources be requested as early as possible. Often the determination regarding additional resources is made within the first few minutes of arriving on the scene.

Once the scene is safe and additional resources are called, the officer approaches the patient. Gaining access to the patient may be as simple as walking up a flight of stairs, opening a car door, or walking down a sidewalk. Or, it could be as complex as crawling up an embankment, safely crossing a busy street, or walking up several flights of steps. Regardless, the LER needs to gain access to a patient safely and possibly use rescue techniques, if trained to do so.

Once at the patient's side, the responder performs a patient assessment. The purpose of a patient assessment is to determine what injuries or illnesses the patient may have and to determine what, if any, treatments need to be performed. A proper patient assessment is a necessity for every patient encountered. A LER should approach a patient assessment in a consistent manner, decreasing the likelihood that components of the assessment will be missed. Although there may be differences regarding what is assessed and how the patient is assessed depending on the circumstances of a particular situation, the basic tenets and principles of patient assessment apply universally.

The number one principle of patient assessment is to determine what is wrong with the patient so that the appropriate treatments and resources can begin. Once the LER performs a patient assessment, treatment should be initiated, especially in circumstances involving injuries in which response (time) is critical (eg, airway, breathing, or circulation problems). Life-saving treatment should begin before EMS transport teams arrive. Patient assessment is discussed in greater detail in the physical assessment and management unit.

While providing emergency medical care and awaiting the arrival of EMS transport teams, you should offer emotional support to the patient, family members, and other affected bystanders. It is important for the LER to provide emotional support to ensure that the difficult situation is not made worse. Emotional support can be offered by simply being present with the injured or ill person, especially at eye level. Being a good listener is also supportive—not just hearing what the person is saying but actually listening and showing that you care and are concerned with his or her well-being. Emotional support should not include unrealistic clichés such as "Everything is going to be okay" or "Don't worry, we won't let you die." Statements like these are not always true, and an uncertain tone of voice makes them sound insincere. Offer unconditional positive support without judging the patient's condition and be empathetic toward the patient.

When other EMS professionals arrive, the LER must inform the arriving responders of his or her assessment findings as well as any treatment that has been provided. This transfer of information is part of the continuum of care and helps prevent duplication of efforts, allowing the subsequent provider to take over where the first provider left off. The LER, trained at the EMR level, is often the first emergency medical professional to provide care to an ill or injured patient. The information they convey to the other EMS professionals will be reported to health care professionals in hospitals and specialty centers. LER, fire, and EMS departments that routinely work together typically have a systematic way in which patient care is transferred from one provider to another and typically work together as a community with local hospitals to ensure that there are seamless transitions of care with appropriate transfer of information. Information transferred should include the patient's age and sex, vital signs, pertinent medical history, and specifics on his or her current condition. Information regarding the patient's condition and the treatment provided should be reported only to the crew members who will be taking over care of the patient. The information should not be provided to others because it may be a violation of the patient's privacy.

Professionalism

It is important for EMS professionals to have up-to-date knowledge in appropriate care and assessment as well as continued competency with skills performed in the prehospital setting. It is also important for EMS professionals to have attributes and characteristics that are consistent with the professionalism expected by the public (**Table 1**).

Table 1

Characteristics of Professionalism

Characteristic	Description
Integrity	Having a sound moral character; honesty
Empathy	Being able to identify with another's feelings, experiences, thoughts, or attitudes
Self-motivation	Being able to undertake or continue tasks without being ordered to do so by supervisors
Appearance and hygiene	Proper dress and a neat, clean appearance
Self-confidence	Having confidence in one's own abilities and skills
Knowledge of limitations	Knowing what you can and cannot do in terms of skills and abilities
Time management	Being punctual and efficient with time
Communication	Being able to effectively listen and respond with pertinent information
Teamwork	Working for the betterment of the team as a group rather than just oneself
Respect	Showing regard for and acceptance of others
Tact	Being able to deal with difficult situations effectively without being offensive
Patient advocacy	Being an advocate for the well-being and needs of the patient
Appropriate delivery of care	Providing the appropriate care when it is needed

In addition to possessing initial competency with knowledge, skills, abilities, and professional attributes, EMS professionals (including LERs) must maintain that competency throughout their careers. As a result, EMS professionals are required to renew their licenses or certifications about every 2 or 3 years, depending on the jurisdiction. To do so, they must obtain continuing education to be updated on the most current medical practices, as well as have their skill proficiencies verified. When applying for initial licensure or certification, EMS professionals may be assessed a fee and will need to answer questions regarding criminal history. They may also be required to undergo a criminal background check to ensure the safety of the public they will be serving.

CONTINUOUS QUALITY IMPROVEMENT

Prehospital emergency medical care, which deals with helping people who are in the midst of difficult situations, requires the absolute highest degree of competency with little room for error. EMS professionals strive to achieve that level of perfection by continually improving their knowledge and skills. Embracing an attitude of **continuous quality improvement** regarding patient care results in improved patient safety, reduction in errors, and sharpened proficiency of skill and knowledge levels.

Continual review of skills, protocols, and knowledge helps maintain a provider's competency level. The old saying "If you don't use it, you lose it" is absolutely applicable here. Errors in treatment can happen as a result of simple human error. No one is perfect, and we all make mistakes. However, these types of mistakes can be minimized by constantly questioning oneself, by using reference guides or decision aids, and by simply asking for help. Other errors occur as a result of inadequate knowledge or poor competency with skills. These errors are preventable with continual practice of skills (especially those that are performed infrequently) and periodic review of didactic information (especially that which is infrequently used). Another way in which errors can be reduced is by getting into a habit of reviewing an EMS incident shortly after it occurs. This habit keeps the information fresh in the crews' minds, and a discussion can be had to determine what was good about the call and what could have been done better. The "what could have been done better" findings will stay in the minds of the responders, and the next time a similar EMS call is encountered, the lessons learned from the previous call will be applied. Taking precautions to minimize errors, as well as properly reviewing EMS calls after they happen, fosters a spirit of continuous quality improvement and ultimately maximizes the quality of care provided to the ill and injured.

EMS AND PUBLIC HEALTH

EMS is part of the medical system as well as the public health system. Throughout the country, EMS systems collaborate with public health entities to promote the health and well-being of people. This is done by providing public education, awareness programs, screening, vaccinations, injury prevention programs, and similar activities. LERs provide public health initiatives by participating in car seat checks (to ensure that car seats are properly installed), by enforcing applicable helmet and seat belt laws, by providing basic medical screenings at public events, by enforcing driving under the influence (DUI) laws, and by promoting prevention of illness and injuries.

Public health initiatives by LER agencies help primarily to reduce disease development and secondarily to reduce disease progression and complications. These are achieved by EMS professionals doing health screenings (eg, blood pressure and diabetes awareness checks) and by educational resources such as pamphlets, videos, and public presentations and discussions. The more obvious public health efforts undertaken by LERs are, however, typically focused on seat belt and helmet enforcement, proper car seat usage, and DUI enforcement. Regardless of what is done, LERs often play an integral role in promoting public health.

Mission Planning

LERs routinely handle a variety of specialized operations and training. These include, but are not limited to, **high-risk warrant service**, barricaded subjects, demonstrations, civil disturbances, and live-fire training exercises (**Figure 8**). Planning for some of these events begins days or weeks prior to the operation. Each of these situations is primarily considered a law enforcement event; however, the overall safety of the responding LERs, as well as the community at large, should be considered when planning for these situations. Unique aspects of intelligence gathering and preplanning for the potential medical problems can accompany such operations (**Figure 9**).

Figure 8 Medical plans should be developed for both operational and training missions including high-risk warrant service.

Figure 9 A tactical team conducts a mission briefing.

THE NECESSITY OF MEDICAL INTELLIGENCE

With the integration of **tactical emergency medical support (TEMS)** into civilian EMS and law enforcement, medical intelligence and mission planning are becoming more widely accepted and used.

The US Department of Defense describes medical intelligence as:

> That category of intelligence resulting from collection, evaluation, analysis, and interpretation of foreign medical, bio-scientific, and environmental information which is of interest to strategic planning and to military medical planning and operations for the conservation of the fighting strength of friendly forces and the formation of assessments of foreign medical capabilities in both military and civilian sectors.

Although most LERs will not be supporting foreign operations, the military's definition emphasizes the importance placed on medical intelligence and mission planning. The use of medical intelligence gives the military command and control function the ability to foresee and plan for unfavorable conditions that may have an adverse operational impact.

These Department of Defense theories on medical intelligence and mission planning are easily translated to the support of civilian law enforcement operations. Since the advent of Special Weapons and Tactics (SWAT) teams in Los Angeles in 1966, intelligence gathering and planning have resulted in the success of thousands of special operations missions. Command staff at these incidents rely heavily on intelligence gathered from a variety of sources, ranging from district patrol officers familiar with a barricaded suspect to counter snipers providing information on a suspect's movements inside a building. The use of sophisticated technology, listening devices, and fiber optic cameras has also supported the intelligence gathering and planning techniques of civilian law enforcement.

Planning the medical mission for civilian law enforcement cannot be shortsighted—this is not merely a plan for the treatment of penetrating trauma. In every military conflict in which the United States has been involved, only 20% of all hospital admissions have been for "combat injuries." Disease and nonbattle injury account for the other 80%. Clearly, the LER, medical director, and supervisors must evaluate a wide range of possibilities when preparing a medical plan for a specific mission.

MISSION PLANNING PRINCIPLES

The US Marine Corps identifies six mission preplanning principles and three medical plan functions. All LERs should be familiar with the six preplanning principles and three medical functions, questioning plans and briefings to ensure that these objectives have been met. A good way to ensure that the preplanning principles and medical functions have been met is to develop forms that specifically call for the planners to speak to the required points. All plans should be reviewed by a senior LER or supervisor prior to implementation. Adhering to these basic principles and medical functions results in effective plans that support the overall mission objective (**Figure 10**).

- **Conformity.** The medical plan must integrate and comply with the commander's plan.
- **Proximity.** The medical plan must provide medical support as close to the operational area as the tactical situation permits.
- **Flexibility.** The medical plan must be capable of adapting resources to a changing situation.
- **Mobility.** The medical plan must anticipate the need to move the sick and injured rapidly during the mission.
- **Continuity.** The medical plan must provide optimum, uninterrupted care from the point of injury to an appropriate medical facility.

Figure 10 Planning for a wide array of law enforcement operations poses unique challenges for the LER.

- **Coordination.** The medical plan must ensure that all resources are used effectively and efficiently in support of the mission.

According to the US Marine Corps, the medical plan must also address the following three functions:

- **Preventive health care.** The identification of those hazards, whether environmental, biologic, plant, or animal, that can be mitigated prior to deployment.
- **Casualty treatment.** The triage and treatment of law enforcement personnel, innocent civilians, and suspects.
- **Casualty evacuation.** The transport and continued care of the sick or injured to appropriate treatment facilities.

INTELLIGENCE GATHERING

Most LERs use the Medical Threat Assessment (MTA) as a tool for gathering intelligence and planning for a mission (**Table 2**). The MTA template allows the LER to assemble a listing of resources and threats that may affect the success of an operation.

If the assignment is a high-risk warrant service, dignitary protection detail, or crowd control at a demonstration, time will be available to gather intelligence and formulate a plan. If, however, you are responding to a barricaded subject, hostage rescue, or explosive ordnance disposal mission, time may be precious. Initially, the responder may not have adequate time to compile all of the required data in a standard MTA. In these situations the responder must rely on his or her baseline knowledge of the area to begin formulating a medical plan.

The standard MTA begins with documenting the date, time, location, and operation type (executive protection mission, demonstration, etc). Before starting the MTA, ensure that no threat assessments have already been completed for a prior mission in the area. Reviewing and updating a previous document is always easier than starting the process from scratch. However, you must always check data for their accuracy.

Medical Facilities

One of the key parts of the MTA is determining which medical facilities are close to the area of operation. The MTA should include at least two local facilities for minor injuries and illnesses, as well as a trauma center and a burn center. Other hospitals with specialty services will be necessary for specific operations. For instance, a hospital capable of handling hazardous material exposures may be necessary if there is a possibility that a clandestine drug lab may be encountered. Officers and agents from local law enforcement offices should become familiar with hospitals in their area. Visiting local hospital emergency departments is the best way to gather needed information. A variety of Internet resources are also available to determine the closest hospital to a given location. In addition, many GPS systems allow the user to locate the closest hospitals to a target address.

Many hospitals in the United States maintain web sites with information valuable for an MTA. Document the address and pertinent phone numbers for each facility. Of particular importance is the direct phone number for the emergency department. Comments can include the number of beds available in the hospital and in the emergency department. Some hospital emergency departments in very rural areas may not be open (or may not be staffed by physicians) 24 hours per day. Such critical information must be documented in the MTA. If an officer is severely injured, time can be wasted by transporting him or her to a facility that is not capable of providing care. The LER should ask whether the hospital has a helipad. Of key importance is the type of aircraft that the pad is capable of holding (**Figure 11**). Smaller rooftop pads may not be capable of holding larger Sikorsky S-70 (the civilian version of the Blackhawk) and Bell 412 (the civilian version of the Huey) aircraft. Additional information regarding the types of specialty services available at the facility can also be included in the Comments section of the MTA.

Tip

Sample Hospital MTA Entry

Johns Hopkins Hospital	410-955-2280	Emergency
600 North Wolfe St.	410-955-5000	Main
Baltimore, MD 21287		

Comments: This is a 918-bed teaching facility well noted throughout the world. Services include Allergy/Immunology, Anesthesiology/Critical Care, Cardiology, Dermatology, Emergency Medicine, Endocrinology, Gastroenterology, Internal Medicine, Nephrology/Neurosurgery, Ophthalmology, OB/GYN, Pediatrics, Radiology, and Surgery. Hopkins is also a level I pediatric and adult trauma center with a rooftop helipad capable of landing large rotary-wing aircraft.

Responders should be aware that a level I trauma center may not always be available and may not be necessary for all traumatic injuries. Rural areas may not have a level I facility

Table 2

Specific Factors for Compiling a Medical Threat Assessment	
Operation Factors	
Date	Date of the operation or training mission
Time	Time of the operation or training mission (operations outside the continental United States should use Coordinated Universal Time [UTC])
Location	Specific address of the target or operation
Latitude/longitude	Latitude and longitude of the target or operation
Weather Temperature, humidity, precipitation, ultraviolet index for the area of operation (AO)	
Fire/EMS	
Agency information	Local fire and EMS agency name(s), addresses, emergency telephone number (eg, 911), administrative telephone number
Capability comments	Advanced life support capabilities, number of response units, proximity to AO, specialized units (eg, hazardous materials unit, dive rescue)
Health Care Facilities Local hospitals, trauma center, burn center, hyperbaric chamber (only necessary if dive mission)	
Hospital information	Name, address, main telephone number, emergency department telephone number
Capability comments	Number of beds in hospital, number of beds in emergency department, MRI and CT scan capability, helipad, emergency department hours of operation, and physician availability (rural hospitals may not be open or have physician staffing 24/7)
Air Medical Resources	
Agency information	Name, address, emergency/dispatch telephone number, administrative telephone number
Capability comments	Number and type of aircraft (fixed wing aircraft, rotary-wing aircraft), staffing (physician, flight nurse, flight paramedic), preferred landing zone size
Disease Risks	
Disease	Common name of the disease
Incubation period	Can be hours to months
Transmission	How the disease is transmitted (eg, vector [mosquitoes, flies, etc], ingestion [food, water])
Countermeasures	How to prevent transmission of disease (eg, drink only bottled water, use insect repellant)

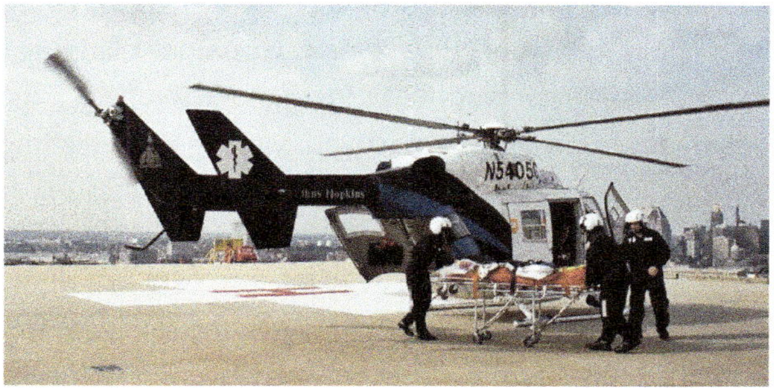

Figure 11 Smaller helipads may not be capable of landing larger rotary-wing aircraft.

in proximity to the operation. A level II center might then be an appropriate resource. In urban areas, a level II trauma center might be used for minor traumatic injuries, especially when heavy patient load could affect the immediate care of an injured officer. Travel times to each facility should be included in the document.

Tip

Trauma Center Designations

Trauma center designations may be assigned by the state or political body that regulates the specific hospital. The fellowship of the American College of Surgeons also evaluates the resources of hospitals and determines if the facility qualifies as a level I or level II trauma center. This evaluation is a voluntary process, and not all states or political bodies subscribe to this credentialing process.

Level I Trauma Center

- Regional center
- Has advanced specialty surgeons and physicians available 24 hours a day
- Maintains specialized clinical staff and facilities dedicated to advanced trauma care

Level II Trauma Center

- Large hospital in a dense population setting where no level I trauma center exists
- Provides advanced definitive care, but without certain specialties or the depth of a level I trauma center

Level III Trauma Center

- A hospital located in an area where no level I or II trauma centers exist
- Provides emergency care, surgery, stabilization, and transfer capabilities

Level IV Trauma Center

- A community or rural hospital or health station in a remote setting
- General practitioners, who have the capability of providing advanced trauma life support prior to patient transfer

If possible, maps highlighting travel routes from the area of operation (AO) to each medical facility should be included in the MTA. Should a transport unit from another section of town be assigned to the mission, it may be unfamiliar with the area. In one instance, an ALS unit was assigned to a police officer's funeral. (The unit was stationed in an area of the county that had a low call volume and thus was selected for assignment to the detail.) The unit was given directions to the place of interment on the opposite side of the county. However, when requested to transport an individual to a local facility, the unit was unfamiliar with both the hospital and the route to the facility.

Fire and EMS Services

Data on area fire and EMS services and their capabilities should be included in the MTA. Information may include whether an EMS service is ALS capable and whether a paramedic is available 24 hours per day. Capabilities of local fire services may include hazardous materials response or an underwater dive rescue unit (in which case the MTA should also include the location of the closest hyperbaric medicine facility).

Many areas of the country rely on volunteer fire and EMS personnel. A single ALS provider may be responsible for hundreds of square miles in rural areas. In other areas, ALS may be available only during specific times of the day. One cannot assume that resources will always arrive on the scene in a timely manner.

Air Evacuation

The use of aircraft to evacuate the sick and injured has become almost routine. The efficiency of air transport cannot be overstated, and it is necessary to have a plan for air evacuation. The LER must first inquire as to whether air assets are available for the AO. Some deployable locations within the continental United States (**CONUS**), as well as those outside the continental United States (**OCONUS**), may be far removed from civilization. Fuel supplies may limit the use of rotary-wing aircraft, thus requiring fixed wing aircraft as the most expedient method of transport for all injuries and illnesses.

A number of factors influence the use of aircraft and the landing zones (LZs) designated for the operation. When contacting the flight service, inquire as to what size aircraft might be deployed, the patient capacity, and the preferred (as well as minimum) size requirements for their LZ. The flight service point of contact (POC) should be queried as to whether firearms or chemical agents are permissible in the aircraft and whether the aircraft will transport prisoners. If you anticipate patients who might be contaminated with a hazardous material, ask what procedures will be required to allow air transport. Many flight services will not transport contaminated patients, even after gross decontamination.

Primary and secondary LZs should be assigned by the lead LER or mission supervisor, with latitude and longitude noted for each site. If there is a possibility of the primary site being compromised, a secondary LZ should be designated nearby. If either LZ requires overflight and landing of civilian aircraft near secure facilities, approval is needed well in advance. Wherever the LZ might be located, the planning stage should include a visual inspection of the site for possible safety hazards. If the AO is in a remote, forested area, the closest LZ may be miles away. Identifying such factors in the planning stage allows for appropriate litters or other evacuation devices to be included in the equipment load-out. Topography maps may be useful to map routes from the mission site to the LZ.

Weather

Weather has a significant effect on the availability of air assets. The MTA should include anticipated weather conditions for the time span of the operation. This information is available through a variety of sources, including the Internet. These sources include the National Oceanic and Atmospheric Administration, University of Michigan Weather, and The Weather Channel. If designated aircraft are down due to a summer thunderstorm or a winter snow squall, the plan should include contingencies. Documentation of temperature, humidity, and winds is also necessary. By consulting heat index or wind chill charts, LERs can anticipate potential heat or cold casualties and make appropriate adjustments to uniforms, hydration, and work cycles.

The LER should be aware that regional weather conditions can vary widely. Desert areas can have drastic temperature swings at different times of day. Some areas can experience high temperature and low humidity in a low-lying desert area, while only a few miles away a mountain range might still have snow at higher elevations. In addition, certain disease processes present in a desert area may not be present in the mountainous areas only miles away. Familiarity with the AO is imperative.

Plant and Animal Life

With familiarity of the AO, responders should also be capable of planning for any plant or animal threats that may be present. The search for suspects or the deployment of counter sniper teams into wooded areas may necessitate planning for bites and stings from various reptiles and **arthropods** (**Figure 12**). Skin reactions from contact with various plant life might also be anticipated. The plan should include the location and quantity of any antivenin that may be required. Underwater operations for the purpose of evidence recovery or explosive ordnance recovery and disposal require special attention to planning for dive injuries. The array of dangerous marine life, both plant and animal, requires specific treatment modalities. Some injuries require a vinegar wash, whereas others require the administration of specific antivenin.

Disease Risks

One of the functions a medical plan must address is preventive health care. There are many diseases that can affect the overall health of officers or agents while on an operation. Some of these diseases may not become apparent until days or weeks following exposure. For instance, agents operating on an OCONUS mission might be exposed to leishmaniasis—a disease transmitted by some species of sand flies—but show no signs until weeks later. The MTA should identify any diseases that may be present in the AO that could have an impact on the short-term or long-term health of responders. In addi-

Figure 12 Plan against any potential plant or animal threats (eg, spiderbites) in the AO.

tion, the assessment should also include the types of countermeasures that can be employed to alleviate exposure. In the previous example, the use of simple insecticides can reduce the potential for exposure to disease. Countermeasures may also include vaccinations for various diseases such as hepatitis, tetanus, or yellow fever.

Tip

Sample MTA Disease Entry

Leishmaniasis (weeks' to years' incubation)

Transmission: Bite from some species of sand flies, but is poorly transmitted and takes hundreds of bites to infect a host.

Countermeasure: Follow personal insect precautions. Wear clothing that covers exposed skin and cover skin with repellants containing DEET 33%. Use 0.5% Permethrin insecticide on clothing. Greatest time of risk is between dusk and dawn.

Of particular interest, whether the operation is CONUS or OCONUS, is the threat of **vector-borne disease**. Insects can carry a variety of diseases (**Table 3**). For CONUS operations, many local health departments maintain information on vector-borne diseases indigenous to their state.

The Centers for Disease Control and Prevention (CDC) and local health departments are valuable assets in determining diseases that may be present in the AO. The regional medical officer located at most US embassies can be of assistance when a mission is overseas.

Table 3

Sample of Insects and the Diseases They Transmit

Insects	Diseases
Mosquitoes	Malaria Yellow fever Dengue fever West Nile virus Ehrlichiosis
Sand flies	Viral fevers Leishmaniasis
Black flies	River blindness
Tsetse flies	Sleeping sickness
Ticks	Lyme disease Tularemia Rocky Mountain spotted fever

OPERATIONAL SECURITY AND THE MEDICAL PLAN

Operational security (OPSEC) is the approach and mechanism applied by a law enforcement agency or military force to ensure that vital mission information remains secure and unavailable to those who do not need the information. OPSEC is a concern with many missions undertaken by law enforcement. As witnessed by the raid on the Branch Davidian compound in Waco, Texas, the loss of operational security can be disastrous. During the Branch Davidian mission, OPSEC was compromised by the procurement of a local ambulance service to stand by at the location (**Figure 13**). Prior to the operation, workers at the ambulance service tipped off the Branch Davidians that they were going to be contacted by federal LERs. When gathering medical intelligence, the LER must be cautious in releasing information that might compromise the mission. The unintended release of any information, such as the date, time, or location of an operation, should be immediately reported to supervisors. Mission supervisors may have to act immediately to carry out the mission or postpone it.

Once the MTA is completed, the LER can begin to develop a medical plan for the upcoming operation. The plan should adhere to the six planning principles noted earlier in this unit.

Figure 13 The loss of operational security at the Branch Davidian compound raid severely compromised the mission.

By examining the intelligence gathered in the MTA, mission supervisors, lead LERs, and the mission medical director can determine which hospital will be used for a given injury or illness. For instance, the 25-bed hospital closest to the operation may be appropriate for an uncomplicated laceration or fracture; however, it may not be appropriate for a team member having chest pain. The next-closest hospital that has a coronary care unit may be more appropriate.

The plan should also include which mode of transport will be used for any medical emergency. Will local EMS be on standby or will a law enforcement vehicle be used to transport the injured to a treatment facility? Operational security necessitates that EMS not be notified prior to the initiation of the operation. Many volunteer fire and EMS services in rural and suburban areas are hubs for community activities. Information regarding a mission may be prematurely leaked if the service is contacted prior to initiation of the operation.

In addition, the plan should document which LZ will be used, its location, and which mode of transportation will be used to move a patient from the site of injury to the LZ. The plan should also note who will provide security for the LZ if necessary and how the aircraft will be contacted.

Communications

Communications in OPSEC

To ensure OPSEC, dedicated agency-supplied resources should be used for emergency responses. Local assets such as ambulances or rescue units should be staged under direct agency supervision at a site near the AO. Care should be taken to prevent excess communications regarding the mission with response personnel until after they are sequestered at the staging area or until after the mission has already begun.

Finally, the LER should determine which countermeasures will be used to reduce any disease risks that may be present in the AO.

Gathering intelligence and preparing a plan for medical threats to an operational or training mission can often determine the success of that mission when officers or agents are injured or become sick. Identifying potential risks and determining countermeasures for those risks can ultimately lead to a successful operation. Knowledge of local resources (eg, hospitals, trauma centers, fire/EMS services) can assist the LER in providing appropriate care quickly and reducing pain and suffering.

Logistics

The roles and responsibilities of the law enforcement community frequently overlap with those of EMS personnel. Gone are the days when law enforcement medical training consisted of the ABCs: ambulance before cop. Aware of the benefits associated with law enforcement emergency response, many agencies and communities are struggling with the logistics necessary to train and equip LERs safely and effectively. Agencies that are not sufficiently prepared can make serious acquisition errors based on the guidance of well-intentioned employees, vendor marketing strategies, and budget constraints.

Individual perspectives and biases can quickly account for logistical mistakes that can damage an agency's performance for a long period of time. Spending a grant or budgeted funds on impractical or expensive equipment may prevent or limit future allocations that could save lives. This is not unfamiliar territory for law enforcement managers. Drawing from past experience, sound policy, and good evidence, many law enforcement agencies consistently acquire, staff, train, and equip law enforcement personnel effectively. The military, EMS, and fire-rescue community can provide outstanding input. Law enforcement emergency managers must be aware that traditional military, fire-rescue, or EMS perspectives applied directly to law enforcement can hamper the LER.

Military medicine is a science and an art unto itself. Strategies and equipment are developed for an incredible range of missions. Many special team medical operators are not held to civilian medical standards and may have a different approach to skill sets, mission duration, and the availability of additional resources. The military perspective on battlefield medicine and care under fire strategies should be considered a primer for developing logistics for law enforcement. However, military approaches regarding provider skill sets, casualty evacuation, and general emergency medicine are not always compatible with traditional EMS regulations and licensure.

Fire-rescue and EMS programs can provide outstanding guidance on traditional trauma and general medical emergencies. EMS programs excel at understanding local standards and medical regulations. They are experienced in working with medical direction, hospitals, and medical supply and equipment vendors. This community is taught to stage away from violent, unsafe scenes. They construct elaborate command structures to deal with the complexities of hazardous materials incidents and mass casualties. Fire-rescue and EMS programs are typically very apparatus and equipment heavy.

MISSION-SPECIFIC LOGISTICS

LERs may work individually or in pairs. Patrol officers' or agents' resources may need to be packaged so they can be carried on their person. The **individual first aid kit (IFAK)**, mentioned earlier in this unit, is a military approach to meeting the needs of the soldier on a battlefield. These kits are often packaged so they can be attached to load-bearing vests. Some law enforcement agencies have adopted the IFAK. Others have altered the IFAK and label it a self-care under fire (SCUF) kit to carry materials used to provide immediate aid for injury from a large-caliber weapon (**Figure 14**).

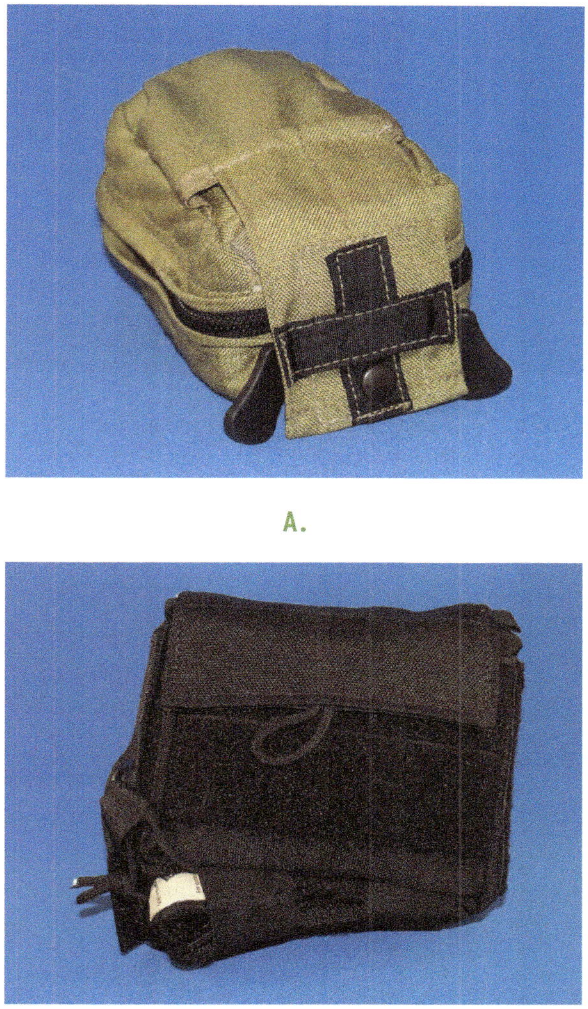

A.

B.

Figure 14 **A.** An IFAK allows packaged materials to be carried on a person. **B.** A SCUF kit carries materials used to provide immediate aid for injury from a large-caliber weapon.

Some vendors offer packaged survival kits that carry traditional EMS supplies in a small, sealed pouch. Many of these smaller packages do not carry sufficient materials to manage the penetrating wounds and severe hemorrhage associated with today's assault weaponry. The officer, agent, or manager should evaluate any of these pouch costs by breaking out the price of the packaged items with a bulk supplier. Using a bulk EMS supplier, the officer, agent, or manager may find that many of the supplies required by the medical director can be purchased individually, then packaged in sealed plastic bags or other waterproof containers. Although not trendy, this plan can save lives at a reduced cost.

Officers or agents operating out of a vehicle or a fixed post may be able to carry additional resources. Medical directors may recommend that a LER have access to oxygen tanks, automated external defibrillators (AEDs), splints, rescue supplies, and fire extinguishers. Care should be taken to secure these items to prevent damage or contamination. Oxygen tanks should be kept away from heat, oil, gases, and dust. They should be stored in such a fashion that they cannot freely move inside the vehicle (**Figure 15**).

The quantity and complexity of items that are being marketed to law enforcement agencies make medical director input a necessity at all levels. Agencies have bought improper equipment, expired supplies, and obsolete AEDs. Unfortunately, these mistakes may go unnoticed until an emergency occurs and the items fail. Managers should ensure that whatever they are purchasing is something that has been medically approved, that the officers or agents are trained in its

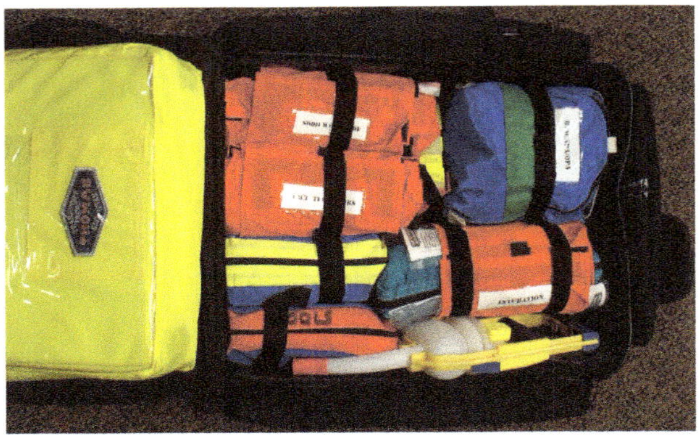

Figure 15 Many commercial bags are available that integrate oxygen storage.

maintenance and use, and that the items are available to the entire staff. Plans should be made with the vendor to ensure that replacement items are quickly available. Some items may require storage to prevent staff from operating without the approved supplies.

Because of the increased number of contents that can be found in the larger response bags, some vendors offer color-coded or labeled pouches to make inspection and use quick and easy. If a program cannot afford to buy premanufactured kits, purchasing medical directed items in bulk and using large, sealable plastic bags or rubberized containers works just as well for a vehicle or fixed post (**Figure 16**).

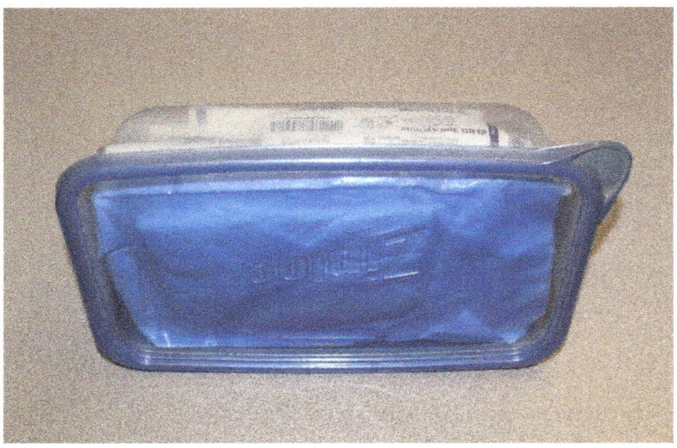

Figure 16 Medical directed items can be purchased in bulk and contained in improvised kits.

Agencies planning to use LERs must also consider the need for personal protective equipment and individual survival supplies. Missions that require exposure to the elements may require sunscreen, insect repellant, bite kits, oral rehydration solutions, water purifiers, and hot and cold protection. Gas masks, nerve agent antidote kits, decontamination supplies, and redress garments are not uncommon in many high-risk law enforcement posts. Many vendors have these items available separately or packaged in kits. Some agencies have packaged the survival supplies with the medical supplies to make a single deployment bag.

Acquisition Strategies

Some vendors are quick to offer an opinion on supplies or equipment. The officer, agent, and manager should assess the market and determine what is available. Make a list of available vendors and items and keep this material accessible as a reference for purchasing. Do not buy whatever the vendor or operator recommends without additional research.

Evaluation Tiers

Management

The point of entry for the procurement of an item should be a designated official in the management structure. Anyone in an agency should be able to freely recommend items for evaluation. Once an item has been recommended for evaluation, a management-guided, structured series of events should occur to ensure that an appropriate evaluation of an item is conducted.

The manager assigned to this task should contact the evaluation tiers in order, starting with the medical director, training staff, and operational providers (**Figure 17**). Each tier should conduct an initial evaluation of the item based on the seven benchmarks and documented with an after-action report. If the item passes the initial assessment and the agency is capable of moving forward with the item, then an operational test phase should occur. The operational test phase should conclude with a second after-action report, which will allow the management team to make an informed decision as to the future deployment of the item.

Medical Director

The medical director should be the first person approached regarding a medical procurement. The agency should provide the medical director a sample or detailed specifications. Be clear in advising the medical director whether this is an urgent

Figure 17 Evaluation of equipment and materials goes through several tiers before approval.

request or a routine evaluation. Some items will require a great deal of research. Something as simple as a pressure dressing can require a lengthy review of published findings.

The agency attempting to procure an item should get a clear approval of the item with documentation of the steps the medical director requires in testing and field evaluation. Each after-action report should be forwarded to the medical director, who has an absolute right to veto any item he or she feels may not meet the mission or the medical director's standards.

Training Officer

Provide a sample to the training program. Ask the training officer to research training programs already in place for the item. Research the item with your regulatory body and determine whether there is a specific training criterion or recertification process required to implement the device. Encourage the training staff to develop scenarios to test providers using the device. Evaluation tools should rate effective application, complications, time to use, and response to environmental conditions.

Provider

Your system may use first aiders, EMRs, EMTs, paramedics, or physicians. If you have a level of care that will be affected by the item you are intending to procure, you should tailor an evaluation form poll or questionnaire to get the input from that group as early as possible. This group will ultimately have to implement use of the device. Encourage an after-action report from providers in light of all seven criteria. If possible, give the providers samples and let them use the items in training scenarios or mock drills. Encourage them to search for alternatives to the item you have provided them.

Benchmarks

Mission

The mission must be clear and concise. Each evaluation tier should be clear about the goals of the mission. A mission statement should be formulated and agreed upon by all four evaluation tiers. If a product fails to meet the mission statement criteria, it should be filed with documentation of why it does not meet the mission at that time.

If a product does meet the mission goals, the evaluation tiers will identify in the after-action report how it meets these goals and research alternative products that may already be in place or are available at a reduced cost.

Environment

The evaluation tiers should list all possible environments and determine the suitability of the product for the given variables. It is not uncommon for products that appear great and intuitive to fail miserably when confronted with routine weather. Batteries, Velcro strapping, and fluid-impregnated dressings may all work in a clinical setting or in an ambulance. In extreme environments and poor weather, however, these items can become useless.

The environment can also change with travel. If your mission requires any degree of transport, you should take into account your expected range of environmental conditions, the environments encountered during your transport, and the environment at your destination (**Figure 18**).

Durability

With the mission and environment identified, the evaluation tiers should evaluate whether the product will be sufficiently durable for the mission. A device that performed admirably

Figure 18 Consider environments you may face and how the equipment will hold up to those environments.

in the desert may function poorly when exposed to cool, wet weather. If there is any concern as to the impact of exposure, the evaluation tiers need to apply the device under extreme conditions to test it.

Certain missions will benefit from single-use, disposable supplies or equipment. Programs with equipment that may be deployed over long durations and in changing environments may benefit from a device that is solidly constructed and can be cleaned and reused. Tourniquets exist in many different configurations, for example, and in some settings an inexpensive, compact, disposable tourniquet may be the best choice.

Weight and Space

Consider whether the items will be carried on the individual at risk in the form of a self-care kit or in a larger deployment bag. Some LERs attempt to carry large quantities of supplies and equipment on their person. Others can be seen carrying large, unwieldy bags. The large personal kit or aid bag can be avoided if the evaluation tiers allot a certain amount of space for these items and adhere to these restrictions.

Common to many rescues is the mining of the bag, resulting in supplies being strewn about in an attempt to find a particular item. Certain bags are designed to compartmentalize and isolate supplies and equipment to reduce the effects of the medical mining operation (**Figure 19**). Well-planned and effective kits and bags effectively secure materials and prevent confusion, loss, and care delays.

Cost

New, cutting-edge products can carry a high price tag. The evaluation tiers should seriously weigh pricing of new items against more traditional items. Some supplies and equipment may come with expiration dates, which can drastically affect replacement costs and place the program in the position of carrying expired items. If staff purchase items with an expiration date, they should take into account future replacement costs and should carefully track expiration dates.

Can you buy in bulk quantities and pack out your own kits, or do you prefer to buy kits already packaged? Some programs will avoid the research necessary to put together their own kits and end up paying several times the value of the contents. To avoid this, work with EMS or medical providers in your area and shop out the specifications of your materials to vendors that supply large quantities of materials. Often a smaller program can link into local contracts or get supplied by local EMS programs.

Training

Consider whether the item you are purchasing corresponds to the training program you currently have. If not, can you alter your training program to teach and evaluate the use of

Figure 19 Bags designed to compartmentalize and isolate supplies and equipment facilitate finding needed equipment and materials.

the item by your staff? Is there a simulator, training aid, or program supplied with the item? Will this item require regular retraining, and if so, can the organization afford all of these costs? Implementation of an item without proper training will result in failure of that item. Looking into this aspect of procurement will prevent unanticipated complications.

Responsibilities

Consider whether the staff to be using the item will be able to maintain proficiency and routinely check batteries and expiration dates on products. Many medical items or kits should be tightly regulated internally, with documentation to record routine inspections.

Investigate the item and ensure that you and your staff are legally able to be trained in the use of the product. Some vendors will sell medically restricted items to agencies and individuals under the caveat that the agency or individual knows whether they can use the item. Document your medical director's approval. If you do not have a medical director, use other agencies and local EMS programs to determine applicability.

After-Action Evaluation

Prior to accepting items for operational use, obtain a sample or purchase small quantities and distribute them for hands-on evaluation. Use them in training scenarios and allow all evaluation tiers to express their opinions in an after-action report. The report should provide information to the leadership of the agency as to the potential acquisition and deployment of the item. Each evaluation tier should be able to veto a specific product if it is able to provide sufficient documentation.

Once you have tested the item and it is acceptable to your agency, implement a testing period with a mandatory review program. A valuable strategy is to purchase limited quantities of new or costly items, train select units, and deploy the items for a limited period of time. All those involved should address an after-action report that speaks to all of the variables. The after-action information should be assembled, and a review board composed of the evaluator tiers should determine whether to continue with the item in full or limited deployment, try another related item, or discontinue this type of item all together.

Good documentation and evaluation can save an agency lives, funding, and time by eliminating the use of inappropriate or poorly performing items. The after-action reports should be filed so they can be available for future use. It is not uncommon for threats to resurface or conditions to change, requiring the reevaluation of some items.

CONCLUSION

The investment in medical equipment or development of medical pre-plans for LERs to treat injuries to themselves or others is somewhat akin to an insurance policy. The likelihood of a LER being involved in an incident leading to injury is relatively low. If the need arises, however, every LER will be better for the preplanning and prepositioning of equipment and training prior to life threat. There is generally no great need for an extraordinary amount of medical equipment or resource investment because the majority of LER duties typically lie elsewhere. However, small and incremental amounts of preparation can improve the outcome for both LERs and their fellow LERs. The life you save may be your own.

Prep Kit

READY FOR REVIEW

- Injuries sustained by LERs may be secondary to blunt trauma, like motor vehicle crashes or falls, and penetrating trauma such as gunshot or stab wounds. Regardless of the mechanism, when a LER encounters major bleeding, it is imperative to stop or minimize the blood loss as quickly as possible.
- The LER may move the body of a patient in an effort to maintain the patency of that patient's airway. The recovery position relies on gravity to move the tongue away from the back of the airway and to assist in clearing the airway of obstructions.
- Knowing one's location at all times is one of the very first skills a trainee must acquire.
- Particularly in medical or rescue situations, LERs must be aware of physical addresses, block ranges, intersections, and well-known landmarks or businesses. Relaying such information verbally is essential for directing aid to themselves or other injured officers.
- During an incident in which an officer is wounded, it is incumbent on LERs to prevent any further injuries from occurring. This may include, but is not limited to, elimination by force of whatever threat is present before casualty injuries can be addressed.
- Moving despite injuries and getting to appropriate cover (most preferred) or concealment (less preferred) is of highest priority.
- Some degree of training is required for officers to become familiar with individual first aid kits (IFAK) or self-care under fire (SCUF) kits and how to use them. Regular retraining is critical to retain this knowledge and to develop understanding of how to deploy these interventions effectively under different circumstances.
- Emergency medical services is a system of care that is provided to acutely injured or ill individuals.
- In the prehospital environment, EMS is provided by personnel from the spectrum of the law enforcement community, fire departments, ambulance and squad services, and hospital-based EMS services.
- The National Highway Traffic Safety Administration Office of EMS's mission is to "reduce death and disability by providing leadership and coordination to the EMS community in assessing, planning, developing, and promoting comprehensive, evidence-based emergency medical services and 911 systems."
- In the prehospital setting, there are typically four levels of providers delivering emergency medical care:
  - Emergency medical responders (EMRs)
  - Emergency medical technicians (EMTs)
  - Advanced emergency medical technicians (AEMTs)
  - Paramedics
- All EMS personnel must maintain a state of readiness, ensuring that they are prepared and able to respond to virtually any emergency when called.
- Embracing an attitude of continuous quality improvement regarding patient care results in improved patient safety, reduction in errors, and sharpened proficiency of skill and knowledge levels.
- EMS systems collaborate with public health entities to promote the health and well-being of citizens. This is done by providing public education, awareness programs, screening, vaccinations, injury prevention programs, and similar activities.
- Medical intelligence and mission planning should be prepared for both operational and training missions.
- Planning for civilian law enforcement missions is not merely a plan for the treatment of penetrating trauma.
- The six principles to consider when planning for a law enforcement mission are conformity, proximity, flexibility, mobility, continuity, and coordination.
- The medical plan should address the preventive health care of the officers or agents, as well as the treatment and evacuation of any injured person on the operation.

- The medical threat assessment should include information on the closest medical facilities; expected weather conditions at the time of the mission; dangerous plant and animal life; disease risks and countermeasures; and available fire, EMS, and air medical resources.
- Drawing from past experience; sound policy; and input from the military, EMS, and fire-rescue community, many law enforcement agencies consistently acquire, staff, train, and equip LERs effectively.
- Managers should ensure that whatever they are purchasing is something that has been medically approved, that the officers or agents are trained in its maintenance and use, and that the items are available to the entire staff.
- Equipment evaluation must be conducted in the following tiers:
  - Management
  - Medical director
  - Training officer
  - Emergency care provider

VITAL VOCABULARY

advanced emergency medical technicians (AEMTs) Intermediate-level prehospital providers who possess the knowledge and skills set of the emergency medical responder (EMR) and emergency medical technician (EMT), as well as additional knowledge and skills.

area of operation (AO) The location where a law enforcement mission or training detail is to occur. The boundaries of that area may be confined to a specific house address when serving a high-risk warrant or may be several city blocks where a demonstration is to occur.

arthropods A class of animals characterized by their exoskeleton and jointed appendages. This class includes scorpions, spiders, centipedes, millipedes, lobsters, crabs, and shrimp.

automated external defibrillators (AEDs) Devices that deliver an electrical shock to patients in cardiac arrest.

cardiopulmonary resuscitation (CPR) The process of manually circulating oxygenated blood in a patient whose heart is not beating.

certification Verification of successfully completing a course or competencies and/or authorization to function at a given prehospital level within a state.

continuous quality improvement A process involving multiple components that results in continual improvement within a given EMS system.

CONUS Refers to an activity occurring within the continental United States.

Coordinated Universal Time (UTC) Also known as Greenwich Mean Time (GMT) or Zulu time; uses 24-hour military time notations and is based on the 0° longitude time meridian, which runs through Greenwich, England. Midnight is 0000 UTC; noon is noted as 1200 UTC.

credentialing The process of acclimation and clearing to function within an EMS system.

emergency medical responders (EMRs) The first responder level of prehospital provider offering basic life support care.

emergency medical technicians (EMTs) Basic life support prehospital providers with the skills and knowledge of an emergency medical responder (EMR) as well as additional knowledge such as performing additional patient care interventions, preparing a patient for transport, and providing transport to a medical treatment facility.

exsanguinating hemorrhage Major, ongoing, life-threatening bleeding.

fixed wing aircraft An airplane.

hemostatic agents Chemical materials, usually in powder form or impregnated into a textile, that are designed to speed the natural clotting process.

high-risk warrant service A law enforcement operation in which an arrest warrant or search/seizure warrant is being served. Determination of "high risk" is made by the individual law enforcement agency.

incubation period The time between first exposure to a disease pathogen and the period when signs and symptoms appear.

individual first aid kit (IFAK) A military approach to a self-care kit that meets the needs of the soldier on a battlefield, often packaged so the kit can be attached to load-bearing vests.

license A privilege and authorization to function as a prehospital provider within a state.

medical director The physician overseeing and responsible for the care provided by prehospital providers functioning in an EMS system.

medical protocols Standards to which EMS professionals must perform given particular emergency situations.

OCONUS Refers to any activity occurring in an area outside the continental United States.

operational security (OPSEC) The approach and mechanism applied by a law enforcement agency or military force to ensure that vital mission information remains secure and unavailable to those who do not need the information.

paramedics The highest level of civilian prehospital provider, who possess the knowledge and skills of the emergency medical responder (EMR), emergency medical technician (EMT), and advanced emergency medical technician (AEMT), as well as additional knowledge to provide advanced life support care.

public safety access points (PSAPs) The access points for police, fire, and EMS services. Throughout most of the United States, PSAPs are accessed by dialing 911.

rotary-wing aircraft A helicopter.

scope of practice The limits and boundaries of what skills and procedures prehospital providers can perform and the care they can provide given their certification or license level.

standard of care The manner in which an individual must act or behave when giving care.

tactical emergency medical support (TEMS) Specially trained emergency medical technicians assigned to law enforcement special operations teams.

tourniquets Constricting bands that reduce or stop blood flow to extremities.

vector-borne disease A disease that is transmitted to humans or other animals.

CHECK YOUR KNOWLEDGE

1. Throughout most of the United States, EMS is activated through:
   A. PSAP centers.
   B. AEMT stations.
   C. NHTSA.
   D. third-party services.
2. Which of the following provides a good example of a LER participating in a public health initiative?
   A. Providing CPR to a fellow officer
   B. Taking care of himself or herself by exercising and getting plenty of rest
   C. Enforcing seat belt usage laws
   D. Stopping a bystander's bleeding
3. After safely accessing a patient, the number one item of focus for the responder is to:
   A. Await the arrival of EMS to initiate prehospital emergency medical care.
   B. Determine what is wrong and ensure that appropriate treatment and resources can be allocated.
   C. Administer lifesaving medications to ill and injured patients in the prehospital setting.
   D. Ensure that adequate resources have been activated.
4. Operational security is generally not considered when contacting hospitals and local fire or EMS services.
   A. True
   B. False
5. Which of the following is the best resource for determining disease risks in an area of operation?
   A. Travel books
   B. Local health department
   C. Local EMS
   D. Local news media

Medical Standards and Responsibilities

Unit 2

Nelson Tang
Joshua Roberts
Kevin Gerold
Nina Bingham

Law Enforcement Responder Objectives

Physical Direction and Oversight

- Discuss the role of medical direction and oversight within a law enforcement agency. (pp 31–33)

Documentation

- List the information that must be documented on the patient care report. (pp 34–38)
- Discuss the legal functions of the patient care report. (pp 38–40)
- Discuss the administrative functions of the patient care report. (p 40)

Ethical and Legal Considerations

- Discuss ethics as they apply to the law enforcement responder. (pp 40–41)
- Discuss the statutory regulations that pertain to responders. (p 41)
- Explain a responder's duty to act and how it is influenced by the standard of care and scope of practice. (pp 41–42)
- Define negligence and discuss the four conditions required to constitute legal negligence. (p 42)
- Discuss Good Samaritan laws. (pp 42–43)
- List and define the various forms of consent. (pp 43–44)
- Explain refusal of care. (p 44)
- Discuss advance directives and living wills. (pp 44–45)
- Define confidentiality and its relationship to the Health Information Portability and Accountability Act (HIPAA). (pp 45–46)
- Discuss statutory responsibilities and mandatory reporting. (p 46)

Forensics

- List the forensic considerations at a crime scene. (pp 46–49)
- List the forensic considerations at the scene of a motor vehicle crash. (p 49)
- List the forensic considerations at a scene of abuse or sexual assault. (p 49)

National EMS Education Standard Competencies

Preparatory

Uses simple knowledge of the emergency medical services (EMS) system, the safety and well-being of the emergency medical responder (EMR), and medical/legal issues at the scene of an emergency while awaiting a higher level of care.

Medical/Legal and Ethics

- Consent/refusal of care (pp 43–44)
- Confidentiality (pp 45–46)
- Advance directives (pp 44–45)
- Tort and criminal actions (p 41)
- Evidence preservation (pp 46–49)
- Statutory responsibilities (p 46)
- Mandatory reporting (p 46)
- Ethical principles/moral obligations (pp 40–41)
- End-of-life issues (pp 44–45)

Research

- Impact of research on EMR care (p 40)
- Data collection (pp 46–49)

Documentation

- Recording patient findings (pp 34–38)

Medical Terminology

Uses medical and anatomic terms.

INTRODUCTION

Law enforcement responders (LERs) face the challenge of providing for the safety of the general public as well as enforcing the law. This noble calling can be a great burden due to the challenges of today's society. The law enforcement role must take precedence over the role of rescuer, and this complex relationship requires a detailed understanding of the many ethical and legal considerations that guide today's rescuer.

The biggest fear many responders have is facing the process of litigation or being subpoenaed as a witness. Legal proceedings, in many cases, do not progress rapidly, allowing a significant amount of time to pass after the event in question. Shootings or other serious crimes may lead the LER to document more carefully than usual. However, you should consider all events significant, leading to more thorough documentation. When called to testify in criminal or civil matters, your ability to recollect the details of an incident that occurred months or even years prior must not be left to chance. The appropriate treatment and documentation of all patient care events, regardless of their severity, should alleviate fears of future legal or civil retribution.

This unit describes established ethical and legal principles that LERs must know to act appropriately and professionally within the bounds of the medical profession, including forensic considerations and documentation. Because laws, regulations, and policies differ from jurisdiction to jurisdiction, LERs must familiarize themselves with the local practices within their jurisdiction.

Physician Direction and Oversight

The concept of physician oversight and medical direction is a familiar one to those responsible for conventional prehospital medical care systems. In fact, comprehensive physician involvement has evolved as a fundamental element of modern emergency medical services (EMS) systems. Qualified physician leadership and medical oversight, as in conventional EMS, is similarly an essential component of law enforcement medical programs. Unique qualifications and special responsibilities exist for physician medical directors of law enforcement medical programs. Potentially enhanced provider scope of practice, adjuncts to conventional EMS operating protocols, and integration with existing emergency medical and law enforcement system infrastructure are important areas of potential physician responsibility.

HISTORICAL PERSPECTIVES

In recent years, significant attention and resources have been directed toward the development of medical support for the law enforcement tactical or special weapons and tactics (SWAT) mission, typically referred to as tactical emergency medical support (TEMS). SWAT operations can be high profile and are often sensationalized in both the media and popular entertainment venues. This interest has been further fueled by military combat experience demonstrating the efficacy of finite medical interventions in treating traumatic injuries likely to occur in the tactical environment.

An apparent unintended consequence of the advancements in TEMS is the frequent misconception that all law enforcement medical programs are tactical in nature. Although posing a high risk for traumatic injury, tactical operations and associated medical response represent a very small subset of all law enforcement operations. Increasingly there is recognition that a broad base of LER training and capability at the officer and agent level is a similarly worthwhile, effective, and complementary endeavor.

QUALIFICATIONS AND RESPONSIBILITIES

There are developmental similarities between EMS and law enforcement agency medical programs. The evolution of civilian prehospital EMS has led to the identification of specific attributes desirable in an EMS medical director. Similar qualifications have been described by both the American College of Emergency Physicians (ACEP) and the National Association of EMS Physicians (NAEMSP). Similar fundamental attributes should be expected of physicians providing medical oversight for law enforcement medical programs. Additionally, specific qualifications of physicians working with law enforcement special operations programs have been described.

Most importantly, the law enforcement agency medical director must have specific and real understanding of the central missions of the agency itself. It is the medical director's responsibility to ensure that every feature and component of the law enforcement medical program is aligned and supports these core missions. Additionally, these physicians must be capable of designing and overseeing effective training in preventive, routine, and emergent medical care as would be expected within agency-specific contexts. Finally, the medical director should be proficient in the formulation of operational medical plans and have a working knowledge of agency-specific operations and procedures.

The responsibilities of a law enforcement medical director are immense. In addition to those of conventional EMS medical oversight, the law enforcement environment creates unique considerations at every level. These include but are not limited to system design, LER training and certification, treatment protocols, communications, transport and evacuation, and interaction with local EMS and receiving facilities.

LEVELS AND SCOPE OF RESPONDERS

Conventional EMS typically does not involve significant direct physician field patient care, a potentially costly and relatively limited resource. Similarly, law enforcement medical support is most often rendered by EMS personnel, including emergency medical technicians (EMTs), paramedics, and prehospital nurses. As extenders of physician practice into the out-of-hospital setting, LERs have a fundamental requirement for appropriately licensed physician medical control and oversight.

A central question for every law enforcement medical program concerns the level of responder to be deployed. Law enforcement medical support is typically provided by either experienced basic life support (BLS) or advanced life support (ALS) providers, each approach with its potential merits. BLS providers are typically more plentiful and the requirements for initial and continuous training are less, whereas ALS providers are generally more costly, less prevalent, and more resource intensive to train and maintain proficiencies. Duly designated medical directors may have the authority to train and deploy BLS providers with specific enhanced skill sets required for agency-specific support, including enhanced training and experience with regards to airway management, intravenous access, pharmacologic interventions, and invasive procedures. Generally, if this approach is to be implemented, physician oversight and authority for such expanded provider training and capability applies as long as care is rendered under the guidelines of the specific law enforcement agency (**Figure 1**).

Figure 1 Physician oversight must adhere with the law enforcement agency's guidelines..

Physicians working with law enforcement medical programs may themselves serve as operational providers, if authorized in that role by the agency. Deployments with physician support add significant medical expertise to the field environment, although this is typically a finite and not widely available resource. Nevertheless, the availability of direct medical control—the real-time communication between field provider and physician—is critical for provider efficacy and mission success. Physicians providing this service must be appropriately qualified to do so. Physician providers who are not the agency medical director must generally adhere to the same policies, protocols, and procedures as all other medical providers.

INTEGRATION WITH LAW ENFORCEMENT OPERATIONS

It is important that a law enforcement agency and its chain of command fully support its medical program and physician medical director. A common obstacle can be misplaced concerns of agency leadership over the physician "directing" law enforcement personnel. An effective approach to program leadership is one in which the physician medical director and a law enforcement commander have shared oversight with complementary responsibilities and consensual decision making.

Law enforcement agencies must also maintain realistic and well-delineated roles for their medical programs. This can be a significant issue for larger agencies, particularly at the state and federal levels, that have multiple divisions with varying intrinsic medical functions. These may include drug enforcement, anti-terrorism, search and rescue, air medical, and homeland security missions. Team safety, provider proficiency, and agency liabilities all mandate clear delineation of medical capabilities and expectations. Physician consultation and input are essential in this process.

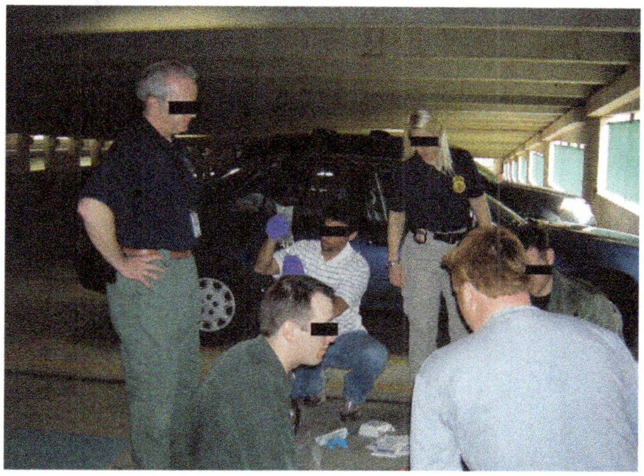

Figure 2 Physicans should be involved in law enforcement medicine training..

PHYSICIAN INVOLVEMENT AND LEADERSHIP IN LAW ENFORCEMENT

As law enforcement medical programs continue to expand in both number and scope, one challenge will be the development and maintenance of qualified physician leadership. Physician involvement in law enforcement remains a relatively rare proposition and unrecognized by established conventional medicine at large. Effective leadership and medical oversight of such programs are highly specialized, and ongoing efforts must be maintained to enhance physician acceptance, experience, and training with respect to law enforcement medicine (**Figure 2**). Physician involvement and medical oversight for law enforcement must be supported as an evolving area of professional practice and expertise.

At the local, state, and federal levels, physicians are playing an ever-increasing role within law enforcement. Historically, many physicians working with law enforcement have been primary care or occupational health providers who have assumed operational medical responsibilities as an ad hoc function, with or without true experience or expertise in this area. There is near universal acceptance today that physicians directing law enforcement medical programs should have strong clinical backgrounds in emergency medicine, trauma, and critical care. A growing number of agencies today have operational physician involvement, either as sworn officers or civilian employees. An extremely effective model has been the acquisition of expert physician services through contractual arrangements. Simple memoranda of understanding have formed the basis of many TEMS programs and remain an important aspect of medical direction services.

FUTURE DIRECTIONS

The integration of emergency medical response capabilities into law enforcement operations is a complex process that requires thoughtful planning and effective physician leadership to ensure successful deployment outcomes. Whether a law enforcement medical program intends to develop robust intrinsic resources for medical support or enlists external support, the fundamental requirement for centralized physician medical direction remains essential.

Physician medical oversight for law enforcement has lacked broad recognition as a distinct area of professional practice and specific guidelines for training, qualifications, and credentialing remain under development. Similarly, essential resources for the appropriate compensation of law enforcement medical directors have historically been either minimal or nonexistent. Rapidly growing evidence for the efficacy and value of LER capabilities will continue to drive the acceptance, integration, and advancement of the law enforcement medical director.

Documentation

Completing a written record of prehospital care is viewed by LERs in different ways, ranging from being something of absolute importance to an afterthought. However, the written record of any patient care is an important part of a patient's chart and **medical record**. This documentation provides a historical record for other care providers to reference. Moreover, it serves as a protection to a LER's reputation and legal standing. This is the best method of legally stating what did or did not occur during an EMS event. The biggest fear many responders have is facing the process of litigation or being subpoenaed as a witness. Legal proceedings, in many cases, do not progress rapidly, allowing for the responder to be involved in numerous EMS incidents after the event in question. Serious events, such as shootings or other serious crimes, may be recognized by the LER as "court worthy," causing him or her to document events more carefully than usual. However, the LER should consider all events as significant, which will lead to more thorough documentation. When called to testify in criminal or civil matters, a responder's ability to recollect the details of an incident that occurred months or even years prior must not be left to chance. The appropriate treatment and documentation of all patient care events, regardless of their severity, should alleviate fears of future legal or civil retribution.

In emergency medicine this document is commonly referred to as a **patient care report (PCR)** and is used to tell other health care providers important information regarding a responder's contact with a patient, including the patient's medical history, the results of the physical examination, the responder's assessment and conclusions relating to the patient's condition, and the care provided. Lawyers and risk managers often suggest that responders document everything. In reality, this is an impossible standard, and such advice is of little help in defining good documentation practices. Rather, good documentation should reflect the relevant observations, impressions, and interventions that affect patient care outcomes.

THE PATIENT CARE REPORT

The medical record, also called a run sheet, should contain the findings that justify the care provided, including pertinent positives and negatives found during the history and physical examination, the impressions of the LER about those findings, and the care provided based on those assessments. Good record keeping is meticulous and should reflect that the LER acted in conformity with his or her protocols and within the standard of care. Most patient encounters are routine, and only basic information is required. Unusual or complex patient encounters that will likely come under scrutiny should prompt more documentation that goes into greater detail.

The PCR provides the primary account of patient presentation and the LER's interaction with the various parties involved at the incident. Information regarding the scene, event, and any information leading up to determining the need for an emergency response should be recorded. This information may be gathered from bystanders, family members, fire department personnel, police officers, or representatives of various government agencies (eg, Office of Aging, Social Services). The PCR should include specific information that identifies the patient, all assessments and interventions provided, and the disposition of the patient. Demographic information is important in ensuring that the patient is positively identified for a financial reimbursement process, if applicable to the agency, and for possible future police, civil, or criminal matters. Important demographic information includes the following:

- Patient's full name
- Date of birth
- Mailing address
- Phone number
- Social Security number

Documentation as it relates to patient care and disposition is an essential component of the PCR because it portrays the event with as much clarity as possible to any outside reader.

States have varying requirements as to how long medical records must be kept; therefore, it is an agency's responsibility to ensure that it is complying with local, state, and federal regulations. Once completed, the PCR may be viewed by a variety of health care professionals, including hospital staff, lawyers, and EMS billing personnel and agencies. Many health care professionals outside EMS use the PCR to monitor a patient's progression of recovery or deterioration. Therefore, the PCR should be easy to read and should provide a detailed description of the events leading up to the call, what was found during the assessment, any and all care provided, and the transfer of care to another health care professional. Nearly all organizations and governing agencies require that a PCR be completed for every patient interaction.

To be used effectively for medical, legal, and administrative purposes, the PCR must contain as much information as possible, providing a thorough reconstruction of the situation presented and all components of the interaction between patient and responder. The EMS document must not be open for interpretation. Therefore, anything that is charted must be clear and concise and not leave any room for doubt or misunderstanding. Medical terms and abbreviations used must be approved and consistent with local protocols. Terms will likely include common prefixes and suffixes (**Table 1**).

An emphasis should be placed on proper spelling, punctuation, and grammar being contained within the PCR. If spellings of the procedures or medications provided for the patient are incorrect, the LER's ability and the quality of care provided may be questioned. Many electronic PCR programs have built-in spelling and grammar checks. If your software does not have this feature, you may wish to use references such as medical dictionaries, which can be found in print or online. If your PCR software permits, you may wish to type your narrative in a document program, such as Microsoft Word, that has the ability to spell-check your writing (**Figure 3**).

Tip

Patient Care and Disposition Considerations

- How did the patient move from his or her original location to the provided transport unit? Did the patient walk, or was he or she assisted in walking or lifted by responders onto an awaiting stretcher?
- What type of transport occurred? Was it emergent, with the use of lights and siren warning devices?
- Where was the patient transported? What factors (and who) made the decision to transport to the documented destination?
- Upon arriving at the receiving destination, where was the patient taken? How did the patient move from the stretcher to the waiting room, bed, or chair? What was the disposition of the patient's personal effects (eg, jewelry)?
- To whom was a verbal care report given, and who assumed patient care?

Consider the following example of a PCR narrative:

Demographics: Patient's Name: Jane Doe, Age: 65, Sex: Female

Subjective:

S—Patient is complaining of a headache for the last 2 hours. Her nose started to bleed 15 minutes ago.

A—No Allergies

M—HCTZ, Trandate, aspirin once a day

P—High blood pressure

L—Ate a meal 4 hours ago

E—Watching TV, talking on phone to daughter

Objective:

Nervous system—Awake, alert, and oriented to person, place, and time. Follows commands. Pupils are equal and respond to light. Moves all extremities. Bleeding from nose stopped. Blood bright red in color.

Skin—Pink, warm, and dry.

Respiratory system—Respirations 18 and good quality. Pulse oximeter—96% on room air, 100% with oxygen. Lung sounds clear in all fields.

Cardiovascular system—Pulse 88, strong and regular, blood pressure 190/106, pulses strong in all extremities

Gastrointestinal/urinary system—Abdomen soft, nontender, no complaints or problems.

Assessment:

Patient presents with high blood pressure with nose bleed and headache.

Plan:

Assess patient, control bleeding, place patient on oxygen 10 liters nonrebreathing mask, give handoff report to paramedic unit 39.

Assessment Findings

All patients should undergo a thorough patient assessment, which includes a general assessment of the entire body and a focused assessment on the area causing the EMS response (discussed further in the patient assessment and examination unit). Because assessment is a major component in providing excellent patient care, it must be thorough, and its documentation must correlate to the findings. A systematic full-body assessment will often prevent omitting objective details relating to the EMS event. The assessment should follow an orderly progression, which is discussed in detail in the unit on patient assessment. **Figure 4** provides a brief outline of the patient assessment process.

Table 1

Common Medical Prefixes and Suffixes	
a-, an-	Without
-algia	Pain
arterio-	Relating to an artery
brady-	Slow
cardio-	Heart
hem-, hema-, hemo-	Blood
hyper-	Above, excessive, or beyond
hypo-	Below, underneath, or deficient
-itis	Inflammation
naso-	Denoting the nose
neuro-	Denoting nerve, nervous system, or nervous tissue
oro-	Denoting the mouth
poly-	Many
retro-	Backward or behind
sub-	Under, moderately
supra-	Above
tachy-	Rapid or swift
therm-	Relating to quantities of heat
trans-	Across
vaso-	Vessel, as in blood vessel

LERs should follow any guidelines for assessment documentation set forth by their organizations and nationally recognized educational training centers. Some agencies have specific formats for narrative portions of the PCR. Some specific methods of documentation include the CHART and SOAP note formats (Table 2). Regardless of which format is used for PCR documentation, writing must be clear and concise and must follow the progression of patient care.

Figure 3 Many LER courses require students to fill out patient care reports as part of the operational training.

Tip

State Documentation Guidelines

Some states have strict guidelines as to how patient care should be documented. Likewise, organizations may have documentation policies to which providers must adhere. These requirements make documentation a standard of care, and failure to perform this function properly can be considered negligent. LERs should check their state and local guidelines.

Continuation of Care

Patient care is a continuous process that involves many players, not just EMS providers. As a result, PCR documentation of interventions performed in the field is very important for the continuation of patient care. If, for example, a medication is provided for pain control, it is important for subsequent health care professionals to know which medication was given, the dose, the route of administration, the time of administration, and the effect the medication had on the patient. This information assists in evaluating medical conditions during the physical examination, in preventing potential overdosing of medications, and in preventing any type of adverse medication reaction. A process of care that is not continuous will place a patient at a higher risk of complications resulting from the health care professionals' actions or inactions.

Documentation of Times

Anything that has an effect on patient care should be carefully and thoroughly documented. Of special consideration

Scene Size-up

- Ensure scene safety
- Determine mechanism of injury/nature of illness
- Take standard precautions
- Determine number of patients
- Consider additional resources

Primary Assessment

- Form a general impression
- Assess level of responsiveness
- Perform a rapid scan
  - Assess the airway
  - Assess breathing
  - Assess circulation
- Update responding EMS units

History Taking

- Investigate the chief complaint (SAMPLE history)

Secondary Assessment

- Systematically assess the patient
  - Full-body assessment and/or focused assessment
- Assess vital signs

Reassessment

- Repeat the primary assessment
- Reassess vital signs
- Reassess the chief complaint
- Recheck the effectiveness of the treatment
- Identify and treat changes in the patient's condition
- Reassess patient
  - Unstable patients every 5 minutes
  - Stable patients every 15 minutes
- Provide a hand-off report

Figure 4 Patient assessment process.

Table 2

CHART and SOAP Documentation

CHART		
C	Chief complaint	The reason for the response
H	History	Subjective information (SAMPLE/OPQRST)
A	Assessment findings	Orderly assessment from head to toe
R	Rx (treatment administered)	Interventions listed in the order in which they were administered Some documentation programs use a flowchart for interventions; if using a narrative as well, make sure that all information matches and does not contradict itself
T	Transport events	How the patient was transported (emergent/nonemergent) Delays in transport Deviations from original/planned destination Transfer of care and belongings
SOAP		
S	Subjective information	Chief complaint SAMPLE/OPQRST Statements from patient, family, bystanders, and others involved at scene
O	Objective information	Physical examination Observations of the scene by documenting responder
A	Assessment	Field impression or differential diagnosis formed by the responder Which protocol/treatment regimen the responder plans on following
P	Plan of care	Document with detailed treatments/interventions provided Treatments/interventions should be listed in the order in which they were performed Document follow-up assessments and evaluations for efficacy of treatment Conclude with patient disposition, and transfer of care and personal effects

are scene times, nationally recognized standards that recommend response times to the emergency, on-scene times, and times to get the patient to definitive care. For example, a LER arrives at the scene of a motor vehicle crash where the victim is entrapped. National trauma organizations and training recommend a 10-minute scene time for these types of patients. If extrication and subsequent packaging of the patient takes 40 minutes, there needs to be an accounting for this delay. Although such accounting does not indicate fault by the responder, it is important to eliminate any questions regarding standards of care. It is necessary to record all related times of the response, which are used by EMS administrators and quality assurance personnel to measure performance. Many EMS agencies participate in localized or widespread studies of various prehospital interventions. Researchers must have accurate timelines for the delivery of care to interpret and deliver quality data and findings. The most common EMS incident times include the following:

- **Time of dispatch to response.** Many jurisdictions and agencies have a standard time by which a dispatched unit must be responding. If there is a deviation from the standard response time, this should be recorded and explained.
- **Time of response to the scene.** There are varying standards for how long it should take the dispatched unit to arrive at the incident. The National Fire Protection Association (NFPA) standard NFPA 1710, *Standard for the Organization and Deployment of Fire Suppression Operations, Emergency Medical Operations, and Special Operations to the Public by Career Fire Departments*, recommends that an EMR or higher-level unit arrive at an emergency within 4 minutes at least 90% of the time. Many factors can affect the response to scene time, such as traffic conditions, weather, or other unforeseen occurrences.
- **Time of initial patient contact.** It may be easy to assume that as soon as the dispatched unit arrives on the scene, contact is made with the patient. However, this is not the case all of the time. For example, if unit X is dispatched to a five-story assisted living nursing facility with over 400 units, it may take several minutes to arrive at the patient's side.
- **On-scene time.** On-scene times that extend beyond the nationally recommended standards for medical and trauma on-scene times should be documented because they may have an effect on patient care and outcome.
- **Transport time.** Transport time is the amount of time from when the unit departs the scene to when it arrives at the destination facility. In many cases, this is a rather routine factor of time. In some instances, it can be affected by weather, traffic, and other occurrences.
- **Transfer time.** This is the time at which care was transferred from the responder to another health care professional. Many EMS systems face the problem of having to wait inside an emergency department for long periods because of overcrowding before patient care is transferred. Patient care does not end once the patient enters the emergency department doors. It is therefore important to continue the documentation of all care and assessments provided while waiting to transfer the patient to a higher-trained provider (**Figure 5**).

FUNCTIONS OF THE PATIENT CARE REPORT

Legal Functions

LERs should be aware of the legal ramifications of the PCR and how the PCR can be used as an official rendering of patient care in different types of legal proceedings. You may be called to crime scenes involving personal injury, child or elder abuse, or dangerous living situations. Intricate details of the scene size-up and assessment must be included in all documentation because these details may be used in future criminal legal actions. When a responder is involved with a patient at a potential or identified crime scene, it is important to include the following information in the PCR:

- How did the scene appear upon your arrival? For example, was the residence or location messy or tidy?
- Where did you find the patient? What was his or her position when you arrived?
- If anyone else was present at the scene, where were they located?
- Was clothing removed from the patient? If so, what?
- Identify all visible markings on the patient.
- Were any objects in the crime scene moved? Where was the patient found initially?
- Record any and all statements relating to the situation at hand provided by outside parties in quotation marks.

Center for Law Enforcement Medicine Johns Hopkins University
CONFIDENTAL: PROTECTED HEALTH INFORMATION
PATIENT CARE REPORT

Reset Form
Print Form

General Incident Information

Incident # | Incident City | Incident State | Incident Date | # of Patients
Less Lethal | Incident Time | Time Pt. Contacted | Time Released / Evac | Physician Consult
Incident Type | Call Type | Patient Disposition | Consult Physician
Transporting Agency | Destination Facility | Weather | Air Temp °f

Patient Demographics

Last Name | First Name | M. Initial | Age | Date of Birth
Address | Other ID# | Phone Number
City | State | Zip Code | Allergies | Pt Weight ◯ Lbs ◯ Kg

Medical Information

Chief Complaint | Triage | Patient Type
History of Present Illness
Past Medical Hx | Medications

Physical Exam

General
HEENT
Pupils
Neck
Chest
Back
Abdomen
Extremities
Neurologic
☐ Cardiac Arrest ☐ Severe Bleeding ☐ Body Armor Worn?

Vital Signs

Initial HR | RR | SBP / DBP | SPO2 % on | Pain#
Final HR | RR | SBP / DBP | SPO2 % on | Pain#
Temp f | GCS | % BSA | Blood Sugar m/dl | IV Fluid Infused mls

Interventions

1st IV Access | 1st IV Location | 1st IV Gauge
2nd IV Access | 2nd IV Location | 2nd IV Gage
Intervention 1 | Medication 1
Intervention 2 | Medication 2
Intervention 3 | Medication 3
☐ Tourniquet Applied | Total Tourniquet Time | ☐ Pt. Defibrillated

Additional Information / Narrative / Progress Note

Provider Name | Provider ID# | Provider Level | Date Submitted

Figure 5 This form is an example of a standardized medical report used by LERs.

PCRs may also be used in civil cases, especially in cases involving negligence or medical malpractice (in the event of a negative patient outcome). For example, if an ambulance becomes lost or is diverted from its intended facility, resulting in a negative outcome for a patient, the transport time contained in the PCR may be used in civil cases against responders and organizations. As a result of this potential liability, the PCR should account for any prolonged periods of time that deviate from the standard practice.

Administrative Functions

The responder's PCR contains multiple pieces of information that can be used for administrative purposes. EMS agency and system managers review response times to ensure that there are an adequate number of appropriate, staffed units available for emergencies. These numbers can be used to justify annual budgets and to request increases in staffing to serve the population effectively. Based on statistics gathered from EMS reports, some organizations use system status management to ensure the availability of an appropriate number of resources in certain areas at peak periods of call volume.

EMS documentation plays a major role in the quality assurance and quality improvement process. Quality assurance and improvement work to improve the existing structure of an EMS system and readily identify needs or performance deficiencies. EMS managers can review existing PCRs to determine which procedures are effective and which are not. System administrators and medical directors use quantitative and qualitative data from documentation in the pursuit of approving or denying potential interventions and medications.

The information obtained from this data collection can also be used in a broader spectrum, such as studies to promote evidence-based medicine in EMS. An example of this is the use of tourniquets by EMS providers. Previously considered dangerous because of loss of blood flow to the limb, research has shown that tourniquets provide better outcomes when used early on for uncontrolled bleeding. A 4-year study in the military prehospital setting showed that the early application of tourniquets that remained in place for up to 305 minutes had no noticeable untoward effects. Studies such as this, with repeated proven results, change the way prehospital care is delivered.

EMS billing agencies have access to the responder's documentation. Information collected and documented by the responder is used to determine billing rates for any care provided to the patient. Many insurance companies and government-funded payers such as Medicare and Medicaid have strict requirements for what is documented in the PCR. It is imperative that the responder document as many demographic items about the patient as possible, along with all assessments and treatments provided, in order to receive the highest level of payment possible.

Ethical and Legal Considerations

ETHICS

LERs are bound by ethical and legal duties to provide care. **Ethics** are the standards that societies, organizations, and professions establish to define expectations for members of that group. They broadly define right from wrong and create expectations of appropriate behavior. Laws, regulations, and policies are used to define ethical behavior more clearly and to impose sanctions for wrongful actions. **Applied ethics** is the use of these ethical values. All persons are governed by their own **morals**, that is, their personal sense of right and wrong. LERs need to internalize the ethical guidelines established by their professional group and use them as the foundation for making decisions relative to integrity. Common decision-making models promote the foundations of doing no harm to the patient, acting in good faith, and performing your duties in the patient's best interest.

LERs should work to maintain the trust of those they serve. Providing impartial aid, honest answers, and professional conduct leads to public acceptance. Examples of general unethical behavior include falsifying documentation, lying or misrepresenting information to patients or coworkers, routinely arriving late to assignments, and avoiding duties and responsibilities that impose additional demands on coworkers. A LER is held in high esteem by the public. Poor ethical or moral actions will tear down that trust and erode public support.

LEGAL CONCEPTS

Working with the public during a crisis can lead to making life-changing decisions. To ensure that all members of the public receive similar care, governments will often develop rules that provide some guidance to responders. Many of these legal concepts are legislated at a state level. **Statutory regulations** are the rules approved by a legislative body. Many of these rules identify the statutory responsibilities as they apply to the responder. Other statutes define specific reporting requirements or actions that must be followed to ensure that the public receives proper care as determined by the legislative body.

A **civil complaint** occurs when a person or group feels that they have not been treated in accordance with a statute. The person or group making a complaint in a civil case is the **plaintiff**. Civil complaints attempt to seek financial damages from the rescuer. This type of legal action is filed to make an argument to a judiciary body that a person or group with statutory responsibilities did not follow the prescribed methods of the statute during a particular incident. The **defendant** is the person or group against whom the complaint is filed. A civil complaint that results in personal injury is often referred to as a **tort**. A negligent act that results in personal injury is an example of a tort.

Some errors result in criminal complaints. The plaintiff in a **criminal complaint** is the government body that maintains oversight of the statute. The defendant is the person or group with statutory responsibilities. Criminal cases occur when the statutes prescribe that error in application of the statute or defiance of the statute should result in the arrest of the alleged offending parties until an argument is made in front of a judiciary body. The judiciary body in a criminal case determines the guilt or innocence of the defendant. If the defendant is found guilty, the judiciary body can assign punishment in the form of damages, fines, or imprisonment.

The LER should identify agency, local, state, and federal rules relative to the following topics:

- Duty to act
- Standard of care
- Negligence
- Abandonment
- Good Samaritan laws
- Consent
- Patient care refusals
- Health Insurance Portability and Accountability Act (HIPAA) of 1996
- Advance directives

DUTY TO ACT

A **duty to act** arises when a responder becomes responsible to the public for rendering aid during a medical emergency. This duty to act is an implied social contract between the person rendering aid and others in society. Police officers, fire fighters, and EMS personnel generally have a duty to provide care because their job includes the provision of emergency medical care within the community (**Figure 6**). When called to assist someone needing medical care, emergency responders are expected to act in a manner consistent with the standard of care. LERs should clarify their agencies' and states' stance relative to their assignment. In some cases, the duty to act may conflict with protection, surveillance, or other law enforcement duties.

Emergency medical responder (EMR) certifications and licenses are routinely governed by state and local laws. Emergency medicine statutes may identify mandatory training content, testing requirements, patient care standards, and

Figure 6 Police officers, fire fighters, and emergency medical personnel generally have a duty to provide care because their job includes the provision of emergency medical care within the community.

medical control responsibilities. The **scope of practice** is often a state or local statute that defines the range of responsibility (eg, types of patients or caseload) and practice guidelines that determine the boundaries within which a health care provider or other professional practices.

The **standard of care** defines the legal obligation of the duty to act within the limits of a practitioner's training, scope of practice, and equipment. It requires a medical provider to render quality care consistent with the level of medical knowledge and practical skill that a minimally competent provider would possess and the medical judgment to render care that is reasonable under the circumstances. Through training and certification programs such as those developed by the US Department of Transportation and the National Registry of Emergency Medical Technicians, EMRs become eligible to provide medical care within their state or jurisdiction through licensing or state certification. The medical provider must also be adept at using equipment and selecting available treatment options. The standard of care for EMRs is defined locally by jurisdictional EMS systems and nationally by organizations such as the National Association of Emergency Medical Technicians. The scope of practice for EMRs is defined by state regulations, which generally limit medical practice to those who are deemed competent to perform it. Providing health care service outside the scope of any license or certification exposes the practitioner to disciplinary or legal sanctions or both.

NEGLIGENCE

A common theme in dictionary definitions of negligence is the failure to provide the level of care that a law requires for a person, resulting in the person being injuriously affected by the lack of prescribed care. **Technical negligence** occurs when a health care provider acts below the standard of care. Even the most competent health care providers periodically make mistakes or act in ways that arguably fall below the standard of care. However, such acts do not normally rise to the level of legal negligence.

Medical negligence (medical malpractice) arises when a person is injured and becomes entitled to monetary compensation because of the negligent actions of a health care provider. For the plaintiff in a medical negligence complaint to receive compensation, he or she must file a civil complaint and prove that **legal negligence** occurred. An emergency responder is legally negligent when he or she fails to use the degree of care and skill that a reasonably competent responder trained to the same level would use in similar circumstances.

Legal negligence requires four elements to be proved in court:

1. The person claiming negligence must have suffered an injury or harm.
2. The care provider must have had a duty to act.
3. The provider must have acted in a manner that falls below the standard of care (a negligent act or a breach of duty).
4. The actions of the provider must have been a substantial factor in causing the injury or harm. Causation must be established.

Gross negligence is a conscious, careless, and reckless disregard for the safety or lives of others. It is more than an unintended or careless error; it represents a voluntary disregard of the need to use reasonable care. Acts of gross negligence are likely to cause foreseeable grave injury or harm to persons, property, or both. These acts may incur both civil and criminal prosecution. An example of gross negligence would be knowingly withholding a prescribed and available patient care item, with the intent of depriving the patient.

Abandonment is a type of negligence that arises when an emergency responder with a duty to provide care prematurely terminates the care and the termination of care results in harm. Once a responder incurs a duty to provide care, he or she is obligated to continue care until the duty is terminated by mutual consent, a competent patient explicitly refuses further care, or care is transferred to another responder with the appropriate skill and competence. Once care is initiated, responders are obligated to exercise reasonable care within their responder's scope of practice until care is transferred to another appropriate provider as directed by the responder's EMS protocols.

GOOD SAMARITAN LAWS

Within common law, a private citizen does not have a duty to rescue or provide care to another person in distress. To encourage medical practitioners to render assistance to those in need of medical care, nearly all states and the District of Columbia have enacted **Good Samaritan statutes**. LERs should make an effort to determine what their jurisdiction dictates relative to Good Samaritan laws. There are wide variations among these laws, but their goal is to shield people without a legal duty to act from civil liability that may arise because of injuries resulting from the care provided. Good Samaritan statutes generally protect responders acting within the scope of their license or training, except for acts of gross negligence.

CONSENT

The ethical principles relating to the provision of care are as follows, in order of priority:

- Autonomy
- Beneficence
- Nonmalfeasance
- Social welfare

The importance of individual **autonomy** was highlighted in 1914 by Supreme Court Justice Benjamin Cardozo when he stated: "Every human being of adult years and sound mind has the right to determine what shall be done with his own body."

Beneficence defines an obligation to act in a helpful or therapeutic manner.

Nonmalfeasance defines an obligation to act in ways that do not cause harm. The principle of social welfare recognizes circumstances in which the right of society takes precedence over the autonomy of an individual. (For example, persons may not yell "Fire!" in a crowded theater or disobey traffic laws without penalty because doing so would place others at risk.)

Consent refers to the patient providing approval or permission for the LER to touch him or her and provide care. Prior to rendering care, LERs have an obligation to obtain consent from patients. Failure to secure consent could lead to charges of assault or battery. **Expressed consent** is the act of the patient communicating to the responder verbally or nonverbally that he or she is willing to let the responder touch or care for him or her. Expressed consent may be identified in literature as actual or informed consent. To allow for **informed consent**, the patient must be given enough information to make an informed choice. The responder should tell the patient the condition needing treatment, the treatment proposed, alternative treatments (including no treatment), and the risks associated with the treatment that a reasonable person would want to know when making an informed choice.

Negligence rarely arises from failing to obtain proper consent but can occur if omitted information would have resulted in a reasonable person refusing consent. Within the context of an emergency medical response, such conditions would be rare. Conversely, allowing a patient to refuse care without providing him with information that would likely cause a reasonable person to consent represents a common source of negiligence.

Tip
Conditions Necessary for Informed Consent

- The patient must be an adult at the age of majority for the jurisdiction where the incident occurs.
- Patients under the age of majority may provide informed consent if they have served in the United States military, are parents to a child, or are otherwise emancipated from their parents. This can vary from state to state.
- The patient must be awake and able to understand the communications relative to the granting of consent.

Exceptions to the rule of informed consent are emergencies and incapacity. Consent is not required in an emergency in which a delay in care would cause harm and consent cannot be provided as a result of a patient's lack of capacity to make an informed decision. Legally, an emergency does not necessarily mean that someone called 911 and EMS responded to the scene. A legal emergency occurs when an exigent circumstance occurs and a reasonable person would believe that prompt action was necessary to prevent physical harm. This is an example of implied consent. **Implied consent** occurs when a responder initiates care and the patient fails to resist. Patients who become unable to make an informed choice as a result of illness, injury, or intoxication are presumed to have consented to the care that a reasonable person would want under similar circumstances.

Patients are deemed to be lacking the ability to make an informed choice (and therefore cannot provide consent) when they are without the mental capacity and maturity to understand their medical condition or are unable to evaluate the relative risks and benefits of their medical condition and the proposed treatment. To protect patients' ethical and legal rights to their autonomy, the legal presumption is that all adults beyond the age of majority are competent to make their own decisions, including decisions that are against their interests. This presumption continues until a patient is deemed incompetent by a court or is determined to lack the capacity to make an informed choice by a physician.

Children below the age of majority are considered incompetent to provide informed consent as a matter of law. This status does not mean that providers should withhold care until a parent or guardian is located and consent is obtained. In cases of emergency, in which a delay in providing care would result in harm, LERs should provide the essential care necessary to prevent the harm (**Figure 7**). If a delay in treatment would not cause harm, then treatment should be postponed until informed consent is obtained from a parent or guardian.

Depending on the complexity of the decision and the consequences that it carries, mentally impaired adults (such as those with mental illness, drug intoxication, acute illness or injury, and elderly patients with dementia) may be incompetent to make some decisions. In some cases, however, the degree of capacity to make decisions may change during the day or during the course of care. A low level of mental capacity is generally required to agree to a treatment option that people in similar circumstances would want. In contrast, a high degree of mental capacity is required to refuse treatment in a situation where most reasonable people would give consent. The rules regarding caring for patients lacking capacity are generally the same as those used to care for children.

LERs should always attempt to obtain informed consent, either expressed or implied, before rendering care. When such consent is impossible to obtain, however, responders can forego consent and provide care in emergency situations when a delay would cause harm or when a patient appears to lack the capacity to make an informed decision and is acting in a manner contrary to that of a reasonable person in similar circumstances.

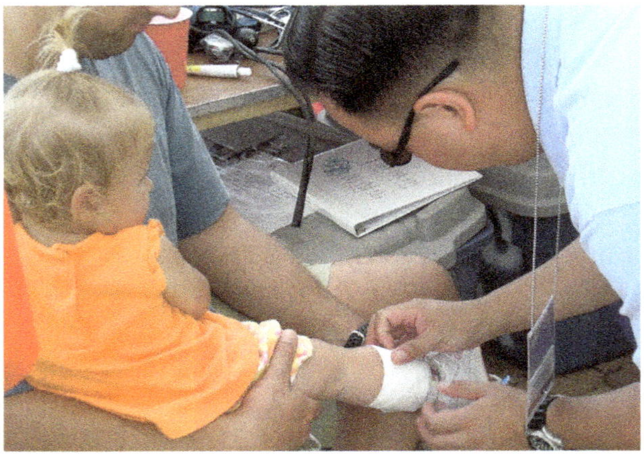

Figure 7 If delaying treatment would cause further harm to a child, begin treatment even without a parent's consent.

PATIENT REFUSAL

All responders will encounter patients who refuse care for their illness or injury. These patients often represent one of the most difficult ethical and legal challenges for responders. Patients have a right to make their own decisions regarding their health, including the refusal of care. However, refusing care places patients at risk for further harm, and they must demonstrate decision-making capacity before they can legally refuse care.

For a patient to legally refuse care, the responder must first provide the patient with enough information to make an informed choice. This requires the responder to inform the patient of his or her condition, what treatment is necessary, why it is needed, the risks of refusing care, and alternative treatment options (including no treatment). Asking a patient to sign a refusal of treatment form alone is insufficient to relieve a responder of the duty to provide care. LERs should clearly review the impact of refusal of care, clearly state what is being offered and refused, and document this effort with witness signatures. In many jurisdictions, statutes and protocols exist that explicitly spell out the steps necessary to obtain a patient care refusal. This may include reminding the patient that he or she should call EMS if the patient changes his or her mind, and notifying medical direction of the refusal. If at any time after the LER received the refusal, the patient's condition deteriorates or the patient changes his or her mind and wants assistance, the responder should immediately act to provide emergency care.

Mentally impaired patients may not refuse care if doing so would place that person at risk for greater illness or injury, resulting in the need for further care. In circumstances in which there is no emergency but a patient is in need of acute care and appears impaired, responders may need to seek assistance from the police to place the patient in protective custody before providing care or transferring the patient to a hospital for further evaluation. You will need to know your jurisdiction's stance on protective custody when caring for patients who present with mental impairment.

ADVANCE DIRECTIVES

Advance directives are legal documents intended to provide guidance to family members, friends, and care providers on how to make medical choices on a patient's behalf in the event of decisional or communicating incapacity. An advance health care directive, or living will, is a binding legal document made by a competent person intending to direct his or her medical treatment in advance of future incapacity. Alternatively, a **durable power of attorney** for health care appoints another person to act as the patient's health care decision maker in the event of future incapacity. Most advance directives are made in writing, but some states permit the creation of advance directives orally by making the directives known to the treating physician. LERs will need to review their jurisdiction's statutes regarding advance directives and durable powers of attorney. In some cases you will need to interact with surrogate decision makers. Such persons may be referred to as health care agents or health care proxies. They may or may not be a relative of the patient. If the documentation does not prescribe a surrogate decision maker, most states will revert to the next of kin for health care guidance.

Patients have legal and ethical rights to refuse medical care, even in the prehospital setting. When EMS units respond to assist someone in a terminal or end-stage condition, it is often difficult for responders to identify patients with advance directives that instruct responders to withhold resuscitative care. In response to this difficulty, many states have enacted "out of hospital" Do Not Resuscitate laws that create a prehospital Do Not Attempt Resuscitation (DNAR) form and, in some states, an identifying bracelet. These provisions help responders rapidly identify patients for whom resuscitation is not warranted. If a patient has a valid prehospital DNAR form or a wrist bracelet, or both, LERs should not initiate resuscitation unless there is evidence to suggest that the DNAR form was revoked, the patient is conscious and requests resuscitation, or a physician directs the responder to disregard the DNAR order. The LER should consider disregarding a DNAR order in the unusual situation in which a patient is unresponsive, a family member requests that resuscitation be initiated, and failing to do so would result in a confrontation with the family member. In this case, implementing the DNAR order can be deferred until the patient arrives at the hospital and the patient's resuscitation status can be determined. Although a DNAR order instructs the withholding of resuscitative care, LERs are still obligated to provide care that will give comfort and minimize suffering.

CONFIDENTIALITY

Responding to emergencies places the LER in the unique position of seeing, hearing, observing, and handling information that is private to the patient or to his or her family. Whenever handling patient information, the LER should protect access to this information from anyone other than parties directly involved in the patient's care who have a right to access the information. The circumstances of the emergency, patient history, assessment, and care given should be disclosed only to the next level of medical care. Reports and documents should be protected and filed as indicated in your agency's policies.

Health Insurance Portability and Accountability Act

The Fourth Amendment to the Constitution provides United States citizens the "right to be secure in their persons, houses, papers, and effects, against unreasonable searches and seizures." In an effort to protect the privacy rights of patients, in 1996 Congress passed the **Health Insurance Portability and Accountability Act (HIPAA)**. The law was intended to establish standards to make the electronic transmission of health information easier and to create procedures to protect the privacy of patients' health information. In addition to HIPAA, many states have passed their own laws further protecting the privacy rights of patients and their medical records.

The portion of HIPAA that affects all health care providers today is the **Privacy Rule**. The Privacy Rule defines protected health information (PHI) as any health information that can identify a person. PHI includes the following information:

- Oral or recorded information
- Information on any past, present, and future physical or mental condition
- All health care treatment
- Past, present, or future payment for health care
- Names, address, date of birth, and Social Security number

Under HIPAA, EMS systems are required to have in place security standards that include administrative procedures to establish and enforce security policies, and physical and technical safeguards to protect computer systems and access to PHI. HIPAA imposes civil monetary and criminal penalties for the following infractions:

- Knowingly disclosing PHI
- Disclosing information under false pretenses
- Disclosing information with the intent to sell, transfer, or use for commercial advantage, personal gain, or malicious harm

In the course of providing care, LERs encounter PHI and are both ethically and legally bound to protect patients' rights to privacy. Your jurisdiction should have a manual and a privacy officer to guide you relative to the limits placed on you and your jurisdiction by HIPAA. To protect a patient's privacy rights, do not disclose PHI to persons not directly involved with the patient's care without the patient's permission. Special situations in which other parties may receive PHI include mandatory reporting, public health, and certain legal situations. Follow your agency's administrative policies regarding the handling of records.

STATUTORY RESPONSIBILITIES AND MANDATORY REPORTING

All medical care providers operate under guidelines established in law, defined in regulations, and implemented through jurisdictional policies and protocols. Because of the wide range of statutes governing medical practice, LERs must fully comply with their jurisdictions' requirements on reporting of statutory information. All information reported must be clear and objective. Failure to report information or attempts to withhold or report incorrect information can result in a criminal complaint leading to damages, fines, and imprisonment.

A LER operating under a state license or certification is obligated to comply with the federal, state, and local laws and regulations and adhere to the policies of his or her agency. Although there is a general intent to protect the privacy of a patient and a patient's medical records, sometimes the safety of the public outweighs the privacy interests of the patient, and a responder is required to report medical conditions or injuries to law enforcement or health department authorities. Examples of conditions that require public reporting include knife wounds, gunshot wounds, motor vehicle crashes with injuries, suspected abuse of vulnerable adults and children, domestic violence, rape, and dog bites. Reportable infectious diseases include suspected cases of anthrax, botulism, rabies, and tuberculosis. Most reporting is done by hospitals and medical clinics, but LERs must become familiar with their statutory obligations for reporting medical conditions.

Forensics

All responders should have a basic knowledge of forensic considerations, including evidence preservation and mandatory reporting. This is particularly true for LERs. Forensics and crime scene investigation are law enforcement specialties; crime scene management as well as the numerous subcategories related to the study and application of forensics requires significant training to master. LERs, whether sworn law enforcement officers or security elements, must at all times strictly adhere to agency protocols specific to crime or death scenes. Response and approach to any scene must be performed in a safe, systematic fashion every time without exception. Adhering to this practice at all times improves investigative outcomes and minimizes the loss of potentially valuable evidence.

Successful outcomes of cases involving forensics are directly related to the responder's approach to documentation, incident management, fire suppression, rescue, and hazardous material response. It is therefore important to establish a thorough understanding and develop good practice habits in these areas.

CRIME SCENE AND EVIDENCE PRESERVATION

There are times when the scene of a medical emergency is also a crime scene. If the scene is unsafe, the responder must take steps to avoid becoming a casualty by weighing the need to provide care against the risk of personal injury. With an unsafe scene, the responder should perform a remote assessment from a position of relative safety to determine potential risks of harm and then attempt to determine the extent of a patient's injuries. Patients who are mortally wounded and those with minor injuries do not require immediate treatment. In circumstances in which the risk of harm to the responder is too great to provide care, attempt to have patients moved to an area of safety or instruct the patients on how to care for themselves until the scene is safe.

In the case of crime scenes involving multiple casualties that include police officers and offenders, ethical dilemmas can arise regarding who gets treated first. All injured persons are entitled to receive care under existing rules for triage. However, applying rules derived from the Geneva Convention, police officers are entitled to the right of first assessment because they are armed, trained to defend themselves using their weapons, and when injured may become a threat to themselves or others if their injuries impair their perceptions and judgments. If a police officer's injuries result in an altered level of consciousness or judgment, as might occur as a result of shock or head trauma, for example, then the officer should be disarmed immediately prior to rendering care. You should follow your agency's policies relative to disarming an injured officer or agent.

Your first obligation is to care for the patient; preservation of the crime scene and any evidence is secondary. When providing care at a crime scene, the LER should make reasonable efforts to avoid disturbing the scene or destroying possible evidence (**Figure 8**). Anything removed from the patient or the scene should be secured, and a responsible party should establish a chain of custody record. LERs should meticulously document what they observe and note anything that was moved or contaminated while providing care.

The term **forensics** is defined as belonging to, used in, or suitable to courts of judicature or to public discussion and debate. Simply put, forensics can be defined as *pertaining to the law*. Using this definition alone, virtually any emergency scene may have the potential to evolve into a case of litigation. Whether a case is identified immediately or delayed, and whether it is criminal or civil, the LER's actions, observations, and subsequent documentation are vital. Early actions and observations are crucial both in terms of providing immediate care to the potentially injured and in terms of gathering and preserving evidence that may eventually be presented in the court of law. It is the LER who sees the scene in its original state and who is often the first person to make the crucial observation that identifies a crime scene and begins the preservation of vital forensic evidence.

Figure 8 When providing care at a crime scene, make reasonable efforts to avoid disturbing the scene or destroying possible evidence.

Regardless of the scene (indoors, outdoors, motor vehicle crash, assault, or unknown injury), the LER should maintain safety of self and others while locating potentially injured victims. Although the first priority is always to render immediate care to obviously injured persons rather than to collect or preserve evidence, the LER should always seek to protect evidence and scene integrity to the best extent possible. Once the LER determines that a serious crime or life-threatening injury has occurred, additional resources should be requested to further assist with medical care of injured persons, scene management, and evidence preservation.

The LER may either remain at a scene to assist further or may be replaced by specialized units. It is not the role of the LER to act as the scene forensic investigator or crime scene technician. You should not provide "expert" opinion or analysis of the scene; expert opinions should be left to the experts.

Victim Location

When a call is dispatched, vital data collection begins immediately and may give clues as to the location of the victim. Note and document the position of injured persons and of objects in the vicinity. Note the victim's appearance and clothing and whether they are appropriate to the scene (season, time of day, etc). If clothing must be cut to render care, avoid cutting through knife tears or bullet punctures in clothes. Observe and document clothing; collect obvious debris that may be lost in transport. If clothing is removed, place individual items in brown paper bags. Observe positioning of pockets and note whether pocket position has been altered (eg, turned out by emergency personnel or as a potential indication of criminal activity) (**Figure 9**).

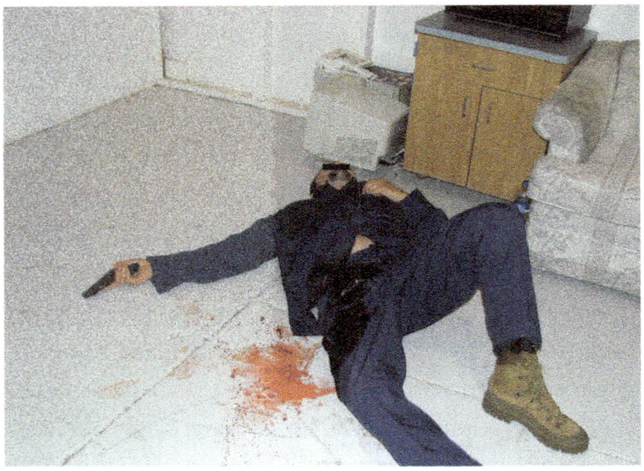

Figure 9 When confronted with a crime scene, LERs must act to save lives as well as consider the needs of protecting the crime scene. Note specific details such as patient position, weapons, and clothing.

If you see potential evidence, document it. Take care to protect and not disturb objects. If weather conditions pose a threat, consider the possibility of covering objects to avoid losing valuable evidence. If objects have been moved to render care, document their original position; do not reposition objects once moved. Responders should take care not to discard medical waste within the scene. Observe the scene for indications of a secondary crime scene.

Note whether the residence is secured and how entry was gained by the LER. Document the position of lights, whether the TV is on or off, whether the windows are open or closed, whether the heat or air conditioning is in use, and so forth. Emergency personnel should not turn on lights, open windows, or turn on heat or air conditioning. Do not use phones or bathrooms at the location or residence.

Note and maintain the scene's entry and exit points, avoiding unnecessary foot traffic. Escort arriving personnel to the victim using the same path. Attempts must be made to minimize responder impact on the scene. Set up a large perimeter. Note any persons or animals at the scene. Establish an entry log and post an officer to maintain a log of all persons entering the area.

Determining Death

When a victim is declared dead, the LER may not be responsible for the subsequent investigation process; however, having an understanding of the necessary information assists in a complete and thorough death investigation. Follow agency protocols regarding declaring persons deceased. A sworn law enforcement officer may be the first person to note obvious signs that death has occurred; however, specific agency policy may preclude the victim from being officially declared deceased. Arriving EMS personnel must therefore officially declare or pronounce the victim as deceased. It is this time that will be recorded as the official time of death. Documentation should include the time the victim was officially pronounced dead and who officially pronounced the victim (name, agency ID number, and contact phone numbers). Determine need and request additional appropriate resources such as crime lab, homicide, and so on. Once the scene is declared safe and jurisdiction of the deceased has been established, notify the medical examiner. The victim, any personal effects, and associated weapons or objects on or near the body (unless posing imminent safety threats) should not be disturbed before arrival of the medical examiner. Identification of the victim should be established. Document how the victim is identified (eg, photo ID or visually by persons present at the scene).

If the victim is unknown, fingerprinting should not take place until the medical examiner has arrived and provided authorization. Fingerprinting performed on scene should take into consideration potential disruption of possible trace evidence that may be present on the fingers or hands. If there is any question regarding potential trace evidence on the hands, the hands should be placed in individual brown paper bags by appropriately trained persons. Subsequent fingerprinting and further examination of the hands will take place at the medical examiner's office. If identification of the victim is established, a check of any previous law enforcement encounters should be done (eg, have there been previous 911 calls to the residence?).

Determine whether next of kin notification must be made. Document names and contact information for next of kin.

A complete accounting of the person's activities leading up to death should be obtained. This may include a full detailed medical history, medications, allergies, occupation, social history, names of treating physicians, and a catalog of medications located in the home with pill counts (specifically noting any medications located near the deceased). Consider when the deceased was last seen alive, and by whom. Is the location of death the same as the location found? Is there a secondary scene? If you are not part of the investigation, pass any information relative to the crime scene to the investigators handling the incident.

Tip

On the Scene of a Death

As a LER, you may be first on the scene of a patient who appears to be dead. These situations are very challenging because there are many things to take into consideration. Is this a crime scene, accident, or death by natural causes? Does the patient have a DNAR that meets local guidelines? Are there signs of obvious death, such as tissue decay (putrefaction), stiffening of the joints (rigor mortis), or settling of blood (dependent lividity), or are injuries so severe that they are not compatible with life (eg, decapitation)? Would attempting resuscitation endanger the life of the responder?

All of these questions may run through your mind as a LER. Safely managing and protecting the scene is a priority while taking into consideration your training as an EMR. For many LERs, those few minutes awaiting the arrival of EMS can be very long minutes.

MOTOR VEHICLE CRASHES

A motor vehicle crash can easily develop into a case of litigation if law enforcement charges are issued; often the onset of a case may be delayed as parties have the time to reflect about events or as injuries either worsen or improve.

When responding to motor vehicle crashes, it is important for the LER to follow all prior training and agency protocols. Scene safety is of utmost importance. Although the LER will most often be replaced by responding EMS units and traffic investigators, his or her initial observations, actions, and subsequent documentation are vital.

As with all scenes, it may be the role of the LER to render basic care until additional personnel arrive to assist with medical management and scene control. During this time, the LER should remain mindful to protect possible evidence to the best extent possible and to minimize impact on the scene. Unless extreme safety hazards exist, vehicles should remain in their original position, and windows and doors should not be broken.

Note the number and position of injured or deceased persons, whether they were inside or outside the vehicle, and the nature of their injuries. If victims are located on the roadway, their position should be marked before they are moved. Deceased victims may have to be moved to save lives. If a deceased person does not have to be moved for rescue operations, however, he or she should not be moved prior to the arrival of the medical examiner.

Note the name and contact information of all injured persons and others involved, as well as vehicle types, makes, and models. Determine whether the vehicle was on or off, as well as the key location (in the ignition, or being held by someone on scene). Also determine whether safety restraints were in use and whether an air bag deployed. The presence or absence of glass debris is also important to note. Injury patterns reflecting dicing injury (small, irregular cuts) may be indicative of occupant position. Dicing injury on the left side of the face may be representative of positioning on the driver side of the vehicle.

Other information regarding the motor vehicle crash should include the position of vehicle(s), road conditions (dry or wet), time of day, position of sun (overhead or setting), and the type of roadway (single lane, double lane, or shouldered).

ABUSE AND SEXUAL ASSAULT

Abuse and sexual assault are sensitive issues that should be carefully managed. Following proper procedures in evidence collection is critical in cases of sexual assault, and evidence must be collected by specially trained personnel. The LER should take care to approach victims in a nonjudgmental fashion and immediately call for assistance. The victim is the crime scene and may carry valuable evidence. The victim should be encouraged not to bathe, wash, or brush his or her teeth, and, if possible, not to urinate until reaching the hospital. Should the victim be exposed, offer him or her a clean sheet from an emergency vehicle for modesty. The location of the assault, if known, should be managed and processed as a crime scene, with care not to disturb items.

CONCLUSION

The documentation process can be difficult for LERs, especially after a difficult call. However, taking a few extra minutes to ensure that your writing is adequate and conforms to state, local, and agency guidelines can spare you months, perhaps years, of future headaches. The role of being "professional" does not simply include dressing appropriately for duty and being respectful to your patients and their families. Many legal and ethical considerations arise in the wake of an emergency. Keeping your priorities and responsibilities in mind can facilitate your response and may improve patient outcomes.

Prep Kit

READY FOR REVIEW

- Qualified physician leadership and medical oversight, as in conventional EMS, are a similarly essential component of law enforcement medical programs.
- Increasingly there is recognition that a broad base of medical responder training and capability at the officer and agent level is a similarly worthwhile, effective, and complementary endeavor.
- A law enforcement medical director must consider system design, responder training and certification, treatment protocols, communications, transport and evacuation, and interaction with local EMS and receiving facilities.
- The written record of any patient care is an important part of a patient's chart and medical record; it provides a historic record for other care providers to reference and serves to protect a responder's reputation and legal standing.
- Patient care reports should be thorough and completed in a timely manner.
- Because assessment is a major component in providing excellent patient care, it must be thorough and its documentation must correlate with the findings.
- Of special consideration in documentation are scene times, response times to the emergency, and times to get the patient to definitive care.
- Responders may be called to crime scenes involving personal injury, child or elder abuse, or dangerous living situations. In such cases intricate details of the scene size-up and assessment must be included in all documentation because these details may be used in future criminal actions.
- The patient care report plays a vital role in the continuous quality improvement and assurance process.
- Information collected and documented by the responder is used to determine billing levels for any care provided to the patient.
- Legal proceedings, in many cases, do not progress rapidly, thus allowing for the responder to be involved in numerous incidents after the event in question. The appropriate treatment and documentation of all patient care events, regardless of their severity, should alleviate fears of future legal or civil retribution.
- The LER needs to internalize the ethical guidelines established by his or her professional group and use them as the foundation for making decisions relative to integrity.
- The duty to act is an implied social contract between the person rendering aid and others in society. Police officers, fire fighters, and emergency medical personnel generally have a duty to provide care because their job includes the provision of emergency medical care within the community.
- Legal negligence requires four elements to be proved in court:
  - Injury or harm
  - Duty to act
  - Breach of duty
  - Causation
- The ethical principles relating to the provision of care are as follows, in order of priority:
  - Autonomy
  - Beneficence
  - Nonmalfeasance
  - Social welfare
- Patients have a right to make their own decisions regarding their health, including the refusal of care.

- An advance health care directive, or living will, is a binding legal document made by a competent person intending to direct his or her medical treatment in advance of future incapacity.
- Whenever handling patient information, the LER should protect access to this information from anyone other than those who have a right to access the information.
- Special situations in which other parties may receive private health information include mandatory reporting, public health, and certain legal situations. Follow your agency's administrative policies regarding the handling of records.
- Examples of conditions that require public reporting include knife wounds, gunshot wounds, motor vehicle crashes with injuries, suspected abuse of vulnerable adults and children, domestic violence, rape, and dog bites.
- Successful outcomes of cases involving forensics are directly related to the responder's approach to documentation, incident management, fire suppression, rescue, and hazardous material response.
- A LER's first obligation is to care for the patient; preservation of the crime scene and any evidence is secondary.

VITAL VOCABULARY

abandonment A type of negligence that arises when an emergency responder with a duty to provide care prematurely terminates the care and the termination of care results in harm.

advance directives Legal documents intended to provide guidance to family members, friends, and care providers on how to make medical choices on a patient's behalf in the event of decisional or communicating incapacity.

applied ethics The use of ethical values in real-life situations.

autonomy The principle that a human being of adult years and sound mind has the right to determine what shall be done with his or her own body.

beneficence An obligation to act in a helpful or therapeutic manner.

civil complaint A legal action that is filed when a person or group feels that they have not been treated in accordance with a statute.

criminal complaint A legal action that occurs when the statutes prescribe that error in application of the statute or defiance of the statute should result in the arrest of the alleged offending parties until an argument is made in front of a judiciary body.

defendant The person or group against whom a complaint is lodged.

durable power of attorney Appoints another person to act as the patient's health care decision maker in the event of future incapacity.

duty to act When a medical responder becomes responsible to the public for rendering aid during a medical emergency.

ethics The standards that societies, organizations, and professions establish to define expectations for members of that group. They broadly define right from wrong and create expectations of appropriate behavior.

expressed consent The act of the patient communicating to the responder verbally or nonverbally that he or she is willing to let the responder touch or care for him or her.

forensics Belonging to, used in, or suitable to courts of judicature or to public discussion and debate; pertaining to the law.

Good Samaritan statutes Laws that shield persons without a legal duty to act from civil liability that may arise due to injuries resulting from the care provided.

gross negligence A conscious, careless, and reckless disregard for the safety or lives of others.

Health Insurance Portability and Accountability Act (HIPAA) A law that establishes standards to make the electronic transmission of health information easier and to create procedures to protect the privacy of patients' health information.

implied consent Occurs when a responder initiates care and the patient fails to object or is unable to object.

informed consent Occurs when a patient is given enough information to make an informed choice regarding his or her treatment.

legal negligence Requires four elements be proved in court: (1) An injury or harm was suffered, (2) there was a duty to act by the health care provider, (3) the provider acted in a manner that falls below the standard of care, and (4) the actions of the provider were a substantial factor in causing the injury or harm.

medical negligence Occurs when a person is injured and becomes entitled to monetary compensation for the negligent actions of a health care provider.

medical record Documentation of care provided to a patient that provides a historical record for other care providers to reference.

morals A person's individual sense of right and wrong.

nonmalfeasance An obligation to act in ways that do not cause harm.

patient care report (PCR) A report containing information regarding an emergency, including patient information, demographic information, patient care information, treatment, and transport and disposition information.

plaintiff The person or group making a complaint.

Privacy Rule Defines protected health information (PHI) as any health information that can identify an individual.

scope of practice The range of responsibility (eg, types of patients or caseload) and practice guidelines that determine the boundaries within which a health care provider or other professional practices.

standard of care Defines the legal obligation of the duty to provide care within the limits of a practitioner's training, scope of practice, and equipment.

statutory regulations The rules approved by a legislative body.

technical negligence Occurs whenever a responder acts below the standard of care.

tort A civil complaint that results in personal injury.

CHECK YOUR KNOWLEDGE

1. You are on patrol and find a man slumped in a stairway, unconscious. You can treat him based on what form of consent?
   - A. Implied consent
   - B. Expressed consent
   - C. Found consent
   - D. None. You do not have consent to treat this man.
2. Which of the following patients would be considered competent to refuse treatment?
   - A. A 4-year-old girl with a broken wrist
   - B. A 32-year-old woman with lacerations on her arm and alcohol on her breath
   - C. An 86-year-old man who is blind and lives alone
   - D. A 21-year-old man speaking nonsense and not responding to his name
3. In which of the following circumstances is it acceptable to move a deceased victim at a crime scene?
   - A. It is never acceptable to move a body.
   - B. Once two medical practitioners have confirmed the death
   - C. To allow access to a potentially live victim
   - D. To look for clues beneath the body
4. Demographic information includes which of the following?
   - A. Patient's date of birth
   - B. Patient's mailing address
   - C. Patient's phone number
   - D. All of the above
5. Which of the following times does not need to be documented on the patient care report?
   - A. Time of response to the scene
   - B. Time your shift ends
   - C. Time of initial patient contact
   - D. Transfer time

Mental and Physical Wellness

Unit 3

Dwight A. Polk

Law Enforcement Responder Objectives

- Define wellness and discuss its value for the law enforcement responder. (pp 55–57)
- List the five components of a healthy lifestyle. (pp 55–57)
- Discuss the importance of routine physical examinations and immunizations. (p 57)
- Identify the key components for preventing exposure to a body substance. (pp 57–60)
- Discuss the procedures used in the event of exposure to body fluids. (pp 59–60)
- List the ways in which a law enforcement responder can be exposed to an infectious disease. (p 57)
- List situations that can be stressful for the law enforcement responder. (p 62)
- List the warning signs of personal stress. (p 62)
- Discuss strategies for managing personal stress. (pp 62–63)
- Describe how to assist grieving patients or family members in the event of death. (pp 63–64)
- Discuss the importance of having a good injury prevention program in place for personnel. (p 61)
- Discuss the risks that police work presents on a daily basis. (p 62)
- Discuss methods for relieving stress. (pp 62–63)
- Discuss the natural reactions to death and dying. (pp 63–64)

National EMS Education Standard Competencies

Preparatory

Uses simple knowledge of the emergency medical services (EMS) system, the safety and well-being of the emergency medical responder (EMR), and medical/legal issues at the scene of an emergency while awaiting a higher level of care.

Workforce Safety and Wellness

- Standard safety precautions (pp 57–60)
- Personal protective equipment (pp 57–59)
- Stress management (pp 62–64)
  - Dealing with death and dying (pp 63–64)
- Prevention of response-related injuries (p 61)

Medicine

Recognizes and manages life threats based on assessment findings of a patient with a medical emergency while awaiting additional emergency response.

Infectious Diseases

Awareness of

- A patient who may have an infectious disease (p 57)
- How to decontaminate equipment after treating a patient (pp 59–60)

INTRODUCTION

A career in criminal justice and law enforcement is one of excitement and danger; however, it also takes hard work, patience, and a balanced, healthy lifestyle to truly succeed. Research suggests a significant correlation between occupational stress and increased alcohol use by law enforcement personnel, resulting in high divorce rates and, sadly, high rates of suicide among police officers. This unit explores one of the areas of the field that can easily be neglected: wellness and safety. Staying fit, both physically and mentally, is just as important as the ability to fire a weapon.

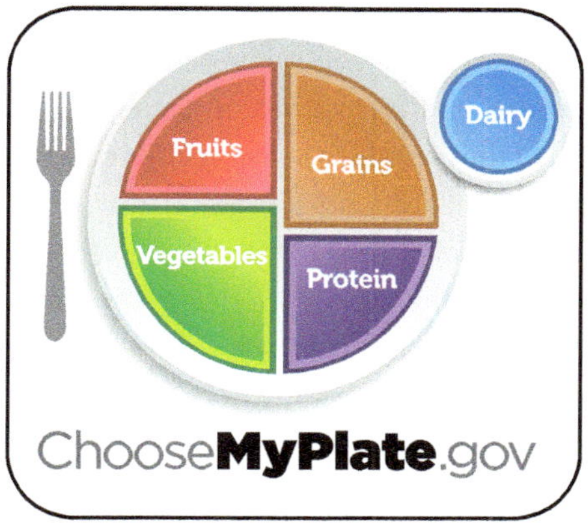

Figure 2 A healthy diet.

THE IMPORTANCE OF WELLNESS

Wellness can be defined in many ways. For the law enforcement responder (LER), wellness (also called **holistic wellness**) relates to a balance in all the components of one's life. In particular, a balance of the following five life components is essential for maintaining a healthy lifestyle: physical, occupational, personal and emotional, family and social, and spiritual health (**Figure 1**).

Physical Health

The life of a LER is stressful and often demands energy and strength far beyond that of other jobs. Physical exercise serves not only to keep the body in good condition, but also as an excellent method for alleviating stress. A mix of cardiovascular and strength exercises helps keep the body in good physical condition. If exercise is something that you do not particularly enjoy, the practice of yoga for 1 hour, three times per week, provides a great alternative. Yoga combines strength, balance, stretching, and endurance exercises along with good mental relaxation.

It is also difficult to maintain good eating habits due to the nature of the job. Meals are often missed or, when they do occur, consist of fast food, which is high in fat and carbohydrates. As a result, extra effort must be made to eat healthily. Consider taking healthy food—including bottled water and fresh fruit and vegetables—on each shift to maintain a proper weight and cholesterol level (**Figure 2**).

Figure 1 Holistic wellness.

Occupational Health

A person's interactions and view of the day-to-day routine in the workplace are classified as his or her **occupational health**. High-stress careers, such as law enforcement, always have two sides. There are aspects of law enforcement that make it a fulfilling career, including helping those in need. However, there are many elements of a law enforcement career that also create high levels of stress. In a paramilitary organization, it is common to experience conflicts in management style and interpersonal relationships. Frontline officers can feel disconnected from the leadership, who are sometimes seen as having forgotten what it is like to be in the field. Additional stress comes from large amounts of paperwork, long hours, and shift work. In many cases, these examples of stress outweigh the stress created by actual police work.

Personal and Emotional Health

Personal and emotional health is essentially who you are—your behavioral and mental health, your personality. It is a component of the lifestyle that affects LERs constantly, both in the workplace and at home. It is also the part of the job that responders may not wish to talk about, especially to someone in the mental health field.

In reality, it is a difficult task to maintain good mental health in a field that sees so many bad things. In the course of a day, LERs may participate in multiple traffic stops, be involved in a chase, pull their service weapon on someone, and work a traumatic scene such as a motor vehicle crash or shooting. As a beginning responder, it is common to consider these events an exciting part of the job. However, for more seasoned officers, these daily activities can be hardening and lead to depression, apathy, burnout, and possibly posttraumatic stress disorder.

In the worst-case scenario, the LER can become overwhelmed and feelings of hopelessness can set in, potentially leading to suicide. Research shows that the rate of police officer suicides may be double that of the general population. It is known that the presence of some form of mental illness (such as depression or bipolar disorder), along with other conditions, increases the chance of suicide in LERs. Relationship problems, access to lethal means, acute crises (job, legal, or financial), changes in physical health, and alcohol or substance abuse are all factors that increase the chance of self-harm.

By understanding the nature of the personality profile of LERs, you can take a proactive approach toward mental health. Working and talking with others, such as professional counselors, who understand the life of a responder can help you maintain positive and stable mental health (**Table 1**).

Table 1

Common Personality Traits of Emergency Personnel

- Type A personality
- Stable sense of self and personal ideology
- Inability to say "no"
- Self-confidence
- Need for autonomous achievement
- Assertiveness
- Increased degree of physical energy
- Common sense rather than theory based
- Helper mentality
- Action orientation
- Thrill seeking
- Empathy
- Restlessness
- "More masculine"
- Difficulty expressing emotions, especially those seen as being weak

Source: Data from Twersky-Glasner A: Police personality: What is it and why are they like that? *J Police Crim Psychol* 2005;20(1).

Family and Social Health

The personal and emotional health of a LER is directly connected to his or her family and social health. Unfortunately, some responders have very stressed family lives, which are often complicated by alcohol abuse and marriages that end in divorce. Although the divorce rate in the general population is around 50%, the rate of failed marriages for LERs is between 60% and 75%, making it one of the highest in the United States.

Although these are grim statistics, addressing any issues of concern before there is a problem is the first step to successful personal and family relationships. The use of family programs that start at the beginning of a responder's career, including spouse and child orientation programs, helps identify areas of concern and stress early on. Although many LERs fear or do not believe in counseling, the use of a mental health professional is an excellent way to address both individual and family issues before they become crises. Administrators or employee assistance programs associated with the agency are one option, but resources can also be sought outside the organization.

Because of the nature of shift work, as well as the general stresses of the job, LERs find it difficult to make friends outside police circles. Many feel that it is difficult to find friends who understand what law enforcement personnel see and do on a daily basis. As a result, friendships are almost always with other officers in the department, which can have mixed social implications. Close personal friendships are very intense and valuable; however, they are often limited to a few intimate friends. Social events often find a LER standing in a corner "talking shop." Responders find it difficult to interact with those outside of police circles, often leaving family members isolated.

Spiritual Health

Many LERs depend on faith and spirituality to get them through each day. In public service organizations such as the police, fire, and emergency medical services (EMS), the department chaplain plays a vital role. A **chaplain** is a person who provides nondenominational spiritual guidance and support to the individual, family, department, or citizens of the community. The department chaplain is able to provide support, resources, a therapeutic presence, and crisis counseling while understanding the pressure and stress associated with the job. In addition to supporting LERs, department chaplains respond to scenes to assist with last rites, death notifications, and family support. Most officers feel that the chaplain is a trusted and invaluable member of the law enforcement team.

WORKING IN A HEALTHY AND SAFE ENVIRONMENT

One of the first rules of working in public safety is scene safety. Although that may sound simplistic, there are many facets to this concept. Safety starts long before arriving on the scene. Rather, it begins with living a healthy lifestyle and with scene management education. This section discusses how you can work in a safe environment and explains standard safety precautions.

Baseline Health Assessment

Every LER should have a **baseline health assessment** when first hired and annually thereafter. This physical examination establishes a responder's baseline health status and subsequently monitors his or her overall health status annually, including an electrocardiogram, blood pressure reading, chest X-ray for tuberculosis, laboratory screening tests, and immunization updates. Because of their constant exposure to the public, it is paramount that LERs maintain current immunizations for the duration of their careers, especially against tetanus; hepatitis B; measles, mumps, and rubella (German measles); chickenpox (varicella); and influenza (flu).

Exposure to Infectious Diseases

LERs are called to provide care to the sick and injured, putting them at risk of being exposed to a variety of contagious diseases. Over the past several decades, much has been learned about infectious diseases and how they are spread. An **infectious disease** is a medical condition caused by the growth and spread of small, harmful organisms within the body. Another common term that is used is **communicable disease**. Although the two concepts are similar, a communicable disease is specifically defined as a disease that can be spread from one person or species to another. For all emergency medical responders (EMRs), including those in law enforcement, it is important to be aware of how to prevent exposure to diseases.

Infectious diseases are commonly transmitted through five methods:

1. Through the air by coughing (droplets)
2. Through direct contact with infected blood or body fluid
3. Through needlesticks
4. Through contaminated food
5. Through sexual transmission

The most common form of transmission for a LER is close contact with a person who has an airborne disease, such as influenza or tuberculosis. Close-quarter areas, such as prisons, are known for a high number of respiratory-related illnesses, especially during flu season.

Exposure to another person's body fluid can occur in various ways. In the process of frisking a person, you might accidentally be stuck by a needle used for shooting heroin, or you might be spat on by someone who has just been arrested. Likewise, a LER might get blood into a cut on the hand while helping the victim of a motor vehicle crash or shooting. An infectious agent (or pathogen) contracted via blood is known as a **bloodborne pathogen**.

Adherence to Standard Precautions and OSHA Regulations

Exposure to diseases spread through blood, body fluids, or respiratory droplets is best prevented by the use of **standard precautions** and **personal protective equipment (PPE)**. Standard precautions are procedures for infection control that treat blood and certain body fluids as capable of transmitting diseases. LERs should always attempt to use PPE. Devices such as gloves, goggles, masks, and gowns can be used as part of standard precautions to prevent the spread of transmittable diseases. Federal regulations issued by the Occupational Safety and Health Administration (OSHA) require that all health care workers, including EMRs, use PPE to prevent possible exposure to body fluids.

Standard Precautions

Standard precautions vary slightly according to the type of patient at the scene. In many cases, wearing medical gloves is all that is needed. Gloves (most commonly latex or nitrile) should be worn to touch any patient when there is a risk of exposure to any kind of body fluid. Proper removal of gloves is important to minimize the spread of pathogens (**Skill Drill 1**):

1. Begin by partially removing one glove. With the other gloved hand, pinch the first glove at the wrist, being careful to touch only the outside of the glove, and start to roll it back off the hand, inside out **STEP 1**.
2. Remove the second glove by pinching the exterior with the partially gloved hand **STEP 2**.
3. Pull the second glove inside out toward the fingertips **STEP 3**. Grasp both gloves with your free hand, touching only the clean interior surfaces, and gently remove the gloves **STEP 4**.

If there is a risk of splashing or spraying of a body fluid (eg, with profuse bleeding or delivery of a baby), you should wear eye protection. Eye protection can be sunglasses, goggles, or a full face shield. Eye protection reduces risk of contamination of the eyes by forms of fluid such as blood, saliva, urine, or feces.

Skill Drill 1

Proper Removal of Medical Gloves

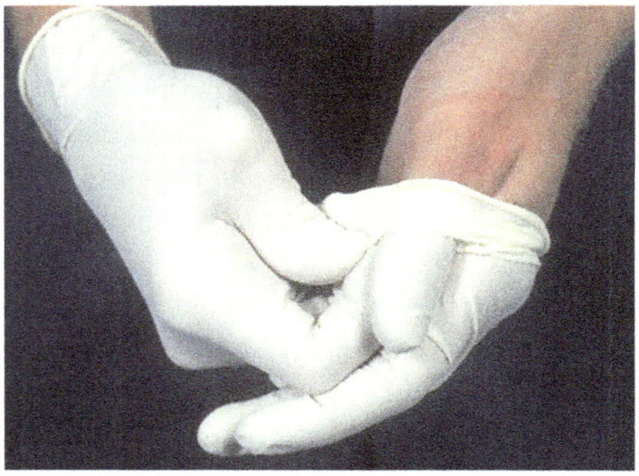

1. Partially remove the first glove by pinching at the wrist and rolling it back off the hand, inside out. Be careful to touch only the outside of the glove.

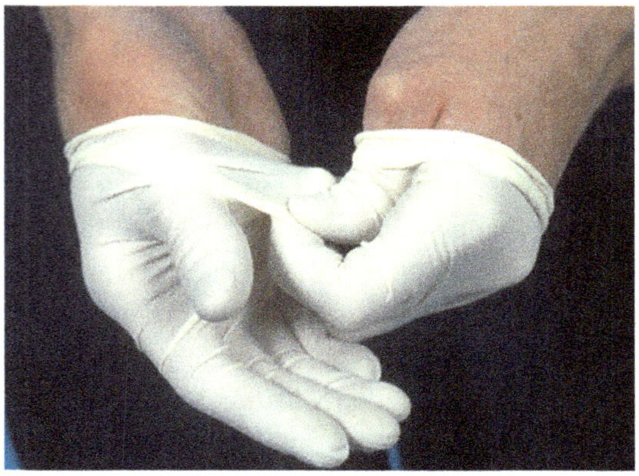

2. Remove the second glove by pinching the exterior with the partially gloved hand.

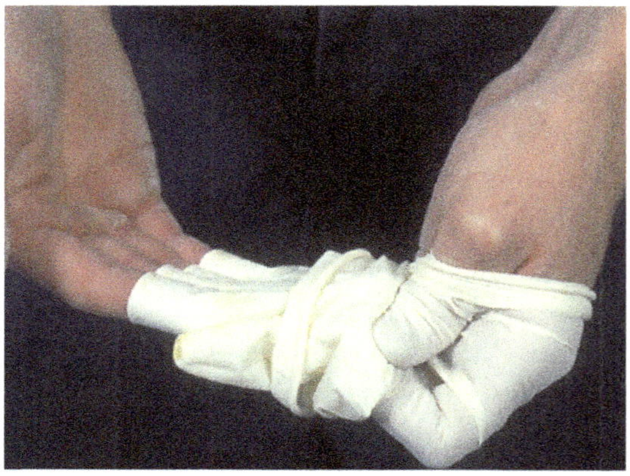

3. Pull the second glove inside out toward the fingertips.

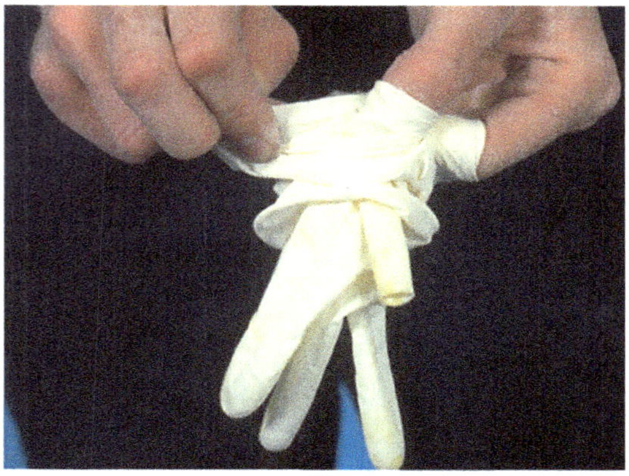

4. Grasp both gloves with your free hand, touching only the clean interior surfaces, and gently remove the gloves.

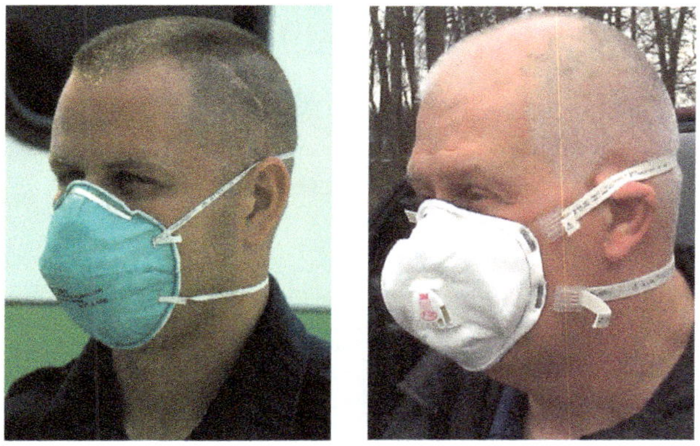

A. B.

Figure 3 These two types of masks reduce the transmission of airborne illness. **A.** N95 mask. **B.** HEPA mask.

Face masks come in various shapes and forms. Some face masks include a paper mask to cover the mouth and nose and have a plastic shield to cover the eyes. When you are caring for a patient with a contagious disease, you may wish to use a high-efficiency particulate air (HEPA) or N95 mask (**Figure 3**). These masks are designed specifically to filter out respiratory contagions. If the patient has a respiratory illness and oxygen is being administered by a nasal cannula, placing a paper surgical mask on the patient is recommended.

Tip

Spitting

When handling persons who are spitting, place a paper surgical mask over the person's mouth and nose to protect you and bystanders from saliva or blood exposure.

The use of a paper gown may be necessary in situations that involve large amounts of blood or body fluids, such as a gunshot, knife wound, or motor vehicle crash. Blood- and fluid-covered PPE should be placed in a red biohazard bag and disposed of according to your agency's policy, usually at the local emergency department.

Frisking, or the "pat down," is one of the most dangerous procedures conducted by the LER. In addition to being in proximity to a potentially violent person, there is always the risk that he or she may be carrying something sharp, such as a needle or razor blade. The disposal of sharp items requires placement of the device into a red, hard plastic container marked "Sharps" or "Biohazard."

It is important to be careful when searching and frisking people, especially when reaching into pockets. It is recommended that LERs wear leather gloves with a puncture-resistant lining (**Figure 4**). When searching vehicles and other places for drug paraphernalia, extra caution should be taken because drug users often hide needles under car seats or in sun visor pockets, glove boxes, or center consoles where they are out of sight. Always use a flashlight and never blindly reach into any place to search for drugs. If a sharp is found, place it on the ground and call out "sharps on the ground" so other officers will know of its whereabouts until it can be properly disposed of.

If an Exposure Occurs

No matter how careful LERs are, there may be a time when they are exposed to some type of body fluid. Although this may be extremely worrisome, remember that most exposures do not result in the transmission of a disease. It is important to continue caring for the patient and to clean the contaminated area immediately after care has been transferred to another responder or EMS crew.

Take the following steps if you are exposed to body fluid:

- Clean the contaminated area thoroughly with soap and water.
- If the eyes are involved, flush them with water for 20 minutes.
- Report the exposure to the EMS providers who take over care of the patient.

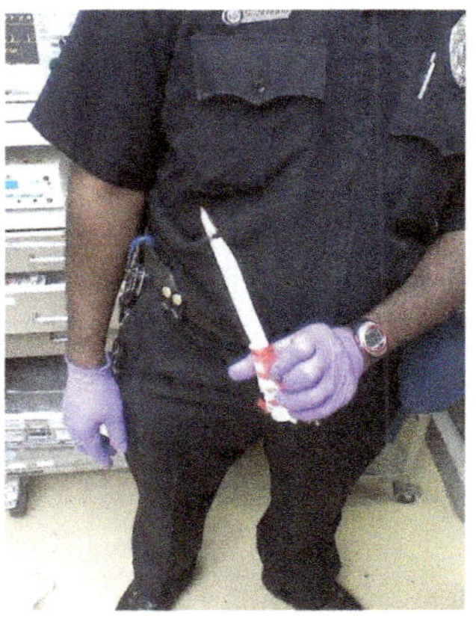

Figure 4 The LER should always wear medical gloves if there may be contact with body fluids. Puncture-resistance leather gloves should be used when searching people, vehicles, and other areas for evidence.

- Report the exposure to the appropriate person identified in your department infection control plan.
- Seek immediate follow-up care as identified in your department infection control plan.
- Document the following:
  - Time and date of the exposure
  - Circumstances of the exposure
  - Actions taken after the exposure
  - Other information required by your department

If your clothing becomes contaminated, remove the clothing and shower as soon as possible. Depending on the type of exposure, work clothes may need to be washed in a separate load or placed in a "red bag" for disposal. If they are washed, they should be washed at the employee's workplace rather than the employee's home. Keep in mind that departmental policy might require that all contaminated clothing and gear be placed in evidence containers for future use in a court case. Blood, saliva, and secretions could be important evidence and used for DNA identification purposes.

In addition to your skin and clothing, your equipment or vehicle may also be contaminated with pathogens. If there was a chance of equipment or vehicle exposure, clean the equipment or vehicle using a soap solution (or similar cleaning agent) and gloves. Then disinfect the item using a spray disinfectant. Dispose of contaminated cleaning supplies properly. Materials covered with blood or other body fluid should be placed in a "red bag" for disposal if they cannot be cleaned.

Hand Hygiene

One of the most important measures for preventing the spread of infection is handwashing. Whether to avoid the flu, the common cold, or exposure to blood, good handwashing is essential. Be sure to wash your hands after working with any patient or suspect, even after removing gloves.

Good hand cleansing requires the use of soap and warm water. Hands should be washed under running water for 30 seconds, or as long as it takes to whistle the theme song from the television show *Jeopardy* (**Figure 5**).

Once washed, dry your hands well using a disposable towel, and then use that towel to open the door as you depart the area. In the field environment, an alcohol-based hand sanitizer can be used until reaching a facility with soap and water (**Figure 6**). You may also wish to carry a container of disposable disinfectant wipes in your car for quick clean-ups, along with a small bottle of hand sanitizer.

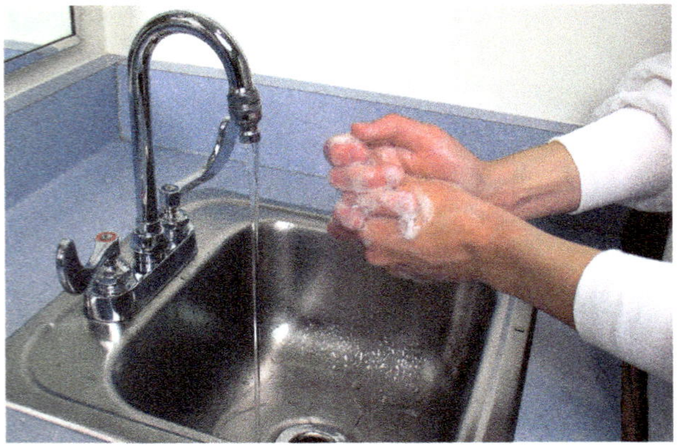

Figure 5 Wash your hands thoroughly with soap and water if you are contaminated with blood or other body fluids.

Frequent handwashing can actually injure the skin. It is common for skin to dry out and lose oils due to frequent washing or use of alcohol solutions. It is advisable to purchase a bottle of hand cream to apply periodically to keep your hands moist and prevent skin from drying and cracking.

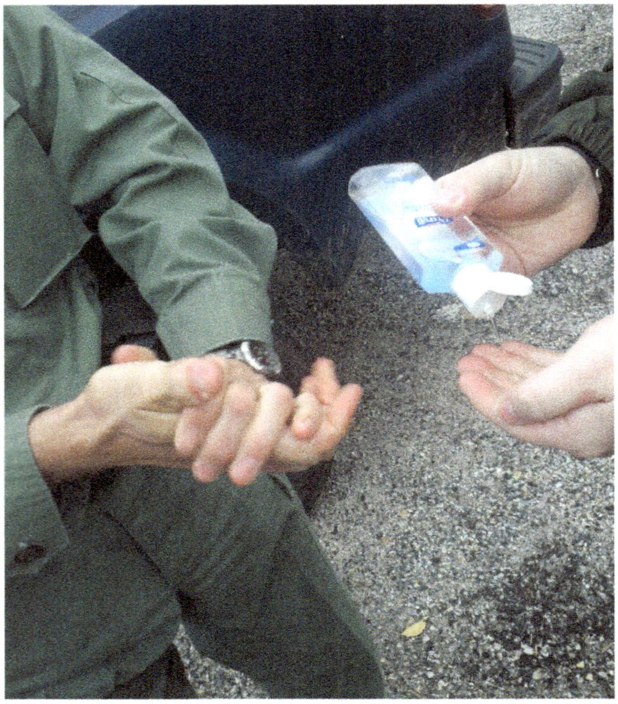

Figure 6 Because soap and water are not always readily available, the LER should have an alcohol-based cleaner on hand for immediate decontamination.

Injury Prevention

Injury prevention must become a daily routine and part of your healthy lifestyle plan. Good personal habits are paramount for injury prevention. Regular check-ups with a physician, maintaining current immunizations, eating well, and getting 7 to 8 hours of sleep per night are all important factors in being healthy. Maintaining the proper body weight and having a good fitness program also help prevent injuries. An exercise program should consist of both a strength and cardiovascular regimen, designed in conjunction with a fitness trainer.

Being physically fit is a key prevention tool for the LER. Law enforcement is dangerous work and has a high risk for interacting with violent persons. You should always be on the lookout for potential violence and be aware of your surroundings. Being aware of a perpetrator's size, mental condition, and access to potential weapons will serve you well. Be cognizant of unusual behavior, biting of the lip, or clenching of the fists, all of which are indicators of potential violence.

One of the skills necessary for a career in law enforcement is the ability to drive aggressively but safely. Although LERs need to respond to a scene or incident as quickly as possible, they also have a responsibility to fellow officers and to the public to respond safely. Every effort should be made to drive safely and to avoid motor vehicle crashes. When driving at a high speed, it is important to be cognizant of traffic hazards, pedestrians, and the vehicle's stability. It is the responsibility of every officer to be constantly aware of his or her surroundings and anticipate potential risks. Depending on the response location, many other factors, such as downed power lines, fire, leaking fluids, and hazardous materials, can be involved.

Hazardous Materials

A **hazardous material** is any material or substance that poses an unreasonable risk of damage or injury to persons, property, or the environment if not properly controlled during handling, storage, manufacture, processing, packaging, use and disposal, or transportation. When responding to a scene, it is your responsibility to assess for signs of hazardous materials. If you suspect that the scene is dangerous, notify dispatch immediately and request a fire department hazardous materials response. Establish a safety perimeter uphill and upwind, and if binoculars are available, look for the presence of placards on trucks or train cars that might indicate the presence of hazardous cargo (**Figure 7**).

Figure 7 Hazardous materials placards.

Chemical placards are usually located on both the side and rear of an 18-wheeler and on the side of a train car. Every chemical has a specific number that identifies it and categorizes it according to its classification and method of handling. If you suspect the existence of a hazardous situation, you must await a specialized response team prior to entering the scene. If possible, attempt to obtain the manifest from the operator of the vehicle and verify the chemical that is being transported. This information should be immediately relayed to the communications center so that other responders, news media, and residents can be notified.

When discussing hazardous materials, it is common to think first of transportation vehicles. In many situations, however, the LER will encounter dangerous situations in a residential or business setting. One of the most dangerous locations to responders is the clandestine drug lab. These chemicals are extremely toxic and dangerous, with the potential for explosion. Other situations that you might encounter could involve cleaning solvents, chlorine gas, swimming pool chemicals, or agricultural products such as pesticides or fertilizers.

Safety is of primary importance. You must be aware and vigilant to the scene. Your senses must be keen and constantly scanning the dynamic and changing environment.

Lifting and Moving Patients

Routine and emergency drags, lifts, and carries place the responder at risk for injury while moving the patient. Restraining patients may also result in physical injuries if the patient resists or struggles. LERs should maintain a high level of fitness, concentrating on the muscle groups necessary to perform patient moves. Refer to the scene management unit for a review of body mechanics and lifting techniques.

STRESS MANAGEMENT

Critical Incident Stress

LERs are not immune to the emotional and psychological consequences of seeing others ill, injured, or dead. Many responders and those involved in extraordinary circumstances can suffer from the emotional and psychological consequences of a critical incident. Symptoms of **critical incident stress** include difficulty concentrating, inability to sleep, repetitive intrusive images of the incident, difficulty with home life, and a variety of symptoms such as avoiding reminders of the traumatic event and experiencing anxiety when exposed to such reminders.

Professional help exists for officers who need it. Many agencies have their own **Critical Incident Stress Management (CISM)** team composed of trained law enforcement peers, mental health professionals, and chaplains. CISM is a comprehensive, integrated, systematic, and multitactic approach designed to help responders cope with the stresses of the job and rapidly return to the workplace. Should you respond to a major event or feel that you are experiencing symptoms of acute stress due to an overwhelming call, ask your command staff for access to the CISM team. All CISM teams work under a system of anonymity and confidentiality.

Events Leading to Stress

Many situations can be stressful for law enforcement personnel; it does not necessarily take a significant traumatic event to cause a stress reaction. On a daily basis, LERs are exposed to a variety of stress-inducing events, including dangerous situations; physical and psychological demands; critically ill or injured people; dead and dying people; overpowering sights, smells, and sounds; multiple-victim situations; or angry or upset victims, family, and bystanders. Although these job-related events become part of our daily lives, it is important to remember that officers also experience stress away from the workplace. Efforts to balance family; work; and financial, physical, and spiritual life can be quite draining for a person. It is important to recognize when life becomes unbalanced, often as a result of the accumulation of stress.

Cumulative stress is the buildup of stress over a period of time that results in symptoms of distress for the person. Common signs of stress seen in LERs are anxiety, irritability, difficulty sleeping, indecisiveness, and physical symptoms (**Table 2**).

Table 2

Warning Signs of Stress

- Difficulty sleeping and nightmares
- Irritability with coworkers, family, and friends
- Feelings of sadness, anxiety, or guilt
- Indecisiveness
- Loss of appetite
- Loss of interest in sexual activity
- Isolation
- Loss of interest in work
- Physical symptoms
- Feelings of hopelessness
- Alcohol or drug misuse or abuse
- Inability to concentrate

Strategies to Manage Personal Stress

There is no one solution for how to manage personal stress because people react to and handle stress differently. Instead you must build a toolkit of techniques that work for you, including knowing when to reach out for help.

While on the scene of an incident, gaining support from and talking with other officers is one of the best ways to cope with immediate or acute stress. Peers are often a great support system. Speaking to someone on a CISM team is another great place to start. In the case of acute stress, most situations of anxiety will resolve within several days following the incident. It is common for a person to experience difficulty sleeping, changes in eating habits, or lack of motivation. Talking about the event helps the person to normalize his or her feelings and return to normal.

If symptoms continue for more than 3 to 4 weeks, seek assistance from a professional counselor. Under these circumstances, the acute stress has not resolved and may be more severe. Often, horrific events or those that drastically affect the responder can result in posttraumatic stress. Do not wait for things to get better. In severe cases, they probably will only get worse unless you reach out for help.

The recipe for success is good self-care. For daily stress involving the job or other issues, lifestyle changes can often reduce stress. Improving your diet, limiting caffeine and alcohol intake, exercising, and using relaxation techniques are often easy ways to regain control and refocus your life. Talking about your situation with friends, colleagues, counselors, or spiritual advisers is also a good way to balance your life.

Dealing With Death and Dying

One of the responsibilities that LERs face on the job is to notify others of the unexpected injury or death of a person. Responses to death and dying are unique to individuals, and you are likely to witness many different reactions during your career. There are many models detailing how people deal with death and dying. The most well-known is based on the work of Elisabeth Kübler-Ross, who in 1969 changed the way the world looked at death. She described five common stages or reactions when a person is faced with the death of a friend or loved one: denial, anger, bargaining, depression, and acceptance.

LERs witness people in different stages of grief, but it is important to recognize that your own personal loss may also follow this model. Denial is generally the first reaction someone has when they hear that a person has died. "I can't believe that she's gone" is a common response. The shock of the death makes people want to deny that the person is no longer with them. Anger is expressed in many different ways. Some people will yell, others will hit a wall, and some will internalize the anger and become quiet or cry.

Bargaining is a reaction to the disbelief that a loved one is dead. It is common to hear statements like, "I'd trade my life if Dad would be here for another day," or "God should have taken me instead because I don't deserve to live." Depression usually comes later in the grieving process after a person has had the time to sit back and realize that a loved one is no longer there and in his or her life. Survivors often feel that their life is empty and void of emotions and love. Acceptance is the last stage described by Kübler-Ross. This is at the end of the grieving process when healing has advanced and the reality of the loss has set in. In most cases, this is the stage at which people move on and return to some type of normal daily functioning.

It is important to recognize that these five stages are not locked in place. In other words, some survivors will move quickly through the stages, whereas others will move forward and then return to a previous stage before ending up at acceptance. In some cases, grieving loved ones may not move through these stages and may become "locked" or "trapped." This unresolved grief may require the help of a licensed counselor who specializes in grief and bereavement.

Although Kübler-Ross describes five stages, there is no particular order or way in which a person must express his or her grief. Some family members may cry uncontrollably and exhibit an extreme outpouring of emotions, whereas others may sit silently and fail to make eye contact. A child's reaction to death depends on developmental age and the child's emotional attachment to the deceased person. Unexpected deaths are more difficult for children to comprehend and manage.

Family members may project feelings of anger toward you because you are a person of authority, or toward others close to them (**Figure 8**). Do not take their anger personally, even though it may seem to be directed toward you. You must remain alert to anger that may become physical and endanger you or others. Often, as you take control of the situation, the family member will gain confidence in your ability to help and will begin to calm down. It is important for such family members to gain control of their emotions while you continue to be empathetic and compassionate.

A safe and supportive environment is important to the healing process from the death of a loved one. Whenever possible, allow affected people to express their feelings and help them understand that these are normal feelings associated with death. It is often helpful to call friends or neighbors to sit with family members or to offer to contact a member of the clergy.

Figure 8 Family members of a deceased person may project feelings of anger toward you or others close to them. Understand that this is a normal reaction, but be alert for any danger that might arise from the anger.

Tip

Reactions to Death

Reactions to death include the following:

- Shock
- Denial
- Feeling overwhelmed and lost
- Mental confusion
- Nausea
- Numbness
- Deep emotional and physical anguish
- Inability to make decisions
- Anger
- Sadness
- Depression

CONCLUSION

Holistic wellness is not a one-day event; it is a lifetime event. Successful careers in law enforcement are built on a healthy way of life that includes exercise, diet, stress management, and peer support. In some situations, it is essential that the officer reach out for professional help to regain balance in his or her personal, family, and occupational life. Whether you are dealing with a stressful event or an exposure to an infectious disease, you must know the resources that are available to assist you.

Prep Kit

READY FOR REVIEW

- Holistic wellness comprises five components: physical, occupational, personal and emotional, family and social, and spiritual health.
- Every law enforcement responder should have a regular fitness program consisting of cardiovascular and strength exercises.
- Job stress can be overwhelming and can carry over to the family environment. It is important to reach out for help when signs of personal stress are prominent.
- Chaplaincy programs for many officers are a vital component of wellness and support.
- Every law enforcement responder should have an annual physical examination by a health care provider that includes an electrocardiogram, blood pressure reading, chest X-ray, laboratory tests, and immunization updates.
- Infectious diseases can spread easily through body fluids, contaminated food, or sexual contact.
- Law enforcement responders should take precautions to prevent exposure to body fluids or infectious diseases, including the use of gloves, eye protection, mask, or gown, or a combination of these, depending on the situation.
- In case of exposure to a body fluid or infectious disease, contact the infection control officer for your agency as soon as possible. Know the procedure for self-decontamination if needed.
- Good handwashing or the use of alcohol-based hand cleaners is the best way to prevent the spread of infectious disease.
- Injury prevention is a continuous process that starts at home and continues in the workplace.
- In the event of a hazardous materials call, set up a safety perimeter that is uphill and upwind until the hazardous materials response unit advises that the scene is accessible.
- Stress can occur acutely in a critical incident or cumulatively over time. Every law enforcement responder and spouse should be aware of the signs of stress so that help can be given early in the process.
- Symptoms of critical incident stress include difficulty concentrating, inability to sleep, repetitive intrusive images of the incident, difficulty with home life, and a variety of symptoms such as avoiding reminders of the traumatic event and anxiety when exposed to such reminders.
- There is no one solution for how to manage personal stress because people react to and handle stress differently. Instead, you must build a toolkit of things that work for you, including knowing when to reach out for help.
- No two people respond to death the same. People grieve differently depending on personality, culture, and the circumstances of the death.
- Children respond to death based on their developmental age and attachment to the deceased person.
- Law enforcement responders should be prepared to provide calm and empathetic support to family members of a deceased person.

VITAL VOCABULARY

baseline health assessment An annual physical examination by a health care provider that includes an electrocardiogram, blood pressure reading, chest X-ray, laboratory tests, and immunization updates.

bloodborne pathogens Microorganisms in the blood that are capable of causing disease.

chaplain A person who provides nondenominational spiritual guidance and support.

communicable disease A disease that can be spread from one person or species to another.

critical incident stress An acute stress reaction that occurs following a significant or traumatic event.

Critical Incident Stress Management (CISM) A comprehensive, integrated, systematic, and multitactic approach designed to help the law enforcement officer cope with the stresses of the job and to rapidly return to the workplace.

cumulative stress Stress accumulated over a period of time that results in symptoms of distress.

hazardous material Any material or substance that poses an unreasonable risk of damage or injury to persons, property, or the environment if not properly controlled during handling, storage, manufacture, processing, packaging, use and disposal, or transportation.

holistic wellness The balance needed in a person's life that includes physical, occupational, personal and emotional, family and social, and spiritual health.

infectious disease A medical condition caused by the growth and spread of harmful organisms within the body.

occupational health A person's interactions and view of the day-to-day routine in the workplace.

personal and emotional health Who you are—your behavioral or mental health, your personality.

personal protective equipment (PPE) Devices such as gloves, eye protection, masks, and gowns, used as part of standard precautions to prevent the spread of transmittable diseases.

standard precautions Procedures for infection control that treat blood and certain body fluids as capable of transmitting diseases.

CHECK YOUR KNOWLEDGE

1. Difficulty sleeping, change in eating habits, inability to concentrate, and feelings of hopelessness are all warning signs of stress.
   A. True
   B. False
2. You are handling a case involving a 14-year-old boy who has just died at home from leukemia. The family is experiencing tremendous grief and emotional pain due to the death of their loved one. Which of the following is your best response to the family?
   A. "This is a horrible thing, but at least you have two other children."
   B. "Don't worry; you'll get over it in a few weeks."
   C. "God just needed another angel."
   D. "I'm very sorry for your loss. I can't imagine the pain that you are suffering right now."
3. Which of the following does *not* exemplify the concept of holistic wellness?
   A. A regular regimen of cardiovascular and strength exercises
   B. Maintaining a proper weight and cholesterol level by eating a balanced diet
   C. Coping with workplace stress by self-medicating with alcohol
   D. Seeking help from a marital counselor to deal with the stressors of raising two teenage children in a law enforcement family
4. A police department chaplain assists only LERs and other emergency responders after an incident.
   A. True
   B. False
5. Hand hygiene includes all of the following elements EXCEPT:
   A. Avoiding hand cream
   B. Washing hands thoroughly after every physical interaction with a patient
   C. Using hand sanitizer when there is no access to soap and water
   D. Using a disposable towel to open the door leaving a handwashing area

Line of Duty Death

Unit 4

Daniel J. McGuire

Law Enforcement Responder Objectives

- Explain the impact that a line of duty death (LODD) inflicts upon any police unit, department, or environment. (p 69)
- Explain the appropriate peer support actions required to stabilize and support the affected unit, department, and so forth after a LODD. (pp 69–70)
- Discuss how to plan for a LODD and a return to normalcy. (pp 70–73)
- Discuss death notification guidelines after a LODD. (pp 71–73)

National EMS Education Standard Competencies

Preparatory

Uses simple knowledge of the emergency medical services (EMS) system, the safety and well-being of the emergency medical responder (EMR), and medical/legal issues at the scene of an emergency while awaiting a higher level of care.

Workforce Safety and Wellness

- Stress management (p 71)
  - Dealing with death and dying (p 71)

INTRODUCTION

Over the course of a year, more than 140 police officers die in the line of duty in the United States. Strangely enough, the majority of line of duty deaths are due to motor vehicle crashes, not gunshot wounds. What is not widely known is that police suicide is also prevalent; it is estimated that every 22 hours a police officer takes his or her life. This phenomenon is commonly known as the **22-hour rule** among police officers.

What exactly is a **line of duty death (LODD)**? Simply put, it is the death of a law enforcement officer while on active duty. Although this definition is used by many agencies, some agencies choose to expand their definition by including several levels of death events, as listed in **Table 1**.

When any department experiences the death of one of its officers, the reverberations quickly travel through the ranks. The news can become a disruptive force that will affect the day-to-day operations of the surviving department.

RESPONDING TO DEATH

Because law enforcement work is inherently dangerous, it takes a toll on the mind, body, and soul of each officer. Facing the fact that, at the end of each shift, there is no guarantee that all officers will return home to their families unharmed can erode officers' resiliency and strength.

Discussions of an officer's death—be it a LODD, an unexpected accidental death, or even a suicide—are not frequently heard or even addressed in an agency until something traumatic happens. The loss of a peer officer is a traumatic and humbling event, both at the individual and departmental levels. However, anticipating and planning for a LODD event is not often a priority within police departments. The reality, however, is that departments need to operate on the assumption that LODDs *will* occur, and the department should have plans and tactics in place prior to a LODD so that discussions can be conducted as a response in a crucial moment of need.

Table 1

Levels of Line of Duty Deaths

Level	Type of Death
1	Officer killed in the line of duty
2	Sudden, unexpected death of a current officer not on duty
3	Death of a retired officer or auxiliary of natural or other causes
4	Unexpected death of a family member of a current officer or a nonline agency staff member

Image Armor

Police officers are typically unwilling to show emotions. This stems from the belief that, in any of the emergency services, expressing emotions, fears, or sadness will be interpreted as a sign of weakness and will mark that person as someone who is "not cut out for this work."

The concept of **image armor** is one to which most, if not all, emergency responders can closely relate: the perceived image of yourself as the flawless responder—in the eyes of peers, the community, and perhaps even your family. The construction of image armor is closely related to the work emergency responders do. In all emergency services, and especially in law enforcement, responders are expected to be capable of handling any emergency they encounter. This expectation can create a troubling friction between what officers expect of themselves and what can reasonably be accomplished.

The fundamental expectation from the community is that when someone dials 911 a responder will arrive at the scene with the skills and experience to bring order to the chaos. Whatever the emergency, emergency responders are expected to bring it under control, and then proceed to the next call without any regard for the reactions and emotions experienced.

The misconception inherent in image armor—namely, that demonstrating emotions signifies weakness—occurs most frequently in law enforcement agencies. This attitude contributes to poor peer-to-peer support, which, in turn, amplifies the inability of an officer to react except in commonly expected ways. Furthermore, this misconception feeds on itself, proliferating through the ranks to the point at which it becomes an unspoken and unwritten law enforced by the bravado and peer pressure that comes with work in law enforcement. If officers are able to set aside their image armor, this action can make the difference in how a LODD-stricken department is able to recover and move forward after such a traumatic loss.

PLANNING FOR LODDs

If a department does not already have guidelines in place for dealing with a LODD, there are two common questions that recur: "Did we do enough?" and "Did we do it right?" In the aftermath of the grief and ceremonies, the ideal circumstance is to find ways to move forward in the **new normal**. As part of that process, it is essential to accept that the officer is now gone forever. Coming to that recognition is part of a natural and balanced grief process. Personnel and agencies need to be able to define their loss and then establish a new environment that includes the gap of the missing officer, all the while understanding that moving on does not mean forgetting.

Contributing to a lack of established LODD procedures is the inability (or unwillingness) to commit the staff, time, and budget dollars required to complete a thorough assessment. Institutional investment is necessary for both evaluating what policies are presently in place and considering where there are significant procedural gaps. Only then is it possible to build a customized LODD response plan that fits the individuality of each department's traditions, formal procedures, and intended outcomes.

A last hurdle to increasing preparedness for LODD responses is acknowledging that creating a LODD response plan is a very difficult, emotional, and complex sequence of tasks. Law enforcement's cultural discomfort with facing end-of-life issues, coupled with the reluctance of police officers to speak about or plan for LODDs, increases the obstacles in creating and continuing a dialogue on LODD response (**Figure 1**).

Preparing an Emergency Contact Form

Key to agency preparation and planning in the event of a LODD is having accurate personal information about the deceased officer. Having a completed **emergency contact form (ECF)** is crucial. Data such as the primary emergency contact and, at a minimum, one backup contact need to be captured within a standardized document that the command staff can easily access for use in a death notification.

The more complete information the ECF contains, the better the department will be able to proceed with caring for the surviving family and avoiding mistakes.

Figure 1 A customized LODD response plan fits the individuality of each department's traditions, formal procedures, and intended outcomes.

All ECFs should include the following basic information about the responder:

- Full name, including any middle name
- Date of birth
- Social Security number
- Religion
- Current physical address (no PO boxes)
- Primary emergency contact person, including a physical address and all phone numbers (home, work, cell, pager, etc)
- Secondary emergency contact person, including a physical address and all phone numbers (home, work, cell, pager, etc)
- Tertiary emergency contact person, if possible
- List of any challenges the death notification team might run into (eg, language barriers, whether sign language is needed, or whether there is a family member in the house with a fragile health state who may be overcome by this traumatic information)
- Whether there are any children at home
- Whether the seriously injured or deceased officer is an organ donor
- Names of any peer officer(s) the stricken officer would like to assist with the death notification (typically someone the surviving family knows)
- Whether there is any supervisor or peer who should not be part of the death notification due to past conflicts or unresolved negativity toward that person

Collecting this information in an organized form for each member of the department helps officers given the task of death notification. Additionally, if the death notification team knows up front about any special circumstances, they will be best prepared to deliver the news to the surviving family.

Solid procedures and supporting information need to be in place in every department. Ad hoc procedures increase the likelihood that mistakes will be made, creating potential embarrassment for the agency and, more important, failing to support the surviving family appropriately.

Reacting to a LODD

In the aftermath of a LODD, it is common for officers to be affected by a cascade of emotions, fears, and thoughts (**Figure 2**). Often what emerges first is anger, hostility, aggressive actions, and the possibility of a "posse mentality" forming, a "Let's get this done right and right now!" mind-set. For those officers who were on scene during the LODD, the sensory impressions of the scene serve to heighten reactions to the event. These responses put the officer in a hyperalert state.

Once the critical portions of the traumatic event begin to wind down, officers may experience confusion, short-term memory difficulties, trouble processing the early stages of the actual event, and physical stress reactions such as the following:

- Increased sweating
- Increased heart rate
- Increased breathing rate
- Body aches
- General exhaustion

Figure 2 After a LODD, members of the department experience a wide range of emotions.

Once the event has begun to stabilize, additional signs and symptoms of acute traumatic stress often continue to be seen. These signs and symptoms include feelings and expression of responsibility guilt, survivor's guilt, or remorse. There may also be circumstances in which past, unresolved events are brought to the forefront of some officers' minds, thus adding to the overall impact on the persons involved and the department as a whole.

Tip

Stress Reaction Warning Signs

If you notice any of the following symptoms in yourself or a peer, see a medical professional for immediate evaluation:

- Shortness of breath
- Chest pains
- Visual disturbances
- Severe pain

STRATEGIC LODD RESPONSE

Once the LODD has occurred, it is critical that all other officers' safety and well-being on scene becomes a top priority, while adhering to the principles of crime scene preservation. A prompt response by a fully trained peer support team and police chaplains at the scene, at the hospital, and at headquarters is essential. Placing these key personnel in these settings allows all staff affected by the news of the death to have someone to depend on during the preliminary stages of traumatic stress reactions and grief. Other important steps in managing these traumatic events include clear and consistent communication of what is being done for the surviving family as well as preliminary wake and funeral details. Any peer department staff feeling "left out" due to poor communication styles or tactics will be a lingering issue for months afterward, prolonging the grief process. It is important to ensure that postincident support services, such as debriefings, are offered and that all officers are broadly encouraged to attend, if not for themselves then to show support for peer officers who need this assistance.

Another top priority is proper death notification of the deceased officer's family. In today's world of instant messaging and e-mail access from hand-held devices, the news of an officer's death will reach the media within minutes. As a result, it is important that death notifications be made as quickly as possible. Time is not on your side when it comes to proper and respectful death notification to the surviving spouse and family.

Finally, there is a widespread lack of suitable death notification training and knowledge of initial grief support in emergency services. Because these topics may only be presented briefly as new officers go through training academies, when it comes time to deliver a death notification, it is often done by officers who lack the appropriate skills and knowledge of the most suitable approach (**Figure 3**).

Communication

Timely Death Notification

The news of an officer's death in the line of duty reaches the media quickly in today's technology-driven society. This makes it more important than ever to notify the deceased officer's survivors as quickly and as respectfully as possible. Do not allow the survivors to hear of their loved one's death from the television or a neighbor.

In the aftermath of a LODD event, the response should be structured using the **Zero Hour Forward** concept, which is defined as beginning the moment the LODD occurs (zero hour), encompassing the next critical minutes, and continuing through the 36 to 48 hours after the event. Careful management of this time frame is essential for mitigating mistakes,

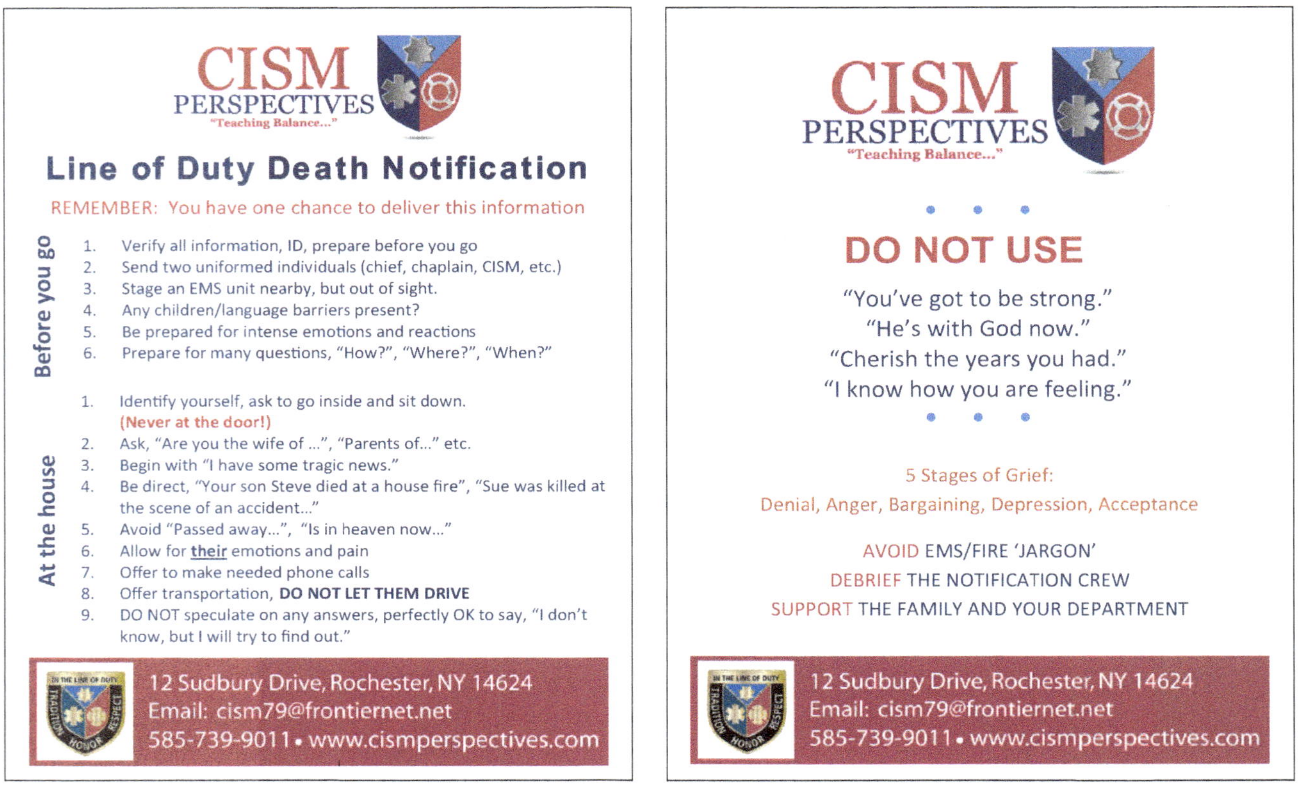
CISM PERSPECTIVES
"Teaching Balance..."

Line of Duty Death Notification

REMEMBER: You have one chance to deliver this information

Before you go

1. Verify all information, ID, prepare before you go
2. Send two uniformed individuals (chief, chaplain, CISM, etc.)
3. Stage an EMS unit nearby, but out of sight.
4. Any children/language barriers present?
5. Be prepared for intense emotions and reactions
6. Prepare for many questions, "How?", "Where?", "When?"

At the house

1. Identify yourself, ask to go inside and sit down. (Never at the door!)
2. Ask, "Are you the wife of ...", "Parents of..." etc.
3. Begin with "I have some tragic news."
4. Be direct, "Your son Steve died at a house fire", "Sue was killed at the scene of an accident..."
5. Avoid "Passed away...", "Is in heaven now..."
6. Allow for <u>their</u> emotions and pain
7. Offer to make needed phone calls
8. Offer transportation, **DO NOT LET THEM DRIVE**
9. DO NOT speculate on any answers, perfectly OK to say, "I don't know, but I will try to find out."

12 Sudbury Drive, Rochester, NY 14624
Email: cism79@frontiernet.net
585-739-9011 • www.cismperspectives.com

CISM PERSPECTIVES
"Teaching Balance..."

DO NOT USE

"You've got to be strong."
"He's with God now."
"Cherish the years you had."
"I know how you are feeling."

5 Stages of Grief:
Denial, Anger, Bargaining, Depression, Acceptance

AVOID EMS/FIRE 'JARGON'
DEBRIEF THE NOTIFICATION CREW
SUPPORT THE FAMILY AND YOUR DEPARTMENT

12 Sudbury Drive, Rochester, NY 14624
Email: cism79@frontiernet.net
585-739-9011 • www.cismperspectives.com

Figure 3 The use of a card with a prepared algorithm provides the officer with a consistent, thorough, and compassionate approach to a death notification. Shown here is an example of a death notification card distributed by CISM Perspectives (www.cismperspectives.com).

managing the mass of issues any LODD event brings about, and maintaining the necessary steps for the dignity of the fallen officer, the surviving family, and the department.

Given the impact that a LODD event has on everyone on scene, the proper procedures can quickly be derailed. The high stakes of the event can rapidly inspire conflicting reactions and priorities. With that in mind, it is essential that the response timetable be kept succinct enough to make it flow with ease but not so brief that critical steps are overlooked. It should be the responsibility of each leadership staff member to know these steps in detail.

With a tactical frame of mind, list the essential tasks, goals, and cautions that must be impressed on every responding officer, supervisor, and leadership staff member who arrives at the scene. Break down the tasks into manageable time frames—the first 15 minutes, the first 60 minutes, the first 2 hours, the first 6 hours, and so on. If the LODD event is handled well from the beginning, it is possible to prevent a traumatic situation from becoming unmanageable and it is even feasible to turn this traumatic incident into a long-term benefit through a timely and compassionate response.

Any agency looking to create a LODD preplan should not be deceived that such a plan is simply a matter of finding pertinent information via the Internet or other sources and then assembling that material into a customized "game plan." Each agency is different, with diverse needs, previously established rituals, and goals of its own; most important, the particular wants and needs of the surviving family differ. Assembling a LODD response guide or plan requires considerable and careful thought, thorough input from all available resources, and a concerted effort on the part of all those responsible.

By making key decisions, arranging priorities, and responding to all the aspects a LODD event generates, a stricken agency can be secure in the knowledge that it took all the right steps in advance, applied the response plan effectively, and did right by all the affected persons and organizations (**Figure 4**).

CONCLUSION

A LODD tests all aspects of responder wellness and can incapacitate a law enforcement officer, regardless of years of experience on the force or personal capacity to deal with traumatic situations. Planning in advance for LODDs facilitates a proper response when confronted with this unfortunate situation. Department protocols for family notifications and peer support create a confidence that all LODD events will be handled correctly.

Figure 4 Proper procedure ensures sound response.

Prep Kit

READY FOR REVIEW

- Law enforcement officers often develop what is known as image armor—that is, the perceived image of oneself as the flawless responder.
- Every law enforcement officer and emergency responder should prepare an emergency contact form detailing how the organization should respond in the case of the responder's death.
- Death notifications to family members must be performed quickly and professionally.
- Peer members should receive professional training on how to make a death notification.

VITAL VOCABULARY

emergency contact form (ECF) A previously prepared, securely maintained document containing information and details pertaining to an officer who has been seriously injured or has died.

image armor The perceived image of oneself as the flawless responder—in the eyes of work peers, community, and family.

line of duty death (LODD) Any death of a law enforcement officer while on active duty.

new normal Creating, setting, and living life following the death of an officer, for family, friends, and peers.

22-hour rule The estimation that every 22 hours, a law enforcement officer ends his or her life by suicide.

Zero Hour Forward Defined as running from zero hour (the moment a line of duty death occurs), through the next critical minutes, and continuing through the 36 to 48 hours after the event.

CHECK YOUR KNOWLEDGE

1. The 22-hour rule refers to which of the following events?
   A. The average time between line of duty deaths
   B. The estimation of how often an officer is killed in a motor vehicle crash
   C. The estimation of how often an officer takes his or her life
   D. The time between fatal police shootings
2. The moment that a line of duty death occurs is commonly known as the zero hour.
   A. True
   B. False
3. Preparing for a line of duty death should be a priority in police and other emergency departments.
   A. True
   B. False
4. Which of the following is not necessary for an emergency contact form?
   A. Full name, including middle name
   B. Former addresses
   C. Religion
   D. Social Security number
5. Which of the following is a physical stress reaction?
   A. Muscle and body aches
   B. Exhaustion
   C. Increased heart rate
   D. All of the above

Assessment in **Action**

SCENARIO

You respond to the scene of a motor vehicle crash where there are several people with obviously life-threatening injuries. A supervisor instructs you to begin caring for those patients while other officers manage the scene. While controlling bleeding on a patient, a small amount of blood splashes you in the face around your protective glasses. EMS arrives on scene and transports the patients to the trauma center. You later learn that the patient you provided care for had died of his wounds.

ACTIONS

1. Which of the following actions would not be appropriate when dealing with being splashed in the face with blood?
   - **A.** Wash the blood away as soon as possible.
   - **B.** Report the possible exposure to the infection control officer.
   - **C.** Ignore it. The hospital would have told you if there was a communicable disease to be concerned with.
   - **D.** Clean or replace the protective eyewear.
2. Several weeks after the incident, you find yourself not wanting to go to work and losing interest in your hobbies. This is a normal response to stress and will dissipate on its own within 3–4 more weeks.
   - **A.** True
   - **B.** False
3. You do not want to share any of your thoughts with coworkers because you are concerned it will impact how they feel toward you. This is known as:
   - **A.** acting tough.
   - **B.** image armor.
   - **C.** CISM.
   - **D.** new normal.
4. You should take a vacation prior to seeking professional help, because it is less intrusive.
   - **A.** True
   - **B.** False
5. Constructive ways to deal with stress include all of the following except:
   - **A.** exercise.
   - **B.** meeting with a counselor.
   - **C.** eating a healthy diet.
   - **D.** drinking alcohol.

SECTION 2

Emergency Response

Section Contents

Scene Management

Unit 5

Bruce Conrad

Law Enforcement Responder Objectives

- Discuss the phases of an emergency medical services (EMS) call. (pp 79–80)
- Discuss steps to assess and ensure scene safety. (pp 80–82)
- Identify methods to ensure personal safety. (pp 82–83)
- Explain the concept of triage. (pp 83–85)
- Describe the priority levels in the START triage system. (pp 83–85)
- List the steps in triaging patients. (pp 83–85)
- Identify the components of the National Incident Management System (NIMS). (pp 85–88)
- Describe how to implement an incident command system (ICS) consistent with NIMS. (pp 85–88)
- Identify strategies to prevent personal injury when moving a patient. (pp 88–89)
- Describe common patient movement techniques. (pp 88–89)
- Describe emergency patient movement techniques. (pp 89, 90–93)
- Identify the types of devices for moving patients. (pp 89, 93–94)
- Discuss how to position patients for movement. (pp 88–89)
- Describe methods for restraining patients for transport. (p 89)
- Identify the risks and responsibilities of emergency apparatus response. (pp 89, 94–95)
- Identify transport methods that are alternatives to ground ambulances. (pp 95–96)

National EMS Education Standard Competencies

Preparatory

Uses simple knowledge of the EMS system, the safety and well-being of the emergency medical responder (EMR), and medical/legal issues at the scene of an emergency while awaiting a higher level of care.

Workforce Safety and Wellness

- Prevention of response-related injuries (pp 80–82)
- Lifting and moving patients (p 88)

EMS Operations

Uses knowledge of operational roles and responsibilities to ensure safe patient, public, and personnel safety.

Principles of Safely Operating a Ground Ambulance

- Risks and responsibilities of emergency response (pp 89, 94–95)

Incident Management

- Establish and work within the incident management system (pp 85–88)

Multiple-Casualty Incidents

- Triage principles (pp 83–85)
- Resource management (pp 83–85)

Air Medical

- Safe air medical operations (pp 95–96)
- Criteria for utilizing air medical response (pp 95–96)

Hazardous Materials Awareness

- Risks and responsibilities of operating in a cold zone at a hazardous materials or other special incident (pp 80–82)

INTRODUCTION

Responding to an emergency scene is both physically and mentally demanding. As a law enforcement responder (LER), you are faced with many challenges. You provide a dual role: providing law enforcement duties and providing emergency medical care. In some cases, the LER will be in the center of an evolving emergency incident. Hostile, violent acts that occur in the presence of the LER may not allow the LER to change into a personal protective ensemble. In many situations, fighting back and searching for cover and concealment will be the primary life-saving actions. In other cases, the LER will have the opportunity to don specialized gear. Emergency scenes are complex and dynamic. You will frequently have to make a split-second decision to determine tactics that have life or death consequences.

Learning what steps are necessary for scene safety, providing emergency care, and integrating law enforcement duties will provide you an advantage over an unprepared responder. Natural and manmade disasters occur without warning, and traditional emergency services responders are often strained thin or not readily available at the early stage of an incident. LERs have worked to triage incidents, transfer patients, and provide immediate care before traditional services arrive.

LERs must have a general awareness of the National Incident Management System (NIMS). As a law enforcement official, you can easily find yourself as the lead government official at various types of disasters. You will need to have an awareness of the other types of emergency responders and transport options. Other responders may include fire, rescue, hazardous materials, ambulance, and public works. Transport options can range from traditional ambulances to water and airborne craft. In many cases, the alternative transport units, such as marine and aviation services, are operated by law enforcement agencies.

LERs who have committed to understanding and practicing all of the components of scene management will stand out as leaders during times of crisis. Not only will their actions reflect well on themselves and their agency or department, but also their often heroic response will save and protect lives.

PHASES OF AN EMS CALL

The phases of an emergency medical services (EMS) call are typically described as reporting, dispatch, first response, EMS response, and hospital care.

Reporting and Dispatch

Reporting is defined as the activation of the EMS system by bystanders or other responders. This usually involves calling the emergency services dispatch center. Civilian phone systems in the United States can use 911 for immediate access to the local dispatch center. In some instances, large properties or campuses will have an internal emergency number. If you are operating on a mission, ensure that you have a direct liaison to emergency services dispatching to prevent errors with communications systems that can occur during large-scale disasters. The dispatch center is the center of communications for responding EMS units. Dispatch center personnel react to information given to them and can pass on only what they have been told (**Figure 1**). If you have an established liaison with a dispatch center, communicate with that center in your planning phase to learn what information the dispatch center requires.

First Response

The first response phase of an EMS call is critical to the success of the call. LERs are heavily involved at this level because of the nature of law enforcement. Law enforcement officers, agents, and security officials are frequently at the point of an attack or quickly available to respond to a public request for help. The LER will have to follow local policy in determining how he or she will balance law enforcement duties with the need for lifesaving decision making and actions. Law enforcement

Figure 1 Dispatch center personnel react to information given to them and can pass what they have been told to the necessary resources.

programs that concentrate only on law enforcement activities disregard the need for LERs to provide a complete response to their service population. Programs that have adopted the most basic levels of responder training—such as cardiopulmonary resuscitation and use of automated external defibrillators (CPR/AED), care under fire, and hazard mitigation—have proven they can save lives and property while maintaining their law enforcement presence.

EMS Response

The EMS response includes basic life support (BLS) or advanced life support (ALS) units. These units should be equipped with medical transport capabilities. LERs traveling to an unfamiliar area should establish a liaison with the EMS units to develop a point of contact and determine what the EMS system's capabilities and expectations are. LERs should establish the same relationship in their routine response area. This relationship should extend to joint training and operational observation exercises for both groups.

Transport of the patient may occur by different mechanisms. Some EMS systems provide ambulances solely operated by their employees, some may share resources, and others contract out for hospital-based or privately operated units. Some systems include water or aviation programs. Others use shared resources.

LERs should make it a priority to understand the basics of EMS systems. In today's security climate, the more departments responding to a security-driven incident, the greater the need to inspect and qualify those who are operating these resources. As a LER, you should be able to quickly identify responding units that do not fit the typical profile of the dedicated EMS responder. If EMS units or personnel look out of place, question them, secure them, and inspect them.

Hospital Care

The last phase of an EMS incident is hospital care. Most EMS systems will understand the types of hospitals available in the area and their capabilities. Although LERs are not routinely involved in patient transport, they should become familiar with the hospitals in their area. Learning routes, parking areas, and emergency entrances can reduce time and confusion during emergencies. LERs should make an effort to establish a liaison with their local hospitals. These relationships can become invaluable assets for training and experience.

SCENE LEADERSHIP

The LER operating as the lead official at the emergency scene may be responsible for taking on a leadership role. Scene management priorities for the LER are scene safety, triage, incident command, and EMS operations.

Scene Safety

Your first consideration at any emergency scene is safety. Your safety is paramount, as is the safety of others on the scene. Some scene safety hazards include the following:

- Fire
- Hazardous materials (HazMat) incidents
- Motor vehicle crashes
- Environmental hazards
- Rescue and extrication incidents
- Multiple-casualty incidents (MCIs)
- Violent or hostile situations
- Animals
- Vehicle and traffic conditions
- Utilities such as gas or electric

If you are responding to an emergency incident, you must evaluate the scene for multiple hazards. You can start this process by evaluating bystander reports to your call center and observing the scene as you approach. You should follow your local protocols relative to scene assessment. A traditional approach is to evaluate for hazardous conditions, fire, damaged utilities, or other hazards that can affect a large area first. Consider the weather, wind direction, and conditions and how they may influence scene management.

As you approach the incident, continue to observe for hazards that are limited to the area of the incident. If you have not identified any hazards at this point, look for potential hazards, such as broken utility poles or uncontrolled traffic. Consider whether you need any additional resources to control the actual or potential hazards. Immediately request resources based on your local protocols (**Figure 2**). Resources can always be returned to service, but if you do not request them, delays in securing some hazards may be detrimental to the survival of victims. As you get deeper into the incident, continue to assess for actual or potential hazards. Look for conditions such as unstable or running vehicles, leaking fuels, or damaged and unstable structures. As soon as possible, assign a safety officer to monitor and manage safety concerns.

If at any time you determine the scene is not safe, limit your access to the incident, evacuate others, and call for addi-

Figure 2 Once you have sized up the scene, request any additional resources you might need. It is better to have too many resources on scene than too few.

tional or specialized resources. As a LER, you may be dealing with law enforcement situations and using your training and use of force protocols to limit or remove violent and hostile threats to civilians and others. Follow your local policies in determining your actions in law enforcement incidents. Controlling a dangerous perpetrator may immediately secure an incident and isolate a threat. Law enforcement is the correct response for these types of situations.

In certain conditions you may be able to control or reduce the impact of hazards on the scene of an emergency incident. Whenever possible, attempt to evacuate people caught inside an affected area to safety. In some cases this may simply mean seeking shelter, sheltering in place, or walking in a safe direction away from a hazard. In other cases you may need transportation devices such as buses, barges, boats, or planes to evacuate an area. Be familiar with the resources you have at a location to help move or protect people from a potential emergency incident.

In some cases, small incipient fires can be quickly extinguished using portable fire extinguishers. The unit on environmental hazards addresses how to assess and manage these types of conditions. Take time to brief the first-arriving units.

Hazardous materials are very difficult to manage and contain. The LER should understand how to assess for these conditions. In some cases you may have already been exposed to hazardous environments, or hazardous substances may be used as weapons to reduce your effectiveness during an attack. The units on hazardous materials and toxicology provide detailed information on hazardous environments and strategies to survive or mitigate exposures.

Whenever you are engaged in a fire, potential fire, explosive, or hazardous materials incident, you should ensure that the local or assigned fire fighters and hazardous materials response teams have been called and understand the conditions. In some cases hostile or violent conditions may exist and must be dealt with prior to placing unarmed emergency service teams at risk of assault. A coordinated effort must be established. LERs should frequently train with local responders and ensure that all those involved can operate within a combined incident management structure.

Some hazardous conditions are not manageable. Electricity, gas, radiation, weather, and natural disasters are typically not controlled by initial responders. Utilities such as gas and electric in small, isolated situations may be easily shut off by unplugging charged appliances or shutting valves. LERs should apply these actions only if they are trained to approach these types of conditions. In most cases you will have to wait for utility companies or building managers to respond.

Weather and disasters such as hurricanes, blizzards, tsunamis, and earthquakes will require the LER to take defensive measures. LERs should always carry weather gear such as insulated coats, waterproof covers and boots, battery-powered lights, drinkable water, and packaged foods to extend survivability. Preplanning for shelter and taking safety precautions for tornados, flooding, blizzards, and lightning provide your best chance to survive these catastrophic environmental threats. In some places weather conditions can change in minutes. Satellite-based weather information sources are a great resource. Local resources and residents are the best sources for weather-related issues, however. Forming a relationship with local resources will prove valuable during these dangerous and unpredictable conditions.

When situations dictate, you must act to defend yourself and others from violence or hostile actions based on your agency's or department's training and policies relative to the use of force. Historically, law enforcement agencies assert that fighting back to neutralize a threat is the best way to limit the impact of a hostile force. Cover can be provided by large, heavy structures or objects that can not only protect you from being seen by the hostile force but can also provide substantial protection from explosive and small arms fire. Concealment, light construction, trees, shrubs, or camouflage can be used to limit the vision of the hostile force on your position. However, concealment will not provide protection against explosives and small arms fire.

Tip

Scene Safety

On-Site

Is this a law enforcement situation requiring the use of force?
If the answer is yes:

- Follow local protocols regarding the use of force and perpetrator apprehension.
- If the incident is hostile, fight, or flee—use cover or concealment.
- If you or other LERs are injured, use care under fire techniques.
- Request additional resources.
- When hostilities have ended or the situation allows, assist others who are injured or caught inside the hostilities.
- Follow local protocols for further actions.

If the answer is no:

- Assess and determine whether there are actual or potential environmental hazards.
- Assess and determine whether there are actual or potential hazards from the area of the incident, such as traffic or unstable structures.
- Assess and determine whether there are hazards specific to the area of the patients.
- Determine whether you will need to evacuate others inside the affected area away from danger.
- Don personal protective equipment (PPE).
- Request additional resources.
- Follow local protocols for further actions.

Responding

- Use bystander reporting and first-arriving unit information to determine whether the scene is safe.
- As you approach the location, systematically do the following:
    - Determine whether this is a law enforcement situation in which you may need to use force and secure perpetrators.
    - Assess and determine whether there are actual or potential environmental hazards.
    - Assess and determine whether there are actual or potential hazards from the area of the incident, such as traffic or unstable structures.
    - Assess and determine whether there are hazards specific to the area of the patients and whether you will need to evacuate others from danger.
- Don PPE.
- Request additional resources.
- Follow local protocols for further actions.

Personal Protective Equipment

LERs are often prepared to defend themselves against hostile threats. Ballistic vests, helmets, and shields are common in today's police force. The LER may also need to consider PPE that includes items traditionally used in fire, rescue, or hazardous materials departments.

Kevlar helmets used for ballistic protection may provide reasonable defense against contact with sharp or hard objects during rescues. Traditional fire rescue helmets are constructed with internal suspensions and securing devices that help absorb blows from falling objects and contact. If a LER decides to use a fire rescue–style helmet, he or she should carefully evaluate construction and styles. Helmets made from a Kevlar-reinforced composite material and that have adjustable chin straps and internal suspensions are a good choice. Fire rescue helmets may contain a rear bill structure designed to channel the flow of water away from the neck of the wearer. These bills can limit the mobility of the wearer. Some fire rescue helmets have integral eye protective shields. If you decide to use this style of eye protection, it should be secondary to safety goggles or glasses that provide protection directly to the area of the eye. Glasses or goggles can protect the eyes from flying shards and debris that may get behind protective shields.

Clothing designed for firefighting is traditionally engineered with an external protective layer made of thick, reinforced fabric and an internal thermal barrier layer designed to prevent the buildup of perspiration during high-heat encounters. This ensemble is commonly referred to as turnout or bunker gear (**Figure 3**). LERs who are routinely exposed to vehicle or structural rescues could benefit from adding this type of gear to their PPE. Some manufacturers provide lighter-weight versions of these suits that provide good exterior protection with less thermal barrier support. These specialized suits are intended for rescue work and not for firefighting.

Figure 3 Turnout or bunker gear is protective clothing designed for use in firefighting.

Gloves are a very important part of the PPE. Leather fire suppression gloves provide good general-purpose protection. They can protect against heat, cold, punctures, and lacerations. These gloves do not provide protection from chemicals or electricity. Some LERs may prefer specialty rescue gloves that are designed for maximum surface adherence and dexterity. Rescue gloves provide minimal protection from heat or cold and do not protect against chemicals or electricity. Gloves used to prevent infection and contamination may be worn under fire suppression or rescue gloves to protect against exposure to blood or body fluids.

Boots used by LERs should have a nonslip sole and should be constructed to provide support to the arch and ankles. Look for boots that provide crush protection to the toes. Puncture-resistant material is available in various configurations. Water-resistant material may benefit responders who may encounter wet conditions or snow. Once you have selected the safety features, your boots should be designed to protect your feet from dirt and grit. Moisture buildup in a boot can limit its effectiveness and lead to tissue damage of the wearer. Boots that can promote ventilation may reduce the risk of moisture buildup. Socks should be padded and fit well. Some rescuers wear two pairs of socks, using a thinner inside sock that will allow moisture to wick into the thicker outer sock. Responders should wear socks and boot combinations to break them in prior to wearing them at work. The break-in period will allow the fabric to relax and conform to the wearer's foot.

TRIAGE

Triage is a French word meaning "the sorting of casualties of war," but the concepts of triage have long been evolving. Today, we think of triage as sorting patients and assigning them to treatment categories associated with their need for care. In modern EMS systems, this occurs with every patient because system-wide priorities are necessary. These assignments are taken into account when hospital access is critical. At incidents where the number of patients can quickly overwhelm the resources of the initial responders, triage can be used to sort which patients need the immediate assets. Those needing lifesaving interventions are of a higher priority than those experiencing only minor injuries. In most triage systems, there is a classification for patients who will not survive or are already dead. The US military uses the term *expectant* to signify someone who is mortally wounded or dead. In the civilian community, EMS systems and local emergency management programs may have triage programs that contain locally specific techniques, content, and language.

The LER should always determine the type of triage program that his or her local or dedicated response system uses. These systems often deploy color-coded markings to identify the triage classification of the patient. Not all EMS systems use the same colors or triage tagging devices. In most systems, red is the highest priority and includes patients who have sustained treatable, life-threatening injuries and are in immediate need of care. Yellow indicates those patients who are seriously injured but whose injuries are not life threatening. The care of yellow-tagged patients can be delayed. Green is assigned to patients with minimal injuries, classically described as the walking wounded. Black is assigned to those patients who are fatally injured or dead.

The sorting and classifying of patients aids those most in need, but it also provides a reasonable way to deploy resources relative to the care and transport of the wounded. At a mass casualty incident (MCI), resources available to treat and transport patients can be more limited than the number of patients that you have to assess and manage. In some instances an MCI can occur with two patients. Usually, we think of an MCI as a large accident, disaster scene, active shooter incident, or a bombing. If the incident overwhelms the available resources, however, it meets the requirements for an MCI. Large-scale MCIs present the challenges associated with incident management and logistics.

As a LER, your initial role at an MCI will typically be to initiate triage. If you are not aware of the local EMS system's triage parameters, you can deploy the **START system**. START stands for "simple triage and rapid treatment." This process is commonly taught as a triage primer at all levels of emergency care in the United States. START uses red ribbons for immediate life threats (priority 1 patients), yellow ribbons for delayed or urgent care (priority 2) patients, green ribbons for delayed care or walking wounded (priority 3) patients, and gray or black ribbons for dead or no-care-required (priority 4) patients (**Figure 4**).

To implement START, first ensure that you are safe and that you have communicated the type of incident with which you are involved to your communications center. Ensure that incident command priorities are being established based on your local protocols. Either assign the task of triage or begin the process yourself. Immediately advise all the people who are involved in the incident to get up and walk to a specific

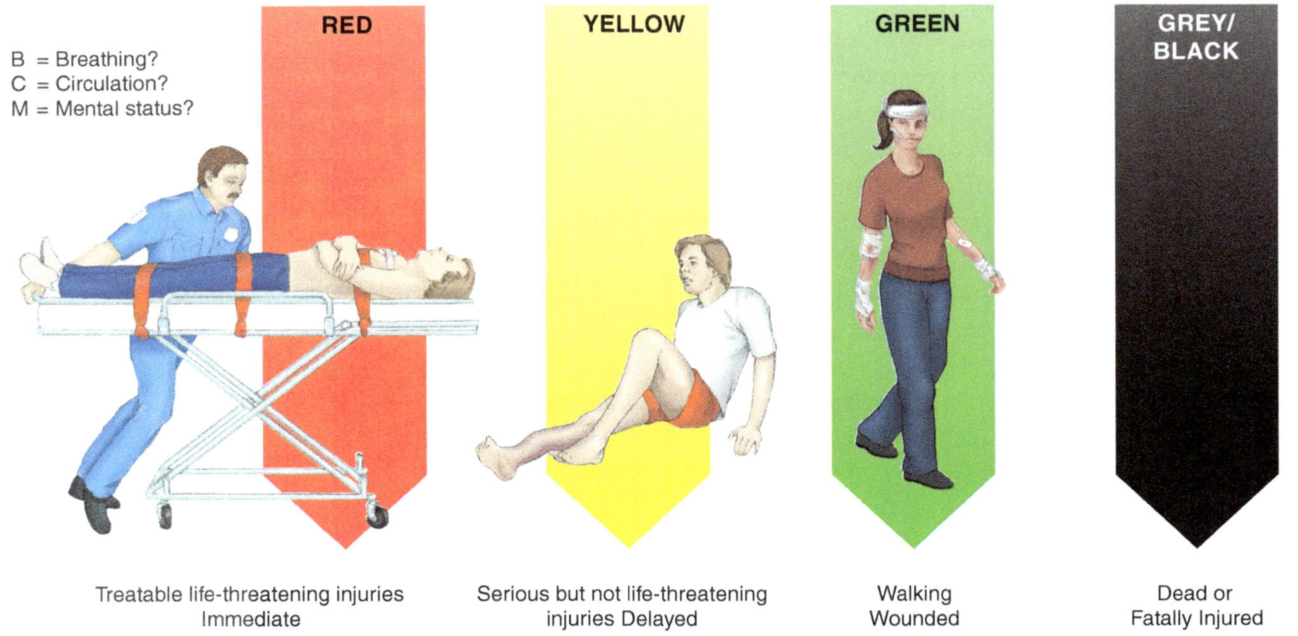

Figure 4 START triage.

safe area. This may require the use of a public address system, bullhorn device, or multiple other responders. Those victims who can move easily are immediately designated as priority 3 patients. The remaining victims will need to be physically sorted. Do not force a patient to move if he or she is unable or is complaining of pain during movement.

The next phase is to move in an orderly and systematic fashion through the area affected. Care should be taken to ensure that the area is covered in a manner such that no patients are missed. Stop at each patient and be prepared to tag each based on the color-coded priority. You should spend no more than a minute at each patient. Your goal is assessment, not care. Getting involved in lengthy treatments will delay care to others and possibly threaten the success of the overall incident.

At each patient, assess for breathing, circulation, and mental status (BCM). To assess breathing, look, listen, and feel the patient for breath sounds. If the patient is not breathing, assess the mouth and remove any foreign objects. If the patient does not breathe, open the airway using the head tilt-chin lift maneuver. If the patient breathes after the airway is open, assign the patient a priority 1 red ribbon. If at any time you think the patient may have trouble maintaining his or her airway or breathing, assign the patient a priority 1 red ribbon. If the patient does not breathe after you have opened the airway, assign him or her a priority 4 black ribbon.

If the patient is breathing at a rate of at least 30 breaths per minute, assign the patient a priority 1 red ribbon. If the patient's breathing rate is less than 30 breaths per minute, move to assess circulation.

Tip

Using the Head Tilt-Chin Lift Maneuver During Triage

The START system at an MCI allows you to use the traditional head tilt-chin lift airway maneuver instead of the modified jaw-thrust maneuver. This is because of the expedient nature of the triage assessment. In all other patient care circumstances, a modified jaw-thrust maneuver should be used to open an injured patient's airway.

Check the patient's circulation by assessing the patient's carotid pulse as described in the assessment and resuscitation units. Check the carotid pulse for 5 to 10 seconds. If the pulse is weak or irregular, assign the patient a priority 1 red ribbon. Consider raising the patient's legs approximately 1 foot to aid in returning blood to the heart and brain. Assess for bleeding. Control major bleeding by instructing the patient to hold direct pressure over the wound, or request walking wounded or bystanders to apply pressure. If the carotid pulse is absent, assign a priority 4 black ribbon.

At this point, you are still assessing patients who are breathing at a rate of less than 30 breaths per minute and have a strong, regular carotid pulse. Evaluate the remaining patients' mental status by asking them to follow a simple command such as "Open your eyes" or "Squeeze my hands." Patients who can comply are considered to have adequate breathing and circulation. These patients should be assigned a priority 2 yellow ribbon. Patients who do not follow commands should be assigned a priority 1 red ribbon.

Remember that patient conditions are frequently changing. LERs must reassess the priority of patients continuously as time passes and additional resources permit. After the initial triage, the scene management will focus on ensuring that incident command has been established according to your local protocols.

NATIONAL INCIDENT MANAGEMENT SYSTEM

At the end of the 20th century, large-scale natural and man-made disasters affected major population centers in the United States. The federal government determined that an incident management framework should be implemented at the federal level that would allow all levels of government and society to provide coordinated approaches to prepare for, respond to, mitigate, and recover from a variety of disruptive incidents. This process developed into a document called the **National Response Framework (NRF)** that provides for the structure and mechanism for a national-level policy of incident response. A companion document, the **National Incident Management System (NIMS)**, provides a template for response to incidents regardless of their size, scope, or cause. These two documents integrate the capabilities and resources of the government agencies, nongovernment agencies, and incident management and emergency response disciplines into a coordinated national framework for domestic incident response.

Prior to the development of NIMS, many different incident control theories were used. Notably, the incident command system (ICS) was developed in the 1970s following a series of catastrophic fires in California's urban interface. Property damage ran into the millions, and many people died or were injured. The personnel assigned to determine the causes of these outcomes studied the case histories and discovered that response problems could rarely be attributed to lack of resources or failure of tactics. Surprisingly, studies found that response problems were far more likely to result from inadequate management than from any other single reason. Entry-level responders are now required to be certified in the use of the ICS and NIMS.

The Incident Command System

The ICS, a key feature of NIMS, is a standardized management tool for meeting the demands of small or large emergency or nonemergency situations. It represents best practices and has become the standard for emergency management across the country. ICS may be used for planned events, natural disasters, and acts of terrorism.

The ICS is designed to increase efficiency by integrating facilities, equipment, personnel, procedures, and communications into a common organizational structure. According to NIMS,

> *"a basic premise of ICS is that it is widely applicable. It is used to organize both near-term and long-term field-level operations for a broad spectrum of emergencies.... ICS is used by all levels of government: federal, state, local, and tribal as well as by many private sector and nongovernmental organizations. ICS is also applicable across disciplines. It is normally structured to facilitate activities in five major functional areas: command, operations, planning, logistics, and finance and administration."*

It is essential to use an ICS at every emergency to help the incident commander (IC) organize, coordinate, and control all the activities that take place at an incident. A one-alarm incident seldom requires a command staff, section positions, or sectoring, so the IC at a single-unit response will generally perform all command staff and section functions. As incidents expand, however, the organization becomes more complex, requiring more staff and apparatus and increasing the need for command staff and section positions (**Figure 5**).

Because few law enforcement agencies do not respond to enough large-scale incidents to become proficient at organizing complex ICS organizations, training and education are needed to fill the experience gap. To maintain proficiency, law enforcement and security programs should regularly apply the ICS to real or simulated large-scale incidents.

A defensive operation at a hostage situation in a building with multiple exposures can provide an example of an

Figure 5 ICS is important at all levels of incident complexity, but becomes more involved as the incident grows in complexity.

operation that requires sectoring, command staff, and section positions. An appropriate training exercise would be the simulation of an incident with the deployment of several units on each side of the building and providing geographic, tactical-level management units for each side.

Discussion should include which command and sections to staff and why. Every member of the agency should be familiar with the ICS terminology and hierarchy, and those who will serve as the IC or in the upper echelon of the ICS organization at larger incidents will need more training in applying the system.

When evaluating your ICS organizational chart, you must answer several critical questions. For instance, does your ICS organizational chart show all your units? Does it use standard ICS terminology? Does the ICS organization follow the standard ICS hierarchy? Are tactical-level management units identified with an intuitive labeling system? Are the areas of responsibility logical? Are necessary command positions staffed? Safety should be staffed at an incident of this magnitude, and more than one incident safety officer may be needed. Are all necessary sections staffed?

By working through such scenarios, ICs will be better prepared to manage any incident safely and effectively. An ICS is developed using a grouping of crucial elements that must be addressed to ensure that the incident will be run without difficulty. The 14 crucial elements of ICS are as follows:

- **Common terminology.** Using common terminology helps define organizational functions, incident facilities, resource descriptions, and position titles.
- **Modular organization.** The ICS organizational structure develops in a top-down, modular fashion based on the size and complexity of the incident and the specific hazards created by the incident (**Figure 6**).
- **Management by objectives.** Establishing objectives will guide the operation. This includes developing and issuing assignments, plans, procedures, and protocols; establishing specific, measurable objectives for various incident management activities; and directing efforts to reach the objectives.
- **Reliance on an incident action plan.** Incident action plans (IAPs) provide a coherent means of communicating the overall incident objectives in the contexts of both operational and support activities.
- **Chain of command and unity of command.** **Chain of command** refers to the orderly line of authority within the ranks of the incident management organization. **Unity of command** means that every responder has a designated supervisor to whom he or she reports at the scene of the incident. These principles eliminate the confusion of multiple, conflicting directives. Incident managers at all levels must be able to control the actions of all personnel under their supervision.
- **Unified command.** In incidents involving multiple jurisdictions, a single jurisdiction with multi-agency involvement, or multiple jurisdictions with multi-agency involvement, unified command allows agencies with different legal, geographic, and functional authorities and responsibilities to work together effectively without affecting any agency's authority, responsibility, or accountability.
- **Manageable span of control.** Within ICS, the span of control of any individual with incident management supervisory responsibility should range from three to seven subordinates.
- **Predesignated incident locations and facilities.** Various types of operational locations and support facilities are established near an incident to accomplish a variety of purposes. Typical predesignated facilities include incident command posts, bases, camps, staging areas, mass-casualty triage areas, and others as required.
- **Resource management.** Resource management includes processes for categorizing, ordering, dispatching, tracking, and recovering resources. It also includes processes for reimbursement for resources,

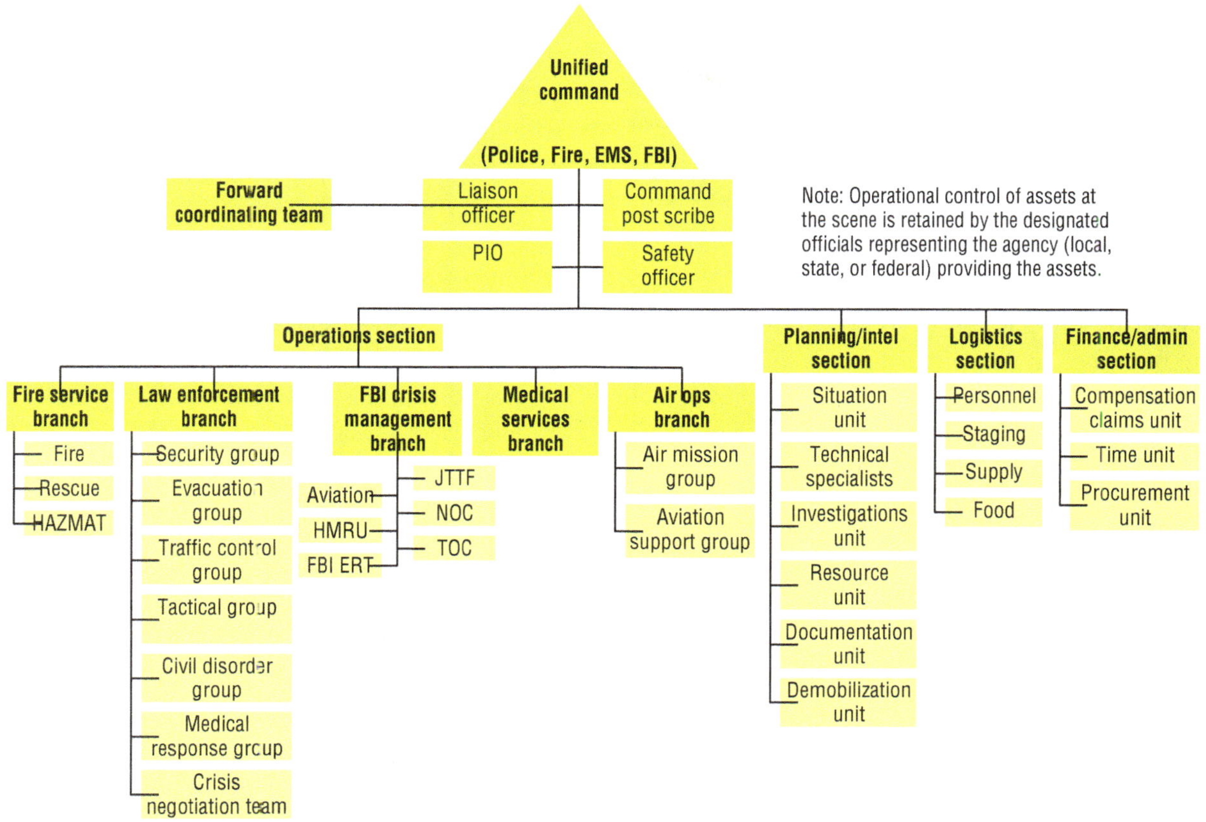

Figure 6 An example of a complete ICS organizational chart.

as appropriate. Resources are defined as personnel, teams, equipment, supplies, and facilities available or potentially available for emergency response.

- **Information and intelligence management.** The incident management organization must establish a process for gathering, sharing, and managing incident-related information and intelligence.
- **Integrated communications.** Incident communications are facilitated through a common communications plan and interoperable communications processes and architectures.
- **Transfer of command.** The command function must be clearly established from the beginning of an incident. When command is transferred, the process must include a briefing that captures all essential information for continuing safe and effective operations.
- **Accountability.** Effective accountability at all jurisdictional levels and within individual functional areas during incident operations is essential. To that end, the following principles must be adhered to:
  - **Check-in.** All responders, regardless of agency affiliation, must report to receive an assignment in accordance with the procedures established by the IC.
  - **IAP.** Response operations must be directed and coordinated as outlined in the IAP.
  - **Unity of command.** Each individual involved in incident operations will be assigned to only one supervisor.
  - **Span of control.** Supervisors must be able to supervise and control their subordinates and to communicate with and manage all resources under their supervision.
  - **Resource tracking.** Supervisors must record and report resource status changes as they occur.
- **Deployment.** Personnel and equipment should respond only when requested or when dispatched by an appropriate authority.

Tip

ICS Timelines and Training

Information on implementation timelines and training can be found at the web site of the Federal Emergency Management Agency (http://www.fema.gov) or through your local emergency management agency.

MOVING PATIENTS

There are many ways and reasons to move patients. LERs will need to be trained in the most basic techniques of moving patients. In some programs the LER may be trained in more advanced forms of moving patients, including the use of transport devices such as flexible stretchers and backboards.

Body Mechanics and Lifting Techniques

If you have not practiced the movement of patients, you will likely use muscles and techniques that can injure you or the patient. You should be physically capable of moving a patient. Injuries to the back and extremities of responders may limit their ability to perform certain movements. Good body mechanics are those lifting techniques in which the lifter uses a straightened natural back while lifting vertically using the large muscles of the legs and pelvis. Your body should remain straight, and your back should not be bent over or twisted. Your arms should be kept close to your body, and your feet should be firmly planted on the floor. Practice lifts so you can determine weights that may be unacceptable for you to move. A responder attempting to lift more than he or she is capable of lifting will soon be a patient.

Safe techniques include all of the lifters operating in unison, with one lead rescuer making the calls to lift and lower. The lead rescuer is typically positioned at the head of the patient. The lead rescuer should observe the positioning and stance of the other lifters and, when satisfied, give instructions on when and where to move. All lifters should communicate and immediately inform the other responders if they are having difficulties or observe unsafe conditions.

Stabilizing Patients

Sometimes the LER may determine that a patient does not need to be moved prior to EMS arrival. In these cases trauma patients with suspected neck or head injuries should lie flat with their neck and head secured to prevent additional movement. This technique of holding the head and neck in place should be maintained until EMS or LERs trained in spinal immobilization arrive. The patient with a head or neck injury may need to be log rolled to assess for life-threatening injuries to the back of the chest or abdomen. To log roll the patient lying on his or her back, follow the steps in **Skill Drill 1**:

1. One responder stabilizes the patient's head and neck with one hand on each side of the head and palms against the patient's face. If you are trained and authorized to apply a cervical collar, it should be applied prior to rolling the patient.
2. Two additional responders position themselves against one side of the patient. The responder closest to the head extends his or her arms over the patient's body and places a hand on the patient's far shoulder and pelvis (STEP 1).

Skill Drill 1

Log Rolling a Patient

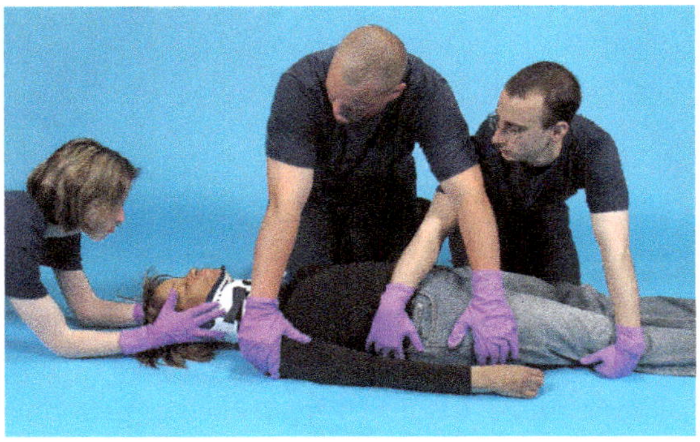

1. One responder stabilizes the patient's head and neck. Two additional responders position their hands on the opposite side of the patient's body.

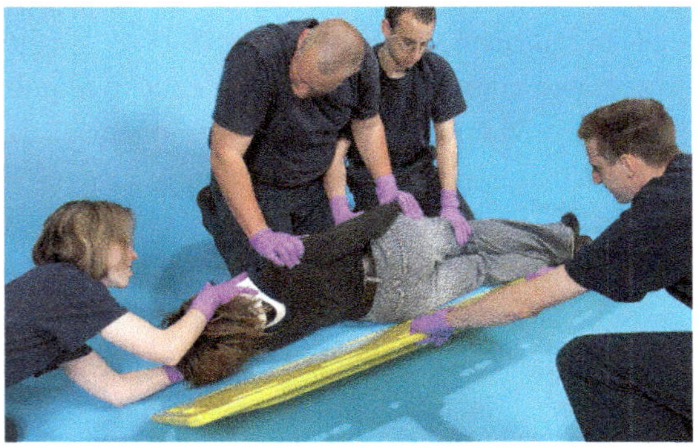

2. Working together, the responders roll the patient toward themselves as a unit.

3. The responder closest to the feet extends his or her arms across the patient's body. The arm closest to the head crosses over the second responder's arm and grabs the patient's far waist. The arm closest to the feet secures the patient's far knee.
4. On command from the responder at the head, the responders roll the patient toward themselves as a unit, allowing access to the patient's back STEP 2. This method can be used to place a long backboard if you are trained and authorized to use this device.

After you have assessed and treated any life threats or placed a backboard, return the patient, as a unit, to the position of lying on his or her back. This movement is completed on command from the responder at the head.

When placing patients on any lifting or moving devices, make sure the patient's weight is centered on the device. The head and arms should be inside the borders of the device. In some cases, the patient's feet and legs may extend past the border of the device. Take care with these exposed limbs and ensure that all other responders are aware of this condition. In some instances you may need to fabricate an extension using another backboard or splint to prevent additional trauma.

Emergency Patient Moves

Local agencies and departments will often provide basic training in patient movement techniques. These emergency movements should be used when a patient needs to be moved away from the area where an injury occurred and there is a danger that a hazard or violent act might occur that could cause additional harm. The quickest way to move a patient with one responder is the drag (**Table 1**). Dragging a patient is done by one person grabbing one part of the patient and pulling the patient away from the unsecured area.

Carries occur when the responder lifts a patient from the floor and moves him or her. The lift can occur with one person or more (**Table 2**).

Transport Devices

Table 3 lists the types of transport devices available for moving patients. LERs should become familiar with the types of patient transport devices their system uses. These devices can range from individual tactical stretchers to functioning ambulance stretchers. Most LER programs use flexible emergency stretchers that can be easily carried on their person or in a vehicle. Certain specialty programs may use backboards and basket stretchers.

Medical Restraints

Whenever you restrain a patient as a LER, you should follow your local policies and protocols relative to the restraint of prisoners or violent subjects. Medical restraints should not replace law enforcement restraints unless your policies authorize this. Conversely, medical restraining of patients to protect themselves and others from injury should not be confused with taking someone into legal custody.

Medical restraining is tightly controlled in EMS systems and is performed only when indicated by protocols or online medical direction. Medical restraints on backboards and stretchers are used much like a seat belt system in a motor vehicle. These systems provide attachment to the device and act as a passive restraint during falls or collisions. Backboard and stretcher restraints can be used in conjunction with commercial limb restraints or restraints made from wide, sturdy material such as cravats or roller gauze. Padding should be used under the constricting material to reduce compression trauma. All of these restraint techniques must be authorized by your medical director, and you should practice them to be able to restrain restless patients expediently without injury.

Restraint systems that constrict the upper airway or provide undue compression against the chest should be avoided. The restrained patient should be positioned in such a manner that the airway can be quickly controlled and, if possible, cleared by gravity. If possible, restraining a nontrauma patient in the recovery position would be optimal. Patients already on backboards for medical purposes must never be left unattended, and suction should be readily available.

AMBULANCE OPERATIONS

Before the LER can begin to manage an emergency scene, he or she must prepare. This preparation extends to the vehicles used to respond to an emergency incident or those used to transport patients from the incident scene to hospitals or casualty care collection points. In some programs, LERs at various levels of licensure may provide ambulance transportation or assist responding ambulances in packaging and transporting patients.

Apparatus Preparation

Ambulances and emergency response vehicles must be inspected regularly and be ready to respond. Some states set

Table 1

Types of Drags		
Clothes drag	Responder grabs clothing or gear vest at the shoulders or neck area.	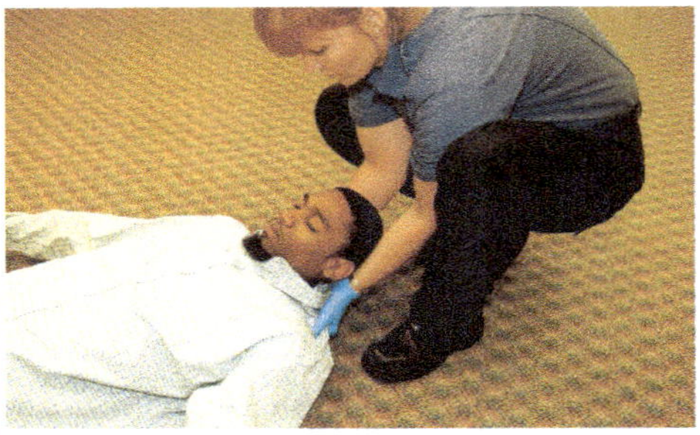
Blanket drag	Patient is wrapped in a blanket or rug, and responder pulls blanket or rug.	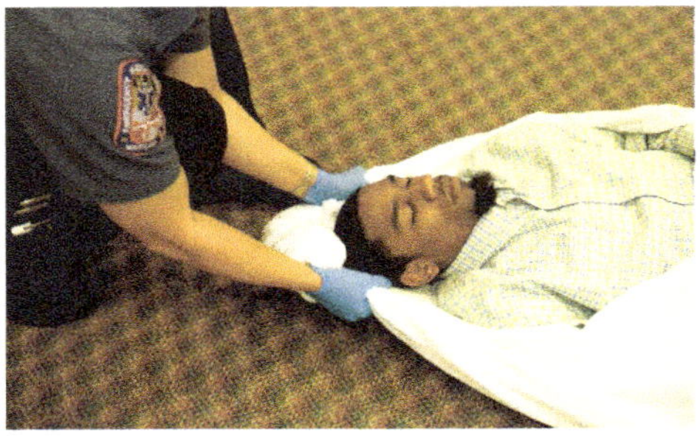
Elevated arm-to-arm drag	Responder positions himself or herself above the patient's head, inserts his or her arms from the patient's back through the armpits, and grabs his or her wrist. Responder lifts with legs and elevates the patient's torso, dragging the patient's feet. This drag will work for patients lying on the floor or from a seated position in a vehicle.	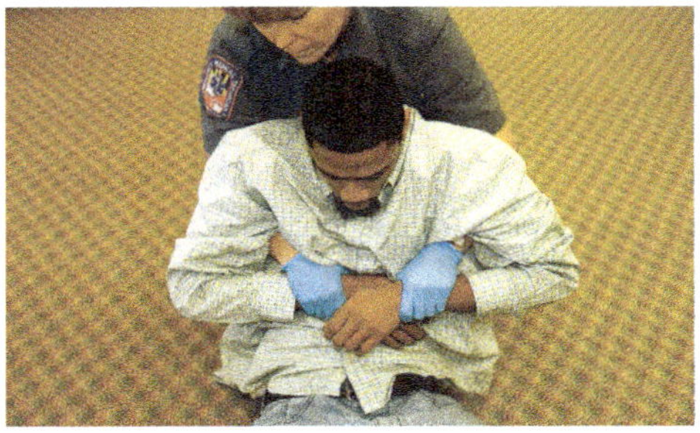
Fire fighter drag	The patient's hands are secured and placed over the responder's neck. Responder drags the patient in a low position face to face. This drag works well for poor-visibility conditions.	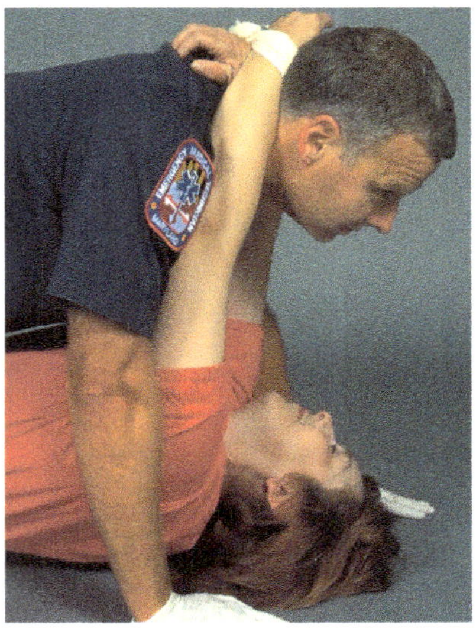

Table 2

Types of Carries

Cradle-in-arms carry	Responder picks up a smaller person or child and carries him or her in front using both arms to support the patient against the responder's body.	
Pack-strap carry	Responder faces away from the patient and pulls both arms over his or her shoulders while bent forward at the waist with knees bent. Responder walks bent at the waist with elevation provided by extension of the legs.	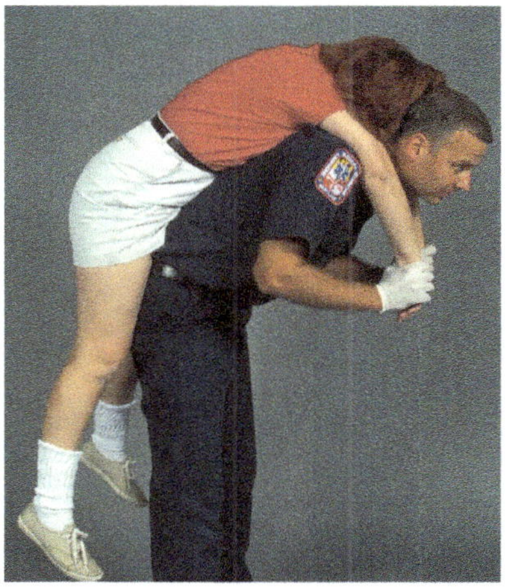
Fire fighter's carry	Facing the patient, the responder grabs the patient by bending down at the knees and placing his or her shoulder into the patient's abdomino-pelvic area. The responder extends his or her legs and brings his or her arm through the patient's legs, securing the patient's arm around the responder's neck.	

(Continues)

Table 2

Types of Carries *(continued)*

Extremity carry	One responder positions himself or herself above the patient's head, inserts his or her arms from the patient's back through the patient's armpits, and grabs his or her wrist. The second responder is positioned between the patient's legs and grabs the patient's thighs. The second responder can face the patient for short-duration carries or face away from the patient for longer-duration carries. Both responders will lift with legs upon command of the responder at the head.	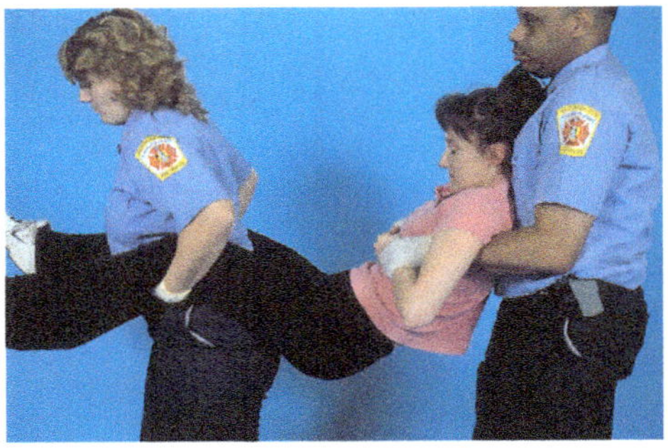
Seat carry	Responders stand side by side, interlock both arms, and scoop up the patient between the arms at the level of the pelvis.	
Chair carry	Using a chair, two responders position themselves at the front and back of the chair. The lift is coordinated and called by the responder at the head.	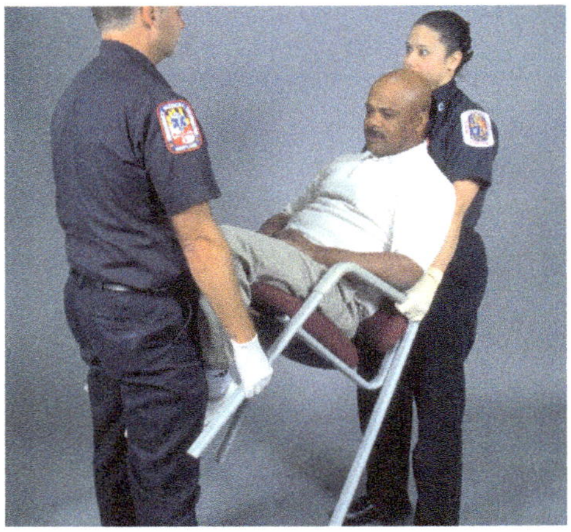

Table 2

Types of Carries *(continued)*		
Supporting carry	One or two responders get under the patient's armpits, securing the patient's arms over their necks and supporting the patient's weight while the patient provides some ambulatory support.	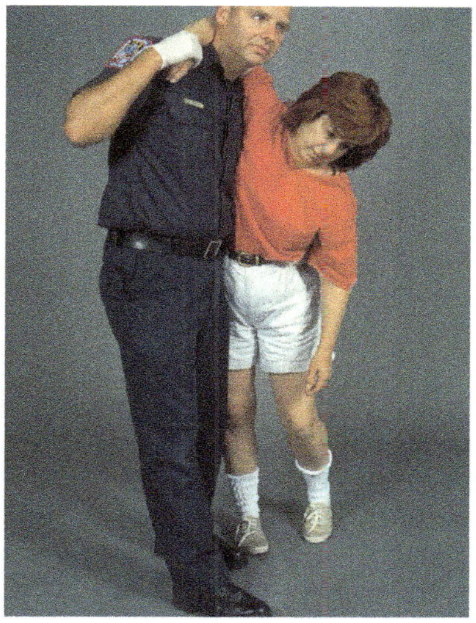

Table 3

Types of Transport Devices		
Portable stretchers	Stretchers may also be referred to as gurneys or litters. They can have wheels and be rolled on flat surfaces, or they may require carrying. Some stretchers are flexible and can be rolled up for storage and transport. All stretchers should have straps or belts to provide fall security to the patient during transport.	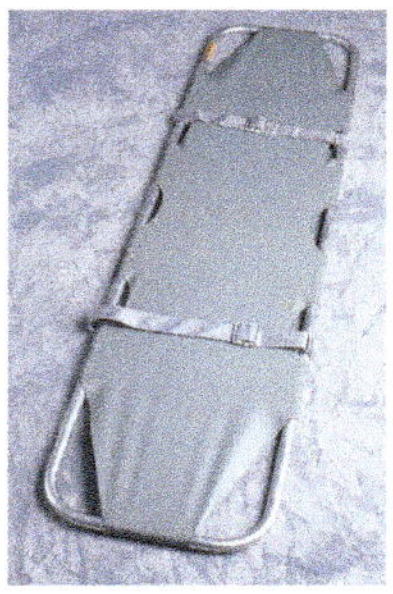 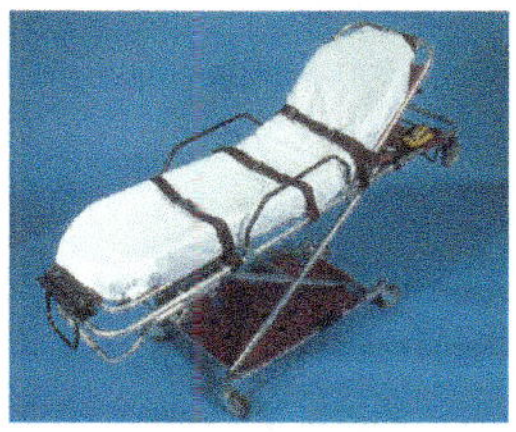
Scoop stretchers	These stretchers can split apart and reassemble under a patient to prevent excess movement prior to lifting.	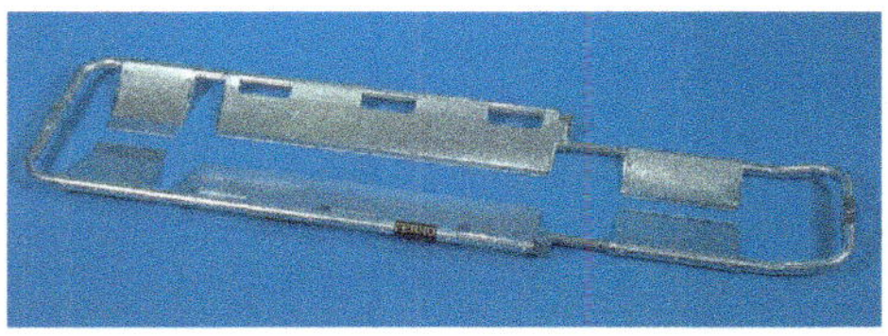

(Continues)

Table 3

Types of Transport Devices *(continued)*

Basket stretcher	These stretchers are commonly referred to as *Stokes* baskets and are used to carry patients securely when there are changes in angles or elevations. They are frequently used in rope rescue incidents.	
Stair chairs	Chairs with small wheels or tracks allow the movement of a patient up or down a stairwell or incline.	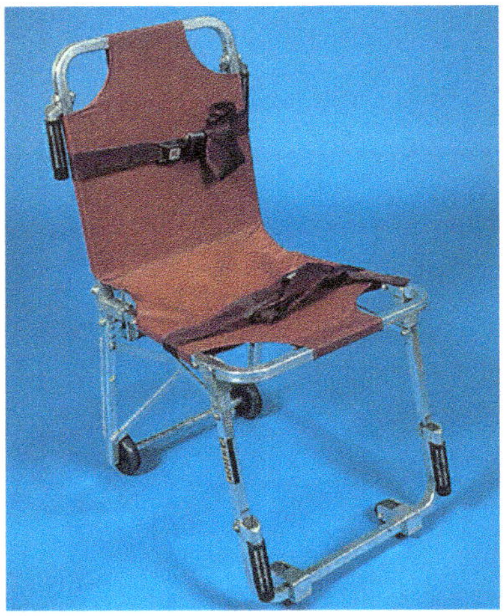
Backboards	Backboards are solid, firm devices that are used to secure a patient with a possible head, neck, or back injury to prevent the injured spine from moving. Short backboards are applied to seated patients to allow safe transfer from vehicles or confined spaces onto a long backboard.	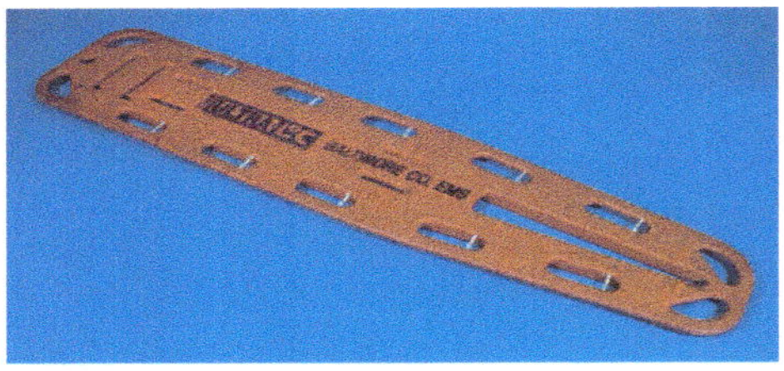

policies regarding the inspection of the unit's engine, brakes, and other vital systems. Regardless of requirements, responders using and operating emergency vehicles should evaluate the apparatus before each shift and throughout a shift to confirm that the unit meets the local operational requirements for tire pressure, engine fluid levels, lights, signals, and vehicle handling and warning devices. Failure to maintain an operational level of apparatus readiness could result in the unit failing to respond.

Safety equipment is typically available on the apparatus. This equipment will include the PPE assigned to you by your agency or department. In some cases, high-visibility traffic gear will be issued for use on or near streets or traffic. Ensure that these items are available and in good working condition prior to placing the apparatus in service.

Prearrival Considerations

When operating the apparatus en route to an incident or hospital, all occupants should use the unit's protective restraints. Protective restraint systems should be designed so the occupants can wear PPE and operate effectively in caring for patients. Because of the large volume of portable equipment associated with EMS apparatus, the responders should confirm that all gear is placed in its normal position and secured prior to the vehicle moving. Equipment has been damaged and lost when unsecured equipment slams into compartment doors, releasing latch mechanisms and exiting the compartment. Loose equipment in the cab and patient compartment can move freely, hitting occupants or interrupting normal vehicle operations. Apparatus operators should follow their local protocols and training relative to the use of emergency devices. In some jurisdictions, units use emergency warning devices when responding and transporting. In other jurisdictions, an apparatus operator is given discretion to use emergency warning devices only when there is a critical need.

When operating an emergency vehicle, it is important to follow all local traffic laws and policies. Apparatus response is typically the most dangerous part of any emergency medical incident. Apparatus should be designed to limit distraction to the apparatus operator from communications systems and patient care.

Scene Safety and Management

Apparatus should be staged in an appropriate location based on incident conditions and needs. Prior to arrival, observe for critical environmental threats. If vehicles are involved or you are in an industrial setting, look for placards or warning signs prior to staging the apparatus.

Ensure that you and your crew leave the vehicle in a safe posture, with wheels chocked or locks engaged based on local protocols. Perform a quick size-up of the incident. Look 360 degrees around the vehicle and the incident, observing for potential or actual threats. Observe for traditional and nontraditional threats. If this is an accidental injury incident, observe for the mechanism of injury. Evaluate whether a patient is trapped or whether you will need any specialized resources.

Leaving the Scene

Prior to leaving an incident, ensure that you have accounted for all possible patients and that all hazards have been identified and, if possible, mitigated. Dispose properly of any disposable supplies and equipment. Clean or, in emergent situations, cover and isolate contaminated areas until you can return and clean the area. Make sure that you have passed appropriate scene and transport information to other public safety officers who are remaining at the location.

Medical Aviation Use and Considerations

Many areas—urban, suburban, and rural—use some form of aviation transport. This is most often accomplished by using rotary-wing aircraft, commonly called helicopters. These aircraft are ideal for moving moderate distances and using small spaces to land and take off vertically. Helicopters can provide a good alternative to lengthy ground transportation for critically ill or injured patients. Some locations may use fixed wing aircraft, commonly called airplanes. These aircraft can transfer a patient over long distances, but they will need runways for landing and takeoff.

Local protocols should be followed for determining who should receive aviation transport. In some locations these protocols may be in the form of state or local statutes. Aviation transport has significant disadvantages. The cost, risk, and inability to travel in poor weather or operate at high altitudes require careful consideration prior to arbitrarily requesting this service. The criteria for use of aviation assets often restrict their use to life-threatening trauma, medical conditions, or specialized populations such as neonates.

LERs must learn the intricacies of the aviation programs which with they may be working. Communication is essential when operating in and around aircraft. Many programs have dedicated radio systems for notification and in-flight communications. If you are communicating face to face you may need to speak inside a vehicle or structure or behind a large vehicle or structure to reduce the noise from the rotors and jet engines. If you are unclear about a communication, stop activity until you are clear.

Helicopters require a dedicated landing zone. These areas range from established pads and designated areas to makeshift landing zones in fields or parking lots. Know the proper requirements for landing zones in your area. With the wide range of aircraft being used and the varied geographical locations, generalized statements about landing zones are not necessarily helpful. Some programs will require light restrictions to keep from blinding pilots when they land. Other programs may require a detailed lighting of the landing zone. Some programs will require fire department assets on location to deal with hazards and to be prepared in the event of a fire. All of these considerations should be addressed with local air services prior to the LER using emergency medical aviation.

Safety of the patient and the flight crew are paramount. To protect yourself and others, never approach a landing aircraft or an aircraft on the ground without authorization from the flight crew. If you are allowed to approach the aircraft, follow the specific instructions from the flight crew. Most programs advise rescuers operating within their landing zone never to go near the tail rotor of the aircraft and always to stay in the pilot's line of sight. If you are in doubt about approaching the aircraft then do not approach the aircraft.

Helicopters are restricted relative to altitude, weather, flight distance, and cabin space. Safety is the key; never approach the aircraft without flight crew permission. Jet engines can easily pull a rescuer into the intake from the front and burn a rescuer severely from the rear. Propellers can be moving so fast that rescuers may not see them and walk directly into the blades. The time it takes to be safe is understood. Rushing to access an air ambulance of any type can result in the death of the rescuer and delay the transport of the patient who required the service.

If you do use medical aviation programs, you should be trained in safe aircraft approach and landing zone requirements and understand exactly what your role is in operating near the aviation unit. Rotors, propellers, and jet engines are all lethal if approached incorrectly. Loading a patient into an aviation unit requires strict adherence to travel paths and flight crew communications.

CONCLUSION

LERs should be prepared to provide scene management at emergency incidents. Scene management should concentrate on the relationship between your role as a law enforcement agent or officer and as an emergency medical responder. In some instances, the LER may never proceed past an initial firefight. Returning fire, managing wounds during a hostile confrontation, and maintaining the safety of the public until local emergency services arrive should be the standard scene management scenario for LERs. With the variety of conditions facing today's LER, however, it is not unreasonable to consider the LER as a vital component at disasters and MCIs. Using concepts of triage, ambulance operations, and NIMS, a LER can bring more than just security to the emergency scene.

Prep Kit

Ready for Review

- LERs must have a general awareness of the National Incident Management System (NIMS). As a law enforcement official, you can easily find yourself as the lead government official at various types of disasters.
- The phases of an emergency medical services (EMS) call are typically described as reporting, dispatch, first response, EMS response, and hospital care.
- The LER operating as the lead official at the emergency scene may be responsible for taking on a leadership role. Scene management priorities for the LER are scene safety, triage, incident command, and EMS operations.
- At incidents where the number of patients can quickly overwhelm the resources of the initial responders, triage can be used to sort which patients need the immediate assets.
- The ICS, a key feature of NIMS, is a standardized management tool for meeting the demands of small or large emergency or nonemergency situations. It represents best practices and has become the standard for emergency management across the country.
- The 14 crucial elements of ICS are as follows:
  - Common terminology
  - Modular organization
  - Management by objectives
  - Reliance on an incident action plan
  - Chain of command and unity of command
  - Unified command
  - Manageable span of control
  - Predesignated incident locations and facilities
  - Resource management
  - Information and intelligence management
  - Integrated communications
  - Transfer of command
  - Accountability
  - Deployment
- You should be physically capable of moving a patient. Injuries to the back and extremities of responders may limit their ability to perform certain movements.
- In some programs, LERs at various levels of licensure may provide ambulance transportation or assist responding ambulances in packaging and transporting patients.

Vital Vocabulary

chain of command A rank structure, spanning the entry-level responder to the incident commander, to manage an incident.

National Incident Management System (NIMS) The structure for managing an emergency incident, which may require a response of many different agencies; designed to provide efficient and effective management from initial response through recovery.

National Response Framework (NRF) A document that provides for the structure and mechanism for a national-level policy of incident response.

START system A system of casualty sorting using simple triage and rapid treatment.

triage The sorting of patients into groups according to the severity of their injuries; used to determine priorities for treatment and transport.

unity of command A characteristic of the incident command system structure that has each individual reporting to a single supervisor and everyone reporting to the incident commander (IC) directly or through the chain of command.

Check Your Knowledge

1. Which of the following is not a phase of an EMS call?
   A. First response
   B. Hospital care
   C. Rescue
   D. Dispatch
2. The LER should not attempt to extinguish small incipient fires using portable fire extinguishers.
   A. True
   B. False
3. Using the START triage method, a patient with minimal injuries would be considered which of the following?
   A. Red
   B. Green
   C. Yellow
   D. Gray
4. How many rescuers are necessary to log roll a patient?
   A. One
   B. Two
   C. Three
   D. Four
5. Which of the following steps is part of the 360-degree scene assessment?
   A. Observe for the mechanism of injury.
   B. Evaluate whether there are any trapped patients.
   C. Observe for nontraditional threats.
   D. All of the above.

Environmental Hazards

Unit 6

Brandon Graham
Robert Yonas
Timothy J. Gabourie

Law Enforcement Responder Objectives

Fire Suppression

- Describe the basic chemistry of fire by explaining the four elements of the fire tetrahedron. (pp 101–102)
- Describe the conditions needed for a fire to occur. (pp 101–102)
- Describe the four methods of extinguishing a fire. (pp 101–102)
- Describe the products of combustion. (pp 102–103)
- Define the five basic classes of fire. (pp 103–104)
- Describe the appropriate use of a fire extinguisher. (pp 104–106)
- Describe the conditions when it is safe for the law enforcement responder (LER) to attempt extinguishment of a fire. (pp 105–106)
- Describe the appropriate use of a fire extinguisher. (pp 106, 107)
- Describe the role of the LER in an integrated incident command system at the scene of a fire incident. (pp 106–107)

Hazardous Materials Accidents and Weapons

- Identify the OSHA standard for a hazardous materials response. (p 108)
- List the content required by a HAZWOPER Hazardous Materials Awareness-level course. (pp 108–110)
- List Department of Transportation requirements and methods for hazardous materials identification. (pp 108–110)
- Identify the purpose of the *Emergency Response Guidebook*. (pp 108–110)
- Discuss National Fire Protection Association (NFPA) guidelines regarding hazardous materials responses. (pp 110–111)
- Identify the NFPA hazardous materials hazard levels, relative to personal risk and personal protective equipment. (pp 110–111)
- Identify types of respiratory protection. (p 111)
- Identify types of hazardous materials clothing ensembles. (p 111)
- List patient care considerations for the hazardous materials patient. (pp 111–112)
- Define decontamination. (p 112)
- List steps and considerations the rescuer should take during decontamination. (p 112)
- Define terrorism. (pp 112–113)
- List and define the types of terrorism. (pp 112–113)
- List and define specific terrorist groups. (pp 112–113)
- Identify the law enforcement response considerations relative to chemical, biological, radiation, nuclear, and explosive threats. (pp 113–117)
- Identify general terrorism response tactics for law enforcement. (p 113)
- Define the purpose of the Department of Homeland Security threat level indicators. (p 113)
- Identify terrorism response safety concerns. (p 115)
- Discuss techniques to preserve evidence after a terrorist incident. (p 115)

Narcotics and Clandestine Labs

- Define clandestine drug laboratory. (pp 117–119)
- Recognize the potential risks and health hazards of a clandestine laboratory. (pp 117–119)
- Recognize the basic materials and chemicals needed in the production of methamphetamine, crack cocaine, and hydroponic marijuana. (pp 117–119)
- Determine the appropriate emergency responder patient management strategies for toxic exposure. (pp 119–121)

National EMS Education Standard Competencies

EMS Operations

Knowledge of operational roles and responsibilities to ensure safe patient, public, and personnel safety.

Hazardous Materials Awareness

- Risks and responsibilities of operating in a cold zone at a hazardous material or other special incident. (p 108)

Mass Casualty Incidents due to Terrorism and Disaster

- Risks and responsibilities of operating on the scene of a natural or manmade disaster. (p 113)

Fire Suppression

Every year in the United States, public safety agencies respond to over 1.6 million fire-related incidents that cause thousands of deaths, tens of thousands of injuries, and billions of dollars in economic loss. Although fire departments are usually responsible for suppression operations at these scenes, law enforcement responders (LERs) play a vital support role in these incidents. During the performance of routine law enforcement activities, it is not uncommon for the LER either to encounter an emergency involving a fire or to be dispatched to assist fire service personnel at the scene of a fire. It is critical that the LER fully understand his or her roles and responsibilities at such incidents—not only to ensure the LER's own safety, but also to protect other public safety personnel and members of the general public.

LERs at an incident involving a fire must quickly respond with appropriate actions that protect life and property without placing themselves in unnecessary danger or obstructing fire department operations. Common roles for a LER operating at a fire incident include assisting with citizen evacuation, traffic control, evidence preservation, and investigation. Additionally, the LER may be in the position to extinguish a fire by properly using a fire extinguisher before the arrival of fire department resources. As with any incident involving multiple-agency response, cooperation and coordination between fire service and law enforcement personnel are critical to successful resolution of the incident.

Every law enforcement agency should have a set of standard operating procedures (or guidelines) that delineate the exact role of its officers and the actions they should take when they encounter a fire during the performance of their duties. These policies and procedures should incorporate the safety, strategic, and tactical considerations detailed in this unit to ensure that officers are operating safely and in a manner that complements the actions of the fire service responders, who are ultimately responsible for resolving fire incidents.

BASICS OF FIRE CHEMISTRY

Fire, also referred to as **combustion**, is simply a rapid chemical process that results in the release of energy in the form of heat and (usually) light. All forms of matter can burn when the right conditions exist, and understanding these conditions is the key to understanding how a fire starts, behaves, and is extinguished. The three basic conditions required for a fire to exist are fuel, oxygen, and heat.

The **fuel** required for combustion can be a solid, a liquid, or a gas. Simply put, fuel is any material that can burn. Although fuels such as gasoline and wood are obvious, in the presence of enough heat and oxygen, almost anything can become a fuel for a fire to burn. Also required for combustion is the presence of sufficient **oxygen**, which is usually present in adequate concentrations in air. As you know, fuel—such as gasoline, wood, or paper—does not spontaneously combust when it is in contact with oxygen. For the process of fire to occur, the fuel and oxygen must be exposed to enough **heat** to start the chain reaction of fire. For a fuel to burn, the fuel must be heated to its **ignition temperature**. For certain common fuels, this temperature is relatively low, such as in the case of gasoline (about 260°C [500°F], depending on grade) or wood (about 302°C [575°F]). For other materials, the ignition temperature can be very high (such as metals, which can be thousands of degrees Fahrenheit).

To understand how these solids burn, it is important to understand that the solids themselves do not burn. When a material is heated to its ignition temperature, it actually releases gases that burn in very close proximity to the solid, giving the appearance that the solid material itself is on fire. The process of a solid releasing gas that can be burned is called **pyrolysis**.

When sufficient fuel, oxygen, and heat are present for the process of combustion, they react with each other in a continuous, uninhibited **chemical chain reaction** that we recognize as fire. It is this chain of continuous chemical reactions that allows a fire to continue to burn as long as the oxygen, heat, and fuel remain. The factors of fuel, oxygen, heat, and the chemical chain reaction collectively compose what is commonly referred to as the **fire tetrahedron** (**Figure 1**).

To extinguish a fire successfully, one simply needs to remove one of the four factors of the fire tetrahedron. The simplest factor to remove is often the fuel. By removing the fuel, there will be nothing left to burn, and the reaction cannot continue. Fire fighters can remove the factor of oxygen by creating a barrier, such as firefighting foam, to prevent oxygen from interacting with a fire. The most common method of extinguishing a fire is by applying water, which lowers the temperature below the ignition temperature so that the fire will not continue to burn. Finally, there are special extinguishing agents (such as Halon and Halon alternatives) that directly interfere with the chemical chain reaction of combustion and stifle the continuation of fire, even in the presence of adequate fuel, oxygen, and heat.

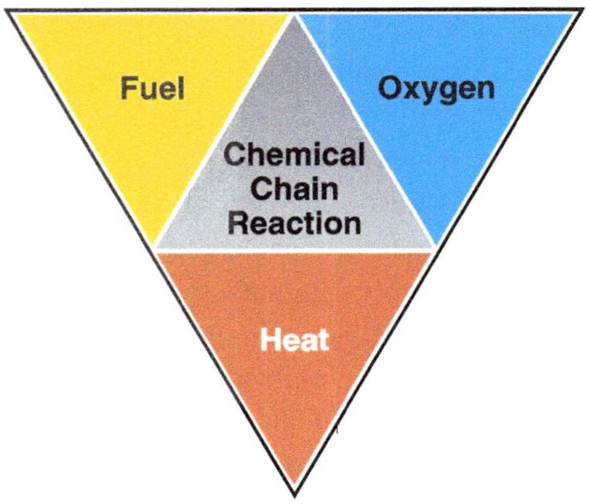

Figure 1 The fire tetrahedron includes fuel, oxygen, heat, and a chemical chain reaction as the essential elements of the combustion process.

Products of Combustion

When materials undergo complete combustion, the major products released are carbon dioxide and water. However, very few fires actually result in complete combustion. In addition to heat and light, most fires typically result in the production of gases, smoke, ash, and other fine solid or vapor materials. These products of combustion vary greatly depending on the type of fuel, atmospheric conditions (how much oxygen is available, for example), and the temperature at which the fire is burning. Many of the compounds found in smoke are very irritating or, in many cases, highly toxic. Dangerous substances such as carbon monoxide, cyanide, phosgene, aerosolized acids, and many other toxic products can be found in even the most routine fire encountered by the LER. Additionally, especially in fires inside buildings or vehicles, smoke can be very hot and can physically burn the upper and lower airways if inhaled. In certain cases, liquid droplets found in smoke can be poisonous if they are absorbed by the skin.

Most people who are victims of fires are affected by the resulting smoke of a fire rather than by flames and burns. Inhalation of smoke from a fire can cause severe injuries or death. Because of this ever-present danger at fire incidents, LERs should use great caution and avoid exposure to smoke. Even after a fire has been extinguished and the air appears to be clean, it is common for toxic gases to be released by partially combusted materials. This is especially important for LERs to consider while conducting investigations following a fire.

Because of the dangers of smoke inhalation, fire fighters always wear respiratory protective equipment while operating at a fire incident. They typically wear self-contained breathing apparatus (SCBA), which provides them with pressurized, breathable air to consume while in a dangerous environment (**Figure 2**). Very rarely is SCBA available for LER use, so avoidance of toxic and smoky environments is the best tactic for a LER to prevent the dangerous effects of smoke inhalation. The use of SCBA requires significant training, certification, and testing to ensure that the user and the equipment are ready for deployment to a potentially hazardous environment.

Tip

When to Use SCBA

Personnel should use SCBA or other personal protective equipment only when they are adequately trained and certified in its proper use.

Figure 2 Closed-circuit SC3A.

Additionally, LERs should not attempt to use their air-purifying respirator (APR, commonly referred to as a "gas mask") in a fire situation, because there is often an oxygen-deprived environment present during fires, and the gas mask does not protect the user from an oxygen-deficient environment.

CLASSES OF FIRE

To extinguish a fire effectively, LERs must recognize the type, or class, of the fire they have encountered. Fires are classified according to the type of fuel that is burning (**Figure 3**). This classification is necessary to determine which method of extinguishment will be the most effective. Extinguishing agents are classified to match the class of fire that they can most effectively extinguish. Certainly, when more than one type of fuel is involved, a fire can be classified into multiple classes.

Class A Fires

Class A fires are very common for the LER. They include fires whose fuel is composed of ordinary solid combustibles such as wood, paper, textiles, and other common solids. Because the most effective method of extinguishing these types of fire is to remove the heat from the fire, the most effective extinguishing agent for class A fires is water.

Figure 3 The icons for classes A, B, C, and K fires.

Class B Fires

Also a routine occurrence for the LER is a class B fire. These types of fire have combustible or flammable liquids as their fuel. Class B fires include such common materials as gasoline, kerosene, and oils. To confront a class B fire effectively, the most success is achieved using an extinguisher that relies on dry chemicals, foams, or carbon dioxide to remove the oxygen from the fire.

Class C Fires

Class C fires are characterized by the presence of energized electrical equipment. Usually the actual fuel for the fire is a class A or class B material, but the presence of electrical hazards requires the fire to be given a special classification for safety purposes. Use of water (or a class A–only fire extinguisher) is strongly discouraged because it presents an electrical hazard to the LER. Carbon dioxide is the extinguishing agent of choice for class C fires. If only water is available when confronted by a class C fire, it is imperative that the electrical equipment be de-energized first. The LER must ensure that all power is shut off before using water on a class C fire. Shutting off the power may be as simple as pulling a cord from a socket, flipping a wall switch to off, or turning off a breaker. If shutting off the power is more complex than these routine measures, the LER may need to wait for assistance from the local fire department or power company.

Class D Fires

Class D fires are distinguished by the presence of a burning metal. For example, magnesium is a metal that can burn at much lower temperatures than most other metals. Lithium and potassium are other examples of metals that are commonly encountered in class D fires. Water should not be used to extinguish class D fires because it will usually only intensify the fire and increase the hazard. Special, salt-based extinguishing agents are specifically designed for class D fires. Class D fire extinguishers will be marked by the letter D on a yellow, five-pointed star. If a class D extinguishing agent is not available, the LER can use dry sand in an attempt to confine or extinguish a class D fire.

Class K Fires

The newest classification of fires is for fires commonly found in kitchen areas. Class K fires involve combustible cooking materials such as cooking oil and grease. There are newer extinguishing agents specially designed for class K fires, and they are commonly found in commercial kitchens and cafeterias.

Figure 4 APW fire extinguisher.

SAFE USE OF FIRE EXTINGUISHERS

As indicated by the different classifications of fire, there are different types of fire extinguishers designed to fight different classes of fires. The three most common fire extinguishers are as follows:

- Air-pressurized water
- Carbon dioxide
- Dry chemical (ABC or BC)

Air-Pressurized Water

Air-pressurized water fire extinguishers contain only water and compressed air. They suppress fire by reducing the heat factor of the fire tetrahedron and should be used only on class A fires such as wood and paper. The numeric rating for this class of extinguisher refers to the water capacity of the extinguisher and the size of the fire it will extinguish. Air-pressurized water should not be used on any other class of fire because it will likely increase the size of the fire and could cause harm to the extinguisher user (**Figure 4**).

Carbon Dioxide

Carbon dioxide fire extinguishers contain compressed carbon dioxide that suppresses class B and C fires by reducing the oxygen factor of the fire tetrahedron. Because the discharge of carbon dioxide is very cold, they also can reduce the heat factor of a fire, but they are usually ineffective on class A fires. These extinguishers should be used on fires involving flammable liquids such as grease, gasoline, and oil. The numeric rating for this class of fire extinguisher refers to the approximate number of square feet of a flammable liquid fire that the user can expect to extinguish (**Figure 5**).

Dry Chemical

Dry chemical fire extinguishers are varied in their types and design. They are filled with a pressurized dry powder agent and can range in size and intended use. ABC models are designed to extinguish class A, class B, or class C fires. The BC versions of dry chemical extinguishers are designed to suppress only class B and class C fires. All of these extinguishers work by insulating the fuel with a thin layer of powder that separates the fuel from the oxygen in air. Because of their diversity of potential uses, these types of extinguishers are commonly found in LER patrol vehicles. They can be used on automobile fires and many other fires encountered by the LER during routine duties (**Figure 6**).

Figure 5 Carbon dioxide extinguishers are heavy because of the weight of the container and the quantity of carbon dioxide needed to extinguish a fire. They also have a large discharge nozzle that makes them easy to identify.

Figure 6 Multipurpose dry chemical extinguisher.

Fire Extinguisher Inspection and Readiness

No matter what type of fire extinguisher you are issued, it is important to ensure its readiness in case you need to use it during an emergency. As is true for all of your other equipment, the usefulness and readiness of the extinguisher is the LER's responsibility before assuming duty or beginning an assignment. The basic elements of a fire extinguisher that should be checked are as follows:

- **Check the gauge.** The pressure indicator on the gauge should be in the "green zone." However, carbon dioxide extinguishers do not have pressure gauges.
- **Check the inspection tag.** The extinguisher should have a current inspection tag, and the date should not be expired.
- **Check the pin and handle.** The pin and handle should be secured in place and are usually sealed with a plastic tab seal.
- **Check the hose.** The extinguisher and hose should be free of any visible damage.

Decision: Fight or Flee the Fire?

When you encounter a situation involving a fire, immediate action is required to save lives and property. The first action should always be to request assistance from the fire department. Even if a fire is small, the fire service should be notified and requested in case the fire spreads or additional fire investigation is required. The next objective is to assist in the removal of any persons in immediate danger from the fire. Whether a fire involves a vehicle or a building, if the LER can safely do so, he or she should attempt to assist those in danger without further risking the LER's own safety.

Once appropriate notification has been made and assistance of those in immediate danger has been accomplished, the LER needs to assess whether it is safe to fight a fire or whether to flee from the immediate danger posed by the fire. The LER should attempt to fight a fire only if:

- **The fire is small and contained.** The best chance at successful extinguishment of a fire is when it first starts. If a fire has already grown out of control, use of a fire extinguisher is not likely to be successful, and the LER is at risk for becoming a victim of the fire by staying in the immediate area. As a rule, if a fire is over your head, you should immediately escape the area. If you are inside a building and it is unsafe to fight the fire, immediately evacuate, and close the doors or windows if possible as you leave. You should not attempt to fight a fire in a confined space.
- **You are safe from toxic smoke.** If a fire is producing thick, black smoke or a chemical smoke, the LER should not attempt to fight the fire. Doing so only puts the LER at great risk for toxic inhalation injury. If you are outdoors, fight a fire with the wind at your back to minimize your exposure to the smoke.
- **You have means of escape.** The LER should fight a fire only if there is a safe passageway to escape the fire if it begins to spread or extinguishment efforts are unsuccessful. Never stay and fight a fire if there is a possibility that you may become trapped inside a building without a safe way out.
- **Your instincts say it's safe.** If you are not completely comfortable fighting a fire, it is time to escape. The fire department will bring the appropriate resources to safely put out the fire. As the saying goes, "Discretion is the better part of valor."

Fighting the Fire

When it is safe to do so, and conditions merit the use of the appropriate fire extinguisher, remember the PASS method (**Skill Drill 1**):

1. Pull the pin STEP 1.
2. Aim the nozzle or hose at the base of the fire from the recommended safe distance STEP 2.
3. Squeeze the lever to discharge the fire extinguishing agent from the extinguisher STEP 3.
4. Sweep the nozzle from side to side while aiming at the base of the fire until the fire is out or the extinguisher is empty. If the fire is not extinguished when the extinguisher is empty, then it is time to escape STEP 4.

SUPPORTING THE FIRE DEPARTMENT

When the public calls 911 to request assistance for a fire, many jurisdictions immediately send law enforcement either to verify the call or to support the fire department. Because of the nature of dynamic law enforcement patrol activities compared with the usual static deployment configuration of most fire departments, it is common for the LER to arrive at the scene of a fire before the fire department. In this scenario, the initial actions of the first-arriving LERs can either provide great assistance or cause major obstacles to the overall response to the incident.

One of the most common mistakes made by LERs when they first arrive at a fire scene is to drive to the address at the fire location and park in front of the building. Law enforcement vehicles serve little purpose in having immediate access to a building on fire, and often are an obstacle for the multiple arriving fire department vehicles that require close proximity to the fire. Although common sense may dictate this simple notion, the first moments of being at the scene of a fire can be very stressful and somewhat chaotic, which can lead to making poor decisions on vehicle placement and resource deployment. LERs should make a conscious effort to park vehicles in a position where they do not obstruct incoming fire department apparatus or fire hydrants that may be needed to supply water to the building that is on fire. Proactive planning should dictate that LERs position their vehicles in locations that will allow them to transition to support duties such as traffic control and incident command support easily.

Common Mission Goals

During an emergency incident, the primary mission of law enforcement personnel is to identify the perpetrators of a crime and to build a case for successful prosecution. The traditional role and priority for LERs consists of activities such as threat analysis and reduction, site security, responder protection, crime scene preservation, and witness interrogation. Even though these skills are often required at the scene of a fire incident, these priorities are not always consistent with those of the responding fire department and other emergency response and support organizations. History has demonstrated that when several agencies converge on a single fire incident, there are often conflicting perspectives on incident response objectives and tactical priorities.

Skill Drill 1

Fighting a Fire Using the PASS Method

1. Pull the pin.

2. Aim the nozzle or hose at the base of the fire from the recommended safe distance.

3. Squeeze the lever to discharge the fire extinguishing agent from the extinguisher.

4. Sweep the nozzle from side to side while aiming at the base of the fire until the fire is out or the extinguisher is empty.

At the scene of a fire, LERs need to recognize the importance of yielding incident command responsibility to the fire department, providing incident support, and successfully maintaining operational authority over their specific tactical responsibilities. Law enforcement agencies and fire service agencies need to recognize this in advance of the incident and address each other's concerns in advance through planning, training, and exercising for small- and large-scale fire incidents. In today's threat environment, law enforcement and the fire service need to work in concert and in harmony under a unified command system that allows maximum cooperation toward maximum preservation of life and property (**Figure 7**).

Figure 7 Law enforcement and the fire service need to work together under a unified command system that allows maximum cooperation.

Hazardous Materials Accidents and Weapons

The LER often comes into close contact with industrial and household substances that are deadly and dangerous. Domestic hazardous materials management has traditionally been a function of the fire department and other emergency service specialized teams. However, the threat of terrorism has forced the law enforcement community to become actively involved in the hazardous materials arena. The abundance of traditional hazardous materials—and the potential for weapons derived from chemical, biological, radiological, and nuclear substances—has changed law enforcement forever.

Consider the following scenario: you are operating in a traffic enforcement squad, and you are alerted to respond to a motor vehicle crash involving a tractor trailer and a car. Local emergency services and other police units are responding to the incident. Units arriving on the scene are no longer communicating with your dispatch center. Other civilian calls to the 911 center are reporting a gas cloud at the incident. You recall your training, stage your unit at a safe distance (in the cold zone), and establish a perimeter with other emergency services units. The first-arriving responders failed to take into account the risk of hazardous material exposure and are now part of the problem.

Tip

HAZWOPER Awareness Competencies

The HAZWOPER Awareness Competencies enumerated in 29 CFR 1910.120: *Hazardous Waste Operations and Emergency Response* include the following:

- Understand what hazardous materials are and their risks
- Understand the potential outcome of a hazardous materials incident
- Recognize the presence of hazardous materials
- Apply traditional identification measures to labeled hazardous materials
- Understand the role of the first responder trained to the HAZWOPER Awareness level in the response plan
- Determine the need for additional resources
- Utilize various communications systems to request additional resources.

Universally, emergency services responders recognize the tremendous potential for death and disability associated with unintentional as well as intentional hazardous materials exposure. Because of the uniqueness of hazardous materials, the Occupational Safety and Health Administration (OSHA) has set mandatory training requirements for first responders in publication 29 CFR 1910.120: *Hazardous Waste Operations and Emergency Response* (HAZWOPER). Emergency responders are required to complete training sufficient to meet the first responder Awareness level as prescribed by HAZWOPER and your employer. Courses focused on OSHA's 29 CFR 1910.120 are intended to provide the background necessary to prevent and contain the threats associated with hazardous materials.

HAZARDOUS MATERIALS IDENTIFICATION

The presence of hazardous materials is easily recognized from warning signs, placards, symbols, or labels on buildings, trucks, railcars, barrels, packages, and boxes. Identifying these items can still be difficult, however, because there is no consistency of use. Some shippers may not even label items as hazardous. Certain quantities are required before the shipment has to be labeled, but even in small quantities, some items are still hazardous in an uncontrolled situation. Substances are not always hazardous by themselves; however, when mixed with another chemical, they can become extremely volatile or toxic. Shippers or handlers routinely place chemicals in proximity to each other without taking into account the consequences of a leak.

In the event of a leak or spill, observe the scene for these indicators of hazardous materials:

- ❑ A visible cloud or strange-looking or colored smoke
- ❑ A visible leak from a tank car, box trailer, or railcar with or without placards
- ❑ An unusual odor or a strong, noxious smell in the area as you approach the scene
- ❑ Patterns of victims who have been overcome by the chemical
- ❑ A scene in which more than one person has collapsed, is unconscious, or is having difficulty breathing

First-arriving units at any emergency should cautiously approach the scene and observe for signs suggesting that a hazardous materials incident has occurred. Using your HAZWOPER Awareness training, you should stop at a safe distance to evaluate the situation. Once you have completed your scene size-up, call for a HazMat assignment per your local protocols. Prevent anyone else from entering the scene until the HazMat team arrives and deems the area safe. If you do not recognize the danger until you have entered too closely, immediately leave the danger zone. Once you are in a safe place—upwind, up hill—try to gather as much information specific to your incident as possible. Try to look for placards, labels, containers, and the sizes and shapes of tanks. Do not under any circumstances reenter the scene, and do not leave the area until cleared by the HazMat team. If you are contaminated, you may worsen the situation by contaminating others.

Even when there are identifiers readily visible, it is often difficult to determine what the exact material is. The driver of a tank or box truck will have a bill of lading that will provide specific information regarding the materials he or she is hauling. If the truck is involved in an accident, these documents may be difficult to access; however, the driver may still be your best source of information. Trains also have a manifest of the tank cars and box cars and what materials are being transported. Planes and ships have similar documents.

The US Department of Transportation Pipeline and Hazardous Materials Safety Administration regulates the transportation of hazardous materials under title 49 CFR and requires specific training, markings, and documentation of these materials. When placed on highway transport vehicles, railroad tank cars, and other forms of hazardous materials transport, these markings are referred to as placards. Labels are smaller versions of the placard and are placed on individual containers. Placards and labels are intended to be placed on all four sides of the specific container. The title 49 CFR identification system gives a general guide to hazardous materials, which are broken down into nine categories of hazards (**Table 1**).

All LERs should have access to the *Emergency Response Guidebook* (**Figure 8**). This publication is updated regularly and jointly provided by the US Department of Transportation, Transport Canada, and the Secretariat of Communications and Transportation Mexico. The latest publication dates are 2008 and 2012. The intent of the publication is to provide emergency responders a listing of all placards and labels. The responder uses the placard or label identification code to identify the hazard (**Figure 9**). After the hazard is identified, the *Emergency Response Guidebook* will provide advice for initial life safety measures, fire hazards, personal protective

Table 1

Categories of Hazardous Materials

Class	Divisions
Class 1: Explosives	Division 1.1: Explosives with a mass explosion hazard Division 1.2: Explosives with a projection hazard Division 1.3: Explosives with predominantly a fire hazard Division 1.4: Explosives with no significant blast hazard Division 1.5: Very insensitive explosives with a mass explosion hazard Division 1.6: Extremely insensitive articles
Class 2: Gases	Division 2.1: Flammable gases Division 2.2: Nonflammable, nontoxic gases Division 2.3: Toxic gases
Class 3: Flammable liquids (and combustible liquids [US])	-
Class 4: Flammable solids; spontaneously combustible materials; and dangerous-when-wet materials and water-reactive substances	Division 4.1: Flammable solids Division 4.2: Spontaneously combustible materials Division 4.3: Water-reactive substances and dangerous-when-wet materials
Class 5: Oxidizing substances and organic peroxides	Division 5.1: Oxidizing substances Division 5.2: Organic peroxides
Class 6: Toxic substances and infectious substances	Division 6.1: Toxic substances Division 6.2: Infectious substances
Class 7: Radioactive materials	-
Class 8: Corrosive substances	-
Class 9: Miscellaneous hazardous materials, products, substances, or organisms	-

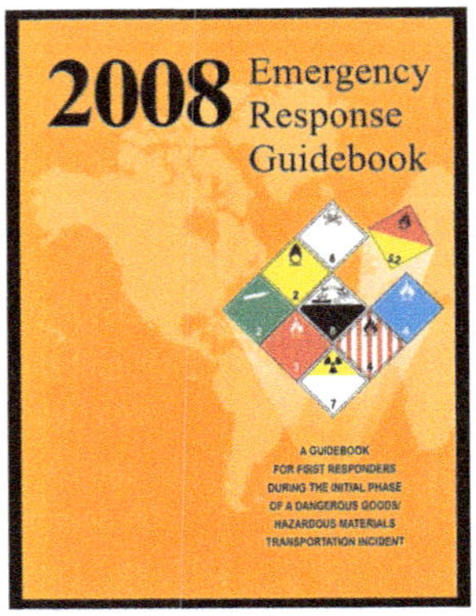

Figure 8 The *Emergency Response Guidebook* is a reference used as a base for your initial actions at a hazardous materials incident.

equipment (PPE) requirements, evacuation requirements, and initial incident management.

HAZARDOUS MATERIALS RESPONSE PLANNING

LERs should determine their role in the hazardous materials emergency response plan. The typical responder, trained to the HAZWOPER Awareness level, will meet the needs of most agencies or departments. In some programs, LERs have to prepare to operate in and around hazardous areas and require additional training. In addition to OSHA, state, local, and agency regulations, the LER should review the National Fire Protection Association (NFPA) guidelines for hazardous

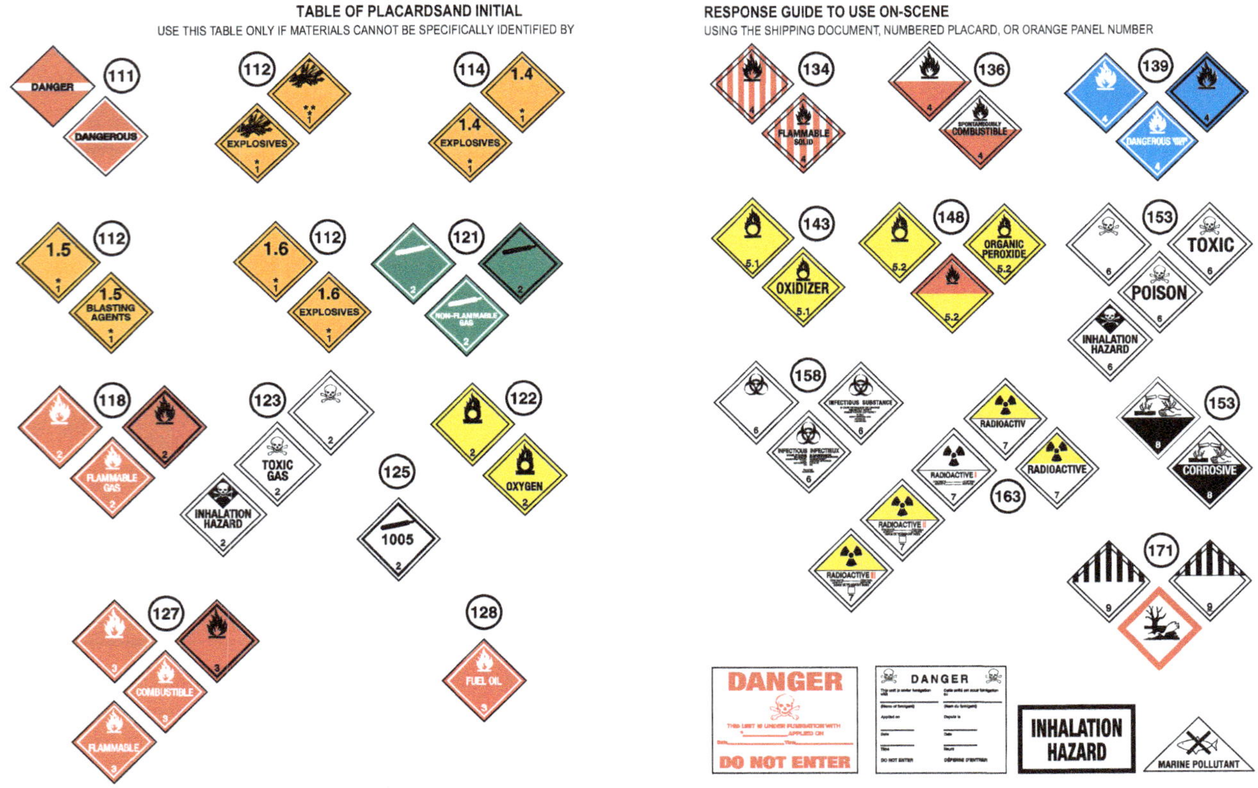

Figure 9 The Department of Transportation uses labels, placards, and markings (such as those in the *Emergency Response Guidebook*) to give a general idea of the hazard inside a particular container or cargo tank.
Source: Courtesy of the US Department of Transportation.

materials response teams (NFPA 472) and emergency medicine hazardous materials response teams (NFPA 473). NFPA 472 is used throughout the United States and is considered to be the correct and safe way to operate during a hazardous materials or weapons of mass destruction incident. This guideline is consistent with 29 CFR 1910.120, addressing many points specific to response, including hazard assessment and requirements for response equipment. NFPA 472 offers hazard assessments at a glance based on a scale of 0 to 4, with 4 being the most dangerous or hazardous.

Tip

NFPA 472 Hazards Scale

Level 0: Little or no health hazard if you came in contact with them.

Level 1: Would cause irritation on contact but only mild residual injury even without treatment.

Level 2: Temporary damage or residual injury without prompt medical treatment. Both level 1 and level 2 are considered slightly hazardous but require the use of SCBA.

Level 3: Extremely hazardous to health; contact requires full PPE so none of your skin is exposed.

Level 4: So hazardous that minimal contact could cause death; requires special gear designed to protect against that hazard.

HAZARD ASSESSMENT AND PERSONAL PROTECTIVE EQUIPMENT

LERs operating at or beyond the OSHA Awareness level should be familiar with the proper PPE. Frequently, law enforcement agencies issue a gas mask or some type of filter respirator to their employees. LERs must understand the limitations of the respiratory protection available to them. A gas mask or filter-type respirator only provides a barrier to prevent the passage of a certain size or type of particle from entering the user's respiratory system. Previous units of this text discussed the respiratory system and what happens when humans breathe. Each time an individual breathes in a toxic atmosphere, he or she brings in contaminants to the respiratory system. A gas mask or respiratory filter will protect an individual against a limited amount of chemicals for a limited amount of time. Your agency must train you in the use and limitations of the device. Determine the type of filter you are issued, what exactly it protects you against, and what the breakthrough time is before the filter fails. Gas masks and respiratory filters will not allow you to function in an oxygen-deprived atmosphere. Only SCBA can provide air with sufficient oxygen in oxygen-deficient atmospheres.

Some law enforcement agencies provide suits, gloves, and other clothing to be used during a hazardous materials or weapons of mass destruction incident. As a LER, you should ensure that you are trained in the use, care, and limitations of the protective ensemble issued to you. NFPA 472 assigns a letter grade to protective clothing for quick recognition of the ensemble's protective limitations.

Tip

NFPA 472 Protective Clothing Grades

All levels require the use of gloves and footwear that are impermeable to the specific hazards.

Level A: The most hazardous materials require fully encapsulated, chemical-resistant, vapor-proof protective clothing that provides full-body protection as well as SCBA and special sealed equipment.

Level B: Requires nonencapsulated PPE: a nonpermeable, splash-resistant suit with SCBA.

Level C: Requires nonencapsulated PPE: a nonpermeable, splash-resistant suit with eye protection and filter mask.

Level D: Work uniform, such as coveralls that afford minimal protection.

Any level of PPE may cause heat stress and can be very difficult to work in. Your field of vision is reduced, your ability to communicate is more difficult, your dexterity and fine motor skills are lessened, and tasks will take longer and be rapidly fatiguing.

HAZARDOUS MATERIALS PATIENT CARE CONSIDERATIONS

General patient care for a patient exposed to hazardous materials is no different from that for a nonexposed patient. The process will be complicated by the need to protect yourself with PPE and the need to decontaminate the patient. Life threats, trauma, burns, and respiratory injuries should all be treated the same. Try to minimize bandages and other splinting materials that may collect and spread contamination. However, bleeding must still be controlled by whatever means necessary.

Special antidotes may be needed for specific types of exposures, such as cyanide and nerve agents. Advanced life support personnel should be standing by and ready to evaluate the contaminated patient. If resources are scarce, the decontaminated patient must be moved toward definitive medical care by whatever means possible.

DECONTAMINATION

A decontamination area will be set up between the hazard zone (hot zone) and the treatment zone (cold zone). **Decontamination** is the process of removing or neutralizing the hazard and properly disposing of materials such as clothing and PPE from patients and rescue personnel.

Anyone who leaves the hazard zone must pass through decontamination prior to exiting the area to prevent the spread of contaminants. It doesn't matter if you think you haven't been exposed—you must still be decontaminated. Simple removal of your clothes can achieve up to 80% of decontamination.

Decontamination can come in many forms. The most common is soap and water. Dish detergent is very effective in releasing many chemicals from the skin's surface. Soap contains surfactant that promotes the chemical to break the attachment to the skin and rise up on the soap bubbles. You must thoroughly clean and rinse all areas of the body, including all the cracks and crevices that a chemical may find its way into. All skin folds, hair, and nails should be thoroughly washed. Hazardous materials technicians operating decontamination systems will sample these areas on patients to confirm that no chemicals remain prior to the patient leaving the contaminated site.

Self and Buddy Decontamination

The following procedure should be used for decontamination:

1. Ensure you are free from the effects of the hazardous chemicals.
2. Remove all clothing.
   a. Protect the airway from further contamination by cutting off clothing that may pass over the face.
   b. Place clothing in a plastic bag if available and seal.
   c. Remove gas mask or respiratory PPE. Be careful not to allow contamination that may be on the mask to fall on or near your airway.
3. Remove external items from contact with the body (such as hearing aids, artificial limbs, jewelry, watches, and wigs). Bag external items in a separate bag from the clothing and seal the bag.
4. Eyeglasses and prosthetic devices can be expediently decontaminated by washing with a detergent soap and warm water solution and rinsing thoroughly with plain water. Replace contact lenses with new ones—do not reuse. If the eyes are contaminated, flush them with large amounts of water for at least 20 minutes.
5. Wash hands, face, hair, and body with soap and water. Do your best to wash and rinse hair, body creases, and folds thoroughly. If possible, use a shower-type setting. In some cases you may have to use fire hoses or exterior water systems.
6. If you are aware that contamination reached a certain body part or area, wash and rinse that area thoroughly.
7. Change into uncontaminated clothing.
8. Follow instructions to proceed to the nearest decontamination station, carrying critical items in a sealed plastic bag if available. You may require multiple decontaminations to be free of certain hazards.

RESPONSE TO TERRORISM AND WEAPONS OF MASS DESTRUCTION

Terrorism is a type of assault that uses surprise or shock tactics to influence or otherwise instill fear into a population (**Figure 10**). Terrorists can act alone or in groups. They can have an international or domestic scope of operations. They can intend to shape policy based on social, religious, economic,

Figure 10 Two days after the 9/11 terrorist attacks, fires still burn in the rubble and debris of the World Trade Center in NYC.

or political ideals. They may attack targets directly related to their perspective, or they may attack civilians, technology, or infrastructure in an attempt to inconvenience or damage a particular society.

Recognizing Terrorist Attacks

LERs have historically been on hand or been the initial responders to terrorist attacks in the United States. Attacks are typically not announced, and the individual efforts of those initially under attack will weigh heavily on the success or failure of the incident. The best way to respond to a terrorist attack is to prevent it. Good police work and diligent community awareness have proven valuable in preventing attacks in various communities.

The LER should always pay attention to the Department of Homeland Security Advisory System. This system is based on intelligence and is designed to spur awareness in LERs when conditions indicate that a particular target, or a specific group, is gaining attention.

Many threats will not be identified by this filter. The emergency responder should look at all incidents and think about how a particular incident matches up to other terrorist events.

Tip

Terrorism Factors

When approaching any incident, assess these factors relative to terrorism:

- Type of location
- Type of call
- Number of patients
- Victims' statements
- Preincident indicators

Terrorism and Weapons of Mass Destruction Response Considerations

The diverse nature of law enforcement should be considered relative to an initial response to terrorism. In some cases, law enforcement personnel will be the object of the attack or already engaged in the fight. Others may be responding into a complex, dynamic situation. If you are engaged in the actual terrorist attack, use all possible law enforcement survival tactics. Consider using shielding, cover, and concealment. If you are approaching an incident, observe for conventional and unconventional threats and stage according to your initial threat assessment.

If you are the initial unit on location or the only operational unit, make notification of the incident, direct responding units, and establish incident command based on your agency's protocols. To extract maximum damage, terrorists may detonate secondary explosives or reengage with another concerted attack. Initial responders to a terrorist incident must be deliberate in establishing a perimeter of control around the initial incident. This perimeter should focus on shielding the persons already under attack and the emergency responders from additional harm.

Tip

Secondary Explosive Devices

LERs should be constantly alert for unusual activity. This activity could occur at any time prior to a terrorist attack. This alertness is often referred to as *situational awareness*. Good situational awareness should be applied universally by all LERs at all times.

Secondary explosives have been used in the United States. Secondary explosive devices are hidden from view or camouflaged by being placed in ordinary objects. The devices can be detonated by a time delay, or remotely by radio-controlled devices or cell phones.

The US Fire Administration (USFA) has made available basic guidelines related to secondary explosive devices that have been modified from those used by the Florida Division of the State Fire Marshal. These guidelines recommend that responders:

1. Anticipate the presence of a secondary device at any suspicious incident.
2. Search for a secondary device before moving into the incident area.
3. Avoid touching or moving anything that may conceal an explosive device.
4. Effectively manage the scene with boundaries, exclusion zones, triage areas, and so forth.
5. Evacuate victims and nonessential personnel as quickly as possible.
6. Preserve the scene as much as possible for evidence collection and crime investigation.

WEAPONS OF MASS DESTRUCTION

Weapons of mass destruction (WMD), also referred to as weapons of mass casualty (WMC), are agents designed to bring about mass death, casualties, and massive damage to property or infrastructure. The agents used for WMD are chemical, biological, radiological, nuclear, or explosive (CBRNE).

Chemical weapons are chemicals that have been identified as lethal to humans and have been engineered to promote lethality through the way in which they are dispersed. These chemicals can be used in weapons as a solid, liquid, or gas. Chemical weapons may be classified according to how long they remain active in an area or on a surface. Chemical agents that will stay available and active for a long time are called persistent or nonvolatile. Conversely, agents that evaporate or break down quickly are called nonpersistent or volatile.

Biological agents include viruses, bacteria, and neurotoxins. When these agents are used as weapons, they often take some time to affect the patient. Early symptoms are often associated with the specific disease process the organisms would create in their natural setting.

Radiation can also be used as a weapon. Radiation is energy that is emitted from a substance in the form of rays or particles. Radioactive substances have varying degrees of energy, typically classified as follows:

- **Alpha:** Weak, often blocked by ordinary material
- **Beta:** More powerful than alpha radiation; can be blocked by heavy clothing
- **Gamma:** Powerful energy that requires lead shielding to block rays
- **Neutron:** Most powerful; easily penetrates lead, requires feet of concrete to stop

Radiation weapons can be in the form of dirty bombs, in which radioactive material is used to enhance the lethality of a routine explosive. They can also be in the form of a nuclear weapon. Nuclear weapons possess devastating energy from explosive force and radiation (**Table 2**).

Table 2

Common Signs and Symptoms of Acute Radiation Sickness

Low exposure	Nausea, vomiting, diarrhea
Moderate exposure	First-degree burns, hair loss, depletion of the immune system (death of white blood cells), and cancer
Severe exposure	Second- and third-degree burns, cancer, and death

LERs need to focus on patient presentations. Terrorists typically do not placard their weapons, and responders will have to sort out what is confronting them. A **toxidrome** is the specific signs and symptoms that a population exposed to a particular type of agent will display. From the toxidromes observed, the responder can try to determine the best course of action for self-survival and patient care (**Table 3**). Regardless of the patient presentations, the LER must always ensure that he or she is using all personal protective measures available to prevent cross-contamination.

Table 3

LER Toxidromes

Speed of Onset	Initial Symptoms	Immediate Responder Care	Type of Weapon
Immediate (minutes after exposure)	Skin irritation Formation of large blisters Swollen, closed, or irritated eyes Possible blindness *If vapors are inhaled:* • Hoarseness and stridor • Severe cough • Coughing up blood • Severe trouble breathing *Specific to lewisite (L) and phosgene oxime (CX):* • Immediate, intense skin pain • Gray skin discoloration	Decontaminate. Assess and manage airway, breathing, and circulation. Cover decontaminated wounds with burn dressings. Promote warmth and safety. Consider transfer to a burn center.	**Vesicant (Blister Agent)** Mustard (H) Lewisite (L) Phosgene oxime (CX)

Table 3

LER Toxidromes *(continued)*

Speed of Onset	Initial Symptoms	Immediate Responder Care	Type of Weapon
Immediate (minutes after exposure)	Upper airway irritation Choking Shortness of breath Hoarseness and stridor Gasping and coughing Odor of bleach *If released as a gas:* • Green haze	Decontaminate immediately. Assess and manage airway, breathing, and circulation. Provide respiratory support, including suction and oxygen if available. Place the patient in a position of comfort. If possible, place the head up but ensure that the patient can have adequate airway drainage. Keep the patient still; activity will increase respiratory distress.	**Pulmonary Agent** Chlorine (CL)
Immediate (minutes after exposure)	*SLUDGEM:* • Salivation/sweating • Lacrimation (excessive tearing) • Urination • Defecation/drooling/diarrhea • Gastric upset and cramps • Emesis (vomiting) • Miosis (constricted pupils)/muscle twitching	Decontaminate immediately. Assess and manage airway, breathing, and circulation. Use nerve agent antidote kits per your local protocol. Position patients to support respiratory drainage.	**Nerve Agent** Tabun (GA) Sarin (GB) Soman (GD) V agents (VX)
Immediate (minutes after exposure)	*Low doses:* • Dizziness • Light-headedness • Headache • Vomiting *High doses:* • Shortness of breath • Gasping respirations • Fast breathing • Flushed skin • Altered mental status • Seizures • Coma • Respiratory arrest • Cardiac arrest	Decontaminate immediately. Assess and manage airway, breathing, and circulation. Ensure the patient is removed from the contaminated environment. Provide supportive care, including resuscitation.	**Metabolic Agent** Hydrogen cyanide (AC) Cyanogen chloride (CL)

(Continues)

Table 3

LER Toxidromes *(continued)*

Speed of Onset	Initial Symptoms	Immediate Responder Care	Type of Weapon
Delayed (hours after exposure)	Limited airway irritation Odor of freshly mowed grass Nausea Chest tightness Severe cough Trouble breathing on exertion	Decontaminate immediately. Assess and manage airway, breathing, and circulation. Provide respiratory support, including suction and oxygen if available. Place the patient in a position of comfort. If possible, place the head up but ensure adequate airway drainage. Keep the patient still; activity will increase respiratory distress.	**Pulmonary Agent** Phosgene
Delayed (hours after exposure)	Dry mouth Intestinal obstruction Urinary retention Constipation Nausea and vomiting Abnormal pupil dilation Blurred vision, double vision Drooping eyelids Difficulty swallowing and speaking Respiratory failure	Decontaminate immediately. Assess and manage airway, breathing, and circulation. Provide respiratory support, including suction and oxygen if available. Place the patient in a position of comfort. If possible, place the head up but ensure adequate airway drainage. Provide ventilation support as needed.	**Neurotoxin** Botulinum toxin
Slow (days after exposure)	Flulike symptoms Fever Trouble breathing Rapid pulse Shock Pulmonary edema Respiratory arrest	Protect yourself and others. Prevent exposure to others. Ensure decontamination has been performed. Assess and manage airway, breathing, and circulation. Provide supportive care until patients can be moved to an emergency care area.	**Anthrax (inhaled)** 1–2 days incubation
Slow (days after exposure)	Fever Headache Muscle pain Tenderness Pneumonia Shortness of breath Severe lymph node pain and enlargement	Protect yourself and others. Prevent exposure to others. Ensure decontamination has been done. Assess and manage airway, breathing, and circulation. Provide supportive care until patients can be moved to an emergency care area.	**Pneumonic plague** 2–3 days incubation

Table 3

LER Toxidromes *(continued)*

Speed of Onset	Initial Symptoms	Immediate Responder Care	Type of Weapon
Slow (days after exposure)	Sudden onset of fever, weakness, muscle pain, headache, and sore throat; followed by vomiting and internal and external bleeding	Protect yourself and others. Prevent exposure to others. Ensure decontamination has been done. Assess and manage airway, breathing, and circulation. Provide supportive care until patients can be moved to an emergency care area.	**Viral hemorrhagic fevers** 4–21 days incubation
Slow (days after exposure)	Severe fever, malaise, body aches, and headaches Small blisters on skin Bleeding of skin and mucous membranes	Protect yourself and others. Prevent exposure to others. Ensure decontamination has been done. Assess and manage airway, breathing, and circulation. Provide supportive care until patients can be moved to an emergency care area.	**Smallpox** 7–17 days incubation

Narcotics and Clandestine Labs

The **clandestine drug laboratory** has become a nationwide problematic phenomenon that has been shown to involve significant health hazards to first responders and law enforcement officers. Most of the laboratories found today by law enforcement operations are centered around the production and manufacture of methamphetamine (meth), a relatively simple drug to produce; the production of crack cocaine (crack) from cocaine base; and the growth and cultivation of marijuana though the use of hydroponics and grow houses.

During the height of production, most clandestine laboratories found and seized by law enforcement officials in the United States were located in the Midwest and Western states, but today, they have become more common in the rest of the country. They can be found in a variety of locations, from the back seat of a car to a hotel room, an empty apartment rented solely for production purposes, a garage, a storage shed, a remote area with good sources of water and utilities, a van, or a trailer.

In today's world, it is imperative that every LER be trained to recognize a clandestine drug laboratory. The safety of all those involved rests on early recognition, proper procedure, and proper training to ensure that no long-term injuries or possible fatalities result as a failure to act properly if confronted with these hazardous situations. All involved with the encounter of these labs should have the specific knowledge and equipment to ensure that the lab is secured properly and is relinquished to a specialized drug laboratory team for assessment, dismantlement, and cleanup.

Because large amounts of money are made from illicit drugs, these labs hold a strong interest for the criminal element. As with all commerce, a supply and demand system is in place for this illicit activity. There is also a huge addiction to the product produced, thereby fueling that demand and encouraging the supply.

It is no secret that the setup and operation of a clandestine laboratory is a relatively easy, inexpensive (considering the profit margin), and extremely dangerous enterprise. The risks and exposure hazards are great and pose an imminent threat to the safety of society.

Precautions should be taken to avoid inhalation injuries and possible booby traps resulting in explosions or fires; the pure volatility of the labs, because of the resources and chemicals needed in production, should be recognized. Only trained personnel should enter the lab and, per procedure, should wear personal protective equipment. The role and actions of LERs are critical to ensure the safety of themselves and the surrounding community.

It is a well-known fact in the law enforcement community that large quantities of illegal narcotics are produced in the United States through the use of clandestine drug laboratories. These labs are often set up, maintained, and monitored by operators with little or no background in chemistry who mix highly dangerous and volatile chemicals. The most common chemicals used to start the meth-making process are over-the-counter cold and asthma medications that contain ephedrine or pseudoephedrine such as decongestants or stimulants. Many of the chemicals involved in meth production are household products that can be readily obtained at the local hardware store and have the capability of producing severe, if not fatal, health problems.

Clandestine drug laboratories range from crude backroom operations to highly sophisticated labs with the ability to be technologically advanced and perhaps even mobile. Often, these labs are hidden in remote areas and contain extensive electronic surveillance equipment to monitor who enters and leaves the locations. The operators of these labs often booby-trap them to destroy any evidence in case of discovery and seizure. Given this fact, responders now must concern themselves with safety as well as health concerns.

Table 4 lists some of the chemicals used in labs for the production of illicit methamphetamine.

One of the most popular clandestinely manufactured drugs is **crack cocaine**. Crack is a highly addictive and powerful stimulant that is derived from powdered cocaine using a simple conversion process. Crack emerged as a popular drug of abuse in the mid-1980s. It is abused because it produces an immediate high and because it is easy and inexpensive to produce, rendering it readily available and affordable.

The production of crack is simple but effective. Crack is produced by dissolving powdered cocaine in a mixture of water and ammonia or sodium bicarbonate (baking soda). The mixture is boiled or heated in a microwave until a solid substance forms. The solid is removed from the liquid, dried, and then broken into chunks (rocks) that are sold as crack cocaine.

This drug typically is produced in the inner city but has been made available to all parts of the nation, including the suburbs. Because of the high demand and relatively low cost and time involved in production, crack continues to be a drug of choice among addicts.

As with other illicitly manufactured drugs, there are health concerns for the LER when encountering crack or cocaine base.

Table 4

Products Used in Methamphetamine Production
Acetone
Alcohol (isopropyl or rubbing)
Anhydrous ammonia (fertilizer)
Ephedrine (cold medications)
Ether (engine starter)
Hydrochloric acid (pool supply)
Iodine (flakes or crystal)
Freon
Kitty litter
Lithium (batteries)
Methanol (gasoline additive)
MSM (nutritional supplement)
Pseudoephedrine (cold medications)
Phenylpropanolamine (Dexatrim)
Red phosphorus (matches or road flares)
Salt (table or rock)
Sodium hydroxide (lye)
Sodium metal
Sulfuric acid (drain cleaner)
Toluene (brake cleaner)
Trichloroethane (gun cleaner)

Data Source: DEA Office of Diversion Control.

Tip

Crack and Cocaine Health Concerns

- Accidental exposure to cocaine via skin
- Accidental inhaling of cocaine
- Accidental ingestion of cocaine

A newer trend in the manufacture of illicit drugs is the indoor cultivation of marijuana using a growing method called **hydroponics**, which is growing plants in a nutrient solution without the assistance of soil or a similar substance (**Figure 11**).

According to the National Drug Intelligence Center, the number of indoor cannabis growing sites seized and indoor cannabis plants eradicated by federal, state, and local law enforcement agencies has increased significantly since 2004. Cannabis growers have frequently moved their operations indoors because indoor conditions reduce the chance of detection and can create higher profit margins because of controlled growing conditions.

These indoor growth operations pose health hazards with which LERs must be concerned.

Tip

Indoor Marijuana Cultivation Hazards

- Exposure to fertilizers
- Respiratory exposure to molds
- The presence of fertilizer and high humidity create an environment that stimulates salmonella growth
- Exposure to other organic organisms

Figure 11 Hydroponics is becoming a more common method of cultivating marijuana.

EMERGENCY RESPONDER STRATEGIES

Assessment

The LER must immediately ensure safety, contain hostile threats, and ensure that proper PPE is in place prior to assessing and managing any exposure. Whenever possible, the LER should plan for decontamination and hazardous substance exposure.

Patient assessment should be performed with an emphasis on exposure as identified in the unit on toxicology.

If there is an exposure to a clandestine drug lab, a general assessment of the severity of that exposure should be performed. The following sections highlight the most common injuries sustained in a clandestine meth laboratory, in a marijuana hydroponic grow house, or due to exposure to cocaine.

Methamphetamine Production Chemicals

Inhalation: Chemical vapors and gases can cause shortness of breath, cough, and chest pain. They can also cause intoxication, dizziness, nausea, disorientation, lack of coordination, pulmonary edema, chemical pneumonitis, and other serious respiratory problems.

Skin contact: Can cause serious chemical contact burns.

Ingestion: Toxic chemicals—or methamphetamine itself—may result in potentially fatal poisoning, internal chemical burns, damage to organ function, and harm to neurologic and immunologic functioning. Maintain awareness for children or others who may have ingested food or drink contaminated by being in the vicinity of the production site.

Hydroponic Marijuana Grow

Inhalation: Airborne mold and mildews, as well as the use and mixture of different organic compounds and liquid fertilizers by nontrained personnel, increase the risk of potentially harmful fumes and gases.

Skin: Organic compounds and liquid fertilizers are caustic and can cause irritation, redness, and burns from prolonged exposure.

Eye contact: Mild irritant.

Aggravation of preexisting conditions: Some people become sensitized from exposure to fertilizers, molds, and fungi and develop coughs, stuffy nose, asthma, and other allergic complaints.

Crack Cocaine

Inhalation: Dilation and immobility of eye pupils, euphoria, and breathing difficulty. Large amounts can cause blindness.

Ingestion: At high levels, intoxication can present with narcotic effects; in cases of excessive ingestion or inhalation, fainting, paleness, breathing arrest, brief convulsions, and death may occur.

Skin contact: Contact numbness. The possibility of absorption under conditions of skin breakage or inflammation exists.

Eye contact: Mild irritant.

Illness or Injury

In the setting of the methamphetamine lab, a patient will, at a minimum, experience inhalation, or skin exposure may result in local injury from **corrosive** substances. The LER who may interdict a methamphetamine lab should be prepared with PPE, a decontamination plan, and emergency medical supplies and equipment to treat severe burns, explosions, respiratory distress, seizures, and cardiac arrest. Acute reactions could occur during or immediately after a drug bust, before the lab has been ventilated. The LER should consider the prestaging of an advanced life support (ALS) emergency medical services unit discretely, as well as a fire rescue unit to help with structure ventilation, decontamination, and the potential for fire. Illnesses and injuries of all types are possible when dealing with illicit drug labs or grows.

Methamphetamine Laboratory Hazards

The possibility of exposure to the following chemicals exists:

- *Pseudoephedrine:* Ingestion of doses greater than 240 mg causes hypertension, arrhythmia, anxiety, dizziness, and vomiting. Ingestion of doses greater than 600 mg can lead to renal failure and seizures.
- *Acetone and ethyl alcohol:* Both are extremely flammable, posing a fire risk in and around the laboratory. Inhalation or ingestion of these solvents causes severe gastric irritation, narcosis, or coma.
- *Freon:* Inhalation can cause sudden cardiac arrest or severe lung damage. Freon is corrosive if ingested.
- *Anhydrous ammonia:* A colorless gas with a pungent, suffocating odor. Inhalation causes edema of the respiratory tract and asphyxia. Contact with vapors damages eyes and mucous membranes.
- *Red phosphorus:* May explode as a result of contact or friction. Ignites if heated above 260°C (500°F). Vapor from ignited phosphorus severely irritates the nose, throat, lungs, and eyes.
- *Hypophosphorous acid:* Extremely dangerous substitute for red phosphorus. If overheated, deadly phosphine gas is released. Poses a serious fire and explosion hazard.
- *Lithium metal:* Extremely caustic to all body tissues. Reacts violently with water and poses a fire or explosion hazard.
- *Hydriodic acid:* A corrosive acid with vapors that are irritating to the respiratory system, eyes, and skin. If ingested, causes severe internal irritation and damage that may cause death.
- *Iodine crystals:* Give off vapor that is irritating to the respiratory system and eyes. Solid form irritates the eyes and may burn skin. If ingested, iodine crystals cause severe internal damage.
- *Phenylpropanolamine:* Ingestion of doses greater than 75 mg causes hypertension, arrhythmia, anxiety, and dizziness. Quantities greater than 300 mg can lead to renal failure, seizures, stroke, and death.

Patient Management

Methamphetamine Lab Exposure

Inhalation: Remove to fresh air. If patient is not breathing, give artificial respiration. If breathing is difficult, give oxygen. Call a physician.

Ingestion: Do not induce vomiting, due to the caustic and corrosive makeup of methamphetamine. Follow the directions of medical personnel.

Skin contact: Immediately flush skin with plenty of water for at least 15 minutes while removing contaminated clothing and shoes. Call a physician immediately.

Eye contact: Immediately flush eyes with plenty of water for at least 15 minutes, lifting lower and upper eyelids occasionally. Get medical attention immediately.

Marijuana Hydroponic Lab

Inhalation: Remove to fresh air. If patient is not breathing, give artificial respiration. If breathing is difficult, give oxygen. Call a physician.

Crack Cocaine

Inhalation: Remove to fresh air. If patient is not breathing, give artificial respiration. If breathing is difficult, give oxygen. Call a physician.

Ingestion: Induce vomiting immediately as directed by medical personnel. Never give anything by mouth to an unconscious person.

Skin contact: Immediately flush skin with plenty of water for at least 15 minutes while removing contaminated clothing and shoes. Call a physician immediately. Wash clothing before reuse.

Eye contact: Immediately flush eyes with plenty of water for at least 15 minutes, lifting lower and upper eyelids occasionally. Get medical attention immediately.

SPECIAL CONSIDERATION FOR LAW ENFORCEMENT RESPONSE

Within the law enforcement community, a risk of the job is the possibility of responding to or accidentally coming in contact with a clandestine drug lab. Whether the drug involved is methamphetamine, cocaine, or hydroponic marijuana, there are special considerations to be taken for the law enforcement response, namely, exposure controls and personal protection. Every effort should be made ahead of time to assess the risk of exposure and the inherent danger that is contained within these labs. First and foremost, the safety of the responding officer, co-officers, and the civilian population takes precedence.

At no time should an officer come in contact with an unknown substance or chemical without using the standard precautions of gloves and eye protection. In cases in which toxic fumes are suspected, the officer, if trained and properly fitted, should don his or her personal respiratory protection.

The LER should have a heightened awareness of the possible volatility of the chemicals involved in the manufacture of these narcotics and should also remember the innate threat of improvised explosive devices used as a means of protection or destruction of the lab.

It is not uncommon for a working lab to have an explosion or a fire as a result of a simple spark, and LERs need not put themselves in danger of becoming a victim of this crime.

CONCLUSION

LERs must plan for the worst conditions. Working in and around explosives, combustibles, and hazardous conditions are routine. Whether these conditions confront the LER as accidental or as a threat, the knowledge and skills required to reduce the danger and survive the incident are not instinctual. Going near fire, assessing its origin, and understanding the options you have to stop the fire during the incipient phase require training and practice. Law enforcement agencies that do not plan to work in and around hazardous chemical leaks, spills, and weapons expose their employees to mortal danger. Respiratory protection and self-decontamination training should become routine basic and continuing education for officers and agents. Awaiting a response from a fire-rescue program to deal with manageable environmental threats will result in body recovery, as opposed to rescues.

Prep Kit

Ready for Review

- LERs at an incident involving a fire must quickly respond with appropriate actions that protect life and property without placing themselves in unnecessary danger or obstructing fire department operations.
- As with any incident involving multiple-agency response, cooperation and coordination between fire service and law enforcement personnel are critical to successful resolution of the incident.
- Fire, also referred to as combustion, is simply a rapid chemical process that results in the release of energy in the form of heat and usually light. All forms of matter can burn when the right conditions exist, and understanding these conditions is the key to understanding how a fire starts, behaves, and is extinguished. Fires require heat, fuel, and oxygen.
- Smoke can be very hot and can physically burn the upper and lower airways if inhaled.
- In Class A fires, fuel is composed of ordinary solid combustibles such as wood, paper, textiles, and other common solids.
- Class B fires have combustible or flammable liquids as their fuel.
- Class C fires are characterized by the presence of energized electrical equipment.
- Class D fires are distinguished by the presence of a burning metal.
- Class K fires involve combustible cooking materials such as cooking oil and grease.
- The use of proper extinguishers is essential for attacking each specific class of fire.
- When it is safe to do so and conditions merit the use of the appropriate fire extinguisher, use the PASS method:
  - **P**ull the pin.
  - **A**im the nozzle.
  - **S**queeze the lever.
  - **S**weep the nozzle.
- The safety of all those involved in the response to clandestine drug labs rests on early recognition, proper procedure, and proper training to ensure that no long-term injuries or possible fatalities result as a failure to act properly if confronted with these hazardous situations.
- The operators of clandestine labs often booby-trap them to destroy the lab and any evidence that may be obtained in case of discovery and seizure of the lab.
- Crack cocaine is produced by dissolving powdered cocaine in a mixture of water and ammonia or sodium bicarbonate (baking soda).
- Many marijuana cultivators have relocated or established their operations indoors because of the reduced risk of law enforcement detection.
- The biggest concern regarding exposure to marijuana grow houses is the airborne unidentified mold and mildews that may be present.
- Red phosphorus is very volatile and may explode as a result of contact or friction.
- For contact of all chemicals with the skin, the procedure is to immediately flush the skin with plenty of water for at least 15 minutes while removing contaminated clothing and shoes.
- In patient management of inhalation exposure to chemicals, the common first responder treatment is to get the patient out of the area and into fresh air.
- Vapors of volatile corrosives may cause eye irritation, lacrimation (shedding tears), redness and inflammation, and corneal injury.
- Exposure controls and personal protection are special considerations to be taken in law enforcement response.

Vital Vocabulary

chemical chain reaction The exothermic (heat-releasing) process that results in maintaining a material at its ignition temperature in order to sustain combustion.

clandestine drug laboratory A secret laboratory in which illicit drugs are manufactured.

combustion A rapid chemical process that results in the release of energy in the form of heat and (usually) light; also known as fire.

corrosive Will destroy or irreversibly damage a substance it contacts.

crack cocaine A solid, smokable form of cocaine. It is a free-base form of cocaine that can be made using baking soda (sodium bicarbonate).

decontamination The process of removing or neutralizing a hazard and properly disposing of materials such as clothing and personal protective equipment from patients and rescue personnel.

fire tetrahedron The four factors necessary for a fire to occur: fuel, oxygen, heat, and a chemical chain reaction.

fuel Any material that is combustible.

heat Added or external energy that causes a rise in temperature in a potential fuel for a fire.

hydroponics A method of growing plants using mineral nutrient solutions, in water, without soil.

ignition temperature The minimum temperature at which a substance will undergo combustion in a normal atmosphere without the additional application of external heat or source of ignition.

oxygen A colorless, odorless gas that comprises approximately 21% of the volume of atmospheric air. It is the element present in air that supports combustion.

pyrolysis The chemical decomposition of a condensed substance, such as a solid or liquid, that occurs at high temperatures and results in the release of combustible gases.

toxidrome The specific signs and symptoms that a population exposed to a particular type of agent will display.

weapons of mass destruction (WMD) Weapons designed to bring about mass death, casualties, and massive damage to property or infrastructure using chemical, biological, radiological, nuclear, or explosive agents; also known as weapons of mass casualty (WMC).

Check Your Knowledge

1. The *most* important aspect in the response to a clandestine methamphetamine laboratory is:
   - **A.** preservation of evidence.
   - **B.** treating the injured.
   - **C.** safety of the responders and other civilians.
   - **D.** proper removal of chemicals.
2. Cocaine base is made into crack cocaine by mixing with boiling water and:
   - **A.** pseudoephedrine.
   - **B.** aspirin.
   - **C.** acetone.
   - **D.** sodium bicarbonate (baking soda).
3. When ingestion of a large amount of methamphetamine is suspected, should you make the patient vomit?
   - **A.** Yes
   - **B.** No
4. The proper procedure for skin exposure to chemicals is to:
   - **A.** remove clothing and wipe material away from the skin.
   - **B.** remove clothing and flush skin with clean water for at least 15 minutes.
   - **C.** wrap the exposed area with sterile gauze with the clothing in place.
   - **D.** remove clothing, expose the skin to air, and check for circulation.
5. Often, clandestine methamphetamine labs are hidden in remote areas and contain extensive electronic surveillance equipment to monitor who enters and leaves the locations. The operators of these labs often booby-trap them to destroy any evidence that may be used in case of discovery and seizure.
   - **A.** True
   - **B.** False

Rescue

Unit 7

Mark G. Falkenhan
Steven M. Kasser

Law Enforcement Responder Objectives

Auto Extrication

- Discuss the role of emergency responders in vehicle extrication. (p 125)
- Identify personal safety measures. (pp 125–127)
- Identify patient safety measures. (p 127)
- Identify situational safety specific to motor vehicle crashes. (pp 127–129)
- Evaluate the need for additional resources. (pp 129–131)
- List and explain access and extrication considerations. (pp 131–133)
- Identify special considerations for patient movement. (p 133)

Water Rescue

- Discuss the difference between water rescue personnel and law enforcement responders and their roles. (pp 133–134)
- Identify the venues in which law enforcement responders may encounter water responses. (pp 134–136)
- Identify environments that increase the hazards of water. (pp 136–139)
- Discuss the elements involved in preparing a water response preplan. (pp 137–138)
- Discuss the different types of drowning. (p 140)

National EMS Education Standard Competencies

Trauma

Uses simple knowledge to recognize and manage life threats based on assessment findings for an acutely injured patient while awaiting additional emergency medical response.

Environmental Emergencies

Recognition and management of

- Submersion incidents (p 140)

EMS Operations

Knowledge of operational roles and responsibilities to ensure safe patient, public, and personnel safety.

Vehicle Extrication

- Safe vehicle extrication (p 127)
- Use of simple hand tools (pp 132–133)

Vehicle Extrication

Every day, law enforcement responders (LERs) respond to, or are involved in, motor vehicle crashes. Motor vehicles are an integral part of our society, but vehicle crashes provide many challenges to the LER. A crash can range from an individual vehicle to multiple vehicles. Most vehicles contain various traditional hazards, such as fuel and electrical systems, but many vehicles also contain additional hazards in the form of alternative power systems, new safety technology, and specialized construction. Although communities are accustomed to having emergency services available to deal with the traditional motor vehicle crash, high-occupancy vehicles such as vans and buses can quickly deplete and overwhelm these resources. The survival of patients in many instances will rely on the quick action of the LER.

Law enforcement agencies and other public safety programs must plan to deal with motor vehicle crashes. Poor planning can result in death or disability of both the victim and the rescuers. The community you serve expects that you have assessed your situation, answered questions, and prepared to respond. Several considerations should be observed in preparing to deal with motor vehicle crashes. The primary consideration is your duty to preserve the life of those involved. To meet this challenge, the LER should develop a response plan that takes into account the following:

- Resources carried on your person or in your vehicle
- External resources available to you
- Accident scene assessment
- Scene stabilization
- Accessibility of the patient for emergency care
- Rapid patient extrication

LER ROLES AT A MOTOR VEHICLE CRASH

The two major roles of the LER at vehicle crash scenes are to provide care to the patients and to determine whether the patient needs extrication from the vehicle.

Providing patient care requires that the LER be able to access the patient who is still inside the vehicle. In some situations, the LER may have to use basic hand tools to gain entry into the passenger compartment of a vehicle. LERs must also take precautions to ensure the safety of the scene, themselves, other rescuers, and the patient or patients. After a patient is reached, simple medical techniques and basic trauma management have proven to be effective in saving lives.

If it is determined that a patient is physically trapped in a vehicle, the LER may be required to perform simple extrication methods to free the patient. Prior to physically removing the patient, consider the dangers posed by leaving the patient in the vehicle versus the dangers associated with moving the patient. Certain issues, such as uncontrollable vehicle fires and unstable terrain, would require rapid extrication. In other instances, a delay in conventional rescue resources as a result of weather, terrain, or response time may require the LER to use basic tools to perform an extrication. The key to extrication is knowing the limitations of your abilities and resources.

PERSONAL SAFETY

When arriving at the scene of a vehicle crash, personal protection is a top priority. Many types of body protection are available and necessary during a rescue (**Figure 1**). In some agencies it may not be possible to wear or have on your person some of these protective measures. It may be more practical to obtain these items and carry them in a gear bag.

Tip

Safety Standards

Agencies should ensure that policies, supplies, and equipment meet or exceed safety standards as required by the Occupational Safety and Health Administration (OSHA). Many agencies will also need to follow other internal, local, or state safety and health mandates. LERs must be familiar with the standards and how these standards affect their work.

Gloves

Proper standard precautions must be in place prior to patient contact. At a minimum, a pair of medical gloves should be worn. The average tactical types of gloves, unless specified,

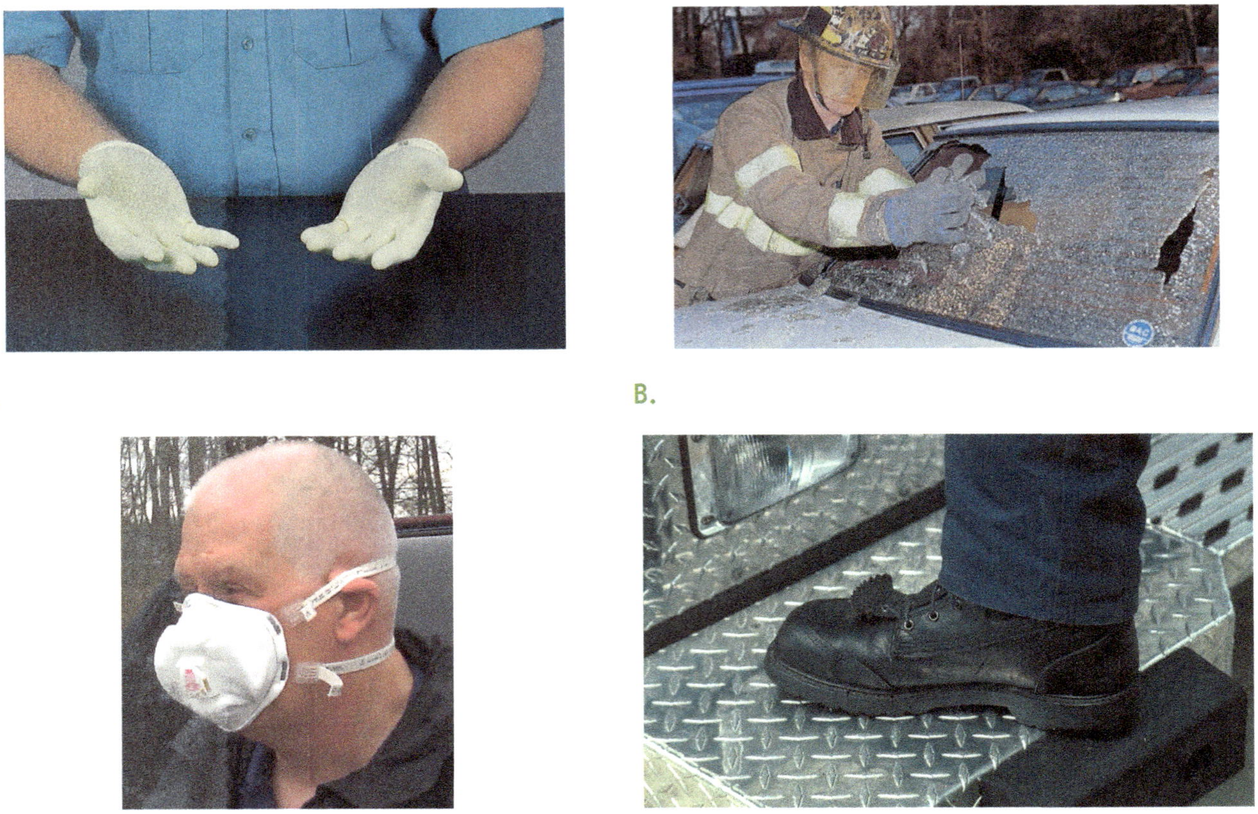

A. B. C. D.

Figure 1 Many types of body protection may be necessary during a rescue. A. Medical gloves. B. Eyewear. C. Respiratory mask. D. Reinforced boots.

normally do not protect the responder from bloodborne pathogens.

Medical gloves are needed as a form of personal protection against body fluids and blood. Medical gloves, however, provide no protection from the physical hazards that may be present. A pair of leather work gloves, at a minimum, will provide protection from sharp edges and broken glass. There are also specific gloves manufactured for automobile rescue. Just like tactical gloves, most of these do not provide protection from body fluids. A LER can, however, don a pair of medical gloves (some prefer two pairs) and then don his or her rescue gloves over them. This is the best way to provide protection of your hands against both physical and bloodborne hazards.

Eyewear

Hazards such as leaking fluids from the vehicle, jagged metal, and broken glass necessitate eye protection. The type of eyewear must be approved by the American National Standards Institute (ANSI). ANSI-approved safety glasses protect the eyes from front and side threats and are rated to different levels of impact. An alternative may be ANSI-approved tactical glasses that also meet the impact requirement. There are many sunglasses that look like safety glasses but are not; be sure your rescue glasses bear the ANSI labeling.

Respiratory Protection

Respiratory protection may also be required at the scene of a vehicle crash. If hazardous materials are involved, self-contained breathing apparatus (SCBA) may be required. This type of respiratory protection requires a tremendous amount of training to be used properly and may not necessarily be a piece of equipment available to the LER. A particulate matter mask, such as an N95 mask, however, should always be available. If the LER is in or around the vehicle while the windshield is being cut, the glass that floats as dust can easily be inhaled and enter the respiratory tract. This in turn can damage the lining of the airway and the lungs. The N95 mask, if properly fitted, will protect the respiratory tract.

When using a filter respirator such as the N95 mask, ensure that the air you are breathing has the proper amount of oxygen. If the atmosphere is deficient in oxygen, SCBA should be used, but only by authorized personnel.

Boots

Agencies will often have footwear policies. It is common for programs to require a boot with a steel or reinforced toe. Boots with toe protection are appropriate during motor vehicle rescues. The most effective rescue boots will be waterproof and have a steel or reinforced shank. If your uniform policy does not allow you to wear protective footwear, consider carrying rescue boots in a gear bag.

Coveralls

Coveralls that have some flash resistance and are marked to comply with ANSI standards relative to traffic are a great asset to the LER. Coveralls add a layer of protection against rigid metal, glass, and dirt. Flash-retardant coveralls provide the extra benefit of reducing injury in and around a flash fire. Although impractical in daily law enforcement use, coveralls can be stored in a gear bag and made readily available.

PATIENT SAFETY

The primary goal for patient safety is to do no further harm to the patient. This includes actions to gain access to the patient, as well as treatment of the injuries found during the patient assessment. During the extrication process, ensure that as the patient becomes disentangled the movement of metal or glass does not add to the patient's injuries or create new ones. The removal and transfer phases, in which the patient is moved from the vehicle to the transport unit, require coordination of all the rescue crews to ensure safe handling of the patient. Methods to aid in patient safety include using coverings, blankets, or tarps to shield the patient from debris. Eye and hearing protection may also be used during lengthy extrications as long as these devices do not aggravate an injury or reduce the effectiveness of medical devices. In situations in which fire may occur and fire resources are scarce, the LER may also want to keep an appropriate fire extinguisher near the location of the extrication.

The extrication process could take several minutes to hours. Communication is a key factor in gaining control and attaining the trust of the patient. Be sure to inform the patient not only of the care you are giving but also of what is happening with the extrication process. The scene will generate noise and confusion for the patient. Make every effort to calm and reassure the patient during all phases of a vehicle rescue. A good practice is to assign one rescuer to act as the primary point of communication with the patient. This same person can monitor the patient's status, provide care, and evaluate the safety of the process relative to the patient.

SITUATIONAL SAFETY

Control Traffic Flow

When arriving at the scene of a vehicle crash with entrapment, the placement of the response vehicles must be considered. Frequently, law enforcement policies are aimed at maintaining an open lane of travel at the scene of an accident, especially if interstate commerce may be impeded. An assessment of the scene may dictate the need to shut down the flow of traffic to ensure that additional resources can respond to the scene and protect the responders operating at the scene.

Strategic placement of apparatus may be needed if the incident involves hazardous materials or to protect the accident scene. If a hazardous materials situation is suspected or known, the responding units should stage upwind and uphill from the hazard. Units may move to other positions once a trained hazardous materials team has determined that it is safe to do so.

A major piece of fire apparatus or large law enforcement vehicles may be used to block the lane of traffic flow (**Figure 2**). The apparatus should be placed at a 45-degree angle to the traffic lane and less than 100 feet prior to the actual incident scene. This offensive measure acts as a wall for the responders operating in the rescue area. The apparatus will act as a blocker if a vehicle loses control and greatly reduces the chance of further injuries to the patient and crew.

Any time an emergency vehicle is stopped at the scene of a crash, it is recommended that all emergency lights be activated to provide warning to oncoming vehicle traffic. In addition, supplemental scene lighting may be needed for

Figure 2 At a crash scene, fire apparatus or large law enforcement vehicles may be used to block the lane of traffic flow.

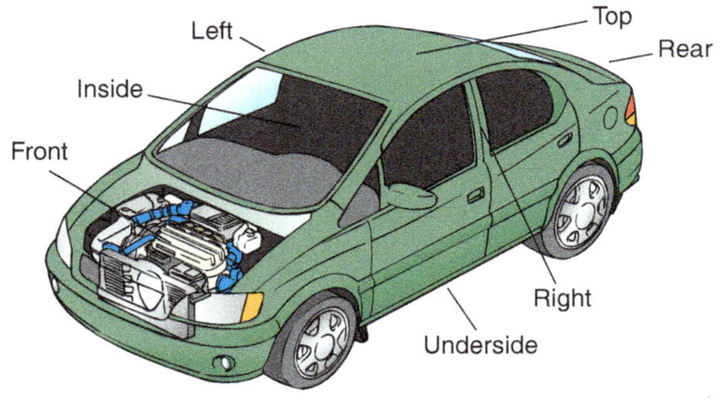

Figure 3 Mentally divide the vehicle into eight sides. The eighth side is the rescue side.

illumination of the rescue ground during rescue operations and during incident reconstruction investigations.

Many states now have rapid traffic response units that respond on interstates and major roadways. They are designed to assist stranded motorists and responding emergency response units. Once at the location of a vehicle rescue, they have the resources to divert traffic away from the incident, including traffic cones and traffic arrow boards.

360-Degree Assessment

After the initial scene size-up, the LER must perform a 360-degree assessment of the incident. This assessment will help the LER narrow down the specific or specialized resources that may be needed. During this assessment, there are several aspects on which to focus.

Focus on the vehicles involved and think of each vehicle as having eight sides (**Figure 3**). Assess the left, front, right, and rear of the vehicle. Then look under the vehicle and at the top of the vehicle. Scan the inside of the vehicle. Once you have looked at these seven sides, the eighth side will be the rescue side. The rescue side is the area of the vehicle where the patient will be disentangled during extrication.

In assessing the scene, the LER should note obvious hazards. Downed power lines are common at the scene of motor vehicle crashes, yet are very seldom noticed until other resources arrive at the scene. A telephone pole supporting the electrical lines may be broken in half with half the pole hanging above the vehicle and the other half under the vehicle. Not all downed power lines arc as they come into direct contact with the metal of a vehicle, but a lack of arcing does not mean that the wire is dead. Downed power lines that are broken are seeking a way to send their electrical energy to ground. If the ground is through an automobile, your first indication of a live power line could very well be when you come in contact with the vehicle and you receive an electric shock. Even if you see a downed line that is contacting the ground some distance from the incident, that line may still transfer electricity to the responders, causing a sudden electric shock and cardiac arrest.

A hidden electrical danger is a transformer box at ground level, which can be hit by a vehicle and displaced. As you arrive at the scene, the actual transformer box may look fine; however, the vehicle is now sitting on high-voltage, open power lines.

If any electrical lines are involved, the incident will require an emergency response from the local electrical utility company. Local electrical utility personnel have the proper training, equipment, and authority to shut down power to the lines in question so the emergency crews can perform the rescue.

As you continue your scene assessment, look for fluids leaking from the vehicle. Antifreeze coolant and oil leaks are often handled by the responding units. Although they are less common, you may also encounter gasoline or diesel leaks. Depending on the amount leaking, a hazardous materials team may be needed to control the leak and offload any remaining fuel safely.

If fire occurs, attempt to extinguish the fire with a fire extinguisher. The most effective extinguisher agent would be a dry chemical ABC type. Unfortunately, the dry chemical extinguishers carried by most LERs have a relatively small amount of extinguishing agent, most commonly 5 pounds.

To have an effective amount of extinguisher agent usually requires a minimum of 20 pounds.

Broken glass can be found around the perimeter of the vehicle. Traditionally the side and rear windows are made of tempered glass, which shatters into hundreds of small pieces when broken. The front windshield is a laminated double-pane design with a thin laminate sheet in the middle holding the panes together. If the windshield is hit, it will break but will not shatter like the tempered glass. If portions of the windshield are broken, the cause may be the front air bags deploying or, in older vehicles, it may be the unrestrained front seat passengers impacting the windshield with their heads.

Scan the interior of the vehicle to determine the number of patients and whether a patient is trapped and requiring extrication. Determine whether all patients are accounted for. Interview the occupants and bystanders and look for clues such as toys, car seats, and other personal items. If it is suspected that patients have been ejected from the vehicle, an immediate search of the area must take place to find those individuals. If it is night and visibility has been reduced, the use of a thermal imaging camera is recommended to assist in the search effort.

An assessment of the mechanism of injury must be made during the 360-degree assessment. Determine what type of impact has occurred. Has the vehicle been hit from the front or the rear? Has the vehicle been impacted from the side or has the vehicle rolled over? Is there intrusion greater than 12 inches into the passenger compartment? Any of these conditions should be a flag for the rescuer to suspect a high potential of severe injuries.

ADDITIONAL RESOURCES

When completing a scene size-up and a 360-degree assessment, the LER must determine what additional resources are needed to support the rescue operation. Because some of the resources may be specialized, it is important to request these specific assets early to secure their response to the incident.

Consider how many patients are involved and the severity of their injuries. Use this information to make a request for resources from the emergency medical system. Request the number of ambulances necessary based on the number of patients. LERs should evaluate the level of care required for treatment and transport of the patients. If a patient is severely injured, air medical support may also be required based on your local protocol.

If it is determined that a patient is physically trapped, the incident will require units with equipment for disentanglement. Some areas have enhanced fire engines or ladder apparatus that carry specific vehicle extrication equipment. Other areas may rely on light-, medium-, or heavy-duty rescue squads that carry a wide array of rescue and extrication tools.

Depending on the severity of the crash, fire suppression units may be responding with you. The firefighting unit will be prepared to address fire, leaking fluids, and other hazards. Firefighting personnel, depending on local protocols, can provide additional manpower for patient care and a blocking vehicle for the accident scene.

Additional law enforcement personnel may be required to assist with scene control and traffic flow. Specialized law enforcement entities such as accident investigators may be required if the incident is complex, especially if a death or serious injury has occurred. Some agencies also have rescue teams that can perform vehicle extrication, responding with their own specialized rescue apparatus.

Large fuel and fluid leaks may require the response of a hazardous materials team. The team may also be called upon if chemicals are contained inside a vehicle or truck. This team is trained to contain and identify the chemicals or fuels involved. They also provide decontamination of the patient at the scene if contamination or exposure has been determined.

Vehicle Stabilization

The vehicle must be stabilized prior to responder access and patient extrication. The term *stabilization* refers not only to the physical act of securing the vehicle so there is no further movement but also to securing the multiple **supplemental restraint systems (SRSs)** found in today's vehicles. Working in a vehicle with a live, armed, undeployed SRS can have disastrous results if the system fires during the extrication.

When approaching the vehicle, listen to see whether the vehicle is running. It you hear the engine running, the vehicle could very well be in gear with the driver's foot still on the brake. Verify that the vehicle is in park, that the parking brake is applied, that the vehicle ignition is in the off position, and that the keys are removed and secured. Keyless ignition systems are becoming more common. They operate from a wireless key fob or smart key that can initiate electrical activity from up to 25 feet from the vehicle. If the vehicle you are working in has one of these types of key systems, it is recommended that you move the key at least 50 feet from the incident to reduce the chance of remotely activating electrical activity within the vehicle. Consider that prior to turning off the key any electric windows should be lowered and electrically operated seats moved back to provide additional room for the patient if needed.

Cribbing, which is blocks that can be supplied in various sizes, should be placed at all four wheels to keep the vehicle from drifting (**Figure 4**). A set of wheel chocks can be used as an alternative to perform the same function. The tire valve stems may also be removed to lower the center of gravity in a controlled manner. Using a knife or another sharp object to puncture the tire is not recommended because the quick release of air from the tire can erupt violently and cause a shift in the overall vehicle load, making the vehicle less stable.

Once the vehicle is stabilized, the batteries must be disconnected. Traditionally, batteries are under the hood of vehicles; however, newer cars may have nontraditional battery locations. Batteries can now be found in the front wheel well, under the rear passenger seats, and in the trunk area. Many of these alternative locations have a disconnect switch that activates if the vehicle is involved in a crash. To confirm that the electrical system is not live, find the battery and cut the negative wire first, and then the positive wire, with a pair of cable cutters or lineman's pliers. Then cut both wires back at least 2 inches. This will greatly reduce the chance that the electrical system can be reenergized.

Figure 4 Cribbing should be placed at all four wheels to keep the vehicle from drifting.

It is important to de-energize the vehicle as soon as possible. The control systems that operate the supplemental restraint systems will have stored capacitized energy for up to 15 minutes once the battery is disconnected. That stored energy could potentially activate an undeployed restraint system during the extrication process. Remove the power to deactivate the stored energy as soon as possible to reduce the chances of further injury to the patient and the rescue crew.

A unique hazard that is growing in popularity is the hybrid vehicle. Although the actual definition of a hybrid vehicle varies from manufacturer to manufacturer, the electric hybrid needs special attention. Identification may prove challenging because many traditional car models have a hybrid option.

Electric hybrid vehicles operate with a high-voltage electric motor that is tied into a combustion engine (**Figure 5**).

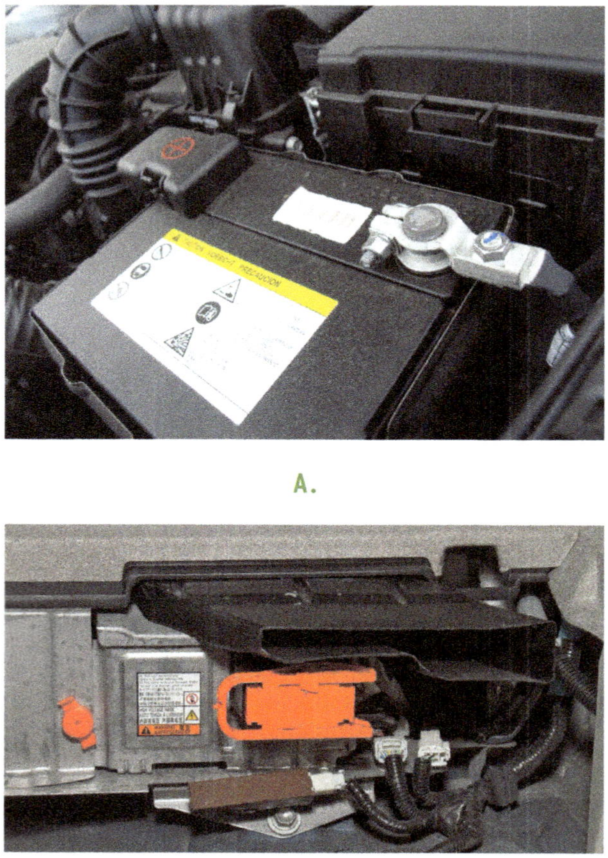

A.

B.

Figure 5 **A.** Traditional car battery. **B.** Hybrid car battery system.

Many do not have a traditional key system, using a key fob instead, and the vehicle is started using an on button located on the front console. As the vehicle idles or operates at low speed (usually under 30 miles per hour [mph]), it will operate with the electric motor. As the vehicle accelerates, the combustion engine engages seamlessly. The challenge is that when you approach the scene of one of these vehicles you may not hear an engine running and you may assume that the vehicle is turned off. In reality, the vehicle may be fully engaged and in gear. This **live load** can shift and move without warning, causing further damage to the patients and the responders.

When approaching these types of vehicles, it is important to ensure that the vehicle is not in gear, that the off button is engaged, and that the parking (emergency) brake is set. The high-voltage battery cells are traditionally in the rear of the vehicle. The high-voltage batteries are encased in a rigid housing that protects the cells during impact. Wiring and connections supporting the battery current are orange; no attempt should be made to cut these wires, because death or serious injury will occur. The 12-volt battery system, once found, can be disengaged in the same fashion as in a traditional vehicle.

ACCESS TO THE PATIENT

Once the vehicle is stabilized, the LER can gain access to the interior of the vehicle. Two major goals of gaining access are to assess the patient and to identify the supplemental restraint systems that have and have not deployed.

The easiest way to gain access is to try to open the vehicle doors in a normal fashion. This may require the patient to unlock the door or lower a window. If a door will not open by the outside door handle, attempt to access the interior handle to open the door.

Tip

Try Doors First

Rescuers should try all doors on a vehicle to make access to the patient. A common error is to attempt only the door where the patient is located. Remember the common saying: "Try before you pry."

Prying tools such as a pry bar or a halligan bar may be needed to open the door. The pry end of the bar is inserted in the gap next to the door handle toward the rear of the vehicle. Pulling on the pry bar while operating the door handle may pop the door off the pin that holds the door in place.

If the windows are intact and the doors cannot be opened, access can be accomplished by breaking the tempered glass. Normally the side and rear windows are made of tempered glass, which shatters into many small pieces once broken. The window used for access should be as far from the patient as possible. A spring-loaded center punch or tactical rescue knife with a window punch option can be used (**Figure 6**). First look for the manufacturer's mark on the window, which is usually in the corner. Place the center punch tip at this mark and activate the punch. The window will then shatter. Next remove the glass from the window frame using an available tool. Do not use your hands to clear the glass. If using the tactical knife, strike the window punch in the same area to break the glass, making sure your wrist rests against the window frame to keep your hand from going through the broken glass.

Once the responder has accessed the vehicle, he or she must further assess the patient's needs. Look for other injuries and determine how the patient may be trapped in the vehicle. Treat injuries based on local protocols. Consider stabilizing the patient's cervical spine. If your system authorizes the LER to carry and use supplemental oxygen, consider providing it to severely injured or trapped patients as soon as possible.

SRS Considerations

Visually inspect the SRSs and determine whether all systems have deployed. If an SRS has deployed, look for SRS-related injuries on the patient. SRSs are designed to increase the survivability of a serious accident; however, this does not mean the patient will be injury free. Some vehicles may have up to 14 SRSs. Most systems are identified by the wording "air bag"

Figure 6 A spring-loaded center punch can be used to break vehicle windows and gain access to victims.

or "SRS." Once the location of a device is known, the LER must immediately relay that information to the rescue crew.

Air bags are the most common SRS. The bags are located in the front steering wheel and the passenger dash area. They are activated by a small explosive charge that deploys and inflates the bag; the bag then deflates rapidly during a frontal impact. Front-facing air bags may also be found for rear-seated passengers. The location of these bags is behind the front driver and passenger seats. Air bags have been suspected of causing fractured arms and wrists and chest trauma.

Knee bolsters may be located under the dashboard on both the passenger and driver sides. The bolster device activates to protect the legs from impacting the underside of the dashboard, thus reducing the chance of lower leg fractures and entrapment during a frontal impact. Bruising and abrasions on the legs, with bleeding, may be present when this device has activated.

Air curtains differ from air bags in many ways. Air curtains are located on the side interior of the vehicle. They may be located in the doors or the outside of the passenger seats and in the outer portion of the interior roof area. They are activated when the vehicle is involved in a side impact or rollover and remain inflated. These devices are activated by a high-pressure gas cylinder. The location of the cylinder can be in one of the posts supporting the windows and doors or along the roof line. The curtains are designed to protect the lateral sides of the body and the head.

Seat belt pretensioners are designed to pull the passenger back into the seat as far as possible just prior to air bag deployment. This feature is designed to lock in the seat belt to keep the patient from moving forward during impact. Activation is from a small charge that pulls a cable tightening the seat belt. These devices are found at either the receiver end of the seat belt or at the base of the seat belt retractor. There may be instances in which the belt has retracted so tightly that the patient is not able to release the seat belt. If this occurs, the belt may be cut. Assess for any type of chest trauma that may occur during deployment.

All SRSs are activated by a small control box, which is usually within the dash assembly or the center console and not readily visible. Within the box is a capacitor that stores energy so that if there is a catastrophic electrical failure the SRS devices can still activate. To deactivate this device, it is important to disconnect the battery as soon as possible, as discussed previously, to reduce the chances of deployment.

EXTRICATION CONSIDERATIONS

Extrication is often defined as the disentanglement of the vehicle to free a trapped patient. Basic extrication may be accomplished by a LER, but a key factor is what resources are available to perform a successful rescue. These incidents are often rescuer and labor intensive and require highly specialized tools and equipment.

Use of Simple Hand Tools

Unless specifically trained and equipped, the LER will most likely not have the proper tools to accomplish patient extrication. Some basic hand tools can assist with gaining access to the patient. A good understanding of the mechanics of basic tools can assist the LER in accessing the patient.

LERs can use a spring-loaded center punch for breaking glass and entering window openings. The pry bar can be used to open doors or to move metal that is impeding patient access or removal. A hacksaw with a bimetal or tungsten blade may be used to cut a door frame or a door post to assist in opening the door for access. It is a good idea to have multiple spare blades available, because they have a tendency to break apart during heavy usage.

A hammer or 5-pound maul can be used in conjunction with the pry bar to expose the **Nader bolt**. Striking the pry bar with the maul will penetrate the pry end deeper into the seam of the door. Once access to the Nader bolt is made, you can attempt to pry the Nader bolt from the door latch.

An excellent mechanical advantage device is the wire rope come-along. A 1.5-ton rated come-along is compact and easy to use (Figure 7). When properly anchored, the come-along device can assist in opening a door that may be jammed.

Socket sets with both SAE and metric sizes can also assist with gaining access. If damage to the Nader pin area is so severe that access may not be possible, attempt to release

Figure 7 When anchored, the come-along device can assist in opening a jammed door.

the door from the hinges. The hinge side of the door can be exposed using your maul and pry bar. Once the bolts can be visualized, they can be removed with the correct socket size and a socket extension. Once all the bolts are removed, the door can be swung out of the way toward the Nader pin.

Tip

Door Control

A note of caution: Once the bolts are removed, the weight of the door will force it downward. Always have control of the door to reduce any sudden movement.

SPECIAL CONSIDERATIONS FOR PATIENT MOVEMENT

Removing the Patient

Accessing the patient will provide the LER an opportunity to accomplish the multiple aspects of patient care. As soon as the patient is assessed and life threats are managed, determine the best route for patient removal. If the LER must move the patient prior to the arrival of EMS resources, he or she should do the following:

- Maintain manual cervical spine stabilization.
- Continue the treatment of life-threatening injuries.
- Move the patient as a unit.
- Determine the safest route to move the patient.

Rapid Extrication

Rapid extrication indicates that the patient is being moved by the rescuer to maintain the patient's life. The LER should consider all the steps identified for removing a patient, but conditions and time may not allow for a methodical, controlled response. Several conditions may require rapid extrication of the patient. Physical conditions may include a vehicle fire that is threatening into the passenger area or instability of the vehicle or the surrounding scene that may compromise the life or condition of the patient. A deteriorating patient condition may also necessitate a rapid extrication.

Water Rescue

Water is essential for life. There is no other substance as critical to sustaining life, or equally as threatening to it. Water can go from constituting a beautiful seascape to being a life-threatening entity in moments. Although water can be extremely destructive, it is unreasonable to live in fear of it. It is imperative to understand the many environments and hazards that water present and to gain a true respect for its power.

According to the Centers for Disease Control and Prevention (CDC), drowning is the second leading cause of unintentional death for children aged between 1 and 14 years. Many water rescue situations will require specialized resources beyond the LER's capability. Although these rescues may be beyond the LER's expertise, it is imperative for the LER to have a basic knowledge of water rescue environments, hazards, and techniques. With this information, the LER can form plans of action and take the appropriate steps to give the victim and rescuers the best possible chance of survival.

WATER RESCUE PERSONNEL

LERs will respond to water-related emergencies, and it is up to the LER to ensure that appropriately trained water rescue personnel are also dispatched. Water rescue personnel are extensively trained and experienced in working in this dangerous environment. Many drowning victims are excellent swimmers, including LERs, and are killed while attempting to rescue a victim in the water. Properly trained water rescue personnel include, but are not limited to, the following:

- Lifeguards
- Beach patrol
- Swift-water rescue technicians
- Dive rescue technicians

It is important to identify the steps you can take until help arrives and to avoid endangering yourself or others. The guideline "Reach, Throw, Row, Go" is an easy way to remember a course of action to assist victims in the water (**Figure 8**).

VENUES

Pools

Pools present unique challenges to the LER. In a private setting, lifeguards will most likely not be present. Unsupervised children, inebriated adults, and skilled and unskilled swimmers may find themselves in harm's way. If you are called to the scene, something unfortunate has already happened. Take steps to mitigate the problem without endangering yourself or others. One's first instinct may be to jump into the problem. Instead, take time to observe the scene. If the victim is still in the water, quickly scan the environment looking for clues to what might have happened. Are there electrical appliances nearby or in the water? Is it possible the victim dived into the pool, striking the bottom and sustaining head or neck trauma or both?

Look for pool tools that may help you retrieve the victim without entering the water—possibly a **shepherd's crook**. Even a pole pool brush may help. If you cannot reach out to the victim, look for something to throw to the victim. Throw him or her a life ring or a rope throw bag; then pull him or her to safety. The last option you should consider is getting in the water, and you should consider it only if you are properly trained in water rescue. If you are so trained, first make sure additional help is on the way and that you take all precautions possible to ensure your safety. Never allow a drowning victim to grab you; many rescuers become victims themselves by being pulled under by panicked victims. Take something to reach out to the victim, keeping distance between you and the victim, and then pull the victim to safety.

If the victim is unconscious, quickly assess the ABCs (airway, breathing, and circulation). If the victim is in cardiopulmonary arrest, get him or her out immediately and begin cardiopulmonary resuscitation (CPR). If the victim still has a pulse but is not breathing, immediately begin rescue breathing. If the victim has a pulse and is breathing, and no life-threatening trauma is noted, move to the shallow area and wait for other rescue personnel to arrive. Position one hand under the patient's back while the other hand stabilizes the patient's head and neck.

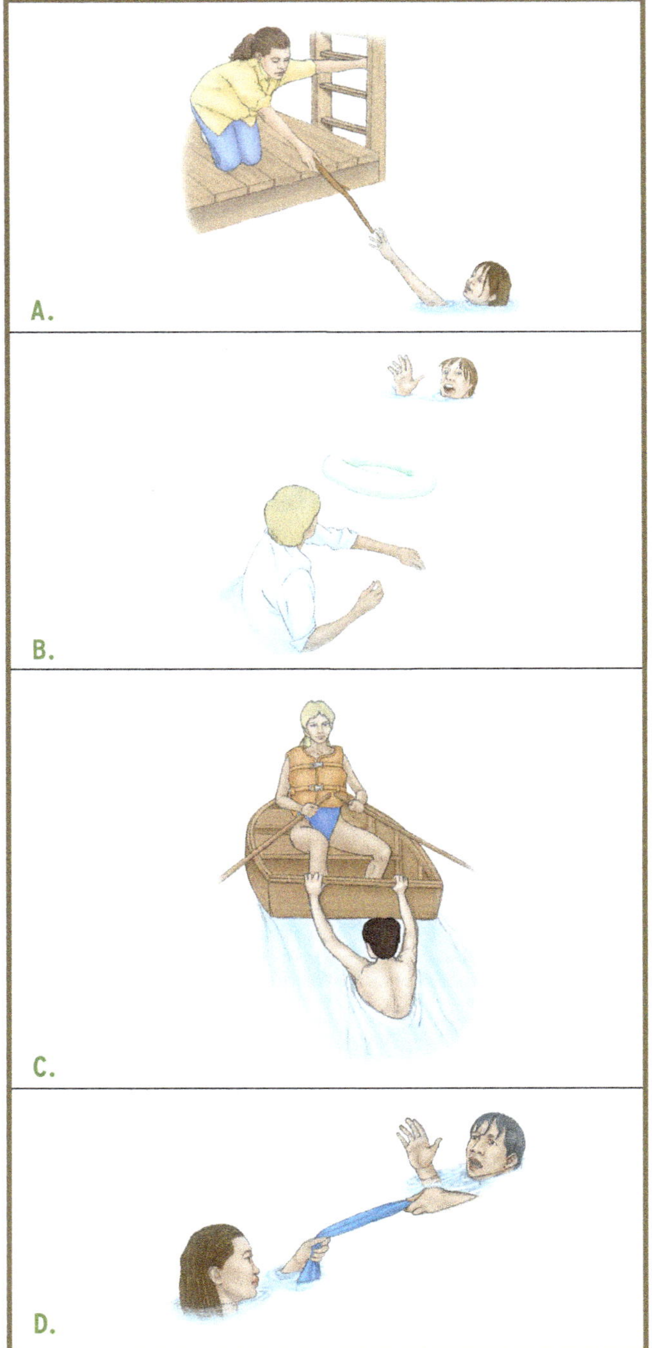

Figure 8 The guideline "reach, throw, row, and go" is an easy way to remember a course of action to assist victims in the water. **A.** Reach. **B.** Throw. **C.** Row. **D.** Go.

Public pools will most likely have trained lifeguards who can facilitate the victim's retrieval from the water. Lifeguards are trained to provide basic first aid and to assist and retrieve a near-drowning victim safely. Do not interfere with their procedures; facilitate additional resources and assist the lifeguards in any way possible. These situations may cause a lot of commotion among bystanders, and you may need to control the environment to allow the lifeguards to do their job.

LERs who patrol an area with swimmers can assist lifeguards by scanning the swim area. Early recognition of the distressed swimmer can save lives. If a distressed swimmer is identified, alert the lifeguards and immediately provide assistance to the swimmer in the form of a throw ring or buoy or the extension of a shepherd's hook or pole. The distressed swimmer will present with a surface struggle and difficulty maintaining buoyancy or forward momentum or both. He or she will appear to be vertical in the water, grasping and flailing, trying to keep his or her head above water, and will not be able to call for help. This will lead to further exhaustion, distress, and the victim gasping for air.

Once the victim is sufficiently hypoxic, he or she will lose consciousness. This may lead to involuntary gasps whereby water may enter the airway. Water that enters the airway may be ingested into the lungs, or **laryngospasm** may occur, closing off the victim's airway and not allowing water to enter the lungs. The victim will slowly submerge and will initially be face down only slightly below the water's surface. These victims need immediate rescue; otherwise, death can occur within minutes.

Beaches

Beach is a generic term we use to describe the water's edge, usually at a large body of water. For this discussion, the term *beach* will be used to describe an ocean beach. There are many factors to consider when evaluating the hazards of an ocean beach, not the least of which is the water's current.

Ocean waves reach the shore, run up the shore, and retreat to the ocean. These continuous motions can create troughs in the shore, which cause the water to run parallel to the shore. The water continues this movement until a common area is reached where the trough is the deepest, allowing the water to be released back out to sea. As the water runs parallel to the shore, a rip current is created (**Figure 9**).

A rip current can easily carry swimmers along its path. Swimmers may be caught in this current and find themselves being quickly carried down the shore, then away from it. The rip current area may appear muddy, foamy, debris-filled, and quickly moving away from shore. The swimmer may be pushed significantly past his or her comfort level, but will not be carried out to sea. The problem is created when the swimmer begins to fight against the current and tries to swim straight to shore against it. Even strong swimmers will be ineffective in swimming against a strong rip current. The caught swimmer begins to panic, swimming harder and quickly tiring, thus becoming susceptible to drowning. The informed swimmer will understand the rip current and know not to swim against it, but to swim parallel to shore until free of the current, then back in toward shore, escaping the current's flow and reaching the shore safely.

Figure 9 The rip current area may appear muddy, foamy, debris-filled, and quickly moving away from shore.

Other natural hazards in the beach environment include indigenous sea life such as jellyfish, coral, sharks, and other dangerous creatures that will be addressed later in this unit.

The ocean surf holds massive power (**Figure 10**). The surf can pick up and throw people easily. Once caught, you have no control over your movement, and you can strike the bottom or other debris very easily. The impact zone is the area near the beach where the surf breaks as the waves reach their highest point. If you are not properly trained, do not enter the surf.

Figure 10 Ocean surf.

Beach recreation can cause hazards of its own. Swimmers on air mattresses can find themselves floating to unsafe distances from shore. Other items, such as surfboards and boogie boards, can become dangerous when they strike a swimmer.

If a swimmer is reported missing, an accurate last known position is essential for quick and efficient rescue and retrieval. This spot can be marked with a marker buoy or dive marker and will assist the rescuers in implementing search patterns.

Rivers, Ponds, and Lakes

Rivers, ponds, and lakes include the same hazards as any other water environment, with some exceptions. A pond or lake may contain unseen bacteria or microbes that may cause illness; it is important to know what hazards exist in your area. If you are unsure, a water sample should be taken to the health care facility along with the patient. Rivers may present hazards due to rate of water flow and currents. Hazards associated with water flow are addressed later in the Swift Water section.

Transient Waters

Water that appears in an area that is not normally submerged can create devastating damage and incredible hazards to responders. Floods occur for many reasons, but primarily because of extremely heavy rains. Floods can occur quickly and can trap people in cars, buildings, or residences. As a LER, it is important for you to understand the hazards you may encounter in this environment so you can protect yourself and prevent harm to others.

Floods cover submerged hazards—everything from cars and fire hydrants to road signs, fences, and power lines—making even boat-assisted rescues dangerous. Perform only those rescues you are trained to perform, and allow the specially trained persons to perform any others. Air assets may be required to rescue victims in extreme situations.

Flood waters can become contaminated with gasoline, heating oils, septic waste or sewage, or any other substance that exists in the covered areas. These contaminants can cause dermal burns or cause the rapid spread of bacteria and disease. Precautions must be taken to minimize exposure to these waters and to decontaminate properly those persons exposed to the water.

Flash floods kill. A flash flood can occur in a matter of seconds in the right environment and has the ability to catch even the experienced responder off-guard (**Figure 11**). Responders must heed warnings of weather officials and take appropriate precautions. Low-lying areas and any areas where minor flooding has already occurred are extremely susceptible. A flash flood can take a minor flood situation and turn it into something that resembles a whitewater rapid. In these situations, avoidance is key. If a rescue must be performed, it is imperative to use responders trained in swift-water rescues. Later in this unit we discuss swift-water environments and describe basic self-rescue techniques to use if you are inadvertently caught in swift water.

Figure 11 Flash floods can occur in just seconds in the right environment and can catch even the experienced responder off guard.

ENVIRONMENTS

Swift Water

Swift water is a body of water with a significant laminar flow (water flowing in parallel layers in the same direction). Although we typically consider swift water a high-velocity situation, keep in mind that even a low-velocity flow can have enough power to push trucks sideways and crush through small buildings. The swift-water environment should be left to professionally trained swift-water technicians.

If you arrive at the scene of a swift-water incident, ensure that properly trained swift-water technicians are en route, and attempt to determine the following:

- Number of victims in the water
- Age of the victims
- What they were wearing

- Personal flotation device (PFD)
- Color of clothing
- Whether the victims know how to swim
- The time and location the victims were last seen

Relay this information to all responders. From a safe location, begin a search of the area for victims. If it is available, you should be wearing a PFD and have a rope throw bag available to assist if a victim is located. Remember, when a victim is found, you should throw the rope bag to him or her. Do not tie yourself to the rope. You should lead the victim, accounting for water flow, and be sure to brace yourself. If the victim can grab the line, the water flow will pull you—be prepared to fight it. Instruct the victim to hold onto the rope and to lie on his or her back. The rope should create a pendulum effect and pull the victim to the side of the water, where he or she can be rescued.

If you are caught in swift water and find yourself being carried away, do not put your feet down. In this type of water, there are hazards called foot entrapments—anything your foot could get stuck under. If you get your foot caught in one of these, you may not be able to withdraw your foot, and you may drown. If you do get caught, look for a stick or something to use as a walking cane. Place the cane in front of you, using it for leverage, and push your body back against the water and attempt to pull your foot backward, removing it from under the entrapment.

Try to float. Lie on your back and pull your knees slightly toward your chest. Keep your feet pointed downstream and use your arms as paddles. You can also use your body to direct your movement. Angle your body slightly left or right, allowing the water to push you where you want to go. Typically, the water will push you in the opposite direction of where you point your feet. Use your arms to paddle and to protect yourself from debris.

Avoid fixed areas of debris in the water, such as fallen trees and poles. The water pressure pushing against you will force you either over or under the debris. These hazards are called strainers, and they are deadly (**Figure 12**). Avoid them at all costs, but if you cannot, do everything possible to let the water carry you over the top of the debris. Make your way to the side of the water flow and exit the water safely.

Figure 12 Strainers, such as fallen trees, present a serious hazard.

Waterborne

If you are called to an emergency on the water, the complexity of the problem can be compounded dramatically. Factors such as weather, distance from shore, available equipment, and sea state will complicate your response and subsequent treatment decisions.

First, LERs must preplan for potential incidents at water-based environments in their jurisdiction. The area will help you identify the emergency resources you will have available to you. If an emergency happens at sea, you need to have a variety of transportation, equipment, medical facility, and specialized resources identified in your preplan. Have a list of contact numbers available to request these additional resources.

Transportation

Water-based rescues will require both water transportation and ground transportation, which must be well coordinated. For water transportation, consider how far the incident is from shore and the expected transport time. The vessel you are on may be sufficient, or you may need a different vessel, depending on the following:

- Where the vessels are coming from
- What resources the vessels have
- A vessel's estimated travel time to the incident and back to shore

LERs must also consider whether air transport should be used and how the patient will get from the vessel to the aircraft.

Ground vehicles may be required to transport the patient to the hospital. Plan where the handoff will take place, including the following information:

- Whether the incident location has been identified on the nautical charts
- The physical address to coordinate ground assets
- Contact information for the marina or handoff dock
- Whether the handoff location is within your jurisdictional boundaries and, if not, the contact number of the receiving jurisdiction's emergency operations center

Equipment

Know in advance what equipment is available on the boat. Consider whether the emergency medical supplies are sufficient to cover the estimated transport times and whether all safety gear recommended by the US Coast Guard is available. Water rescue equipment should include the following:

- Rope throw bag
- Throw rings
- Marker buoys
- Spare PFDs
- Hand-held VHF radio
- Personal Locator Beacon (PLB)/Emergency Position-Indicating Radio Beacon (EPIRB)

Medical Facilities

Many factors will help the LER determine the medical facility to which the patient should be transported. Among these factors are the following:

- The handoff location
- Whether the hospital has a helipad (if air transport is being used), and whether that helipad would support the weight and size of the transport aircraft
- The capabilities of the receiving facility
- The patient's needs:
  - Trauma center
  - Cardiac center
  - Brain center
  - Pediatric center
  - Hyperbaric medicine center

Consider how the receiving medical facility will be notified.

Identify Specific Hazards

When responding to an incident on the water, the weather and sea state will affect your emergency transportation plan significantly. LERs should keep up with local marine weather forecasts and National Oceanic and Atmospheric Administration (NOAA) marine watches and warnings, as well as local water currents and submerged hazards to navigation. Refer to current marine charts, water temperature (for exposure considerations), and the ambient air temperatures (for hyperthermia or hypothermia).

The type of water (eg, salt, fresh, brackish) will also affect the kinds of hazards responders will encounter. Any pollutants in the water, or indigenous wildlife or marine life, will also create unique hazards for which the LER must prepare.

If someone has fallen into the water, consider the following potential mechanisms of injury (MOI):

- Propellers or other propulsion mechanisms
- Speed of the vessel from which the patient fell and the resulting torque on the patient's head and neck
- Depth of water for bottom strikes
- Submerged and floating debris
- Striking the side of the vessel

Frozen Water

In many areas, water outside can freeze. Water can freeze thick enough to carry the weight of a vehicle or thin enough to allow even a small animal to fall through. Never assume that ice thickness is universal in an environment. Even if the ice is thick in one area, it may be extremely thin just a few feet away. If a victim falls through the ice, call for appropriately trained personnel to perform the rescue. Such personnel are equipped and experienced in this deadly type of rescue. If specialized personnel are not available, the following guidelines may be helpful in attempting a rescue:

- Never work alone.
- Throw a line to the victim and attempt to pull him or her out from a safe distance.
- If throwing a line fails, consider moving closer if the level of risk allows:
  - Put on a PFD and tether yourself on a line to shore.
  - Spread out your body weight. One technique is to use a small boat to approach the break in the ice, sitting on the rail with one foot in the boat, and using the foot outside to push yourself to the edge of the ice hole. Another technique is to place a long ladder horizontally on the ice, keeping your body weight on the ladder while crawling to the ice hole.

- Once closer, use a rope, stick, or similar item to reach out to the victim and pull him or her to safety.

If you find yourself falling through the ice, remember to focus. Your first instinct will be an involuntary gasp. Instead, catch your breath and quickly focus—you have only a few minutes before you become too weak to rescue yourself. The edges of the ice around the hole into which you fell may be weak and break if you attempt to grab them. Use a pocket knife or metal pen to try to spike the ice and pull yourself out. Kick forcefully, pushing your upper body as far out of the water as possible. When you reach your highest point, reach over the edge of the hole as far away from the edge as possible and stab the knife or pen spike into the ice. If you have another item, stab that as well. Slowly pull yourself out of the hole. This process may need to be repeated several times for success. Do not give up.

Underwater

Scuba diving accidents can be life threatening and challenging to the LER. Scuba diving accidents can occur as a result of improperly trained participants, improperly maintained or malfunctioning gear, or simply as a result of unforeseen circumstances. This section will not address the retrieval of submerged victims because such rescues require personnel with specialized skills and equipment beyond the scope of this book. Once the victim is on the surface, you may see evidence of specific injuries common to scuba diving victims. As the scuba diver descends under the water, the pressure exerted on the body and equipment is increased. The further the descent, the greater the pressure. This increased pressure is the primary culprit in many of the injuries encountered and may be referred to as **barotrauma**.

Pressure-Related Injuries

Pressure-related injuries in an underwater environment include the following:

- **Ear squeeze:** As the diver descends, he or she must equalize the pressure between the inner and outer ear. Otherwise, the diver may experience severe pain and eardrum rupture.
- **Mask squeeze:** If the diver fails to relieve the pressure inside his or her mask during descent, the additional pressure may injure the eyes or the area around the eyes. This usually presents as bruising around the eyes or red eyes because of damage to the vessels in the eyes.
- **Sinus squeeze:** If the diver is unable to equalize pressure properly, he or she develops sinus squeeze. This condition may present as a bloody nose or as blood presenting as a postnasal drip. The diver should stop diving activity because sinus squeeze may take several days to resolve and may lead to sinus infections.
- **Lung overpressure:** Lung overpressure may develop if the diver ascends too rapidly or fails to exhale as he or she ascends. The air inside the lungs at depth is under pressure, and is therefore in a compressed state. As the diver ascends, the compression of the air is relieved, and if the diver fails to exhale, the expanding air inside the lungs may rupture the alveolus or the lungs themselves. This can be a life-threatening injury. It may present in many ways, depending on what ruptured, but most cases will include elements of the following presentation:
  - New-onset pain to the chest or throat; voice changes
  - Shortness of breath; cyanosis
  - Subcutaneous or mediastinal emphysema

These victims need advanced life support (ALS) as soon as possible and may need to go to a hyperbaric chamber.

Decompression Sickness

Decompression sickness occurs when a diver ascends too quickly, not allowing the appropriate amount of time for gases in the blood to go from a soluble phase to a gas phase safely. This allows gas bubbles to form in the bloodstream and tissues. These bubbles have many effects on the body, including creating embolisms (blockages) in the vasculature. The patient may present with any of the following signs and symptoms:

- Joint pain
- Skin rash; itching
- Weakness or paralysis
- Difficulty with balance or hearing
- Visual disturbances
- Fatigue; flu-like symptoms
- Headache; difficulty concentrating; mood changes

Patients who present with signs and symptoms of decompression sickness need to be evaluated at a medical facility and may need to be transported to a hyperbaric chamber. If the condition presents as extreme, medical consultation should be made, and direct transport to a hyperbaric facility may be warranted.

WATER-RELATED MEDICAL EMERGENCIES

Drowning

Drowning is a condition caused by suffocation as a result of water submersion. You may hear a victim who survives referred to as having experienced a "near drowning." Drowning can be categorized as either a wet or dry drowning. A **wet drowning** occurs when a person is submerged and attempts to breathe, drawing water into the lungs. A **dry drowning** occurs when a person is submerged and attempts to breathe, but, as water enters the upper airway, laryngospasm occurs, closing the airway and preventing water from entering the lungs. Death in drowning is primarily caused by inadequate oxygenation of the brain and vital organs.

The possibility of **secondary drowning** must be recognized. Secondary drowning is a postimmersion respiratory problem that can kill. It is characterized by the decreased ability to deliver proper oxygen and gas exchange in the lungs. It may present as early as 1 hour or as late as 48 hours after the submersion incident in a victim who initially appeared to be fine. It is important to have all submersion victims assessed by health care professionals.

An unresponsive patient with a history of water submersion may be in respiratory or cardiopulmonary arrest and may have abdominal distension. A responsive patient may present with coughing; difficulty breathing; cyanosis; chest pain; cool, pale skin; irritability; lethargy; and vomiting.

To manage a submersion victim, first assess the victim's ABCs and send someone to call for EMS and request advanced life support. Be prepared to use suction for secretions or vomitus. Do not press on the patient's abdomen in an attempt to relieve distension. If the patient is breathing, apply supplemental oxygen if available. Assess the scene for possible clues of a spinal injury. Many near-drowning victims have spinal injuries secondary to diving into shallow water and striking their head or neck. If spinal injury is not suspected, place the patient in the recovery position. If spinal injury is suspected, manually stabilize the cervical spine.

Remove wet clothing and cover the patient with a blanket to prevent heat loss. If possible, send a water sample with the victim to the hospital. Remember that resuscitation attempts should be made even after a prolonged submersion, especially in the case of children and cold water.

Sea Sickness

Motion sickness is caused by conflict among body receptors regarding movement. This conflict, which includes the eyes, ears, and other organs, can lead to an uncomfortable feeling that includes nausea and vomiting. The best treatment for motion sickness is avoidance. Most people can avoid motion sickness by planning ahead and taking over-the-counter antihistamines such as meclizine or dimenhydrinate 30 to 60 minutes before travel. Alternatively, prescription scopolamine is available as a patch.

Care for motion sickness after symptoms have started includes having the patient do the following:

- Focus vision on a faraway fixed object or the horizon.
- Do not eat greasy foods.
- Sit in a chair, resting the head and keeping it still.
- Do not smoke or drink caffeine.
- Drink a soda and eat crackers to calm the stomach.

Marine Life

Jellyfish

Jellyfish is a generic term for many different creatures characterized by a jelly-like appearance and containing stinging cells (nematocysts) that attack with toxin-soaked stingers (**Figure 13**). They usually have long tentacles that can

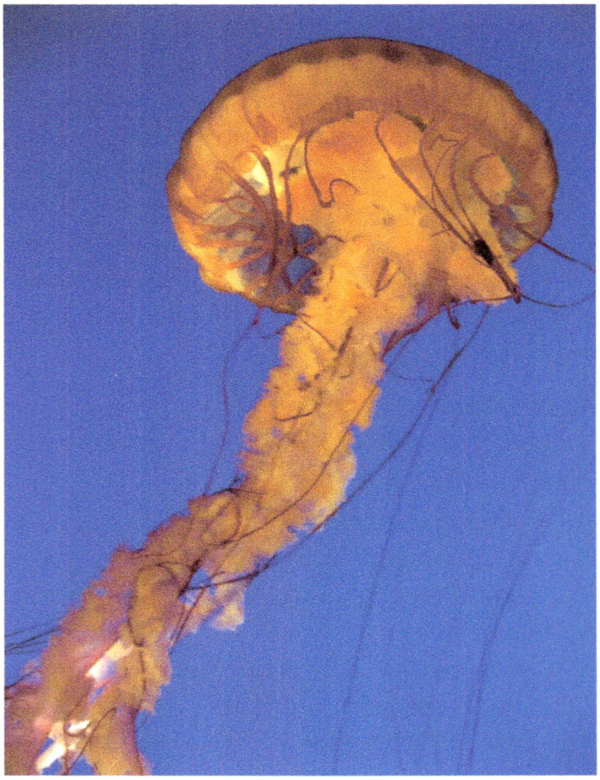

Figure 13 Jellyfish contain stinging cells.

wrap around the victim. Depending on the type of jellyfish involved, the sting may be mild (moon jelly) or life threatening (man o'war). Victims should have the tentacles carefully removed and the area rinsed with sea water (do not use fresh water). LERs should use caution and protect themselves and the patient from further contamination when removing the jellyfish. Gloves or a thick plastic bag should be used to protect your hands. If possible, use another object (towel, sand, clothing) to remove the tissue from the patient. Place the patient in a position that will allow the tissue to fall free and not drop back on the patient or others. Rinsing the area with vinegar can help relieve the pain by denaturing the toxin. Severe stings may induce anaphylaxis and should be treated at a medical facility.

Stingrays

Stingrays may strike a victim if stepped on while a person is wading or swimming. The tail is a hard, barbed shaft that is coated with a protein-based toxin. Injuries can be very painful. Move the patient to a safe location and keep him or her still. Control any associated bleeding with direct pressure. If the stinger is still present and is superficial, attempt to remove it to minimize further toxin exposure if doing so will not cause further injury. If no pain is present, clean and disinfect the area with soap and water. The patient may develop pain, nausea, and faintness and become diaphoretic as the toxin is absorbed. If transport times are significant, pain management can be initiated by immersing the affected area in hot water (approximately 45°C [113°F]) as tolerated, being careful not to burn the victim. This will begin to neutralize the toxin. Even minor injuries need to be seen at a medical facility for treatment, including a possible tetanus booster.

Sharks

Most sharks are timid, but some sharks may attack humans. The best treatment is avoidance. If you are responding to an attack, however, prepare for massive bleeding that may be hard to control. Although sharks' teeth can be razor sharp, they tend to tear tissue. Torn tissue creates difficulties managing blood loss. Apply direct pressure to the wound. If an extremity is involved and bleeding cannot be controlled quickly, immediately apply a tourniquet proximal to the zone of injury and tight enough to make the bleeding stop completely. Remember that estimating blood loss in a water environment is difficult because of how the blood dissipates. A trauma center would be the best facility for a victim with a significant wound. Treat the victim for shock, including high-flow oxygen, removal of wet clothing, and use of a blanket to prevent heat loss.

Puffer Fish

Puffer fish is a generic term used to describe a family of fish that engorge themselves with water to warn off predators. These fish are toxic to eat. They also have a very strong bite and can be quite aggressive. Bites may take small chunks of flesh, and although bites are not toxic, they can be quite painful. Treatment includes controlling the bleed, treating shock, and transporting for evaluation. These victims may need antibiotic therapy.

Scorpion Fish

Scorpion fish are equipped with poisonous, prickly fins that can sting (**Figure 14**). A sting can be very painful and cause swelling at the injection site. The edema from the sting can spread rapidly, causing edema to the entire extremity within minutes. The toxin may also cause the following:

- Altered mental status; fainting
- Gastrointestinal issues such as nausea, vomiting, and diarrhea
- Cardiovascular effects such as tachycardia or bradycardia and blood pressure changes
- Difficulty breathing
- Paralysis or seizure activity

Stings from scorpion fish may be life threatening. Call EMS and request advanced life support. A rapid transport may be required. Initial therapy may include treating for shock and washing the injection site with soap and water. If transport times are significant, pain management can be initiated by immersing the affected area in hot water (approximately 45°C [113°F]) as tolerated, being careful not to burn the victim.

Figure 14 Scorpion fish are equipped with poisonous, prickly fins that can sting. Stings may be life threatening.

Coral Cuts

Contact with coral can lead to lacerations that may be contaminated with small pieces of coral or debris. Lacerations may quickly become infected because of this debris. The wound may become red, swollen, and festering. The redness around the wound may begin to spread, indicating infection and the need to seek immediate medical attention.

Initial care of coral wounds should include the following:

- Cleaning with soap and water
- Rinsing with vinegar or isopropyl alcohol if the wound stings and may contain nematocysts (like a jellyfish)
- Flushing wound with a mixture of 50% water and 50% hydrogen peroxide to remove debris, then rinsing with fresh water
- Applying antibiotic ointment to decrease the risk of infection during healing

CONCLUSION

LERs must plan to perform rescues. You will be exposed to people who need your help, and whether you work in a patrol setting, as a detective, in security, or on a special team, you will be the person turned to during a rescue. Vehicles create dangers that kill and injure tens of thousands of people every year in the United States. No segment of the population is immune to their threat. LERs must plan to deal with these incidents for their own survival as well as those they protect. Frequent training and review of the dangers associated with rescuing a patient form a crashed vehicle can improve your performance and prevent injury to yourself and others. Evaluating the tools you need to perform such maneuvers and obtaining simple inexpensive hand tools can allow the LER to safely gain access to a patient and stabilize them before EMS arrives. LERs should consider practicing with these tools with a qualified rescue instructor on vehicles at salvage yards or at fire-rescue training programs.

Water is historically a major threat to human survival. Drownings occur daily, in all areas of the country and to all populations. As a LER, you may find yourself dealing with a partner who has broken through the ice or fallen from a dock. If you work in and around the ocean or major waterways, you run the risk of exposure to poisonous animals, boats, or floating debris that can debilitate you or others performing your law enforcement duties. LERs must plan for and consider the dangers associated with the water. Practicing basic water rescue techniques, such as throwing rope bags or extending a pole, have been proven as lifesaving measures. Equipping your vehicle or detail with approved life vests and training in water survival can make the difference to you or your partner returning from an assignment.

Prep Kit

Ready for Review

- A motor vehicle crash can range from an individual vehicle to multiple vehicles. Most vehicles contain hazards such as fuel and electrical systems. Newer vehicles may contain alternative power systems, new safety technology, and specialized construction.
- Two major roles of a LER at the scene of a motor vehicle crash are to provide care to the patients and to determine whether a patient needs extrication from a vehicle.
- At the scene of a motor vehicle crash, personal protection is a top priority and includes gloves, eye protection, boots, respiratory protection, and clothing.
- Always make sure that traffic and other safety issues are managed.
- Prior to attempting access to the passenger compartment of a crashed vehicle, the vehicle should be properly stabilized, the battery disconnected, and other features that may harm the patient or responders should be disarmed.
- Various tools and techniques, such as a pry bar, hand tools, come-alongs, or hydraulic rescue equipment may be needed to extricate a patient.
- Hybrid vehicles may not sound as if they are on when only the electric engine is engaged, so responders must ensure there is no chance the vehicle may move prior to initiating activities around the vehicle.
- Drowning is a condition of suffocation caused by water submersion. Its symptoms include possible cardiac or respiratory arrest or both, coughing, difficulty breathing, vomiting, and cyanosis.
- The dangers of water can be increased in environments that include swift water, frozen water, cold water immersion, and underwater or waterborne elements.
- LERs may encounter water in many venues, including pools, beaches, rivers, ponds, and lakes.
- Floods and flash floods affect areas not typically covered by water and may appear quickly.
- As a LER you have many skills and know many lifesaving techniques, but you are not trained as a water rescue technician. Acting as if you are a water rescue professional will endanger your life and the lives of others.
- In preparing a waterborne preplan, address the following elements: transportation, equipment, medical facilities, and specific hazards.

Vital Vocabulary

barotrauma Injury caused by increased pressure exerted on the body by deep water.

cribbing Blocks of wood or other materials used to immobilize a vehicle.

dry drowning Suffocation that occurs when a person is submerged and attempts to breathe, but laryngospasm occurs, closing the airway and preventing water from entering the lungs.

extrication The disentanglement of the vehicle to free a trapped patient.

laryngospasm A closing of the larynx preventing anything (air, water, etc) from entering the trachea.

live load An energized vehicle that may be in gear and poses a significant threat to rescuers.

Nadar bolt A pin or latch added to car doors to prevent them from opening during a crash. Ralph Nadar, a consumer activist, pushed for the addition of this mechanism in the United States.

rapid extrication Technique used to remove a patient from a vehicle when there is an immediate life threat and time is a significant factor for survival.

secondary drowning A postimmersion respiratory problem characterized by the decreased ability to deliver proper oxygen and gas exchange in the lungs.

shepherd's crook An extendable pole with a blunt-end life hook large enough to encircle a victim safely.

supplemental restraint systems (SRSs) High-pressure curtains, bolsters, or bags that deploy when sensors detect a vehicle has been impacted at a certain speed. The devices are meant to protect the occupants of the vehicle, but can also cause certain injuries. These devices also are a potential threat to responders if they are not properly disconnected.

wet drowning Suffocation that occurs when a person is submerged and attempts to breathe, drawing water into the lungs.

Check Your Knowledge

1. A water environment that appears quickly, may have extremely quick moving water, and creates extreme dangers to victims and rescuers alike is called:
   - **A.** flood.
   - **B.** swift water.
   - **C.** flash flood.
   - **D.** river.
2. A patient with altered mental status presents with coughing, vomiting, cyanosis, difficulty breathing, and soaked clothing. You suspect:
   - **A.** nerve agent poisoning.
   - **B.** heat stroke.
   - **C.** snake bite.
   - **D.** drowning.
3. A dangerous water condition known as a rip current can present itself in which water venue?
   - **A.** Flash flood
   - **B.** River
   - **C.** Pool
   - **D.** Beach
4. As part of your waterborne preplan, you should make sure which emergency equipment is carried onboard the vessel?
   - **A.** Rope throw bag
   - **B.** Spare personal flotation devices
   - **C.** US Coast Guard safety equipment
   - **D.** All of the above
5. A water rescue professional is properly trained and equipped to perform water rescues. Which of the following is not an example of these professionals?
   - **A.** Swift-water technician
   - **B.** Technical rescue personnel
   - **C.** Law enforcement responder
   - **D.** Lifeguard

Assessment in **Action**

Scenario

You arrive on scene of a motor vehicle crash where one of the vehicles is precariously perched on the edge of an embankment. Twenty feet below the embankment is a river flowing quickly. Other officers have blocked the road and moved bystanders to a safe distance. You have been tasked with patient care.

Actions

1. The gloves and some of the other protective equipment you wear to perform basic extrication should be approved by which entity that establishes guidelines for safety equipment?
   A. OSHA
   B. NFPA
   C. ANSI
   D. DOT
2. If the fuel tank of the vehicle were to catch fire, which type of extinguisher should be used?
   A. Class A
   B. Class B
   C. Class C
   D. Class ABC
3. The following information would be essential to relay back to dispatch, to allow other responding units situational awareness, EXCEPT:
   A. patients' name.
   B. specialty equipment needed for rescue.
   C. number of patients.
   D. findings of the 360-assessment.
4. You check down the embankment and see that one of the vehicle's occupants was ejected into the river. The patient is conscious and screaming for help. The best method for rescuing this patient from the river is:
   A. Run down the embankment and enter the river.
   B. Throw a line to the patient from a safe location.
   C. Instruct the patient to tread water until a rescue boat arrives.
   D. Run down the embankment to give a PFD to the patient.
5. One of the vehicles is carrying a box with a placard that reads "DANGEROUS." What should you do with this box?
   A. Open it to check the contents.
   B. Douse it with water to render it safe.
   C. Evacuate the area and request a hazardous materials team.
   D. Ask the driver of the vehicle what the contents might be.

SECTION

3

Patient Assessment

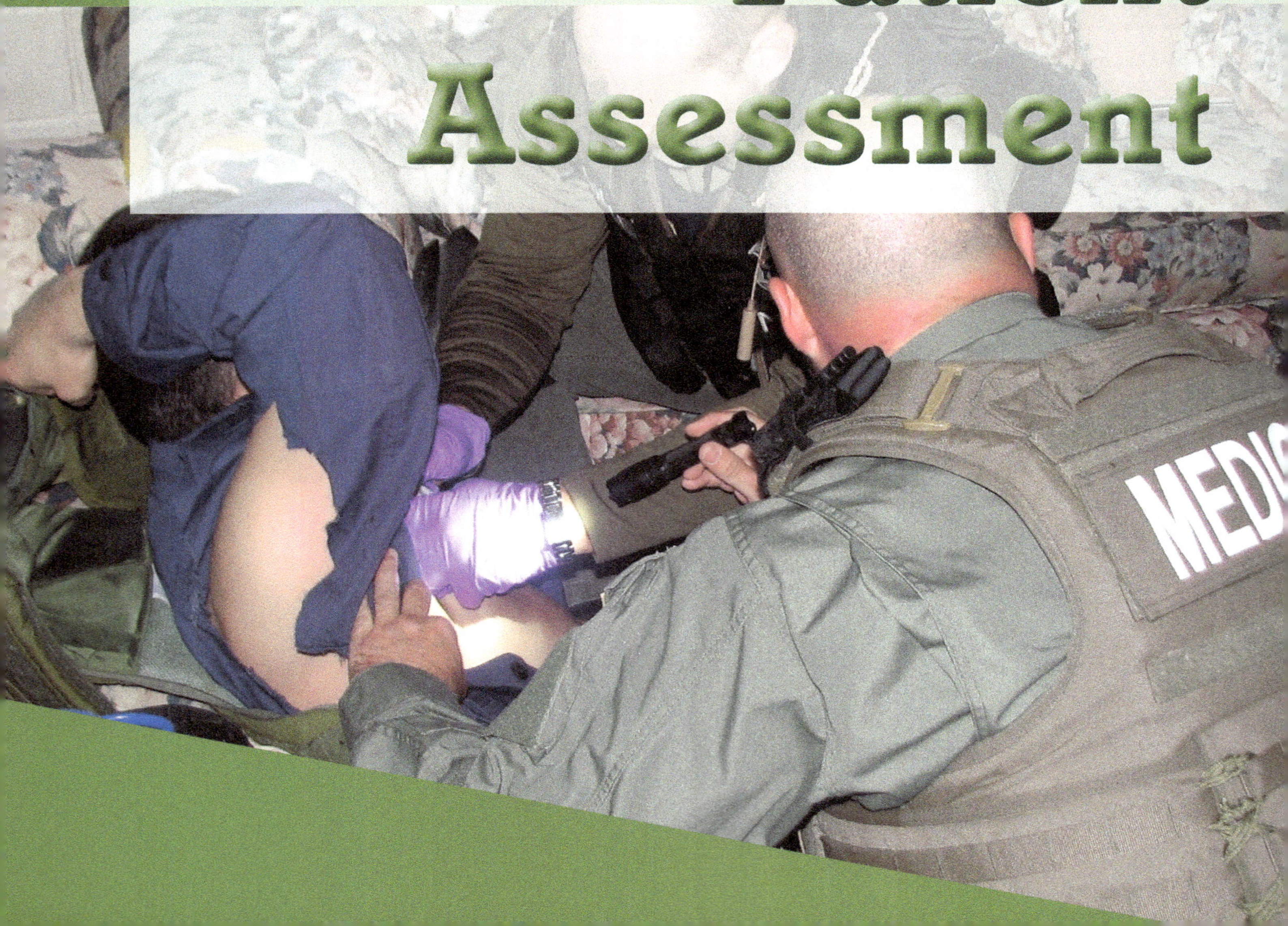

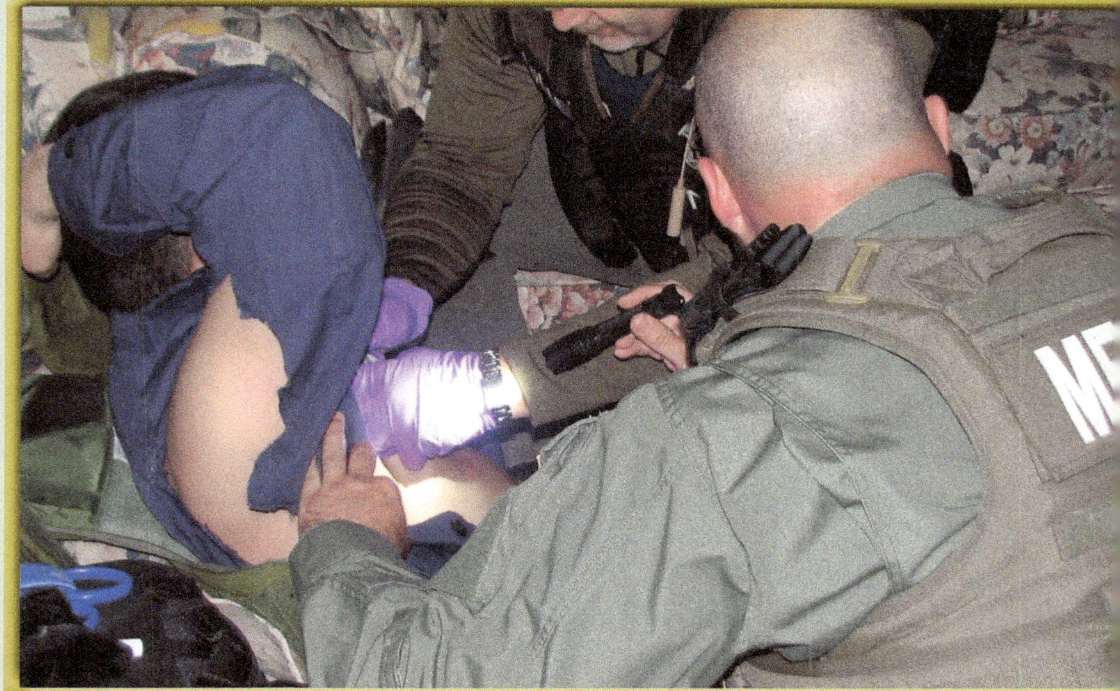

Section Contents

Anatomy and Physiology

Unit 8

Randy Stair

Law Enforcement Responder Objectives

- Define standard anatomic terms used by emergency medical responders. (pp 149–150)
- Identify and define the anatomic components of the human body. (pp 150–152)
- Discuss the composition and function of organs, tissues, and cells. (pp 150–152)
- Explain how body systems function in a normal state. (pp 152–153)
- Discuss the roles of oxygenation, perfusion, and fuel efficiency within the body. (pp 152–153)
- Explain the life support chain and identify its components and their functions. (pp 152–153)
- Identify the major structures and the importance of the following organ systems:
  - Skeletal (pp 154–157)
  - Muscular (p 157)
  - Respiratory (pp 157–158, 160)
  - Circulatory (pp 158–160)
  - Skin (p 160)
- Identify the major structures and general function of the following organ systems:
  - Nervous (pp 160–162)
  - Digestive (pp 162)
  - Genitourinary (pp 162–163)
  - Endocrine (pp 163)
- Discuss age-related anatomic variations for children and the elderly. (pp 163–164)
- Outline and explain the stages of life span development. (pp 163–164)

National EMS Education Standard Competencies

Anatomy and Physiology

Uses simple knowledge of the anatomy and function of the upper airway, heart, vessels, blood, lungs, skin, muscles, and bones as the foundation of emergency care.

Life Span Development

Uses simple knowledge of age-related differences to assess and care for patients.

INTRODUCTION

A law enforcement responder (LER) must be able to understand medical terms and use correct terminology when speaking about the anatomy of a patient. Medical responders at all levels must learn to identify the parts of the human body and understand how they function. Knowing how the human body works in a disease-free state—in normal function—will help you to identify and manage abnormal function.

This unit seeks to address anatomy and physiology in the following ways:

- Discussing anatomic positions of the body
- Discussing medical terminology
- Identifying the critical functions that take place within the body
- Discussing body systems

Communication

Knowing How to Communicate

It is important that LERs know how to communicate using medical terminology, whether they function in an isolated manner with local emergency medical services or as part of a team.

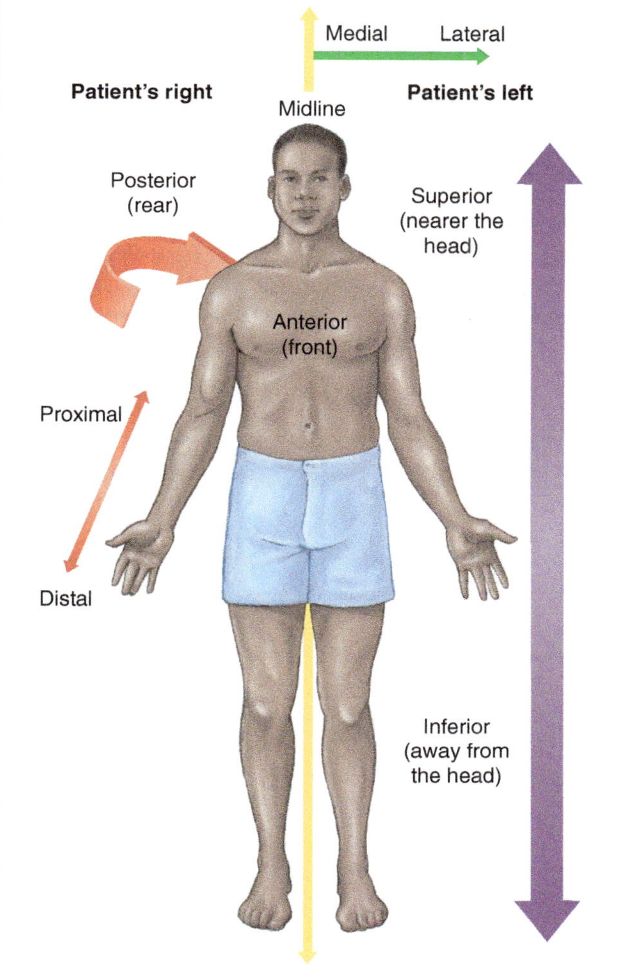

Figure 1 Referring to the human body using the anatomic position simplifies medical discussion.

ANATOMY

Anatomy refers to the study of parts of a particular **organism** (a living being). **Topographic anatomy** refers to the superficial landmarks on the body that help in locating structures under the surface. For example, by stating that the patient was stabbed to the left of the belly button, a physician will understand that injuries may have occurred to the organs found in the left side of the abdomen.

Anatomic Terminology

To standardize medical terminology, medicine teaches students to observe patients in the anatomic position. The **anatomic position** occurs when the human body is pictured as standing facing forward with the palms of the hands turned forward (**Figure 1**). Always refer to the patient's right and left when describing location. You can also use the directional terms in **Table 1** when the patient is in the anatomic position.

Other anatomic terms are used to describe body positioning (**Figure 2**). A patient lying on his or her back is considered **supine**. A patient lying face down is considered **prone**. A patient lying on his or her side is often referred to as **laterally recumbent** or in the **recovery position**.

Many body structures appear on both sides of the body, making them **bilateral**. Bilateral structures can be internal to the body (such as the kidneys) or external to the body (such as the ears). Other body structures are referred to as **unilateral** because they exist on only one side of the body (such as the spleen).

The body contains different cavities. The thoracic cavity, or **thorax**, comprises the area from the shoulders through the

Table 1

Anatomic Terminology

Term	Meaning	Example
Superior	Closer to the head	The eyes are superior to the lips.
Inferior	Closer to the feet	The ankle is inferior to the kneecap.
Anterior	The front	The nose is on the anterior surface of the head.
Posterior	The back	The vertebrae of the neck are posterior to the trachea.
Medial	Closer to the middle of the body	The eye is medial to the ear.
Midline	Imaginary vertical line drawn from head to toe	The nose is midline on the face.
Lateral	Away from the midline	The nipple is lateral to the sternum.
Proximal	Closer to the center of the body	The armpit is proximal to the elbow.
Distal	More distant from the center of the body	The wrist is distal to the elbow.

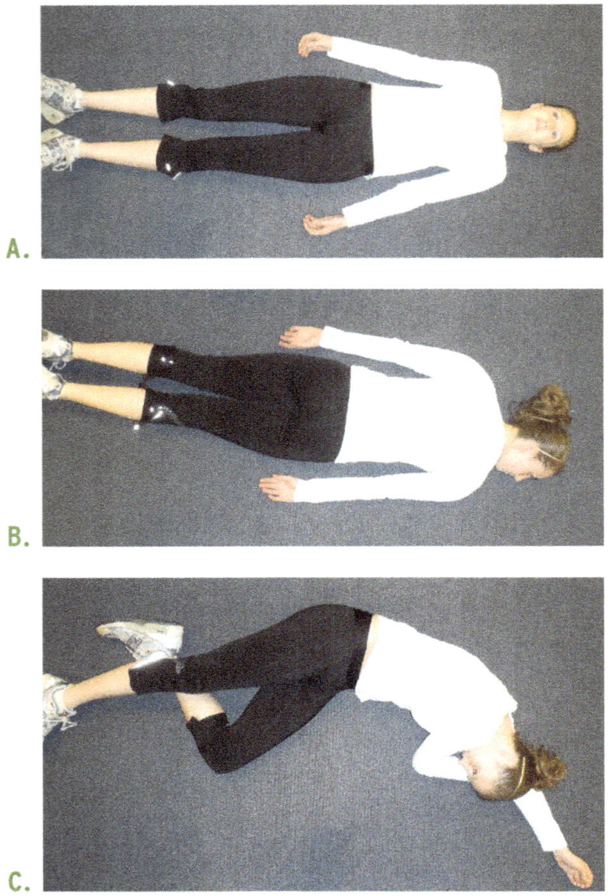

Figure 2 Body positioning. **A.** Supine. **B.** Prone. **C.** Laterally recumbent (recovery position).

rib cage. The abdominal cavity, or **abdomen**, starts at the bottom of the rib cage and extends into the pelvis. The abdomen can be further subdivided into smaller portions by drawing imaginary horizontal and vertical lines through the belly button, separating the body into right and left halves and top and bottom halves. This creates four quadrants: the right upper quadrant (RUQ), the left upper quadrant (LUQ), the left lower quadrant (LLQ), and the right lower quadrant (RLQ) (**Figure 3**).

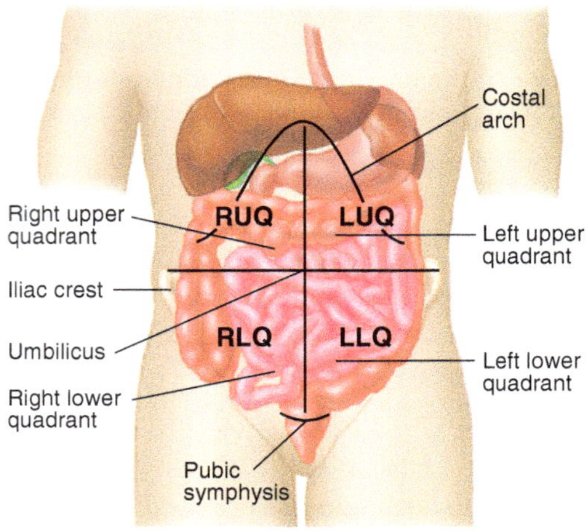

Figure 3 Using quadrants is the easiest way to identify areas of the abdomen.

Organ Systems

Injury and illness are commonly seen as something happening to a specific part of the patient. For example, a leg is broken or a heart is damaged. However, all components of the human

Table 2

Organs and Their Functions

Organ	Function
Brain	Controls the nervous center and commands selected organs to respond
Heart	Blood pump
Kidneys	Filter blood for waste and remove the waste as urine
Lungs	Respiration (exchange of oxygen and carbon dioxide)
Liver	Filters blood chemicals and helps store glucose
Pancreas	Glandular organ that secretes insulin and digestive enzymes
Spleen	Breaks down old red blood cells, prevents infections, releases small amount of blood when patient is in shock
Stomach	Holding area where food is broken down
Small intestine	Receives food from the stomach and absorbs nutrients
Large intestine	Receives food from the small intestine, removes water, and expels waste

Table 3

Tissues and Their Functions

Tissue	Function	Types
Muscle	Supports movement	Skeletal Cardiac Smooth
Nerve	Creates and transmits messages	Brain Spinal cord Nerves
Connective	Supports and binds other tissues together	Bone Blood Fat
Epithelial	Serves as a lining or covering	Skin Lining of blood vessels Lining of the digestive tract Airway

body are linked together, and damage to any one of them can have profound effects on the entire body. Therefore, when caring for a patient, it is necessary to treat the entire person, not just the damaged part.

The human body can be divided into subsystems called organ systems. **Organ systems** comprise groups of organs that come together to provide a certain function. **Organs** are individual structures that provide a specific function within an organ system (**Table 2**).

Organs are made of **tissue**, which is a group of like cells. Tissue is the building element that the body uses to form larger structures. Tissues can exist in thin layers to create a body lining such as skin, or they can exist in mass bundles to create structures such as skeletal muscle (**Table 3**). Different tissues combine to form an organ serving a specific purpose in the body. The heart is an excellent example of many different types of tissue coming together to make an organ. The heart muscle provides the core structural material, nerve tissue provides the electrical system that runs the heart, cartilage is used to develop the valves, and epithelial tissue is used to line the surfaces.

Cells are considered the basic units of life. These are the smallest living structural elements. Cells have specialized functions (**Table 4**). Nerve cells, called **neurons**, have the ability to create, send, and receive messages. Heart muscle cells are able to contract like other muscle cells, but they have the additional capacity to generate electrical impulses that can trigger other cardiac cells. Because cells are the basic building blocks of an organ, injury or death of cells can seriously affect the entire body.

Inside cells are smaller structures called **organelles** (little organs), which provide a specific function in the cell, similar in function to the organs in our bodies:

- Nucleus—Controls cellular function and holds genetic information
- Mitochondria—Control cellular respiration
- Cell membrane—Covering around cell that controls access to cell

Table 4

Cell Types and Functions

Cell	Function
Neuron	Nerve tissue; creates, sends, and receives messages
Cardiocyte	Heart muscle; contracts to pump blood and can create and respond to impulses
Epithelial	Covers body (eg, skin cells) and organs
Red blood cell	Carries oxygen in blood
White blood cell	Controls infection
Platelet	Creates clots
Osteocyte	Bone cell

Table 5

Breaking the Life Support Chain

Alteration	Example
Composition of ambient air	Not enough oxygen
Patency of the airway	Choking
Mechanics of ventilation	Hole in chest wall and collapsing lung
Regulation of respiration	Breathing too slowly
Transport of gases	Poison not allowing oxygen to be moved
Blood volume	Uncontrolled bleeding
Effectiveness of the heart as a pump	Abnormal heart rhythms
Blood vessel size and resistance	High blood pressure

PHYSIOLOGY

Physiology refers to how an organism functions. The human body has a very complicated physiology, and certain basic, critical functions must exist to support life. All emergency medical techniques are designed to keep the patient alive by supporting these critical functions. The goal of the organism is to maintain a state of **homeostasis**, a stable state of equilibrium between the external environment and the internal environment. Although this may sound complex, it simply refers to the body keeping all the internal components running by taking what it needs from its surroundings. The fundamental elements to maintain homeostasis are oxygenation, perfusion, and fuel efficiency. Emergency medicine often addresses the relationships among oxygenation, perfusion, and fuel efficiency as the life support chain. An alteration in any of these fundamental elements will result in illness or death. **Table 5** lists situations that can alter the performance of the fundamental elements, resulting in an alteration of the life support chain.

Oxygenation

Oxygenation is the process of moving oxygen into an area. This occurs in the blood when air with a higher concentration of oxygen comes into contact with blood containing a lower concentration of oxygen. The higher concentration diffuses toward the lower concentration in an attempt to equalize concentrations. The lungs are where the exchange of oxygen and carbon dioxide occurs with the inhaled air. This process is typically called **respiration**. The actual sites on the lung where this occurs are small grapelike sacs called the **alveoli**. The alveoli are made up of a very thin piece of tissue, similar to a tiny balloon, covered with thin blood vessels called **capillaries**. Because of the thinness of the tissue, oxygen moves into the blood, and carbon dioxide (a waste product from the cell) moves out of the blood and into the air within the lung. This process, in which a natural chemical moves from an area of higher concentration to an area of lower concentration until it is equally dispersed, is called **diffusion**. For the lung to do its job, air containing the proper concentration of oxygen must enter the alveoli. Room air is typically 21% oxygen.

Once the blood is loaded with oxygen and the carbon dioxide has been released, the heart pushes the blood to the rest of the cells in the body. When the cells receive the blood at the capillaries, an exchange happens: oxygen is moved from the blood to the cells, and carbon dioxide is moved from the cells to the blood.

Perfusion

Cells, our basic living structures, must have an adequate supply of oxygen, glucose (sugar), and waste removal to survive.

A. B. C. D.

Figure 4 Medical responders can assist patients in maintaining good perfusion. **A.** Oxygen administration. **B.** Cardiopulmonary resuscitation (CPR). **C.** Glucose administration. **D.** Bleeding control.

When these conditions are met, the human body has good **perfusion**. Any reduction in oxygen, glucose, or removal of waste can have a negative impact on the cell and cause it to die. When illness or injury occurs, medical responders apply lifesaving techniques to avoid or limit poor perfusion (**Figure 4**).

Fuel Efficiency

Humans need fuel in the form of glucose for energy. We get this energy by eating food, which is broken down into glucose that is absorbed into the body. The glucose moves throughout the body in the blood. When the blood reaches the cells, the glucose must be able to pass into the cells. This requires the body to produce a hormone called **insulin** that opens a channel into the cell, allowing the glucose to go inside. When the glucose is inside the cell, it is broken down into energy units that the cell uses for fuel. To best use the glucose, the cells need oxygen to help break it down. If the cells do not receive enough oxygen, the breakdown of glucose can produce acid, which can cause injury.

BODY SYSTEMS

Skeletal

The purpose of the skeletal system is to support the body, protect vital structures, and develop blood cells. Bones make up part of the skeletal system and are often thought of as the rigid structures that are seen in skeletal diagrams (**Figure 5**). However, **bones** are actually complex living tissue. There are 206 bones in the human body, which are divided into long bones, short bones, flat bones, and irregular bones. Inside these bones are cavities that contain bone marrow. **Bone marrow** is used by the body to create red blood cells, white blood cells, and platelets.

Tip

Bones

Long bones are used like levers by the body and are found in the thigh, leg, arm, and forearm.

Short bones are found in the wrist and ankles.

Flat bones are broad and flat and are used for protection. Examples include the ribs, sternum, and the sides of the skull.

Irregular bones do not fit into the other categories—for example, vertebrae.

Also making up the skeletal system is **cartilage**. Dense and fibrous, cartilage supports structures like the nose or in between joints. **Joints** are where bones meet. Typically, joints allow for some type of movement (**Figure 6**). Hinge joints, such as elbows and knees, are examples of joints that allow for movement in one plane. Ball-and-socket joints, such as shoulders and hips, allow for movement in more than one

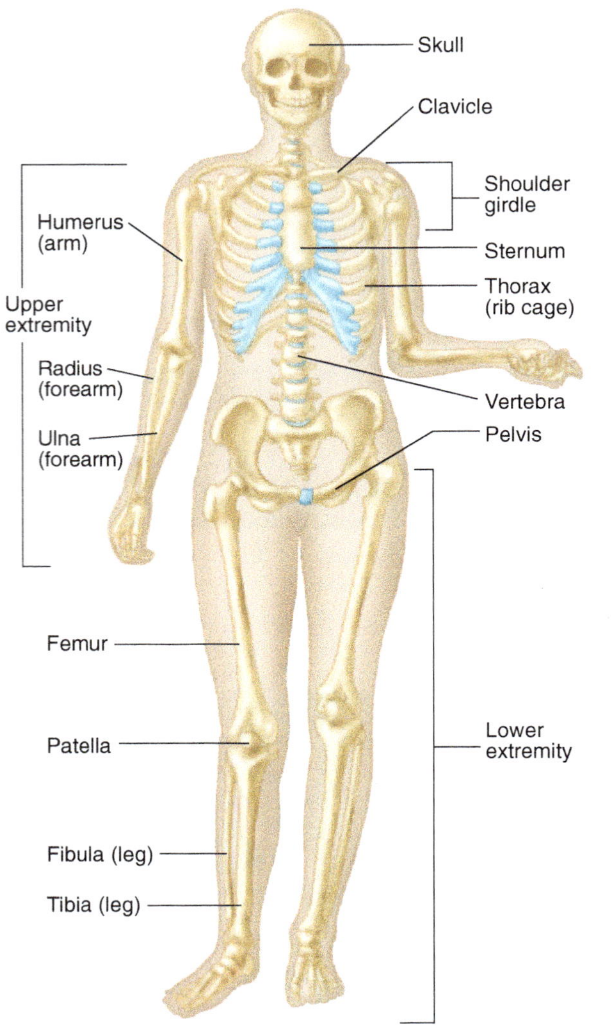

Figure 5 The human skeleton.

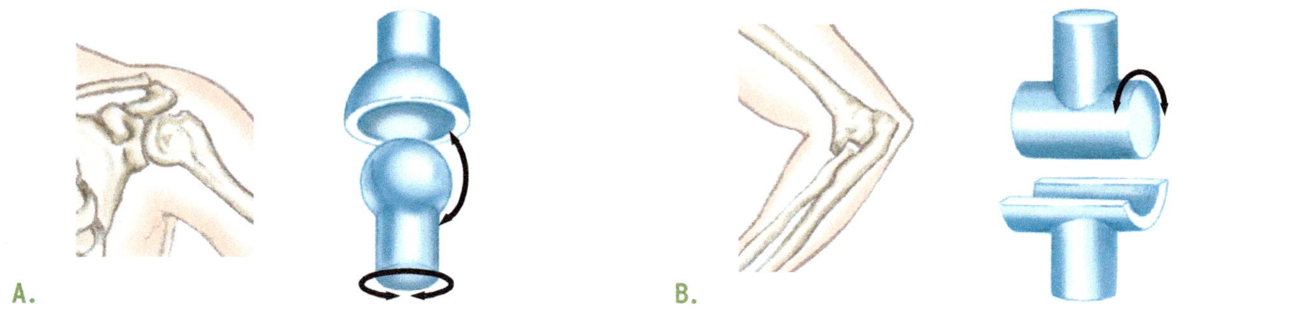

Figure 6 Different types of joints. **A.** The shoulder is a ball-and-socket joint. **B.** The elbow is a hinge joint, which allows motion in only one plane.

Table 6

Parts of the Skull

Bone(s)	Location
Mandible	Lower jaw
Maxilla	Upper jaw
Nasal	Base of the nose
Orbits	Around the eyes
Mastoid process	Behind the ear
Sinuses	Hollow cavities behind the nose and around the eyes
Ethmoid bone	Portion of the skull that protects the portions of the brain that lie behind the nasal bones and sinuses
Foramen magnum	The large opening at the base of the skull where the brain stem terminates and the spinal cord begins
Frontal bone	The portion of the skull that sits above the facial bones and protects the anterior portion of the cerebrum
Occipital bone	The portion of the skull that protects the posterior part of the cerebrum and the cerebellum
Parietal bone	The portion of the skull that protects the side and top of the brain behind the ears
Sphenoid bone	The portion of the skull that protects the base of the brain and lies behind the oral cavity
Temporal bone	The portion of the skull that protects the area of the brain that lies behind and to the side of the frontal bone; includes the areas around the ears

plane. However, some joints do not move at all, such as where the bones of the skull fuse together. Bones are connected to another through tough, fibrous cords of tissue called **ligaments**. **Tendons** are the terminal end of a skeletal muscle and are used to attach the muscle to the bone.

The Skull

LERs commonly map the skeletal system by working from head to toe, using a skeletal diagram or model. The human head is supported by the bones that come together to make the skull. **Table 6** lists important parts of the skull. The skull is very important because it makes up the cranial vault where the brain is stored (**Figure 7**).

Other functions of the skull bones include supporting the airway tissue and forming the space called the foramen magnum (Latin for "big hole"), where the spinal cord passes from the brain into the spine.

The Spine

Moving down the body, the next major area of the skeletal system is the spine. The function of the spine is to protect the spinal cord and to provide support and movement for the body. The **vertebrae** make up the protective covering of the spinal cord and are collectively referred to as the spine. There are five distinct sections to the spine (**Figure 8**):

- **Cervical:** Neck
- **Thoracic:** Upper back/chest
- **Lumbar:** Lower back/abdomen
- **Sacrum:** Base of the spine/pelvis
- **Coccyx:** Tailbone

The Shoulder Girdle and Upper Extremity

The shoulder girdle is made up of the collarbone (**clavicle**), shoulder blade (**scapula**), and the first bone of the upper arm (**humerus**). The upper arm includes the humerus and extends to where the bones of the forearm (**radius** and **ulna**) meet the elbow joint. The radius and ulna cross over each other, providing the distinct movement found in the wrist. The hand bones (**carpals** and **metacarpals**) make up the structures between the wrist and the fingers, the **phalanges**.

The Rib Cage

The shoulder girdle, spinal cord, and rib cage come together to make the chest, or thorax (**Figure 9**). The thorax, often called the thoracic cavity, contains the structures of the lower airway, the heart, large blood vessels, some of the digestive organs, and the lungs. The ribs are connected to the spinal column in the back. The upper five pairs of ribs attach in the front to the breastbone (**sternum**). Ribs 6 through 10 attach to each other with cartilage at the bottom front of the thorax. Ribs 11 and 12 are free floating off the spinal column. The sternum is the typical location for hand placement for chest compressions during cardiopulmonary resuscitation.

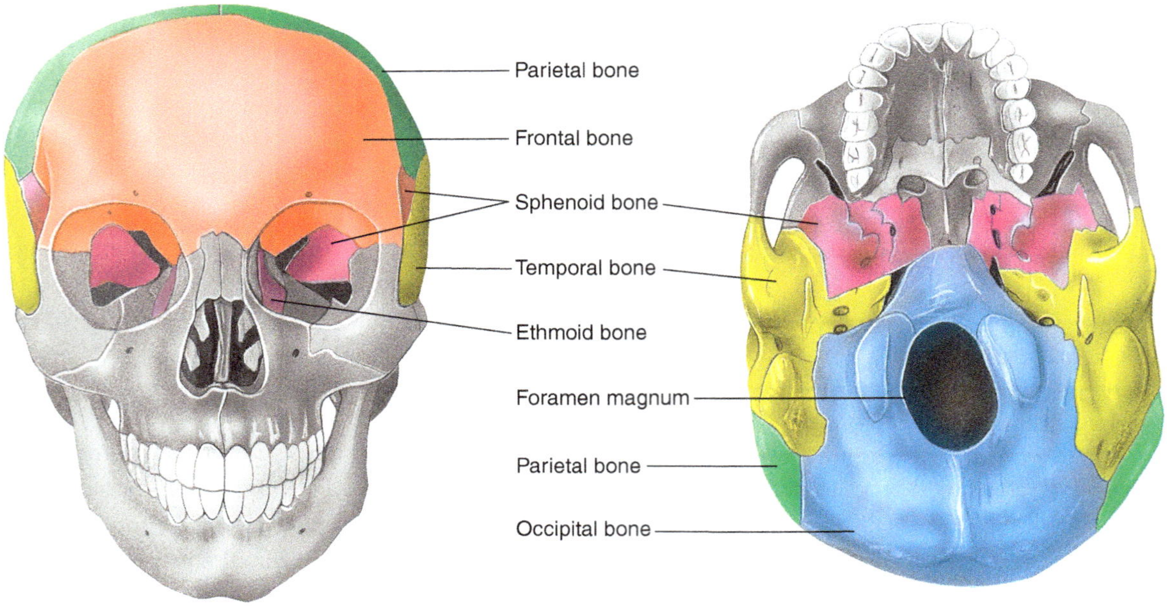

Figure 7 Cranial vault and foramen magnum.

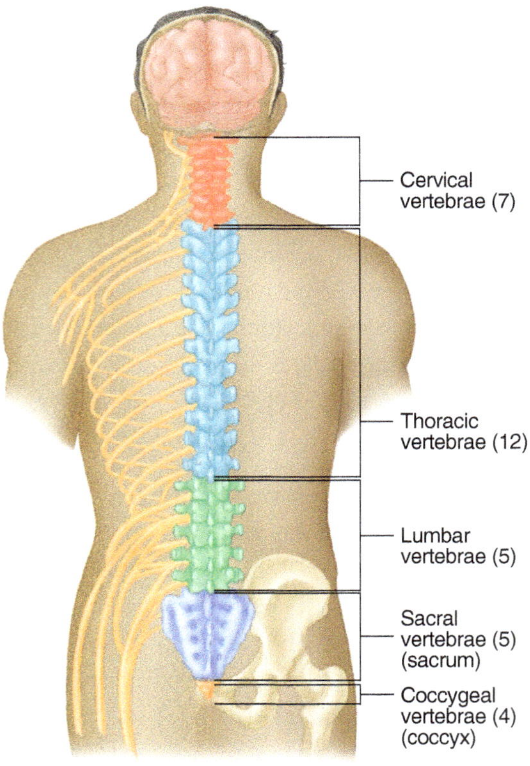

Figure 8 The five sections of the spine.

At the tip of the sternum is the **xiphoid process**. Because the xiphoid process is made up of bone, improper hand placement near or over this process during chest compressions can cause digestive organ damage.

The Pelvis

The abdomen connects the thorax to the pelvis. The digestive organs and genitourinary organs are located in the abdomen,

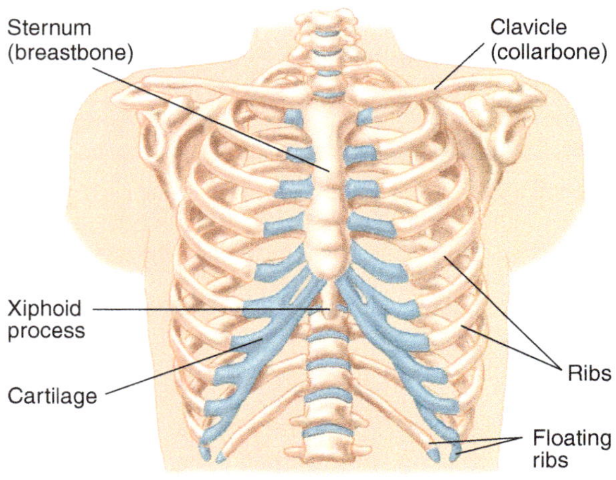

Figure 9 The rib cage.

with some protruding into the pelvis. Along with the bones of the sacrum, the **pelvis** makes up a bony ring of protection around the organs found in the lower abdomen. The pelvis creates the structural link between the trunk and the lower extremities, the final area of the skeletal system.

The Lower Extremities

The large thighbone (**femur**) extends from within the pelvis down to the knee. The kneecap (**patella**) stabilizes the knee joint. The lower leg (**tibia** and **fibula**) lies between the knee and ankle. The tibia primarily supports the lower extremity, and its relationship with the fibula provides for linkage with the ankle. The ankle is the joint between the tibia and the **talus**. The **calcaneus** is the heel bone. The foot extends off the ankle and is made up of a collection of small bones called the **tarsals** and **metatarsals**. The toes, like the fingers, are called phalanges.

Muscular

You may have heard reference to the *musculoskeletal system*. This term applies to the grouping of the skeletal muscle with the bones for discussions of anatomy and physiology. **Muscles** provide support and motion in the body through the process of shortening (contraction) and lengthening (relaxation). There are three types of muscles in the human body: skeletal muscle, smooth muscle, and cardiac muscle (**Figure 10**).

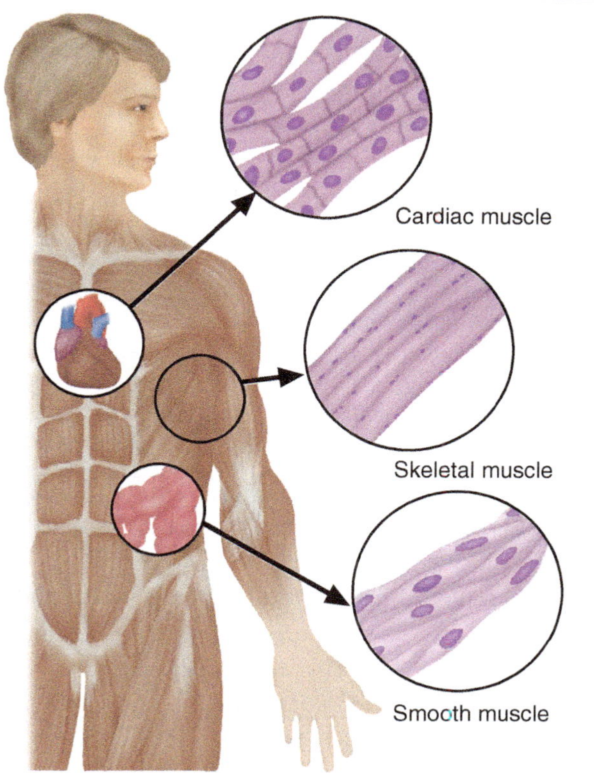

Figure 10 The three types of muscle are skeletal, smooth, and cardiac.

Controlled voluntarily, **skeletal muscles** are attached to the bones and provide motion. Skeletal muscles are made up of protein chains that move back and forth over each other. These protein chains are made of pink and white fibers, creating the striped or striated appearance of skeletal muscle.

Smooth muscle is made of short, powerful protein strands that wrap involuntary organs (eg, the digestive tract) and the sides of airways and blood vessels. Unlike skeletal muscles, smooth muscles work involuntarily.

Cardiac muscle (also called myocardium) is found only in the heart. The cardiac muscle is involuntary (like smooth muscle) and is striated (like skeletal muscle). Cardiac muscle requires a continuous flow of oxygenated blood and must work without rest.

Respiratory

The respiratory system is one of the most important systems in the body. If the respiratory system is compromised, the organism will have difficulty getting oxygen and eliminating carbon dioxide. The major organs associated with the respiratory system are the lungs. There are two lungs, a left and a right. Alveoli are the functional units of the lungs where oxygen and carbon dioxide exchange takes place via inhaled air (**Figure 11**). Alveoli are round, thin, balloonlike structures wrapped in thin blood vessels.

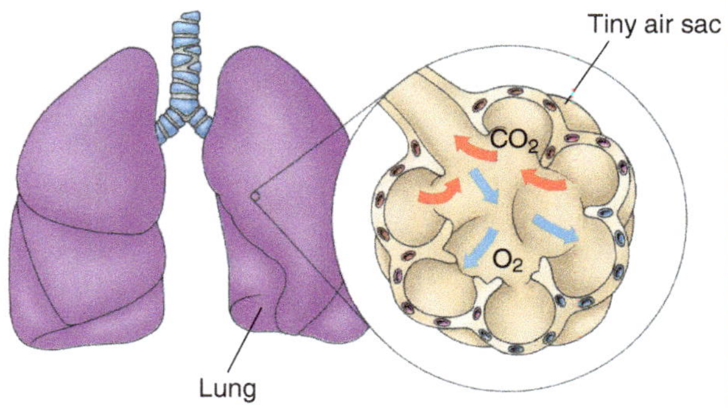

Figure 11 The exchange of carbon dioxide (CO_2) and oxygen (O_2) in the lungs.

Lungs do not have muscle. They rely on the muscles between the ribs (**intercostal muscles**) and the diaphragm. The intercostal muscles move the chest off the shoulder girdle, and the **diaphragm** pushes down into the abdomen. This action expands the chest, creating a vacuum that allows air to run into the alveoli of the lungs.

Tip

Pleural Space

To maintain the vacuum seal in the chest, the space between the rib cage and the lungs has a lining. One piece of clear tissue lines the inside of the ribs, and another wraps around the lung surface. Between the linings is a small amount of clear fluid that acts as a lubricant during ventilation. The space between the linings is called the **pleural space**. Damage to either layer can allow air or blood to rush into the space and impair the vacuum needed to expand the lungs.

When the rib muscles and diaphragm relax, they create positive pressure that forces the air out. The process of breathing in is called **inspiration**. The process of breathing out is called **expiration**. **Ventilation** is the process of both inspiration and expiration (**Figure 12**).

Ventilation and respiration are the two components of **breathing**. Breathing is affected if the airway is partially obstructed or closed. The **airway** comprises the structures that take air from the nose or mouth down to the alveoli (**Figure 13**). As the air travels through the airway, it is warmed, humidified, and cleansed as it comes in contact with the lining of the airway. The lining of the airway is made up of a special type of tissue called **mucous membranes**. This tissue secretes **mucus**, a sticky substance to aid in cleaning and humidifying the air. The mucous membranes are full of small blood vessels and can swell to accommodate temperature changes in the air.

The upper airway is designed to cleanse, humidify, and regulate the temperature of the air being inhaled. The lower airway structures allow for the passage of air to the capillaries, where oxygen and carbon dioxide are exchanged in the blood. The upper and lower airways include the structures listed in **Table 7**.

Circulatory

The circulatory system, like the respiratory system, must always operate effectively or the organism will die. The circulatory system moves blood throughout the body using a central pump (the **heart**); outgoing blood vessels (**arteries**); thin blood vessels where the blood can exchange gases, nutrients, or waste (capillaries); and vessels that return blood to the heart (**veins**) (**Figure 14**). Without this simple process, the cells in the body cannot receive nutrients or oxygen and cannot eliminate waste or carbon dioxide. If the cells of the body are not able to use the available fuel properly, acid builds up and the cells die. Problems associated with the circulatory system are true emergencies.

Blood, the solution that is moved by the circulatory system, is made primarily of **plasma**, a fluid containing important proteins that help the body regulate fluid. The plasma is where many nutrients and carbon dioxide are found; it contains the red and white blood cells and platelets necessary for keeping the body healthy. **Red blood cells** (**erythrocytes**) float in the blood and carry oxygen. Red blood cells contain **hemoglobin**, a chemical to which oxygen attaches. **White blood cells** (**leukocytes**) are also transported through the body in the blood and are used to fight infection. Some white blood cells label foreign organisms for attack, and other white blood cells physically attack the foreign organisms. **Platelets** (**thrombocytes**) are tiny structures in the blood that are drawn toward wounds to create a plug or clot.

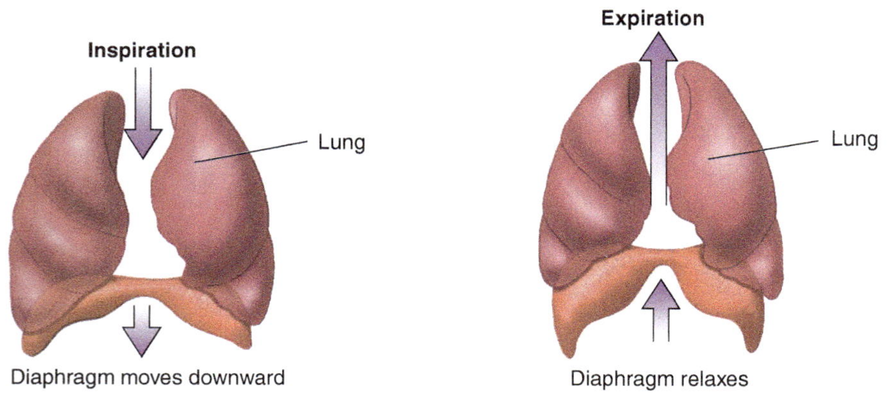

Figure 12 Mechanisms of breathing.

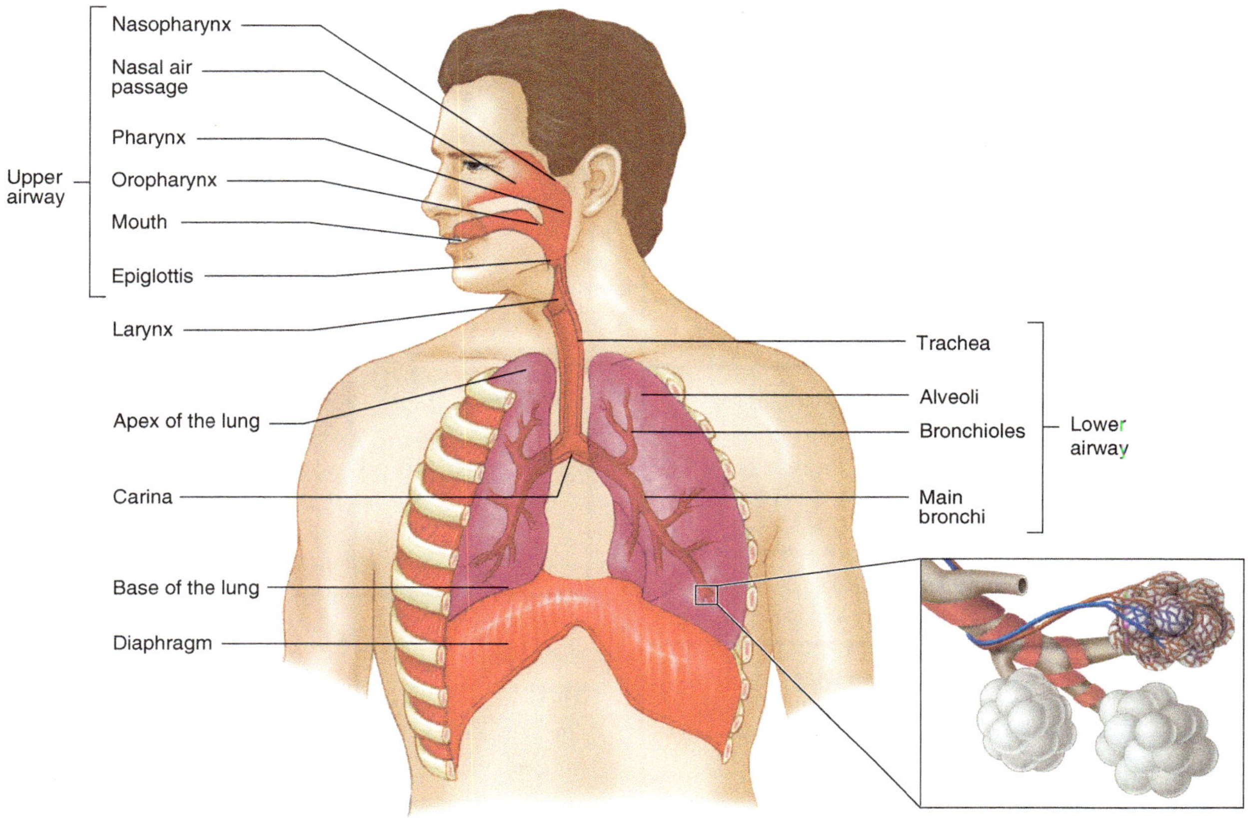

Figure 13 The respiratory system consists of all structures of the body that contribute to the process of breathing.

The blood moves away from the heart through the arteries, which are thick and lined with muscle to absorb the pressure that the heart places on them when it pumps. Capillaries are very thin blood vessels (of single-cell thickness) that allow for nutrients, waste, and gases to move through them. Veins, blood vessels that return blood to the heart, are also lined with muscle. Veins are not as thick as arteries, and they use gravity, skeletal muscle contraction, and valves to help move blood back to the heart. Arteries and veins have the ability to constrict or dilate, allowing the organism to change blood pressure or to deal with blood volume loss.

The heart receives deoxygenated blood from the body through two large veins: the inferior and superior vena cavae (**Figure 15**). The **inferior vena cava** is a large vein that brings blood back from the lower part of the body. The **superior vena cava** brings blood back from the upper part of the body. These blood vessels empty into the right-side top portion of the heart. The chambers at the top of the heart (**atria**) receive the blood coming into the heart, provide some storage, and pump the blood into the bottom chambers of the heart. The bottom chambers of the heart (**ventricles**) pump blood away from the heart. The right ventricle pumps the deoxygenated blood it received from the right atrium to the lungs, where carbon dioxide is released to the air and oxygen is absorbed for transport to the body's cells. This blood is called oxygenated blood. The left atrium receives the oxygenated blood from the lungs and then moves it toward the left ventricle, which pumps the blood out to the rest of the body through the largest artery, called the **aorta**. The heart receives its oxygenated blood from the first branch off the aorta. The vessels that bring blood directly to the heart muscle are called the **coronary arteries**.

Table 7

Structures of the Airway

Structure	Description
Upper Airway	
Nares	The openings into the nose.
Nasal cavity	The opening inside the nose.
Lips	The opening into the mouth.
Oral cavity	The opening inside the mouth, behind the lips.
Pharynx	The cylindrical cavity between the nasal cavity (nasopharynx), oral cavity (oropharynx), and larynx (laryngopharynx).
Tongue	The muscle in the bottom of mouth used for speech, taste, and movement of food.
Epiglottis	The muscular flap at the base of the tongue that acts as a valve to cover the lower airway.
Esophagus	Located in the bottom of the pharynx, this tube takes food to the stomach. In an unconsciious person it can also release vomitus into the structures of the upper airway. This can lead to a blocked airway or aspiration of the vomitus into the lungs, severely compromising breathing.
Lower Airway	
Larynx	The opening into the trachea; it is made of cartilage and contains the vocal cords.
Trachea	The breathing tube that travels down the neck into the chest.
Bronchi	The tubes (one for the right lung and one for the left lung) that come off the trachea in the chest. Bronchi are wrapped by smooth muscle that allows the tubes to get larger (dilate) or smaller (constrict).
Bronchioles	Smaller tubing that branches off the bronchi and joins to the air sacs.
Alveoli	The air sacs, which are wrapped with capillaries. These air sacs are the location where oxygen from the air enters the blood in the capillaries, and carbon dioxide leaves the blood for the air in the air sac.

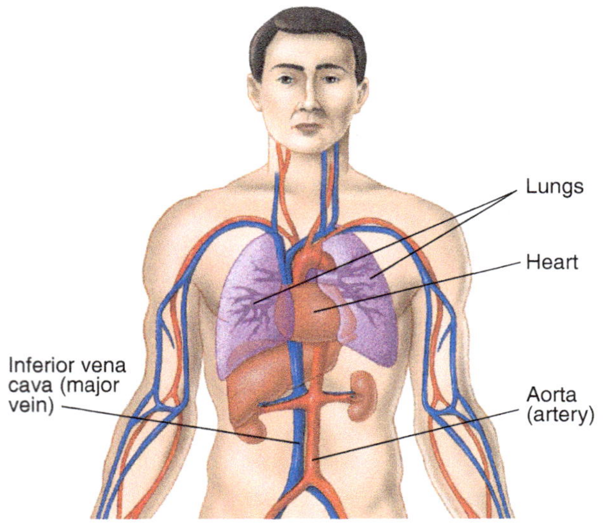

Figure 14 The core circulatory system.

Skin

The **skin** is the largest organ of the body. The skin affects the survival and well-being of the organism by protecting the organism against harmful substances, regulating temperature, and receiving information from the outside of the body. The skin has an outer layer called the epidermis that is made up of cells that progressively die off and renew. The next layer beneath the epidermis is the dermis (*epi-* meaning "above"). The dermis contains capillaries, glands, nerves, and hair follicles. The dermis sits above a subcutaneous layer that contains fat and covers the muscles (**Figure 16**).

Other Systems

Many other organ systems are important for the survival of the patient. The LER may need to manage illnesses or injuries to these systems as well.

Nervous

The nervous system is composed of the brain and the spinal cord (**Figure 17**). The **brain** is the control center of the body and is protected by the skull. It receives and interprets input from the outside world, regulates all other organ systems, and controls thought and movement. The **spinal cord**, which is protected by the vertebrae, transmits the sensory information from the peripheral nerves (sensory nerves located throughout the body) to the brain and carries messages from the brain back down to the rest of the body.

The brain and the spinal cord are protected by the **meninges**, which comprise three separate layers of tissue. The first layer, lying directly under the skull, is the dura mater (Latin for "tough mother"), a very tough fibrous layer. The second layer is the arachnoid, which resembles a spider's web. The third layer is the pia mater (Latin for "small mother"), a very thin layer that adheres to the brain tissue. **Cerebrospinal fluid** is created in the brain by the filtering of blood. The cerebrospinal fluid is clear and watery and fills the void between the pia mater and the arachnoid to aid in absorbing shock.

The smallest functional unit of the brain is the nerve cell, or neuron. Neurons create impulses and transmit them to other nerves or muscle. It is easy to think of the neurons in the body as electrical wiring like we find in homes. We conceptualize that electrical impulses travel from nerve to nerve in the same manner as electricity conducts across copper wire. However, this is not how the neurons work. Neurons generate impulses and transmit them to each other or to muscle cells across a space called the synaptic cleft. Because nerves do not come in direct contact with other nerves or muscle cells, the sending nerve releases a chemical called a **neurotransmitter**. This chemical floods the space and activates specialized places on the receiving nerve or muscle called **receptors**. When these receptors are activated, the receiving nerve or muscle responds. The neurotransmitter that floods the space is broken down by other chemicals called **enzymes**, break-

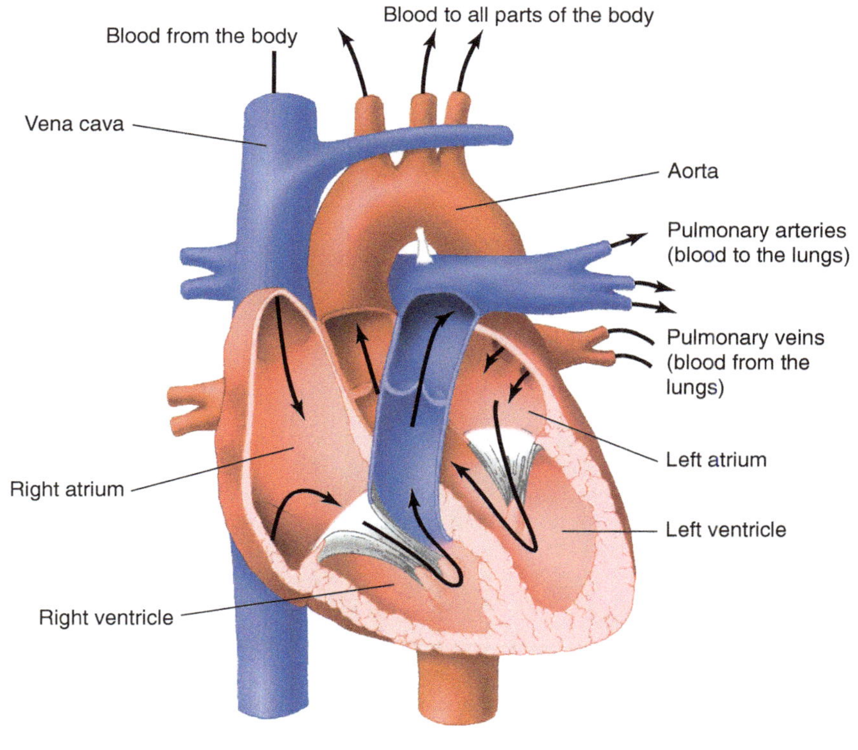

Figure 15 Schematic representation of the functions of the four chambers of the heart.

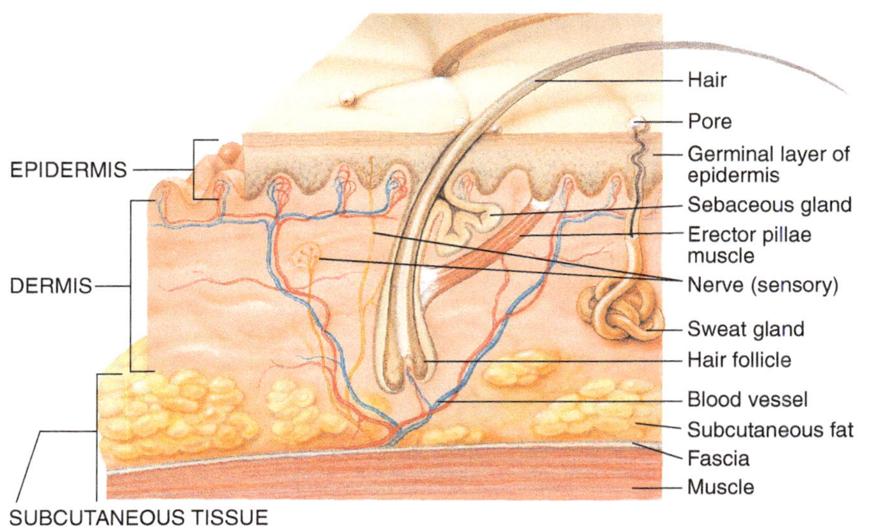

Figure 16 The skin.

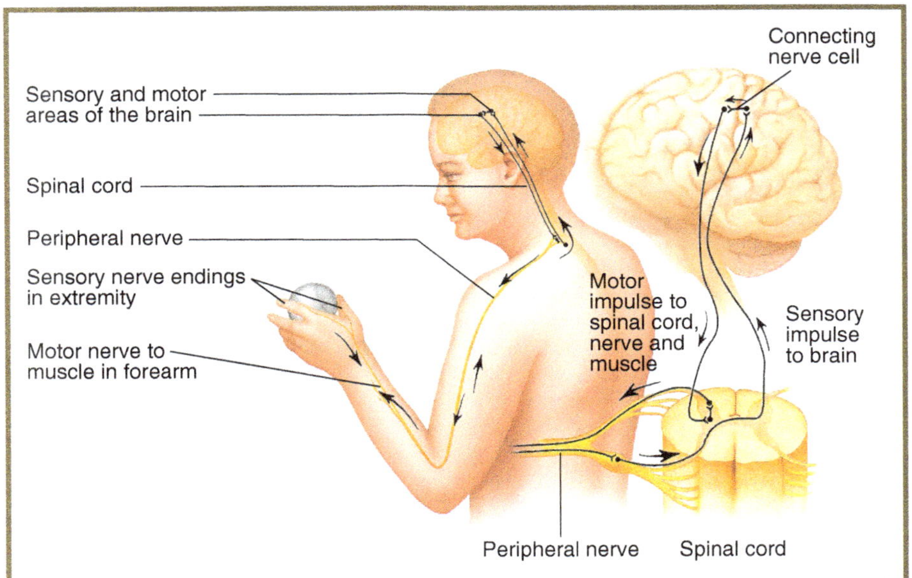

Figure 17 The nervous system.

ing the message. If the enzymes were not there to remove the neurotransmitter, the message would continue to be sent.

Medications can be used to activate receptors in the nerve, or in some cases to compete with the neurotransmitters and block the message from being sent. For example, the body sends a message to the smooth muscle of the bronchioles (larger airways) to constrict (make them smaller) during an asthma attack. Albuterol is a drug that can be administered to block the receptors on the smooth muscle, helping the muscle to relax and making the airway larger, curtailing the asthma attack.

The **central nervous system** maintains life through a control center called the **autonomic nervous system**. This system functions independently, involuntarily controlling body functions and responding to stress. The autonomic nervous system is made up of the **sympathetic nervous system**, which controls our response to stress or emergencies, and the **parasympathetic nervous system**, which controls our daily organ functions.

Tip

Fight or Flight; Feed or Breed

The sympathetic nervous system uses adrenaline as its neurotransmitter and is often called the "fight or flight" system.

The parasympathetic nervous system uses a chemical called acetylcholine as a neurotransmitter and is often called the "feed or breed" system.

Digestive

The digestive system is made of hollow and solid organs (**Figure 18**). Hollow organs include the stomach, gall bladder, large intestine, and small intestine. These organs receive food, break it down, absorb the nutrients, and expel the leftover waste. The solid organs, the liver and pancreas, secrete chemicals that aid in breaking down the food, or act to filter the blood containing the absorbed food.

Food is taken into the digestive system through the mouth, where it is immediately broken down by the mechanical action of chewing and the chemical action of saliva. The food bolus is swallowed and passes through the pharynx, down the esophagus, and into the stomach. The stomach is a holding tank filled with acid that acts to break down the food so it can be pushed into the small intestines, where nutrient absorption occurs. The pancreas and liver support digestion in the intestines by producing digestive enzymes and fluids that specialize in breaking down the food components. The food is pushed through the intestines by a rhythmic muscular contraction called **peristalsis**. When most of the nutrients have been pulled from the food bolus, it travels into the large intestines. Bacteria that live in the large intestine absorb nutrients from the food bolus, break down the food, and release essential vitamins.

Genitourinary

The genitourinary system is responsible for removing waste products from the bloodstream and for reproductive functions.

The kidneys filter blood to remove toxins, waste, and extra chemicals. The fluid from the kidneys creates urine, which is stored in the urinary bladder in the pelvis. The urine is excreted from the bladder through a tube called the urethra.

The major organs of male reproduction are the testes, which produce sperm, and the penis, which delivers sperm to fertilize the female egg. The major female reproductive organs are the ovaries, which produce eggs, and the uterus, which holds the fertilized egg as it develops during pregnancy. The egg released by the ovaries travels to the uterus through the fallopian tubes. The external opening of the female reproductive system is the vagina.

Endocrine

The endocrine system functions as a chemical messenger system in the body and is regulated by the brain (**Figure 19**). Endocrine organs are glands that excrete chemicals called **hormones** directly into the blood. These hormones aid in body function, glucose processing (insulin), and response to stress (adrenalin).

AGE-RELATED CONSIDERATIONS

Generally, the standard presentation for anatomy and physiology involves early and middle adulthood. However, as LERs, you will have to care for patients at all age levels. LERs need to understand how age has an impact on human beings. Throughout a person's life, the body constantly changes. It is important for LERs to understand how these changes affect the treatment of patients. **Table 8** lists the typical age-related categories.

Children's bodies change continuously as they develop, and certain anatomic considerations should be applied when treating children (**Table 9**).

Patients are considered part of the elderly population when they are older than 65 years. Changes that occur in the elderly population often result in a decrease in the body's general function. The elderly typically do not respond well to a sudden onset of severe illness or injuries. In addition, the elderly may be compromised by the use of various types of medications to control cardiovascular functions. One such

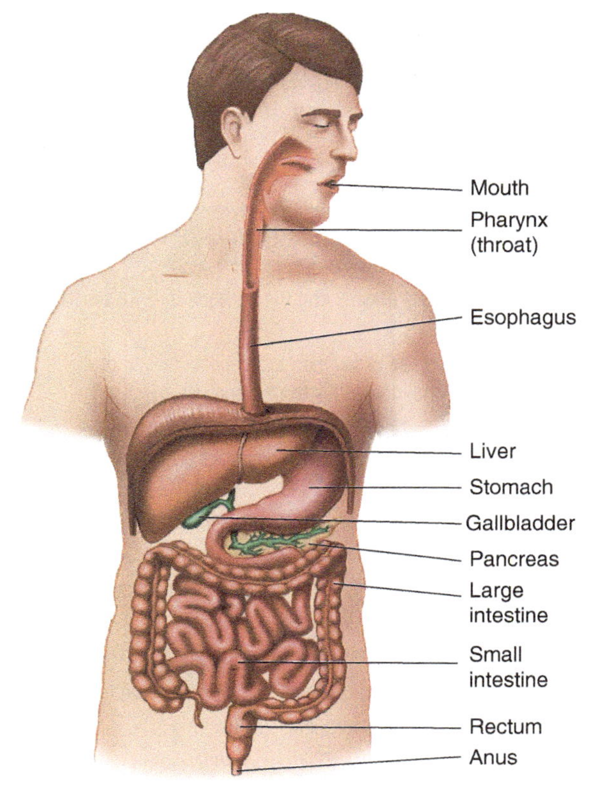

Figure 18 The digestive system.

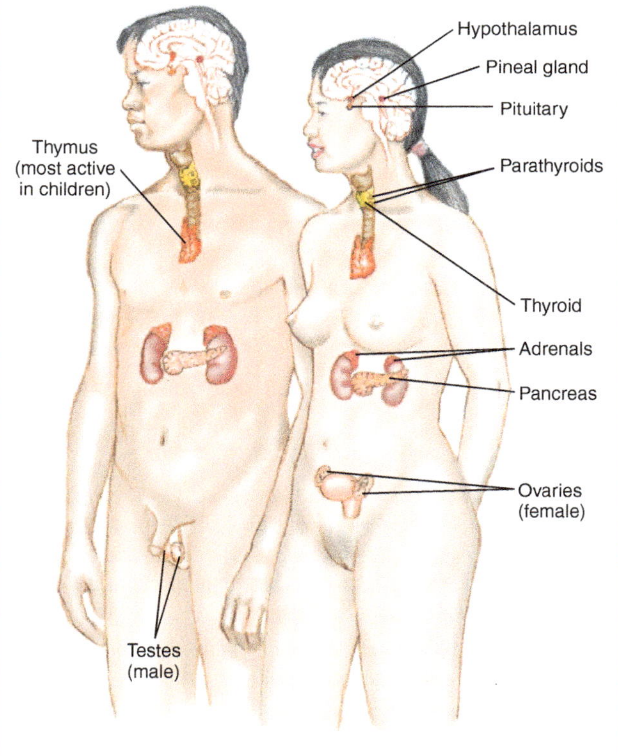

Figure 19 The endocrine system controls the release of hormones in the body.

Table 8

Age Categories

Category	Age
Infant	0-12 months of life (during the first month of life, the infant is commonly referred to as a neonate)
Toddler	1-3 years
Preschool age	3-5 years
School age	6-12 years
Adolescent	13-18 years
Early adult	19-39 years
Middle adult	40-59 years
Late adult	60+ years (elderly patients are typically identified as being older than 65 years)

medication is a beta-blocker, which controls a patient's heart rate, not allowing it to rise; therefore, when a stressor is placed on a patient who is taking a beta-blocker, the heart cannot increase its rate to compensate. Another common medication is a calcium channel blocker, such as nifedipine (Procardia), which does not allow blood vessels to constrict. This medication reduces the body's ability to increase blood pressure.

Table 10 lists anatomic changes to consider when treating elderly patients.

Table 9

Anatomic Considerations for Pediatric Patients

- The head of an infant or toddler is large in proportion to the body.
- An infant's skull has depressions (fontanelles) where the bones have not fused.
- An infant's or toddler's tongue is proportionately larger than an adult's.
- An infant's or toddler's trachea is smaller and narrower than an adult's.
- A neonate breathes primarily through the nose until age 4 weeks.
- An infant's or toddler's spinal column is not as well developed as an adult's. The child can have damage to the spinal cord without obvious damage to the vertebrae.
- An infant's or toddler's chest is more flexible than an adult's and may have thoracic organ damage without obvious injuries to ribs.
- An infant's or toddler's abdominal organs are larger and less protected than an adult's.
- An infant's, toddler's, or school-age child's bones are weaker than the ligaments, resulting in more fractures than in adults. The growth plate in the bones of a child is also a weak point.

CONCLUSION

Anatomy and physiology provides the foundation necessary for the LER to understand all emergency medicine care. Concentrating on this unit will improve your ability to process information gathered in a patient assessment, allowing you to reach life-saving conclusions quickly. Understanding normal body functions and their limitations such as those associated with breathing or bleeding will reinforce the need to act quickly when these normal responses are damaged.

LERs operating in and around other health care professionals will benefit from understanding basic medical terminology. After reading this unit the LER will have encountered many of the basic anatomic terms used routinely in emergency medicine. Failure to grasp these concepts and terminology can result in confusion and poor patient care.

Table 10

Anatomic Considerations for the Elderly

- Lungs become less elastic, and the rib cage becomes brittle and fragile.
- The alveoli decrease in number and become larger, often preventing all the inhaled air from being used.
- **Arteriosclerosis**, hardening of the blood vessels, makes the blood vessels stiff and unable to constrict or dilate as well when the body is stressed.
- The heart's electrical system can shrink, increasing irregular heart rhythms.
- The heart muscle becomes enlarged after experiencing years of stress.
- Nerve speeds tend to slow, altering perception and response.
- The brain tends to shrink, becoming more susceptible to damage.
- Bones tend to lose strength, muscles lose mass, and joints stiffen.
- The spinal column can become distorted, creating curvatures or humps.
- The kidneys reduce in size, losing the ability to filter blood as effectively.

Prep Kit

READY FOR REVIEW

- Anatomy refers to the structures that make up a body. Physiology refers to the function of a body.
- Topographic anatomy allows the LER to make an assessment of how an illness or injury has affected the structures below it.
- Anatomy and physiology require an understanding of commonly used terminology.
- The body is made up of a hierarchy of units that affect survival: cells, tissue, organs, organ systems, and the organism.
- Humans, like all other organisms, must maintain homeostasis—a state of equilibrium between the external environment and its own internal environment.
- Oxygenation, perfusion, and fuel efficiency are vital components to the life support chain. Alteration or damage to these components can lead to the death of the organism.
- The major organ systems are as follows:
  - Skeletal
  - Muscular
  - Respiratory
  - Circulatory
  - Skin
  - Nervous
  - Digestive
  - Genitourinary
  - Endocrine
- Children and older adults have variations to the standard presentation, and LERs must consider these differences when caring for these patients.

VITAL VOCABULARY

abdomen The cavity that lies between the thorax and the pelvis and contains the digestive organs.

airway The structures that allow the passage of air from the outside environment to the functional units of the lungs.

alveoli Small, grapelike sacs surrounded by capillaries; considered the functional unit of the lungs.

anatomic position The position used to study the body. The person is standing, facing forward, with palms turned forward.

anatomy The study of the parts of the body.

anterior The front of the body.

aorta The main artery that receives blood from the left ventricle of the heart and delivers it to all the other arteries that carry blood to the tissues of the body.

arteries The blood vessels that take blood away from the heart. They can constrict and dilate, are under pressure, and have a thick muscle layer.

arteriosclerosis Hardening of the blood vessels, which makes the blood vessels stiff and unable to constrict or dilate as well when the body is stressed.

atria The chambers at the top of the heart that receive the blood coming into the heart, provide some storage, and pump the blood into the bottom chambers of the heart.

autonomic nervous system The part of the central nervous system that controls involuntary body functions.

bilateral On both sides of the body.

blood The fluid contained in the blood vessels, consisting of plasma, formed elements (red blood cells, white blood cells, and platelets), dissolved gases, nutrients, and waste.

bone marrow The substance inside certain bones that is responsible for developing red blood cells, white blood cells, and platelets.

bones Complex living tissue that helps to make up the skeletal system.

brain The primary organ of the central nervous system, comprising millions of neurons separated into specialized functional units.

breathing The process of ventilation and respiration.

bronchi The large tubes in the lower airway that connect to the trachea and channel air through the lungs.

bronchioles The smaller tubes in the lower airway that connect to the bronchi and channel air to the alveoli.

calcaneus The heel bone.

capillaries Blood vessels that are a single cell in thickness and allow for the exchange of gases, nutrients, and waste.

cardiac muscle The muscle that makes up the heart. Made of protein chains that give it a striated appearance, it functions involuntarily and is also called the myocardium.

carpals The irregular bones in the wrist. These bones are relatively large and extend from the radius and ulna toward the metacarpals.

cartilage The dense, fibrous material used in the skeletal system to cover joints or create flexible structures.

cells The basic units of life; contain tiny structures called organelles that maintain the cell's regulation and function.

central nervous system Composed of the brain and spinal cord.

cerebrospinal fluid The fluid in the skull that is made from blood plasma and used to help cushion the brain.

clavicle The collarbone.

coronary arteries The arteries that take blood to the muscle of the heart.

diaphragm The large muscle used to create a vacuum in the chest and to promote the movement of air in the lungs; separates the lungs from the abdominal organs.

diffusion The process in which a chemical moves from a higher concentration to a lower concentration until it is equally dispersed.

distal Away from the center of the body.

enzymes Chemicals that promote a reaction in the body; often used to break down other chemicals.

epiglottis The flap that lies behind the tongue and covers the trachea when a person swallows.

erythrocytes Red blood cells.

esophagus The smooth muscular tube that takes food and fluid from the throat to the stomach.

expiration Pushing air out of the lungs.

femur The large bone of the thigh.

fibula The outer and smaller bone of the two bones of the lower leg.

flat bones Broad and flat bones that are used for protection. Examples include the ribs, sternum, and the sides of the skull.

heart A two-stage pump that takes blood from the body, pushes it to the lungs for an exchange of gases, and then pushes the blood back out to the body.

hemoglobin A chemical made with iron that lies in the red blood cells. Oxygen attaches to this chemical, allowing it to be transported in the blood.

homeostasis The process in nature by which an organism maintains equilibrium between the internal and external environment.

hormones Substances formed in specialized organs or glands and carried to another organ or group of cells in the same organism. They regulate many body functions, including metabolism, growth, and body temperature.

humerus The bone of the upper arm.

inferior Lower than another point on the body (closer to the feet).

inferior vena cava The large vein that brings blood from the lower body to the heart.

inspiration Pulling air into the lungs by contracting the diaphragm to create negative pressure.

insulin The hormone that is necessary to get glucose into a cell.

intercostal muscles The muscles between the ribs that contract to expand the chest. In conjunction with the diaphragm, these muscles create a vacuum in the chest, allowing air to rush into the lungs.

Irregular bones Bones that do not fit into the other categories—for example, vertebrae.

joints The parts of the skeletal system where bones meet.

larynx The opening into the trachea; it is made of cartilage and contains the vocal cords.

lateral Away from the midline.

laterally recumbent The patient is lying on his or her side. The recovery position is an example of a laterally recumbent position.

leukocytes White blood cells.

ligaments Tough, fibrous cords of tissue that connect bones to bones across a joint.

lips The exposed covering of the oral cavity.

long bones Bones that are used like levers by the body and are found in the thigh, leg, arm, and forearm.

mandible Lower jaw.

mastoid process Bony points behind the ear.

maxilla Upper jaw.

medial Closer to the middle of the body.

meninges Coverings inside the skull and spinal column that protect the brain and spinal cord.

metacarpals The small bones in the hands that attach to the fingers.

metatarsals The small bones in the foot that attach to the toes.

midline An imaginary vertical line drawn from head to toe.

mucous membranes The tissue that lines body openings and contains specialized cells that create mucus.

mucus A sticky, thick fluid secreted by specialized cells in the body; aids in humidification, temperature control, and air filtering.

muscles The tissue created out of protein that the body uses to perform work or motion.

nares The openings in the nose.

nasal bones The bony structures that make up and support the nasal cavity. Cartilage extends past the nasal bones to make the tip of the nose.

nasal cavity The large opening behind the nose, lined with mucous membranes.

neuron The smallest functional unit of nervous tissue; neurons create impulses and transmit them to other nerves or muscles.

neurotransmitter The chemical that floods the space between nerves and activates specialized places on the receiving nerve or muscle.

oral cavity The opening behind the lips, below the nasal cavity.

orbits Openings that create the cavities for the eyes.

organelles The small structures in the cell that are used to maintain cellular function.

organism A living being supported by many different subparts.

organ systems Groupings of organs that together perform a certain body function.

organs Structures that provide a specific function within an organ system.

oxygenation The process of moving oxygen into an area. This occurs in the blood when air with a higher concentration of oxygen comes into contact with blood containing a lower concentration of oxygen. The higher concentration diffuses toward the lower concentration in an attempt to equalize concentrations.

parasympathetic nervous system The part of the autonomic nervous system that controls the vegetative functions of the body.

patella The kneecap.

pelvis Ring of bone at the bottom of the trunk; attachment point for legs and spinal column.

perfusion The process by which cells obtain oxygen and nutrients and use them to sustain life.

peristalsis Rhythmic muscular contraction of the intestines.

phalanges The fingers and toes.

pharynx The cylinder-like tube that lies between the nasal cavity, oral cavity, and the larynx.

physiology The study of how the body functions.

plasma A fluid containing important proteins that circulate throughout the body.

platelets Small cells that fill holes in blood vessels, creating a clot; also called thrombocytes.

pleural space A space between the lining of the ribs and the lungs.

posterior Toward the back.

prone Lying on the front of the body.

proximal Closer to the center of the body.

radius The bone on the thumb side of the forearm.

receptors Specialized places on nerve or muscle cells that attach to a chemical messenger and send the message forward.

recovery position Placing the patient on his or her side, with an arm supporting the head and the legs positioned so the patient cannot roll onto his or her back or front. The intent of the recovery position is to allow the unconscious person to lie flat while allowing the airway an opportunity to drain secretions or vomit (see **lateral recumbent**).

red blood cells Specialized cells containing hemoglobin that move oxygen through the body; also called erythrocytes.

respiration The process of exchanging carbon dioxide and oxygen at the cells and in the lungs.

scapula The shoulder blade.

short bones Bones that are found in the wrist and ankles.

sinuses Hollow cavities in the skull, behind the nose and around the eyes.

skeletal muscles Tissues made of protein chains that are used to move bones. Skeletal muscle is under the voluntary control of the person.

skin The outer covering of the body, consisting of the epidermis, dermis, and subcutaneous layers.

smooth muscle Short muscle fibers that are used to move, open, or close structures in the body. Smooth muscle movement is involuntary.

spinal cord Specialized grouping of nervous tissue used to move messages to and from the body and the brain.

sternum The flat breastbone that sits in the center of the chest.

superior Closer to the head.

superior vena cava The large vein that brings blood to the heart from the upper body, head, and neck.

supine Lying on the back facing upward.

sympathetic nervous system Part of the autonomic nervous system that controls the stress response.

talus The bone at the ankle joint that connects the foot to the lower leg.

tarsals The irregular bones in the ankle and foot. These bones are relatively large bones extending from the ankle to the metatarsals.

tendons Fibrous cords that are the terminal end of a skeletal muscle and attach the muscle to the bone.

thorax The cavity surrounded by the ribs and spinal column; contains organs from the cardiovascular and respiratory systems.

thrombocytes Platelets.

tibia The shin bone; the larger of the two bones of the lower leg.

tissue A group of like cells that come together for a specific purpose.

tongue The muscular structure in the oral cavity used for speech, taste, and movement of food.

topographic anatomy The superficial landmarks on the outer surface of the body that help in locating structures under the surface.

trachea The cartilaginous windpipe connecting the larynx to the bronchi.

ulna The bone on the little-finger side of the forearm.

unilateral On one side.

veins Blood vessels that carry blood back to the heart.

ventilation The process of inspiration and expiration.

ventricles The bottom chambers of the heart, which pump the blood away from the heart.

vertebrae The irregular bones that loosely connect to make the spinal column. The vertebrae consist of the cervical, thoracic, lumbar, sacrum, and coccyx sections.

white blood cells Specialized cells in the blood that identify and attack threats from invading chemicals or infections; also called leukocytes.

xiphoid process The tip of the sternum that protrudes over the bottom of the thorax and over the abdomen.

CHECK YOUR KNOWLEDGE

1. In order for an organism to survive, it must be able to maintain a state of equilibrium between its internal environment and the external environment. This is an example of:
   A. anatomy
   B. ventilation
   C. homeostasis
   D. hemoglobin
2. Which of the following is not part of the life support chain?
   A. Blood pressure
   B. Fuel efficiency
   C. Oxygenation
   D. Ventilation
3. Which of the following structures are tough, fibrous cords that attach bones to bones across a joint?
   A. Tendons
   B. Capillaries
   C. Ligaments
   D. Cartilage
4. Alveoli are considered the:
   A. functional unit of the lungs where gas is exchanged
   B. functional unit of the kidney where blood is filtered
   C. functional unit of the cell where sugar is used
   D. largest arteries of the body
5. ____________________ carry blood away from the heart.
   A. Hemoglobins
   B. Arteries
   C. Capillaries
   D. Veins

Physical Examination and Assessment

Unit 9

Geoffrey Shapiro

Law Enforcement Responder Objectives

- List the stages of a patient assessment. (p 171)
- Discuss the components of a scene size-up. (pp 171–173)
- Discuss the purpose and components of the primary assessment. (pp 173–175)
- Explain history taking and its role in the patient assessment. (pp 175–176)
- Discuss the purpose and components of the secondary assessment. (pp 176–180)
- Explain the purpose of the reassessment. (p 180)
- List the information that should be addressed in a handoff report. (p 180)
- List the differences between performing a patient assessment on an adult and performing one on a child. (p 180)

National EMS Education Standard Competencies

Preparatory

Uses simple knowledge of the emergency medical services (EMS) system, the safety and well-being of the emergency medical responder (EMR), and medical/legal issues at the scene of an emergency while awaiting a higher level of care.

Therapeutic Communication

- Principles of communicating with patients in a manner that achieves a positive relationship
  - Interviewing techniques (pp 173–175)

Assessment

Uses scene information and simple patient assessment findings to identify and manage immediate life threats and injuries within the scope of practice of the EMR.

Scene Size-up

- Scene safety (p 171)
- Scene management
  - Impact of the environment on patient care (p 171)
  - Addressing hazards (p 171)
  - Violence (p 171)
  - Need for additional or specialized resources (p 171)
  - Standard precautions (pp 171–172)

Primary Assessment

- Primary assessment for all patient situations
  - Level of consciousness (p 173)
  - ABCs (pp 174–175)
  - Identifying life threats (p 173)
  - Assessment of vital functions (pp 174–175)
- Begin interventions needed to preserve life (pp 174–175)

History Taking

- Determining the chief complaint (p 175)
- Mechanism of injury or nature of illness (p 175)
- Associated signs and symptoms (p 176)

Secondary Assessment

- Performing a rapid full-body scan (pp 176–179)
- Focused assessment of pain (p 180)
- Assessment of vital signs (p 179)

Reassessment

- How and when to reassess patients (p 180)

Life Span Development

Uses simple knowledge of age-related differences to assess and care for patients.

INTRODUCTION

As a law enforcement responder (LER), your first priority should be safety—both your own and that of your patients and any bystanders. Your efforts may never go beyond attempting to secure the scene and activating emergency medical services (EMS) resources if deemed appropriate, but you may also be expected to render medical care. Knowing what to do begins with assessing the situation and patient. Every patient you encounter will need to be assessed; assessments vary based on the situation, but be ready to perform some type of patient assessment on all patients you encounter. Performing a complete patient assessment will require you to use most of your senses (touch, sight, smell, and hearing). Even during situations where you may be concentrating your efforts on law enforcement duties, you may need to perform a patient assessment to provide direction to others on scene who may be able to provide medical assistance and to update responding medical teams.

PATIENT ASSESSMENT

There are several stages to completing a thorough patient assessment: the scene size-up, the primary assessment, history taking, the secondary assessment, the reassessment, and the handoff report. Using a systematic approach will enable you to gather the appropriate information and render good care. It is important to be comprehensive when performing the patient assessment because certain subtle findings can be difficult to assess but may have a significant impact on patient condition and outcome.

SCENE SIZE-UP

The scene size-up may begin prior to physically arriving at the location of the emergency. Dispatch information should be reviewed by the LER so he or she can consider what may be found and what actions may need to be taken. Keep in mind, however, that dispatch information may be incomplete or inaccurate, so it is important to react to what you actually find upon arrival. Other factors that should be taken into account during the emergency response include weather, traffic, time of day, additional resources, number of reported patients, and special considerations. Once you have confirmed that patient care is required, be sure to verify that EMS resources have been dispatched and are responding appropriately.

Scene Safety

When you arrive on scene, safety is the first priority. If the scene is not safe, it is the responsibility of the LER to attempt to make the scene safe or to evacuate to a safe location. Traditionally, fire department or EMS personnel will stage away from a scene that is unsafe because of unsecured weapons or violence until notified by law enforcement that the scene has been secured and it is safe for them to approach (**Figure 1**).

Common scene hazards include environmental conditions (rain, snow, extreme temperature), the presence of hazardous substances (chemical, biologic, or explosive agents; clandestine lab indicators), violence, and crowds. Other special circumstances may include the presence of a crime scene, rescue situations, unstable structures, confined spaces, traffic, or other scenarios in which specialized personnel or equipment may be needed.

If the LER cannot safely secure or manage the scene, he or she should wait until the appropriate resources arrive to assist. If injured, the LER will not do the patient any good and will just add to the overall problem. The LER must ensure that the scene remains safe throughout the entire event, not just during the beginning stages of the event.

Personal Protective Equipment

Ensure that the proper personal protective equipment (PPE) is available and used when appropriate. Examples of PPE

Figure 1 Evaluate the scene for hazards as soon as you arrive.

include uniforms and footwear, reflective vests, respiratory protection, and standard precaution equipment. It is up to the individual responder to use the protective equipment that is both appropriate and available.

Standard precautions should always be used when there is a chance that you may come in contact with any body fluids. The concept of standard precautions states that all body fluid should be considered contaminated and may pose a threat if it is introduced into the responder's body via a break in the skin, mucosal membranes (eyes, nose, mouth), or injected through the skin. To reduce the risk of contamination, the LER should, at a minimum, wear medical examination gloves whenever touching a patient. Additional PPE may include protective eyewear, a face mask, and a splash-resistant overgarment.

In addition to protecting the responder, using standard precautions reduces the risk of the responder contaminating the patient. Waterless hand sanitizers should be available so a LER can properly disinfect after removing his or her gloves. The LER must also wash his or her hands with soap and water as soon as possible, even if waterless hand sanitizers were used, because handwashing remains the most effective way to prevent the spread of disease. It is also important that contaminated or potentially contaminated equipment be properly cleaned, and that disposable equipment be placed in the appropriate containers.

Number of Patients

Determine how many patients are present at an emergency scene, whether triage will be necessary, and which resources are needed. As few as two patients can pose a problem to a single emergency responder; if there are more patients than responders present at an emergency, the responders will need to triage (sort) the patients to identify those who need to receive care prior to others. (Triage is discussed in the scene management unit.)

Trauma or Medical Patient

One of the first pieces of information instrumental in determining the appropriate care of a patient is determining whether the patient is sick (a medical patient) or injured (a trauma patient) (**Figure 2**). If the patient is experiencing a medical emergency, try to determine the **nature of illness (NOI)**. If the patient has been injured, try to determine the **mechanism of injury (MOI)**. There are some patients for whom it is difficult to determine whether the issue is medical or trauma. Other patients may fall into both categories—for instance, a patient who has a heart attack while driving, causing him to crash his car.

The NOI is the general type of illness of which the medical patient is complaining. Examples of NOI include chest pain, shortness of breath, headache, weakness, and nausea. Knowing the NOI can help the LER narrow down the type of medical emergency the patient is having and determine the proper interventions.

Tip

Example of Information Regarding a Mechanism of Injury

You respond to a patient who was pushed from a roof. All law enforcement duties and scene safety responsibilities have been initiated. You are beginning to complete your patient assessment and treatment while waiting for EMS to arrive. What information regarding the MOI would be important to determine and include in your report to EMS, and subsequently to the hospital? Mechanism-specific information includes the following:

- Distance fallen
- Cause of fall
- Patient position on landing
- What, if anything, the patient hit while falling (multiple impacts)
- What surface the patient hit

Specific MOIs and treatments are discussed in the trauma units.

The MOI is what caused the trauma patient to become injured. Examples of MOI include a motor vehicle crash,

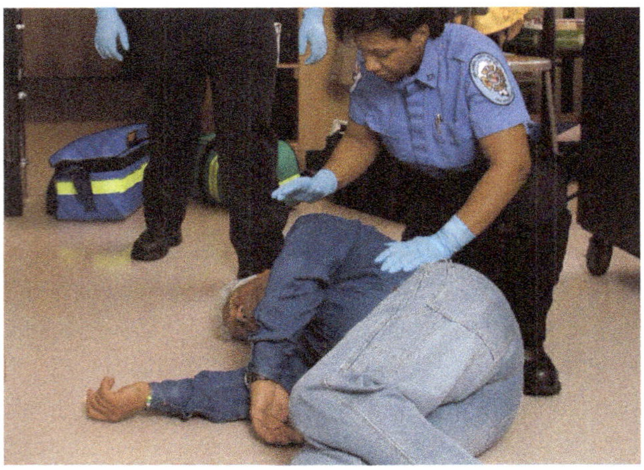

Figure 2 It is not always easy to determine whether you have a medical patient or a trauma patient.

fall, gunshot, stabbing, and explosion. Determining the MOI can assist the LER and all other levels of health care providers in knowing what injuries the patient may have sustained based on the energy transferred to the body. Some MOIs are so significant that patients may need to be transported to an appropriate trauma center even if there are no overt injuries noted during the patient assessment. If the patient has sustained a significant MOI, the LER should assume there is a cervical spine injury and take appropriate actions to protect and manually stabilize the head and neck.

PRIMARY ASSESSMENT

The purpose of the primary assessment is to identify and treat life-threatening problems, including major bleeding, airway obstructions, respiratory difficulties, and circulation issues. Techniques for correcting these life threats are discussed later in the text. As the LER approaches the patient, he or she should form a general impression. Some of the information used to form the general impression includes the following:

- Patient's age
- Patient's gender
- Overall patient appearance
- Patient's position
- Any obvious bleeding or injuries
- Whether cervical spine control is indicated

When making contact with the patient, introduce yourself and ask for consent to begin assessment and treatment. This helps in determining the patient's mental status and level of responsiveness. It also explains to the patient that you are trained to provide medical care and are there to help. Remember to position yourself in a defensive fashion that is not threatening to the patient. It is also helpful to position yourself so that you are at the same eye level as the patient.

Your first contact with the patient sets the tone for your assessment and treatment. It is important to be open and honest with information about the patient's illness or injury, and to put the patient at ease. When interviewing patients, format your questions into a conversation and ask just one question at a time. The patient may be distressed, and a calm manner from the LER could help comfort the patient. However, do not ask leading questions or provide false reassurance. Honesty and simplicity are best.

Determine Mental Status

The first step in determining mental status is to see whether the patient is conscious (awake) or unconscious (not awake). Regardless of consciousness, the next step is to determine the patient's level of responsiveness using the AVPU scale:

- **Alert.** The patient is conscious and responding appropriately to all of your questions. Standard questions that can be used to determine if the patient is alert and oriented include the following: "What is your name?" "What is the date today?" "Where are you?" "What happened?" If the patient is not alert, check to see if the patient responds to verbal stimulus.
- **Verbal stimulus.** The patient responds only to commands or your voice but is unable to answer your questions. Examples of questions to ask the patient include the following: "Can you wiggle your fingers or toes?" "Can you open your eyes?" If the patient responds to your voice, he or she is said to be responsive to verbal stimulus or voice commands. If the patient is not responsive to verbal stimulus, he or she does not respond to your voice or loud noises. Check to see if the patient responds to painful stimulus.
- **Painful stimulus.** Various ways to assess for painful response include pinching the patient's ear or fingertip, placing a nasopharyngeal airway (if indicated), or carefully performing a sternal rub. If the patient withdraws from the painful stimulus or grimaces, he or she is said to be responsive to pain. If the patient is not alert and does not respond to either verbal or painful stimulus, he or she is said to be unresponsive.
- **Unresponsive.** Remember that unresponsive patients may still be able to hear your voice and what is going on around them, so always explain what you are doing and encourage the patient to respond.

Assessing the Airway

The next step in the primary assessment is ensuring that the patient has a patent or open airway. The airway is clear if the patient is conscious, talking without difficulty, and not exhibiting signs that the airway may be obstructed (the tongue and foreign bodies are common airway obstructions). If the patient is unconscious, the airway must be opened and maintained. Two techniques used to open the airway are the head tilt-chin lift maneuver (if there is no suspected cervical spine injury) and the modified jaw-thrust maneuver (if there is suspected cervical spine injury). An airway adjunct, such as an oropharyngeal, nasopharyngeal, or King-LTD airway, can also be placed to assist in maintaining the airway if the LER is trained to use such devices. Suctioning the airway if there is blood, saliva, or other fluids present in the nose or mouth is also important. Foreign bodies or substances, including food, broken teeth, chewing tobacco, or chewing gum, may need to be manually removed from the mouth.

Assessing Breathing

Once a patent airway is established, the LER should assess the adequacy of breathing. Just because a patient appears to be breathing does not mean that the movement of air in and out of the body is adequate to support life. To determine whether breathing is adequate, the LER must look, listen, and feel to assess rise and fall of the chest, respiratory rate (one breath is a complete inspiratory and expiratory cycle), the patient's ability to talk, the patient's position or body language, sounds or noises of breathing, accessory muscle use, mental status, and skin color.

A patient who is breathing adequately will have a respiratory rate that is not too slow or too fast (approximately 12–20 breaths per minute in an adult, 20–30 breaths/min in a child, and 30–60 breaths/min in an infant). Other characteristics of adequate breathing include the ability to speak in full sentences, visible equal rise and fall of the chest, no abnormal sounds such as wheezing, and minimal work of breathing.

If the patient is having breathing difficulty, the LER should administer supplemental oxygen and look for possible causes of the difficulty. Specific causes may include traumatic injuries such as sucking chest wounds, flail segments, or broken ribs. Medical causes such as smoke inhalation, asthma, or chronic obstructive pulmonary disease (COPD) may need to be treated medicinally.

Assessing Circulation

Assessment of airway and breathing is followed by assessment of circulation. There are several assessment steps when checking circulation. First, check for major bleeding; if major bleeding is present, immediately take the appropriate steps to stop the bleeding. Be sure to complete a blood sweep underneath the patient. Second, check for pulses; check both the carotid (neck) and radial (wrist) pulses (**Figure 3**). The carotid pulse is found on either side of the neck (only check one side of the neck at a time) and can be checked by placing your index and middle finger on the larynx and sliding them into the groove on the side of the neck. The radial pulse is found in the groove on the thumb side of the wrist. The LER should be able to consistently find pulses within 5 seconds of beginning to look for them; this requires practice. Once the pulses are found, note the rate (normal, fast, or slow), strength (normal, weak, or bounding), and rhythm (regular or irregular). If there is no pulse, immediately begin cardiopulmonary resuscitation (CPR).

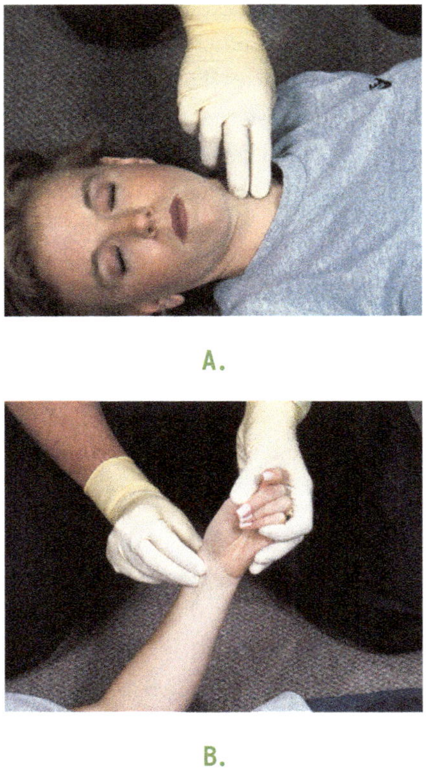

Figure 3 When assessing a patient's circulation, check both the carotid **(A)** and radial **(B)** pulses.

Next, assess the patient's skin for color, temperature, and moisture. Skin color should be pink and can be checked in the nail beds or mucous membranes around the eyes (conjunctiva) or lips. Abnormal skin color may be pale, cyanotic (blue), jaundiced (yellow), or flushed (red). Skin color abnormalities may indicate a problem with perfusion. Skin temperature should be warm to the touch—not too hot or too cold. Cool skin may indicate shock, whereas hot skin may indicate fever or heat emergency. The skin should be dry or slightly moist. Clammy skin or profuse sweating may indicate problems such as severe pain, shock, or environmental emergency.

Tip

Treat for Shock

Indications of shock include cool, clammy skin; profuse sweating; very fast or slow heart rate; and unresponsiveness to verbal stimuli. If a patient exhibits these signs, stop your assessment and treat him or her for shock. Lay the patient flat and administer oxygen at 15 liters per minute via nonrebreathing mask.

Capillary refill time is particularly helpful is assessing circulation in children. Capillary refill is assessed by pressing on the skin, especially in a nail bed, and seeing how long color takes to return (**Figure 4**). Normal capillary refill time is less than 2 seconds. The LER should be aware that temperature and environment may affect capillary refill time.

In completing the primary assessment, the LER should have identified and corrected any immediate life threats. You should also have enough information to decide whether the patient's condition is emergent, urgent, or stable.

Emergent conditions are those that will cause significant morbidity or death unless treatment is provided immediately. Conditions considered emergent include any problem maintaining an airway, difficulty breathing, circulation compromise (especially from major internal or external bleeding), and altered mental status.

Urgent, or unstable, conditions are those that will result in significant morbidity or death unless effective treatment is given within several hours. Examples of conditions considered urgent include fractures, wounds requiring surgical repair, or abdominal pain without signs of shock.

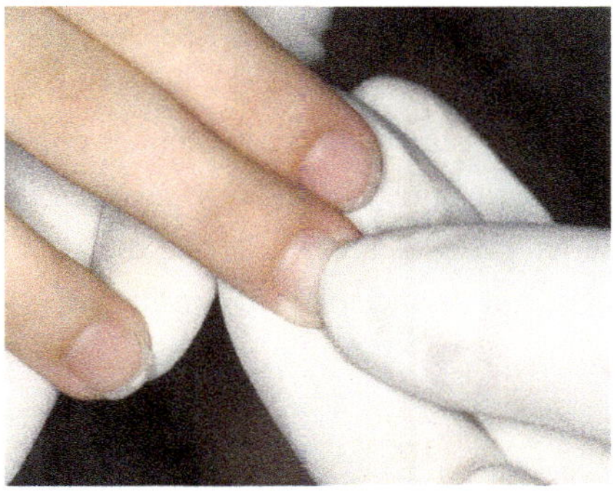

Figure 4 Capillary refill is assessed by pressing on the skin, especially in a nail bed, and seeing how long color takes to return.

Stable conditions may require treatment, but a delay in providing that treatment will not result in increased mortality or morbidity. Examples of conditions considered stable include a sprain or strain, dental pain, and minor burns.

The primary assessment should take the LER only a few minutes to complete. The length of time to complete the assessment is not as important as the thoroughness of the assessment. It is more important to check everything that needs to be checked and to identify and treat those identified life threats than to go through the motions quickly.

HISTORY TAKING

While the LER is completing the physical elements of the patient assessment, he or she must also gather information that will help paint a complete picture as to what is going on with the patient. Most of the time the patient will be the best source of information; however, if the patient is unable or unwilling to communicate, other sources such as bystanders, medical alert jewelry, family members, or clues at the scene can provide valuable information.

The first piece of information in the history is the chief complaint. The chief complaint is the reason why medical assistance was summoned to the scene. The LER can ask the patient, "Why did you call for help?" or "What seems to be the problem?" When documenting the chief complaint, the LER should use the patient's actual statement and not editorialize. For instance, if the patient states, "It feels like an elephant is sitting on my chest," the LER should repeat that exact statement as the chief complaint and not change it to "The patient has chest pain."

If not already determined during the scene size-up, or to verify information, the MOI or NOI should be confirmed. Once background information has been obtained—such as the patient's name, age, and contact information—specific information relating to the patient's medical problem should be ascertained. Use open-ended questions and allow the patient to give the information he or she feels is relevant. If the patient is not answering questions appropriately, the LER should then use more specific or pointed questions. It is more important for the LER to have a conversation with the patient than it is for him or her to just go down a list of questions.

There are two acronyms the LER can use to obtain a complete patient history. The first acronym, SAMPLE, should be used on all patients:

- **Signs and symptoms.** A sign is something the LER can see, such as flushed or pale skin, vomiting, or the patient using accessory muscles to breathe. A symptom is something the patient will tell you that he or she is feeling, such as dizziness, nausea, chest pain, or a headache.
- **Allergies.** Determine anything the patient is allergic to, such as medications, environmental allergens, foods, or insect bites. Also determine what happens if a patient is exposed to a particular allergen. For instance, if a patient says he is allergic to bee stings, ask him what happens when he is stung by a bee. Reactions can be mild, such as localized pain or swelling, to severe, such as complete swelling of the airway and significant drop in blood pressure. Previous reactions are a great indicator of future reactions, so if someone has had a severe reaction in the past, the LER should anticipate having to manage the same level of reaction.
- **Medications.** Determine whether the patient is taking any medications, including prescription medications, over-the-counter medications, home remedies, or other holistic remedies. Also determine whether the patient has been compliant with his or her medications and how long the patient has been taking the medications.
- **Pertinent medical history.** Determine whether the patient has any medical conditions currently under the care of a physician. Also determine whether the patient has experienced the same type of complaint he or she currently is experiencing in the past.
- **Last oral intake.** Determine when the patient last had something to eat or drink. This information may have an impact on anesthesia, or even a direct impact on the patient's current condition. For example, if the patient has a history of diabetes, has taken his or her insulin, but has not had anything to eat since then, the medical emergency can be explained and treated.
- **Events.** Determine what the patient was doing leading up to the current problem. For instance, was the patient performing physical activity or was he at rest when his chest pain began?

In addition to the SAMPLE history, if the patient is complaining of any type of pain, the OPQRST history should be completed:

- **Onset.** Similar to the "events" category in the SAMPLE history: what was the patient doing when the pain started?
- **Provocation/palliation.** Does anything the patient does make the pain feel better or worse?
- **Quality.** Ask the patient to describe the pain. What does the pain feel like? Common descriptions of pain include the following: dull, throbbing, sharp, stabbing, crushing, burning, and tearing.
- **Radiation.** Ask the patient if the pain moves anywhere; in other words, if the pain is worse in one area but is also felt in other parts of the body.
- **Severity.** This is a subjective finding but can aid the LER in determining the efficacy of interventions. Ask the patient how bad the pain is, on a 0 to 10 scale. For instance, someone with excruciating pain may respond that her pain is a 10, whereas someone with little pain may respond that his pain is a 1 or 2.
- **Time.** Determine when exactly the pain started. Interventions may be based on how long the injury or illness has been present.

Even though much of the information may not have a direct impact on the LER, or may even seem superfluous, it is important to complete a very comprehensive history. The LER may be the only medical responder present fast enough to get this information before a patient becomes unconscious as a result of the medical condition. If this information is not retrieved, other medical providers such as EMS or the hospital physicians may not have the information needed to treat the patient effectively. The LER should also take notes regarding the information gathered during the patient assessment and history so that this information can be included in the hand-off report. Keep in mind that history-taking will likely take longer in older patients because of the higher likelihood of multiple medications and medical conditions.

SECONDARY ASSESSMENT

Once the primary assessment has been completed and all obvious life threats have been treated, it is time to begin the secondary assessment—a systematic exam of the entire body to identify any other injuries that have not been discovered during the primary assessment. During this exam, particular focus should be on areas determined to be of concern based on the patient's complaints. As you discover specific signs, symptoms, or injuries, there may be specific relevant questions to ask or interventions to perform that will be discussed in later units of this book.

Performing the secondary assessment can be challenging for the LER because it involves exposing, inspecting (looking at), and palpating (touching) the patient's body. To ease some of the patient's concerns, the LER should explain everything that he or she is going to do before doing it and not leave the patient exposed any longer than necessary. For instance, when examining the chest, it is important to remove all clothing from that area of the body, but as soon as you are done assessing the chest, it should be immediately covered up. It may also be beneficial to place a barrier between the patient and any onlookers prior to completing the assessment. It is essential to maintain professionalism throughout the entire exam and to display compassion toward your patient and his or her family members.

Some of the physical findings for which the LER is looking can be summarized by the acronym DOTS:

- **Deformities.** Does anything appear to be misshapen or not look as it should?
- **Open wounds.** Are there any openings in the body that should not be there?
- **Tenderness.** Does anything hurt when touched or pressed?
- **Swelling.** Is there any swelling noted on the body or extremities?

Other physical findings will be assessed based on the specific body part that is being examined. It is important to document if a finding is *not* noted, because this may provide information regarding pertinent negatives. While performing the secondary assessment, it is important not only to look at the body part you are assessing, but also to watch the patient for any grimacing or other reactions he or she may have. Assess the areas of the patient's body systematically by following the steps in **Skill Drill 1**:

1. **Assess the head.** Gently feel the skull and facial bones. Note whether there are any indentations, soft spots, crepitus (bones grating together), swelling, bumps, lumps, bruises, Battle's sign (bruising behind the ears), or raccoon eyes (discoloration around the eyes) STEP 1. Also check the eyes to see if the pupils are round, equal in size, and reactive to light (both pupils should respond when a light is shone into one eye) (PEARL) STEP 2. It is important to note any blood or fluid draining from the ears, nose, and mouth, as well as any fluid or obstructions in the mouth and airway STEP 3. If any interventions were started during the primary assessment, reassess to make sure they are still providing the desired result.
2. **Assess the neck.** Feel the back of the neck for any "step-offs"—vertebrae that are not aligned on top of one another. Also feel for any tenderness or pain that the patient experiences when you touch the neck STEP 4. Check the trachea to make sure it is midline. Also look at the jugular veins to see if they are distended.
3. **Assess the chest.** Start by palpating the clavicles (collarbones) one side at a time. Then run the side of your hand down the sternum (breastbone). Feel each side of the chest to make sure the ribs are stable, attached to the breastbone, and rise and fall equally STEP 5. Also look for any bruising, flail segments, or open chest wounds. Be sure to check as far under the patient as you can access while the patient is in a supine position. You will check the remainder of the back when the patient is log rolled later in the assessment. If trained to do so, assess lung sounds at this time.
4. **Assess the abdomen.** Divide the abdomen into four sections, or quadrants, using the umbilicus (belly button) as the diving line (**Figure 5**). Palpate each quadrant, starting in the midline and moving outward. Feel for rigidity, pulsatile masses, or tenderness STEP 6. Also look for any bruising and rebound tenderness (the patient does not complain of pain when you push down on an abdominal quadrant, but does complain of pain after you release the pressure).
5. **Assess the pelvis and genitalia.** If there is no obvious injury, the pelvis should be palpated for stability by placing one hand on each pelvic bone. Gently press together, if there is no crepitus or pain, and then apply gentle pressure in a downward motion STEP 7. The external genitalia should be assessed for trauma or bleeding. In males, assess for priapism (an erection caused by a spinal injury).

Skill Drill 1

Secondary Assessment

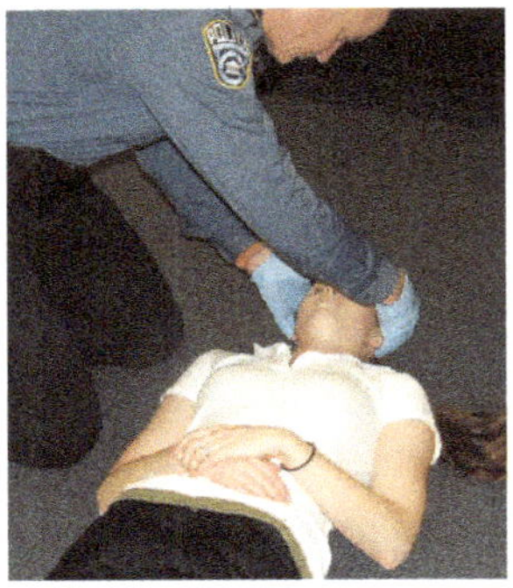

1. Observe and palpate the head.

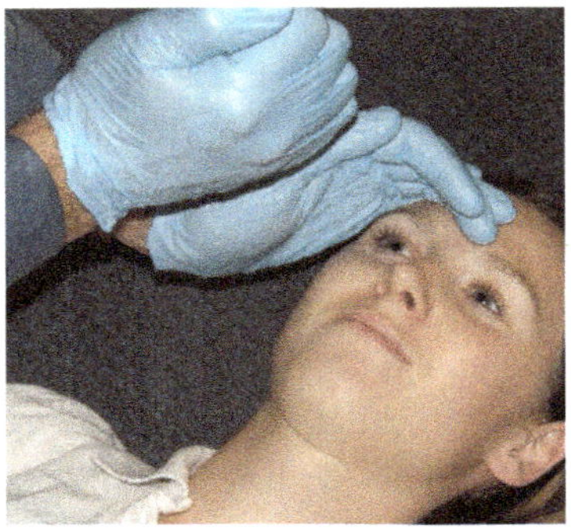

2. Assess the eyes.

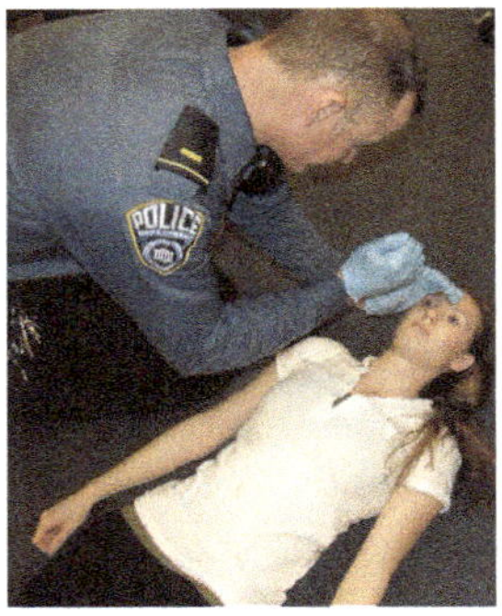

3. Check the nose and mouth for blood and drainage.

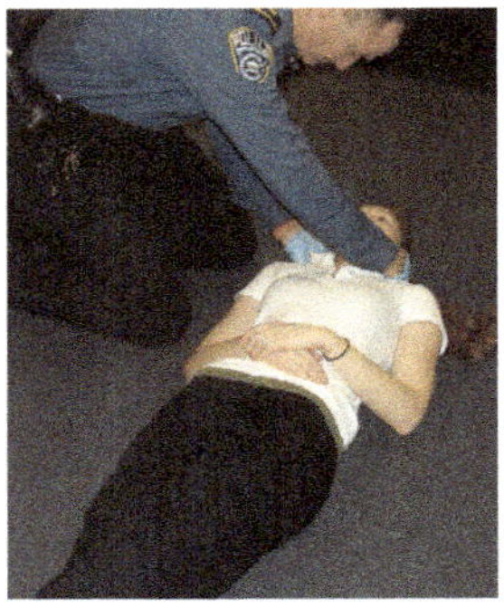

4. Assess the neck.

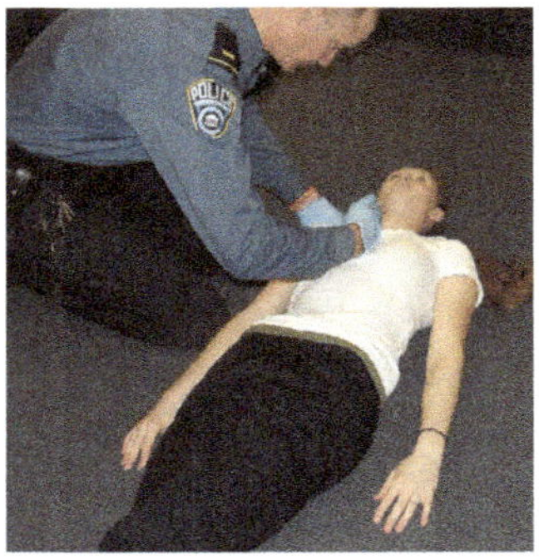

5. Assess the chest.

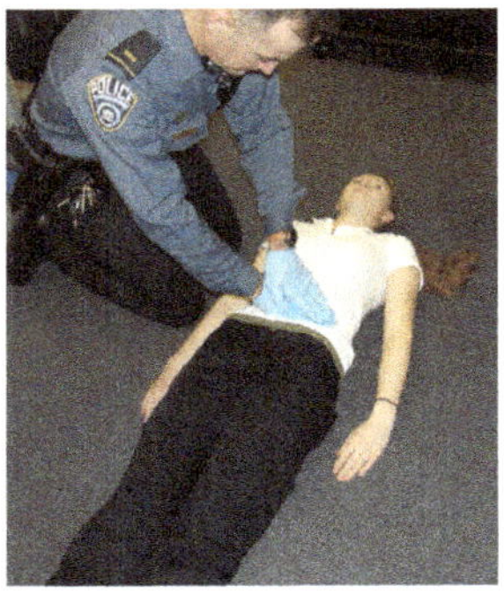

6. Assess the abdomen.

6. **Assess the legs.** Assess each leg by wrapping your hands around the leg and squeezing as you work your way down the extremity STEP 8. Feel for stability and crepitus. Check for a distal pulse, movement, and sensation in each leg.

7. **Assess the arms.** Assess each arm by wrapping your hands around the arm and squeezing as you work your way down each extremity. Feel for stability and crepitus. Check for a distal pulse, movement, and sensation in each arm.

Skill Drill 1

Secondary Assessment *(continued)*

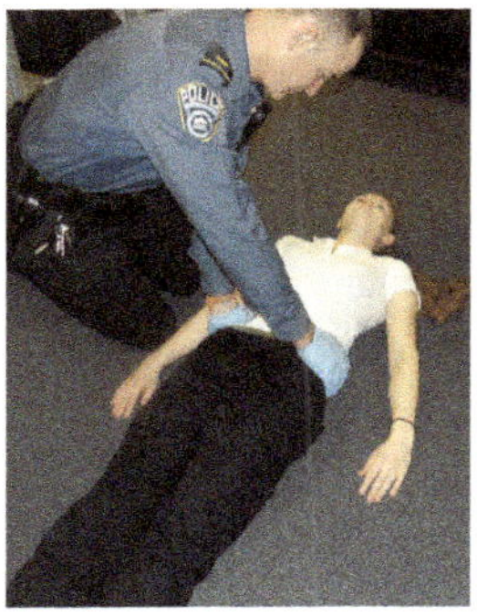

7. Gently press on the pelvic bones.

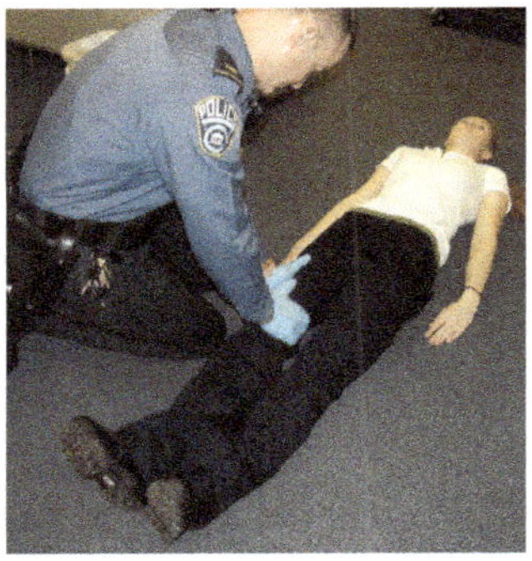

8. Assess the legs.

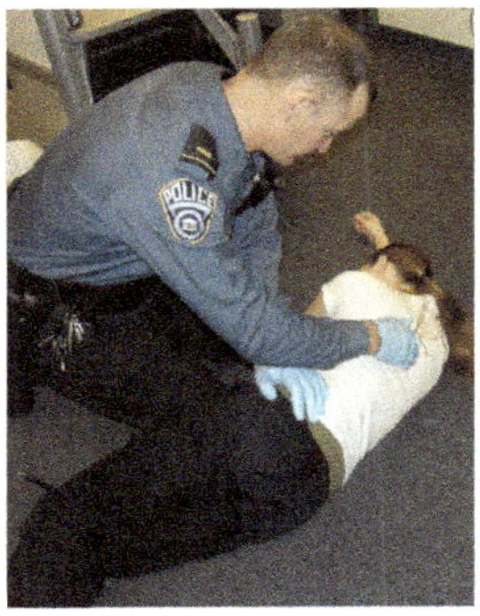

9. Log roll the patient and assess the back.

8. **Assess the back.** If there are enough rescuers available, a log roll should be performed and the posterior side of the patient should be assessed STEP 9. Ideally, the patient would be rolled directly onto a long backboard at this time.

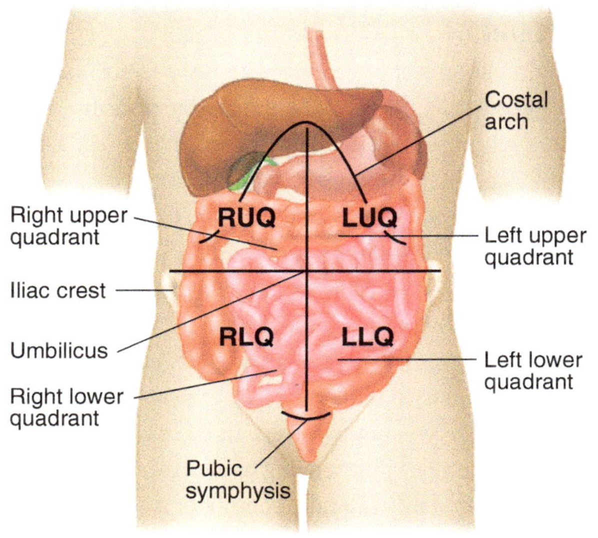

Figure 5 The four quadrants of the abdomen.

Interventions should be performed as needed. If any interventions were completed during the primary assessment, they should be reassessed during the secondary assessment to make sure they are still working and appropriate. If trained to do so, the LER should also get a full set of vital signs, including pulse rate, respiratory rate, lung sounds, pulse oximetry, blood glucose level, and blood pressure (see the units on pediatric patients and elderly patients for more information on vital signs in those populations) (**Table 1**). Upon completing the secondary assessment, the LER can also form or reaffirm the patient's status of being either stable or unstable and update responding EMS assets.

Table 1

Normal Adult Vital Signs

Assessment	Average Value
Heart rate	70 beats/min
Respiratory rate	16-20 breaths/min
Blood pressure	80/120 mm Hg
Blood glucose	70-100 mg/dL
Pulse oximetry	95-100%

Focused Assessment and Detailed Assessment

In certain circumstances a complete head-to-toe exam may not be appropriate. Some of these circumstances may include a patient who has sustained an isolated injury (eg, a person who rolls an ankle during a basketball game) and is able to communicate that there is nothing else wrong with him or her. Another circumstance that may allow the LER to forgo a complete head-to-toe exam would be a medical patient who is able to describe his or her problem.

These patients still require a physical exam; however, the exam may be focused to just the part or parts of the body the patient is telling you are involved. In the case of the patient who rolled an ankle while playing basketball, it is appropriate to check the injured leg and to compare it with the noninjured leg. It may not be appropriate, however, to assess the chest or abdomen. If there is any doubt whether a complete head-to-toe exam should be completed, the LER should do a more thorough exam.

Additionally, if an injury is found in a particular part of the body, then the LER should complete a detailed assessment of that area. A detailed assessment would involve assessing for specific findings before and after an intervention is completed.

REASSESSMENT

Once the primary and secondary assessments are completed, it is imperative that the LER consistently reassesses the patient and any interventions that have been completed. Vital signs should be assessed approximately every 5 minutes for an unstable patient and every 15 minutes for a stable patient. Compare all reassessments to the baseline status obtained during the initial assessments. Reassessing the patient's vital signs will establish a trend that will allow other medical providers to see whether a patient's condition is stable or deteriorating. It is not uncommon for an intervention to work (eg, a bandage stopping bleeding) when first put in place but to become ineffective over time. The LER should be able to identify that the intervention needs to be redone or another method of treatment put in place.

HANDOFF REPORT

All the information obtained during the secondary assessment and SAMPLE history should be recorded by the LER. Once EMS arrives, a verbal report should be given to the responding personnel or hospital, followed by a written report or record (**Figure 6**). Information to be provided in the report includes the following:

- Patient's name
- Patient's age
- History of present illness
- Medical history
- Assessment findings
- Interventions performed
- Intervention outcomes
- Vital signs
- Other pertinent information

PEDIATRIC CONSIDERATIONS

Contrary to popular belief, children are not just small adults. Anatomically, physiologically, and developmentally, they differ in many ways that are discussed specifically in the pediatrics unit. Because of these differences, the LER may need to alter his or her approach to completing a thorough patient assessment on a pediatric patient.

Some issues that need to be overcome include children's inability to understand what is wrong with them, communication, fear, and modesty. The best source of information regarding a pediatric patient may be a parent or primary caregiver. It is also helpful to have someone the child knows and trusts present while performing the assessment, unless having that individual present is upsetting to the child or is unsafe.

Despite possibly being uncomfortable performing a physical assessment on a child, the LER must do so if appropriate. If a young child is conscious, he or she may fight the LER touching them. One approach to make it less intrusive on the child is to complete a toe-to-head exam instead of a head-to-toe exam. Letting the patient have a familiar toy or stuffed animal during the exam may also make it easier for the LER to complete the assessment (**Figure 7**). Always let the child know when you are about to touch him or her or if you think something might hurt when touched, because it may be less traumatizing for the patient.

CONCLUSION

Patient assessment is one of the more important skills requiring LER proficiency. To determine what is wrong with a patient and what interventions are appropriate, the LER must perform

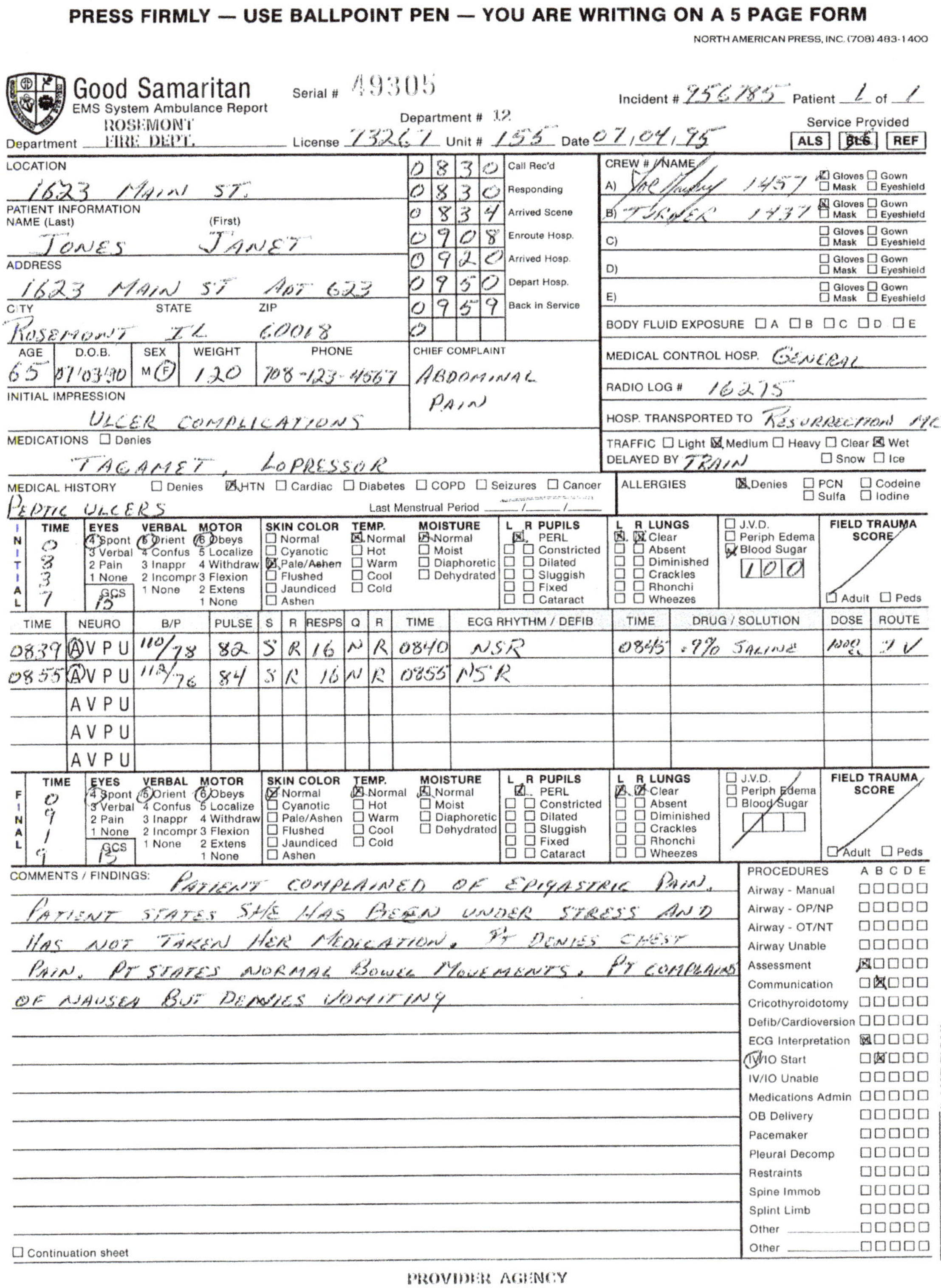

PRESS FIRMLY — USE BALLPOINT PEN — YOU ARE WRITING ON A 5 PAGE FORM

NORTH AMERICAN PRESS, INC. (708) 483-1400

Good Samaritan EMS System Ambulance Report

Serial # 49305 — Incident # 256785 — Patient 1 of 1

Department # 12

Department ROSEMONT FIRE DEPT. — License 73267 — Unit # 155 — Date 07/04/95

Service Provided: ALS / BLS / REF

LOCATION: 1623 MAIN ST.

0830	Call Rec'd
0830	Responding
0834	Arrived Scene
0908	Enroute Hosp.
0920	Arrived Hosp.
0950	Depart Hosp.
0959	Back in Service

CREW # / NAME:
A) [signature] 1457 — ☒ Gloves ☐ Gown ☐ Mask ☐ Eyeshield
B) TURNER 1437 — ☒ Gloves ☐ Gown ☐ Mask ☐ Eyeshield
C) — D) — E)

BODY FLUID EXPOSURE ☐ A ☐ B ☐ C ☐ D ☐ E

PATIENT INFORMATION
NAME (Last) JONES (First) JANET
ADDRESS 1623 MAIN ST APT 623
CITY ROSEMONT STATE IL ZIP 60018

AGE	D.O.B.	SEX	WEIGHT	PHONE
65	07/03/30	F	120	708-123-4567

CHIEF COMPLAINT: ABDOMINAL PAIN

INITIAL IMPRESSION: ULCER COMPLICATIONS

MEDICAL CONTROL HOSP. GENERAL
RADIO LOG # 16275
HOSP. TRANSPORTED TO RESURRECTION MC
TRAFFIC ☐ Light ☒ Medium ☐ Heavy ☐ Clear ☒ Wet ☐ Snow ☐ Ice
DELAYED BY TRAIN

MEDICATIONS ☐ Denies: TAGAMET, LOPRESSOR

MEDICAL HISTORY ☐ Denies ☒ HTN ☐ Cardiac ☐ Diabetes ☐ COPD ☐ Seizures ☐ Cancer: PEPTIC ULCERS

Last Menstrual Period __/__/__

ALLERGIES ☒ Denies ☐ PCN ☐ Sulfa ☐ Codeine ☐ Iodine

INITIAL: TIME 0837; GCS 15 (4 Spont, 5 Orient, 6 Obeys); SKIN COLOR ☒ Pale/Ashen; TEMP. ☒ Normal; MOISTURE ☒ Normal; PUPILS ☒ PERL; LUNGS ☒ ☒ Clear; ☒ Blood Sugar 100; FIELD TRAUMA SCORE ☐ Adult ☐ Peds

TIME	NEURO	B/P	PULSE	S	R	RESPS	Q	R	TIME	ECG RHYTHM / DEFIB	TIME	DRUG / SOLUTION	DOSE	ROUTE
0837	(A)VPU	110/78	82	S	R	16	N	R	0840	NSR	0845	.9% SALINE	1000	IV
0855	(A)VPU	112/76	84	S	R	16	N	R	0855	NSR				
	AVPU													
	AVPU													
	AVPU													

FINAL: TIME 0919; GCS 15 (4 Spont, 5 Orient, 6 Obeys); SKIN COLOR ☒ Normal; TEMP. ☒ Normal; MOISTURE ☒ Normal; PUPILS ☒ PERL; LUNGS ☒ ☒ Clear; FIELD TRAUMA SCORE ☐ Adult ☐ Peds

COMMENTS / FINDINGS: PATIENT COMPLAINED OF EPIGASTRIC PAIN. PATIENT STATES SHE HAS BEEN UNDER STRESS AND HAS NOT TAKEN HER MEDICATION. PT DENIES CHEST PAIN. PT STATES NORMAL BOWEL MOVEMENTS. PT COMPLAINS OF NAUSEA BUT DENIES VOMITING

PROCEDURES (A B C D E): Assessment ☒ (A); Communication ☒ (B); ECG Interpretation ☒ (A); IV/IO Start ☒ (B)

☐ Continuation sheet

PROVIDER AGENCY

Figure 6 The LER must complete a written report for each patient.

a methodical assessment. Information gathered during the assessment will follow the patient through his or her entire treatment pathway, both out of hospital and in hospital, so it must be complete and concise. Using a tiered approach to patient assessment will ensure that life-threatening issues are corrected first, followed by anything else that the LER may do to have a positive impact on the patient. Each patient will be unique and present challenges, but by having a similar approach with each patient the LER should not miss any life threats.

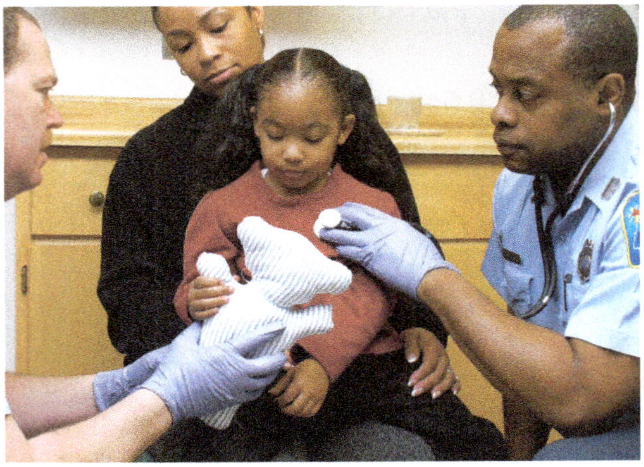

Figure 7 Letting a child have a familiar toy or stuffed animal during the exam may make it easier for the LER to complete the assessment.

Prep Kit

READY FOR REVIEW

- Every patient you encounter will need to be assessed; assessments vary based on the situation, but be ready to perform some type of patient assessment on all patients you encounter.
- There are several stages to completing a thorough patient assessment: the scene size-up, the primary assessment, the secondary assessment, history taking, the reassessment, and the handoff report.
- Factors that should be taken into account during the emergency response include weather, traffic, time of day, additional resources, number of reported patients, and special considerations.
- If the scene is not safe, it is the responsibility of the LER to attempt to make the scene safe or to evacuate to a safe location.
- Standard precautions should always be used when there is a chance that you may come in contact with any body fluids.
- One of the first pieces of information instrumental in determining the appropriate care of a patient is determining whether the patient is sick (a medical patient) or injured (a trauma patient).
- The purpose of the primary assessment is to identify and treat life-threatening problems, including major bleeding, airway obstructions, respiratory difficulties, and circulation issues.
- The airway is clear if the patient is conscious, talking without difficulty, and not exhibiting signs that the airway may be obstructed (the tongue and foreign bodies are common airway obstructions).
- Once a patent airway is established, the LER should assess the adequacy of breathing. Just because a patient appears to be breathing does not mean that the movement of air in and out of the body is adequate to support life.
- There are several assessment steps when checking circulation. Check for major bleeding; carotid and radial pulses; and skin color, temperature, and moisture.
- While the LER is completing the physical elements of the patient assessment, he or she must also gather information that will help paint a complete picture as to what is going on with the patient.
- There are two acronyms the LER can use to obtain a complete patient history:
    - SAMPLE (signs and symptoms, allergies, medications, pertinent medical history, last oral intake, events)
    - OPQRST (onset, provocation/palliation, quality, radiation, severity, time)
- The secondary assessment is a systematic exam of the entire body to identify any injuries not discovered during the primary assessment. Particular focus should be on areas determined to be of concern based on the patient's complaints.
- Once the primary and secondary assessments are completed, it is imperative that the LER consistently reassesses the patient and any interventions that have been completed.
- Once EMS arrives, a verbal report should be given to the responding personnel or hospital, followed by a written report or record.
- Because of anatomic, physiologic, and developmental differences, the LER may need to alter his or her approach to complete a thorough patient assessment on a pediatric patient.

VITAL VOCABULARY

mechanism of injury (MOI) The way in which traumatic injuries occur; the forces that act on the body to cause damage.

nature of illness (NOI) The general type of illness a patient is experiencing.

CHECK YOUR KNOWLEDGE

You arrive at the scene of a motor vehicle crash and are tasked with patient care until EMS arrives. The crash involved a single vehicle that drove into a tree at relatively high speed. There is significant front-end damage to the car. The scene has been secured by other officers.

1. During which phase of the assessment would you determine how many patients were involved in the crash?
   - **A.** Scene size-up
   - **B.** Primary assessment
   - **C.** Secondary assessment
   - **D.** Reassessment
2. While you are assessing the driver of the vehicle, he tells you that his right leg hurts, and you can see that it is deformed. This patient's chief complaint would be noted as:
   - **A.** possible loss of consciousness from the impact.
   - **B.** reckless driving.
   - **C.** right leg injury.
   - **D.** right leg injury secondary to motor vehicle crash.
3. The purpose of the primary assessment is to identify and treat life-threatening injuries.
   - **A.** True
   - **B.** False
4. Which acronym should be used to ascertain the patient's medical history?
   - **A.** OPQRST
   - **B.** DOTS
   - **C.** SAMPLE
   - **D.** SLUDGEM
5. What information should NOT be included in the hand-off report to EMS?
   - **A.** Speed of the vehicle during impact
   - **B.** Citations issued
   - **C.** Restraints, such as seatbelts and airbags, in use
   - **D.** Treatments performed

Assessment in **Action**

SCENARIO

Upon arrival to a single-family residence to assist during a medical emergency, you find a 56-year-old woman who is sitting in the tripod position in a chair and working hard to breathe. She appears to be pale, is breathing fast, and is restless.

ACTIONS

1. This initial gathering of information would have been done during which phase of the assessment?
   - **A.** Scene size-up
   - **B.** Primary assessment
   - **C.** Secondary assessment
   - **D.** Focused assessment
2. Which assessment should be performed next?
   - **A.** Scene size-up
   - **B.** Primary assessment
   - **C.** Secondary assessment
   - **D.** Reassessment
3. Which body system would probably not be involved in this emergency?
   - **A.** Cardiovascular
   - **B.** Respiratory
   - **C.** Digestive
   - **D.** Nervous
4. Based on the information on hand, you can say this patient is unstable.
   - **A.** True
   - **B.** False
5. What would be another indicator that the patient is in respiratory distress?
   - **A.** Delayed capillary refill
   - **B.** Unequal pupils
   - **C.** Accessory muscle use
   - **D.** Difficulty swallowing

SECTION 4

Resuscitation

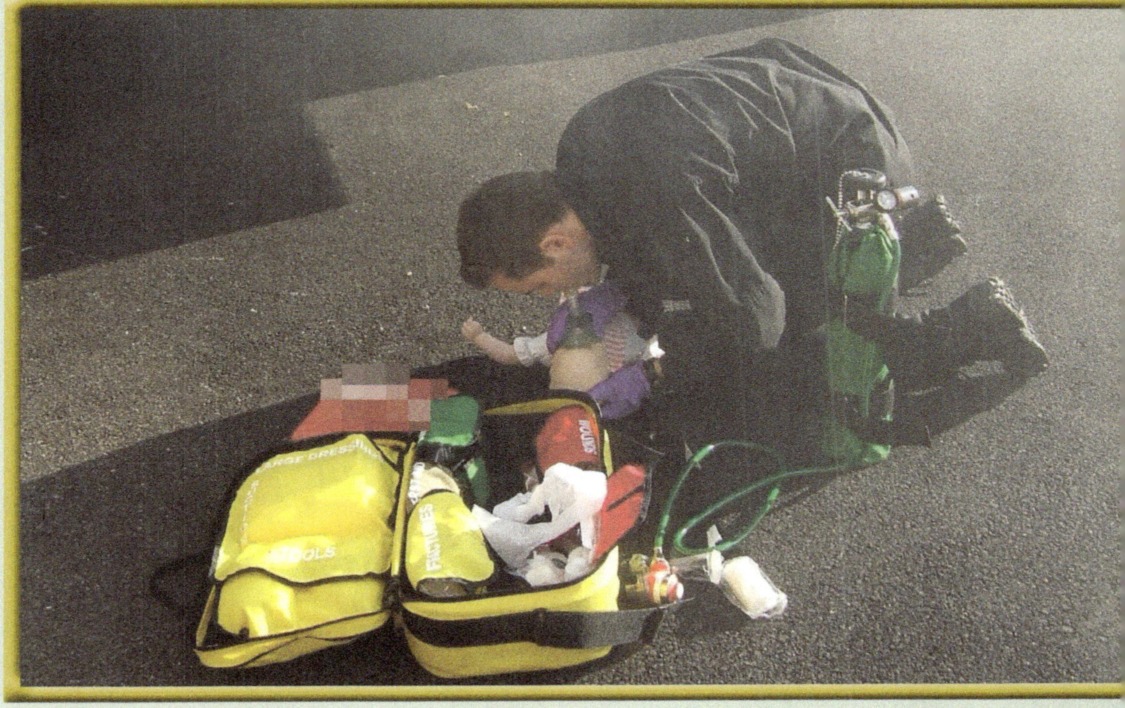

Section Contents

Airway, Breathing, and Oxygenation

Unit 10

Michael Hite

Law Enforcement Responder Objectives

- Describe the anatomy and physiology of the respiratory system. (pp 189–190)
- Identify initial steps to assess and manage an airway. (pp 190–198)
- Discuss how to identify and treat blocked airways. (pp 192–194)
- List common airway obstructions. (pp 192–193)
- Describe manual airway maneuvers. (pp 194–196)
- Identify basic adjuncts available to maintain the airway. (pp 196–197)
- Discuss the types of advanced airway management available to EMS. (p 198)
- Identify initial steps to assess and manage breathing. (pp 198–206)
- Define the role of oxygen in emergency medicine. (p 200)
- Discuss the proper storage and use of oxygen in the field. (pp 200–204)
- Compare normal ventilation to positive pressure ventilation. (p 206)
- Discuss age-specific considerations regarding airways, breathing, and oxygenation. (pp 206–207)

National EMS Education Standard Competencies

Airway Management, Respiration, and Artificial Ventilation

Applies knowledge (fundamental depth, foundational breadth) of general anatomy and physiology to ensure a patent airway, adequate mechanical ventilation, and respiration while awaiting additional emergency medical services (EMS) response for patients of all ages.

Airway Management

- Airway anatomy (pp 189–190)
- Airway assessment (pp 190–192)
- Techniques of ensuring a patent airway (pp 194–198)

Respiration

- Anatomy of the respiratory system (pp 189–190)
- Physiology and pathophysiology of respiration (pp 189–190)
  - Pulmonary ventilation (pp 189–190)
  - Oxygenation (pp 189–190)
  - Respiration (pp 189–190)
    - External (pp 189–190)
    - Internal (pp 189–190)
    - Cellular (pp 189–190)
- Assessment and management of adequate and inadequate respiration (pp 200–204)
- Supplemental oxygen therapy (p 200)

Artificial Ventilation

Assessment and management of adequate and inadequate ventilation:

- Artificial ventilation (p 204)
- Minute ventilation (pp 189–190)
- Alveolar ventilation (pp 189–190)
- Effect of artificial ventilation on cardiac output (p 204)

Medicine

Recognizes and manages life threats based on assessment findings of a patient with a medical emergency while awaiting additional emergency response.

Respiratory

Anatomy, signs, symptoms, and management of respiratory emergencies, including those that affect the:

- Upper airway (pp 189–207)
- Lower airway (pp 189–207)

INTRODUCTION

The movement of air in and out of the body, and the transfer of gases at the cellular level, is crucial to life. Adequate breathing requires a patent airway and functioning respiratory system. Without the delivery of oxygen to the brain, irreversible damage can occur in as few as 4 to 6 minutes. Maintaining an open airway may seem simple, but failure to take action to open an airway can result in death. Law enforcement responders (LERs) routinely provide airway assistance to save the lives of those they serve. LERs who understand how to open and maintain an airway, support breathing, and operate an oxygen system will give ill and injured patients their best chance of survival.

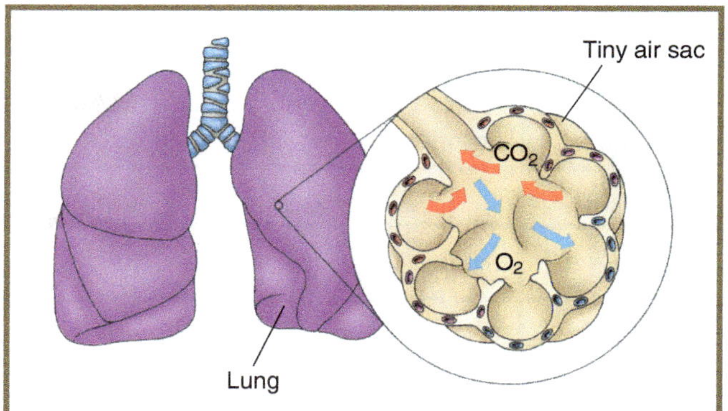

Figure 1 The exchange of carbon dioxide (CO_2) and oxygen (O_2) in the lungs.

RESPIRATORY ANATOMY AND PHYSIOLOGY

The respiratory system is one of the most important systems in the body. If the respiratory system is compromised, then the organism will have problems getting oxygen and eliminating carbon dioxide. Movement of air in and out of the body is called **ventilation**, whereas the exchange of gases in the lung or cellular level is called **respiration**. Respiration cannot take place without ventilation of air that has adequate amounts of oxygen. Once good gas, oxygen, is exchanged for waste gas, carbon dioxide, in the lungs, the circulatory or cardiovascular system can deliver nutrient-rich blood to the rest of the body, so that the nutrients can be used by the cells (cellular respiration).

The major organs associated with the respiratory system are the lungs. There are two lungs, a left and a right. **Alveoli** are the functional units of the lung in which oxygen and carbon dioxide exchange takes place via inhaled air. Alveoli are round, thin, balloonlike structures wrapped in thin blood vessels (**Figure 1**).

Lungs do not have muscle; they rely on the muscles between the ribs (intercostal muscles) to move the chest off the shoulder girdle, and the **diaphragm** to push down on the abdomen. When the diaphragm pushes down on the abdomen, the chest expands, creating a vacuum and allowing air to run into the alveoli of the lungs. To maintain the vacuum seal in the chest, the space between the rib cage and the lungs has one piece of clear tissue lining the inside of the ribs and another wrapping the lung surface. Between the linings is a small amount of clear pleural fluid. This space is called the pleural space. Damage to either layer can allow air or blood to rush into the space and impair the vacuum needed to expand the lungs.

When the rib muscles and diaphragm relax, they create a positive pressure that forces the air out. The process of breathing in is called **inspiration**; the process of breathing out is called **expiration**. Ventilation is the process of inspiration and expiration (**Figure 2**). The exchange of oxygen and carbon

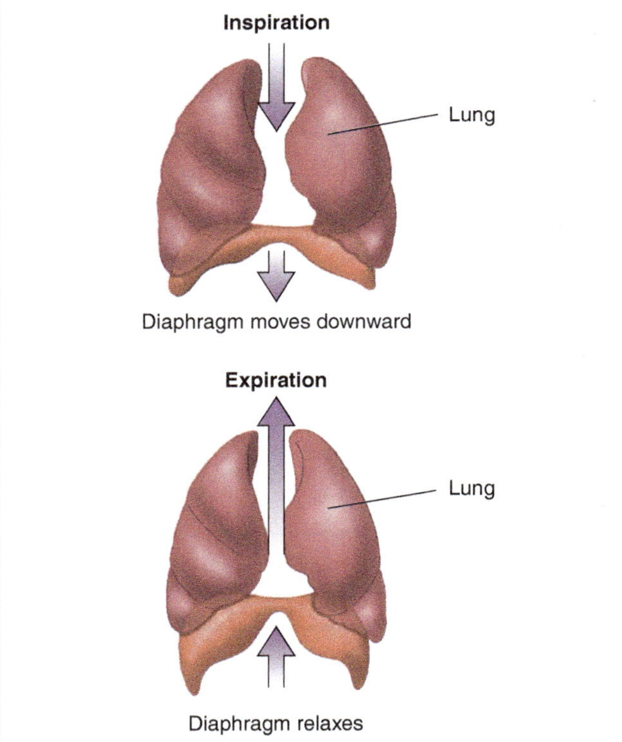

Figure 2 Mechanism of breathing.

Table 1

Structures of the Airway

Structure	Description
Upper Airway	
Nares	The openings into the nose.
Nasal cavity	The opening inside the nose.
Lips	The opening into the mouth.
Oral cavity	The opening inside the mouth, behind the lips.
Pharynx	The cylindrical cavity between the nasal cavity (nasopharynx), oral cavity (oropharynx), and larynx (laryngopharynx).
Tongue	The muscle in the bottom of the mouth used for speech, taste, and movement of food.
Epiglottis	The muscular flap at the base of the tongue that acts as a valve to cover the lower airway.
Esophagus	Although not part of the upper airway, it originates in the back of the mouth and is the tube that takes food to the stomach.
Lower Airway	
Larynx	The opening into the trachea; it is made of cartilage and contains the vocal cords.
Trachea	The breathing tube that travels down the neck into the chest.
Bronchi	The tubes (one for the right lung and one for the left lung) that come off the trachea in the chest. Bronchi are wrapped by smooth muscle that allows the tubes to get larger (dilate) or smaller (constrict). They are also supported by cartilage.
Bronchioles	Smaller tubing that branches off the bronchi and joins to the air sacs.
Alveoli	The air sacs that are wrapped with capillaries. These air sacs are the location at which oxygen from the inhaled air enters the blood in the capillaries and carbon dioxide leaves the blood for the air in the air sac.

dioxide that occurs in the alveoli is called **alveolar ventilation**. The amount of air pulled into the lungs and removed from the lungs in one minute is called **minute ventilation**.

Ventilation and respiration are the two components of breathing. If the airway is closed or even partially obstructed, breathing is affected and an emergency responder must ensure that the airway is open and that the patient is either breathing on his or her own or is being ventilated. The **airway** comprises the structures that take air from the nose or mouth down to the alveoli (**Table 1**). As the air travels through the airway and comes in contact with the lining, it is warmed, humidified, and cleansed (**Figure 3**). The lining of the airway is made up of specialty tissue called **mucous membranes**. This tissue secretes **mucus**, a sticky substance to aid in cleaning and humidifying the air. The mucous membranes are full of small blood vessels and can swell to deal with temperature changes in the air.

AIRWAY ASSESSMENT AND MANAGEMENT

Airway Assessment

LERs can rapidly assess the patency of an airway through minimal interaction, and such interaction can provide valuable information on a patient's condition. Medical providers assess an unconscious patient's airway by looking for an unobstructed airway and for equal and full chest rise and fall, listening for air movement and respirations, and feeling for air movement from the mouth or nose (the look, listen, and feel technique).

Conscious patients are assessed with the same look, listen, and feel methodology, but the assessment process is slightly different. A conscious patient who can speak in full sentences with no difficulty has a patent airway and is moving adequate amounts of air. During conversation, LERs should also assess the tone and quality of a patient's voice. Although some abnormal sounds will be obvious to the LER, asking awake and alert patients if their voice sounds normal to them can offer insight to prevent missing more subtle clues of impending airway obstruction.

Signs of an Inadequate Airway

Patients who are unconscious or have an altered level of consciousness present the greatest likelihood for having an inadequate or unsecured airway. Focus your assessment on the

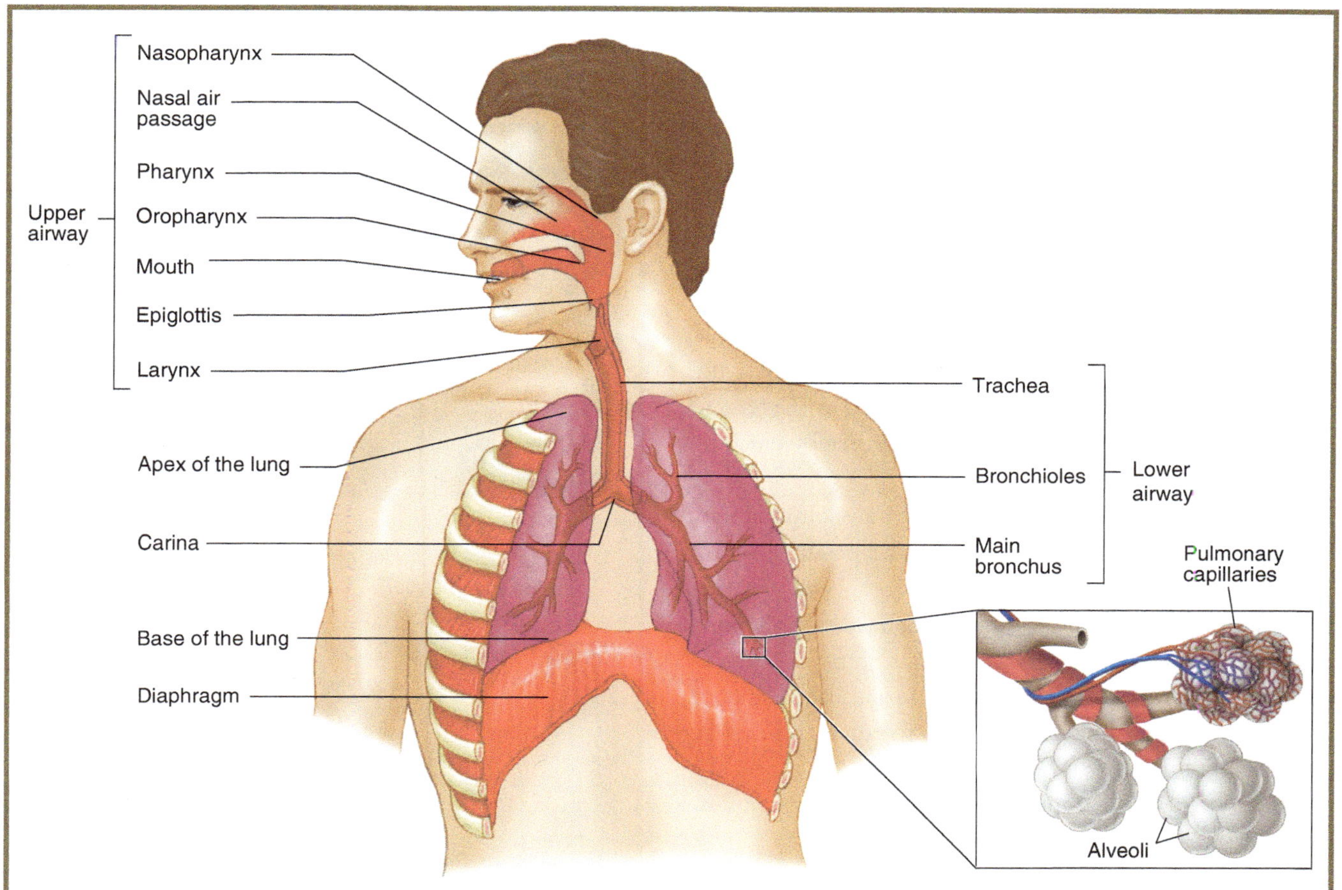

Figure 3 The upper and lower airways contain the structures in the body that help us breathe.

same look, listen, and feel premise as described previously. Early indicators of an inadequate or partially obstructed airway are abnormal noises heard during the process of ventilation. A high-pitched noise heard mainly with inspiration is called **stridor** and represents a narrowing of the upper airway. Causes of stridorous respiration include allergic reactions, inhalation injuries, foreign body obstructions, and croup with children. Snoring respirations are present most frequently in patients with a significantly decreased level of consciousness or patients who are unconscious, caused when the tongue relaxes and partially obstructs the airway. This scenario can be treated by repositioning the patient in the recovery position, opening the airway with the head-tilt chin lift or modified jaw thrust maneuver, or by using airway adjuncts as appropriate.

Patients who are awake, alert, and able to speak may be able to inform responders that their voice sounds different, or that their throat feels suddenly and abnormally hoarse. These signs can be indicative of increased swelling found with smoke or steam inhalation injuries. Consider any other potential causes of sudden-onset swelling, and take a history of preceding events from patients who can speak. Doing so will assist you in finding the cause of the problem.

Unconscious patients with complete airway obstruction, as a result of either medical or traumatic etiologies or inappropriate positioning, will not be moving air. The chest wall may make minimal movement or no movement at all, depending on the scenario. If this scenario continues unresolved, the patient will quickly become **apneic** (not breathing). This is a true emergency and must be treated and resolved quickly to ensure there is no progression to full cardiac arrest.

Airway Obstruction

Airway obstruction can have a number of different causes, all of which require immediate assessment and potential intervention. Common obstructions include the tongue, food, vomit, blood, teeth, and foreign bodies.

The tongue is a frequent cause of airway obstruction. In unconscious patients, muscle relaxation causes the tongue to move freely inside the mouth. If these patients are lying supine, the airway can be completely occluded by the relaxed tongue as it falls backward into the throat, thereby blocking air passage into the trachea and lungs.

Regardless of how well dissolved or how soft food may be, any and all food substances create the potential for an airway obstruction. Pieces of food may completely obstruct the airway and may not be visible to the responder looking for a quick resolution. LERs should focus on quick and correct identification of the possibility that food caused complete airway obstruction and should attempt to rapidly resolve the situation with the use of the Heimlich maneuver. To assist a conscious patient with a complete airway obstruction, follow the steps in **Skill Drill 1**.

1. Ask, "Are you okay? Can you speak? Can I help you?" If there is no verbal response, assume that the airway obstruction is complete **STEP 1**.
2. Stand behind the patient and position the thumb side of your fist just above the patient's navel **STEP 2**.
3. Grasp the fist with your other hand and press into the patient's abdomen with quick inward and upward thrusts **STEP 3**. Repeat the abdominal thrusts until either the foreign body is expelled or the patient becomes unresponsive.
4. If the patient is obese or in the late stages of pregnancy, use chest thrusts instead of abdominal thrusts. Chest thrusts are done by standing behind the patient and placing your arms under the patient's armpits to encircle the patient's chest. Press with quick backward thrusts.
5. If the patient becomes unresponsive, perform CPR.

Vomit can rapidly occlude the airway, especially if there is a high volume of vomit. As with food, however, complete airway obstruction can occur with a minimal amount of vomit. Vomit and other foreign objects and fluid can be cleared using a mechanical suction device if available, although something as simple as a gloved finger sweep can clear significant quan-

Skill Drill 1

Performing the Heimlich Maneuver

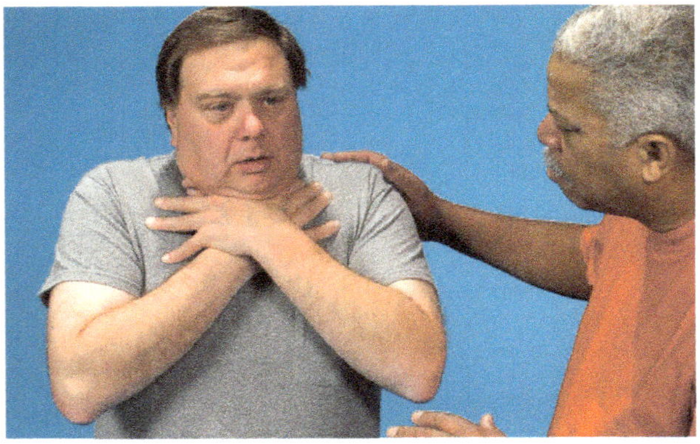

1. Look for signs of choking and ask, "Are you okay? Can you speak? Can I help you?"

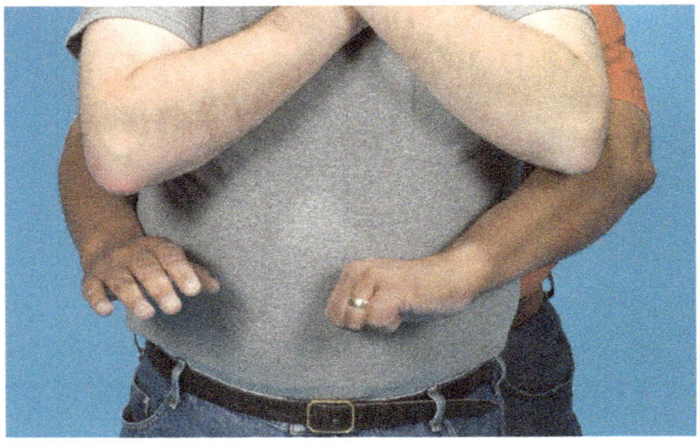

2. Place your fist with the thumb side against the patient's abdomen, just above the navel.

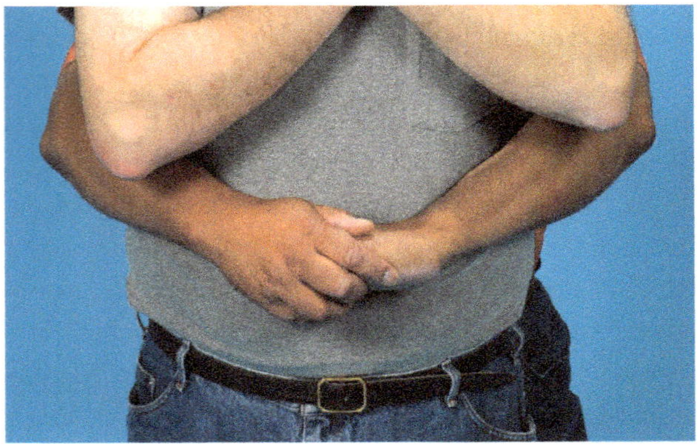

3. Grasp the fist with your other hand and press into the abdomen with quick inward and upward thrusts.

tities of foreign material. It is important to use caution when performing a gloved finger sweep, because the patient can bite down unexpectedly and injure you. Always place a bite block of some sort prior to putting a finger in a patient's mouth.

As with food and vomit, a small amount of blood can occlude an airway and hinder effective ventilation. Of special consideration for LERs is the cause of the bleeding, because the bleeding may be difficult to control in the prehospital environment. In addition to clearing the airway to allow for ventilation, you should focus on positioning the patient in a manner that will facilitate drainage of blood away from the airway. For example, in immobilized patients, angling the backboard slightly can facilitate drainage and the continued patency of the airway.

Teeth that have been knocked loose create a significant problem for medical responders, creating a scenario with a foreign body obstruction and the potential for uncontrollable bleeding. In addition to clearing the airway of active obstructions, you should focus on patient positioning for continued maintenance of a patent airway. Further, it is important to evaluate the oral cavity for other teeth that are loose and that have the potential to cause additional obstruction. Remember to keep the cervical spine immobilized when clearing or protecting an airway in a patient with facial trauma or head or neck trauma.

Any foreign body that can fit inside the mouth has the potential to completely obstruct the airway. As with all other obstructions, responder interventions should be focused on clearing the obstruction and subsequently maintaining a patent airway.

Swelling as a result of trauma or infection can also obstruct a patient's airway. Traumatic etiologies include both penetrating and nonpenetrating injuries. Nonpenetrating blunt trauma can cause internal bleeding and bruising that creates occlusive swelling (swelling that will block the airway). For example, patients in motor vehicle crashes may have direct injury to their trachea, causing constriction due to crush injury and disruption of the tracheal rings, or swelling of soft tissue around the upper airways. Penetrating injury tracts can encapsulate bleeding, creating pockets of rapidly swelling tissue that can hinder airflow. These injuries are often seen with small-diameter stab wounds to the throat or small-caliber rounds that may or may not exit the body.

Medical causes of tissue swelling can include epiglottitis (swelling and inflammation of the epiglottis), asthma, allergic reactions, or other reactive airway illnesses or can be related to masses resulting from cancer. Injuries and infections such as those described here create significant problems for responders because there is little effective treatment short of definitive surgical intervention.

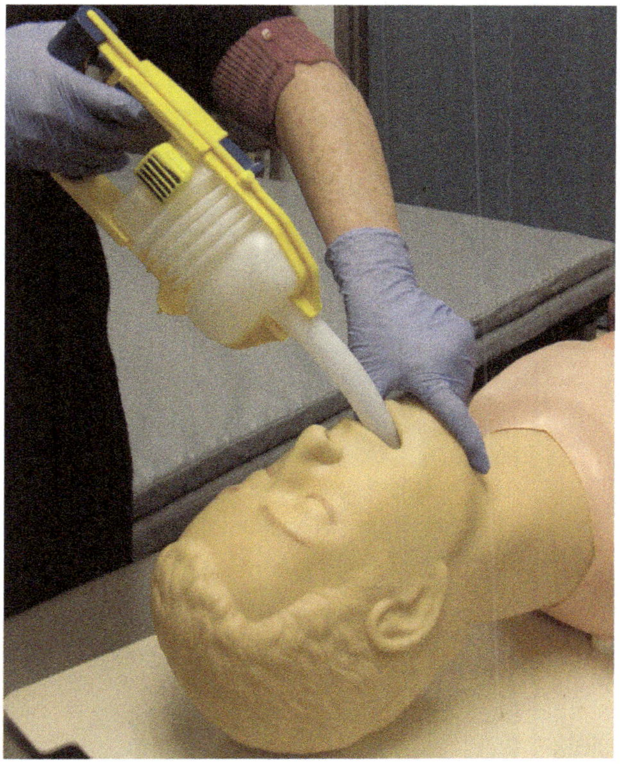

Figure 4 Suction units provide a means to clear airways of liquids, vomit, partially digested foods, and other soft substances.

Managing the Airway

LERs must be familiar with other techniques to clear airways of obstructions, and a frequently used skill is upper airway suctioning. Suction units provide a means to clear airways of liquids, vomit, partially digested foods, and other soft substances (**Figure 4**).

Although there are a variety of suction units and catheters that can be used in patients, the technique is the same (**Skill Drill 2**):

1. Turn on the assembled suction unit **STEP 1**.
2. Measure the suction catheter by holding it up against the side of the patient's face and noting the distance between the earlobe and corner of the mouth **STEP 2**. Use only the measured amount of catheter when placing it in the airway.

Skill Drill 2

Suctioning a Patient's Airway

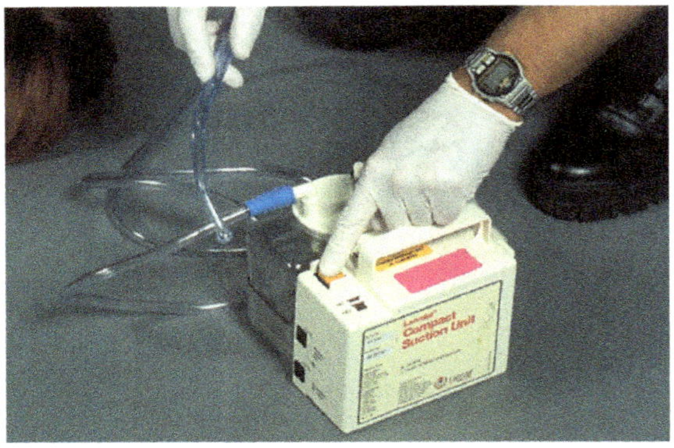

1. Make sure the suctioning unit is properly assembled and turn it on.

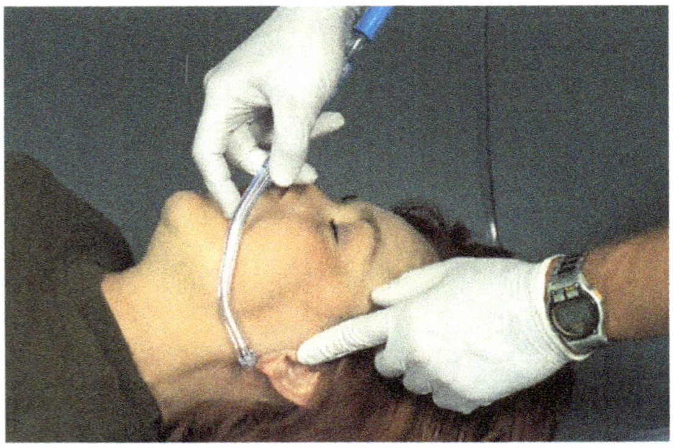

2. Measure the suction catheter from the corner of the mouth to the earlobe or angle of the jaw.

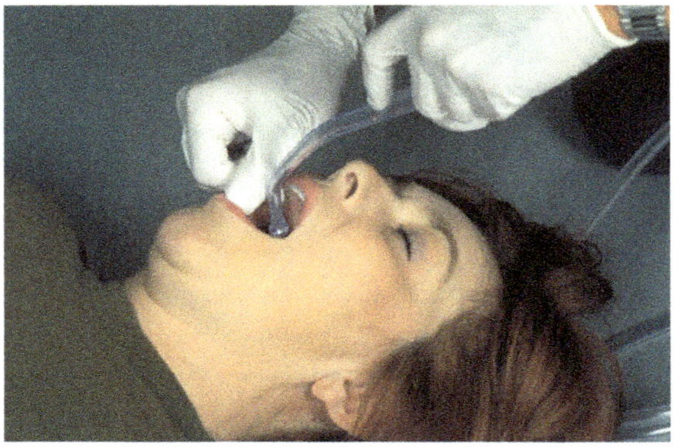

3. Open the patient's mouth and insert the suction catheter to the depth measured.

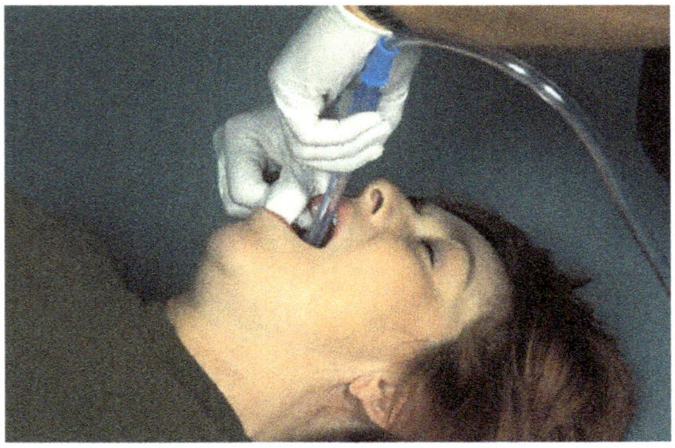

4. Apply suction in a circular motion as you withdraw the suction catheter. Do not suction an adult for more than 15 seconds.

3. Place the suction catheter to the depth measured into the patient's mouth STEP 3 and then apply suction while withdrawing the suction catheter STEP 4.

Many catheters used with mechanical suction devices have a hole that must be covered to apply the suction. When the hole is not covered, the catheter will not be actively suctioning material. Manual suction units require suction to be created by squeezing the handle of the device. Suction should not be applied for more than 15 seconds at a time in patients who do not have total airway obstruction. In patients whose airways are completely obstructed, the priority is to clear the airway in the shortest amount of time possible.

Suction catheters that are rigid plastic can cause damage to the fragile oral tissue if used too vigorously by medical providers. The softer, more flexible catheters, however, frequently become obstructed when suctioning large amounts of vomit (**Figure 5**). Use your discretion when choosing suctioning equipment, based on the scenario at hand.

Airway Management Techniques

Manual Airway Maneuvers

Head Tilt-Chin Lift Maneuver

The head tilt-chin lift maneuver is used in unconscious patients whose airway is blocked or occluded, potentially by the relaxed tongue displaced over the trachea. A simple and easy maneuver for one responder, this technique can be used quickly and easily to open the airway by lifting the tongue from the posterior airway, permitting spontaneous respiration in patients who are

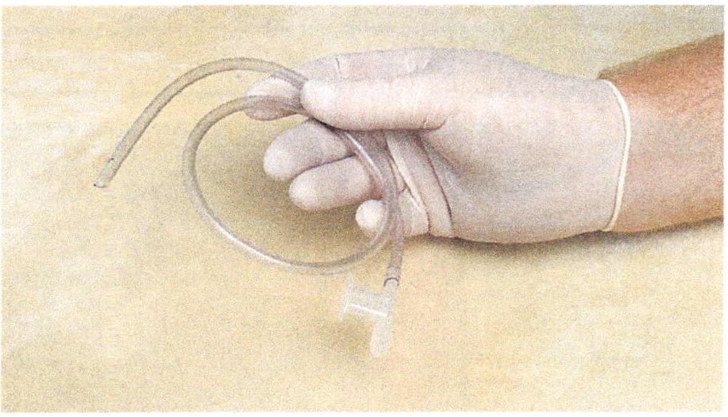

Figure 5 Softer, more flexible catheters can be helpful in certain situations where a rigid catheter is not ideal, but they may be more likely to be obstructed during suctioning.

able to breathe on their own. In patients who are in full respiratory arrest, this procedure will maximize the opening of the airway, allowing for effective ventilation through mechanical means. It is important to note that this procedure should be attempted on those without evidence or mechanism of injury that could have resulted in trauma to the head or neck, because it involves moving the neck and the potential for greater injury of the spinal cord in the event of a cervical spine fracture.

The procedure for performing the head tilt-chin lift maneuver begins with the supine positioning of the patient. After taking position next to the head of the patient, place one hand on the forehead of the patient and two fingers of the other hand on the bony prominence of the chin. At the same time, tilt the chin upward while pushing down on the forehead (Figure 6). Pay close attention to ensure that the mouth is not being pushed closed in the process and that the procedure opens the airway. The jaw-thrust maneuver allows for the airway to be opened without moving the neck and also enables the responder to hold manual C-spine stabilization while performing the technique.

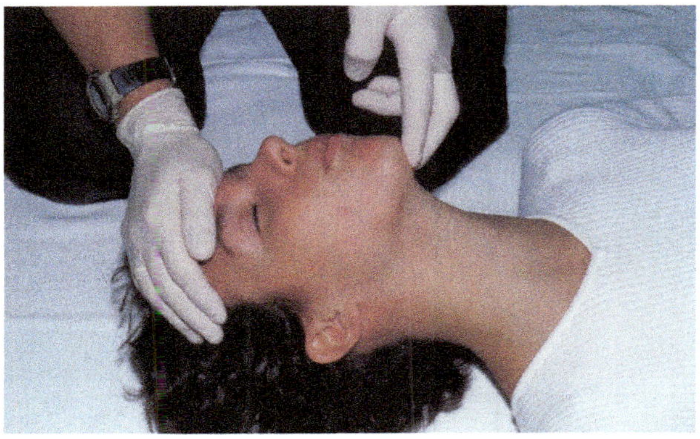

Figure 6 Open the patient's airway using the head tilt-chin lift maneuver.

Jaw-Thrust Maneuver

The jaw-thrust maneuver is another method to open the patient's airway. This technique should be used instead of the head tilt-chin lift maneuver when the patient is suspected of having an injury to the cervical spine. For example, in scenarios involving motor vehicle crashes, diving injuries, or significant falls where there is high potential for a neck injury, the jaw-thrust maneuver should be the first technique used to open the airway.

To perform the jaw-thrust maneuver, position yourself at the head of the supine patient. Using both hands to maintain cervical spine alignment, place your index fingers at the angle of the jaw (Figure 7). Apply upward pressure to the angle of the mandible. As the mandible moves upward, the tongue is lifted

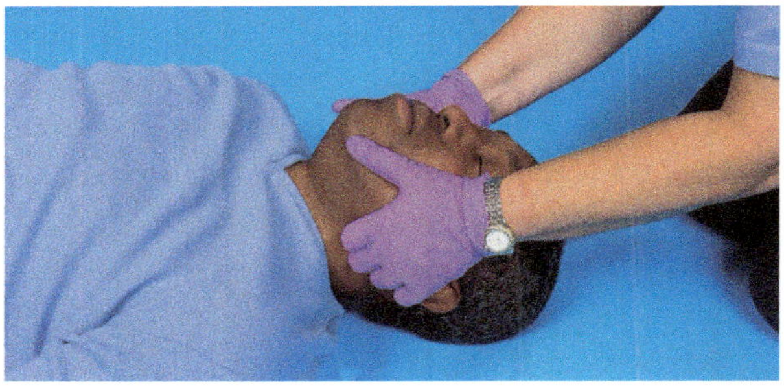

A.

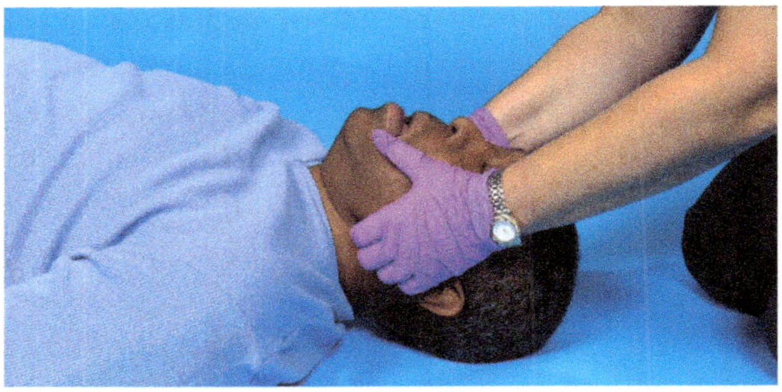

B.

Figure 7 The jaw-thrust maneuver should open the patient's airway without extending the neck. A. Kneeling above the patient's head, place your fingers behind the angles of the lower jaw and push the jaw upward. Use your thumbs to help position the lower jaw. B. The completed maneuver should look like this.

with the mandible and displaced from the posterior airway, allowing for respiration or for ventilation support.

In the event that you cannot open the airway using this technique, attempt the head tilt-chin lift maneuver even in the presence of a suspected cervical spine injury. Opening the airway takes precedence over maintaining C-spine control.

Mechanical Airway Devices

Oropharyngeal Airway

An **oropharyngeal airway (OPA)** is a rigid plastic device designed to prevent the tongue from falling back in the posterior oropharynx in patients who are unconscious or obtunded and unable to manage their own airway. As the tongue falls back in the unconscious patient, the tongue blocks the opening of the trachea, preventing the movement of air. The jaw-thrust maneuver lifts the jaw and the tongue, resolving the airway occlusion. Correct placement of the OPA accomplishes the same thing by holding the tongue away from the posterior airway. Once the OPA is properly in place, the responder may not need to continue pushing on the mandible to maintain the open airway. The device will hold the tongue off the trachea. After opening the airway using either the head tilt-chin lift or modified jaw-thrust maneuver, follow these steps to insert an OPA (**Skill Drill 3**):

1. The OPA is sized from the corner of the patient's mouth to the tip of the earlobe **STEP 1**.
2. Once it is correctly sized, insert (the OPA) upside down along the roof of the patient's mouth until you feel resistance **STEP 2**.
3. Rotate the airway 180° until the flange comes to rest on the patient's lips or teeth **STEP 3**.

When placed using the 180° technique, the tip of the OPA runs along the roof of the patient's mouth until posteriorly placed, at which point the OPA is rotated to align with the patient's anatomic curvature. This method limits the chances of pushing the tongue further back into the oropharynx, thereby compounding the occluded airway.

The OPA should not be used in patients who have an active gag reflex. Placement of the OPA in patients with a gag reflex may elicit an episode of vomiting, potentially creating a further airway obstruction and clinical issues as a result of aspiration of the vomit.

The OPA, as with other airway adjuncts, can cause bleeding in a patient's mouth if placed roughly or incorrectly, compounding airway obstruction. Additionally, incorrect sizing of the OPA can result in incorrect seating of the OPA and further airway obstruction.

Skill Drill 3

Inserting an Oropharyngeal Airway

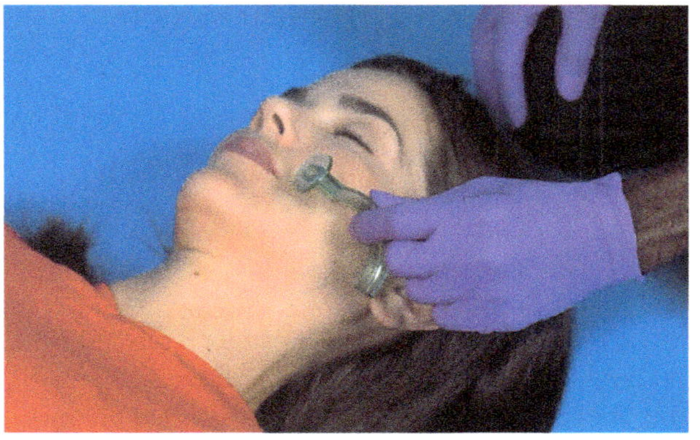

1. Size the OPA by measuring from the patient's earlobe to the corner of the mouth.

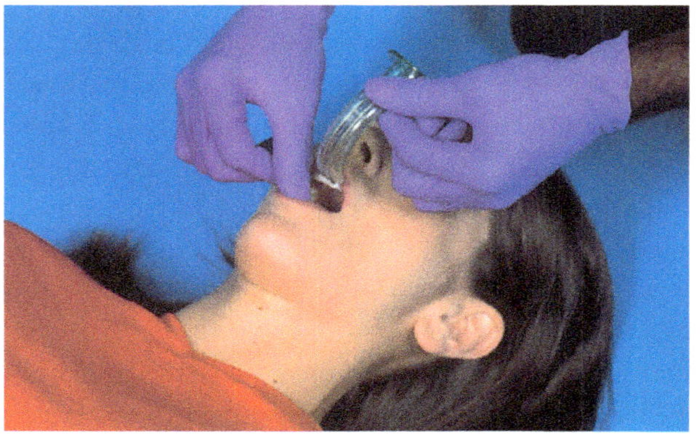

2. Insert the OPA upside down along the roof of the patient's mouth until you feel resistance.

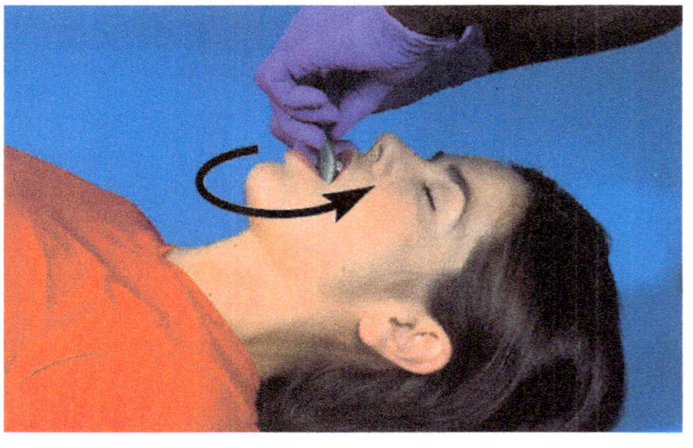

3. Rotate the airway 180° until the flange comes to rest on the patient's lips or teeth.

It is important to note that the OPA is not a definitive airway, meaning it neither prevents aspiration nor isolates the trachea from the esophagus. The OPA's role is to lift the tongue from the posterior airway, thereby allowing the passage of oxygen with mechanical ventilation. Patients who tolerate an OPA must have some form of definitive airway placed upon reaching either advanced life support (ALS) providers or an emergency department.

Nasopharyngeal Airway

The **nasopharyngeal airway (NPA)** is a semirigid rubber tube that is placed in a patient's nare to facilitate the flow of supplemental oxygen. The NPA can be placed in all patients, although those who are awake find the procedure uncomfortable and are unlikely to tolerate placement.

The NPA is used frequently in patients who have an altered level of consciousness or are lethargic and who have a gag reflex, thereby making it impossible to use an (OPA). Although the NPA creates a passage that facilitates the intake of supplemental oxygen, it does not secure the airway. Like the OPA, the NPA does nothing to limit or prevent aspiration.

The NPA is contraindicated in patients with known nasal septal structural deficits and should be used cautiously with patients who are known to be on blood thinners because there is a possible risk of traumatic injury with insertion. Never use an NPA in a patient with a head injury who has fluid or blood draining from the nose or evidence of severe fantail trauma, as the device could penetrate the patient's brain, causing severe injury.

Placement of the NPA is relatively straightforward and made significantly easier by the use of a sterile water-based lubricant or jelly. Follow the steps in **Skill Drill 4** to insert an NPA:

1. Size the NPA by measuring the distance from the patient's nare to the tip of the earlobe STEP 1.
2. Apply lubricant to the NPA, then insert it along the right nare with the bevel side sliding against the septal wall STEP 2. The right nare is larger than the left in a majority of the population; however, this is not a guarantee that NPA placement in the right nare will be successful. If you cannot place the NPA in the right nare, attempt to place it in the left nare.
3. As you advance the NPA through the nare, turn it so the NPA's curvature follows the natural curvature of the nasal anatomy STEP 3.

Skill Drill 4

Inserting a Nasopharyngeal Airway

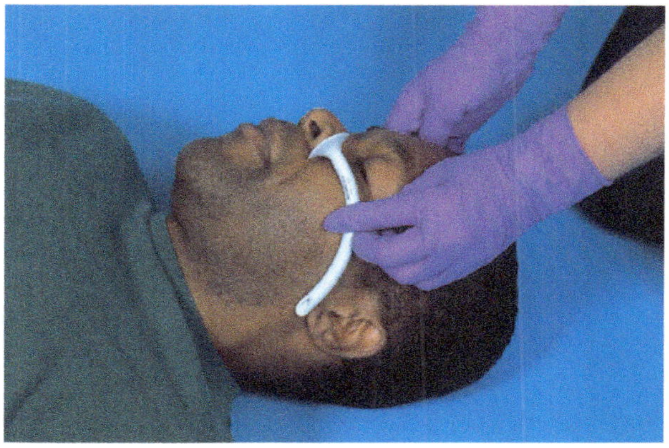

1. Size the airway by measuring the distance from the patient's earlobe to the tip of the nose.

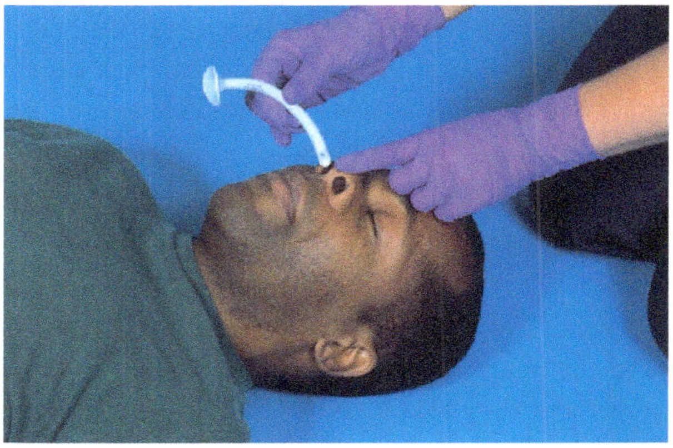

2. Insert the lubricated airway into the right nostril.

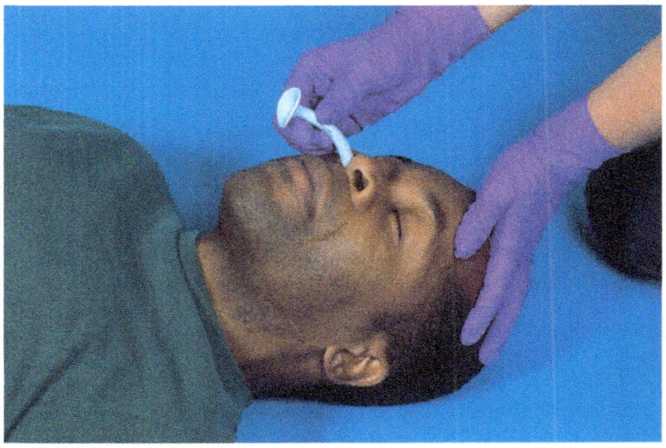

3. Advance the airway until the flange rests against the nose.

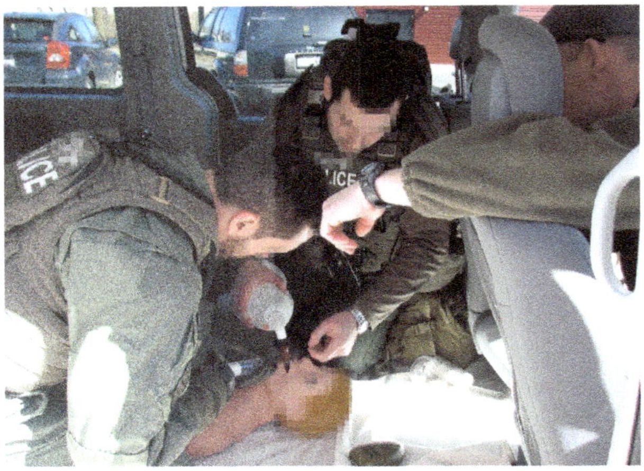

Figure 8 The King LT-D is one example of a blind insertion device used by certain BLS and ALS providers.

Advanced Airways

Advanced airways are not considered a part of the LER skill set, but LERs work with other responders who use advanced airways and may need to assist during placement or use of these devices after they are placed.

Blind Insertion Devices

A blind insertion device is designed for rapid insertion into the airway of a patient without respiratory effort and without a gag reflex (**Figure 8**). These devices are used in hospitals and in emergency medical systems throughout the country as either a primary adjunct airway management device or a **failed airway device**, meaning that an ALS provider has been unsuccessful in attempts to secure the airway through endotracheal intubation (a tube placed directly into the trachea). Blind insertion devices such as the King LT-D can be inserted without direct visualization of the trachea, secured via the single-fill air bladder, and used to ventilate a patient regardless of location in the airway. For this reason, these devices are frequently referred to as "rescue airways," rescuing a previously unsuccessful attempt to secure a patient's airway.

The air bladders on rescue devices all serve the same purpose: to block the esophagus to prevent reflux of gastric contents into the trachea and to allow air and oxygen to pass directly into the trachea and lungs.

Rescue devices should only be placed in patients without a gag reflex. Placement of the device in patients with a gag reflex may induce vomiting and will significantly increase the risk of aspiration of stomach contents. Additionally, these rescue devices should not be placed in patients who have ingested caustic materials.

Blind insertion devices have a number of limitations. They are generically sized for a range of patient heights and do not take into account the specificity of each individual's anatomic differences. Also, given that patient sizes are grouped, there is a minimum and maximum patient size for which the device is either too big or too small and therefore should not be used. Blind insertion devices are not as effective as endotracheal intubation at securing the trachea, meaning that there is always a risk of aspiration of stomach contents. Also, blind insertion devices require additional equipment, such as syringes, which increases the complexity of the procedure.

Blind insertion devices are relatively simple to insert. In a supine patient who has no respiratory effort or gag reflex, the lower jaw and tongue are lifted, either with a laryngoscope or by grabbing the jaw in hand and lifting in an upward motion. With the patient's head positioned in a midline fashion, the properly sized blind insertion device is inserted to the device-specific marking point, usually a line on the device itself. With devices that have sequential air bladders that are filled, air is injected in the correct order. In single-lumen (one tube), single-balloon devices such as the King LT-D, the balloon is filled and the syringe used to inject the air is disconnected. Patient ventilation is performed after attaching the bag-mask device to the blind insertion device, by squeezing the bag at the appropriate ventilation rate (determined by the patient's needs). Once the device's position has been confirmed, usually by the presence of lung sounds, the blind insertion device is secured with either tape or a commercial airway holder.

BREATHING ASSESSMENT AND MANAGEMENT

LERs can gain valuable information regarding their patients' respiratory status from an initial look at the patient. When not in any respiratory distress and breathing normally, patients have equal inspiration and expiration times, are able to speak in full sentences, and appear comfortable.

When breathing abnormally, patients may present with a respiratory rate that is too fast or too slow. Speech may be limited to short sentences; occasionally, only one-word answers may be possible. When sitting, patients in respiratory distress may appear shifty or fidgety, trying to find a position that allows for maximum air passage through the respiratory tract. These visual cues give responders an early idea about a patient's respiratory status. Similarly, breathing can be diminished as a result of secretions in the upper airway or in the lungs themselves. When conditions such as these are present, patients can present with gurgling sounds on inspiration, expiration, or both.

All patients who are exhibiting difficulty breathing or respiratory distress should receive supplemental oxygen. The degree of respiratory difficulty and the environment dictate the amount of supplemental oxygen that is administered by the responder.

Supplemental oxygen for patients breathing adequately on their own is primarily provided by nasal cannula or nonrebreathing mask. Patients who have minimal or no inherent respiratory effort and who are cyanotic and/or unresponsive should be considered candidates for mechanical ventilatory support via bag-mask device.

Assessment of Respiration

Assessment of the respiratory status of a patient should include a thorough evaluation that can be performed in less than 30 seconds as a rapid scan. The first indication of whether and how a patient is breathing can be noted from across the room or at a distance as responders enter the scene. Responders are quickly able to determine whether the respiratory rate is fast, slow, or nonexistent. Additionally, poor oxygenation causes a patient to have a pale or bluish tint around the lips and eyes, on the palms, and in the oral mucosa. This condition is known as **cyanosis**. Decreased oxygenation can lead to an altered mental status and abnormal behavior. Accordingly, patients with altered mental status must receive supplemental oxygen, and responders should ensure that oxygenation and ventilation problems are not the root cause of the altered mental status.

Patients find a physical position that permits the easiest breathing and permits the greatest amount of air passage. A patient who is positioned in a sitting, tripod position is having difficulty breathing. A patient with difficulty breathing will frequently be flaring his or her nostrils in an attempt to increase the passage of oxygen.

Although a talking patient is a breathing patient, breathing may not be adequate. The speech pattern of a patient gives significant information about his or her respiratory status. A patient who is able to speak in only short, one- or two-word sentences is exhibiting difficulty breathing. This is an appropriate time to evaluate the use of accessory muscles in the neck and the chest. If the patient is using muscles in these areas to assist in breathing, LERs should administer supplemental oxygen, perform a more thorough evaluation of the event at hand, and plan for patient transport to the hospital. Patients in respiratory distress may also use abdominal muscles in an attempt to move more air in and out of their lungs. The greater the degree of accessory muscle usage, the greater the degree of respiratory distress the patient is experiencing. LERs should keep in mind that if not treated promptly, patients experiencing significant respiratory distress eventually tire and may lose all respiratory effort.

During evaluation for accessory muscle use, evaluate the chest wall for integrity, making sure it is in one piece, any abnormal movement, or other signs of trauma or abnormal functionality. Areas of the chest wall that move in the opposite direction as the rest of the chest wall indicate an area of multiple rib fractures known as a flail chest and represent a significant problem for respiration. During inspiration, one side of the chest may move while the other side does not, indicating asymmetric chest wall movement. Patients or LERs may use a pillow or a blanket, or even their hand, to effectively splint areas of injury. Previous blunt injuries may present with bruising. Penetrating injuries may not always be readily obvious during a rapid scan, but must be considered, especially in cases where patients are unconscious or unresponsive. Regardless of the mechanism of injury, pain and deformity hinder respiration and the movement of air in and out. These are important findings and must be addressed.

Additionally, LERs can gain significant information on the respiratory condition of the patient from any noises that are present during respiration. Gurgling noises can represent secretions or other fluids in the upper airway, or a partial obstruction. **Wheezing** is a high-pitched, continuous whistling sound produced when air is moved under pressure through the narrow bronchi or bronchioles in the lower airways. The narrowing of these airways often occurs from asthma, an allergic reaction, inflammation, or deep airway burns. Wheezing is best heard when listening to breath sounds using a stethoscope. Wheezing can be representative of both upper and lower airway constriction. Both sounds require further investigation and treatment. Other abnormal sounds are also indicators of respiratory distress or airway problems.

Patients who are found unconscious and occasionally gasping for air should be treated as if they were not breathing at all. They require prompt initiation of mechanical ventilation with supplemental oxygen (**Figure 9**).

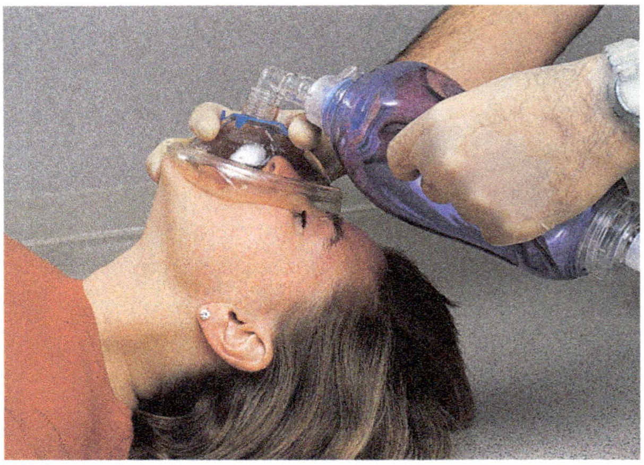

Figure 9 An unconscious patient who is occasionally gasping for air should receive mechanical ventilation with supplemental oxygen.

Management of Adequate and Inadequate Respiration

LERs must assess patients rapidly to ensure a patent airway. Using manual techniques such as the head tilt-chin lift maneuver in unconscious and unresponsive patients helps responders secure the airway. Patients found to be apneic (not breathing) and unresponsive are candidates for a more secure method of airway management, including a blind insertion device or other ALS intervention. LERs should always assess the environment for hazards. In some cases, inadequate respiration may be a result of toxic or oxygen-deficient atmospheres. If you are concerned about the integrity of the environment, consider removing the patient from the potentially hazardous atmosphere.

Supplemental Oxygen Therapy

Supplemental oxygen therapy is a standard among emergency medical services (EMS) systems in the United States. Illness or injury always places patients at risk for a reduction in oxygen in the cells in their body. If these cells do not receive enough oxygen, they will not perform properly and may actually build up acids that decrease the patient's chance of survival. If the affected cells are part of the cardiovascular system or central nervous system, the damage may be devastating to the patient's survival.

Oxygen makes up about 21% of the gases found in air. Altitude also plays a role in the amount of oxygen available to the body. Many respiratory diseases make it difficult for the patient to receive enough oxygen from the normal amount found in air. Injuries and other illnesses may require more oxygen from the blood than is normally available. Supplemental oxygen applied early by emergency responders is thought to help correct these deficits. Supplemental oxygen is also indicated for patients who have been rescued from low-oxygen environments such as confined spaces and fires. LERs should never enter a low-oxygen environment without the proper protective equipment and training.

Oxygen Cylinders

LERs should be trained to use supplemental oxygen. In the law enforcement setting, oxygen tanks may not be readily available. Advance planning on oxygen tank placement and oxygen delivery strategies should be a part of any high-risk program. Oxygen cylinders may not be readily available during forward operations (**Figure 10**). In some cases the medical director may indicate that oxygen should be available in high-risk areas, and the LER will need to obtain special packaging and devices.

Tip

Access to Oxygen

Never withhold oxygen from any patient who might benefit from it, especially if you must assist ventilations.

Oxygen increases the rate of combustion. It does not explode or burn. If oxygen comes in contact with any heat source, it may create a larger fire or an explosion of the material that is already burning. A small, smoldering fire can dramatically turn to a roaring fire in an oxygen-rich atmosphere.

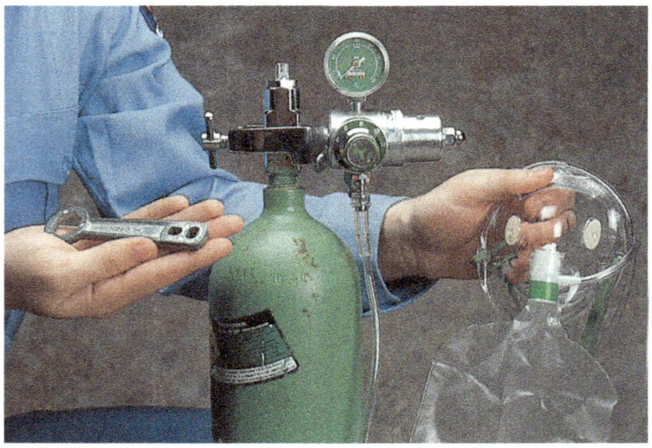

Figure 10 Oxygen administration equipment.

Oxygen should never be used around any ignition source. Avoid use in poorly ventilated areas; areas where hazardous materials are present; and near or around open flames such as cigarettes, candles, or cooking appliances.

Oxygen is a compressed gas and must be transported in cylinders. These cylinders are usually charged to a level of 2,000 psi. To contain this pressure, the cylinder must be made of strong materials, the most common of which are steel and aluminum. Medical aircraft often use a special tank—an aluminum tank wrapped with polycarbon fibers—designed to reduce weight. Never leave a tank standing upright where it is susceptible to falling. Tanks should always be stored safely to prevent falls; crushing; accumulation of grease, oil, gasoline, or dust; punctures; and exposure to heat.

Oxygen cylinders in the United States are painted green. When determining whether the oxygen cylinder you have should be used, look for a label indicating that the cylinder contains medical-grade oxygen. If your agency does not label the cylinders, ensure that you purchase only medical-grade oxygen. Industrial oxygen does not receive adequate screening for impurities and is not ideal for human use. Oxygen cylinders receive a hydrostatic test to determine whether they can safely hold up to the pressures required to compress gas within them. If a cylinder has not been tested or its test date has expired, oxygen suppliers cannot safely fill the cylinder. To determine whether your cylinder is compliant with testing, look at the collar for a series of letters and a date stamp.

The neck of the cylinder, which sits above the collar, is where the responder accesses the gas inside. Most EMS or health care systems use a neck on small portable cylinders that contains a gas outlet with a series of two pins that ensures that only regulators built for use with oxygen can be used on the cylinder (**Figure 11**). This pin-indexing system was developed by the compressed gas industry to prevent the mistakes that can occur when using odorless, colorless, tasteless, volatile gases. Larger cylinders use a threaded port on the neck that is known as the American Standard System. Responders should take time to familiarize themselves with their local practices because there is some variation of these systems in the United States.

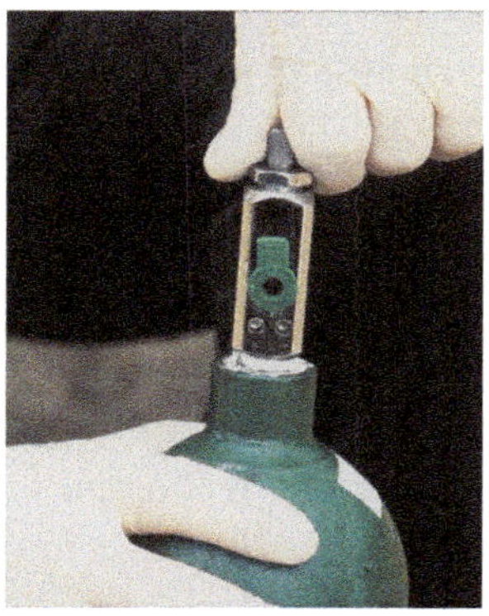

Figure 11 A valve stem with pin-index holes.

Oxygen cylinders come in many different sizes. They are assigned a letter from A through K to rate their volume (**Table 2**). The most common in EMS programs are the D, super D, and E cylinders. Some law enforcement programs use the small A tank in rapid response kits. M and larger tanks are typically found secured for use in ambulance or vehicle oxygen systems. Tanks that are free-standing should always be mounted with approved safety hardware provided by the compressed gas industry.

Regulators

It is not appropriate to use the gas directly from the cylinder. The pressure must be controlled so that the gas may be delivered in the desired dose to the patient you are treating. To ensure proper delivery of this gas, a **regulator** is applied to the neck of the cylinder (**Figure 12**). A regulator is a device that takes the cylinder pressure (2,000 psi) and reduces it to 40 to 70 psi. The gas is channeled through the regulator and distributed in various ways using different ports. Some regulator ports use the pressure to operate resuscitators or suction units. Other ports are reduced so they can be adjusted to administer oxygen at liters-per-minute (LPM) doses. Typically, the LPM range goes from 1 to 15 or from 1 to 25. Some EMS systems configure their regulators to provide a wider range of LPM settings. If you operate inside an emergency vehicle that has an onboard oxygen system, flowmeters are typically

Table 2

Oxygen Cylinder Sizes

Size	Volume in Liters
D	350
Super D	500
E	625
M	3,000
G	5,300
H, A, K	6,900

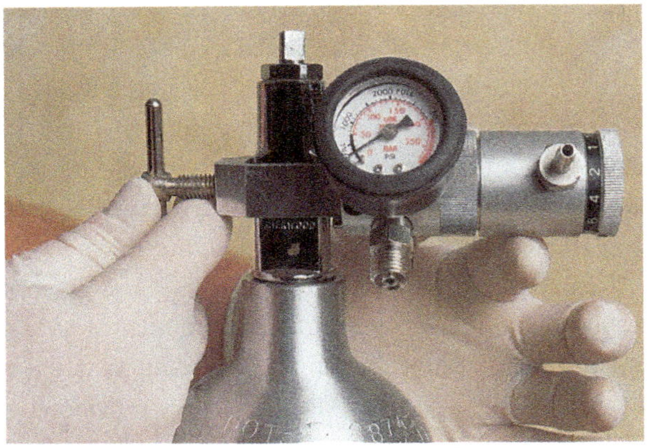

Figure 12 The regulator/flowmeter attaches to the outlet of the oxygen cylinder.

attached to wall ports and allow the rescuer to adjust the LPM dose. Some EMS systems attach small tanks of water to their flowmeters to humidify the oxygen. The LER should become familiar with his or her routine equipment.

Operating Procedures

To place an oxygen cylinder into service, follow the steps in **Skill Drill 5**.

1. Inspect the cylinder and its markings. If the cylinder was commercially filled, it will have a plastic seal around the valve stem covering the opening in the stem. Remove the seal, and inspect the opening to make sure that it is free of dirt and other debris. The valve stem should not be sealed or covered with adhesive tape or any petroleum-based substances. These can contaminate the oxygen and can contribute to combustion when mixed with pressurized oxygen.

   "Crack" the cylinder by slowly opening and then reclosing the valve to help make sure that dirt particles and any possible contaminants do not enter the oxygen flow. Never face the tank toward yourself or others when cracking the cylinder. Open the tank by attaching an oxygen wrench to the valve and rotating the valve counterclockwise. You should be able to hear clearly the rush of oxygen coming from the tank. Close the tank by rotating the valve clockwise **STEP 1**.
2. Attach the regulator/flowmeter to the valve stem after clearing the opening. On one side of the valve stem, you will find three holes. The largest one, on top, is a true opening through which the oxygen flows. The two smaller holes below it do not extend to the inside of the tank. They provide stability to the regulator. Following the design of the pin-indexing system, these two holes are very precisely located in positions that are unique to oxygen cylinders. Above the pins on the inside of the collar is the actual port through which oxygen flows from the cylinder to the regulator. A metal-bound elastomeric sealing washer (also called a gasket) is placed around the oxygen port to optimize the airtight seal between the collar of the regulator and the valve stem **STEP 2**. In the past, crush gaskets made of plastic and nylon were used, but they are no longer recommended. If used, crush gaskets can be used only once and then must be replaced.
3. Place the regulator collar over the cylinder valve, with the oxygen port and pin-indexing pins on the side of the valve stem that has the three holes. Open the screw bolt just enough to allow the collar to fit freely over the valve stem. Move the regulator so that the oxygen port and the pins fit into the correct holes on the valve stem. The screw bolt on the opposite side should be aligned with the dimple depression. As you hold the regulator securely against the valve stem, hand-tighten the screw bolt until the regulator is firmly attached to the cylinder. At this point, you should not see any open spaces between the sides of the valve stem and the interior walls of the collar **STEP 3**.
4. With the regulator firmly attached, open the cylinder completely, check for air leaking from the regulator–oxygen cylinder connection, and read the pressure level on the regulator gauge. Most portable cylinders have a maximum pressure of approximately 2,000 psi. Most EMS systems consider a cylinder with less than 500 psi to be too low to keep in service. Learn your department's policies in this regard and follow them. The flowmeter will have a second gauge or a selector dial that indicates the oxygen flow rate. Several popular types of devices are widely used. Attach the selected oxygen device to the regulator flowmeter by connecting the universal oxygen connecting tubing to the "Christmas tree" nipple on the flowmeter. Most oxygen delivery devices come with this tubing permanently attached; however, some oxygen masks do not. You must attach this tubing to the oxygen delivery device if it is not already attached **STEP 4**.

Skill Drill 5

Placing an Oxygen Cylinder Into Service

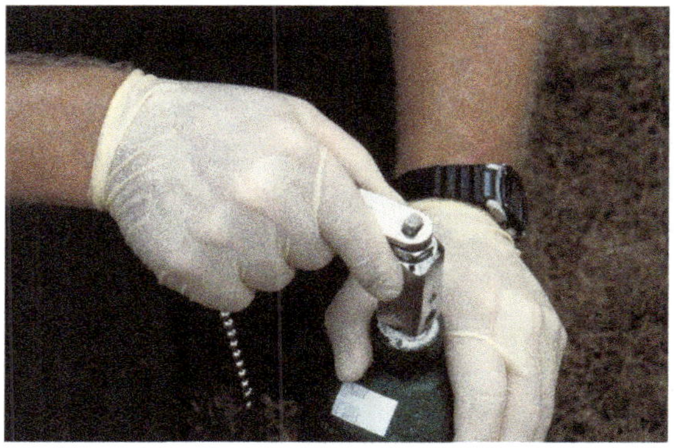

1. Using an oxygen wrench, turn the valve counterclockwise to slowly "crack" the cylinder.

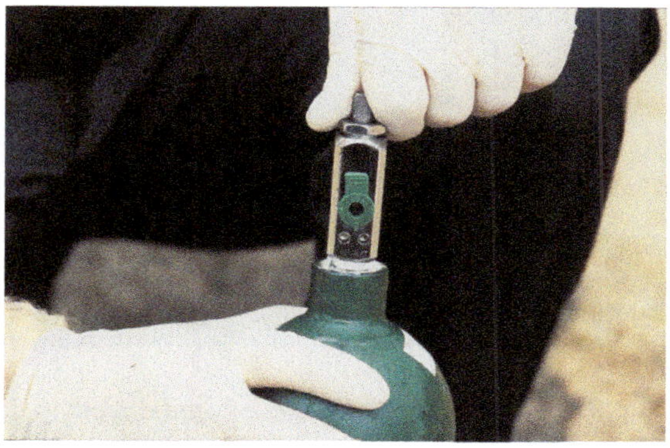

2. Attach the regulator/flowmeter to the valve stem using the two pin-indexing holes and make sure the washer is in place over the largest hole.

3. Align the regulator so the pins fit snugly into the correct holes on the valve stem, and hand-tighten the regulator.

4. Attach the oxygen connective tubing to the regulator flowmeter.

Supplemental Oxygen Delivery Devices

The nasal cannula offers the ability to provide supplemental oxygen at a flow rate of 1 to 6 LPM to patients with adequate spontaneous respiration (**Figure 13**). The nasal cannula is an appropriate delivery device for patients who are not experiencing significant difficulty breathing, are not exhibiting signs of hypoxia (low oxygen levels) or altered mental status, and have no additional traumatic injuries.

The nasal cannula is essentially flexible oxygen tubing with prongs that are positioned in the patient's nares for inhalation through the normal process of respiration. Use of the nasal cannula requires patients to be breathing spontaneously and capable of breathing through their nose. Patients who are unable to breathe through their nose should be considered candidates for a nonrebreathing mask instead of the nasal cannula.

The nonrebreathing mask delivers a higher concentration of oxygen than the nasal cannula (**Figure 14**). Its reservoir is filled from the oxygen tank via the flexible tubing connected directly to the oxygen tank, and it is capable of delivering 100% oxygen, making it the intervention of choice for patients experiencing difficulty breathing along with traumatic injuries or altered mental status or both.

Prior to placing the nonrebreathing mask on the patient, you must ensure that the reservoir is filled with oxygen. After the nonrebreathing mask is placed on the patient, you

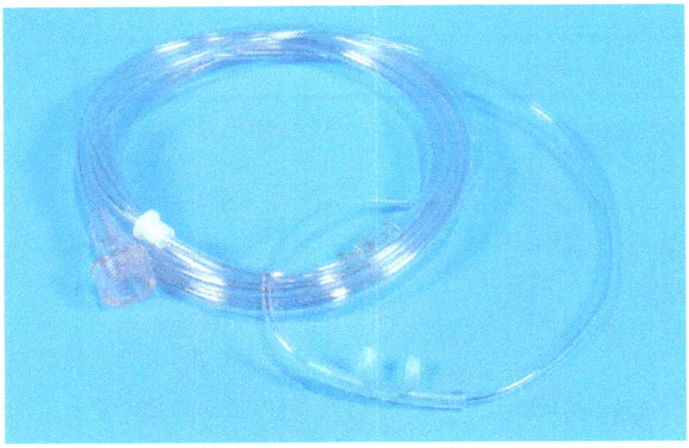

Figure 13 The nasal cannula delivers oxygen directly through the nostrils.

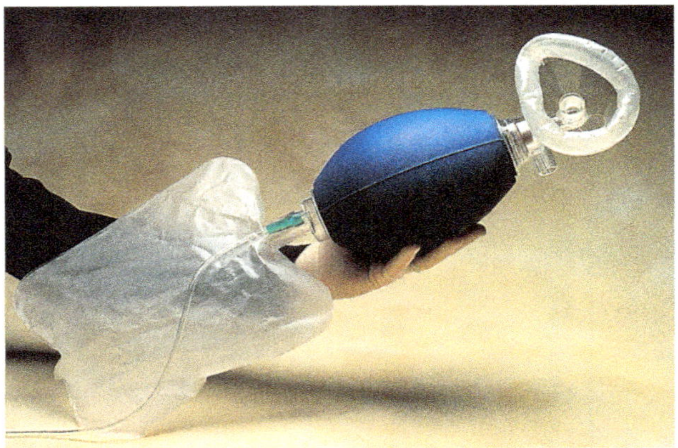

Figure 15 Bag-mask device.

should ensure the tightest possible fit around the bridge of the nose to prevent shifting of the mask and to minimize loss of oxygen.

Although the nonrebreathing mask delivers a substantial amount of oxygen to patients, it is of no clinical benefit to patients who are not spontaneously breathing or to patients whose breathing is ineffective.

Bag-Mask Ventilation

The **bag-mask device** is used to ventilate patients who have lost their respiratory drive. It is used in conjunction with one of the other airway adjuncts, frequently the OPA. The bag-mask device consists of a squeezable bag designed for one-handed operation (**Figure 15**). The second piece of the bag-mask device is a rigid face mask with an air-filled cushion that acts as a seal around the patient's mouth and nose. The bag-mask device connects via tubing to an oxygen source, allowing the device to deliver nearly 100% oxygen with each ventilation.

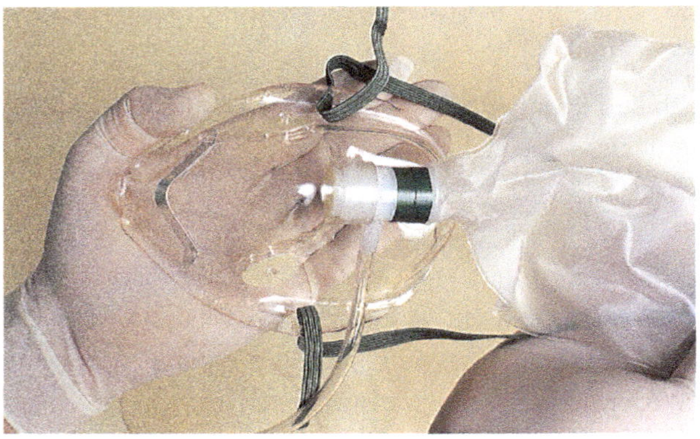

Figure 14 The nonrebreathing mask contains flapper valve ports at the cheek areas of the mask to prevent the patient from rebreathing exhaled gases.

Patients who require ventilatory support are those who have lost their respiratory effort completely or for whom the respiratory effort is insufficient to actually move air. Patients may be conscious if intervention is started early; however, the majority of patients will be unconscious. The bag-mask device should not be used in patients who are breathing spontaneously and are generating sufficient air movement.

A common complication with bag-mask device ventilations is **gastric insufflation**, in which air is forced into the stomach through the **positive pressure ventilation (PPV)**. Gastric insufflation significantly increases the likelihood of regurgitation (vomiting), of decreased lung space available for ventilation, and of a resulting decrease in cardiac output that can lead to insufficient blood pressure. Complications can result from a lack of maintenance of an adequate seal around the face, causing insufficient ventilatory support and decreased air movement. Inappropriate mask placement can also distort facial anatomy and can cause an airway obstruction.

Management of Adequate and Inadequate Ventilation

Patients who have adequate spontaneous respiration and are ventilating well may or may not require supplemental oxygen. Responders must continue to reassess a patient's condition because the patient can deteriorate and may need additional intervention.

Patients with inadequate ventilation may be conscious or unconscious. LERs must rapidly intervene to correct episodes of respiratory distress or respiratory failure through supplemental oxygen delivery with mechanical ventilation.

When a bag-mask device is unavailable, the LER can use a pocket mask to create a protective barrier to facilitate mechanical ventilation (**Figure 16**). LERs should lift the jaw to the mask, using the last three fingers to manipulate the patient's jaw. The thumb and index finger should hold the mask in place by making a "c" shape and securing the top of the mask around the bridge of the nose. Responders should exhale slowly and steadily into the port while securing a patent seal and watching for steady and even chest rise. Air escaping from under the face mask indicates an incomplete seal and requires a readjustment of either finger placement or mask placement around the patient's face.

The pocket mask is a useful tool for emergent initiation of mechanical ventilation in situations in which medical equipment may be limited, or in situations in which responders are alone. A one-way valve on the pocket mask prevents transmission of infectious disease to the responder and eliminates the need for mouth-to-mouth ventilation. However, in cases in which a patient vomits during mechanical ventilation, the one-way valve can become occluded with gastric contents, subsequently preventing further use. Responders must remain cognizant of the limitations of their equipment.

Some pocket masks have an outlet where supplemental oxygen can be attached through tubing, augmenting the percentage and amount of oxygen delivered to the patient. When supplemental oxygen is available for use, it should be used.

Figure 16 Barrier devices such as a pocket mask are necessary in providing artificial ventilations.

Ventilation of an Apneic Patient

LERs will, during their primary assessment, identify patients in need of ventilatory support. Patients in need of this support can present with either no respiratory effort at all or very minimal or ineffective respiratory effort. Accordingly, patients with ineffective or insufficient respiratory effort can exhibit gasping or gurgling or can present with extremely shallow regular or irregular breathing. LERs should consider their knowledge of what regular respiratory effort is and should be ready to assist any respiratory effort that is insufficient. Responders must use mechanical ventilation to move oxygen into the lungs of the patient who is not breathing spontaneously, effectively taking control of the process of ventilation.

Monitoring the Patient

LERs must frequently reassess patients in their care, especially when interventions are being performed, to gauge the effectiveness of the treatment(s). While providing mechanical ventilation to a patient, evaluate the rise and fall of the chest wall during ventilation. Adequate rise and fall indicates ventilation is occurring. Additionally, reassessing OPA or NPA placement and the face-mask seal is key to ensuring appropriate delivery of ventilatory support. Hissing noises or air felt escaping from beneath the mask during ventilation indicates an ineffective face-mask seal that must be adjusted and corrected immediately.

Responders should also continuously monitor the color of a patient during ventilation; a bluish or pale tint indicates further problems with oxygenation and requires immediate attention. Mottling, or a splotchy appearance, can also indicate breathing and/or circulation problems, especially in pediatric patients. During the course of treatment, it is also possible that patients' conditions will improve. As patients become more responsive, they may start to fight against the mechanical ventilation. At this point, you should stop ventilatory support and reassess the patient.

Limitations

Mechanical ventilation is a resource-intensive treatment. At best, bag-mask device ventilation requires one person who does nothing else. At worst, securing an appropriate seal with the face mask can require two responders to hold the mask in place and a third to squeeze the bag reservoir.

PPV also has some adverse effects. Air is frequently forced into the stomach, causing the stomach to expand. This leads to the patient vomiting, thereby increasing the potential for aspiration in a patient who already has no gag reflex or inherent respiratory effort. This increased air trapping in the stomach also puts pressure on the diaphragm, limiting full expansion of the lungs during ventilation, which in turn limits the full effectiveness of mechanical ventilation. To combat this effect, properly trained emergency responders should consider an orally or nasally placed gastric tube that can be attached to suction to decompress the stomach of air and gastric contents, limiting the potential for aspiration.

As with any mechanical intervention, mechanical ventilation is less effective than spontaneous ventilation, creating a scenario in which a critical patient is receiving less oxygen than in a normal state. Because all cells and tissue require oxygen to survive, any deprivation of oxygen creates an environment prone to further adverse issues.

Normal Ventilation and Positive Pressure Ventilation

During the normal process of ventilation, as the diaphragm pulls downward and the intercostal muscles pull the chest upward, the volume inside the chest and lungs increases. This creates negative pressure inside the chest and causes air to be sucked into the lungs. Additionally, this process helps pull blood back to the heart from the rest of the body.

PPV forces air into the lungs, thereby increasing the volume of the lungs and causing the chest wall to rise and the diaphragm to be pushed downward. During this process, blood return to the heart is decreased due to the nature of positive pressure forcing air into the lungs. This reduction in blood flow to the heart equates to less circulating oxygen in the system, further compounding the medical emergency at hand. Additionally, there is a decrease in the amount of blood circulated with each heartbeat and a decrease in blood pressure.

LERs must keep in mind that mechanical ventilation that is either too fast or too deep may worsen the loss of returning blood flow. Similarly, overventilation leads to gastric insufflation (expansion of the stomach) and vomiting that may potentially create an airway obstruction.

AGE-SPECIFIC CONSIDERATIONS

Emergency responders must consider the differences in airway anatomy among different age groups. Techniques for airway management can vary greatly depending on anatomy.

Pediatric Patients

Pediatric patients require consideration not only for age-related anatomic differences but also for special circumstances leading to the airway emergency. For example, toddlers frequently pick up small items from the ground and place them in their mouths, creating a high potential for an airway obstruction.

Anatomically, pediatric patients have a proportionately larger head than adults. Similarly, pediatric patients also have less muscle mass in their shoulders and backs compared with adults. These physical traits result in a hyperflexion of the neck when laying pediatric patients supine, creating a scenario in which the unaware responder could actually occlude the airway while trying to assess the pediatric patient (**Figure 17**). To address these issues, LERs should consider placing padding under a pediatric patient's shoulders to assist in opening the airway while maintaining proper in-line immobilization.

The oral cavity of pediatric patients is also physically smaller than in adults, limiting the space in which emergency responders have to treat airway obstructions. Compounding the smaller area is a proportionally larger tongue than in adults, further limiting available space. Accordingly, these

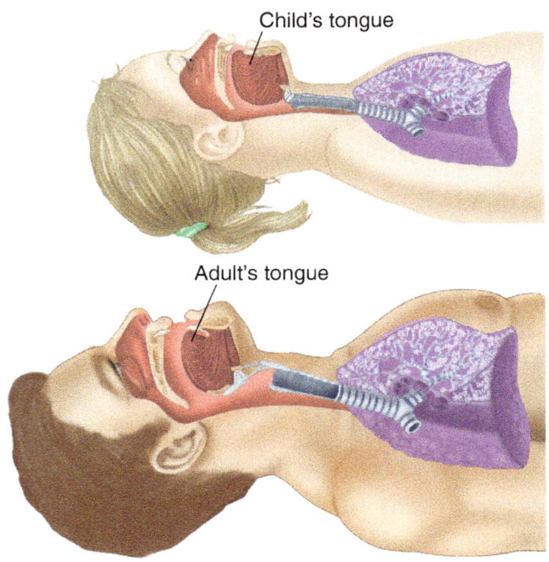

Figure 17 The anatomy of a child's airway differs from that of an adult. The tongue is proportionally larger and can more easily block the airway. Also, the back of a child's head is larger, so head positioning requires more care.

patients are at risk for an airway obstruction resulting from a smaller foreign object or a significantly smaller amount of fluid than with adults.

Given the positioning and anatomic differences in pediatric patients, LERs should focus on positioning and packaging pediatric patients. Trauma patients who are immobilized can easily be turned as a unit to facilitate the spontaneous clearing of vomit from the airway. Medical patients who are breathing spontaneously will find the position of comfort that allows for the maximum amount of air passage. Responders should, as clinically and safely as is appropriate, allow breathing patients to find their comfort position to help facilitate respiration.

Geriatric Patients

Geriatric patients have a number of age-related concerns that differ from other patients. Geriatric patients may have dentures as a replacement for missing teeth. Dentures can be removed for cleaning by the patient but also create a potential for airway obstruction. Dentures can be different sizes, ranging from two or three teeth (also known as a bridge) to the entire upper or lower layer of teeth (or both layers). When opening the airway of an unconscious elderly patient, you should quickly evaluate the mouth for the presence of dentures or bridges. If present, dentures should be removed prior to treatment to eliminate the possibility of accidentally dislodging the dentures and subsequently creating an airway obstruction. In the event that there are bridges or dentures that are missing, LERs should be prepared to remove any pieces of dental equipment that may have been lodged in the upper airway.

For geriatric patients with no respiratory drive, the lack of teeth or dentures will make it difficult for responders to get an adequate seal using a bag-mask device for mechanical ventilation. A thinning facial shape as one ages can also make a proper seal difficult. When possible, emergency responders should use the two-responder method for mechanical ventilation to ensure an adequate seal between face and mask and to maximize the delivery of oxygen.

Related to the problem of missing teeth is the possibility of airway obstructions caused by incompletely chewed food. Dehydration is a common side effect of the aging process, which has a direct correlation with the amount of saliva produced at any given time. With less saliva, the process of food breakdown is slowed, increasing the chances for inhalation of a piece of food and subsequent airway obstruction.

CONCLUSION

Management of the airway and breathing is paramount to sustaining a patient. Many techniques and devices exist to help an emergency responder keep a patent airway and ensure that the patient is receiving adequate amounts of oxygen. With techniques ranging from using gravity all the way through placement of OPAs, NPAs, and blind-insertion devices, responders need to able to open an airway, keep it open, and make sure oxygenated air is flowing in and out of the lungs.

Prep Kit

READY FOR REVIEW

- The respiratory system (airway, lungs, and associated organs) is responsible for getting oxygen into the body and for the removal of waste gases such as carbon dioxide. Maintaining an open airway and adequate breathing is essential for life.
- Lungs do not have muscle; they rely on the muscles between the ribs (intercostal muscles) to move the chest off of the shoulder girdle, and the diaphragm to push down on the abdomen. When the diaphragm pushes down on the abdomen, the chest expands, creating a vacuum and allowing air to run into the alveoli of the lungs.
- Assessing for a patent airway and adequate breathing requires looking for equal chest rise, listening for air moving in and out of the body, and feeling for adequate air movement.
- Patients who are unconscious or have an altered level of consciousness present the greatest likelihood for having an inadequate or unsecured airway.
- Not being able to speak in full sentences and abnormal sounds such as wheezing, snoring, or stridor indicate an issue with the respiratory system.
- Airway obstruction can have a number of different causes, all of which require immediate assessment and potential intervention. Common obstructions include the tongue, food, vomit, blood, teeth, and foreign bodies.
- Manual techniques, such as the head tilt-chin lift maneuver or modified jaw-thrust maneuver, and airway adjunct devices (OPA, NPA, King LT-D airway, suction) can be used to maintain an open airway.
- The jaw-thrust maneuver should be used instead of the head tilt-chin lift maneuver when the patient is suspected of having an injury to the cervical spine.
- Poor oxygenation causes a patient to have a pale or bluish tint around the lips and eyes, on the palms, and in the oral mucosa. This condition is known as cyanosis. Decreased oxygenation can lead to an altered mental status and abnormal behavior.
- Patients who are found unconscious and occasionally gasping for air should be treated as if they were not breathing at all. They require prompt initiation of mechanical ventilation with supplemental oxygen.
- Oxygen is a compressed gas and must be transported in cylinders. These cylinders are usually charged to a level of 2,000 psi.
- Oxygen cylinders come in many different sizes. They are assigned a letter from A through K to rate their volume. The most common in EMS programs are the D, super D, and E cylinders. Some law enforcement programs use the small A tank in rapid response kits. M and larger tanks are typically found secured for use in ambulance or vehicle oxygen systems.
- Any patient who is exhibiting signs and symptoms of respiratory distress should receive supplemental oxygen.
- Oxygen delivery devices such as the nasal cannula, nonrebreathing mask, pocket mask, and bag-mask device are attached to the oxygen tank regulator and are used in different circumstances to deliver various amounts of oxygen or to ventilate a patient.

- Mechanical ventilation is a resource-intensive treatment. At best, bag-mask device ventilation requires one person who does nothing else. At worst, securing an appropriate seal with the face mask can require two responders to hold the mask in place and a third to squeeze the bag reservoir.
- Normal breathing efforts and respiratory rates will differ with patient age.

VITAL VOCABULARY

airway The passages from the openings of the mouth and nose to the air sacs in the lungs through which air enters and leaves the lungs.

alveolar ventilation The exchange of oxygen and carbon dioxide that occurs in the alveoli.

alveoli The air sacs of the lungs where the exchange of oxygen and carbon dioxide takes place.

apneic Not breathing spontaneously.

bag-mask device A device with a face mask attached to a ventilation bag containing a reservoir and connected to oxygen; delivers more than 90% supplemental oxygen.

cyanosis Bluish coloration of the skin resulting from poor oxygenation of the circulating blood.

diaphragm A muscular dome that separates the chest from the abdominal cavity. Contraction of the diaphragm and the chest wall muscles brings air into the lungs; relaxation expels airs from the lungs.

expiration The movement of air out of the lungs.

failed airway device A device that is used after an advanced life support provider has been unsuccessful in attempts to secure the airway through endotracheal intubation.

gastric insufflation A condition in which air fills the stomach as a result of high volume and pressure or airway obstruction during artificial ventilation.

inspiration The movement of air into the lungs.

minute ventilation The amount of air pulled into the lungs and removed from the lungs in one minute.

mucous membranes The lining of the body cavities and passages that communicate directly or indirectly with the environment outside the body.

mucus The opaque, sticky secretion of the mucous membranes that lubricates the body openings.

nasopharyngeal airway (NPA) An airway adjunct that is inserted into the nostril of a patient who is not able to maintain a natural airway.

oropharyngeal airway (OPA) An airway adjunct that is inserted into the mouth to keep the tongue from blocking the upper airway.

positive pressure ventilation (PPV) The process of forcing air into the lungs using an external device.

regulator A device applied to the neck of a gas cylinder that takes the cylinder pressure (2,000 psi) and reduces it to 40 to 70 psi.

respiration The exchange of gases in the alveoli or at the cellular level.

stridor A high-pitched noise heard primarily on inspiration.

ventilation The movement of air in and out of the lungs.

wheezing A high-pitched, continuous whistling sound produced when air is moved under pressure through the narrowed bronchi or bronchioles in the lower airways. The narrowing of these airways often occurs from asthma, an allergic reaction, inflammation, or deep airway burns.

CHECK YOUR KNOWLEDGE

1. While assessing your patient, you notice the following signs and symptoms. Which sign or symptom would indicate normal breathing?
   - **A.** Cyanosis
   - **B.** Patient not able to speak in full sentences
   - **C.** Equal rise and fall of the chest
   - **D.** Wheezing
2. You are attempting to manage the airway of a patient who was riding a motorcycle when he was struck by another vehicle and thrown through the air. Which manual technique should be used to open the airway?
   - **A.** Head tilt-chin lift maneuver
   - **B.** Oral airway
   - **C.** Nasal airway
   - **D.** Modified jaw-thrust maneuver
3. Your patient has stopped breathing. Which device should be used to move oxygen into the lungs?
   - **A.** Bag-mask device
   - **B.** Nonrebreathing mask
   - **C.** Suction device
   - **D.** King LT-D
4. Which of the following is not part of the respiratory system?
   - **A.** Esophagus
   - **B.** Trachea
   - **C.** Epiglottis
   - **D.** Alveoli
5. An oral pharyngeal airway (OPA) is measured from:
   - **A.** earlobe to nares.
   - **B.** earlobe to corner of mouth.
   - **C.** mouth to nose.
   - **D.** base of skull to mouth.

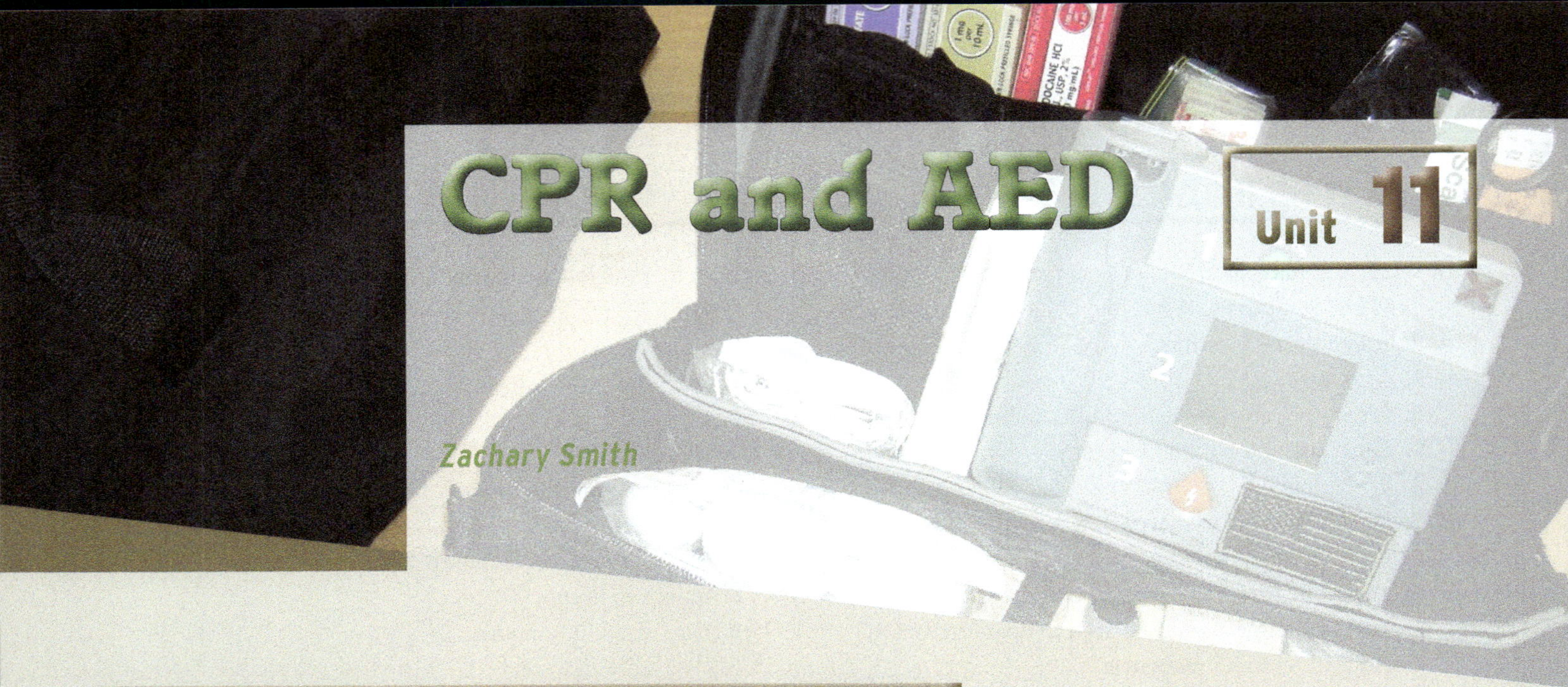

Zachary Smith

CPR and AED

Unit 11

Law Enforcement Responder Objectives

- Identify the basic pathophysiology of cardiopulmonary resuscitation (CPR). (p 213)
- Describe the purpose of cardiopulmonary resuscitation CPR and use of an automated external defibrillator (AED). (p 213)
- Discuss the chain of survival. (p 214)
- Discuss the roles and responsibilities of the law enforcement responder in terms of CPR and AED use. (p 214)
- Perform high-quality CPR, using adequate compressions. (pp 214–218, 219)
- Operate an AED correctly. (pp 218, 220, 221)

National EMS Education Standard Competencies

Shock and Resuscitation

Uses assessment information to recognize shock, respiratory failure or arrest, and cardiac arrest based on assessment findings and manages the emergency while awaiting emergency response.

Assessment

Uses scene information and simple patient assessment findings to identify and manage immediate life threats and injuries within the scope of practice of the emergency medical responder.

Primary Assessment

- Primary assessment of all patient situations (p 214)
  - Level of consciousness (p 214)
  - ABCs (p 214)
  - Identifying life threats (p 214)
  - Assessment of vital functions (p 214)
- Begin interventions needed to preserve life (pp 214–218, 219)

Anatomy and Physiology

Uses simple knowledge of the anatomy and function of the upper airway, heart, vessels, blood, lungs, skin, muscles, and bones as the foundation of emergency care.

Pathophysiology

Uses simple knowledge of shock and respiratory compromise to respond to life threats.

INTRODUCTION

Performing cardiopulmonary resuscitation (CPR) and operating an automated external defibrillator (AED) are invaluable skills for all health care providers, law enforcement responders (LERs), and prehospital personnel. Emergency medical services (EMS) treat approximately 300,000 cardiac arrest patients annually. Of those patients, fewer than 8% survive. The number of lives saved can be doubled or even tripled by the initiation of prompt, quality CPR, early defibrillation, and early access to medical care.

The year 2010 marked the 50th anniversary of modern CPR. Over the years, there have been tremendous developments in resuscitative efforts, but what has been shown to be the most effective skill to improve outcomes is the ability to perform quality chest compressions. Providing compressions of an adequate rate and depth, allowing complete chest recoil, and minimizing interruptions in chest compressions are the focus of CPR.

This unit emphasizes that high-quality CPR should be the foundation of an improved health care system. CPR will not only increase the number of patients who return to spontaneous circulation (ROSC) after sudden cardiac arrest but also will improve their quality of life and functional state of health.

ANATOMY AND PHYSIOLOGY

CPR is an effort to create artificial circulation by manually pumping blood through the heart to restore oxygenated blood to vital organs. During circulatory failure, the heart is unable to provide sufficient cardiac output to satisfy tissue metabolic requirements. Blood flow is restricted to all vital organs but least restricted to the brain and heart.

The purpose of CPR is to maintain adequate circulation, oxygenation, and tissue perfusion. During cardiac arrest, blood circulation throughout the body ceases. Anaerobic metabolism (cells inefficiently using energy without oxygen) starts almost immediately, followed by a complex cascade of metabolic events.

Neurologic function is the most susceptible to circulatory compromise. Without adequate brain tissue perfusion, irreversible damage occurs within 5 minutes of an arrest state. Recovery of prearrest neurologic function rarely occurs after 10 minutes of untreated cardiac arrest. The heart is the second most susceptible organ to circulatory arrest. Although **cardiac output** (the amount of blood pushed out of the heart with each beat) is difficult to measure, studies suggest that cardiac output is severely compromised, to approximately 30% to 40% of normal, during high-quality chest compressions. CPR directs blood flow to the brain and heart, restoring organized myocardial electrical activity and minimizing ischemic brain injury.

TYPES OF ILLNESS OR INJURY

Circulatory failure may result from a failure of the heart to contract, heart valve damage, heart dysrhythmias, extremely fast or slow heart rates, blood loss, cardiac tamponade, tension pneumothorax, or a variety of less common conditions. In most cases, regardless of the cause, the initiation of high-quality CPR will provide the best chance for ROSC and ultimately increase survival rates.

Tip

Cardiac Arrest Situations

The American Heart Association (AHA) has identified, reviewed, and expanded on 15 specific cardiac arrest situations:

Asthma
Anaphylaxis
Pregnancy
Morbid obesity
Pulmonary embolism
Electrolyte imbalance
Toxic ingestion
Hypothermia
Avalanche
Drowning
Electrical shock
Lightning strike
Percutaneous coronary intervention (PCI)
Cardiac tamponade
Cardiac surgery

These special circumstances may be infrequent and unique to certain situations. They may call for rapid invasive intervention, which may be beyond the scope of the law enforcement responder.

ASSESSMENT OF CARDIAC ARREST

LERs should use a systematic approach when initiating CPR. Previous American Heart Association (AHA) guidelines used the ABC (airway, breathing, circulation) sequence of steps for starting CPR on adult and pediatric patients. However, as of 2010, the AHA has recommended changing those guidelines. The CAB (circulation, airway, breathing) approach is now considered the standard method to minimize time to first chest compressions.

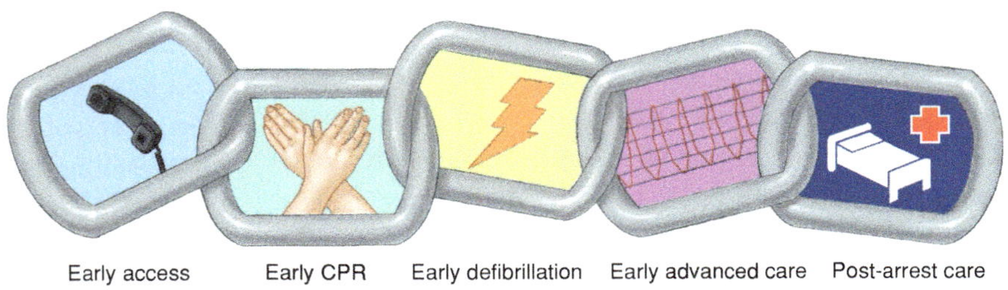

Figure 1 The five links of the chain of survival. Adapted from American Heart Association.

> **Tip**
> ### Recognition of Cardiopulmonary Arrest
> Ensure that the scene is safe, determine that the victim is unresponsive and either is not breathing or has abnormal breathing, and call for help. If you are trained to the AHA healthcare provider level, check for a carotid pulse (infants check brachial pulse) for no more than 10 seconds. If the patient has no pulse, immediately start chest compressions and call for an AED. Provide rescue breathing of one breath every 6-8 seconds.
>
> Rescuers should provide a ratio of 30 compressions to 2 rescue breaths. If there are two rescuers for an infant or child, the ratio should change to 15 compressions to 2 rescue breaths.

Experts agree that the highest survival rate occurs in those who suffer cardiac arrest with a rhythm of ventricular fibrillation or pulseless ventricular tachycardia. The crucial steps that contribute to the survival of these patients during CPR are chest compressions and early defibrillation.

> **Tip**
> ### Ventricular Tachycardia and Fibrillation
> Ventricular tachycardia and ventricular fibrillation are lethal electrical rhythms that interrupt the normal function of the heart, resulting in a decreased pumping of blood to the body.

Assessment of a patient experiencing cardiac arrest continues to be the essential lifesaving principle of basic life support (BLS) and the chain of survival. Fundamental aspects include recognition of sudden cardiac arrest, activation of the emergency response system, initiation of early high-quality CPR, and defibrillation in the appropriate setting.

MANAGEMENT

The assessment of the patient and initiation of CPR remain the foundation for saving lives of victims who suffer cardiac arrest. Recognizing cardiac arrest, activating EMS, performing prompt high-quality CPR, and defibrillating when appropriate will give patients the best chance of survival. It is important for the LER to implement the **chain of survival** and the new BLS guidelines in practice (**Figure 1**). For all ages, determine that the patient is unresponsive and not breathing or gasping. Then proceed to the CPR method appropriate for the patient.

> **Tip**
> ### Key Features of CPR
> Assess CAB (circulation, airway, breathing).
>
> Assess patient's responsiveness (no breathing, gasps).
>
> Activate EMS.
>
> Deliver prompt, high-quality chest compressions, with minimal interruptions, at a rate of 100 compressions per minute and a depth of 2 inches for adults and 1.5 inches for infants.
>
> Use a compression-to-ventilation ratio of 30:2 for one- or two-person rescue.

Infant CPR

Respiratory disease and airway compromise can affect the infant or child's health to the point of cardiopulmonary arrest. Infants and children can experience sudden cardiac arrest, but this is not a common occurrence. Respiratory compromise that can lead to cardiopulmonary arrest extends from a variety of causes, including:

- Blunt and penetrating injuries
- Respiratory and systemic infections

- Foreign body in airway
- Near drowning
- Poisoning and drug overdoses
- Sudden infant death syndrome (SIDS)

Infants are children under 1 year of age. Infants under 1 month of age are considered neonates. When rescuing an infant or neonate, emphasis should be placed on attempting to establish the level of consciousness. Avoid shaking or slapping an infant or neonate to establish responsiveness. The best method to arouse the patient is to tap on the shoulder or rub the back vigorously while speaking loudly. If the infant or neonate does not respond, immediately move forward with the resuscitation.

For neonates, check the airway, suction if needed, and check for breathing. If rescue breathing is required, administer two ventilations. Check for a pulse at the brachial artery in the patient's upper arm for no more than 10 seconds. If there is no pulse or you are uncertain whether there is a pulse, start CPR at a ratio of three compressions to one breath. Compressions should be delivered using two fingers on the bottom one third of the sternum. An alternative method that is preferred for neonates or small infants is the two thumbs/hands encircling chest method, which has been shown to improve perfusion (**Skill Drill 1**).

1. Find the proper hand position—one finger width below an imaginary line drawn between the nipples on the middle third of the sternum **STEP 1**.
2. Place both hands around the neonate so that your thumbs are side by side, resting on the middle third of the sternum, and the rest of your fingers encircle the thorax.
3. Press the two thumbs gently against the sternum. The neonate's chest is easy to compress. Use only enough force to compress the sternum to a depth of approximately one-third the diameter of the chest **STEP 2**.

The LER should try to get 100 compressions per minute to the neonate. The depth of compressions should be one third the diameter depth of the infants chest, or roughly 1.5 inches (4 cm).

If your medical director considers you a health care provider, your protocols may advise you to check a pulse for no more than 10 seconds. For infants, check the brachial pulse (**Figure 2**).

Skill Drill 1

Performing Chest Compressions on a Neonate

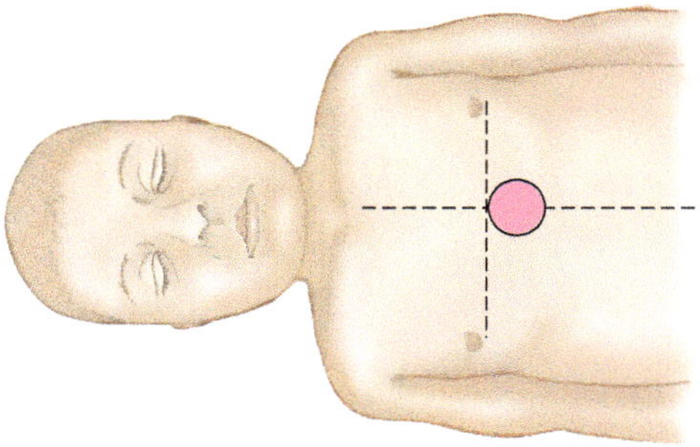

1. Find the proper hand position: just below the nipple line, middle of the lower third of the sternum.

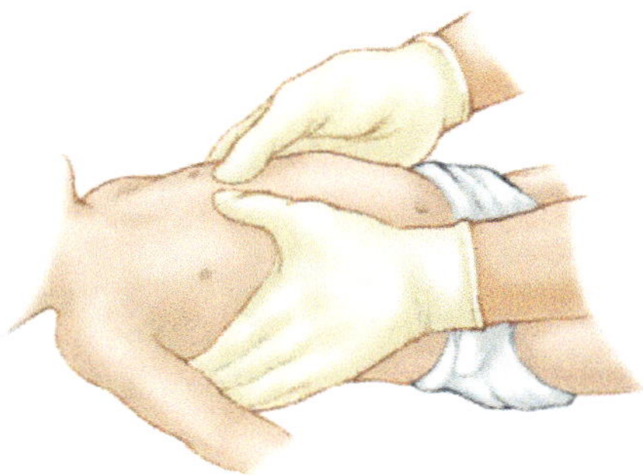

2. Wrap your hands around the neonate, with your thumbs resting at that position. Press your thumbs gently against the sternum, compressing to a depth of one third the diameter of the chest.

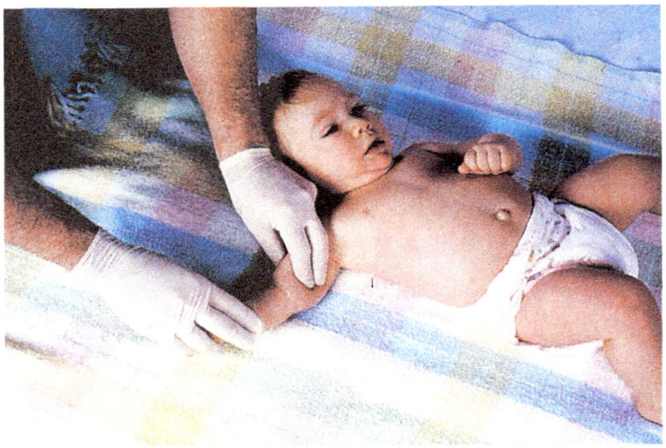

Figure 2 To assess the pulse in an infant, palpate the brachial artery on the inner side of the arm, midway between the elbow and shoulder.

As with neonates, compression depth for older infants should be one third the diameter of the chest, roughly 1.5 inches (4 cm). Follow the steps in **Skill Drill 2**:

1. Place the infant on a firm surface, using one hand to keep the head in an open airway position.
2. Imagine a line drawn between the nipples. Place two fingers in the middle of the sternum, about one finger width lower than the imaginary line STEP 1.
3. Using two fingers, compress the sternum at least one third the depth of the chest (about 1.5 inches in most infants). Compress the chest at a rate of at least 100 per minute.
4. After each compression, allow the sternum to return briefly to its normal position. Allow equal time for compression and relaxation of the chest. Do not remove your fingers from the sternum, and avoid jerky movements STEP 2.

Child and Adult CPR

If you are trained to the AHA health care provider level you should assess an unresponsive patient's pulse, check the carotid pulse in children and adults. If you are unable to feel a pulse, start chest compressions at a rate of 100 per minute. If you are a health care provider, you should rotate compressors every 2 minutes. Interruptions to chest compressions should not take longer than 10 seconds. If you are not trained to ventilate the patient, you should just maintain compressions at a rate of 100 per minute until EMS arrives.

If you are trained to ventilate, the airway should be maintained using the head tilt–chin lift maneuver. If you suspect trauma, and your medical direction allows, use the jaw-thrust maneuver to keep the airway open.

Skill Drill 2

Performing Infant Chest Compressions

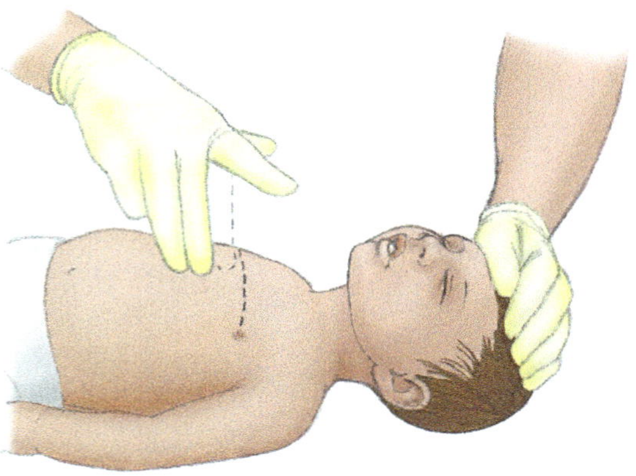

1. Position the infant on a firm surface while maintaining the airway. Place two fingers in the middle of the sternum just below the nipple line.

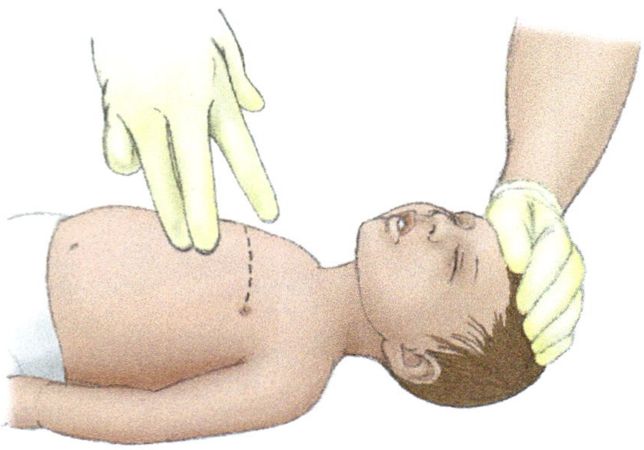

2. Use two fingers to compress the chest one third the anterior-posterior diameter of the chest at a rate of at least 100 per minute. Allow the sternum to return to its normal position between compressions.

Follow the steps in **Skill Drill 3** to perform CPR on a child:

1. Place the child on a firm surface. Locate the center of the chest, in between the nipples STEP 1.
2. Place the heel of one or two hands in the center of the chest. Compress the chest at least one third the diameter of the chest (approximately 2 inches in most children) at a rate of at least 100 per minute STEP 2.
3. In between compressions, allow the chest to recoil fully. Compression and relaxation time should be the same duration. Use smooth movements. Hold your fingers off the child's ribs and keep the heel of your hand(s) on the sternum.
4. Coordinate rapid compressions and ventilations in a 30:2 ratio for one rescuer and 15:2 for two rescuers, making sure the chest rises with each ventilation. At the end of each cycle, pause for two ventilations STEP 3.
5. Continue cycles of compressions with ventilations until an AED becomes available, EMS arrives, or the patient shows signs of spontaneous breathing.
6. If the child resumes effective breathing, place him or her in a position that allows for frequent reassessment of the airway and vital signs during transport STEP 4.

Skill Drill 3

Performing CPR on a Child

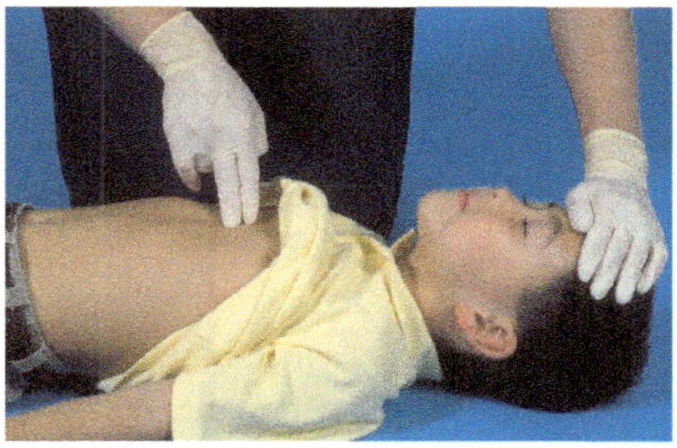

1. Place the child on a firm surface. Locate the center of the chest between the nipples.

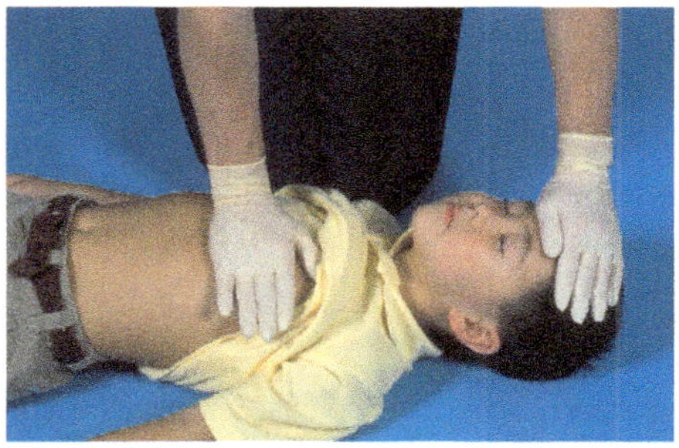

2. Place the heel of one or both hands in the center of the chest. Compress the chest one third the anterior-posterior diameter of the chest at a rate of at least 100 per minute.

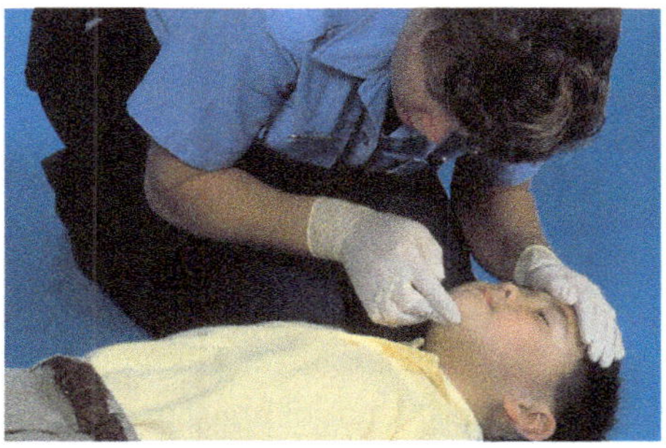

3. Coordinate compressions with ventilations in a 30:2 ratio (one rescuer) or 15:2 ratio (two rescuers), pausing for ventilations. Open the airway and deliver two rescue breaths.

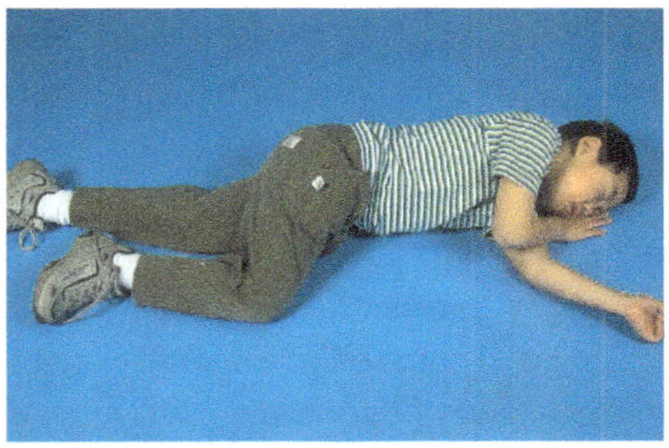

4. If the child resumes effective breathing, place him or her in a position that allows for frequent reassessment of the airway and vital signs during transport.

Providing CPR to an adult includes similar steps as providing CPR to a child. Follow the steps in **Skill Drill 4** to perform CPR on an adult:

1. Determine unresponsiveness, and then call for additional help (STEP 1).
2. Position the patient supine on a firm surface.
3. Determine pulselessness by checking the carotid pulse (STEP 2). If there is no pulse, you have an AED, and you believe the down time has been only a few minutes, apply the AED now. If the down time was more than 4 to 5 minutes, begin chest compressions for 2 minutes, then apply the AED.
4. If the patient has no pulse and there is no AED, begin compressions. Place your hands in the proper position for delivering chest compressions—the heel of one hand on the sternum between the patient's nipples, and the heel of the other hand over the first hand.
5. With your arms straight, lock your elbows and position your shoulders directly over your hands. You may choose to interlock your fingers, but be sure to keep your fingers off the patient's chest.
6. Give 30 compressions at a rate of at least 100 per minute. Each set of 30 compressions should take about 20 seconds. Using a rhythmic motion, apply pressure vertically from your shoulders down through both arms to depress the sternum at least 2 inches, then rise up gently and fully (STEP 3).
7. Open the airway according to suspicion of spinal injury.
8. Determine breathlessness. If the patient is unresponsive but breathing adequately, place him or her in the recovery position and maintain the open airway (STEP 4).
9. If the patient is not breathing, begin rescue breathing by delivering two breaths, each lasting one second (STEP 5).
10. Perform five cycles of compressions and ventilations, then reassess the patient for no more than 10 seconds. If there is no change, resume CPR. If the patient is breathing adequately but still unresponsive, place the patient in the recovery position and closely monitor his or her condition.
11. If the patient is not breathing spontaneously after five cycles, consider transport to the hospital while continuing CPR.

If two rescuers are available, one rescuer can provide the chest compressions and the other can provide ventilations. Every 2 minutes the rescuers should switch tasks so the rescuer providing chest compressions does not get tired as quickly.

CPR With an Advanced Airway

If you are rescuing an infant, child, or adult patient and an advanced airway device has been placed, deliver chest compressions steadily at a rate of 100 per minute without interruptions. Ventilations should be administered asynchronously at a rate of 8 to 10 breaths per minute.

AUTOMATED EXTERNAL DEFIBRILLATION

Early defibrillation via AED remains an integral part of resuscitation of those who suffer from cardiac arrest. Patients with implanted defibrillators/pacemakers should not delay use of AED. Single-shock methods have also continued to be recommended by the AHA.

If an AED becomes available during CPR, immediately turn it on and follow the prompts from the AED for application to the patient. Typically, AEDs will prompt the rescuers to expose the chest, apply the electrode pads to the bare chest, and stand by without touching the patient while the AED analyzes the electrocardiogram (ECG) of the patient and determines if a shock is necessary.

If the AED determines that the patient should receive an electrical shock to correct the cardiac rhythm, the AED will charge and tell you to "clear" everyone from touching the patient. When the AED is charged, it will tell you so and advise you to push the shock button to deliver the electrical shock to the patient. Ensure that no one is touching the patient, then press the shock button. The cycle of shocks is dictated by the programming of the AED. Once it is applied and operating, CPR should be performed only when the AED advises.

Follow the steps in **Skill Drill 5** to use an AED on an adult patient:

1. Assess responsiveness while continuing to perform CPR if it is already in progress (it is important to limit the amount of time compressions are interrupted). If the patient is responsive, do not apply the AED.
2. If the patient is unresponsive and CPR has not been started yet, begin providing chest compressions and rescue breaths at a ratio of 30 compressions to 2

Skill Drill 4

Performing CPR on an Adult

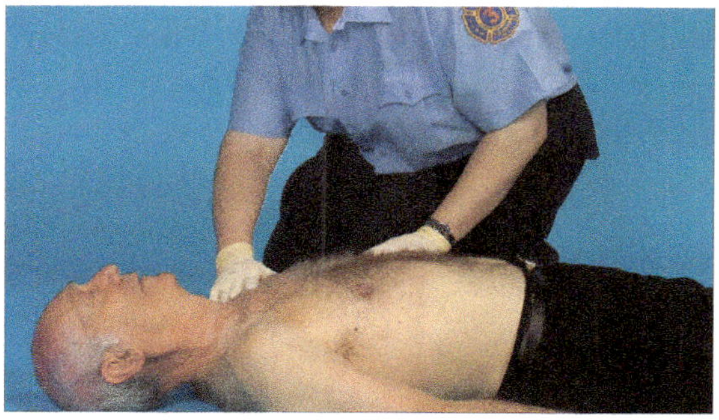

1. Confirm that the victim is not breathing or is breathing abnormally (gasping). Determine unresponsiveness and call for help.

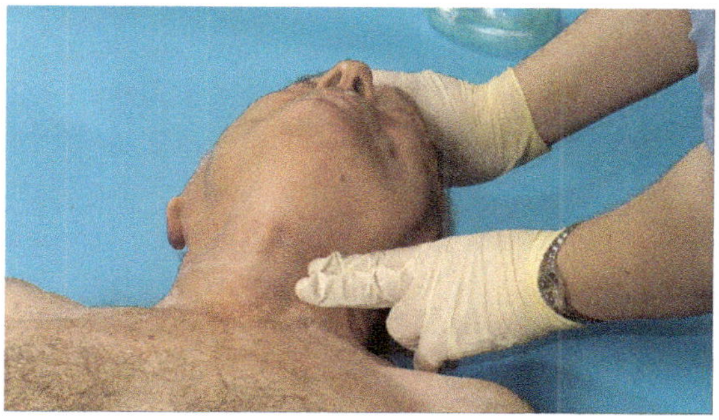

2. Check the carotid pulse for no more than 10 seconds. Call for an AED, apply it as soon as it is available, and follow prompts.

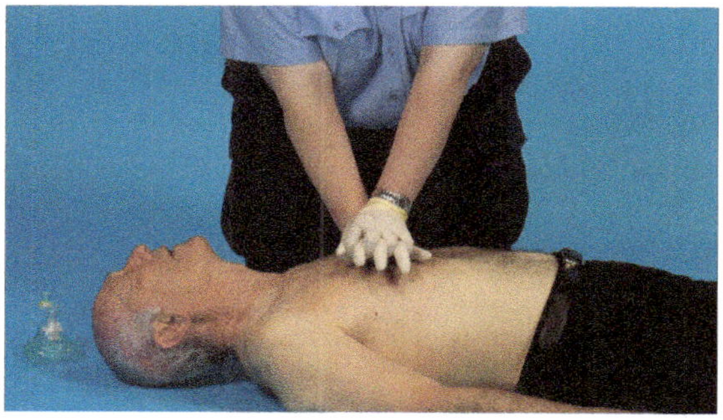

3. If there is no pulse and an AED is not available, place your hands in the proper position for delivering chest compressions. Give 30 compressions at a rate of at least 100 per minute.

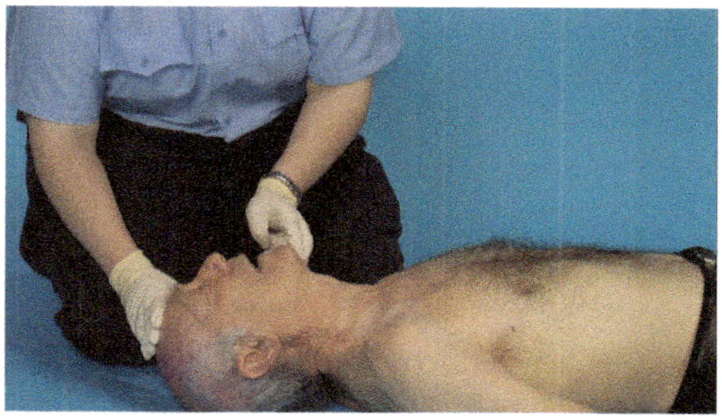

4. Open the airway. If breathing is adequate, place the patient in the recovery position.

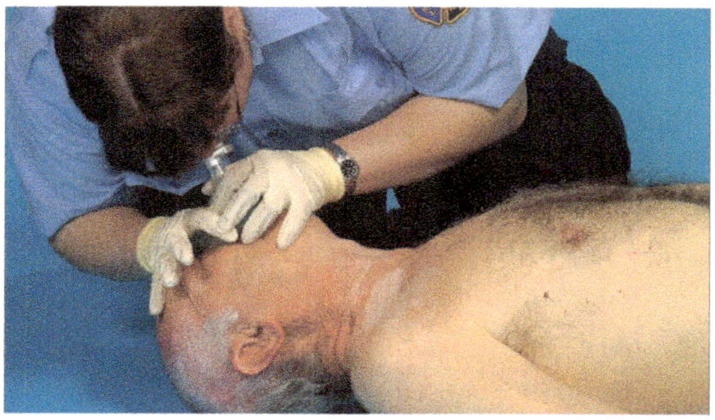

5. If the patient is not breathing, give two rescue breaths lasting 1 second each.

breaths, continuing until an AED arrives and is ready for use STEP 1.

3. Turn on the AED STEP 2. Remove clothing from the patient's chest area. Apply the AED pads to the chest: one just to the right of the breastbone (sternum) just below the collarbone (clavicle), the other on the left lower chest area with the top of the pad 2" to 3" below the armpit. Do not place the pads on top of breast tissue. If necessary, lift the breast out of the way and place the pad underneath. Ensure that the pads are attached to the patient cables (and that they are attached to the AED in some models). Plug the pads connector into the AED.
4. Stop CPR.
5. State aloud, "Clear the patient," and ensure that no one is touching the patient.
6. Push the Analyze button, if there is one, and wait for the AED to analyze the cardiac rhythm.
7. If no shock is advised, perform five cycles (2 minutes) of CPR beginning with chest compressions and then reanalyze the cardiac rhythm. If a shock is advised, reconfirm that no one is touching the patient and push the Shock button.
8. After the shock is delivered, immediately resume CPR beginning with chest compressions STEP 3.
9. After five cycles (2 minutes) of CPR, reanalyze the cardiac rhythm STEP 4. Do not interrupt chest compressions for more than 10 seconds.
10. If the AED advises a shock, clear the patient, push the Shock button, and immediately resume CPR compressions. If no shock is advised, immediately resume chest compressions.
11. Gather additional information about the arrest event.
12. After five cycles (2 minutes) of CPR, reanalyze the cardiac rhythm.
13. Repeat the cycle of five cycles (2 minutes) of CPR, one shock (if indicated), and 2 minutes of CPR.
14. Transport, and contact medical control as needed STEP 5.

Tip

Key Features of AED Use

- Early use and rhythm recognition
- Proper pad placement in any of the four positions
- No delay in patients with implanted devices
- Single shock with resumption of CPR

POST-CARDIAC ARREST CARE

Post-cardiac arrest care is equally as important as initiation of CPR and AED use. Once ROSC is accomplished, it is imperative to take a multi-disciplinary approach to patient care to improve outcome and maximize neurologic recovery. The goals following ROSC include optimizing cardiopulmonary function and organ perfusion, transportation to a comprehensive postresuscitation setting (hospital or critical care unit), temperature control, and treatment of multiple organ dysfunction.

SPECIAL CONSIDERATIONS FOR LAW ENFORCEMENT RESPONSE

LERs encounter unique situations that present hazardous obstacles to patient care. The primary concern is always scene safety. Ensure the scene has been cleared prior to initiation of patient care. Any situation requiring direct patient contact should prompt the use of standard precautions. Assume that all patients are potential carriers of bloodborne pathogens. Use proper barriers, including medical gloves, gowns, and face protection. It is also important to activate the emergency response system. Ensuring maximum medical support in a timely manner will improve patient outcome and survival rates. Finally, rapid triage of wounded or ill patients will maximize resources and identify those in need of emergent intervention.

CONCLUSION

Over the years, resuscitative techniques have continued to evolve as more research and data have become available. One major change from the 2005 guidelines in the 2010 guidelines is the emphasis on the CAB sequence in CPR. This focus shows that high-quality chest compressions are the foundation of resuscitation.

It is important for every agency and community to place an emphasis on continuing education of their rescue personnel. Be sure every rescuer in your agency has completed his or her recertification for BLS and advanced cardiac life support (ACLS) every 2 years. Provide feedback to your fellow LERs to ensure continuous quality improvement and help bridge the gap between ideal training scenarios and actual resuscitation.

Skill Drill 5

Using an AED

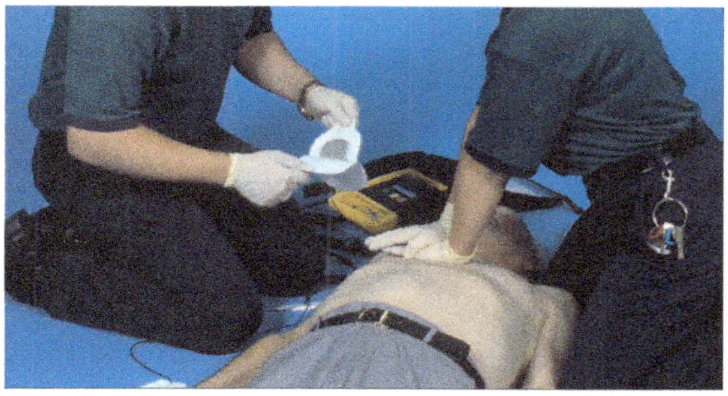

1. If the patient is unresponsive and CPR has not been started yet, begin providing chest compressions and rescue breaths at a ratio of 30 compressions to 2 breaths, continuing until an AED arrives and is ready for use.

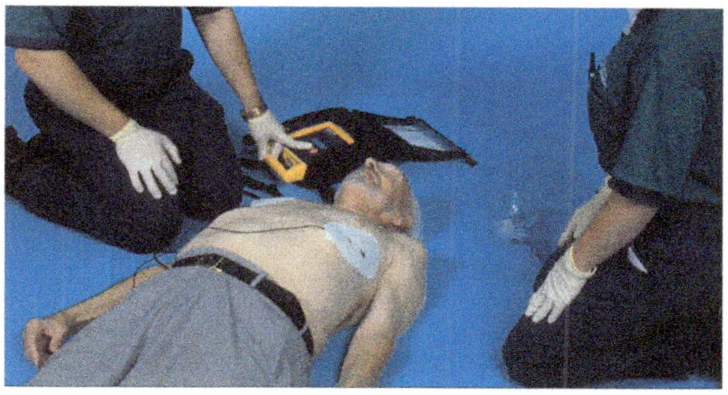

2. Turn on the AED. Apply the AED pads to the chest and attach the pads to the AED. Stop CPR.

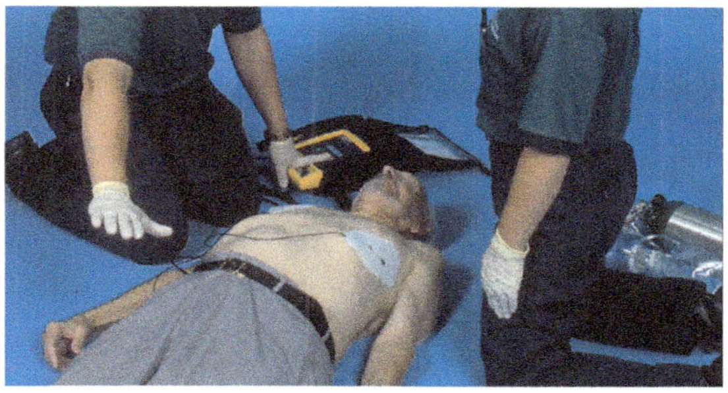

3. Verbally and visually clear the patient. Push the *Analyze* button, if there is one. Wait for the AED to analyze the cardiac rhythm. If no shock is advised, perform five cycles (2 minutes) of CPR and then reassess the cardiac rhythm. If a shock is advised, recheck that all are clear, and push the *Shock* button. After the shock is delivered, immediately resume CPR beginning with chest compressions.

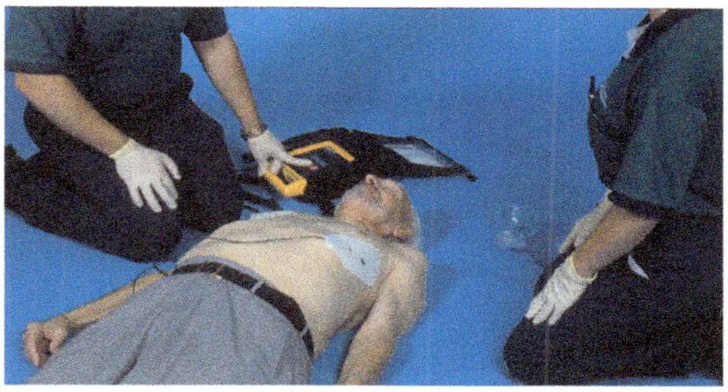

4. After five cycles (2 minutes) of CPR, reanalyze the cardiac rhythm. Do not interrupt chest compressions for more than 10 seconds.

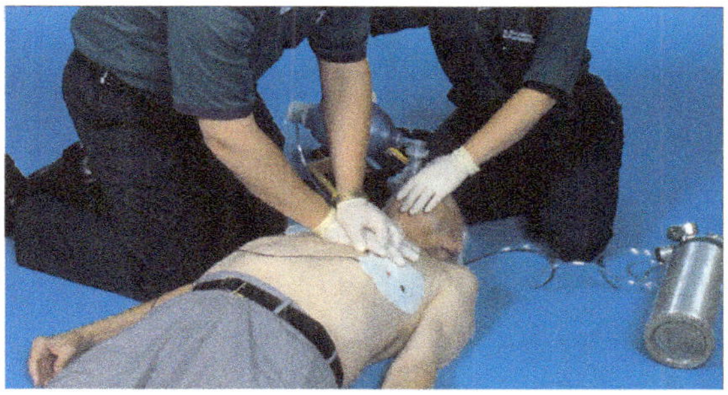

5. If shock is advised, clear the patient, push the *Shock* button, and immediately resume CPR compressions. If no shock is advised, immediately resume chest compressions. After five cycles (2 minutes) of CPR, reanalyze the cardiac rhythm. Repeat the cycle of five cycles (2 minutes) of CPR, one shock (if indicated), and 2 minutes of CPR. Transport, and contact medical control as needed.

Prep Kit

READY FOR REVIEW

- CPR will not only increase the number of patients who achieve return of spontaneous circulation (ROSC) after sudden cardiac arrest, but also will improve their quality of life and functional state of health.
- CPR is an effort to create artificial circulation by manually pumping blood through the heart to restore flow of oxygenated blood to vital organs.
- Circulatory failure may result from a failure of the heart to contract, heart valve damage, heart dysrhythmias, extremely fast or slow heart rates, blood loss, cardiac tamponade, tension pneumothorax, or a variety of less common conditions.
- The CAB (circulation, airway, breathing) approach is now considered the standard method to minimize time to first chest compressions.
- The assessment of the patient and initiation of CPR remain the foundation for saving lives of victims who suffer cardiac arrest. Recognizing cardiac arrest, activating EMS, performing prompt high-quality CPR, and defibrillating when appropriate will give patients the best chance of survival.
- Post-cardiac arrest care is equally as important as initiation of CPR and AED use. Once ROSC is accomplished, it is imperative to take a multidisciplinary approach to patient care to improve outcome and maximize neurologic recovery.

VITAL VOCABULARY

cardiac output The amount of blood pushed out of the heart with each beat.

chain of survival The five-link sequence for cardiac arrest care: early access, early CPR, early defibrillation, early advanced care, and post-arrest care.

CHECK YOUR KNOWLEDGE

1. Which of the following is the most important skill in resuscitative efforts?
   - **A.** Use of an AED
   - **B.** Performing high-quality chest compressions
   - **C.** Activating the emergency response system
   - **D.** Effective advanced life support
2. The compression-to-ventilation ratio for two-person rescue is 30:2.
   - **A.** True
   - **B.** False
3. Which organ is most susceptible to injury from cardiac arrest?
   - **A.** Lungs
   - **B.** Heart
   - **C.** Brain
   - **D.** Liver
4. Which of the following is not included in the American Heart Association's chain of survival?
   - **A.** Early defibrillation
   - **B.** Activation of the emergency response system
   - **C.** Effective advanced life support
   - **D.** Adequate oxygenation and ventilation
5. Adult chest compressions should be performed at a rate of 100 compressions per minute.
   - **A.** True
   - **B.** False

Assessment in **Action**

SCENARIO

You arrive on scene of a motor vehicle crash involving a single car. The driver appears to have been thrown from the vehicle and lands several feet away from the car. As you approach the patient, you hear gurgling every time the patient takes a breath. The patient is unconscious and his breathing also seems irregular and gasping, at a rate of approximately 8 breaths per minute.

ACTIONS

1. The most appropriate way to open this patient's airway is:
   - **A.** the head tilt–chin lift with cervical spine control.
   - **B.** the modified jaw-thrust with cervical spine control.
   - **C.** to place the patient in the recovery position.
   - **D.** any way possible; the patient's life is at stake.
2. The gurgling sound is most likely being caused by:
   - **A.** fluid in the upper airway.
   - **B.** fluid in the lower airway.
   - **C.** foreign body airway obstruction.
   - **D.** the tongue.
3. Which of the following would not be an acceptable method to manage ventilations?
   - **A.** Nasal cannula with supplemental oxygen
   - **B.** Positive pressure ventilator
   - **C.** Bag-mask device
   - **D.** Suction and recovery position
4. An oral airway adjunct will be more effective than a nasal airway adjunct for this patient.
   - **A.** True
   - **B.** False
5. If you use a bag-mask device to assist this patient, the supplemental liter flow should be set to which rate?
   - **A.** 2 LPM
   - **B.** 6 LPM
   - **C.** 8 LPM
   - **D.** 15 LPM

SECTION 5

Illness

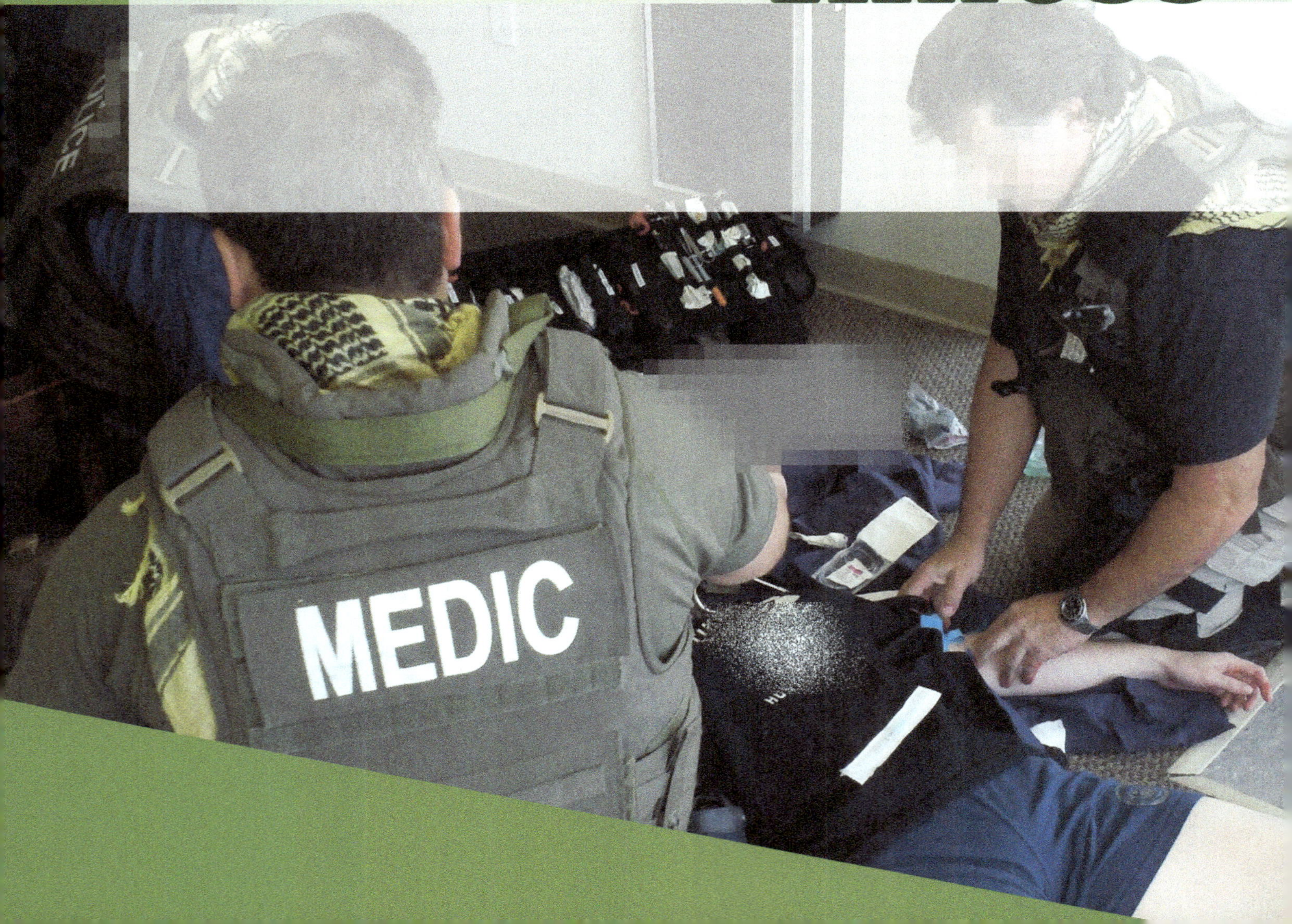

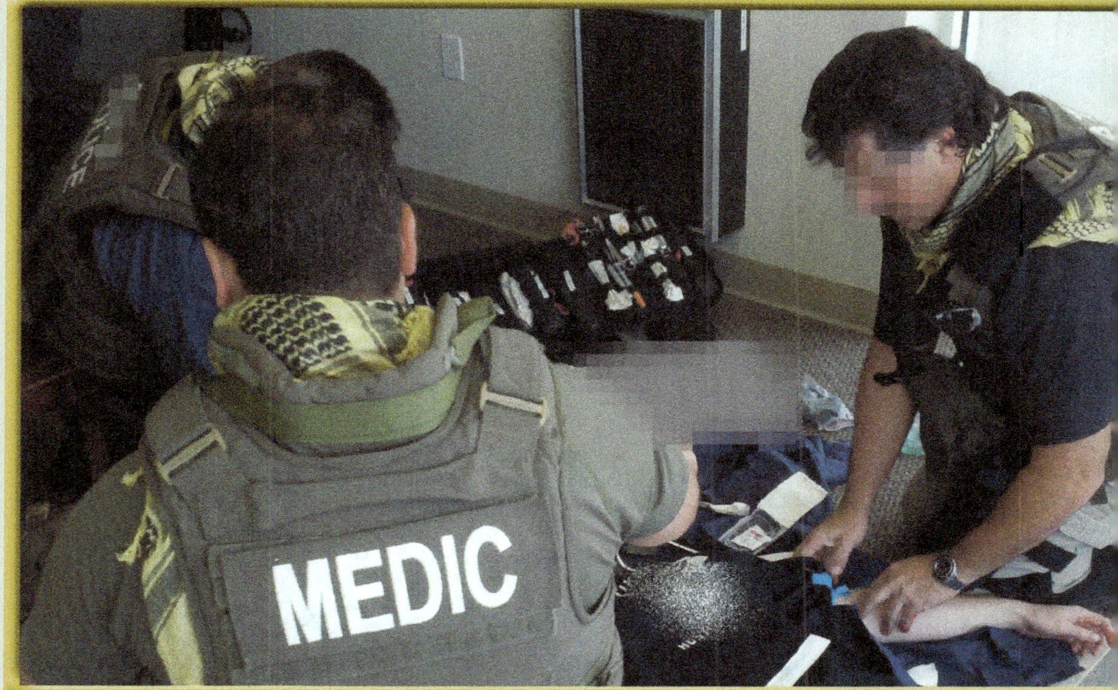

Section Contents

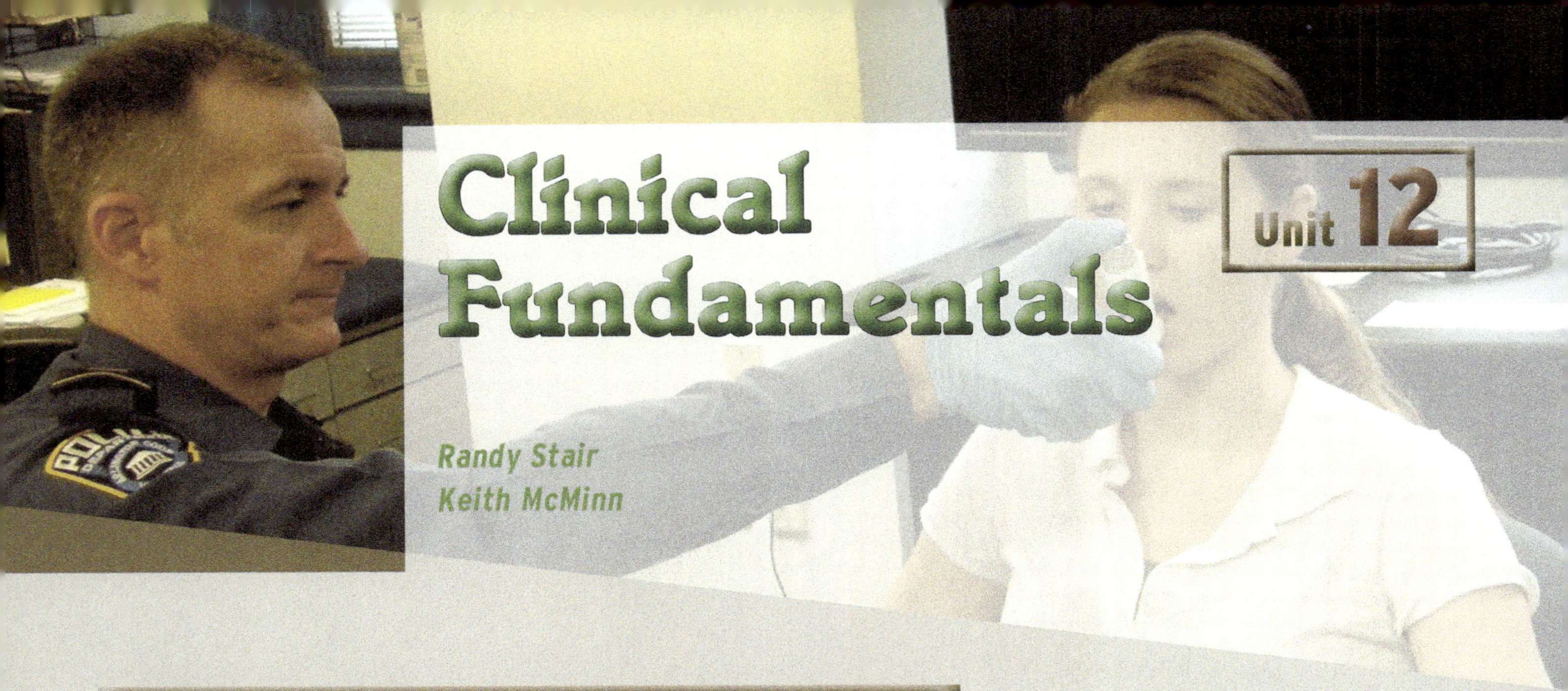

Clinical Fundamentals

Unit 12

Randy Stair
Keith McMinn

Law Enforcement Responder Objectives

Pathophysiology

- Define pathophysiology. (p 227)
- Discuss the effects of respiratory compromise on the body. (pp 227–228)
- Discuss the possible types of shock and how they are caused. (pp 228–231)
- Identify the stages of shock. (pp 228–231)
- Identify a plan for general shock interventions. (pp 228–231)

Pharmacology

- Explain how medications work. (pp 232–233)
- Explain the process by which a drug interacts with the human body. (pp 232–233)
- Discuss medication delivery options available to the emergency responder. (pp 233–235)
- Discuss the advantages, disadvantages, and techniques of auto-injector administration. (pp 236–237)
- Identify common medications that patients take during a medical emergency. (pp 235–237)

National EMS Education Standard Competencies

Pathophysiology

Uses simple knowledge of shock and respiratory compromise to respond to life threats.

Pharmacology

Uses simple knowledge of the medications that the emergency medical responder (EMR) may self-administer or administer to a peer in an emergency.

Medication Administration

Within the scope of practice of the EMR, how to

- Self-administer medication (pp 233–235)
- Peer-administer medication (pp 233–235)

Emergency Medications

Within the scope of practice of the EMR

- Names (pp 232–233)
- Effects (pp 232–233)
- Indications (pp 232–233)
- Routes of administration (pp 233–235)
- Dosages for the medications administered (pp 232–233)

Pathophysiology

Law enforcement responders (LERs) are often called to provide rescue or emergency medicine to the general public. Law enforcement emergency medicine programs will quickly embrace the principles of tactical emergency medicine (based on military medicine), only to realize that this material does not adequately address the wide range of medical emergencies that officers and agents encounter. Many of these medical emergencies require a basic understanding of how the body normally works, what can go wrong, and what care is needed urgently to stabilize the patient. In many law enforcement agencies, the focus on preparing LERs to assess and manage medical conditions provides an added service, making the officer or agent a valuable asset to the community. Arriving on scene first and leaving last, the LER must concentrate on treating life-threatening injuries and illnesses. In particular, he or she must consider respiratory compromise and shock. Severe medical emergencies can benefit greatly from critical emergency interventions such as oxygen administration or assisting with prescribed medications.

Building on the anatomy and physiology already presented, it is important to have a basic understanding of pathophysiology. **Pathophysiology** refers to a functional change associated with, or resulting from, disease or injury. In other words, pathophysiology means "abnormal function."

RESPIRATORY COMPROMISE

Respiratory compromise occurs when a patient suffers an impairment of the airway, ventilation, or respiration. The primary goal of breathing is to transfer oxygen from the air into the blood that is passing through the blood vessels surrounding the lung tissue. The second goal of breathing is to move the carbon dioxide from the blood to the lungs and finally into the external air.

The oxygen that travels from the air into the lungs passes through the capillaries and attaches itself to the hemoglobin on the red blood cells for movement throughout the body. This oxygen is released throughout the body. The cells use the oxygen to maximize their breakdown of glucose. When cells break down glucose with oxygen, they receive the greatest amount of energy from the glucose for cellular fuel. The gas released from breaking down glucose with oxygen is carbon dioxide. The carbon dioxide is released by the cells and absorbed in the blood. The venous blood vessels return the deoxygenated blood, rich with carbon dioxide, to the lungs, where an exchange of these gases takes place.

If the patient's airway is open, there is an adequate amount of oxygen in the air, and the patient is able to breathe air in and out, the gas exchange will occur and the oxygen-rich blood will return to the body, repeating the process. The LER should be familiar with the oxygenation and perfusion process explained in the units on anatomy and physiology and airway, breathing, and circulation.

Airway

The airway includes all of the structures of the upper and lower airway. If these structures are damaged or blocked, then air cannot move in and out of the alveoli and blood cannot exchange carbon dioxide for oxygen (**Figure 1**). The inability to exchange oxygen for carbon dioxide will lead to inadequate tissue perfusion, and cells will begin to die. A LER dealing with an incompetent airway should assess for blockage and manage per local protocols.

The following conditions can result in a blockage of the airway:

- Foreign body airway obstruction
- Tongue blocking the airway in an unconscious patient
- Blood or secretions
- Swelling
- Trauma to the neck

Ventilation

Ventilation refers to the process of actively pulling air into the lungs (inspiration) and letting it flow out (expiration). Inspiration rate and depth are usually controlled by the autonomic nervous system. The structures of the thorax and the diaphragm must work properly to exchange the air.

After ensuring that the airway is open, ensure that the patient is breathing. If the patient is not breathing, or is breathing too slowly or too quickly, the patient may not be able to get an adequate amount of oxygen into the lungs or an adequate amount of carbon dioxide out of the body.

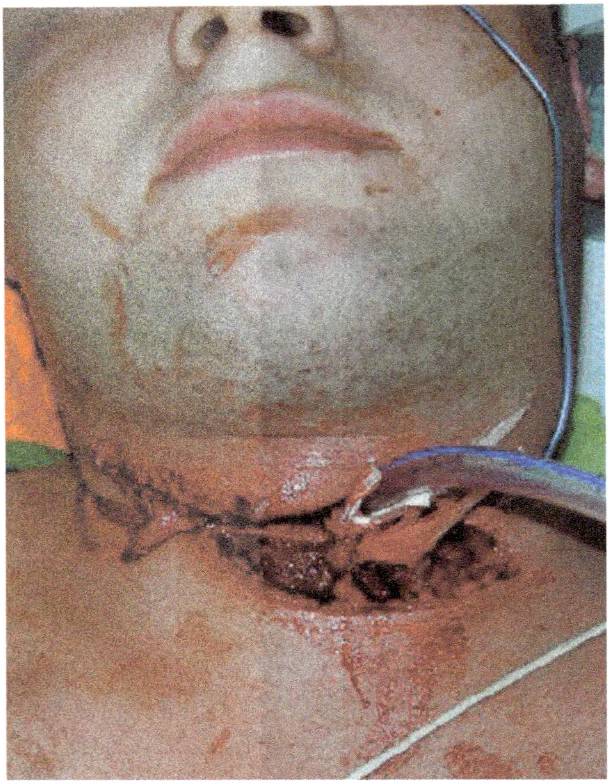

Figure 1 If airway structures are damaged or blocked, air cannot move through effectively.

This lack of gas exchange is a major threat to the patient's survival.

The following conditions can alter ventilation:

- Unconsciousness or altered level of consciousness
- Injury to the chest
- Poisoning or overdose
- Disease

Respiration

Respiration occurs when the airway is open, oxygenated air reaches the alveoli, and the capillaries on the alveoli are receiving blood flow from the circulatory system. LERs who are confident that the airway of the patient is open and that the patient is ventilating on his or her own or with assistance should immediately address other factors that can alter respiration. Be aware that some environmental threats, such as a low-oxygen environment or poisonous gases, may threaten the responder as well as the patient. If the LER thinks that he or she is being exposed to these environmental threats, he or she should immediately move the patient to a safe location.

If the patient presents with a respiratory condition that can block the exchange of gases, the LER must immediately understand the seriousness of this condition. These patients will benefit from immediate actions such as supplemental oxygen and access to the local emergency medical services (EMS) system or higher levels of care.

The following factors can alter respiration:

- Low-oxygen environment
- Poisonous gases (Figure 2)
- Infection of the lungs
- Illness that narrows the airway and causes wheezing
- Excess fluid in the lungs
- Excess fluid between the lungs and blood vessels
- Poor circulation

SHOCK

Laypersons frequently use the phrase *in shock* to describe anyone who does not act normally after a tragic event. Medically, however, shock is a condition that occurs when a patient suffers a severe illness or injury that has altered the patient's ability to move oxygenated blood to the cells and take deoxygenated blood from the body. This situation leads to a state of inadequate tissue perfusion because large numbers of cells cannot efficiently use glucose with oxygen to produce energy. This alteration in cell perfusion is a result of a diminished circulatory system. The LER must take immediate action to limit the effects of shock. Failure to stabilize the components of the circulatory system can lead to inadequate perfusion that is so severe it can destroy organs and ultimately kill the patient.

LERs should understand that treating medical patients suffering from shock requires quick, definitive measures. Just

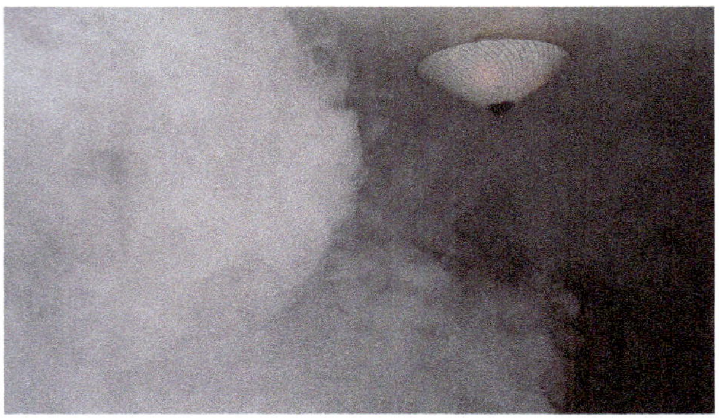

Figure 2 Smoke and gases can affect respiration.

as the rapid, appropriate use of a tourniquet can save lives in trauma patients by preventing hemorrhage, the appropriate deployment of an **epinephrine auto-injector** can save a life by reducing the effects of anaphylaxis. All illnesses and injuries are capable of creating shock. If left untreated, any medical condition that affects the patient will at some point negatively affect the circulatory system and place the patient in jeopardy of shock.

Conditions Affecting the Circulatory System

When the circulatory system is compromised by an illness or injury, it will not work properly. This failure of the heart or blood vessels or loss of blood will quickly be identified by the patient's body. When cells do not get the oxygen they need, carbon dioxide builds up in the blood. The body will identify this increase in carbon dioxide and make changes to the body's respiratory and circulatory systems. If the blood pressure starts to drop, the patient's body will identify this drop in pressure and will make changes in the circulatory system. If the patient is going into shock and the patient's normal corrective actions will not work, the patient's body will stimulate the sympathetic nervous system. Activation of the sympathetic nervous system will cause a release of adrenaline to counteract the lethal effects of shock on the body.

Heart disease, poisoning, and excessive rate or depth of artificial ventilation can affect the circulatory system. The pulse rate may be too slow or very fast, reducing the total amount of blood pumped per minute. Additionally, ventricular contractions may be too weak to pump blood effectively. **Table 1** lists types of shock and their causes.

Tip

Pump, Pipes, and Fluid

Because the different types of shock can be confusing, some LERs may find it useful to think of the heart as a pump, the blood vessels as pipes or hoses, and the blood as water.

Analogy: A fire truck uses a pump to pull water from a water tank or hydrant, it pushes water out through hoses toward a fire.

- If the fire truck pump fails, it is unable to push the blood properly (cardiogenic shock).
- If the water runs out, there is not enough blood to pump (hypovolemic shock).
- If the fire fighters switch from small-diameter hoses to large-diameter hoses. This drops the pressure in the hoses (sepsis, anaphylactic, psychogenic).
- If the fire fighters cannot switch to small-diameter hoses, the pressure on the hoses remains low (spinal shock).

Table 1

Types of Shock and Their Causes

Shock Type	Cause
Cardiogenic shock	Heart failure
Spinal shock	Brain cannot send the message to shrink the blood vessels
Septic shock	Toxins from infection open the blood vessels
Anaphylactic shock	Allergic reaction opens the blood vessels
Psychogenic shock	Emotional stress opens the blood vessels
Hypovolemic shock	Loss of blood or fluid

Neck fractures with spinal cord injury, infections, and anaphylaxis can lead to shock when blood vessels are unable to constrict, dropping blood pressure and reducing the effectiveness of the heart to pump blood.

Bleeding, vomiting, diarrhea, and burns decrease the amount of blood or its components in the blood vessels. This can reduce blood pressure, reduce the ability of the blood to carry oxygen, or create clots (**Figure 3**).

Types of Shock

Adrenaline is a hormone released by the adrenal glands, which are located above each kidney. Adrenaline increases the heart rate and shrinks the blood vessels. Patients who have lost a lot of blood from wounds or who have lost body fluid as a result of conditions such as burns or dehydration will suffer from a condition called hypovolemic shock. Hypovolemic shock is a loss of blood or fluid that decreases the ability of the heart to effectively circulate blood.

When a patient with hypovolemic shock receives adrenaline, the blood vessels constrict to maintain pressure on the blood left inside them, and the heart rate increases to circulate the blood faster. This response creates a situation in which the patient looks and functions near normal. This stage of shock is called **compensated shock**. If the patient continues to lose blood or fluid, the adrenaline will not be able to keep the patient operating at normal levels, and drastic changes in the patient's activity and functioning

Figure 3 There are three basic causes of shock and impaired tissue perfusion.

will occur. This stage is called **decompensated shock**. If the patient's condition continues to get worse, the patient will enter the final stage of shock, called **irreversible shock**. This last stage of shock will lead to death as organs die from a lack of oxygen.

Depending on the type of shock, the effect of adrenaline may or may not be beneficial. If the cause of the shock is a damaged heart, the patient will go into pump failure and adrenaline can stress the heart and worsen the patient's condition. If the patient has a condition that causes the blood vessels to open up (dilate), constriction of blood vessels by adrenaline may not be strong enough for long-term survival. In some cases that involve damage to the spine or the brain, the patient's body may not be able to send a message to release adrenaline.

The signs and symptoms of shock are often influenced by the stage of shock the patient is in and the cause of the condition. In the patient with hypovolemic shock, the release of adrenaline often causes the peripheral blood vessels to constrict, resulting in a paleness of the patient's skin tone, known as pallor. Moving the blood toward the important inner organs will also result in the patient feeling cooler, delaying capillary refill times. Because adrenaline is released when a person is under stress, signs and symptoms associated with the stress response will occur. The patient will become sweaty, restless, anxious, and possibly confused. The patient can complain of nausea, weakness, shortness of breath, and a racing heart. These symptoms are all associated with compensated shock. When the patient's body is still releasing adrenaline but is unable to compensate for the large amount of blood loss, the patient's blood pressure will drop. This is often noticed through a loss of peripheral pulses, such as the radial pulse in the wrist, while the carotid pulse in the neck weakens or remains present. If the patient can talk, he or she may complain of thirst and lose the ability to think clearly. As the patient continues to proceed into decompensated shock, he or she will become unconscious (**Figure 4**).

Tip

Signs and Symptoms of Shock

Signs and symptoms of shock include the following:

- Confusion, restlessness, or anxiety
- Cold, clammy, sweaty, pale skin
- Rapid breathing
- Rapid, weak pulse
- Increased capillary refill time
- Nausea and vomiting
- Weakness
- Low blood pressure
- Thirst
- Unconsciousness
- Decreased urine output

Although shock may be a dire condition, the LER who understands the seriousness of this condition and the steps associated with slowing or stabilizing shock can drastically improve the patient's chances for survival. LERs should consider the types of illnesses that can lead to shock and how they can best have an impact on them. If you understand that the patient who is passing out and has a very slow heart rate with chest pain is at risk for shock, and you understand that shock will lead to the patient's death, you will have the edge you need to respond quickly to calls for advanced levels of care and provide interventions approved by your local protocols to treat shock.

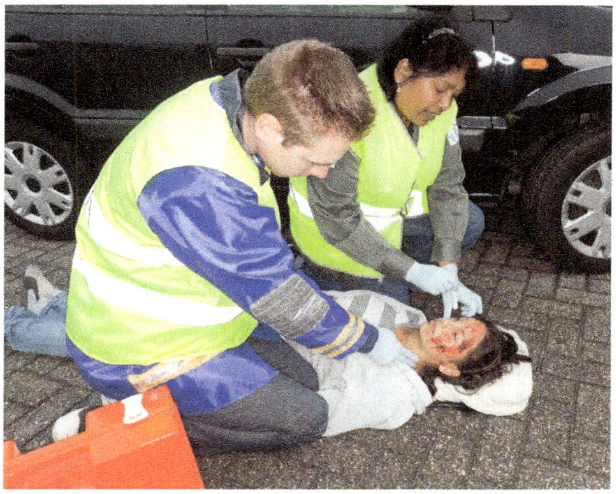

Figure 4 A patient in shock may be unconscious, with cool, sweaty skin.

Tip

General Interventions for Shock

Here are some general interventions for patients in shock. Remember to follow your local protocols when treating shock patients.

- Call for EMS.
- Position the patient.
  - If a head or neck injury is present, keep the patient flat and control the cervical spine.
  - If a heart or breathing problem is involved, position the patient for ease of breathing.
  - For all other conditions, lay the patient flat and consider elevating the feet, if in keeping with local protocols.
- Assess and manage airway, breathing, and circulation.
- Give supplemental oxygen.
- Treat the cause of shock as approved and authorized by your local protocols.
  - If shock is caused by blood loss, control bleeding.
  - If shock is anaphylactic, assist with patient's epinephrine auto-injector if available.
  - Seal open chest wounds.
  - If shock is heat related, assist with cooling and rehydration.
  - If shock is diabetic, administer oral glucose.
- Preserve the patient's body heat.
- Protect the airway by preventing oral intake. If the patient is vomiting, place the patient in the recovery position.
- Confirm EMS response or arrange for immediate transport to a medical facility.

Pharmacology

You arrive at the location of a noise complaint to find people fleeing the location and one civilian lying on the floor with a needle and syringe in his arm. He is unconscious and barely able to breathe. Scenarios similar to this have confronted many LERs at some point in their career. Unfortunately, this patient has succumbed to the use of street drugs. Many LERs face situations in which early arrival requires them to administer medications to save a life. The LER must learn to respect the power of medications and to understand when and how to use them.

A drug is a substance that in some way creates or blocks an effect in the body. Some drugs can be used to provide fuel or other substances the body needs. Drugs should never be handled carelessly. Even drugs that are very familiar may produce a dangerous response to a patient. Today, we encounter many different types of drugs. Emergency medicine drugs such as nitroglycerin are used to reduce the workload of the heart in cardiac patients. Epinephrine is used to fight off the effects of anaphylaxis. Glucose paste may be used for fuel in diabetic patients, and oxygen is a drug that is frequently used to maintain good perfusion.

In the early part of the 20th century, the United States started to use medications in a variety of fashions. Sometimes, the response was terrific, such as the invention and use of penicillin. Other times, people developed addictions, suffered disabilities, or died. Realizing the dangers that the public faced, the US government sought to regulate drugs. After many attempts, the **Food and Drug Administration (FDA)** was developed to provide oversight and regulation to the drug industry. The **Drug Enforcement Agency (DEA)** was established under the Department of Justice to become the lead federal law enforcement agency for drug law enforcement.

HOW MEDICATIONS WORK

Pharmacology is the study of the properties and effects of drugs and medications. Although the terms *drugs* and *medications* are used interchangeably, most people associate drugs with illegal substances, and medications with substances that have the ability to treat illness, relieve pain, and prevent disease. The **US Pharmacopoeia (USP)** is a scientific, not-for-profit organization that sets standards for medicines, foods, and dietary supplements. There are many drug reference texts and Web sites that provide drug information that may be helpful to the LER. It is important to understand that each medication actually has three names: the chemical name, the generic name, and the trade name given by the manufacturer.

Tip

Medication Names

Generic name: Original chemical name, which is not capitalized and is most commonly used

Trade name: Brand name assigned by the manufacturer and marketed for sale

Chemical name: Technical formula used by scientists

Medications may be prescription drugs or over-the-counter (OTC) drugs. Prescription drugs are dispensed by a pharmacist under a physician's order. OTC medications can be purchased directly from a wholesale or retail store without a physician's order. A "street" drug, such as heroin or cocaine, lacks pharmacologic purity but has active chemical properties and will cause an effect.

Tip

Medication Forms

Medications come in many different forms:

- Compressed powders or tablets
- Liquids that can be injected
- Gels and creams that are applied topically onto the skin or absorbed through mucous membranes
- Suspensions
- Fine powders or gases for inhalation
- Sublingual forms
- Liquid that vaporizes

In the United States, drugs and medications are classified based on how safe and effective they are. Certain drugs containing chemicals that have a history of abuse and the potential for drug dependence are assigned a rating on a schedule of controlled dangerous substances (Table 2).

A drug's interaction with the human body follows a particular process. It is absorbed into the body, distributed to the tissue, metabolized, and excreted. The introduction of the drug into the body's bloodstream is called **absorption**. When a drug is absorbed, it can be pushed out into the rest of the body through a process called **distribution**. As soon as the drug enters the body, it begins to be metabolized. **Metabolism** is the

Table 2

Controlled Substances

Schedule	Abuse Potential	Accepted Medical Use	Dependence
I	High	None	High
II	High	Yes	High
III	Less than I/II	Yes	Moderate/Low
IV	Less than III	Yes	Limited
V	Less than IV	Yes	Limited

process of breaking down the drug so it can be released from the body. Finally, the body rids itself of the drug through a process of **excretion**.

As a LER, you will be authorized to give patients certain medications. Physicians develop drug orders and protocols that include drug dose and indications for use. The physician takes into account the drug's actions, contraindications, side effects, route of administration, and time to give and repeat a drug dose to achieve the desired effect. Your medical director should have policies and protocols in place to guide you. The protocols for giving medications often include the following information:

- **Dose**. The amount of a particular drug that the medical director has authorized you to give. For example, if you are authorized to use glucose paste for diabetic emergencies, the dose may be 15 grams.
- **Indications**. The therapeutic uses for which a medication is prescribed and used. In the case of glucose paste, a typical indication would be for diabetic patients who have signs and symptoms of low blood glucose levels.
- **Contraindications**. When a medication should not be given to a patient because of harmful effects. For example, many medical directors avoid using glucose paste in patients who are unconscious.
- **Side effects**. The undesirable actions, both predictable and unpredictable, of a drug. Side effects can occur even if the medication is taken or administered properly. For example, nitroglycerin can cause a headache when properly administered. The headache will not harm the patient, but it is uncomfortable. Not all drugs have side effects.
- **Action**. The therapeutic effect a drug has on the body. For example, nitroglycerin reduces the workload of the heart by making the blood vessels dilate, reducing the amount of blood returning to the heart.

MEDICATIONS USED BY EMERGENCY RESPONDERS

Some medications work by activating or blocking certain mechanisms in the body called receptor sites. Receptor sites are found in nerves and muscles. When they are activated, they stimulate the tissue where they are located to perform a certain function. An example of this type of activity is the receptors found on the smooth muscle of the airways in the lungs. When stimulated by a medication such as epinephrine, the muscles relax and the airways open, making it easier to breathe.

Some drugs are used for energy or as enzymes. Glucose paste is often administered by responders to patients with diabetes whose blood glucose levels are low. The glucose is easily absorbed in the mouth and made available to the blood for transport to vital organs. Other medications may provide a boost in electrolytes required for certain body functions. Electrolytes are often delivered in emergency medicine through intravenous fluids or oral rehydration solutions.

Local protocols and medical direction will dictate the type of drugs and the way the LER can use them. LERs are often able to assist patients with their own prescribed medications. This is commonly done with nitroglycerin, epinephrine auto-injectors, and albuterol inhalers. Some LERs carry glucose paste, nerve agent antidote kits, and oxygen for delivery based on patient conditions. Some law enforcement EMT programs allow EMTs to carry epinephrine auto-injectors, aspirin, nitroglycerin, and intravenous solutions. Tactical-oriented EMTs may be allowed to carry a host of OTC medications that can be used to manage minor symptoms during long operations.

Special Populations
Medication Considerations

- Children and elderly patients may need different doses of medications than those used by adults. This is due to their slower ability to absorb and excrete medications.
- Pregnant patients are unable to take certain medications because they can harm the fetus.
- Some medications are delivered based on the patient's weight. Epinephrine auto-injectors and metered-dose inhalers deliver a fixed dose of drug. LERs should use only those drug delivery systems authorized by their local protocols and medical direction.
- Elderly patients may take a large number of different drugs. LERs should attempt to determine all of the drugs available to elderly patients, including OTC and herbal remedies.

ROUTES OF ADMINISTRATION

Medication can be delivered to the bloodstream by several means. Almost all of these routes of administration travel through body tissue before entering the bloodstream. Certain medications can be given to a patient by only one route of administration, whereas other medications can be given many different ways.

Typical Emergency Medication Routes

Emergency medication routes are as important as the drugs themselves. Oral medications are rarely used in emergency medicine because of decreased blood flow to the gastrointestinal system during shock and the potential for oral medications to become an airway issue. Intravenous routes are often reserved for advanced life support (ALS) providers because the drugs are directly available in the bloodstream as soon as they are administered. Giving drugs intravenously requires a great deal of training and experience to prevent life-threatening complications.

LERs often use medication routes that result in quick access to the blood with minimal risk. Routes such as intramuscular, inhalation, and sublingual can provide LERs quick, low-risk access to the bloodstream with minimal training.

Emergency medications are commonly administered via the following routes:

- **Inhalation**. Medication is inhaled into the lungs either to work on the lungs or to be absorbed into the bloodstream quickly.
- **Intravenous (IV) injection**. Medication is injected directly into a vein. This method provides the fastest way to deliver a chemical substance.
- **Intramuscular (IM) injection**. Medication is injected into the muscle and absorbed quickly because of the vast blood supply to the muscles. This route is less effective in people who are experiencing decreased tissue perfusion and shock.
- **Oral (PO)**. Medication is taken by mouth and enters the bloodstream through the digestive system. This process can take up to an hour.
- **Sublingual**. Medication is absorbed through the oral mucous membranes under the tongue.

Tip: Intramuscular Auto-injectors

Intramuscular auto-injectors have become a routine way to deliver life-saving medications that must access the blood in a relatively short period of time. Auto-injectors require minimal training and preparation and can be used quickly. Epinephrine auto-injectors and nerve agent antidote kits are packaged with a dose of medication that is specific for the condition. These auto-injectors can be carried relatively easily on the person who may need them.

Auto-injectors are helpful not only in assisting patients, but also in administering self and buddy aid. Ensure you know how and when to administer these medications to yourself and to your partner.

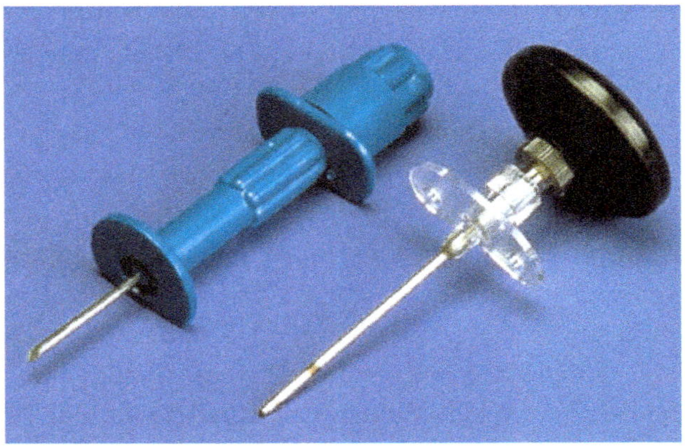

Figure 5 Intraosseous (IO) injection allows medication access to the bloodstream from the bone marrow.

Alternative Emergency Medication Routes

Some medical programs use alternative medication routes for specific medications or complications. **Intraosseous (IO) injection** is an excellent backup route for ALS providers if intravenous access cannot be obtained; medication is injected into the bone and travels to the bloodstream through the bone marrow (**Figure 5**). In some cases, the **rectal** route can be used to administer anticonvulsive medications (in the form of a suppository) to seizing children.

LERs in some programs may use **subcutaneous (SC) injection** instead of IM injection for certain drugs. In SC injection, medication is injected into the tissue between the muscle and the skin. The absorption rate for this delivery method is slower than other methods because of the decrease in blood supply in the area being injected.

Tip: Five Rights

When determining whether a medication is acceptable to use at an emergency scene, you should confirm the following information:

1. Right patient: Is this the correct patient?
2. Right medication: Is this the correct medication for this patient?
3. Right dose: Is this the correct dose of the correct medication for this patient?
4. Right route: Is this the right route to give the patient the correct dose of the medication?
5. Right time: Is this the correct time to give the patient the correct dose of the medication via the correct route?

The **transcutaneous** route may also be used for medications that can be absorbed through the skin. Some law enforcement programs use pain medication and motion sickness patches that can be placed on the skin allowing for long duration delivery of the medication.

COMMONLY PRESCRIBED MEDICATIONS

It is common for a LER to encounter a patient with an illness that requires a metered-dose inhaler for breathing problems, nitroglycerin for chest pain, or epinephrine for anaphylaxis. Knowledge of these commonly prescribed medications and the illnesses associated with them will improve your ability to assist patients on scene.

Metered-Dose Inhaler Medications

Most metered-dose inhaler (MDI) medications are taken for the respiratory condition asthma. The medications prescribed in an inhaler are focused on treating and improving the lungs and easing breathing. Taking an MDI medication may require a great deal of coordination, which can be difficult if a patient is having trouble breathing. In some cases, a doctor will prescribe a spacer to assist with directing the medication into the lungs. Once the MDI or spacer with MDI attached is placed into the mouth, the spray is released when the canister is pressed into the adaptor (**Figure 6**). Patients often take two puffs of their inhaler in an attempt to get the needed relief.

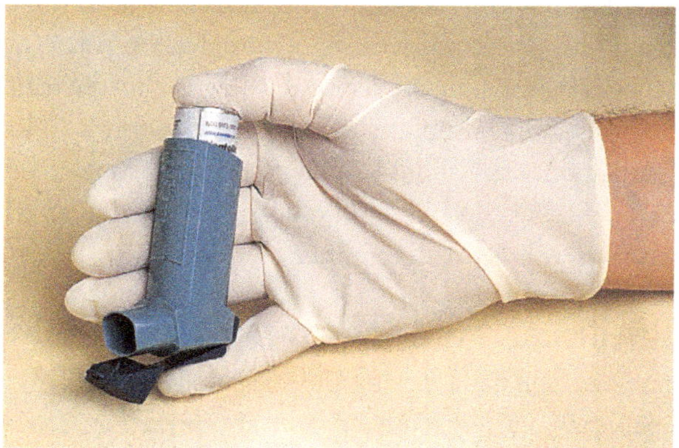

A.

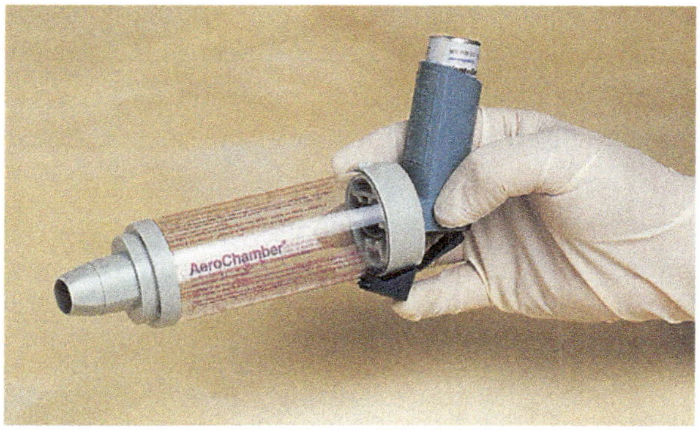

B.

Figure 6 **A.** Metered-dose inhaler. **B.** Metered-dose inhaler with a spacer.

Nitroglycerin

Many patients that you will encounter have conditions such as recurrent chest pain (angina, ischemic heart disease) or a history of heart disease. These patients will take nitroglycerin pills or spray to help dilate the blood vessels, reducing the amount of blood returning to the heart. This reduces the work load on the heart, thus reducing the heart's need for oxygen. A patient who develops chest pain and is already prescribed this medication will be instructed to take a nitroglycerin pill or spray in an attempt to resolve the pain (**Figure 7**).

Patients should not take nitroglycerin unless it is prescribed for them by their physician. A serious and unsafe interaction can occur if nitroglycerin is taken after a patient has taken an erectile dysfunction medication (eg, Viagra, Cialis).

Erectile dysfunction medications act by dilating the blood vessels. Combined with the dilating effects of nitroglycerin on the blood vessels, the patient's blood pressure can drop drastically.

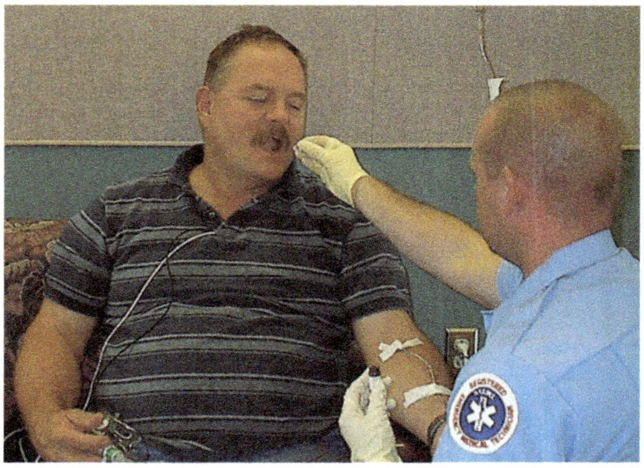

Figure 7 Nitroglycerin in the form of pills, ointments, patches, and sprays is used for the relief of chest pain.

LERs should determine whether a patient who is prescribed nitroglycerin is wearing a nitroglycerin patch. Some local protocols require the removal of the patch if the patient's blood pressure is dropping or the patient requires CPR and defibrillation. Care should be taken handling these medication patches. Use gloves and do not allow yourself or others to come in contact with the drug.

Epinephrine Auto-injectors

When a person has a serious and potentially lethal allergy, an epinephrine auto-injector (such as an EpiPen) is often prescribed to counter the effects of an allergic reaction should one occur (**Figure 8**). Epinephrine auto-injectors are commonly carried by people who have a known allergy to bee stings, shellfish, or to a medication such as penicillin. Epinephrine constricts the blood vessels and relaxes the airway passages during an allergic reaction episode. In patients with these severe allergies, epinephrine must be injected quickly. The auto-injector device is a spring-loaded syringe that, when depressed, releases and injects epinephrine into the muscle.

Depending on your protocols and medical direction, you will have to select a site for the auto-injector to deliver its medication into the muscle. The thigh, gluteus, and deltoid are common sites for application. Because these medication systems must be administered quickly, the clothing does not have to be removed over the site of injection. Take care that other objects, such as wallets and keys, are not in the needle's path.

The person applying the auto-injector will have to determine if there is a need to deliver the medication. Once need has been established, a safety device must be removed to arm the needle. The needle is housed inside one end of the plastic tube. The needle end contains a rubber stopper mounted in a plastic tube that is placed against the patient's body. When pressure is applied to the auto-injector, the needle end is pushed toward the patient's body, setting off the spring-loaded needle and pushing it through the rubber stopper and into the patient's muscle. Once the auto-injector has fired, it will push all of its contents out of the needle. The needle will remain exposed through the rubber stopper.

Care should be taken to prevent accidental needlestick from the exposed needle. An appropriate sharps container should be used (**Figure 9**). Because most of these auto-injectors are used away from routine medical environments, sharps containers may need to be improvised. A variety of alternatives exist in dealing with the exposed needles. Some systems break off the needle; others shove the needles into the ground, plastic jugs, or other devices that can accept the needle without providing additional risks.

Auto-injectors are notorious for accidental discharges. You should never play with an auto-injector. Never remove the safety device unless you are ready to inject the drug. Some programs train the responders to hold the needle in their

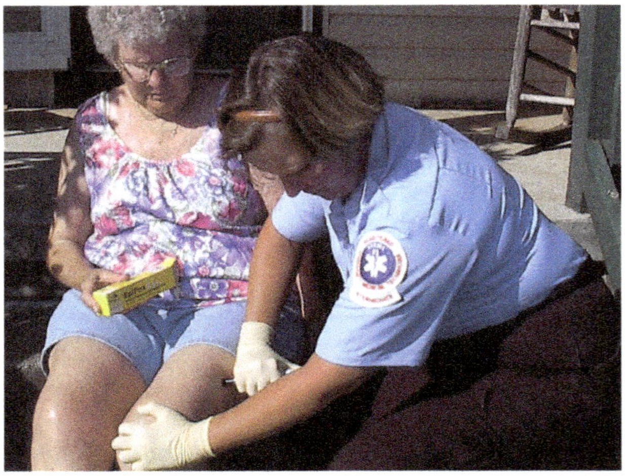

Figure 8 An Epi-Pen auto-injector may be used to administer a preset dose of epinephrine.

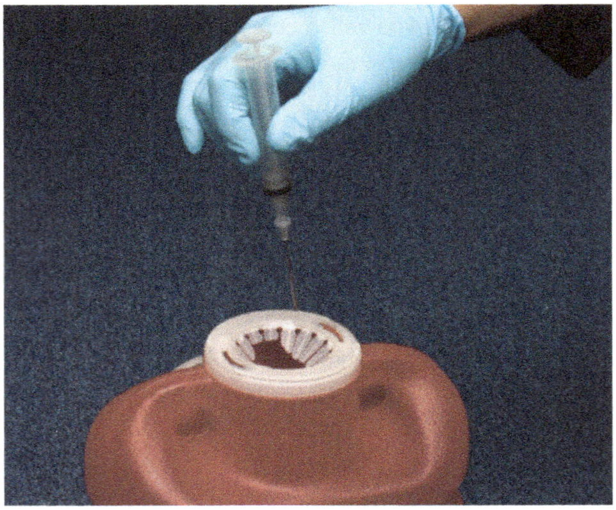

Figure 9 Properly dispose of any sharps (including epinephrine auto-injectors) in a closed, rigid, marked container.

hand with their thumb wrapped around their fingers. Too often this method results in the thumb falling on the injector end of the auto-injector. A better method is to hold the auto-injector between a thumb and two fingers like a writing marker or piece of chalk. This method prevents the thumb from slipping in front of the needle.

CONCLUSION

Respiratory compromise and shock are the major threats to both trauma and medical patients' survival. Through tactical EMS programs, LERs are indoctrinated into the importance of tactical priorities that address the stabilization of respiratory compromise and shock in the battlefield patient. Expediency in treating medical patients who are experiencing respiratory compromise or shock will save lives. Because of the large number of severe medical conditions that affect children, adults, and the elderly, the LER's ability to assess and manage respiratory compromise and shock provides the greatest benefit to the public he or she serves.

LERs will continue to expand their scope of practice and use lifesaving medications to aid people who rely on them. Medications, when administered according to local protocol, can be used quickly and safely.

Prep Kit

READY FOR REVIEW

- LERs must understand normal anatomy and physiology to understand pathophysiology (abnormal physiology).
- A primary goal of LERs should be to assess and manage the life threats of respiratory compromise and shock.
- Respiratory compromise can result from a problem with the airway, ventilation, or respiration.
- Shock is inadequate perfusion as a result of a diminished circulatory system.
- Many illnesses and injuries are capable of creating shock.
- The body's response to shock is to use the sympathetic nervous system to release adrenaline, causing an increased heart rate and shrinking blood vessels.
- To understand the circulatory system, the LER should think of the heart as the pump, the blood vessels as pipes, and the blood as the fluid being pumped.
- There are several types of shock:
  - Cardiogenic
  - Spinal
  - Septic
  - Anaphylactic
  - Psychogenic
  - Hypovolemic
- Shock exists in three phases: compensated, decompensated, and irreversible.
- Shock signs and symptoms can vary based on the type of shock. Typically, the shock signs and symptoms are related to the effects of adrenaline and how the patient responds to it.
- Treatment of shock should be driven by local protocols for specific conditions.
- The Food and Drug Administration (FDA) was developed to provide oversight and regulation to the drug industry, and the Drug Enforcement Agency (DEA) was established under the Department of Justice to become the lead federal law enforcement agency for drug law enforcement.
- Pharmacology is the study of the properties and effects of drugs and medications.
- *Medication* and *drug* are interchangeable terms.
- Drugs can have at least three different names: chemical, generic, and trade.
- In the United States, drugs and medications are classified based on how safe and effective they are.
- Certain drugs containing chemicals that have a history of abuse and the potential for drug dependence are assigned a rating on a schedule of controlled dangerous substances.
- A drug's interaction with the human body follows a particular process. It is absorbed into the body, distributed to the tissue, metabolized, and excreted.
- Medication can be delivered to the bloodstream by several different means. Certain medications can be given to a patient by only one route of administration, whereas other medications can be given in multiple ways.
- Typical emergency medication routes include inhalation, intravenous injection, intramuscular injection, oral, and sublingual.
- Alternate emergency medication routes include intraosseous injection, rectal, subcutaneous injection, and transcutaneous.
- It is common for a LER to encounter a patient with an illness that requires a metered-dose inhaler for breathing problems, nitroglycerin for chest pain, or epinephrine for anaphylaxis.
- Many law enforcement special operations teams use tactical emergency medical support guidelines in emergency care.

VITAL VOCABULARY

absorption The introduction of a drug into the bloodstream.

action The therapeutic effect that a medication has on the body.

adrenaline Hormone released by the adrenal gland that causes the blood vessels to constrict and the heart rate to increase.

anaphylactic shock Shock caused by an allergic reaction so severe that patients experience dilated blood vessels and airway constriction, altering their perfusion.

cardiogenic shock Damage to the heart that prevents it from being an effective pump, reducing blood flow and decreasing perfusion.

chemical name Technical formula used by scientists to identify a substance.

compensated shock A stage of shock in which adrenaline keeps the patient operating and functioning at near normal levels.

contraindications When a medication should not be given to a patient because of harmful effects.

decompensated shock A stage of shock in which the effects of adrenaline are not able to keep up with the problem causing the shock (eg, blood loss, toxins).

distribution The act of the body pushing the drug to the rest of the body after absorption.

dose The amount of a particular drug that the medical director has authorized you to give.

Drug Enforcement Agency (DEA) Organization established under the Department of Justice to become the lead federal law enforcement agency relative to drug law enforcement.

epinephrine auto-injector A device that administers medication similar to adrenaline that is used to fight the effects of severe allergic reaction.

excretion (The process of eliminating) a drug or its components from the body to the external environment. Excretion can occur through urination, defecation, sweating, breathing, and lactation.

Food and Drug Administration (FDA) Organization developed to provide oversight and regulation to the drug industry.

generic name Original name of a drug, which is not capitalized.

hypovolemic shock Loss of blood or fluid, which decreases the ability of the circulatory system to maintain adequate perfusion.

indications The therapeutic uses for which a medication is prescribed and used.

inhalation Breathing in a substance. As a medication route, medication is inhaled into the lungs either to work on the lungs or to be absorbed into the bloodstream quickly.

intramuscular (IM) injection Route of medication administration in which medication is injected into the muscle and absorbed quickly because of the vast blood supply to the muscles.

intraosseous (IO) injection Route of medication administration in which medication is injected into the bone, reaching the bloodstream through the bone marrow. Used when an intravenous route is needed and cannot be accessed.

intravenous (IV) injection Route of medication administration in which medication is injected directly into a vein. This is the fastest way to deliver a chemical substance.

irreversible shock The last stage of shock, in which organs are damaged and the body is near death.

metabolism The process of breaking down a substance so it can be released from the body. Starts as soon as the substance enters the body.

oral (PO) Route of medication administration in which medication is taken by mouth and enters the bloodstream through the digestive system.

pathophysiology Abnormal function of the body.

pharmacology The study of the properties and effects of drugs and medications.

psychogenic shock A temporary type of shock in which the blood vessels are dilated by an emotional stress response.

rectal Route of medication administration in which medication is absorbed through the rectum in the form of a suppository.

septic shock A type of shock created by the toxins from a severe infection, causing the blood vessels to dilate.

side effects The undesirable actions, both predictable and unpredictable, of a drug. Side effects can occur even if the medication is taken or administered properly; not all drugs have side effects.

spinal shock Inadequate blood flow caused by damage to the brain or neck that prevents the central nervous system from controlling the size of the blood vessels.

subcutaneous (SC) injection Route of medication administration in which medication is injected into the tissue between the muscle and the skin. The absorption rate for this delivery method is slow because of the low blood supply in the area being injected.

sublingual Route of medication administration in which medication is absorbed through the oral mucous membranes under the tongue.

trade name Brand name of a drug assigned by the manufacturer and marketed for sale.

transcutaneous Route of medication administration in which medication is absorbed through the skin, creating a slower, long-lasting effect.

US Pharmacopoeia (USP) A comprehensive government publication that lists every drug and medication by its generic name.

CHECK YOUR KNOWLEDGE

1. Your patient is experiencing chest pain and trouble breathing. Which of the following is the most likely cause of shock?
   A. Cardiogenic
   B. Hypovolemic
   C. Spinal
   D. Septic
2. Your patient is bleeding from a gunshot wound to the leg. Your best course of action would be to:
   A. Call EMS, assess and maintain ABCs, control bleeding, and give supplemental oxygen.
   B. Control bleeding and, when bleeding has stopped, reassess.
   C. Call EMS, apply oxygen, and lay the patient flat, elevating his or her legs.
   D. Place the patient in a vehicle and rapidly transport to a medical facility without wasting time with treatment.
3. Your partner and mentor for 5 years has developed chest pain. He advises you he is going to take his prescribed nitroglycerin spray. Nitroglycerin
   A. will make him hyperactive.
   B. acts to numb the heart.
   C. reduces the workload of the heart.
   D. should be injected into the leg.
4. Which of the following agencies is responsible for the oversight and regulation of the drug industry?
   A. DEA
   B. USP
   C. HHS
   D. FDA
5. __________ is the emergency medicine administration route that is used when an auto-injector is activated and discharged into a patient's thigh.
   A. Sublingual
   B. Intramuscular
   C. Inhalation
   D. Intravenous

Unit 13

Medical Emergencies

Michael Fayer
Bruce Walz

Law Enforcement Responder Objectives

General Medical Emergencies

- Conduct a thorough assessment of an ill patient. (pp 243–244)
- Discuss the causes, assessment findings, and management of neurologic emergencies. (pp 245–249, 250)
- Discuss the causes, assessment findings, and management of respiratory emergencies. (pp 249–253)
- Discuss the causes, assessment findings, and management of cardiovascular emergencies. (pp 253–256)
- Discuss the causes, assessment findings, and management of abdominal and gastrointestinal emergencies. (pp 256–259)

Special Medical Emergencies

- Discuss the causes, assessment findings, and management of renal emergencies. (p 259)
- Discuss the causes, assessment findings, and management of gynecologic emergencies. (pp 259–260)
- Discuss the causes, assessment findings, and management of immunologic emergencies. (pp 260–262)
- Discuss the causes, assessment findings, and management of endocrine emergencies. (pp 262–264)

National EMS Education Standard Competencies

Medicine

Recognizes and manages life threats based on assessment findings of a patient with a medical emergency while awaiting additional emergency response.

Medical Overview

Assessment and management of a

- Medical complaint (pp 243–245)

Neurology

Anatomy, presentations, and management of

- Decreased level of responsiveness (p 245)
- Seizure (pp 245, 248–249)
- Stroke (p 249)

Abdominal and Gastrointestinal Disorders

Anatomy, presentations, and management of shock associated with

- Gastrointestinal bleeding (pp 258–259)

Immunology

Recognition and management of shock and difficulty breathing related to

- Anaphylactic reactions (p 260)

Endocrine Disorders

Awareness that

- Diabetic emergencies cause altered mental status (p 262)

Cardiovascular

Anatomy, signs, symptoms, and management of

- Chest pain (pp 253–256)
- Cardiac arrest (p 255)

Genitourinary/Renal

- Blood pressure assessment in hemodialysis patients (p 259)

Gynecology

Recognition and management of shock associated with

- Vaginal bleeding (pp 259–260)

INTRODUCTION

Law enforcement responders (LERs) encounter a wide variety of medical emergencies affecting family, coworkers, and the citizens they protect. Many LERs find these situations stressful and difficult to control. However, knowledge of how to assess and manage medical emergencies using a standardized approach can help LERs perform calmly and effectively. A systematic approach to assessing a patient, recognizing life threats, and providing emergency interventions allows stabilization of the incident and has a positive effect on the survival of the patient. After immediate life threats have been addressed, it is important to collect crucial information from a patient interview. Additional information can be gathered from family members and friends, as well as any bystanders.

This unit focuses on both general and specific medical conditions. The general conditions covered have a number of different causes that can present with similar signs and symptoms. Although it is unlikely that you will be able to diagnose the underlying causes of an altered mental status or a seizure in a patient, your ability to treat the presenting symptoms and stabilize the patient is an important step in the patient's care.

This unit also covers a number of specific and often very serious medical conditions, including heart disease, stroke, respiratory emergencies, diabetes, kidney failure, abdominal emergencies, gastrointestinal bleeding, allergic reactions and anaphylaxis, and infection. Collectively, these medical conditions affect millions of people in this country. According to the Centers for Disease Control and Prevention (CDC), heart disease alone affects over 26 million adults in the United States. As a LER, you will no doubt encounter people with these conditions first-hand in the line of duty. Sometimes the patient or the patient's family will tell you that the patient has a particular medical condition. Other times you will suspect a certain condition based on your assessment of the patient and your medical knowledge, allowing you to provide more tailored intervention.

LERs are often the first ones on scene for medical emergencies. Through careful study of the material in this unit, you will be prepared to provide these patients with reassurance and maybe even lifesaving care.

General Medical Emergencies

GENERAL MEDICAL COMPLAINTS

General medical complaints can vary as much as the medical problems that cause them. When responding to a medical call, most of the information you collect will be from talking to the patient, his or her family and friends, and any bystanders who witnessed the medical emergency. However, be aware that this information is subjective and must be supplemented with your own direct observations and assessments.

Assessing the signs and symptoms of your patient will help you determine the illness that you will be treating. A **sign** is anything that you can see or feel, such as labored breathing or a weak pulse, or anything that you can measure, such as an elevated temperature. A **symptom** is something that your patient tells you he or she is experiencing. Another way of looking at it is that signs are objective because you see them, and symptoms are subjective because they are from the patient's perspective.

Some common examples of medical signs you might observe are a patient's blood pressure reading, heart rate, respiratory rate, temperature, vomiting, and blood in the feces. Chest discomfort, shortness of breath, nausea, dizziness, numbness, tingling, or abdominal pain are all examples of symptoms a patient would express to you.

General Assessment of the Medical Patient

When assessing a medical patient, it is important that you use a systematic approach, which will help you be consistent and provide the highest level of care for your patient. LERs should use the medical assessment guide as a template for interacting with medical patients (**Table 1**). As soon as a life-threatening problem is discovered, however, you must stop your assessment and treat that problem.

When performing a patient assessment on a medical patient, remember to use a standardized approach. Using

Table 1

Medical Assessment Guide

Medical Assessment Guide	
Consider scene safety.	• If the scene is not safe, remove the patient to cover or concealment. • Consider toxic or environmental threats. • Assess and manage life threats.
Does the patient look sick?	• Look for signs of distress. • Look for a medical identification tag.
What is the patient's mental status?	• Assess AVPU (alert, verbal, pain, unresponsive).
Interview the patient and/or bystanders.	• Determine the nature of the illness.
Take SAMPLE history.	• Signs and symptoms • Allergies • Medications • Past medical history • Last oral intake • Events prior to incident
Obtain vital signs.	• Check pulse, **respiration**, skin status, and pupil status. • Monitor blood pressure; use pulse **oximetry** if approved.
If you believe the patient is seriously ill, repeat the primary assessment and obtain vital signs every 5 minutes. For noncritical patients, reassess the patient and vital signs every 10 minutes.	

the same sequence will ensure that you don't miss any key information or problems. Start with the scene size-up, noting the number of patients, scene safety, and additional resources that might be needed.

Once the scene size-up is completed, you can proceed to the primary assessment and evaluate the airway, breathing, and circulation (ABCs) of the patient. Correct life-threatening problems as you identify them. Once the primary assessment is complete, take a thorough medical history and begin completing your detailed secondary assessment. In the secondary assessment, you complete a head-to-toe evaluation, while identifying and treating non–life-threatening conditions.

The reassessment is vital but varies among patients. In critically ill patients, reassessment is performed every 5 minutes, or more often if needed. With non–life-threatening conditions, the LER should reassess the patient every 10 minutes.

General Management of the Medical Patient

The management of a patient with a medical condition can be complicated by the nature of the illness. You will encounter a number of medical situations in the prehospital environment. Patient management in many of these cases is reviewed in this unit. However, there are some general principles that you can always use with patients who have a sudden illness.

First and foremost, everyone must be safe. Once the scene is secure, you may approach the patient, conduct your assessment, determine a treatment plan, and if necessary, reassess the patient at regular intervals (**Figure 1**). Maintain a professional demeanor at all times and work within your abilities to stabilize the patient prior to the arrival of emergency medical services (EMS).

Every effort should be made to ensure that the patient has an open and clear airway (also called a **patent airway**), that he or she is breathing adequately, and that any issues with bleeding and circulation have been addressed. If pulse and respirations are absent, begin cardiopulmonary resuscitation (CPR) and call for an automated external defibrillator

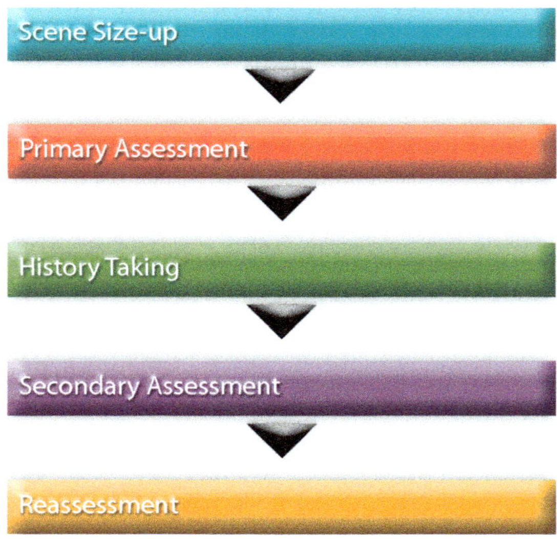

Figure 1 Patient assessment sequence.

Figure 2 The recovery position for an unconscious patient.

(AED) if one is available. If the patient has shortness of breath or exhibits signs of respiratory distress, administer oxygen. If the patient is vomiting, be sure to place the patient in the **recovery position** (on his or her side) so that vomit will not obstruct the patient's airway (**Figure 2**).

Frequently with medical emergencies, supportive care is all that is needed. Talking with patients, making them comfortable, and listening to their needs will often suffice until emergency medical technicians (EMTs) or paramedics have arrived on the scene. Good patient management prior to the arrival of EMS is critical and can be lifesaving. Continue to reassess the patient every 5 to 10 minutes as you wait for the arrival of EMS.

NEUROLOGIC EMERGENCIES

For the LER, patients experiencing emergencies associated with the nervous system can be very challenging. Unlike illnesses that present with a very specific or narrow range of symptoms; illnesses involving the brain are complicated and present with a wide variety of signs and symptoms. In most cases, neurologic emergencies focus on changes in the brain because of oxygen supply, blood flow, or unusual electrical activity. For example, many patients you encounter will present with dizziness, nausea, or confusion. It will be your task as a LER to take a thorough history and to assess the scene to determine a field diagnosis and plan for treating the patient.

This section will focus on some of the most common neurologic emergencies seen by responders.

Altered Mental Status

Altered mental status (AMS) is defined as a change in mentation, or responsiveness. AMS can range from confusion or anxiety to unresponsiveness or coma. As a LER, determining that your patient has an AMS is usually the easy part. Determining why can be a challenge.

Assessment

There are many causes for AMS. The main source of information about a patient's condition may not be available because the patient may be unable to communicate. Working with family members, friends, and bystanders will usually enable you to gather enough information to assess and treat a patient who is not responding appropriately or at all. Patients with AMS should not be allowed to refuse treatment and transport to a medical facility for further evaluation.

The airway is always the primary concern with a patient who has AMS. Poor oxygenation or inadequate **ventilation** will cause a decreased oxygen supply to the brain, which in turn causes **hypoxia**, a dangerous and potentially life-threatening condition in which the cells and tissues of the body do not have enough oxygen to survive.

There are many ways to explore why people have altered responsiveness. One easy way to remember the different possible causes of AMS is to use the mnemonic **AEIOU TIPS** (**Table 2**).

Communication

Possibility of Diabetes

When assessing a patient presenting with altered mental status, it is important to check for evidence of diabetes. If the patient is responsive, ask the following questions:

- Are you a diabetic?
- Did you take your insulin today?
- Have you eaten today?

Seizure

A seizure is a disruption of the normal electrical activity of the brain. There are many common causes of seizures. In adults, the most common cause of seizure is a failure by patients with a history of seizure disorder to take their antiseizure medication.

For infants and children, the most common cause of seizure is a high fever or sudden increase in body temperature. This kind of seizure, called a febrile seizure, is caused

Table 2

AEIOU TIPS Mnemonic

A	Alcohol abuse	Alcohol abuse is a widespread problem in many societies. Alcohol intoxication can be found in patients of any age, from teenagers to the elderly. It is important to remember that alcohol is a **depressant**, meaning it decreases the activity of the central nervous system. People under the influence of alcohol can experience AMS, nausea, vomiting, and unsteady gait. If you have a patient involved in a motor vehicle crash or a fall, use extra caution when assessing your patient because alcohol can mask injuries or underlying medical problems. Alcohol abuse can be acute or chronic. A person can ingest too much alcohol over a short period of time—acute abuse—resulting in what is called alcohol poisoning. This is a life-threatening condition because excessive alcohol decreases one's drive to breathe. Thus, a patient with alcohol poisoning can die of hypoxia to the brain. Furthermore, a severely intoxicated patient is unable to manage his or her airway and may die if the contents of the stomach are inhaled into the lungs (aspirated) after vomiting. Chronic alcohol abuse presents a different set of problems. Alcohol can cause malnutrition, liver disease and failure, gastrointestinal disorders, esophageal erosion, and life-threatening bleeding. When a patient has abused alcohol for an extended period of time and decides to stop drinking "cold turkey," it may be necessary to treat the patient for alcohol withdrawal. Over a long period of time, the body becomes dependent on alcohol. Within 24 to 72 hours after their last drink, chronic alcohol abusers may present with signs and symptoms of alcohol withdrawal, delirium tremors (DTs), hallucinations, and even **seizures**. This form of alcohol withdrawal is considered a life-threatening emergency and requires immediate attention in the emergency department.
E	Epilepsy (seizures)	**Epilepsy** is a common cause of seizures, which can be as mild as a person staring off into space with no noticeable signs other than a failure to respond to the care provider. The most severe seizure is a **grand mal seizure**, which presents with total body convulsions. Widespread muscle spasms disrupt breathing patterns and can cause hypoxia. Other common causes of seizures are tumors, diabetic problems, trauma, **stroke**, hypoxia, poisoning, and a specific complication of pregnancy called eclampsia.
I	Insulin (diabetes)	In a healthy person, the **pancreas** produces the hormone **insulin**, which enables **glucose** in the blood to enter the body's cells, where it is used as fuel. **Diabetes** is an endocrine system disease that disrupts this process. **Hypoglycemia** (low blood sugar) is the most common cause for AMS in a diabetic patient. Severe hypoglycemia, called **insulin shock**, can progress rapidly, often within a few minutes. If insulin shock is not diagnosed and corrected by the rapid administration of glucose in some form, the patient may die. If a patient presents with AMS, be sure to assess for insulin shock. Keep in mind that a person experiencing insulin shock may appear drunk, making it easy to misdiagnose. The section on diabetic conditions covers hypoglycemia and other diabetes-related issues in more detail.
O	Oxygen or overdose	Oxygen: Of all the organs in the body, the brain is the most sensitive to changes in oxygen levels in the blood. If the body lacks oxygen, the brain will become affected within minutes. If hypoxia is caused by an unsafe environment, it is imperative to remove the patient from the scene. If the patient is in a confined space, specialized resources will be necessary to remove the patient from the scene safely. If you respond to a lab or an area that you suspect has a depleted oxygen supply, be sure to assess for scene safety first. Look through a window or door to see if anyone is in the area. If you have more than one person down or see a vapor cloud, do not enter the area under any circumstances. If you suspect a fire in the room, feel the doorknob or door for heat prior to entering. Overdose: A drug overdose can be intentional or accidental and can result from over-the-counter medications, prescription medications, or illicit drugs. The improper administration of nearly any medication can cause overdose. Drugs are often classified as stimulants or depressants. Cocaine, PCP, and caffeine are examples of **stimulants**, meaning they increase the activity of the central nervous system. Persons taking stimulants present with signs and symptoms such as agitation, increased activity, nervousness, increased heart rate, dilated pupils, or aggressiveness. These patients can become violent and dangerous in some situations. Depressants—such as alcohol, opiates (morphine, heroin), or barbiturates—suppress the central nervous system and cause AMS. Common signs and symptoms include drowsiness, confusion, decreased heart and respiratory rates, and lethargy. If taken in sufficient quantity, opiates can suppress the respiratory system to the point at which the patient stops breathing. If not corrected, the patient will go into cardiac arrest due to hypoxia. If you get dispatched for a "young" person in cardiac arrest, immediately assess the patient for shallow respirations. If respirations are shallow, assess for pinpoint pupils. This is a classic sign of narcotic overdose. If you maintain the airway and ventilate the patient until EMS arrives, the patient's condition can often be reversed with the drug naloxone (Narcan), which is carried by most paramedic ambulances.

Table 2

AEIOU TIPS Mnemonic *(continued)*		
U	Uremia (kidney problems)	**Uremia** is a condition that results from kidney failure. The nonfunctioning kidneys are unable to remove waste products from the blood, resulting in a high level of toxins in the body. Signs and symptoms of uremia can range from decreased appetite, weight loss, and lethargy in the early stages to AMS and coma in the late stages. Other symptoms include nausea, vomiting, muscle cramps, bone pain, itching, cold, shortness of breath, and seizures. This is not a disease process that is treated by LERs in the field. Patients should be stabilized with oxygen and a good airway and placed in a position of comfort until EMS arrives.
T	Trauma or temperature	Trauma: Trauma as a cause of AMS is most commonly associated with traumatic brain injury. Trauma to the head can be life threatening. Even if the patient is conscious when you arrive at the scene, ask bystanders if they observed a period of AMS or unconsciousness in the patient. All trauma patients with altered mentation should be considered candidates for cervical spine immobilization and transport to a trauma center. Temperature: Patients can experience AMS in situations where their temperature becomes too high or too low. Assess both the medical and the environmental situation.
I	Infection	An infection in the body, accompanied by high fever, can often cause altered mentation. In these situations, it is common for the body to build up toxins and become septic. Attempt to control the patient's fever by gradually cooling the body. Cooling is done by wiping the patient down with towels soaked in tepid or room temperature water or by placing ice packs in the arm pits and groin areas. Be sure to wrap the ice packs in a towel so they do not freeze the skin. Remember that cooling the body too quickly causes the body to shiver. (Shivering is the body's mechanism for generating heat.) As a result, you risk actually increasing the patient's temperature.
P	Psychiatric or poisoning	Psychiatric: Psychiatric causes for AMS are many. Patients with psychiatric conditions can exhibit a wide range of behaviors—from mania to depression to psychosis—where they appear to be out of touch with reality. Behaviors can vary from being withdrawn and reclusive to being aggressive and demanding. Attempt to calm and reassure the patient while maintaining a safe distance. Always be alert to any sudden moves. Speaking to the patient in a professional manner and letting the patient talk is important. It is paramount to be honest and never mislead or lie to patients. Do not agree with patients' delusions simply because you think it will make them feel better or make your job easier. In the end, it will generally cause you more complications. Poisoning: A poison is any substance or chemical that causes a potentially toxic reaction in the body. As a LER, you will experience many patients who have been exposed to drugs, kitchen cleaners, antifreeze, and many other substances that may cause a life-threatening condition to occur. These chemicals can result in burns, respiratory distress, vomiting, or unresponsiveness. Scenes involving poisoning are often chaotic due to the urgency of what is happening with the patient. It is important that the emergency responder remembers to see the "big picture" in this situation. Is the chemical that poisoned your patient a risk to you? Is it a gas, liquid, powder, or other form? Scene safety is paramount. Your treatment will depend on the presentation of the patient. Managing the ABCs will serve you well until the arrival of EMS.
S	Shock or stroke	Shock: Shock is defined as inadequate tissue perfusion. This means that the body is not able to push the blood throughout the body with enough force to provide oxygenated blood to the tissues adequately. There are several types of shock, all of which affect one of three systems: the heart, the blood vessels, or the blood. Our bodies maintain perfusion by the heart pumping at the correct rate and pressure. Meanwhile, the blood vessels maintain the right size to hold the volume. When the blood vessels are filled and pumping properly, there needs to be enough volume to transport the oxygenated blood to all the body tissue. If the blood can't get to the brain with enough pressure to perfuse the brain, an altered level of consciousness will occur. Stroke: A stroke is a condition affecting the brain that is caused by either a blood clot in an artery in the brain or a hemorrhage within the blood vessels or brain itself. Strokes range in severity from mild to severe and can result in death or permanent disability. The onset of signs and symptoms occurs suddenly and is often very pronounced. Patients can experience AMS, high blood pressure, facial drooping, drooling, loss of bowel and bladder control, and difficulty speaking. These patients need rapid administration of high-flow oxygen, airway maintenance, and rapid transport to an emergency department for further evaluation and treatment.

primarily by how *fast* a child's body temperature rises, not necessarily how *high*. An infant or child whose body temperature rises to 104°F over a 24-hour period is less likely to have a seizure than an infant or child whose body temperature rises to 104°F in a few hours.

Seizures are often a sign of an underlying condition. The most common causes of seizures are as follows:

- Brain tumor
- Hypoglycemia or hyperglycemia (diabetes)
- Trauma
- Stroke
- Hypoxia
- Poisoning
- Seizure disorder
- Alcohol or drug withdrawal
- Eclampsia
- Heat stroke

Assessment

There are several different types of seizures. A less serious type of seizure is called a partial complex, or petit mal, seizure. This type of seizure usually lasts only a few seconds and is not accompanied by uncontrolled muscle spasms. In fact, a person who has a petit mal seizure may perceive it as simply a momentary lapse of consciousness or a blank stare.

Generalized seizures, also called grand mal seizures, are the most dramatic and severe type of seizure. They include loss of consciousness and uncontrolled muscle spasms, which can cause the jaws to clench shut and can disrupt the body's ability to breathe. Sometimes patients who are seizing may bite their tongue or cheek, causing bleeding, which can in turn compromise the airway. It is also common for patients who are seizing to become incontinent, meaning they lose control of their bowel or bladder.

Generalized seizures can be dramatic and often draw a crowd. As you approach the area, complete a scene size-up. Ensure that the scene is safe to enter, evaluating safety for yourself and the seizing patient. Standard precautions are always needed. If the patient is actively convulsing, place a jacket or padding under the patient's head to decrease the possibility of head trauma without occluding the airway. Move the crowd back as soon as possible and try to protect the patient's privacy. Do not restrain or hold down the patient. Doing so could actually harm the patient and possibly fracture bones. Attempt to loosen any restrictive clothing and observe the patient's airway. Because the patient may not be breathing, it is common for the patient to become cyanotic, meaning the skin takes on a bluish tinge due to poor oxygenation of the circulating blood. Most seizures stop within 1 to 2 minutes and the patient starts to breathe again spontaneously.

Tip

During a Seizure

Do not attempt to put anything in the patient's mouth during a seizure. Objects such as wallets, spoons, or bite sticks are not helpful and may result in bleeding from the soft tissue or broken teeth.

Status epilepticus is a life-threatening condition in which a patient has a series of three or more seizures without regaining consciousness or a seizure that lasts longer than 30 minutes. Such seizures are potentially fatal because the patient does not breathe during the actual seizure activity, resulting in hypoxic injury to the patient's brain and other vital organs.

Tip

Multiple Patients Having a Seizure

Remember your weapons of mass destruction training. If more than one patient is having a seizure, there may be a chemical agent involved.

Management

Protect the patient from harming himself or herself by moving objects away and supporting the patient's head. As soon as the seizure activity stops, assess and manage the patient's airway. Clear the airway of any blood or secretions, using suction if needed and available. Do not force anything into the patient's mouth. Roll the patient over into the recovery position and complete a rapid patient assessment. During this time, the patient will become more oriented but will be exhausted and will want to rest. Try to get a SAMPLE history from those at the scene and give this information to EMS when they arrive.

Tip

Clearing the Patient's Airway

It is common for seizure patients to bite their tongue or lips during a grand mal seizure. Be prepared to clear the airway and move the patient to the recovery position as soon as the seizure ends.

Special Consideration for Law Enforcement Response

LERs should always maintain a high level of suspicion when responding to a seizure call, especially when responding to a public area. En route to the scene, contact dispatch and request the number of patients on location who are seizing. If there is more than one patient, you may have a different issue to deal with upon arrival, such as a hazardous material or dirty bomb. Securing the scene would then become your highest priority.

Stroke

Stroke is a leading cause of brain injury and disability in adults. Each year about 700,000 adults experience strokes, and approximately 158,000 of them die. Although some strokes are caused by hemorrhage in the brain, most strokes (70%) are caused by a blood clot that lodges in an artery of the brain. The clot blocks the blood supply to part of the brain. Without treatment, that part of the brain will be damaged or die. Think of a stroke as a "brain attack," similar to a heart attack. People with high blood pressure have an increased risk of having a stroke.

A stroke is a medical emergency, and the LER has a critical role in the patient's outcome. If a stroke can be identified within the first 2 hours of the onset of signs and symptoms and the patient is transported to a specialty stroke center, current treatment can often reverse the effects on the brain.

Assessment

There are many signs and symptoms of stroke, and they can be similar to the signs and symptoms of a head injury, insulin shock, or seizures. Signs and symptoms of stroke include the following:

- Headache (often described as "the worse headache I've ever had")
- Confusion or AMS
- Unresponsiveness
- Difficulty speaking or slurred speech
- One-sided weakness
- Loss of bowel or bladder control
- High blood pressure
- Dizziness or weakness
- Loss of facial muscle control (one sided, sometimes presenting as facial droop)
- Loss of vision or vision that is doubled or blurred
- Combative, uncooperative, or restless behavior
- Inability to swallow, or tongue deviation

The **Cincinnati Stroke Scale** is an accurate way to determine whether a patient is having or has had a stroke. It consists of three tests that are easy for you to administer and easy for the patient to perform. **Table 3** outlines how to conduct this exam. If the patient is not able to complete one or more of these tasks, suspect a stroke.

Management

Many stroke patients are unable to maintain a clear airway due to paralysis or weakness. Open the airway and provide high-flow oxygen if available. Constantly evaluate the airway. If the patient appears to be having difficulty maintaining an open airway—such as coughing, gagging, or becoming cyanotic—you must take action immediately. You may have to position the patient in the recovery position until the arrival of EMS. If the patient is sitting in an upright position, move him or her safely to the floor (with assistance) and roll the patient onto his or her side. If the patient is lying down on a bed or sofa, quickly roll the patient into the recovery position. Provide reassurance to the patient because most stroke patients are scared and feel helpless due to their sudden illness.

Communication

Do Not Add to Anxiety

A stroke patient may be able to hear you even if he or she cannot speak or appears to be unconscious. Be careful not to say anything that would increase the patient's anxiety.

RESPIRATORY EMERGENCIES

The respiratory system performs two functions: ventilation and respiration. Ventilation is the act of moving air in and out of the lungs, achieved through the use of the primary respiratory muscles. These muscles, the diaphragm and the intercostal muscles of the chest, are controlled by the brain.

In a healthy person, the brain monitors the level of carbon dioxide (CO_2) in the body. As carbon dioxide levels increase, the brain sends a message to the respiratory muscles to contract, resulting in an increase in the volume of the chest. As the volume increases, the pressure in the lungs decreases. Once the pressure inside the lungs decreases below the atmospheric pressure, air rushes into the lungs. This is called **inhalation** and is the active phase of breathing.

Once the lungs are full of air, the opposite occurs. The respiratory muscles relax and return to their normal position, the volume of the chest decreases, and air is forced out of the lungs. This is called **exhalation** and is the passive phase of breathing.

Table 3

The Cincinnati Prehospital Stroke Scale

Facial Droop	**Have the patient show teeth or smile.**	
Normal	Both sides of the face move equally.	
Abnormal	One side of the face does not move as well as the other side.	
Arm Drift	**Patient closes eyes and holds both arms straight out for 10 seconds.**	
Normal	Both arms move the same or both arms do not move.	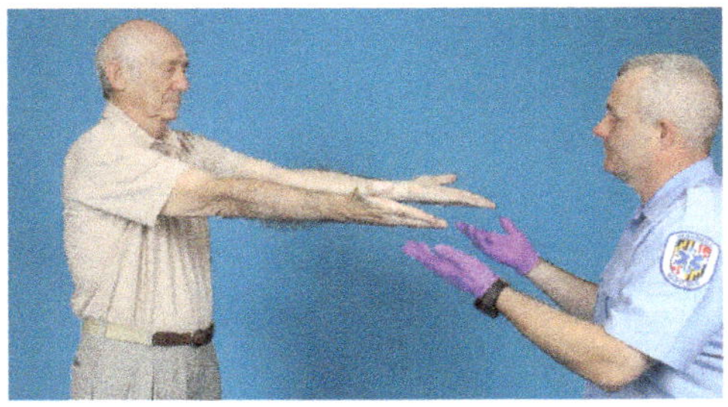
Abnormal	One arm does not move or one arm drifts down compared with the other.	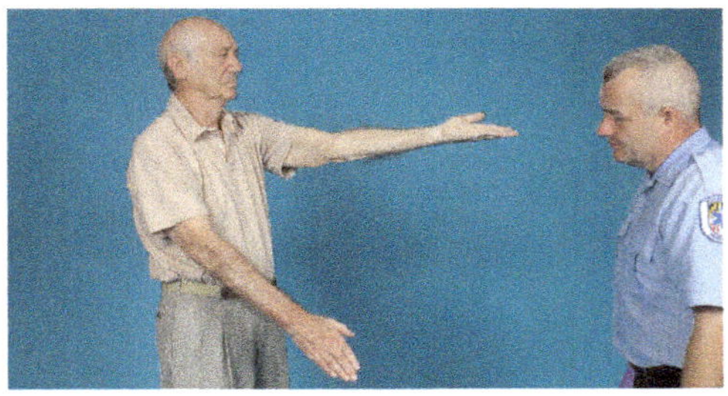
Speech	**Have the patient say, "You can't teach an old dog new tricks."**	
Normal	Patient uses correct words with no slurring.	
Abnormal	Patient slurs words, uses the wrong words, or is unable to speak.	

The second function of breathing is respiration. Respiration occurs once the alveolar sacs fill with air. During inspiration, the sacs stretch, allowing oxygen to transfer into the blood and carbon dioxide to transfer from the blood to the alveolar sacs. After this process occurs, the red blood cells in the blood are full of oxygen and the alveolar sacs are full of carbon dioxide. Then, during exhalation, carbon dioxide is breathed out of the system and removed from the lungs.

General Assessment

The assessment of a patient in respiratory distress starts with determining the adequacy of the patient's breathing. To assess adequate breathing, first assess the respiratory rate and determine whether it is within the normal limits for the patient (**Table 4**).

Next, determine whether the breathing is regular or irregular. Regular breathing is a sign of adequate breathing, whereas irregular breathing is a sign of inadequate or problematic breathing. Skin color is another indicator of adequate breathing. Normal skin color is a sign of adequate breathing, whereas pale or bluish skin color is a sign of inadequate breathing.

The signs and symptoms of respiratory distress can be pronounced and frightening for both the patient and the LER. Patients may present with respiratory distress, shortness of breath, restlessness, increased pulse rate, or changes in respiratory rate or rhythm. It is also common to observe skin color changes, abnormal sounds of breathing, inability to speak, accessory muscle use, AMS, use of the abdominal muscles to assist breathing, coughing, or sitting up in a tripod position.

Dyspnea is a term used to describe the sensation of shortness of breath, as experienced by the patient. It is subjective and therefore is specific to the individual who is having difficulty breathing. There are many causes of dyspnea in adults, such as **asthma**, heart attack, **emphysema**, anxiety, and shock.

Pediatric patients can also present with dyspnea. Distress in children can be caused by problems with either the upper or the lower airway. Upper airway obstruction can occur when children have respiratory infections or a blockage of the airway due to mucus or choking on a foreign object. Congenital birth problems or infections are common causes of complication in the lower airway.

Table 4

Normal Respiratory Rates Based on Age

Age	Respirations (breaths/min)
Infant (newborn to 1 year)	25–50
Child (1 to 8 years)	15–30
Adult	12–20

To be thorough, we can say that hypoxia, or the lack of oxygen in the system, causes a person to experience dyspnea. **Table 5** reviews some of the more common causes of hypoxia.

Asthma

Asthma is a condition caused by a sudden constriction, or tightening, of the airway. It can be triggered by stress, exercise, sudden exposure to cold air, or an allergic reaction to something. During an asthma attack, the patient experiences severe shortness of breath, trouble getting air out of the lungs, and aggressive coughing. There is also a swelling of the cells lining the airway and excess mucus production. An easy way to remember what happens during an asthma attack is the three Ss of asthma: *spasm, swelling, and secretions.*

Approximately 6 million Americans are affected by asthma each year, and of those affected, 4,000 to 5,000 people die. Patients of all age groups experience asthma. It is particularly common in children and is often outgrown in late adolescence. However, asthma can be seen in adults. It is important to remember that asthma attacks are serious and life threatening.

Most asthma patients are familiar with the disease and know how their body responds to treatment. They usually have

Table 5

Common Causes of Hypoxia

- Coronary arterey disease
  - Angina, myocardial infarction, congestive heart failure
- Repiratory disease
  - Emphysema, bronchitis, asthma
- Drug overdose (prescription or illegal)
- Trauma
- Stroke
- Alcohol intoxication
- Toxic chemical or smoke inhalation
- Seizures
- Shock
- Infection (sepsis)
- Psychological causes
  - Anxiety, stress reaction, panic attack
- Acidosis
  - Hyperglycemia, antifreeze overdose

their own inhaler containing a prescription bronchodilator. If an asthma patient calls 911 for help, he or she is usually in crisis.

Assessment

Asthma patients generally present with a loud wheeze that can be heard without a stethoscope. This wheeze is caused by air passing through a tight or partially closed airway. In worst-case scenarios, the airway may be completely collapsed and no air will be moving, so you will not hear the wheezing sound. Additionally, asthma patients are usually seated in an upright position and appear to be in respiratory distress. They will report dyspnea and may be cyanotic if they are in crisis. The heart rate will be elevated in most cases.

Management

Asthma patients need immediate and aggressive treatment with bronchodilators. As a LER, you may assist an individual in taking his or her prescribed medication if requested (**Figure 3**). You may also administer oxygen while waiting for the arrival of EMS. Be aware that taking too much of the bronchodilator can trigger the opposite effect and cause bronchoconstriction, or tightening of the airway. This is one situation where more is *not* better.

Figure 3 You may assist an individual in taking his or her prescribed medication if requested.

Chronic Obstructive Pulmonary Disease

Chronic obstructive pulmonary disease (COPD) is a group of diseases that affect the condition of the alveoli and lungs over a long period of time. The end result is an airway, alveoli, and blood vessel system that are permanently damaged due to exposure to irritants such as chemicals, gases, or smoke. Approximately 10% to 20% of the adult population of the United States suffers from some form of COPD. The two most common types of COPD are emphysema and **bronchitis**.

COPDs all have one thing in common. Over a period of years, they cause a gradual increase in the body's carbon dioxide levels. Recall how the brain monitors the body's carbon dioxide level to breathe. Over time, in patients with emphysema or chronic bronchitis, receptors in the body realizes that they can no longer effectively monitor the carbon dioxide level because it keeps rising, so the brain starts to monitor the oxygen level instead. As their condition worsens, patients with COPD may need to be on home oxygen.

Emphysema is a condition caused by the destruction and loss of elasticity of the air sacs (alveoli) of the lungs. The most common cause of emphysema is cigarette smoking. However, the condition can be seen in patients who have never smoked. In a healthy person, the alveoli use their elasticity to stretch, helping to move air into and out of the system. Once the alveoli are damaged, this elasticity is limited; air easily moves into the alveoli but has difficulty getting out. In patients with emphysema, many of the alveoli are eventually completely destroyed. The result is lungs that do not have the full capability to exchange gases.

Patients with chronic emphysema adapt over the years to living with lower levels of oxygen in their systems, allowing them to maintain a normal skin color even though they may be low in oxygen.

Bronchitis is a respiratory condition that can be either acute or chronic. In most cases, acute bronchitis is secondary to some type of respiratory irritant or infection. This type of bronchitis is a one-time event, and the patient recovers following treatment. However, chronic bronchitis is a disease process that develops following repeated irritation of the trachea and major airways.

Bronchitis is identified by excessive production of mucus. Unlike asthma and emphysema, which tend to affect the smaller airways and alveoli, bronchitis is a disease of the larger airways (the bronchi and bronchioles) and the trachea. Following years of exposure to foreign irritants, the protective mechanisms of the lungs that would normally remove mucus are destroyed.

Assessment

Patients with emphysema often present with severe dyspnea, a long exhalation phase, and wheezing resulting from poor oxygen exchange. They will nearly always be sitting upright and using the accessory muscles of the neck, chest, and abdomen to help them breathe (**Figure 4**). Part of the assessment phase for these patients is determining a history of the condition. These patients are usually able to tell you a lot about their condition. It is common for them to be on low-flow home oxygen at 1–2 liters per minute (LPM) and to take inhalers several times a day to help them breathe more easily. Although short of breath, patients may be "puffing" through their lips, which often have a pink color.

Patients suffering from bronchitis present with a deep, raspy cough and produce significant amounts of mucus when they cough. Patients with the disease are often cyanotic because it is difficult for oxygen to reach the alveoli as a result of the thick secretions in the bronchi and bronchioles. This bluish color commonly gets them the name of "blue bloaters."

Management

Management of patients with COPD involves supportive care and assisting patients in using their prescription inhalers. It is important to provide a calm environment and to encourage the patient to relax and breathe as easily as possible. In all cases of respiratory distress, high-flow oxygen should be administered via a nonrebreathing mask until EMS arrives.

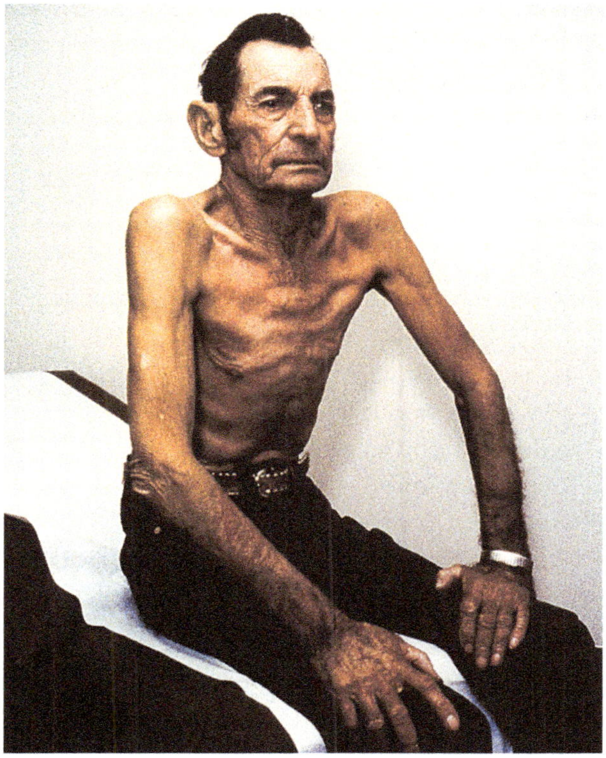

Figure 4 Patients with COPD often use accessory muscles for breathing. Notice, also, that this patient with emphysema is sitting in the tripod position.

> **Tip**
>
> **Every 5 Minutes**
>
> Patients who are short of breath or receiving oxygen should have their breathing and pulse monitored at least every 5 minutes. Underlying illness or trauma may cause certain patients to stop breathing and require you to begin rescue breathing.

CARDIOVASCULAR EMERGENCIES

The heart is a muscle that is made up of very special cells known as cardiac muscle. The heart is the only place in the body that has this specialized muscle tissue. The reason the muscle is unique is that it can generate its own electrical impulses and beat without direction from the brain.

However, the heart is like other muscles in that it needs a constant supply of oxygen to work properly. The heart is very sensitive to oxygen levels. The coronary arteries are responsible for supplying the heart with the oxygenated blood it needs to beat effectively. As we age, deposits of calcium and fibrin, also known as plaque, start to accumulate in these arteries.

The buildup of plaque in the coronary arteries is known as coronary artery disease (CAD) or coronary heart disease (CHD). When the plaque builds up in the arteries to the point at which signs and symptoms of cardiac problems are noticeable, it is said that the patient has ischemic heart disease (IHD).

Risk factors for CAD are divided into two categories—those that we can change and those over which we have no control. For example, people have the ability to monitor and control their blood pressure and to stop smoking. They cannot, however, control their age or family history.

> **Tip**
>
> **Risk Factors for Coronary Heart Disease**
>
> - Older age
> - Male sex
> - High blood pressure
> - High cholesterol level
> - Smoking
> - Diabetes
> - Obesity
> - Sedentary lifestyle
> - Stress
> - Genetics or family history

General Assessment

Chest pain is the first symptom to look for with someone who might be having a cardiac event. The chest pain is usually dull and throbbing, although the pain can be sharp or burning. The location of the pain is usually substernal, meaning just below the breastbone, and may radiate to different areas of the body, including the arm, back, neck, jaw, or stomach. Use OPQRST to collect more information about the pain. Be aware that a small group of patients, often females or diabetic patients, will not present with chest pain but will still be having a cardiac event. They may present with atypical symptoms such as weakness or fainting, with no classic signs such as chest pain or pain radiating into the arm.

Other signs and symptoms of a cardiac event are shortness of breath that can come during activity or at rest. Moreover, the shortness of breath can get worse when the patient is in a supine position. The patient's skin may be pale, cold, and sweaty, and he or she may also experience nausea, vomiting, and light-headedness. Blood pressure and heart rate may be high or low, depending on the location of the heart muscle affected. The patient's respiratory rate will vary as well.

Ischemic Heart Disease and Angina Pectoris

As CAD obstructs the coronary arteries, the amount of oxygenated blood reaching the tissue is reduced. Eventually, the blockage reaches a point at which the artery is unable to provide the oxygenated blood the heart needs during an increased demand. The heart demands increased oxygen any time it has to work harder. In essence, any time there is an increase in heart rate or blood pressure, the heart needs more oxygen. A clogged artery is not able to provide oxygen-rich blood, depriving that part of the heart of oxygen.

The heart often tells us that it needs more oxygen by creating chest pain. Although initially the cells of the heart do not die from a lack of oxygen, they will die eventually if either the heart cannot reduce the demand for oxygen or the artery cannot increase the supply of oxygen. This condition is known as **angina pectoris**, or simply angina. Angina is chest pain caused by a lack of oxygen to a part of the heart that results in no permanent damage to the cells. Failure of the heart to be reoxygenated, however, can result in the patient experiencing a heart attack or myocardial infarction.

Assessment

Keep in mind that it can be difficult, even for physicians in hospitals, to distinguish between the pain of angina and the pain of a myocardial infarction. Patients experiencing chest pain, therefore, should always be treated as if they are having a myocardial infarction.

Management

Treatment for angina requires reducing the heart's demand for oxygen or enlarging the coronary arteries so that more oxygen can travel to the cells. Most patients diagnosed with angina or IHD are prescribed a medication called **nitroglycerin**. Nitroglycerin is a vasodilator and is supplied as either a tiny white pill or a spray and is placed under the tongue. This medication causes the coronary arteries to enlarge for a short period of time, allowing more oxygenated blood to flow to the cells and giving patients time to stop what they are doing and rest. Nitroglycerin and rest bring the heart rate and blood pressure down and cause the chest pain to stop.

Myocardial Infarction or Heart Attack

When the cells of the heart muscle start to die from a lack of oxygen, it is said that an individual is experiencing a **myocardial infarction**, commonly called a heart attack. The term *infarction* means death of tissue. A heart attack can occur at rest or during any kind of activity.

The signs and symptoms of angina and those of a heart attack are much the same, but not all patients present with the warning sign of chest pain. A patient experiencing a heart attack commonly presents with the following symptoms:

- Chest pain below the breastbone that may radiate to the jaw, left shoulder, or left arm
- Elevated or irregular heart rate
- A drop in blood pressure
- Pale, sweaty skin
- Nausea and vomiting
- Feeling of impending doom or that they are going to die

Special Populations

Silent Heart Attacks

Not everyone having a heart attack has chest pain. The elderly, older women, and people with diabetes are more likely to have "silent" heart attacks. People experiencing silent heart attacks may report vague feelings of discomfort and not feel the classic chest pain associated with heart attacks. Do not discount vague complaints, such as weakness and dizziness, in these patients. The only way to rule out a heart attack is via a thorough examination by a physician.

Assessment

It is important to obtain as much information as possible from the patient. Even if the patient has an altered mental status or is having a hard time communicating, no one else can describe subjective symptoms like pain or shortness of breath as well as the patient can. Obtain the patient's vital signs, which will give you a primary picture of the severity of your patient's condition. These findings can be used as a measure against the ongoing assessment of the patient.

Management

Patients experiencing chest pain are often scared and will need you to be calm and reassuring. Ask patients to relax and to breathe easily as you administer high-flow oxygen. Help patients get into a comfortable position and ask if they are taking any medications for pain, in particular nitroglycerin or aspirin. Assist patients in taking a dose of nitroglycerin if they are currently taking this medication and have not taken any already. Patients can have a maximum of three doses of nitroglycerin. More than three doses without proper monitoring by a paramedic or physician could cause a sudden drop in blood pressure and be life threatening.

Aspirin is a commonly prescribed medication for cardiac patients. If you are permitted by your local protocols, you may also help patients take an aspirin. Always call EMS, even if the patient feels better after resting or taking his or her nitroglycerin or aspirin.

Sudden Cardiac Death

Sudden cardiac death, commonly called **cardiac arrest**, is caused by a sudden interruption in the electrical activity of the heart. The majority of adult patients who experience sudden cardiac death have what is called ventricular fibrillation, or an uncontrolled vibrating of the heart muscle. During ventricular fibrillation, no blood is pumped from the heart to the body. This condition can often be corrected by providing an electric shock, or defibrillation, from an AED.

Cardiac arrest can occur following the warning signs of a heart attack. In some situations, however, the patient will immediately develop ventricular fibrillation and collapse without warning.

Assessment

Patients can be in cardiac arrest prior to your arrival or they may collapse in your presence. The absence of breathing and a pulse are the key signs to recognize a significant cardiac event. If the patient arrested prior to your arrival, you should attempt to determine the amount of time the patient has been in cardiac arrest. Are there any signs that the patient has been dead for an extended time? Is the patient cold, stiff, or cyanotic (which might indicate a prolonged death)?

Management

As a LER, you have many tasks to perform in this situation, all of which are important. You must immediately call for help, both EMS and someone to help you perform CPR. If an AED is available, you must apply and operate it. The AED will tell you either to shock the patient or to begin CPR. Good basic life support is paramount until the arrival of EMS. Be sure to review in your mind how you will respond to these types of calls and practice using the AED.

Congestive Heart Failure

Congestive heart failure (CHF) is a condition commonly seen in elderly patients with a history of heart disease. CHF occurs when the muscles of the lower chambers of the heart, or ventricles, that pump out blood can no longer keep up with the blood coming into the heart. As a result, there is a backlog of blood in the system.

The heart is essentially composed of two pumps: one on the left side that pumps oxygen-rich blood out to the body, and one on the right side that pumps oxygen-depleted blood to the lungs. Either side of the heart can fail, and symptoms will depend on which side is failing.

Right-sided heart failure occurs when blood returning from the body is not pumped out to the lungs. As a result, blood backs up in the vascular system and the patient presents with swollen feet and legs. This condition is known as **dependent edema**. In most cases, right-sided heart failure is a chronic condition and is not life threatening.

Left-sided heart failure has a dramatic presentation and is a life-threatening emergency. When the left side of the heart fails, the blood returning from the lungs fails to get pumped out efficiently by the left ventricle. As a result, blood backs up in the lungs and creates a condition known as **pulmonary edema**. Once this blood backs up into the pulmonary system, it spreads out over the lungs, filling the alveoli with fluid, which then inhibits oxygenation from occurring (**Figure 5**).

Assessment

Patients with right-sided CHF do not present as critically ill as do their counterparts in left-sided CHF. Right-sided failure patients will generally not have shortness of breath, but instead have swollen ankles and fluid in the legs and lower part of the back.

Left-sided CHF presents with pulmonary edema, acute dyspnea, and AMS because of poor oxygen supply going to the brain. Patients are often agitated and may unconsciously reach and grab at you as though they are begging for help. Because of the fluid in the lungs, patients commonly report that they feel as though they are drowning. Often they will be coughing up pink, frothy sputum from the lungs. If you listen to the lungs with a stethoscope, you will hear noisy breathing as air moves through the fluid. In severe cases, patients may collapse or experience cardiac arrest.

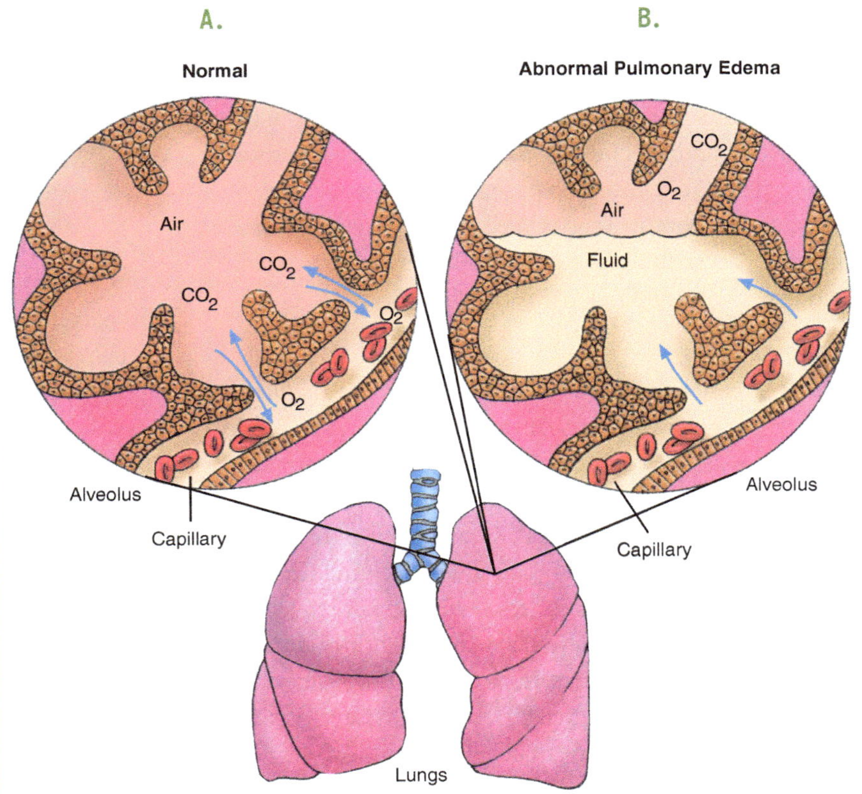

Figure 5 **A.** Normal exchange of oxygen and carbon dioxide between a capillary and an alveolus. **B.** Left-sided congestive heart failure causes fluid to leak from the capillaries and build up in the alveolus, resulting in pulmonary edema.

Management

All patients with acute CHF should be transported to an emergency department by EMS. The role of the LER is supportive. Provide a calm, supportive environment as you wait for the paramedics. If available, provide high-flow oxygen via nonrebreathing mask at 15 LPM. Remember that nearly all of these patients will want to remain in a seated, upright position because of the extra fluid in their body.

Special Populations

Pediatric Cardiac Arrest

Pediatric patients can present with unusual variations during assessment for cardiac compromise. Heart problems are not common and are often related to congenital heart conditions. Cardiac arrest is rare but when it occurs, it is usually caused by respiratory failure.

ABDOMINAL EMERGENCIES

The organs of the abdominal cavity are divided by function. The digestive tract includes the stomach, small intestines, large intestines, and the appendix. The accessory organs for digestion are the liver, gallbladder, and pancreas. One organ that is not actually a digestive organ but is located in the abdominal cavity is the spleen.

Adjacent to the abdominal cavity are organs of the urinary system. These organs—which include the kidneys, ureters, and bladder—are located behind the abdominal or pelvic cavity. Problems with organs of the urinary system are usually associated with flank pain as opposed to abdominal pain.

The organs of the reproductive system are also located in the abdominal cavity. For female patients who are of childbearing age and present with abdominal pain, pregnancy must always be considered. In particular, ectopic pregnancies (in which the fetus begins to develop outside the uterus) are a serious and potentially life-threatening concern. In the United States, ectopic pregnancies are the leading cause of pregnancy-related maternal death during the first trimester.

Acute abdominal pain can be a symptom of a number of abdominal illnesses. As a LER, your task is to assess the patient and determine the severity of the pain. Unfortunately, in most cases, it is not possible to diagnose the cause of abdominal pain in the field. Most patients will need to be transported to the hospital for further evaluation. EMS should be called, and these patients should be transported to an appropriate facility.

Acute Abdomen

One condition you may encounter is an **acute abdomen**. Acute abdomen is not a specific diagnosis but a set of signs and symptoms, often very pronounced and dramatic, that can be caused by a variety of potentially serious underlying medical conditions. Signs and symptoms can include abdominal pain; back pain; pain that starts in the center of the abdomen and moves to the patient's lower right; nausea and vomiting; signs of shock; blood in the stool or urine; guarding or protecting the abdomen; shortness of breath; fever; and an abdomen that is distended, hard as a board, or pulsating.

Assessment

As always, identify and correct any immediate life threats first. With most conscious patients, you can perform a secondary assessment on the abdomen. If you have an unconscious patient, however, a thorough and rapid patient assessment is required. Complete a SAMPLE history and use OPQRST to gather information about the pain.

Tip

A Sample OPQRST Assessment

O – Onset: What were you doing when the pain started?

P – Provokes: Is there anything you do that makes the pain feel better or worse?

Q – Quality: Describe the pain. Is it sharp, dull, or burning? Does it come and go or is it constant?

R – Radiation: Does the pain radiate or is it located in one spot?

S – Severity: On a scale of 1 to 10, 10 being the worst pain you have ever felt, how would you rate this pain?

T – Time: What time did the pain start or how long have you had the pain?

When performing the secondary assessment, first expose the abdomen. Look for any bruising, marks, or swelling (**Figure 6**). It is important to identify anything that is visually abnormal or unusual, for example, signs of trauma or bleeding.

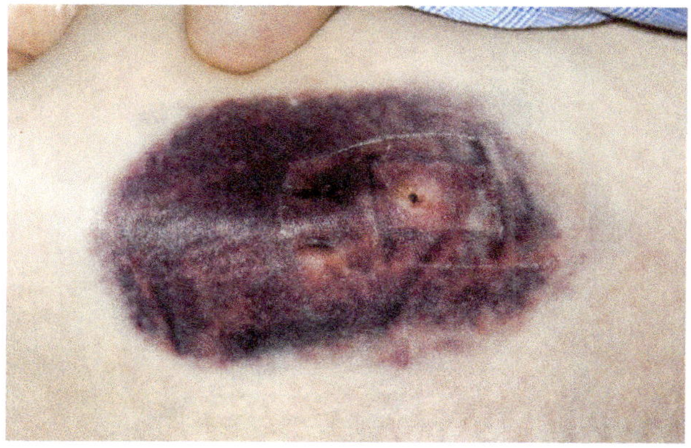

Figure 6 Assess the abdomen for bruising, marks, or swelling.

Tip

Check the Back

Don't forget to examine the posterior side of the body, especially in the case of trauma. Important information may be hidden on the back.

Next palpate the abdomen. Using the belly button as the center, divide the abdomen into four quadrants (**Figure 7**). Place one hand over the other and push together to palpate each quadrant. The two-hand method provides you with stability while pushing and a better sense of the tone of the abdomen wall. Start palpating in the farthest quadrant from any identified area of pain. In most cases, once you palpate over an area where the patient is having pain, you will be unable to palpate the other quadrants because of the severe pain and uncooperativeness of the patient. A healthy abdomen will feel soft and will not be tender to the touch. Abnormal findings include pain; excessive nausea, vomiting, and diarrhea; blood in emesis or stool; fever; and signs of shock.

Management

Management of the patient with an acute abdomen is mostly supportive in the prehospital environment. As is common practice, begin with evaluating the scene for safety, ensuring that the cause of the pain is not due to trauma, altercation, or some form of weapon. Evaluate the patient's airway and breathing and administer high-flow oxygen. Oxygen is helpful in these patients in that severe pain often limits

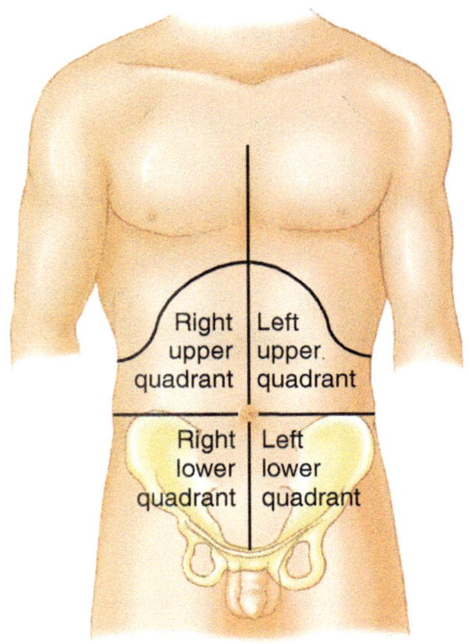

Figure 7 The abdomen is divided into four general quadrants.

breathing efforts, and they may have an underlying low oxygen level.

Check pulses and the condition of the skin. A patient with severe abdominal pain typically has a fast heart rate and moist skin, especially in the presence of shock.

For the LER, providing comfort and supportive care is a valuable treatment plan. Patients will usually want to be on their side in a knee-tuck or fetal position. This position alleviates pressure on the abdominal wall and diminishes pain. Emotional support is also very valuable to those experiencing extreme abdominal discomfort.

Gastrointestinal Bleeding

The GI tract is very long, reaching from the esophagus to the rectum. Along these many feet of tissue are many places where bleeding can develop. Common causes of bleeding are ulcers, chronic alcohol abuse, and trauma. **Gastrointestinal bleeding** can be a difficult call for the LER to evaluate and manage because of the location and severity of the bleed.

The vomiting of bright red blood indicates active bleeding in the upper GI tract. If the blood remains in the stomach, it becomes partially digested and becomes darker, looking more like coffee grounds.

If the bleeding is coming from the lower GI tract, blood will be discharged from the rectum. Acute bleeding in the lower portion of the large intestine or rectum can be bright red. However, blood that has been digested in the small intestine or upper portion of the large intestine will be black and tarry and have a very strong odor.

Assessment

Assessing for bleeding may be difficult. In the case of upper GI bleeding, there is often a lot of vomit mixed with bright red blood. Vomiting can be severe and retching. Patients with lower GI bleeding often use the bathroom and flush evidence of the injury.

Be sure to observe the patient for signs and symptoms of shock. Bleeding may be internal and not obvious. Complete a secondary assessment of the abdomen. Look for rigidity and pain on palpation. If the patient complains of a sharp, stabbing pain that radiates directly to the lower back and you palpate a pulsating mass around the belly button, the patient may have an **abdominal aortic aneurysm (AAA)**, a condition that results in the bulging of the aorta in the abdominal cavity. Patients with diabetes, high blood pressure, or atherosclerosis, as well as heavy smokers, are at high risk for developing AAA. Although the signs and symptoms of AAA are present in the abdomen, this condition is really a cardiovascular emergency.

Management

All patients with GI bleeding should be given high-flow oxygen and treated for shock. Position the patient supine with legs elevated, maintain body temperature, and provide oxygen per your local protocols. If the patient is actively vomiting, you may need to place him or her in the recovery position to maintain an open airway. Under no circumstances should you give the patient anything to eat or drink.

Age-Related Variations

Vomiting and diarrhea are very common in pediatric patients, but they can be a serious condition. When assessing a child with vomiting and diarrhea, look for signs and symptoms of shock, which can develop very rapidly: cool, clammy skin; rapid breathing and heart rate; and sunken fontanelles on infants. Fontanelles are the soft spots on an infant's head. Sunken fontanelles are a sign of dehydration. If you suspect the child has lost a lot of fluid due to vomiting and diarrhea and may be going into shock, immediately administer high-flow oxygen, maintain the child's airway, and advise the EMS unit upon its arrival.

It is very difficult to determine the cause of abdominal pain in geriatric patients. Treat the patient's signs and symptoms and complete a secondary assessment and a thorough SAMPLE history. Do not rule out a heart attack or other cardiac event; abdominal pain and heartburn are common complaints among older patients experiencing a cardiac emergency.

Special Populations

Potential Cardiac Event

Assess for a heart attack if an elderly patient complains of abdominal pain or heartburn.

Special Medical Emergencies

KIDNEY FAILURE AND DIALYSIS

When kidney failure occurs, the kidneys can no longer filter toxins and waste out of the blood. As a result, patients need some form of artificial filtration to survive. **Hemodialysis**, commonly called **dialysis**, is a procedure that cleanses the blood for patients who are in kidney failure. Most patients travel to a dialysis center several times per week to have their blood filtered. However, some patients have portable dialysis machines in their homes.

Most dialysis patients have a special device called a shunt implanted in their arm or leg. The shunt is used to connect the patient to the dialysis machine and looks like a raised bump on the patient's arm or leg. Always take a blood pressure reading on an arm without a shunt or you could damage the device.

Another method of filtering the blood is known as **peritoneal dialysis**. Peritoneal dialysis cleanses the body of toxic waste by placing a concentrated fluid into the abdominal cavity via a rubber tube or catheter. Patients perform this procedure at home on a nightly basis, making it unnecessary to go to a dialysis center.

Assessment

Complications following dialysis are common. When assessing a dialysis patient, be aware of some life-threatening problems. The patient may experience low blood pressure as a result of volume loss following his or her treatment. Nausea and vomiting, as well as an irregular pulse, may be common. Bleeding from a shunt is hard to manage because these patients are given a blood-thinning drug during their treatment. Sudden onset of shortness of breath may be a sign of a blood clot. These patients always require rapid transport to a hospital.

Management

Providing care for a dialysis patient usually involves supportive treatment. Maintain the airway and follow your local protocol for oxygen administration. If indicated, assist with ventilations using a bag-mask device. Bleeding from a shunt can be life threatening and must be controlled as soon as possible. Apply direct pressure over the site using layers of gauze or a clean towel. If that does not control the bleeding, use a tourniquet above the dialysis device. If signs and symptoms of shock are present, position the patient supine, provide oxygen and elevate the legs per local protocol, and maintain body temperature. If a patient is experiencing difficulty breathing, keep the patient in an upright position.

VAGINAL BLEEDING

On rare occasions, the LER may be called to a scene where a female patient is experiencing vaginal bleeding. Vaginal bleeding can occur for many reasons, all requiring an evaluation by a physician. Bleeding can be a natural occurrence in females experiencing menstruation, but that seldom requires the intervention of the LER. In cases such as miscarriage, sexual assault, gynecologic emergency, or pregnancy, however, you may be requested to assist until the arrival of EMS.

Assessment

Other than situations involving active childbirth, the need for visualization or inspection of the vaginal area is rare in the field environment. Note whether the patient is experiencing abdominal pain, along with its onset, location, and severity. If hemorrhage is obvious, attempt to note the amount and color of the blood that is present.

Management

If hemorrhage is present, clean vaginal napkins or towels may be placed over the opening of the vaginal canal to control bleeding. Ask the patient to attempt to hold her legs together, putting pressure on the towel. Administer high-flow oxygen and provide emotional support.

Special Populations

Sexual Assault and Trauma

Remember your role as a LER. Provide care to the patient experiencing vaginal bleeding. In the case of trauma or sexual assault, you will be required to use your investigative skills as well and to document the situation. Control of bleeding must take priority.

ALLERGIC REACTIONS AND ANAPHYLAXIS

The human body is constantly being attacked by outside agents such as germs, foreign bodies, irritating substances, and chemicals. To ward off these attacks, the body has developed a defense mechanism known as the **immune system**. When a foreign body or substance contacts the skin or mucous membranes, is inhaled or ingested, or penetrates the skin, the body reacts by mounting an immune response. Such a response is commonly known as an **allergic reaction**. An example of an allergic reaction is the redness and itching experienced when the skin comes in contact with poison ivy. The redness results from increased blood flow to the area, which brings special blood cells to the site that isolate and destroy the invading substance. The itching results from the release of the protein **histamine** from the irritated cells. Histamine stimulates nerve endings in the skin, causing redness and itching. Histamine is also responsible for the swelling seen in allergic reactions. Common over-the-counter allergy relief medicines, such as diphenhydramine, are called **antihistamines** because they reduce the release of histamine. Allergic reactions are generally minor to moderate and resolve themselves over time.

More severe allergic reactions can develop into a serious medical emergency known as **anaphylaxis**. In anaphylaxis, the foreign substance not only creates a localized effect as just described, but also creates the same reaction throughout the whole body. It is this systemic reaction that makes anaphylaxis so dangerous. Some parts of the body, such as the airway passages, are more susceptible to the effects of histamine. Increased swelling and narrowing of the air passages as a result of histamine cause anaphylaxis patients to have trouble breathing and make audible breathing sounds called wheezing. If left untreated, the air passages may close completely, suffocating the patient. The massive release of histamine may also affect the heart (rapid pulse and low blood pressure) and the skin (itchy pale or red skin, hives).

Allergic reactions and anaphylaxis can be caused by many different sources that enter the body. Common allergens include poison ivy, bee sting, seafood, and medications such as penicillin.

Assessment

As with any response, scene safety is your first concern. Because irritating or chemical substances may bring on anaphylaxis, you should make sure the environment is safe. You should also make sure the patient is not contaminated by some hazardous substance and is safe to handle. If the patient is contaminated, isolate the patient and advise your dispatch center of the need for a special hazardous materials response. In most situations, decontamination may be as simple as washing the skin. In the worst cases, you may need to evacuate people from the area. If it is safe to proceed, your immediate actions should be to assess the ABCs, paying special attention to the airway. Look for obvious swelling around the mouth or nose. Remember that anaphylaxis patients may be irritated or combative as a result of poor blood and oxygen flow to the brain. If a patient is unconscious, check that the airway is open and clear of fluids.

Tip

Poison Control

If you are not sure what to do, a good resource is the National Poison Control centers. The phone number is 1-800-222-1222.

Check the patient's pulse. The pulse will likely be rapid and weak. If you can take a blood pressure reading, it will likely be low, with the systolic reading below 100 mm Hg. The patient's skin will likely be pale, red, or cyanotic. The patient may also exhibit hives or experience itching and swelling, especially around the mouth, tongue, and eyes (**Figure 8**). Other signs and symptoms can include nausea, vomiting, and AMS.

Management

It is important to maintain the patient's airway because the main cause of death in anaphylaxis is suffocation due to clo-

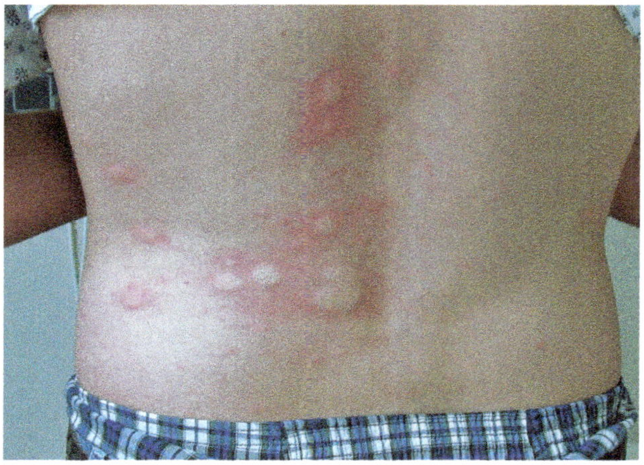

Figure 8 The presence of hives is one sign of an allergic reaction.

sure of the air passages. You can maintain the airway using manual methods such as the jaw-thrust maneuver, or use a simple airway adjunct, such as an oropharyngeal airway. If you use an adjunct, be sure to place it early because of the ongoing swelling of the air passages. Once the airway has been opened, check for breathing. If the patient is not breathing, begin either mouth-to-mask ventilation or another means of assisted ventilation. Check for a pulse and begin CPR if needed. If the patient is breathing adequately, continue to maintain and monitor the airway and place the patient in either the recovery position or in a position that facilitates adequate breathing. If available, administer high-flow oxygen.

Because the body's response in anaphylaxis is caused mainly by the release of histamine, the prompt administration of an antihistamine may reduce the swelling and the airway compromise. If your service authorizes the use of an **epinephrine auto-injector** such as the EpiPen or the Twinject, you should use it according to established guidelines (**Figure 9**). An epinephrine auto-injector is a spring-loaded device that administers a preset dose of epinephrine to a patient experiencing an anaphylactic reaction. If the patient is conscious, ask if the patient has used his or her own auto-injector before, and if not, assist as necessary.

Once you have ensured adequate respirations and pulse, vital signs should be taken and noted every 5 minutes. Depending on the nature of the substance that has caused the allergic reaction, you may be able to remove or eliminate it, such as the stinger from an insect bite.

Removing an insect stinger is done by taking something like a plastic credit card and gently scraping on top of the skin to push the stinger and venom out of the site. A common mistake is to try to grab the stinger with a pair of tweezers or your fingers, which only pushes any remaining venom into the wound.

Age-Related Variations

For pediatric patients, the signs and symptoms of anaphylaxis are similar to those of adults. However, children may not be

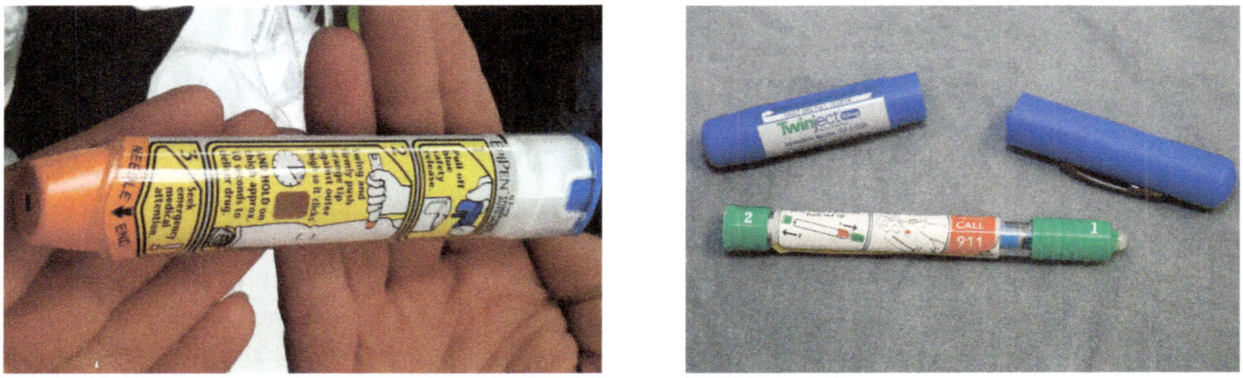

A. B.

Figure 9 Patients who experience severe allergic reactions often carry their own epinephrine, which comes predosed in an auto-injector or a standard syringe. **A.** EpiPen auto-injectors. **B.** Twinject auto-injector.

aware that they are having an allergic reaction and thus not be able to express this clearly to you. They may not be aware of the trigger, such as a specific type of food, that caused the reaction. For newborns and infants, anaphylaxis is especially critical because the air passages are very small and even minor swelling can cause closure. Young children also have an immature immune system that has not developed specific defenses against foreign substances. Pediatric-appropriate EpiPens are available and should be used as directed. Use of an adult-dose pen on a child should be avoided as it could cause severe complications.

Geriatric patients in anaphylaxis also present special challenges. Older patients often have other medical conditions that can be triggered or made worse by anaphylaxis. Of special concern are respiratory conditions such as emphysema that may already be limiting air passages. The release of histamine affects the heart as well, and an increased strain on the heart, such as increased heart rate or drop in blood pressure, may lead to cardiac complications or failure. The potential for such complications may limit or preclude the use of an epinephrine auto-injector for older patients. Poor blood flow due to clogged or blocked blood vessels may be further decreased by the low blood pressure brought on by anaphylaxis, resulting in an AMS or unconsciousness. In these situations, the epinephrine auto-injector should not be used without consulting paramedics or an emergency department physician.

DIABETES

Almost all of the body's cells require a simple sugar called glucose to function. Glucose is derived either from food that has been digested by the body or from the breakdown of stored body fat. Either way, glucose is released into the bloodstream to be available to all the body's cells. However, a cell cannot absorb glucose without insulin, a naturally occurring hormone that breaks down large molecules of glucose. In healthy individuals, specialized cells in the pancreas produce insulin. In some people, the pancreas either does not produce insulin or does not produce enough insulin. In others, insulin is produced in the proper amount, but for some reason the cells cannot use the insulin. Someone with either of these conditions suffers from diabetes and is known as diabetic. Other terms associated with diabetes are diabetes mellitus, juvenile diabetes, insulin-dependent diabetes, type I diabetes, and type II diabetes.

Emergencies involving diabetics can be broadly classified into two conditions: high blood glucose levels (**hyperglycemia**, also called **diabetic coma**) and low blood glucose levels (**hypoglycemia**, also called **insulin shock**). In hyperglycemia, there is plenty of glucose present in the blood, but the cells do not absorb it. This condition is usually caused by the body's inability to produce insulin, an insufficient amount of insulin, or failure by the patient to take an insulin injection.

In hypoglycemia, cells cannot function properly because of the lack of glucose. Hypoglycemia often results from patients failing to eat, overexercising, taking too much insulin, or experiencing stress. Hypoglycemia is a serious medical emergency. If it is not diagnosed and corrected by the rapid administration of glucose in some form, the patient may die. The onset of changes in mental status, along with other changes in condition, is rapid and pronounced. This rapid onset of signs and symptoms is one of the key ways to differentiate between diabetic emergencies that are caused by low blood glucose levels versus high blood glucose levels.

Tip

Altered Mental Status in Diabetic Emergencies

It is important for LERs to make a careful assessment of any patient who presents with an AMS or seems combative or drunk, because the patient may be suffering from a diabetic emergency, which could result in death if it is not treated appropriately.

Assessment

When assessing a patient presenting with AMS, it is important to check for evidence of diabetes. If the patient is responsive, ask the following questions:

- Are you a diabetic?
- Did you take your insulin today?
- Have you eaten today?

Patients with diabetes frequently wear medical identification jewelry. During your initial physical check of the patient, you may find a small, pager-like device worn at the waist and connected to a very small tube. This is an insulin pump, which administers a controlled release of insulin. It should not be removed because it is connected via the tube to a needle inserted into the abdominal skin or another location in the body (**Figure 10**). Commonly, patients assess their blood glucose at regular intervals using a glucometer. To test their blood glucose they place a test strip in the glucometer and obtain a blood sample to place on the test strip.

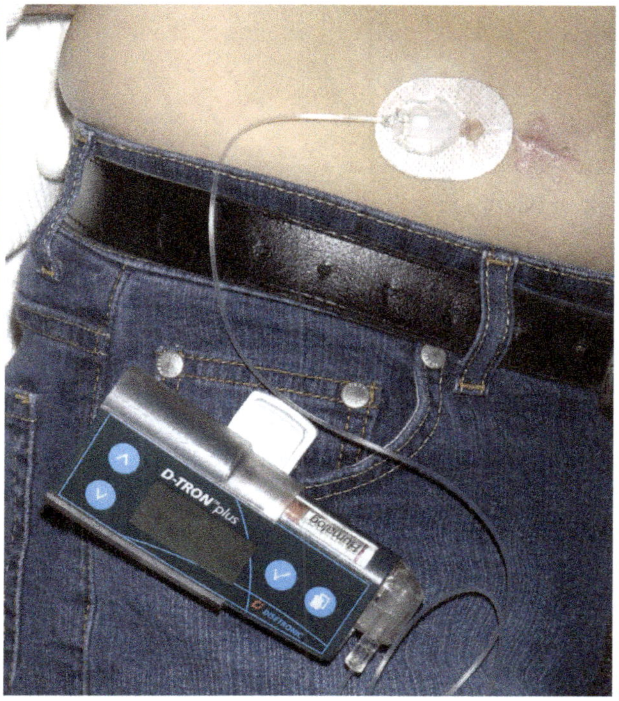

Figure 10 If the patient is wearing an insulin pump, do not remove it.

A patient with a low blood glucose level presents with a rapid decrease in mental status leading to seizures and coma. This progression may be preceded by bizarre behavior, tremors, and shaking. The skin may be moist from sweating. Respirations will be rapid and shallow while the pulse is rapid and full. If the patient is conscious, he or she may complain of hunger.

In contrast, a patient with a high blood glucose level may present with a normal or slightly depressed mental status that will change slowly over time. Breathing is often rapid, with a noticeable fruity or sweet smell on the breath. This odor is often confused with that of "old alcohol." The pulse is weak and rapid. The skin appears pale, warm, and very dry. The patient may complain of weakness and nausea. Vomiting and urination may be present. The patient may exhibit an increased appetite or thirst, making repeated requests for something to eat or drink.

It is not always easy to tell the difference between diabetic emergencies involving high and low blood glucose levels. Signs and symptoms other than mental status are much more likely to help you in your assessment of the patient (**Table 6**).

Table 6

Comparing Hypoglycemia (Insulin Shock) and Hyperglycemia (Diabetic Coma)

Hypoglycemia	Hyperglycemia
Pale, moist, cool skin	Warm, dry skin
Rapid, weak pulse	Rapid pulse
Normal breathing	Deep, rapid breathing
Dizziness or headache	–
Confusion or unconsciousness	Unresponsiveness or unconsciousness
Rapid onset of symptoms (minutes)	Slow onset of symptoms (days)

Again, a thorough patient history is most helpful in determining the patient's condition.

Management

As with any medical emergency, your first concern should be checking and maintaining the ABCs. This response is especially critical in a patient showing signs of decreased mental status. If the patient is unresponsive, take steps to maintain an open airway. If circulation is adequate, place the patient in the recovery position and continue to monitor the ABCs. Administer high-flow oxygen if available.

For the responsive patient, ensure adequate respirations and a clear airway, especially if the patient has vomited. Place the patient in a comfortable position and administer oxygen. If the scene is public or semiprivate, provide emotional support, because diabetic patients often soil themselves and are embarrassed if they have a seizure or exhibit some other odd behavior. Diabetics can often tell you if they are suffering from low blood glucose levels. As long as a patient is responsive enough to maintain his or her own airway, administer accessible sources of sugar, such as orange juice or oral glucose paste from a first aid bag (**Figure 11**). Do not administer any fluids or solids to an unresponsive patient!

Age-Related Variations

Diabetic children are more at risk for diabetic emergencies than adults. Children often have difficulty controlling their

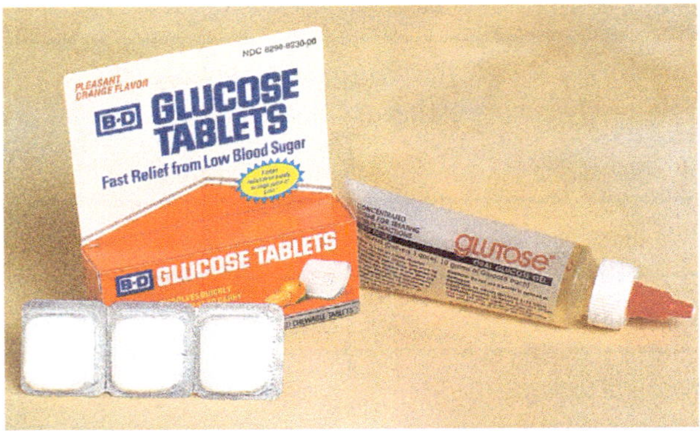

Figure 11 Instant glucose provides high concentrations of sugar.

sugar and insulin intake. A child who has been out playing or participating in sports may use up more glucose than normal. Children also tend to be less mindful about adhering to good eating habits and may have trouble remembering to eat or to take their insulin on time. In addition to many of the signs and symptoms listed previously, pediatric patients may present with seizures when their blood glucose levels drop to a dangerously low level.

In the geriatric patient, other medical conditions may stress the body and lead to a change in glucose usage. A slowing down of body functions may also contribute to a change in the level of blood glucose or insulin. A diabetic emergency in an older patient may lead to a stroke or other serious medical condition.

Special Considerations for Law Enforcement

Any patient presenting with what looks like simple intoxication should be assessed for a diabetic emergency, because the presentation is often similar. The presence of alcohol on the breath may mask the sweet-smelling odor characteristic of a high blood glucose level. Diabetics who are alcoholics often do not eat regularly or take their insulin as prescribed. There have been many stories in the press about law enforcement responding to a belligerent or intoxicated person and transporting the subject to jail, only to find the subject unresponsive or dead a few hours later. If you cannot definitively rule out a diabetic emergency, request an EMS response. Keep in mind that law-abiding citizens may react in bizarre or uncharacteristic ways while experiencing a diabetic emergency, only to recover and not recall their actions or behavior.

INFECTIONS

Almost everyone has had an infection at some point in his or her life. Infections come in various levels of severity. They can be as simple as a splinter in a finger that has become inflamed to a generalized infection of the body, which can be life threatening. Infections are often caused by bacteria, although they can also be caused by a virus or a fungus.

When an infection spreads to the entire body, it is known as **sepsis** and the patient is considered "septic." These types of infection spread through the bloodstream. Sepsis in its most severe form leads to septic shock, which is a medical emergency in which the blood is full of toxins that cause the blood vessels to dilate. If the body cannot compensate for this, blood pressure starts to drop. This situation is very dangerous and can be fatal.

Assessment

Common signs and symptoms of isolated infections, such as an infected laceration, are localized redness and pain. The site may be warm or hot to the touch and often has a discharge or pus draining from the infected area. Some local infections develop red streaks as they worsen, which is an indication that the infection may be spreading. In this case the patient should seek medical care.

A septic patient generally presents with a variety of signs and symptoms, including the following:

- Increased body temperature or fever
- Chills and shaking
- Rapid heart and respiratory rate
- Normal or low blood pressure
- Confusion
- Agitation
- Dizziness
- Decreased urine output
- Rash
- Joint pain

Management

Most isolated infections are managed at home or by the patient's primary care physician. It is uncommon for a LER to be asked to manage this type of case unless it occurs at your workplace, where you may be seen as the medical authority.

You may, however, be called to assist a patient in septic shock. Treating a patient for septic shock includes three steps:

1. Lay the patient flat with the legs elevated 8 to 12 inches.
2. Give the patient high-flow oxygen at 15 LPM via nonrebreathing mask.
3. Maintain the patient's body temperature and manage it appropriately.

Although a patient in septic shock may be shivering and probably has a fever, he or she does not need to be covered with blankets. Do not give the patient fluids to drink even though he or she may be dehydrated. Water or other liquids may cause vomiting and block the airway. Paramedics will be able to give the patient intravenous fluids, which will go directly into the venous system. Be sure to monitor the patient continuously until EMS arrives.

CONCLUSION

As a LER, you are likely to encounter persons who are having medical emergencies. Taking the time to assess an ill patient properly will greatly increase the chance of survival and decrease the risk of complications. By identifying the signs and symptoms of medical emergencies, understanding the potential risks for further complications, and following basic care procedures such as checking and maintaining the ABCs, you will be able to properly assess and manage a patient with a potentially serious and life-threatening emergency. Remember that it is better to transport the patient to the emergency department for evaluation than to wait and see what will happen. When in doubt, call EMS and transport.

Prep Kit

READY FOR REVIEW

- Assessing a patient's signs and symptoms will help you determine the illness that you will be treating.
- When assessing a patient, using a standardized approach will help stay consistent and organized, and provide the highest level of care.
- A special medical emergency involves a condition that is either severely life threatening or of an unusual or infrequent nature and requires special attention by the LER.
- When confronted with an individual with a medical emergency, always follow a standard protocol of ensuring scene safety and then evaluating the patient's airway, breathing, and circulation.
- Your role as a LER is to stabilize the patient prior to the arrival of EMS.
- Proper LER management for many medical conditions is often supportive care and the administration of oxygen until EMS arrives.
- Altered mental status can range from confusion or anxiety to unresponsiveness or coma.
- An easy mnemonic for remembering the causes of altered mental status is AEIOU TIPS.
- Seizures are a disruption of the normal electrical activity of the brain.
- The most common reason for an adult patient to experience a seizure is the failure to take his or her antiseizure medication.
- The most common cause for a child to experience a seizure is a sudden increase in body temperature.
- Generalized or grand mal seizures are the most dramatic form of seizures but are not life threatening unless they are poorly managed or develop into status epilepticus.
- A stroke occurs when part of the brain is deprived of oxygen as the result of an obstructed or ruptured cerebral blood vessel.
- LERs can use the Cincinnati Stroke Scale to assess a patient suspected of having a stroke.
- Asthma is a condition in which the patient is experiencing a tightening of the airways and increased mucus production. The LER should always remember the three S's of asthma: spasm, swelling, and secretions.
- Two types of chronic obstructive pulmonary disease are emphysema and bronchitis.
- Emphysema is caused by destruction and loss of elasticity of the alveoli of the lungs.
- Bronchitis is excessive mucus production in the larger airways of the respiratory system and can be either acute or chronic.
- The buildup of plaque in the coronary arteries is known as coronary artery disease or coronary heart disease.
- Ischemic heart disease or angina occurs when the demand for oxygen in the heart exceeds the supply. Patients with a known history of angina often take nitroglycerin to decrease their chest pain.
- A myocardial infarction, or heart attack, occurs when heart muscle dies due to a lack of oxygen.
- Sudden cardiac death, also known as cardiac arrest, can occur without warning.
- There are two types of congestive heart failure (CHF). Right-sided CHF presents as a fluid overload with dependent edema in the feet and legs of the patient. It is usually not life threatening. Left-sided CHF presents suddenly as pulmonary edema in the patient's lungs and is a life-threatening emergency.
- In most cases, it is not possible to diagnose the cause of abdominal pain in the field. EMS should be called, and these patients should be transported as a high priority to the closest appropriate hospital.
- For female patients who are of childbearing age and present with abdominal pain, pregnancy must always be

considered. In particular, ectopic pregnancies are a serious and potentially life-threatening concern.

- Acute abdomen is not a specific diagnosis but a set of often pronounced and dramatic signs and symptoms that can be caused by a variety of potentially serious underlying medical conditions.
- Gastrointestinal (GI) bleeding can be classified as either upper or lower GI bleeding, depending on the location of the hemorrhage.
- Vomiting of bright red blood indicates active upper GI bleeding. If the vomit looks dark and has the texture of coffee grounds, the blood is partially digested.
- Bright red blood in the stool indicates an active lower GI bleed. If the stool is black and tarry, the bleeding site is probably higher in the GI tract and the blood has had time to digest.
- Patients in kidney failure need assistance in filtering out toxins in their system. Artificial filtration of the blood is called hemodialysis. Placing a concentrated fluid into the patient's abdomen is known as peritoneal dialysis.
- The body's immune system is constantly being attacked by outside agents such as germs, foreign bodies, irritating substances, and chemicals.
- In some cases, an allergic reaction occurs in response to a foreign body or substance that has come in contact with the body.
- A severe or life-threatening allergic response is known as anaphylaxis, or an anaphylactic reaction.
- Many of the signs and symptoms of an allergic or anaphylactic reaction occur as a result of the release of histamine. Patients may present with itching, swelling, and redness.
- Some patients with a history of allergic reactions have their own epinephrine auto-injector, commonly called an EpiPen.
- Diabetes is a common condition resulting from either the lack of production of insulin from the pancreas or the body's inability to use the insulin produced.
- There are many common names for diabetes, including diabetes mellitus, juvenile diabetes, insulin-dependent diabetes, type I diabetes, and type II diabetes.
- Hypoglycemia is a condition in which the body has a low blood glucose level. A high blood glucose level is known as hyperglycemia.
- No food or drink should ever be given to a person who is unable to control his or her own airway, even if that person is having a diabetic emergency.
- People with hypoglycemia commonly present as though they are intoxicated.
- An infection that spreads throughout the entire body is known as sepsis.
- Infections can be caused by bacteria, viruses, or fungi.

VITAL VOCABULARY

abdominal aortic aneurysm (AAA) A condition that results in a bulging of the aorta in the abdominal cavity. It is usually identified by the presence of a pulsating mass around the midabdomen and a sharp, stabbing pain that radiates directly to the lower back.

acute abdomen Not a specific diagnosis but rather a set of signs and symptoms, often very pronounced and dramatic, that can be caused by a variety of potentially serious underlying medical conditions.

AEIOU TIPS A mnemonic for recalling the causes of altered mental status.

allergic reaction The body's immune system reaction to a foreign substance, which is usually localized. An allergic reaction can result from contact with the skin or mucous membranes, inhalation, ingestion, or penetration of the skin. Allergic reactions are generally less severe than anaphylaxis.

altered mental status (AMS) A change in a person's mental activity, state of mind, or responsiveness.

anaphylaxis A more severe allergic reaction to a foreign substance that not only creates a localized effect but also creates the same reaction throughout the whole body. Anaphylactic reactions may be life threatening in some situations.

angina pectoris A type of cardiac disease resulting from coronary artery plaque buildup that causes chest pain when cardiac oxygen demand exceeds oxygen supply.

antihistamine A category of medications that work by reducing the release of histamine.

asthma A condition caused by a sudden constriction of the airway, usually triggered by stress, exercise, cold air, or allergic reaction to something.

bronchitis A form of chronic obstructive pulmonary disease that is characterized by excessive mucus production in the larger airways and trachea.

cardiac arrest See *sudden cardiac death.*

chronic obstructive pulmonary disease (COPD) A group of diseases, most commonly emphysema and chronic bronchitis, that affect the condition of the alveoli and lungs over a long period of time.

Cincinnati Stroke Scale A diagnostic test used to identify the signs of a stroke.

congestive heart failure (CHF) A form of cardiac disease that results when one side of the heart fails to pump blood out at the same rate as the other side.

dependent edema Fluid collection in the feet and legs of individuals with right-sided congestive heart failure.

depressant A classification of drug that depresses or decreases the activity of the central nervous system.

diabetes A medical condition in which the pancreas either fails to produce insulin or does not produce enough insulin. In some people, insulin is produced in the proper amount, but for some reason the cells cannot use the insulin.

diabetic coma See *hyperglycemia.*

dialysis See *hemodialysis.*

dyspnea Shortness of breath.

emphysema A form of chronic obstructive pulmonary disease that is characterized by the destruction and loss of elasticity of the alveoli of the lungs.

epilepsy A disease manifested by seizures, caused by an abnormal focus of electrical activity in the brain.

epinephrine auto-injector A spring-loaded device, such as the EpiPen, that administers a preset dose of epinephrine to a patient experiencing an anaphylactic reaction.

exhalation The passive phase of breathing in which air is pushed out of the lungs.

gastrointestinal bleeding Bleeding that occurs along the digestive tract.

generalized seizure See *grand mal seizure.*

glucose A simple sugar needed by cells. Glucose is derived either from food that has been digested by the body or from the breakdown of fat stored in the body.

grand mal seizure The most dramatic type of seizure, which presents with uncontrolled muscle contractions and loss of consciousness.

hemodialysis A method of filtering toxins from the blood of patients with kidney (renal) failure by removing blood from the body, cleaning it, and returning it to the body.

histamine A protein released by the body during allergic and anaphylactic reactions that causes swelling, redness, and itching of the skin.

hyperglycemia A condition in which a high blood glucose level prevents normal cell function.

hypoglycemia A condition in which a low blood glucose level prevents normal cell function.

hypoxia A dangerous and potentially life-threatening condition in which the cells and tissues of the body do not have enough oxygen to survive.

immune system The body's defense mechanism that responds to outside agents such as germs, foreign bodies, irritating substances, and chemicals.

inhalation The active phase of breathing in which air is pulled into the lungs.

insulin A naturally occurring hormone secreted by the pancreas that is used by the body to break down large molecules of glucose.

insulin shock A life-threatening condition of severe low blood glucose levels that occurs in a diabetic patient who has taken too much insulin or has not eaten enough food.

myocardial infarction A form of cardiac disease that occurs when a lack of oxygen causes the death of heart muscle. Commonly called a heart attack.

nitroglycerin A medication that is taken by patients with angina pectoris for the purpose of dilating the coronary arteries and allowing more oxygen to reach the heart muscle.

oximetry Measuring the concentration of oxygen in arterial blood using a device called an oximeter.

pancreas An organ of the digestive and endocrine systems that releases several important hormones, including insulin and glucagon, in response to a person's intake of nourishment. These chemicals break down proteins, carbohydrates, and fats.

patent airway An open and clear airway.

peritoneal dialysis A method of filtering out toxins from patients with kidney (renal) failure by infusing a concentrated solution into the abdomen.

pulmonary edema The collection of fluid in the lungs of individuals with left-sided congestive heart failure.

recovery position A side-lying position that helps an unconscious patient maintain an open airway.

respiration The process of gas exchange at the alveolar level.

seizures Disruptions of the normal electrical activity of the brain.

sepsis A generalized infection that has spread throughout the body.

sign Something that you are able to observe or measure in a patient, such as blood pressure, bleeding, or deformity.

status epilepticus A life-threatening condition that occurs when a patient experiences three or more seizures without regaining consciousness, or any seizure lasting more than 30 minutes.

stimulant A classification of drug that increases the activity of the central nervous system.

stroke A disruption in the supply of blood to any part of the brain. A stroke is a medical emergency that can cause disability or death.

sudden cardiac death A form of sudden death that results from an interruption in the electrical activity of the heart. Also known as cardiac arrest.

symptom Something subjective that a patient tells you, such as "My belly hurts" or "I feel like I'm going to throw up."

uremia A buildup of waste products in the blood caused by renal failure.

ventilation The process of moving air in and out of the respiratory system.

CHECK YOUR KNOWLEDGE

1. From the following list, select the answer that is a sign.
   - **A.** "I feel sharp abdominal pain that radiates into my back."
   - **B.** Indigestion or feeling the need to burp
   - **C.** High blood pressure
   - **D.** "My chest hurts like a vise is squeezing me."
2. You respond to a call to assist EMS for a medical emergency. You are first on the scene, and EMS has a 6-minute estimated time of arrival. Upon entering the house, you find an elderly man sitting in a chair with obvious dyspnea. He is frail looking and sitting in front of a fan that is blowing air directly into his face. His shirt is removed and you can see he is using his accessory muscles and diaphragm. He is using home oxygen at 2 LPM via nasal cannula and speaks using two-word phrases. He tells you that he has been a chain smoker for 60 years. You suspect which of the following conditions?
   - **A.** Angina pectoris
   - **B.** Emphysema
   - **C.** Chronic bronchitis
   - **D.** Left-sided congestive heart failure
3. You are working at your part-time job providing security at a local nightclub. Near closing time, a man in his 20s walks out of the bar and collapses onto the ground. He begins shaking violently for approximately 30 seconds, stops, and becomes motionless on the sidewalk. There is blood coming from his mouth from what appears to be a bite wound. He starts to breathe spontaneously after about 60 to 90 seconds. You suspect which of the following conditions?
   - **A.** Stroke
   - **B.** Alcohol intoxication
   - **C.** Generalized seizure
   - **D.** Overdose of methamphetamines
4. You are dispatched to assist EMS with a medical emergency call at the local seafood restaurant, where a family has just started eating their dinner. When you arrive, you find a 26-year-old man complaining of severe shortness of breath. His respirations are labored and he is obviously in distress. You notice that his face is flushed, and he is scratching red-colored hives that appear over both of his arms, face, and chest. You suspect which of the following conditions?
   - **A.** Anaphylaxis
   - **B.** Hyperglycemia
   - **C.** Heat exhaustion
   - **D.** Allergic reaction
5. For a LER, the greatest concern when assisting an individual experiencing an anaphylactic reaction is:
   - **A.** Development of a nosebleed
   - **B.** Low blood pressure
   - **C.** Loss of a clear, open airway
   - **D.** Being sued by the family

Toxicology

Unit 14

Zhanna Livshits
Lewis S. Nelson

Law Enforcement Responder Objectives

- Discuss the patient assessment process at the scene of a suspected poisoning. (pp 271–272)
- Describe the clinical findings of a potentially poisoned patient. (p 271)
- Discuss when to notify the poison control center. (pp 271–272)
- Identify the routes of exposure to various toxins. (p 272)
- Explain the causes and effects of carbon monoxide toxicity. (pp 272–274)
- Discuss the management of a patient with carbon monoxide toxicity. (pp 273–274)
- Describe the key clinical features and management of nerve gas poisoning. (pp 274–276)
- Understand how to use DuoDote antidote auto-injector kit. (pp 275–276)
- Identify common drugs of abuse and their forms.
- (pp 276–281)
- Discuss the differences in the manifestations and management of toxin exposure among the pediatric, adolescent, adult, and geriatric populations. (pp 281–282)
- Describe the clinical findings and field management of scorpion, snake, and spider envenomations common to the United States. (pp 282–285)

National EMS Education Standard Competencies

Medicine

Recognizes and manages life threats based on assessment findings of a patient with a medical emergency while awaiting additional emergency response.

Toxicology

- Recognition and management of
  - Carbon monoxide poisoning (pp 272–274)
  - Nerve agent poisoning (pp 274–276)
- How and when to contact a poison control center (pp 271–272)

INTRODUCTION

The definition of the term **poison** has evolved over centuries. It first appeared in English literature around the year 1230 CE and referred to a "potion or draught that was prepared with deadly ingredients." Poison is now considered any chemical substance that has the potential to injure, harm, or kill in variable amounts and by various routes of exposure such as inhalation, ingestion, and/or skin contact. In this unit, the terms *poison* and *toxin* are used interchangeably.

This unit provides guidance for the recognition and management of specific toxins. The network of Poison Control Centers across the United States is both an informational resource as well as a surveillance tool, staffed by trained health professionals. Poison control should be contacted at (800) 222-1222 when faced with any potential toxin exposures.

Law enforcement responders (LERs) should pay special attention when they arrive on scene and as they patrol the area. Exposure to a toxin should be suspected if multiple people are experiencing the same symptoms.

PATIENT ASSESSMENT

Assessing the Scene

As in all emergency situations, you must first determine the safety of the scene and ensure your own safety. If an environmental toxin is suspected, wear personal protective equipment (PPE) and adhere to standard precautions at all times. Your supervisor or medical director should determine the appropriate PPE for special circumstances. At a minimum, you should always wear gloves when touching a poisoned patient and, if possible, a particulate mask and eye protection.

> **Tip**
> **Standard Precautions for Poison**
> Always use standard precautions before approaching a patient. In some situations, standard precautions may not be enough. If you are at risk, do not enter the scene. Call for hazardous materials specialists per your local protocols.

Assessing and Managing the Patient

Once you have determined that the scene is safe, assess the patient, provide lifesaving interventions, and decide whether the patient needs further medical attention. You should suspect a poisoning if:

- There are empty bottles or scattered pills at the scene.
- There is an odor surrounding or emanating from the victim.
- The person's immediate environment has the potential to contain certain toxins (eg, working in a sewage plant or chemistry laboratory).
- The person is drowsy or comatose.
- The person is agitated and uncooperative.
- The person is not breathing or does not have a pulse.

Assess and manage the poisoned patient using your agency's protocols. The most important part of your initial contact is assessing the patient's airway, breathing, and circulation (ABCs) (**Figure 1**). Call the regional Poison Control Center to report the exposure. Transport the patient to the nearest hospital, using EMS if available, based on your local protocols.

> **Tip**
> **Containers and Paraphernalia**
> It is important to look for pill bottles, containers, and other paraphernalia at the scene and to bring them to the nearest healthcare facility.

When to Call the Poison Control Center

When you suspect that a person may be poisoned, after assessing and addressing the ABCs (and if allowed by local protocol), call your regional Poison Control Center for guidance. (The national number is 1-800-222-1222.) The calls are answered by specialists in poison information (SPIs) who have access to an extensive information database which can

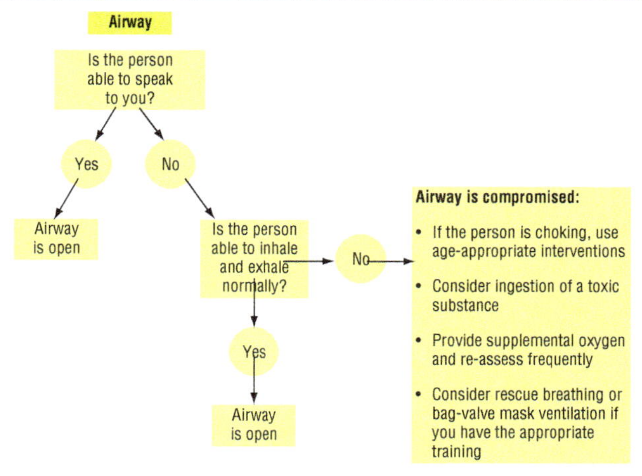

Figure 1 Assessing the airway of a potentially poisoned patient.

be used to contact board-certified medical toxicologists. SPIs are trained to distinguish exposures that may be managed at home versus those which require referral to the emergency department. In addition, poison control centers collect epidemiologic data on the incidence and severity of poisoning. This information may alert the public to the emergence of new toxic threats.

Special Considerations

Following initial assessment and management of the airway, breathing, and circulation, it is important to address decontamination strategies. While skin and eye decontamination should be performed as quickly as possible, gastrointestinal decontamination or evacuation of toxic substance from the stomach needs special consideration and is treated on a case-by-case basis. The following possibilities must be considered:

- Gastrointestinal (GI) decontamination
- Skin exposure and decontamination
- Eye exposure and decontamination
- Drowsy patients
- Pregnant patients

Gastrointestinal (GI) Decontamination

When dealing with gastrointestinal decontamination, do not attempt to evacuate the toxin that the person has ingested. Inducing vomiting mechanically or via syrup of ipecac is almost never recommended in either the prehospital or hospital setting. It is not safe to induce vomiting in a drowsy or comatose person because vomit can be inhaled into the lung (aspiration) and lead to pneumonitis (lung inflammation). A poisoned awake patient has the potential to decompensate quickly, depending on the substance ingested.

Syrup of ipecac causes rapid projectile vomiting. Syrup of ipecac can create an airway problem in some patients and should be used only if approved by your medical protocols. Syrup of ipecac may be used on a case-by-case basis in an alert patient following a life-threatening ingestion, but only when hospital transport time is greater than 1 hour. It takes about 20 minutes for syrup of ipecac to induce vomiting. It should never be administered without prior discussion with a poison control center or medical control physician.

Activated charcoal can be used as an absorbent in the stomach because it can bind certain poisons. Due to its taste and consistency, it can also stimulate vomiting. Activated charcoal can create an airway problem in some patients and should be used only if approved by your local protocols. Activated charcoal is generally administered in a healthcare facility, under close monitoring.

Skin Exposure and Decontamination

If the patient has been exposed to a chemical, decontaminate the patient on scene, according to the protocols based on the type of substance. Contact your medical director for specific instructions.

Eye Exposure and Decontamination

In cases of chemical or toxic eye exposure, irrigate the eyes with normal saline for 15 minutes during hospital transport. If normal saline is not available, use tap water.

Drowsy Patient

If the patient is drowsy but is breathing and has a pulse, the patient's ABCs are stable. Turn the patient on his or her side (recovery position) to prevent aspiration of vomit into the lungs. Continue to administer oxygen if available.

Pregnant Patient

Keep a pregnant patient on her left side (left lateral recovery position) at all times in order to enhance blood return to the heart.

CARBON MONOXIDE POISONING

Carbon monoxide poisoning is the leading cause of poisoning **morbidity** and **mortality** in the United States. It is vital that the signs of carbon monoxide toxicity are recognized, because delayed treatment may lead to a poor neurologic outcome. Failure to recognize signs of toxicity and continued exposure to carbon monoxide may result in death.

Carbon monoxide poisoning impairs oxygen delivery to all the cells in the body and prevents these cells from using glucose as an energy source. As a result, most cellular processes are disrupted. Carbon monoxide sources that may lead to poisoning include the following:

- Burning of carbon-containing fuel sources
  - Fire
  - Charcoal grills
  - Gasoline-powered equipment (automobiles, boats, generators, power washers)
  - Propane-powered equipment (ice resurfacing machines, forklifts)
  - Natural gas–powered equipment (water heaters, gas ranges, ovens, furnaces)

- Metabolic conversion to carbon monoxide following ingestion, inhalation, or skin absorption
  - Methylene chloride, which is found in paint strippers, cleaning and degreasing agents, and aerosol propellants

Exposures most commonly occur during winter months given the increased use of heat-generating equipment that burns carbon-containing fuel. Additionally, many people attempt suicide by closing themselves in a garage or other enclosed location while running a car engine or other device. The LER should immediately have someone open the doors or windows while caring for the patient and awaiting the arrival of EMS, thus ensuring that the LER does not succumb to carbon monoxide poisoning. If possible, move the patient outside to obtain fresh air.

Assessment

The earliest symptoms of carbon monoxide poisoning are headache, dizziness, and nausea. The brain and central nervous system are very sensitive to the toxic effects of carbon monoxide. Mild exposure may manifest as a headache and dizziness. Severe and prolonged exposures may result in loss of consciousness, seizures, coma, or may mimic a stroke. The heart is also sensitive to carbon monoxide-exposure, manifesting as myocardial ischemia (lack of oxygen in the heart muscle), life-threatening dysrhythmia, and cardiac arrest. Lung injury, kidney failure, cherry-red skin color, or large blisters (known as bullae) are rare complications of carbon monoxide poisoning.

People with significant carbon monoxide poisoning may develop delayed neurologic or psychiatric symptoms, 2 to sometimes as long as 40 days after the initial exposure. These findings are collectively referred to as the **delayed neurocognitive sequelae**. Delayed neurologic symptoms range from mild memory loss to dementia, **amnestic syndrome**, peripheral neuropathy, movement problems, and paralysis. Delayed neuropsychiatric sequelae can include personality changes to symptoms of psychiatric illness. Those who lose consciousness and are over the age of 30 are predisposed to developing these delayed effects.

Management

When arriving at the scene, follow the general rules for assessing and managing a poisoned patient. Victims of smoke inhalation during a fire may have difficulty breathing and have cutaneous burns or soot on their skin. However, none of these signs or symptoms needs to be present for the patient to have sustained carbon monoxide poisoning. Those with severe carbon monoxide poisoning may be drowsy, comatose, and sometimes in cardiac arrest.

If you suspect carbon monoxide poisoning, the fire department or other appropriate agency should be alerted to assess the carbon monoxide levels at a given location and to prevent carbon monoxide toxicity in other inhabitants of the facility. Since carbon monoxide is odorless and colorless, it is undetectable except with specialized equipment, and suspicion is based on the circumstances of the exposure, number of victims, location and surroundings, and clinical findings. Detectors are readily available to confirm the presence of excess ambient concentrations of carbon monoxide.

Tip

Carbon Monoxide

Carbon monoxide is odorless and may present with a variety of clinical findings. Prompt recognition and removal of a person from the source of exposure is life saving.

Following the primary assessment, rapidly move the patient outside into the open air. If readily available, place a nonrebreathing mask on the patient and provide high-flow oxygen. Stabilize the ABCs according to your local medical protocols.

If a patient has mild symptoms of carbon monoxide poisoning, call EMS and arrange transport per your local protocols. Some EMS systems use a facility that has a hyperbaric oxygen chamber (**Figure 2**). Although the degree of benefit

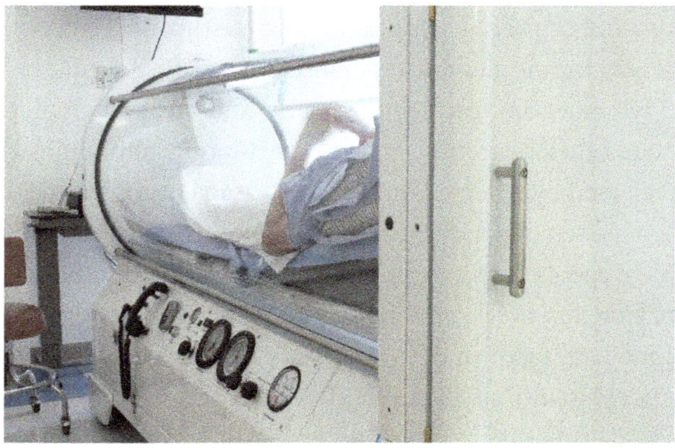

Figure 2 A patient with carbon monoxide poisoning can benefit from hyperbaric oxygen therapy at a medical facility. This photo shows a monochamber; multiplace chambers may also be used.

of hyperbaric therapy is disputed, it may reduce the risk of developing delayed neurocognitive sequelae following carbon monoxide poisoning.

Hyperbaric oxygen therapy subjects a person to an elevated atmospheric pressure as well as high concentrations of oxygen, effectively increasing the amount of dissolved oxygen in the blood by more than 10 times. Raising the oxygen concentration in the blood allows for a significantly faster clearance of carbon monoxide from the body. It also works on the molecular level to decrease the inflammatory cascade caused by carbon monoxide in the brain. This has only been shown in an animal model, and there is conflicting evidence of benefit of the hyperbaric therapy in humans. Thus, the decision to use it in the treatment of carbon monoxide poisoning is state and medical center-dependent.

Tip

Removal to Safety

The primary goal for LERs is to remove the victim safely from the carbon monoxide-filled environment.

NERVE AGENTS

Nerve agents are very powerful chemical weapons. Chemical weapons are designed to kill, injure, or incapacitate by the use of toxic or noxious chemicals. Nerve agents are dispersed in liquid, aerosol, or vapor forms. The most frequently considered nerve agents are tabun, sarin, soman, and VX.

Nerve agents are extremely potent, meaning that very small doses can have substantial clinical effects. They are organophosphorus compounds that disrupt the function of the autonomic nervous system (ANS), which regulates the body's functions through the release and breakdown of molecules called neurotransmitters. A neurotransmitter molecule is released by a nerve onto its target, leads to an effect, and is then broken down by a functional molecule called an enzyme. Nerve agents bind to and inactivate acetylcholinesterase, the enzyme that breaks down acetylcholine. This process occurs rapidly after exposure to a nerve agent, thus leaving a small window to introduce the antidote. An excess of acetylcholine then disrupts the regulation of muscle contraction, level of consciousness, glandular secretions, heart rate, lung function, pupil size, urination, and digestion.

Pure nerve agents are odorless and colorless liquids. Tabun, however, has a fruity odor. Soman odor has been described as fruity, sweet, musty, spicy, nutty, or camphor-like. Nerve agents may be aerosolized or vaporized by heating to produce rapid-onset toxic effects via inhalation.

Tip

Acetylcholine Excess: Muscle Fiber Example

Acetylcholine release from a nerve onto a muscle fiber results in contraction. In the presence of a nerve agent, the body is not able to break down acetylcholine and the muscle continues to contract without being able to relax. This first leads to muscle fasciculations, then to weakness and paralysis.

Exposure Routes

Nerve agents come in contact with and have a direct effect on the eyes, mouth, nose, throat, lungs, and skin. Exposure may occur via the following routes:

- Inhalation of a nerve agent in a gaseous form
- Absorption via the skin or mucous membranes through either gaseous or liquid forms
- Ingestion in either a liquid form or from food contaminated with organophosphorus-containing pesticides

Assessment Findings

Nerve agents are absorbed very quickly into the body and produce clinical effects within seconds or minutes of exposure. Exposure to and toxicity from nerve agents can result in the following clinical symptoms:

- Constricted pupils (may persist for several weeks)
- Nausea and vomiting
- Blurred or dim vision
- Tearing (lacrimation)
- Excessive urination
- Excessive defecation
- Excessive sweating
- Excessive drooling, pulmonary (lung) secretions creating the sensation of drowning
- Difficulty breathing
- Slow or fast heart rate
- Slurred speech
- Muscle twitching
- Muscle weakness or paralysis
- Seizures
- Loss of consciousness
- Death

These symptoms may be best memorized with mnemonics SLUDGE (salivation, lacrimation, urination, defecation, gastrointestinal distress, emesis) and DUMBBELS (defecation, urination, miosis, bronchospasm, bronchorrhea, emesis, lacrimation, salivation). Although miosis is the most common physical manifestation of nerve agent exposure, the "Killer Bs" (**bronchorrhea**, bronchospasm, bradycardia) and paralysis lead to death.

> **Tip**
>
> **Nerve Agent Patients**
>
> Patients with organophosphate or nerve agent exposure typically die of paralysis.

Even following treatment, the neurologic and psychiatric symptoms may persist for weeks to months for example **Ataxia**, **peripheral neuropathy**, and posttraumatic stress disorder have been described in victims of sarin exposure in the Tokyo subway in 1995.

Management

When arriving at the scene, follow the general rules for assessing and managing a poisoned patient. All responders should wear PPE prior to entering the scene. Failure to wear PPE may result in exposure to toxins and rapid toxicity. Remove the victim from the contaminated environment as soon as is safely possible. Decontamination should be performed by appropriately trained and protected personnel before or during the treatment with an antidote, unless the patient is critically ill. If possible, the victims should remove all their liquid-contaminated clothing to avoid the possibility of cross-contaminating the emergency responders.

The assessment of the ABCs is critical. Toxicity from nerve agents often leads to copious salivation and secretion of fluid into the lungs. When combined with muscular **fasciculations** (muscle twitching) or paralysis, the person's airway and breathing becomes compromised. The sensation is similar to that of a person drowning. All victims with labored breathing, copious salivation, or fasciculations/paralysis require supplemental oxygen via a nonrebreathing mask. A victim should have the head elevated at 30 degrees above a flat surface. Immediate administration of the nerve agent antidote auto-injector kit is indicated as well. One of the components of the antidote kit, atropine, dries up secretions and helps the person breathe. In cases of paralysis or muscle fasciculation, a victim may need supplemental ventilation. All victims need immediate hospital transport. If you, the LER, begin to develop any symptoms of nerve gas toxicity, consider self-administration of the nerve agent antidote auto-injector kit per existing protocols.

Nerve Agent Antidote

Treatment of patients with nerve agent poisoning consists of the administration of two antidotes: atropine and pralidoxime chloride (2-PAM). Although atropine reverses some of the minor clinical effects seen with nerve agent poisoning (such as drooling), it is not effective in reversing paralysis and fasciculations. Pralidoxime chloride helps reactivate the enzyme acetylcholinesterase that was inactivated by the nerve agent. Atropine most importantly dries saliva and secretions in the lungs, improving the victim's ability to breathe. Atropine has the following effects:

- Increases the heart rate
- Decreases vomiting and diarrhea
- Dilates pupils

Pralidoxime chloride reactivates the ability of cholinesterase to break down acetylcholine and also prevents the irreversible binding of the nerve agent to this enzyme. It improves muscle twitching and weakness, and eases breathing difficulties. It is not as effective in soman or tabun exposure.

The nerve agent antidote DuoDote was approved by the Food and Drug Administration (FDA) in 2007. It includes both atropine and pralidoxime chloride in one syringe. Administer a nerve agent antidote auto-injector kit if:

- You are authorized to do so by medical direction or protocol.
- You are called to the scene of nerve agent exposure and the patient has compromised breathing, excessive drooling, seizure activity, low heart rate, and/or dangerously low blood pressure.
- You or your peers develop consistent signs or symptoms of nerve gas toxicity.

Make sure to administer the medication as quickly as possible after the onset of symptoms.

Do not administer a nerve agent auto-injector kit if the patient has only mild signs and symptoms, such as tearing or a runny nose.

Take the following steps to administer DuoDote:

1. Wear PPE and follow standard precautions.
2. Confirm that serious signs and symptoms of nerve agent poisoning are present.
3. Confirm that you have the correct drug and check the expiration date.
4. Hold the syringe with your dominant hand.
5. Remove the gray protective cap.

6. Press the green end of the injector very firmly against the outer side of the patient's upper leg (thigh) at a 90° angle. Hold for 10 seconds.
7. Check for the presence of a needle at the green tip to ensure the drug was injected.
8. Dispose of the syringe appropriately.
9. Reassess the patient's signs and symptoms.

Administer a nerve agent antidote auto-injector kit before transporting the victim to the healthcare facility. Although the nerve agent antidote is not always effective, failure to administer it rapidly may lead to death of the victim. If the person continues to have severe symptoms of toxicity such as drooling, difficulty breathing, muscle weakness, confusion, or slow heart rate, administer two more doses of the antidote kit. The use of benzodiazepine agents such as intramuscular lorazepam by trained personnel should be considered if the victim has seizure activity (**Figure 3**).

Tip

Attention to Nerve Agent Signs

It is important for LERs to recognize the signs and symptoms of nerve agent poisoning and to alert medical personnel. It is absolutely vital to wear PPE at all times.

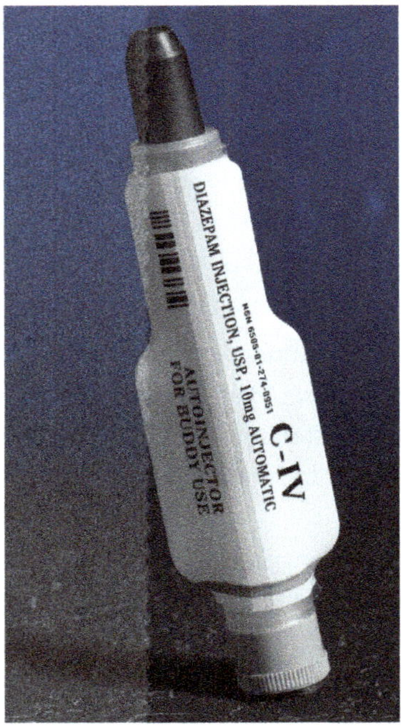

Figure 3 A convulsant antidote for nerve agent (CANA) injector.

COMMON DRUGS OF ABUSE

The term *drugs of abuse* encompasses an extensive list of toxins. This section highlights the following substances: cocaine, amphetamines, heroin, opiates, phencyclidine, ketamine, sedative-hypnotic agents, and gamma-hydroxybutyric acid.

Assessment

Cocaine and Amphetamines

Cocaine is an alkaloid extracted from the leaves of *Erythroxylum coca*. Cocaine hydrochloride, a white powder, is otherwise known as coke, blow, snow, and nose candy. It can be inhaled or dissolved in a liquid and injected. Alternatively, cocaine may be smoked in the nonhydrochloride (also called alkaloidal) form, such as crack cocaine or free base. Regardless of route, it is rapidly absorbed. It prevents the termination of physiologic reactions generated by dopamine, serotonin, epinephrine and norepinephrine molecules, which create a sense of euphoria and fight-or-flight response.

Amphetamines are a group of excitatory substances which include the commonly used methamphetamine (also known as meth, speed, yaba, go, and ice) and 3,4-methylenedioxymeth amphetamine (MDMA) (also known as ecstasy, E, Adam, and XTC), as well as other less commonly encountered agents.

Amphetamines release dopamine, norepinephrine, and epinephrine, which are endogenous substances responsible for the fight-or-flight response.

Methamphetamine is created from ephedrine or related compounds such as over-the-counter pseudoephedrine. It is a white or off-white bitter-tasting substance that is distributed in a powder or crystal form. It may be inhaled, smoked, ingested, or injected.

MDMA is available in colorful tablets with unique branded inscriptions. It is commonly sold at dance clubs and raves. It is less stimulating than methamphetamine but more euphoric.

Signs and symptoms of cocaine and amphetamine toxicity are consistent with the "fight-or-flight" response. Neurologically, cocaine and amphetamines produce agitation, hallucinations (both tactile and visual), and bizarre, irrational behavior. Although seizures have resulted from cocaine and amphetamine toxicity, these patients require a detailed neurologic evaluation to look for a seizure focus. Intracranial hemorrhage is another life-threatening sequelae of stimulant toxicity and often manifests as a change in behavior or severe headache. Stroke has also been reported.

Agitation may lead to life-threatening hyperthermia (body temperature greater than 100.4°F (38°C). Extreme elevation of body temperature leads to multisystem organ failure and death. Be aware that core temperature, typically obtained via either rectal thermometer or esophageal probe, is the most accurate measurement of body temperature. A mildly elevated body temperature obtained by oral or tympanic thermometer may markedly underestimate the degree of hyperthermia.

Severe agitation often leads to muscle breakdown and impaired kidney function. Increased respiratory rate (tachypnea) and profuse sweating (diaphoresis) are commonly seen features of stimulant toxicity.

Cocaine inhalation or insufflation may lead to life-threatening pneumothorax (trapped air in the thorax outside of the lung), **pneumomediastinum** (trapped air in the chest cavity), or **pneumopericardium** (trapped air in the pericardial sac). This often prevents effective lung expansion and oxygen exchange and affects heart function. Users often bear down against a closed epiglottis (**Vasalva maneuver**), a maneuver used to facilitate bowel movement, which increases pressure inside the chest cavity. Crack cocaine use may precipitate acute lung injury known as "crack lung," with symptoms of fever, difficulty breathing, cough with bloody sputum (**hemoptysis**), and potential for progression to respiratory failure.

Cocaine and amphetamines stimulate the cardiovascular system and produce elevated blood pressure (hypertension), fast heart rate (tachycardia), abnormal heart rhythm (dysrhythmia), and constriction of blood vessels (vasoconstriction). Severe hypertension or tachycardia leads to increased oxygen demand of the heart, manifesting as chest pain, and may progress to a heart attack. It may also lead to a life-threatening tear (dissection) of a blood vessel wall. Dysrhythmia compromises the blood flow to vital organs and may deteriorate into cardiac arrest.

Severe constriction of blood vessels may affect many organ systems and lead to life-threatening complications. In addition to stroke and heart attack, a person may experience acute paralysis from injury to the spinal cord, death of lung tissue (pulmonary infarction), intestinal injury and death (intestinal ischemia), renal and splenic infarction, and disruption of placental blood flow in pregnant women.

Although MDMA falls into a methamphetamine class, low doses of the drug produce a sense of euphoria. Adverse effects may include hyperthermia and low blood sodium (hyponatremia), which may result in seizures. Large doses of the drug may produce stimulant effects similar to amphetamines.

Heroin and Opioids

Opioids are a class of agents capable of producing opium-like effects. In therapeutic doses, they modulate pain, induce euphoria, and suppress bowel function and the cough reflex. In excessive doses, they are associated with respiratory depression, which may be lethal if breathing is not supported.

Heroin is a semisynthetic opioid derived from morphine and is known as dope, smack, junk, horse, H, and chiva. The common forms include a sticky, black, tarlike substance or a powder that is brown, tan, or white in color. Heroin is mostly injected, smoked, or inhaled.

Street heroin may be produced with adulterants and contaminants. Adulterants are substances added to heroin to decrease the amount of pure drug in the batch and increase the dealer's profit. Contaminants are additive substances responsible for epidemic deaths. Some of the historic contaminants of heroin included quinine, thallium, lead, cocaine, methaqualone, phenobarbital, amphetamines, scopolamine, and clenbuterol.

Other opioids include the following:

- Morphine
- Codeine
- Oxycodone (Percocet, OxyContin)
- Dextromethorphan (Robitussin DM, Coricidin)
- Fentanyl (Duragesic patch, Sublimaze injection)
- Hydrocodone (Vicodin, Hycodan)
- Hydromorphone (Dilaudid)
- Methadone (Dolophine)
- Buprenorphine (Buprenex, Subutex, Suboxone)
- Meperidine (Demerol)
- Propoxyphene (Darvon, Darvocet)
- Tramadol (Ultram)

Opioids are analgesic agents whose toxicity leads to sedation and respiratory depression. Decreases in both respiratory rate and ventilation impair a person's ability to inhale oxygen and exhale carbon dioxide. It is the most common cause of death from opioid toxicity. Acute lung injury, which manifests as shortness of breath and hypoxia, may be seen with both use of and precipitated acute withdrawal from opioids following reversal agents such as naloxone (Narcan). Release of catecholamines, or fight-or-flight neurotransmitters such as epinephrine and norepinephrine, are thought to contribute to lung injury seen with abrupt reversal of opioid toxicity. Animal models demonstrate that higher blood concentrations of carbon dioxide prior to reversal with naloxone are associated with higher levels of catecholamine release. Extrapolating this information to humans implies that artificial ventilation in patients with a low respiratory rate prior to administering naloxone may reduce lung injury.

Constricted pupils (miosis) are among the most evident opioid effects. However, constriction often lasts long after the life-threatening opioid effects have worn off. Furthermore, the co-exposure to other agents that dilate pupils, such as "speedball" (cocaine and heroin) or presence of hypoxic brain injury, may change the pupillary size. Miosis is therefore not a reliable sign of opioid toxicity.

Low blood pressure and low heart rate are rarely observed. Methadone interferes with electrical conduction of the heart and may lead to dysrhythmias. Propoxyphene, an agent rarely used, may lead to arrhythmias and seizures in a setting of an overdose. Seizures are also seen in the setting of tramadol and meperidine toxicity.

Phencyclidine and Ketamine

Phencyclidine (PCP) was originally developed as an anesthetic agent. Laboratory investigations of PCP led to the discovery of ketamine. Both agents can produce the effect of dissociation between perceptions and their interpretation by the brain. This is most relevant in the ability to dissociate the sensation of pain from the interpretation of the pain as harmful, accounting for its use as an anesthetic.

PCP is also known as angel dust, sherms, embalming fluid, crystal, rocket fuel, wet, water, fry, amp, formaldehyde, and hog. It is distributed in the form of crystals, powder, tablets, and liquid. Recently, it has been available on the underground market in the form of cannabis (marijuana) or tobacco cigarettes, termed *illy*, dipped in a solvent containing PCP.

Ketamine is also known as K, special K, vitamin K, and lady K. Recreationally, ketamine is inhaled as a white powder or injected into the muscle.

PCP and ketamine effects produce dissociation from reality. These drugs may produce a spectrum of psychological effects ranging from calm to hostile and wild agitation. People under the influence of these agents often perceive that they have super-human strength and may sustain serious injuries. These are the people seen running naked on a highway or trying to lift a car. They may experience auditory hallucinations more frequently than visual, paranoia, disordered thought process, and **dysphoria** (restlessness, depression). Loss of balance, involuntary and oscillatory eye movements (nystagmus), and gait instability have been described. Ketamine use may produce unpleasant psychological and somatic experiences such as buzzing, ringing, or whistling sounds; sensation of traveling through a dark tunnel; intense visions; and out-of-body or near-death experiences otherwise referred to as "k-hole."

Agitation may lead to life-threatening hyperthermia. PCP and ketamine are cardiovascular stimulants but rarely lead to life-threatening emergencies. Similar to cocaine and amphetamines, effects such as hypertension, tachycardia, intracranial hemorrhage, and severe blood vessel constriction have been reported.

Sedative-Hypnotics

Sedative-hypnotic agents include benzodiazepines and barbiturate agents. They produce sedation in therapeutic dose or overdose. Oral overdose of sedative-hypnotic agents produces an effect of mild to severe sedation with normal blood pressure, heart rate, respiratory rate, body temperature, and oxygen saturation.

Respiratory depression may result from a rapid large intravenous injection of sedative hypnotic agents or when taken in combination with drugs such as alcohol or opioids.

Table 1 includes a list of commonly used sedative-hypnotic agents.

Gamma-Hydroxybutyric Acid

Gamma-hydroxybutyric acid (GHB) has a very strong depressant effect on the central nervous system, similar to sedative-hypnotic agents and alcohol. It is generally available as a powder that is diluted in water or prediluted in aqueous form.

Table 1

Sedative-Hypnotic Agents

Benzodiazepines	Barbiturates
Alprazolam (Xanax)	Phenobarbital (Luminal)
Clonazepam (Klonopin)	Secobarbital (Seconal)
Diazepam (Valium)	Pentobarbital (Nembutal)
Lorazepam (Ativan)	
Restoril (Temazepam)	
Zolpidem (Ambien) behaves like a benzodiazepine	

GHB is also known as G, Liquid X, and Gamma-OH. GHB is typically abused in the following settings:

- By athletes who aim to increase their muscle mass at bodybuilding gyms and fitness centers
- As a sleep aid
- For recreational use at nightclubs and raves
- During criminal, drug-facilitated sexual assault

Once diluted, GHB is a clear liquid. Blue food coloring is often added to help identify it as GHB and prevent the ease of slipping it into someone's drink without notice. A person under the influence of GHB often appears lethargic or stuporous and undergoes rapid complete awakening. Vomiting, jerking movement of the arms and legs (myoclonus), low heart rate, and low body temperature (hypothermia) are also effects of GHB. Respiratory depression has been described as well, but occurs mostly with concomitant use of other agents.

Management

When arriving at the scene, follow the general rules for assessing and managing a poisoned patient. People who display a change in behavior (including lethargy or agitation, abnormal blood pressure, heart rate, respiratory rate, and oxygen saturation) need to be transported to the hospital as quickly as possible. When apprehending a suspect for bizarre and disruptive behavior, do not forget that these people need to be evaluated by a physician. They may die in custody from complications of drug use without immediate medical attention.

Hyperthermia is associated with high morbidity and mortality. Follow local protocols under medical direction, which may direct you to treat hyperthermia aggressively by submerging or packing the torso of the affected individual in ice. The use of a standard fan, air conditioning, or a cooling blanket is not as effective as ice submersion. It is important to cool the patient to at least 102.2°F (39°C) in less than 30 minutes to reduce mortality.

In the event of a seizure, it is important to provide supplemental oxygen and to place patients on their side to prevent aspiration. Authorized personnel may administer benzodiazepine to control the seizures during hospital transport. Be sure to assess for hypoglycemia and to treat it if needed.

People with opioid toxicity appear sedated and have respiratory depression or apnea. If the patient is not breathing or if the respiratory rate is below 10 breaths per minute, it is important to initiate artificial breathing, such as with a bag-mask device connected to a 100% oxygen supply. Naloxone is an antidote for opioid toxicity and may be administered by authorized personnel. When using naloxone, avoid using large doses for complete reversal. Ventilate a person with respiratory depression before administering naloxone. When dosing naloxone per protocols, consider starting with a very small dose. You should not use doses of greater than 0.4 mg naloxone prior to discussing the case with your medical doctor. A dose of 0.4 mg of naloxone is a large dose and in most cases sufficient to reverse opioid-induced respiratory depression. Higher doses are indicated in only a few circumstances. Remember that you can redose naloxone every minute for a goal respiratory rate of greater than 11 breaths per minute and adequate chest rise (ventilation). Slow reversal of opioid toxicity is safe and will prevent acute opioid withdrawal. Remember that precipitated opioid withdrawal can lead to life-threatening acute lung injury.

Special Considerations for Law Enforcement

Restraining an Agitated Person

Patients with significant agitation typically require restraint for hospital transport. When applying restraints, do not place the patient in the prone position. There have been reports of death from agitation, hyperthermia, and positional asphyxia (suffocation) when patients were restrained in this manner. It is unclear whether patient positioning is the most important contributor to death. It is important that a restrained, agitated patient be positioned to enable adequate ventilation. Avoid placing the incapacitated patient in a nonporous body bag, due to the risk of developing hyperthermia. Follow the steps in **Skill Drill 1** to restrain an aggressive patient:

1. Assemble four or five rescuers and have the stretcher or carrying device and soft restraints nearby. Designate a leader STEP 1.
2. Assign positions to each team member: head and four extremities STEP 2.
3. If possible, corner the patient in a safe area STEP 3.
4. On the direction of the team leader, move together toward the patient STEP 4.
5. Each team member should grasp the assigned body part and carefully, with the least amount of force, bring the patient to the ground STEP 5.

Skill Drill 1

Restraining an Agressive Patient

1. Assemble four or five rescuers and have the stretcher or carrying device and soft restraints nearby. Designate a leader.

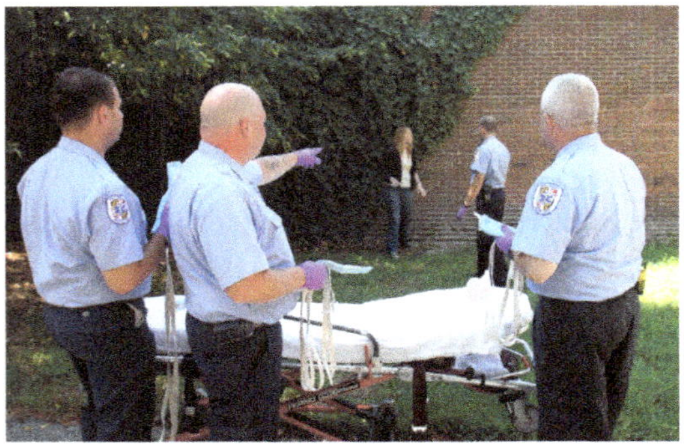

2. Assign positions to each team member: head and four extremities.

3. If possible, corner the patient in a safe area.

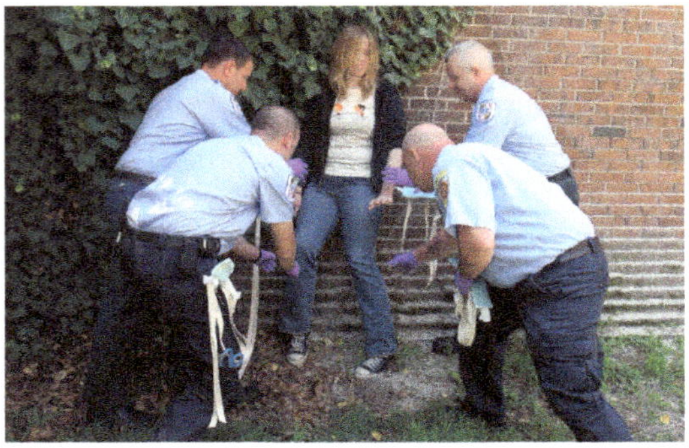

4. On the direction of the team leader, move together toward the patient.

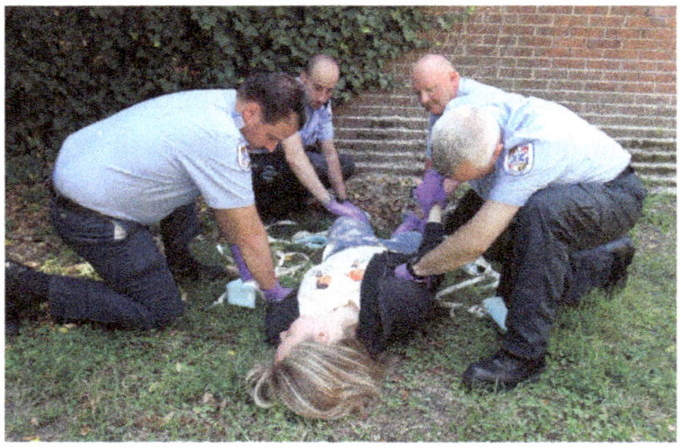

5. Each team member should grasp the assigned body part and carefully, with the least amount of force, bring the patient to the ground.

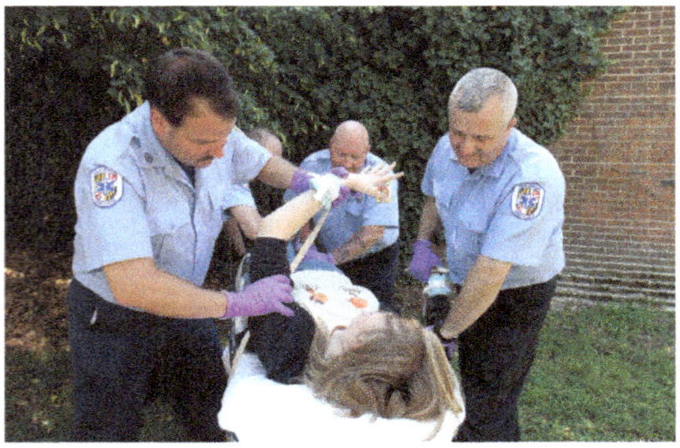

6. Carefully place the patient on a stretcher or carrying device in a face-up position.

Skill Drill 1

Restraining an Agressive Patient *(continued)*

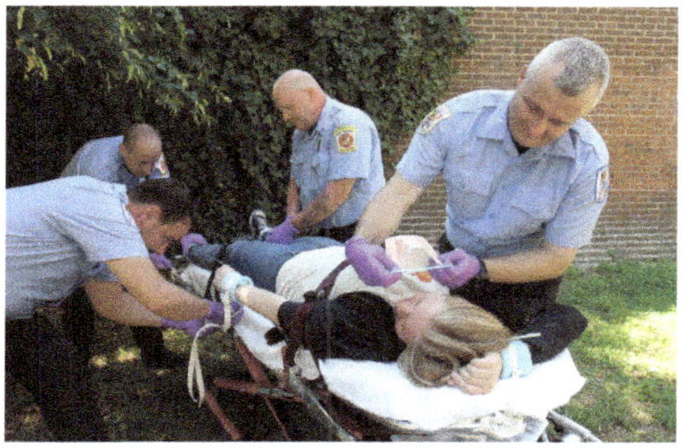

7. Tie the patient with soft restraints at each wrist and ankle as well as the chest and pelvis with sheets. If the patient is spitting, place the oxygen mask or surgical mask on the patient's face.

6. Carefully place the patient on a stretcher or carrying device in a face-up position STEP 6.
7. Tie the patient with soft restraints at each wrist and ankle as well as the chest and pelvis with sheets. If the patient is spitting, place the oxygen mask or surgical mask on the patient's face STEP 7.

Body Stuffers/Packers

In an attempt to conceal evidence during an arrest, people may swallow cocaine or heroin that is not appropriately packaged. This phenomenon is known as body stuffing. It is important to bring these people to the hospital as soon as possible, before questioning or taking them to the police station. Ingestion of cocaine or heroin that is not well packaged may be deadly in a matter of minutes in the absence of appropriate medical attention. Conversely, some swallow carefully packaged drugs for illegal transport. Any physical complaints should be rapidly addressed by immediate transport to the hospital.

VARIATIONS FOR PEDIATRIC AND GERIATRIC PATIENTS

Pediatric Patients

All children and adolescents who ingest a toxin need to be transported to the nearest medical facility. Toddlers often inadvertently ingest toxins within their reach, including medications, common household products, and substances that are not secured by their caretakers (**Figure 4**). An ingestion that would be nontoxic in an adult may be life threatening or deadly in a child, given the child's smaller size. Additionally, a young child's physiology and metabolism differ from that of an adult. For an example, a child who drinks a small quantity of ethanol (alcohol) may develop life-threatening hypoglycemia (low blood glucose level) and develop coma if untreated. Many medications are now flavored and sweetened for children, resembling candy or juice. Children may seek these medications and consume them for the taste.

Special Populations

Intentional Poisoning and Child Abuse

Intentional poisoning is a significant form of child abuse. Any suspicion of child abuse requires a full investigation involving law enforcement and child protective services after the child is stabilized at the nearest healthcare facility.

Adolescents experience an intense period of social growth. They may feel the desire to "fit in" with their peers or a "need to escape." Although their ingestions may involve medications or products accessible at the home or from a nearby store, they also experiment with drugs of abuse.

Figure 4 Toddlers often inadvertently ingest toxins within their reach, including medications, common household products, and substances that are not secured by their caretakers.

Geriatric Patients

The elderly population is at an increased risk of unintentional poisoning and adverse drug events. Medication errors are common for many reasons and may result in life-threatening conditions. Age-related factors such as impaired vision, hearing, and/or memory can contribute to a medication error, often resulting in overdose. In addition, prescribed medications may have prolonged effects and may not be readily eliminated from the body because of the age-related reduction in kidney function.

Elderly patients may present late after a poisoning, especially if they live alone and cannot call for help. In addition, it may be challenging to assess toxicity in a person with a significant cognitive decline. All elderly people with suspected poisoning or toxicity should be transported to the nearest healthcare facility by EMS.

ENVENOMATIONS

Not all toxins are created by humans as drugs or weapons. Many more exist naturally in plants and animals. LERs should have a basic understanding of the natural toxins found in their jurisdictions and how to assess and treat exposure to these toxins.

Snakes

Fortunately, the United States does not contain many kinds of snakes. There are two groups of snakes whose envenomations lead to toxicity: the crotalinae and the elapidae.

Some crotalinae snakes are also known as pit vipers, named for the depression behind their nostrils that houses a heat-sensing organ. These snakes have characteristic triangular-shaped heads, paired with fangs that retract into the roof of the mouth following envenomation, and vertically elliptical eyes (**Figure 5**). Crotalinae genus includes the following species of snakes: rattlesnakes, water moccasins (cottonmouths), and copperheads (**Figure 6**).

The elapidae snakes are brightly colored snakes, with color patterns of red followed by yellow, and then black (**Figure 7**). The nonvenomous look-alike is the King snake, which has red color followed by black. The following phrase has been used to differentiate venomous from nonvenomous elapids: "Red on yellow kills a fellow; red on black, venom lack." The coral snake is a venomous elapid indigenous to the United States.

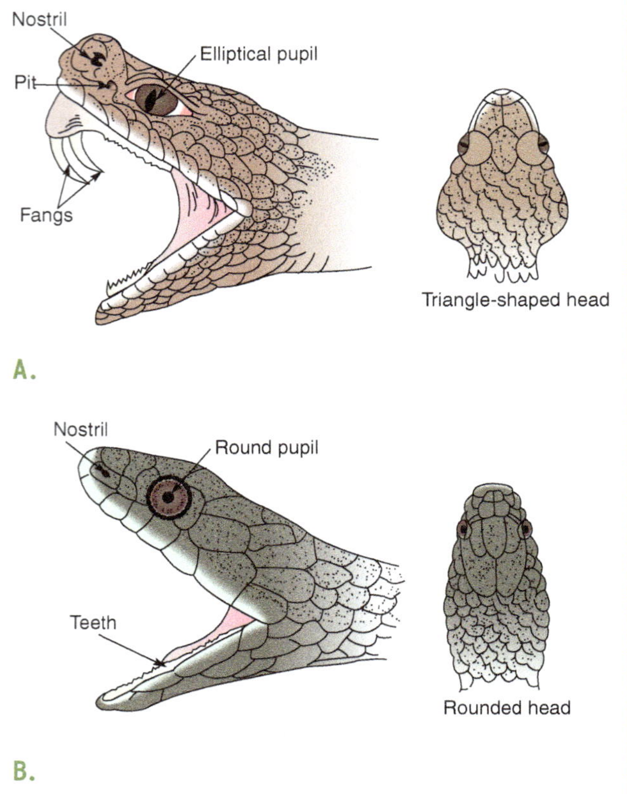

Figure 5 Characteristic features of **A.** venomous snakes (pit vipers) and **B.** nonvenomous snakes.

Assessment

Venom is injected through a bite, and the amount of venom may depend on the depth of the bite and the number of strikes. Pit vipers produce a characteristic bite due to their distinctive needle-like fang marks. Coral snakes have small fangs and may not produce a visible bite mark following envenomation. Systemic spread of venom occurs through venous and lymphatic drainage.

Crotaline snakes kill their prey by a hematologic toxin. Venom is a complex mixture of molecules with specific functions. Some of the components prevent the blood from clotting effectively (anticoagulants), and others enhance blood clotting (procoagulant). There are additional components that destroy tissue at the site of the bite. Some crotaline snakes, such as the Mojave rattlesnake, produce a neurotoxin as well.

The composition of venom varies by snake species, and, therefore, clinical effects vary as well. Physical examination may reveal fang marks with significant local tissue destruction such as redness, swelling, hemorrhagic blistering, and tissue death (necrosis). There may be a significant delay in symptom

Figure 6 **A.** Rattlesnake. **B.** Water moccasin (cottonmouth). **C.** Copperhead.

Figure 7 Coral snake.

onset. However, the person may not have visible injury, but instead may develop significant platelet and clotting abnormalities. The neurotoxin in the Mojave rattlesnake may produce nerve weakness that may progress to paralysis. Although rare, some patients may experience a life-threatening allergic reaction (anaphylaxis) that is characterized by swelling of the airway, itchy rash, and low blood pressure.

Coral snake venom contains a neurotoxin meant to paralyze the prey. Clinical effects typically include muscle weakness that may progress to paralysis. Be aware that the clinical effects may be delayed.

Management

Field approach to a patient bitten by a snake is simple. If the person has significant weakness or paralysis, you may need to provide rescue breathing with a bag-mask device if trained to do so.

If the hospital is a few hours away, immobilize the affected body part if possible and rapidly transport the patient to the hospital. The use of a pressure bandage, tourniquet, or constriction band is not advised in the setting of crotaline envenomation. These methods may increase the chances of local tissue injury or death associated with crotaline venom.

Do not attempt to incise and drain or suck out the venom with your mouth. This procedure is often unsafe because it can damage the underlying nerves, tendons, and blood vessels.

Transporting the patient to the hospital by ambulance, instead of performing heroic unproven and potentially unsafe procedures, is the most important thing you can do for the bitten patient. In the hospital, a physician will decide if the patient requires antivenin therapy.

Spiders

Given the incredible diversity of spiders, discussion in this text is limited to the *Latrodectus mactans*, otherwise known as the black widow spider, and *Loxosceles reclusa*, otherwise known as the brown recluse spider (**Figure 8**).

A.

B.

Figure 8 **A.** Black widow spider. **B.** Brown recluse spider.

The black widow spider is found in Canada and New England and in the states including Florida, Texas, Kansas, and Oklahoma. It is well recognized for its black color and distinctive, ventrally-located, red hourglass shape. The spiders are nocturnal and bite when provoked or threatened. The venom is neurotoxic.

The brown recluse spider is a shy and nocturnal arthropod that has a characteristic dorsally-located brown marking in the shape of a violin. The brown recluse is common to the southeast and southwest United States. Similarly to the black widow spider, they bite only when provoked. The venom is cytotoxic, leading to cell injury and death around the bite.

Assessment

The black widow spider may leave very small puncture marks on the skin that sometimes progress to a wheal surrounded with a halo. Envenomations typically progress from pain to neuromuscular symptoms within 15 to 60 minutes following the bite. Painful muscle cramping may start shortly after the bite and persist for days, commonly involving muscles of the chest, abdomen, and face. Patients may have prominent facial effects, most notable for grimacing, sweating, inflammation of the eye (including eyelid and conjunctiva), and spasm of the masseter muscle that's responsible for chewing. The bite victims may also experience nausea, vomiting, and headache. Hypertension, breathing difficulty (respiratory distress), heart attack, and gangrene are life-threatening signs and symptoms and need immediate medical attention. After resolution of acute symptoms, people often suffer for weeks to months from muscle spasms and weakness.

Clinical effects following envenomation by a brown recluse spider, otherwise known as loxoscelism, can be divided into three categories: mild skin reaction, cytotoxic reaction, and systemic loxoscelism. Mild local skin reaction, such as redness or minimal swelling, occurs when a very small amount of venom is injected. Cytotoxic reaction refers to the skin swelling, discoloration, and cell death in the area surrounding the bite (**Figure 9**). The area affected by the bite may blister and ulcerate, attaining a violet color. This area may become surrounded by a circle of blanched or whitish skin, followed by a circle of redness. This pattern is termed "red, white, and blue," and is seen following a brown recluse spider envenomation. The progression of symptoms occurs within 2 to 8 hours following the envenomation. The blister may then become blackened and form an eschar in 5 to 7 days after the bite. Skin lesions may grow very large, and may take months to heal. The systemic loxoscelism occurs 24 to 72 hours after the bite. Its development may be independent of presence or absence of skin findings. The clinical findings range from nausea, vomiting, and fever to multisystem organ dysfunction, bursting of red blood cells (hemolysis), organ failure, and death.

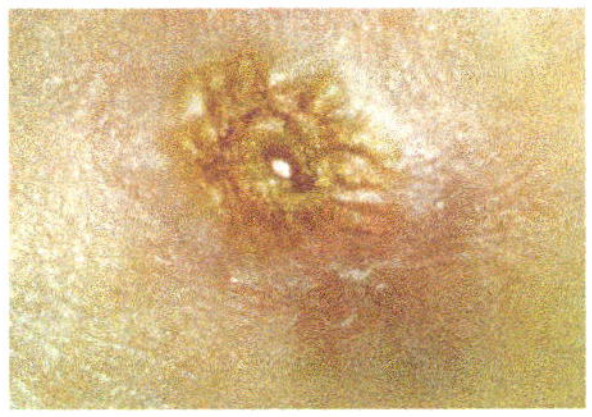

Figure 9 Bite from a brown recluse spider.

Management

People with suspicion of a black-widow spider envenomation should be transported to the nearest hospital. If they are asymptomatic, they may need an observation period under medical supervision. Supplemental oxygen may be warranted in patients who appear to be in pain or have respiratory symptoms. There is a crude antivenin, derived from horse serum. However, it carries a risk of a life-threatening allergic reaction. Although the envenomation produces severely painful effects, the mortality is low. Only an experienced clinician should decide whether the risks of antivenin administration are worth taking.

If you are treating a suspected brown recluse spider bite, evaluate the wound and assess for presence or absence of systemic symptoms. If you believe that the patient is experiencing systemic symptoms from a spider bite, have the patient transported to the hospital for medical evaluation. Patients with skin blistering, discoloration, or systemic symptoms necessitate transport to the nearest hospital. Only patients without symptoms or mild skin findings (such as a small area of swelling without discoloration) could remain at home. These people need to receive strict instruction to go to the nearest emergency department if their symptoms progress.

Scorpions

Scorpions are arthropods that envenomate humans by stinging with their tail. Fortunately, there are only two venomous scorpions in the United States: *Centuroides exilicauda* (bark scorpion) and *Centuroides vittatus* (striped bark scorpion). We will focus on the bark scorpion *C. exilicauda* for the remainder of the discussion (**Figure 10**). The venom is a neurotoxin.

Assessment

A person who sustains a scorpion bite will typically have pain, redness, burning, tingling sensation, numbness, or skin discoloration at the site of the bite. Sometimes there is a lack of skin findings with only numbness and tingling. The symptoms may progress to involuntary jerking movements of the arms and legs, roving eye movements, and increased salivation.

Muscle weakness may occur from nerve dysfunction and may involve the face, airway and breathing muscles, or the torso and extremity muscle groups.

Furthermore, people envenomated by *C. exilicauda* may experience cardiac dysrhythmias and various electrocardiographic abnormalities, and may deteriorate quickly. Some people have experienced acute lung injury, inflammation of the pancreas (pancreatitis), blood coagulation abnormalities, and seizures.

Management

People who have minor symptoms such as pain and swelling, numbness, or tingling confined to the site of the bite need to be transported to the nearest hospital for medical evaluation and observation.

Figure 10 Bark scorpion.

If a person has any neurologic signs, provide supplemental oxygen, preferably via a nonrebreathing mask. If the person has labored breathing or hypoxia, be prepared to provide ventilation with a bag-mask device if trained to do so.

All people experiencing *C. exilicauda* or *C. vittatus* envenomation need to be transported quickly to the nearest hospital.

CONCLUSION

When approaching a poisoned patient, it is important to maintain standard precautions. In a poisoned patient, it is vital to initially assess the ABCs and to immobilize injuries prior to moving the victim. Ensure your own safety prior to helping a patient. If appropriate, wear PPE. The majority of poisoning patients will improve with good supportive care, including adequate oxygenation and ventilation, cardiovascular support with intravenous fluids, removal from toxin exposure, and prompt transfer to the nearest healthcare facility.

Prep Kit

READY FOR REVIEW

- Poison is now considered any chemical substance that has the potential to injure, harm, or kill in variable amounts and by various routes of exposure such as inhalation, ingestion, and/or skin contact.
- Before entering a scene with a poisoned victim, initiate standard precautions.
- When approaching a poisoned victim, assess ABCs (airway, breathing, and circulation) first.
- Following primary assessment and management of the airway, breathing, and circulation, it is important to address decontamination strategies.
- Carbon monoxide is the leading cause of poisoning morbidity and mortality in the United States.
- Patients with carbon monoxide poisoning may present with symptoms varying from headache to cardiac arrest.
- If a patient has mild symptoms of carbon monoxide poisoning, consider transport to a facility that has a hyperbaric oxygen chamber.
- The most important intervention in carbon monoxide poisoning is to remove yourself and the patient from the environment and administer high-flow oxygen.
- Nerve agents may produce significant toxicity with very small exposures.
- The most common signs and symptoms of nerve agent toxicity are increased oral and lung secretions, sweating, muscle twitching, and paralysis.
- Administer the DuoDote nerve agent antidote kit to a person with serious nerve agent toxicity in the field.
- Cocaine and amphetamine toxicity manifest with symptoms of agitation and elevated blood pressure and heart rate.
- PCP and ketamine can produce the effect of dissociation between perceptions and their interpretation by the brain.
- In therapeutic doses, opioids modulate pain, induce euphoria, and suppress the cough reflex. In excessive doses they are associated with respiratory depression, which may be lethal if breathing is not supported.
- Street heroin adulterated or contaminated with various substances may lead to a mixed presentation of toxicity and may be deadly.
- Sedative-hypnotic toxicity manifests as sedation progressing to coma.
- GHB toxicity is marked by a rapid onset of coma followed by sudden awakening.
- Patients with significant agitation typically require restraint for hospital transport. When applying restraints, do not place the patient in the prone position.
- All children and adolescents who ingest a toxin need to be transported to the nearest medical facility.
- Age-related factors such as impaired vision, hearing, and/or memory can contribute to a medication error, often resulting in overdose.
- Immobilize the extremity that has been bitten by a snake and transport to the hospital as quickly as possible. Avoid applying pressure bands.
- Crotaline envenomations produce blood clotting abnormalities, and elapid envenomations produce neurologic symptoms.
- Black widow spider bites lead to severe muscle spasms mimicking other medical conditions.
- Brown recluse spider bites affect the skin and may lead to skin necrosis.
- Scorpion envenomation is associated with movement abnormalities and cardiac effects.

VITAL VOCABULARY

amnestic syndrome A syndrome that involves a transient or a permanent memory loss.

ataxia Lack of coordinated movement; unsteadiness with movement of the limbs.

bronchorrhea Excessive secretion production from the bronchioles; can result in copious amounts of sputum.

delayed neurocognitive sequelae Neurologic or psychiatric symptoms that occur 2 to 40 days after the initial insult. Symptoms may include mild memory loss, dementia, amnesia, and problems with peripheral nerves and movement.

dysphoria Restlessness, disquiet, depression.

fasciculations Muscular twitching involving the simultaneous contraction of contiguous groups of muscle fibers.

hemoptysis Coughing up blood.

morbidity State of disease.

mortality State of death.

peripheral neuropathy Situation where the peripheral nerves are not working properly.

pneumomediastinum Air trapped in the portion of the chest that sets between the lungs and behind the sternum.

pneumopericardium Air trapped in the pericardial sac.

poison Chemical substance that has the potential to injure, harm, or kill in variable amounts and by various routes of exposure such as inhalation, ingestion, and skin contact.

vasalva maneuver A maneuver, conducted by advanced medical providers, in which the patient is instructed to force air out against a closed airway while forcibly contracting the abdominal muscles, bearing down in the abdomen and pelvis. This increases the pressure in the trunk and places pressure against the vagus nerve. The vagus nerve is the primary nerve of the parasympathetic nervous system. Employing this maneuver will promote a parasympathetic response in the body.

CHECK YOUR KNOWLEDGE

1. Carbon monoxide works by which of the following mechanisms?
   - **A.** Interfering with oxygen delivery to the body
   - **B.** Directly preventing the contraction of the heart muscle
   - **C.** Is a gastrointestinal irritant, causing nausea and vomiting
   - **D.** Preventing oxygen delivery and use by the cells
2. When approaching a poisoned patient, it is important to do the following:
   - **A.** Enlist the help of interested observers.
   - **B.** Assess the patient's airway, breathing, and circulation and then look for signs of trauma.
   - **C.** Shock the patient with an automated external defibrillator prior to initiating cardiopulmonary resuscitation. Induce vomiting.
   - **D.** Look for signs of trauma prior to assessment of the patient's airway, breathing, and circulation.
3. The symptoms of carbon monoxide poisoning may include:
   - **A.** bloody vomiting.
   - **B.** headache.
   - **C.** diarrhea.
   - **D.** violent behavior.
4. Which of the following are signs of nerve agent toxicity?
   - **A.** Skin blistering
   - **B.** Paralysis
   - **C.** Sedation
   - **D.** Bloody diarrhea
5. You arrive at the scene and see an agitated man running naked in the traffic, hitting the passing cars with a bat. It takes six men to restrain him prior to hospital transport. Which of the following agents did he likely ingest?
   - **A.** PCP
   - **B.** Benzodiazepine
   - **C.** Heroin
   - **D.** Marijuana

Environmental Threats

Unit 15

Horace Liang
Joy Crook

Law Enforcement Responder Objectives

- List factors that predispose patients to heat-related emergencies. (pp 289–290)
- Identify various types of heat emergencies based on presenting signs and symptoms. (pp 289–290)
- Treat various heat-related emergencies. (pp 289–290)
- List factors that contribute to cold emergencies. (pp 291–293)
- Discuss hypothermia and differentiate levels of severity based on signs and symptoms. (pp 291–292)
- Treat different stages of hypothermia. (pp 291–292)
- Identify and treat frozen tissue injuries. (pp 292–293)
- Discuss altitude and its effect on the body. (pp 293–295)
- Discuss the assessment and management of acute mountain sickness (AMS). (pp 295–296)
- Discuss the assessment and management of high-altitude cerebral edema (HACE). (p 296)
- Discuss the assessment and management of high-altitude pulmonary edema (HAPE). (p 297)
- Discuss prevention considerations to limit altitude-related illness. (p 297)

National EMS Education Standard Competencies

Trauma

Uses simple knowledge to recognize and manage life threats based on assessment findings for an acutely injured patient while awaiting additional emergency medical response.

Environmental Emergencies

Recognition and management of

- Temperature-related illness (pp 289–293)

INTRODUCTION

Law enforcement responders (LERs) frequently encounter environments and conditions that are not routine. All experienced officers and agents can relate stories of extreme temperatures. Because of the variations associated with geography, many LERs will have to travel to experience altitude changes or endure changing temperature and temperature extremes.

Heat and Cold Exposure

Injuries from environmental exposures are preventable. Dressing appropriately for extremes in temperature and weather, adequate hydration and nutrition, and limitation of physical activity with appropriate rest periods may diminish the occurrence of illness or injury during heat and cold exposure.

Poor planning for missions exposes LERs to environmental insults. LERs frequently respond to incidents involving environmental emergencies and should understand the extremes that may affect them or those under their responsibility.

HEAT EXPOSURE

Maintaining core temperature relies on heat production minus heat loss. Heat production is a by-product of a person's **basal metabolic rate**. The basal metabolic rate is the rate at which humans use energy at complete rest. It is measured by the amount of heat produced and is the primary source of human heat production. At high temperatures, heat loss occurs primarily through evaporation (sweating). Less effective heat dissipation mechanisms include radiation (heat moving away from the body into the environment), convection (a surrounding layer of warm air being replaced by cooler air), conduction (direct contact with a colder surface), and minimally via respiration losses. This balance of heat production and heat loss is **thermoregulation**. The human body uses energy to create heat or to lose heat through sweating to maintain a stable core temperature. When environmental conditions are very hot and humid, sweating as a primary mechanism for cooling may be impaired. Failure of thermoregulation results in several types of heat-related illnesses.

Tip

Assess the Environment

After the primary assessment, the LER should act immediately to assess and manage the environmental needs of the patient, whether the issue is medical or traumatic.

Heat Cramps

Heat cramps may occur after working or exercising in a warm environment (**Figure 1**). They are characterized by involuntary, spastic contractions of isolated muscles. The person experiencing heat cramps, however, has a normal body temperature and mental status. The cause is thought to be a relative deficiency of fluids and electrolytes. Although painful, the condition is usually self-limiting, and the treatment consists of gentle stretching, fluid replacement, and rest. Massaging heat cramps is not recommended because it may cause the muscle to release more acids into the system.

Figure 1 Heat cramps may occur after exercise in a warm environment.

Heat Exhaustion

When physically active in a hot and especially humid environment, a person may experience nonspecific symptoms such as light-headedness, dizziness, headache, fatigue, and nausea. The patient with **heat exhaustion** will also have a rapid pulse, be pale with profuse sweating, have a normal to slightly confused mental status, and usually have a normal temperature. Heat exhaustion is a heat illness brought on by dehydration and electrolyte losses.

Initial treatment of heat exhaustion includes moving the patient to a cooler, less humid location and removing excess clothing. If the patient is conscious and can swallow, careful administration of oral fluids is appropriate. If the person has continued symptoms, he or she should be transported for further medical care. Heat exhaustion may progress to heatstroke, which is a medical emergency. If in doubt, treat the patient as a possible heatstroke victim.

Tip

Oral Rehydration

If a patient is conscious and able to drink, follow your local protocols regarding the use of oral rehydration solutions. Water or electrolyte drinks, such as those provided by Cera Products, should be utilized. Avoid sodas, tea, alcohol, and coffee.

Heatstroke

When a person is subjected to a hot environment with high humidity for a prolonged period of time, his or her ability to maintain a normal core temperature may become overwhelmed and the person may experience **heatstroke** (Table 1). In such an environment, the person's ability to radiate, evaporate, convect, or conduct heat away from the body is decreased. This is commonly seen in episodes of seasonal heat waves, during which the extremely young, the elderly, or those who are not able to care for themselves are most vulnerable. Heatstroke may also occur during physical training in extremely hot and humid environments, even if the person is physically fit, or in children left unattended in vehicles during the summer.

Heatstroke is an absolute emergency. The illness is characterized by an elevated temperature (greater than 104°F [40°C]), hot skin with decreased sweating or dry skin, rapid pulse rate, confusion, lethargy, seizures, or unconsciousness.

To treat heatstroke, move the patient to a cooler, less humid environment. Remove the victim's clothing and begin externally cooling the patient with cool (not cold) water (Figure 2). Use a fan, if available, to enhance evaporative and convective heat loss. If ice is available, place ice bags on the groin and armpit areas. Arrange for rapid transport to a medical facility. Delays in treatment may result in organ failure, permanent disability, or death.

Heatstroke is preventable. Training activities should not be held when there is a period of extreme temperature and humidity. During seasonal heat waves, it has been shown that heat illness and death can be effectively prevented when people spend even a few hours in an air-conditioned environment.

Table 1 Heat Exhaustion Versus Heatstroke

Heat Exhaustion	Heatstroke
Normal or slightly elevated temperature	Significantly elevated temperature
Sweating	Less sweating or dry skin
Cool and clammy skin	Hot and flushed skin
Alert or slightly confused	Lethargic; seizures or unconsciousness

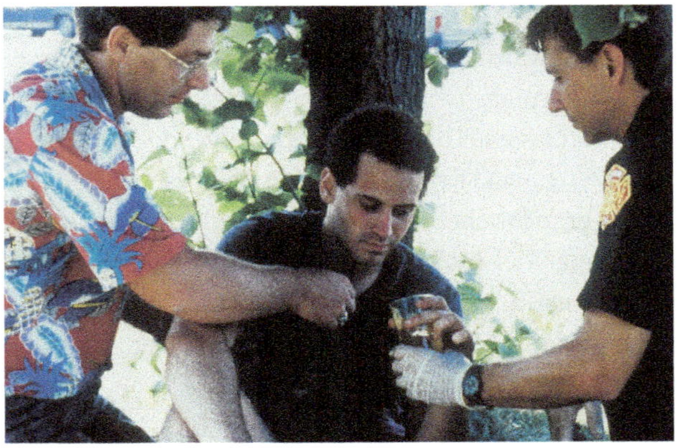

Figure 2 To treat heatstroke, move the patient to a cooler environment and begin externally cooling the patient.

COLD EXPOSURE

Cold emergencies can occur in various ways. Most people are aware that cold, wet, and windy environments can deplete heat from patients and place them at risk for cold-related emergencies. Gradual exposure to cool temperatures in wet environments, however, can place an unsuspecting person at risk for cold injury. Too often, a LER encounters rescues where civilians and law enforcement personnel are exposed to gradual cooling, unsuspected changes in weather, or situations where warming devices have failed. LERs who are aware of the progression of cold-related injuries have the best chance of surviving these conditions or treating others with cold-related injuries.

Figure 3 Hypothermia can happen to anyone who is exposed to cold, even in urban areas. Hypothermia often results from exposure to cold temperatures over hours.

Hypothermia

Hypothermia occurs when the body can no longer maintain its core temperature, with a resultant fall in body temperature (below 95°F [35°C]). Environmental hypothermia may occur to people involved in outdoor activities, but the greatest numbers of hypothermia cases are reported in the urban setting. Hypothermia can happen to anyone who is exposed to cold, but most often occurs in infants; the elderly; and persons with poor circulation, in overall poor health, who suffer from chronic diseases, and who are homeless (**Figure 3**). Certain medical conditions, alcohol, drugs, and poisons can also predispose a person to hypothermia.

A mild decrease in body temperature initially triggers constriction of blood vessels to decrease heat loss through radiation and initiate shivering to produce more heat. If the degree of heat loss exceeds the capability of heat conservation or heat generation, hypothermia will occur. Acute hypothermia can occur within minutes of a severe cold water immersion because the human body loses heat faster in a wet environment. More commonly, subacute hypothermia results from a generalized exposure to a lower environmental temperature over hours. This process is accelerated for people wearing wet clothing for any length of time in the cold, especially if there is also wind.

Clinical hypothermia caused by environmental exposure is generally classified as mild, moderate, or severe (**Table 2**).

As a compensatory mechanism to cold exposure, people shiver to increase heat production. As their core temperature decreases, they may appear less alert and have decreased motor skills. As hypothermia progresses, shivering ceases and there is a slowing of metabolic functions, such as a decreased heart rate, weaker pulses, and slowing respiration. In severe hypothermia, people may become unresponsive to the point of appearing dead. If not promptly treated, they will ultimately succumb to cardiac arrest.

To treat hypothermia, first check the patient's airway, breathing, and circulation (ABCs). This may be difficult because profound hypothermia may produce coma, muscle

Table 2

Classification of Hypothermia

Mild Hypothermia	Moderate Hypothermia	Severe Hypothermia
95°-90°F (35°-32°C)	90°-82°F (32°-28°C)	< 82°F (< 28°C)
Apathy; impaired judgment; shivering preserved	Progressive depression of level of consciousness; loss of coordination; muscle stiffness; decreased shivering	Unresponsive; weak pulse; slowed respiration

rigidity, and severe slowing of the pulse rate. After assessing the ABCs, assess for any associated trauma that may necessitate immobilization of the patient. Injuries should be treated according to your local protocols. Be careful to maintain warmth and handle severely hypothermic patients gently. Patients who are able to drink and can swallow without difficulty can receive sugary drinks (warmed, if possible) based on your local protocols and medical direction.

Tip

Hypothermia Assessment Cues

- Skin and muscle
  - Pallor increases with drop in temperature. Extremities may become mottled or blue.
  - The patient has a low core temperature. If a thermometer is not available, the patient's abdomen may be cold when checked with the back of your hand.
  - The patient experiences shivering. As body temperature decreases, muscle rigidity occurs and you may see erratic, jerky movements. As the body continues to cool, muscles maintain a rigid state.
  - The patient experiences clumsiness and uncoordinated movement.
- Nervous system
  - The patient experiences confusion.
  - The patient has difficulty making decisions.
  - The patient is drowsy.
  - The patient experiences lethargy.
  - The patient is apathetic about his or her condition.
  - Consciousness decreases and the patient may fall into a coma
- Cardiovascular system
  - The pulse is weak and may become very slow and only accessible at the carotid artery.
  - The patient experiences shallow breathing.

Automated external defibrillators (AEDs) should be applied based on your local protocols and medical direction. Some programs will not use defibrillation on severely hypothermic patients. Others may restrict defibrillation to three attempts.

Regardless of the severity of hypothermia, the first step is to stop further heat loss. Remove the patient from the cold environment. Remove any wet clothing and provide a dry, insulating covering (eg, a windproof vapor barrier) to decrease further heat loss by radiation and convection. If the patient cannot be immediately removed from the scene, additional insulation should be provided between the ground and the patient to decrease conductive heat loss (**Figure 4**). Once the patient is extricated from the scene, provide a warm, draft-free environment and transport the patient to the closest hospital or casualty collection point. Warm fluids may be administered orally to a conscious, stable, mildly hypothermic patient who has not suffered any associated trauma.

Tip

Treating Hypothermia

Take the following steps to care for a patient with hypothermia:

- Remove the patient from the environment.
- Protect the patient from further heat loss.
- Remove wet clothing.
- Cover the patient with a sleeping bag, blanket, or the like.
- Provide protection from wind.
- Handle the patient gently.
- Transport the patient in a supine or recovery position.

If the patient is unresponsive and is not shivering, handle him or her gently, especially in cases of presumed moderate or severe hypothermia. Such patients are more prone to suffer cardiac arrhythmias. Transport the patient in a supine or recovery position. Do not attempt to administer warm fluids or stimulants by mouth.

Frostbite

Frostbite commonly affects the ears, face, hands, and feet (**Figure 5**). It is the cooling of the body's tissue to the point at which injury occurs to the tissues. The skin may initially become reddened, may blister, and then appears mottled and pale. Once this occurs, the affected area becomes numb.

Figure 4 Consider adding insulation between the ground and the patient to decrease conductive heat loss.

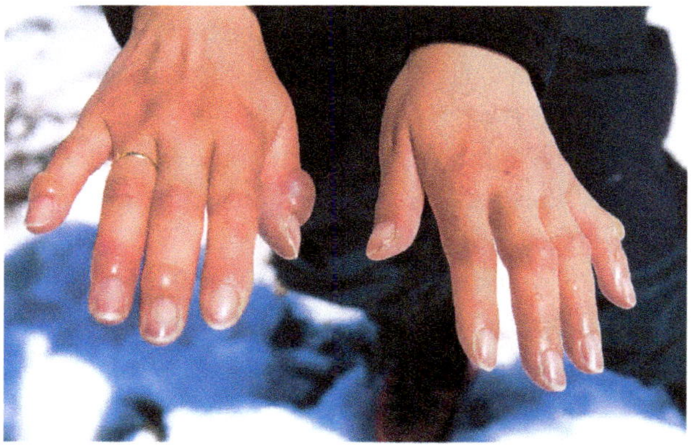

Figure 5 Frostbite most commonly affects the ears, face, hands, and feet.

Handle potentially frostbitten areas gently. Do not rub or massage the extremity; doing so may cause additional tissue injury. Remove any potentially constricting clothing or jewelry from the extremity. Leave blisters intact and, if possible, cover them lightly with a dry dressing. Protect the patient from further heat loss. Frostbitten tissue will have to be warmed to return to normal function. If the tissue is left frozen, it will eventually have irreparable damage. Thawing the extremity may be quite painful to the patient. If thawing is necessary, immerse the extremity in a warm-water bath of 100°F (37.8°C). Do not attempt to warm the extremity with a direct heat source (campfire, heat lamp, hair drier) because these heat sources may result in thermal burns. Avoid giving the patient food or drink. This may decrease blood flow to the affected areas, increasing the chance of tissue damage. Ensure that the patient is covered to maintain body heat and protect against hypothermia.

It is important that a thawed extremity not be allowed to refreeze because refreezing would create greater tissue damage. It is best to treat this injury in a hospital setting. Frostbite patients are best managed at a hospital where there is no chance that the freshly thawed tissue will refreeze. Hospitals also can provide supportive care and pain medication to make the process more comfortable. If you decide to transport your patient with frostbite or a frozen limb, pad around the frozen areas and protect them from damage. Nonsteroidal anti-inflammatory medications such as ibuprofen may be helpful in the field depending on local protocols because they can potentially limit some of the body's inflammatory cascade. Maintaining a normal body temperature and adequate hydration is important. It is never recommended to open or drain blisters, either clear or bloody, in the field. Again, the key factors are to recognize that frostbite has occurred and to transport the patient to medical attention immediately, not undertaking rapid rewarming unless under medical supervision and there is no chance for refreezing of the injured body part.

Hypothermia and Cardiac Arrest

A patient with severe hypothermia may appear to have frozen to death (cold, stiff, cyanotic, dilated pupils). If there is a pulse present, do not perform chest compressions. Unfortunately, it may be difficult to detect a pulse or respirations, which may be slow, weak, and shallow. Take at least a minute to palpate a pulse. If you suspect cardiac arrest due to severe hypothermia, begin cardiopulmonary resuscitation (CPR) and follow your agency's resuscitation protocols. There are reported cases of successful recovery after prolonged CPR and appropriate hypothermic resuscitation. Hypothermic patients should not be considered dead until they have had their core temperature corrected in an appropriate medical facility. Therefore, the treatment goals are to remove the patient from the cold environment, examine the patient, and initiate CPR if you are unable to detect respiration or pulse. The next steps are to insulate the patient and to provide rapid transport.

High-Altitude Illness

Law enforcement officers and agents frequently find themselves in settings of high elevations. Many people are aware that the highest mountains in the continental United States are found in the Rocky Mountain range. Many are unaware, however, that mountains classified as high altitude (taller than 4,950 ft) exist throughout the country. The highest summit east of the Mississippi is Mount Mitchell in North Carolina at 6,684 feet. Because of the geographic extremes in many regions of the United States, LERs can find themselves going from near sea level to a high altitude within hours.

Elevation in altitude triggers a multitude of normal and abnormal physiologic responses that can result in medical complaints. More than 100 million people worldwide live at elevations in excess of 2,500 m (8,200 ft), and still more travel to these areas for work, recreation, or religious reasons. In the United States, many national park, ski, and recreational areas are located in areas of high elevation; therefore, it is critical to be able to recognize people at risk for high-altitude illness as well as to identify those already suffering from the effects of altitude.

High altitude is defined by land elevation above sea level and takes into consideration the physiologic responses triggered in the body when these altitudes are attained (Table 3).

There is a common belief that the percentage of oxygen in the atmosphere declines at higher elevations. This is not the case. The percentage of oxygen in the air remains a constant 21%; rather, it is the barometric pressure of oxygen that changes. Decreases in oxygen's barometric pressure result in less oxygen being available in the air to breathe. This results in less inspired oxygen and produces the hypoxia (low levels of oxygen in the blood) that exists in the human body at altitude. At altitudes approaching 3,000 m (9,842 ft), which are not uncommon in the United States, the barometric pressure of oxygen is almost one third less than it is at sea level. These decreases are not linear, meaning that at very high and extremely high altitudes, a small change in altitude results in a large drop in the availability of oxygen to breathe.

PHYSIOLOGY AND ACCLIMATIZATION TO ALTITUDE

The human body is very sensitive to changes in the barometric pressure of oxygen and the resulting hypoxia. Although this hypoxia is a normal physiologic response to altitude, mechanisms are triggered in an attempt to limit the adverse effects on the body and to prepare the body to go to even higher altitudes. Collectively, these mechanisms are referred to as **acclimatization**.

Table 3

Altitude Classifications

Classification	Elevation Above Sea Level in Meters (Feet)
High altitude	1,500-3,500 (4,920-11,500)
Very high altitude	3,500-5,500 (11,500-18,050)
Extremely high altitude	5,500-8,850 (18,050-29,035)

As low as 1,500 m (4,921 ft) and in as quickly as a few hours of exposure to these altitudes, the human body senses changes in the barometric pressure of oxygen in the atmosphere, which results in increased respiratory rates. The increased respiratory rate allows the body to decrease carbon dioxide levels because each breath blows off more of the carbon dioxide by-product made by the body. This response also serves to minimally increase the oxygen levels in the blood.

Tip

Human pH Level

pH is an abbreviation that indicates the concentration of hydrogen. The pH is used to describe how acidic or alkaline a substance is. A pH of 7 is considered neutral. The normal human body pH is 7.35-7.45.

The body uses various physiologic mechanisms to maintain this fragile pH. To do this, the body controls the amount of bicarbonate (buffer that binds to hydrogen reducing acid levels) and carbon dioxide (the more carbon dioxide the body keeps, the more acidic the blood will be; the less carbon dioxide the body keeps, the more alkaline the blood will be) in the blood.

The bicarbonate levels are maintained through the kidneys; carbon dioxide levels are maintained through the lungs. The brain works to control both of these organs, keeping the pH where it should be.

This entire respiratory process affects the acid-base balance in the body, raising the body's pH into the alkalosis end of the spectrum. However, the human body does not tolerate alkalosis very well. Therefore, in an effort to bring the pH back to a normal, or neutral, range (around 7.4), the kidneys will excrete bicarbonate, or base, into the urine to lower the body's pH. If the kidneys cannot accomplish this task, the alkalosis created by breathing faster will halt the process, and no further increases in respiratory rate can occur. This will stop acclimatization. As long as the kidneys continue to excrete bicarbonate into the urine, the brain will continue to signal to the body to breathe faster, thus allowing more increases in the respiratory rate and better oxygenation of the blood. This process is maximally effective in about 4 to 7 days at a given altitude.

How efficiently this entire process takes place plays a role in how well an individual person acclimatizes to altitude. It should be noted that there is a prescription medication called acetazolamide that facilitates the excretion of bicarbonate from the kidney, with the ultimate result being faster, more efficient acclimatization. Although acclimatization allows a person to continue to ascend in altitude without becoming ill, this process does not represent perfect compensation, and levels of oxygen in the blood will never reach those seen in the same person at sea level until descent.

As previously mentioned, low levels of oxygen in the blood are expected at altitude. In addition, there are normal decreases in exercise tolerance and increased breathing rates even at rest. Much of the following discussion of illness related to high altitude is focused on diseases that contain these two symptoms, only in a more profound state. This is to say that it is important to recognize that these phenomena may be a normal response to altitude, or they may be the first symptoms of a very serious and life-threatening disease. Distinguishing between the two may be difficult even for a medically trained person. The key is to be aware of potential problems related to altitude.

Altitude causes other physiologic changes in the body. The lower oxygen level in the blood triggers a mechanism in the lungs called vasoconstriction, which is constriction of the blood vessels in the lungs where oxygen is transported into the blood. This causes an abrupt rise of the blood pressure in the lungs, a phenomenon called **pulmonary hypertension**. This sudden change in the blood pressure of the lung blood vessels helps initiate the cascade of events that leads to **high-altitude pulmonary edema (HAPE)**, or excessive fluid buildup in the lungs, which will be discussed later in this unit. Mental acuity, especially the ability to complete complex functions such as mathematics, is diminished at altitude. In the short term, over a few minutes, this can be compensated for with increased concentration, but this compensation is lost over the long term. Night vision has also been noted to decline even at the lower end of the high-altitude spectrum.

Another normal response to low blood oxygen levels is a more chronic change that takes several weeks to develop. There is a rise in the body's production of red blood cells, which are the oxygen carriers in the body. The natural response to low blood oxygen levels is to increase the number of oxygen carriers in an effort to raise the overall oxygen levels. The bone marrow begins to produce more red blood cells after a more prolonged exposure to altitude, a condition that is called **polycythemia**. People who live at high elevations have chronically elevated red blood cell counts compared with those who do not.

Some responses to altitude are very common but cannot be placed easily into either the category of normal or that of disease. Sleep disturbances are incredibly common, thought to be caused in part by hypoxia in the brain. As a person ascends in altitude, he or she may experience frequent nighttime awakenings and an overall lack of feeling rested. Another phenomenon, called periodic breathing, may also play a role. While sleeping, a person may be noted to breathe rapidly for several seconds, followed by a period of apnea. When carbon dioxide levels build up in the blood as a result of not breathing, the brain triggers breathing again. This often results in a gasp, which wakes up the person. Although disturbing to witness and experience, overall these two occurrences are not harmful. These phenomena are the basis of the recommendation that a person should not sleep at the highest altitude achieved when climbing. "Climb high, sleep low" is a common phrase among mountaineers to try to prevent these problems.

ACUTE MOUNTAIN SICKNESS

Acute mountain sickness (AMS) is a spectrum of disease that ranges from the benign **high-altitude headache (HAH)**—which consists of a headache only, with no other symptoms—to life-threatening **high-altitude cerebral edema (HACE)**, a swelling of the brain. In 1993, the Lake Louise Consensus Group at the International Hypoxia Symposium defined AMS as involving the recent arrival of an unacclimatized person to altitude and the presence of a headache, plus one or more of the following symptoms:

- Gastrointestinal symptoms (nausea, vomiting, anorexia [decreased appetite])
- Insomnia or difficulty sleeping
- Dizziness, light-headedness, or lassitude
- Fatigue

The symptoms usually begin within 2 to 3 hours of arrival at altitude and rarely start more than 36 hours after arrival. Most people will be better within 3 days; however, a small subset will continue to worsen despite no further gains in altitude.

Wide variability exists among studies looking at the incidence rates of AMS in persons traveling to altitude. Several studies suggest rates among unacclimatized individuals close to one person in every four developing symptoms when traveling to altitudes of greater than 2,000 m (6,562 ft). AMS has been recognized in people at altitudes as low as 1,500 m (4,921 ft). Because the incidence rates increase as elevation increases, more people will develop AMS the higher the elevation achieved.

The risk factors for developing AMS include the rate of ascent, the ultimate altitude reached, the sleeping altitude, and individual susceptibility. Of these, the rate of ascent seems to play the most important role. By achieving high elevations quickly, the body's acclimatization mechanisms do not have time to fully compensate for the hypoxia, thus putting the person at risk for developing an altitude-related illness. Individual susceptibility to altitude is very complex. An individual's personal history of prior exposures to altitude is very important. A history of prior AMS in a person means that person is at increased risk for developing it again upon exposure to altitude. Other factors, such as the altitude of a person's permanent residence and the person's medical history, including certain blood diseases such as sickle cell anemia and underlying heart and lung disease, all play a role. Physical fitness is not protective against developing altitude-related illnesses and generally does not correlate with how well someone will acclimatize to altitude.

People who experience only a headache are not considered to have AMS; rather, they simply are experiencing HAH, which can be treated with rest, hydration, stopping the ascent, over-the-counter pain medications such as acetaminophen or nonsteroidal anti-inflammatory drugs (NSAIDs), and the administration of oxygen if medical personnel are available. Starting the prescription medication acetazolamide (Diamox) prior to ascent may prevent HAH; acetazolamide is also used to treat it. The headache is usually self-limiting and improves with the treatments just described or on its own. As with all of the altitude-related illnesses discussed here, ascent should not continue until the symptoms resolve. If they do not resolve within 24 hours, or if they worsen, then descent of at least 500 m (approximately 1,600 ft) is mandatory.

The development of AMS (altitude exposure plus headache plus one or more of the other symptoms listed previously) is more serious because it represents a movement along the spectrum of disease that leads to HACE. The key is recognition; many people will not feel well but will attribute their symptoms to other things or not realize that it is not a normal response to altitude. Once AMS is suspected, ascent should be halted immediately and medical personnel should be contacted. Medications such as oxygen and acetazolamide alone may be enough to treat the symptoms. However, descent of between 500 m to 1,000 m (1,000 to 3,200 ft) rapidly improves the condition. This may be achieved by physically descending in elevation or by simulated descent in a portable hyperbaric chamber, such as a **Gamow bag**. Continuing ascent once AMS has begun or before the symptoms have resolved may be life threatening.

Tip

AMS Risk Factors

The risk factors for developing AMS include the following:

- Rate of ascent
- Altitude reached
- Sleeping altitude
- Individual susceptibility

High-Altitude Cerebral Edema

The endpoint of the disease spectrum of AMS is HACE, swelling in the brain as a result of the altitude itself. Some new research indicates that all persons who travel to higher altitude have some amount of brain swelling, although most people do not develop HACE. It is possible this is a result of how well an individual compensates for the brain swelling. Overall, this disease is rare, with only 1% to 2% of people traveling over 4,500 m (14,700 ft) suffering from it.

The hallmark symptoms of HACE are confusion and **ataxia** (unsteady and uncoordinated movements or a staggering gait). People with more serious cases develop depressed mental function, which may result in coma and death. People may also experience a phenomenon called **lassitude**, which is characterized by weakness, exhaustion, or lethargy. Rarely, hallucinations have occurred. Other physical symptoms such as headache, nausea, and vomiting may also be present. Although people typically develop HACE after experiencing AMS, there is a subset of people who will directly develop HACE without a clear diagnosis of AMS first. These symptoms can develop and progress rapidly, sometimes within a few hours of arrival to a new altitude. Therefore, altered mental status, confusion, or ataxia should be considered to be HACE until proven otherwise. Once this diagnosis is considered, medical assistance should be sought immediately.

The mainstay of treatment for HACE is descent, either actual or simulated in a portable hyperbaric chamber. In general, a descent of more than 1,000 m (3,200 ft) is necessary, but the total descent necessary will be dependent on the individual's symptoms and overall health status. Medications such as oxygen and steroids should be given immediately; acetazolamide and other **diuretics** (medications that produce greater urination and lower blood volumes) may also be beneficial and used if descent or evacuation is delayed. Symptoms usually begin to improve rapidly with descent. It is not advisable to restart a climb or ascent after an individual has suffered from HACE, even after the symptoms have resolved.

HIGH-ALTITUDE PULMONARY EDEMA

HAPE is a disease involving the lungs and the blood vessels in the lungs. Fluid fills up the air sacs, making it difficult to breathe and to take oxygen into the bloodstream. It accounts for more deaths at altitude than any of the other high-altitude illnesses and is most commonly seen above 3,000 m (9,843 ft). Although the mechanism of how it occurs is not perfectly understood, it is closely related to a sudden onset of elevated blood pressures in the lungs called pulmonary hypertension. As previously mentioned, the hypoxia induced by altitude causes the blood vessels in the lungs to vasoconstrict, which results in higher blood pressures in the lungs. When this occurs rapidly, the body does not have time to compensate for it, and fluid leaks into the lung's air sacs. This fluid acts as a barrier to oxygen coming into the blood and leaves a person short of breath and coughing.

HAPE most commonly occurs the second night at a new altitude and rarely occurs after 4 to 5 days at the same altitude because the body has compensated for the new blood pressures in the lungs by that time. This clock will reset once a new altitude is attained. The early symptoms of HAPE are often difficult to distinguish from normal adjustments to altitude because decreased exercise tolerance and shortness of breath are common to both. It can be helpful to compare an individual to the group with which he or she is ascending. If one person is doing much worse, struggling to breathe, or a cough has developed, then HAPE should at least be considered. In general, a dry cough develops first, and then it becomes wet, with people often coughing up blood or pink, frothy sputum. Tachypnea (increased breathing rate) is also noted. Interestingly, about half of the people who experience HAPE also experience AMS, and a smaller percentage will experience both HAPE and HACE.

As with all high-altitude illnesses, early recognition is very important. The disease may progress rapidly and become severe, with the person being unable to compensate on his or her own. Treatment for HAPE begins with stopping ascent and notifying medical personnel. Oxygen therapy and descent, again either actual or simulated, of 500 m to 1,000 m (1,000–3,200 ft) should be instituted immediately. Additional medications have been used to treat HAPE successfully, including medications to lower the blood pressures in the blood vessels of the lungs, and albuterol, which is also used to treat asthma. All medications should be implemented in conjunction with oxygen and descent. If the person is no longer able to keep breathing on his or her own, medical personnel may have to provide artificial breathing for the patient. Because descent is so effective at treating HAPE, however, additional medication is usually not necessary. Again, it is not advisable to restart an ascent after surviving HAPE, even if the symptoms have resolved. Someone who has had HAPE on a previous exposure to altitude is at greater risk for the disease again.

PREVENTION CONSIDERATIONS

The main way to prevent any high-altitude illness is to ascend slowly. It is recommended that at elevations over 3,000 m (9,800 ft), a person should not increase his or her sleeping altitude more than 300 m to 500 m (1,000 ft to 1,600 ft) per day. Furthermore, a day of rest, or acclimatization, during which the sleeping altitude does not change even if you ascend during the day, should occur with every 1,000 m (3,200 ft) in elevation. The axiom "climb high, sleep low" is protective in that the body will be exposed to higher elevations, thus pushing the natural acclimatization process, whereas sleeping at a lower altitude will allow more oxygen in the bloodstream and brain (**Figure 6**). Acetazolamide, discussed throughout this section, is a medication that has been shown to stabilize breathing at high altitudes. There has been a lot of interest in the herb ginkgo biloba being used to prevent AMS as well; however, recent larger studies have not proved its efficacy in this capacity, and thus there is no current recommendation for its use as such.

Tip

Descent is Key

The treatment for unknown altitude illness is alwasy descent, descent, descent!

EXPOSURE-RELATED ILLNESSES

It is important to recognize that other illnesses occur at altitude, often related to activities that are being done there and to exposure to the elements rather than directly related to the altitude itself. High altitudes often mean colder temperatures, increased wind, and less shelter to protect an individual. Hypothermia is not uncommon and may occur at temperatures well above freezing, particularly if high winds or rain are part of the weather mix. Another problem encountered,

Figure 6 Climbing high and sleeping low pushes the natural acclimatization process during climbing but allows sleeping at an altitude that will ensure more oxygen in the bloodstream and brain.

although less expected, is hyperthermia (elevated core body temperatures). Often clothing is layered or water resistant in an effort to deal with expected weather elements. However, at high altitude on a clear, sunny day, temperatures can rise quickly. This rapid rise coupled with physical exertion may make an individual susceptible to heat-related illnesses such as heat exhaustion or the life-threatening condition of heatstroke. Of note, temperatures inside tents on Mount Everest during the day have been recorded at well over 100°F (37.8°C). Wearing breathable, moisture-wicking clothing and layering clothing as well as maintaining good hydration practices will help prevent heat-related complications.

Though not common and often preventable with adequate clothing and shelter, frostbite is a serious problem that plagues individuals who are left exposed to cold temperatures for extended periods of time. The amount of time it takes to develop frostbite is dependent on the air temperature, wind, and the amount of moisture in the air. Once this diagnosis is suspected, it is critical to get the individual sheltered from the elements and to notify medical personnel for evacuation immediately. Attempting to rewarm the frostbitten area in the field should be undertaken only with medical supervision.

CONCLUSION

Regardless of these extreme and frequently dangerous situations, the LER must work through these extremes to carry out missions. LERs must train for these situations. In some cases, preparation time will not be possible, and LERs will have to meet these challenges using their knowledge, experience, and ingenuity.

Prep Kit

READY FOR REVIEW

- Environmental injuries are preventable. Plan appropriately by dressing for temperature and weather. Make sure you plan for adequate hydration and nutrition and limit physical activity with periods of rest.
- At high temperatures, heat loss occurs primarily through evaporation (sweating). When environmental conditions are very hot and humid, sweating may be impaired. Failure of thermoregulation results in several types of heat-related illnesses.
- Heat cramps are characterized by painful spastic contractions of isolated muscles.
- Heat exhaustion often presents with nonspecific symptoms of exhaustion. The patient may have a rapid pulse, pale and profusely sweating skin, normal to slightly confused mental status, and a normal temperature.
- Heatstroke occurs when the patient is no longer able to maintain a normal core temperature. Heatstroke patients have hot skin, failing sweating mechanisms, rapid pulse, and confusion, lethargy, seizures, or unconsciousness.
- Hypothermia occurs when the body can no longer maintain its core temperature, with a drop below 95°F (35°C).
- Hypothermia can happen to anyone who is exposed to cold but most often occurs in infants; the elderly; and persons with poor circulation, in overall poor health, who suffer from chronic diseases, and who are homeless.
- Remove hypothermia victims from the cold environment, remove wet clothing, and provide a dry, windproof covering.
- If hypothermic patients are unresponsive and not shivering, handle them gently to prevent cardiac dysrhythmias.
- If you suspect a cardiac arrest caused by severe hypothermia, begin CPR. Follow your agency's resuscitation protocol.
- Frostbite commonly affects the ears, face, hands, and feet. The skin may initially become reddened, blister, and become mottled.
- In the United States, many national parks, ski, and recreational areas are located in areas of high elevation.
- The percentage of oxygen in the air remains a constant 21% at all altitudes, but the barometric pressure of oxygen changes. These decreases in the barometric pressure of oxygen effectively result in less oxygen available in the air to breathe.
- Acute mountain sickness (AMS) is a spectrum of disease that ranges from the benign high-altitude headache (HAH) to life-threatening high-altitude cerebral edema (HACE), or swelling of the brain.
- Risk factors for developing AMS include the rate of ascent, the ultimate altitude reached, the sleeping altitude, and individual susceptibility.
- The hallmark symptoms of HACE are confusion and ataxia. Patients with more serious cases develop depressed mental function, which may result in coma and death. The mainstay of treatment for this is descent, either actual or simulated in a portable hyperbaric chamber.
- High-altitude pulmonary edema (HAPE) is a disease involving the lungs and the blood vessels in the lungs that results in fluid filling up the air sacs, making it difficult to breathe and take up oxygen into the bloodstream. It accounts for more deaths at altitude than any of the other high-altitude illnesses.
- The main way to prevent any high-altitude illness is to ascend slowly. The treatment for unknown high-altitude illness is descent.

VITAL VOCABULARY

acclimatization A mechanism triggered in an attempt by the body to limit the adverse effects on the body and to prepare the body to go to even higher altitudes.

acute mountain sickness (AMS) Range of illnesses affecting unacclimatized persons; these illnesses include a headache and one or more of the following symptoms: gastrointestinal complaint (nausea, vomiting, anorexia, or decreased appetite), insomnia, dizziness, light-headedness, or lassitude and fatigue.

ataxia Unsteady and uncoordinated movements or a staggering gait.

basal metabolic rate The rate at which humans use energy at complete rest.

diuretics Medications that produce greater urination and lower blood volumes.

frostbite Cooling of the body's tissue to the point at which injury occurs. The skin may initially become reddened, may blister, and then appears mottled and pale.

Gamow bag A portable hyperbaric bag.

heat cramps Involuntary, spastic, and very painful contractions of isolated muscles occurring after physical activity in a warm environment.

heat exhaustion A heat illness brought on by dehydration and electrolyte losses. Patients appear with generalized exhaustion symptoms.

heatstroke An emergency characterized by an elevated temperature, hot skin with decreased sweating, a rapid pulse rate, and confusion, lethargy, seizures, or unconsciousness. Heat stroke is fatal if untreated.

high-altitude cerebral edema (HACE) Swelling of the brain as a result of altitude, with the hallmark symptoms of confusion and ataxia.

high-altitude headache (HAH) An initial symptom associated with developing cerebral edema without any other symptoms.

high-altitude pulmonary edema (HAPE) A disease involving the lungs and the blood vessels in the lungs that results in fluid filling up the air sacs, making it difficult to breathe and take up oxygen into the bloodstream.

hypothermia Condition in which the body can no longer maintain its core temperature, with a resultant fall in body temperature below 95°F (35°C). Blood vessels constrict to decrease heat loss through radiation and initiate shivering to produce more heat. The degree of heat loss eventually exceeds the capability of heat conservation or generation.

lassitude A condition characterized by weakness, exhaustion, or lethargy.

polycythemia When bone marrow begins to produce more red blood cells after a prolonged altitude exposure.

pulmonary hypertension Increased blood pressure in the lungs.

thermoregulation The balance of heat production and heat loss.

CHECK YOUR KNOWLEDGE

1. Which of the following is a mechanism that allows the patient to lose body heat while lying on a cold surface?
   - A. Radiation
   - B. Convection
   - C. Conduction
   - D. Sweating
2. Which of the following is an example of an appropriate treatment for heat cramps?
   - A. Pack armpits, groin, and neck with cold packs.
   - B. Allow for gentle stretching.
   - C. Allow patient to rehydrate as tolerated.
   - D. Have the patient rest.
3. Which of the following best describes the way to treat a patient who you think is in cardiac arrest from hypothermia?
   - A. Start cardiopulmonary resuscitation (CPR) immediately.
   - B. Warm patient to 95°F (35°C) and then start CPR.
   - C. Transport without CPR and rewarming to a medical facility.
   - D. Delay CPR until an automated external defibrillator (AED) is available.
4. Massaging affected tissue is the best way to treat frostbite.
   - A. True
   - B. False
5. The best way to treat high-altitude cerebral edema (HACE) is to:
   - A. Continue the ascent, because it will improve with altitude.
   - B. Stay at the present altitude, because moving an affected individual can make him or her worse.
   - C. Ascend slowly, utilizing supplemental oxygen and hydration.
   - D. Descend immediately.

Assessment in **Action**

SCENARIO

You have been dispatched to a shopping center for a report of a "person down." When you arrive you find a middle-aged woman sitting on a curb. She appears to be confused, has very sweaty skin, and is wearing a medical identification bracelet that states "DIABETIC." The patient's daughter is with her, and states that her mother recently took insulin but has not eaten. The daughter also has a tube of glucose paste and is requesting you help her mother.

ACTIONS

1. It would be indicated to administer glucose to this patient (if local protocols permit).
   A. True
   B. False
2. Which route would you use to administer glucose paste?
   A. Oral
   B. IM
   C. IV
   D. Rectal
3. Which information should be checked on the package of the medication?
   A. Dose
   B. Expiration date
   C. Name
   D. All of the above
4. The patient is not willing to take the medication orally and asks that you load the medications into one of her insulin syringes so it can be injected. Is this acceptable for you to do?
   A. Yes, because the route of a medication does not matter
   B. Yes, because it is important for the patient to receive the medication as soon as possible so the condition does not get worse
   C. No, because medications should be administered by the intended route
   D. No, because LERs are not permitted to give injections
5. Once the medication is administered, the patient's condition improves. She is now alert and oriented. She does not want to be transported to the hospital. What should you do?
   A. Cancel the responding EMS unit
   B. Notify your supervisor
   C. Ask the daughter for her opinion
   D. Have EMS continue responding

SECTION 6

Trauma

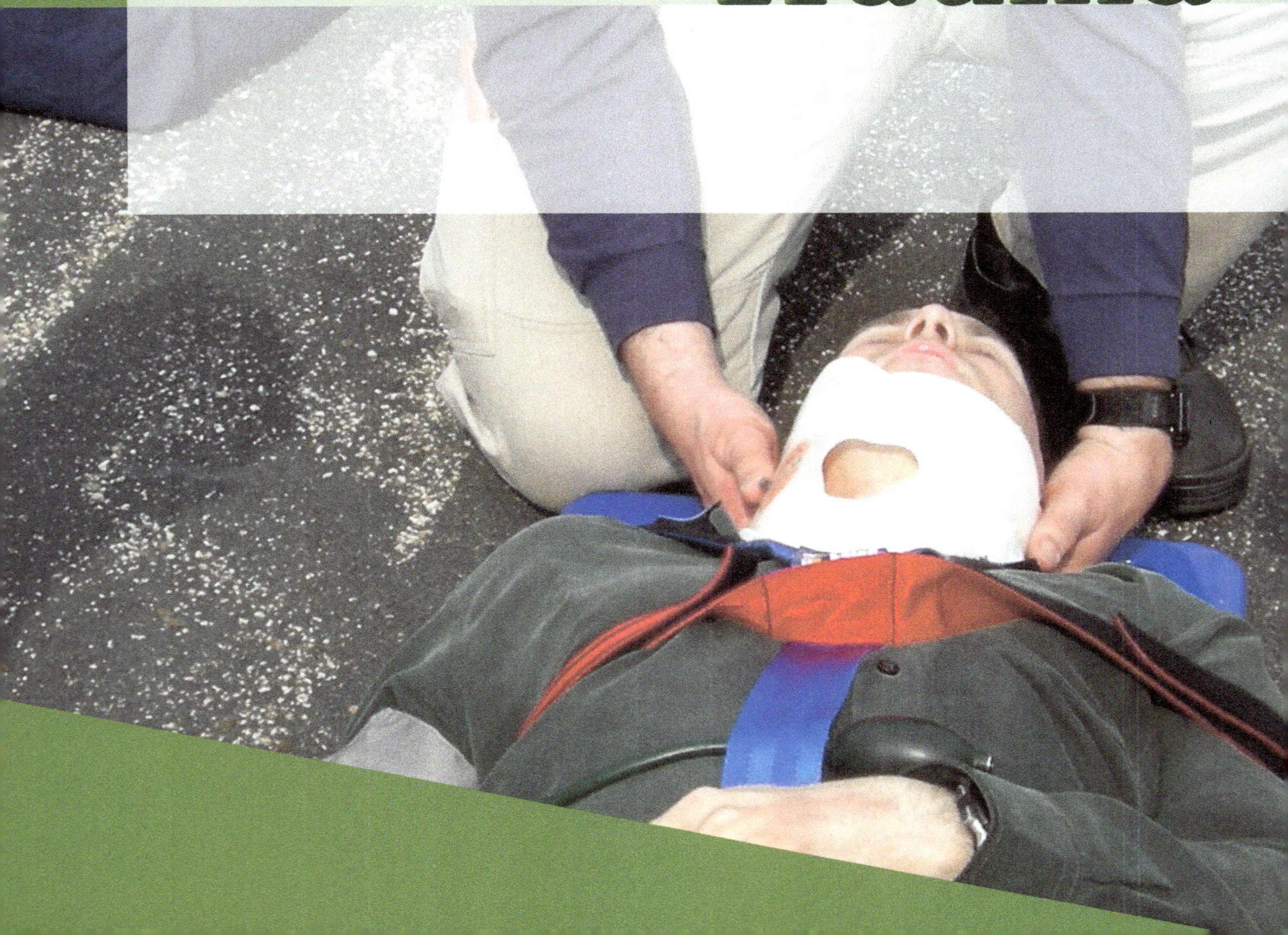

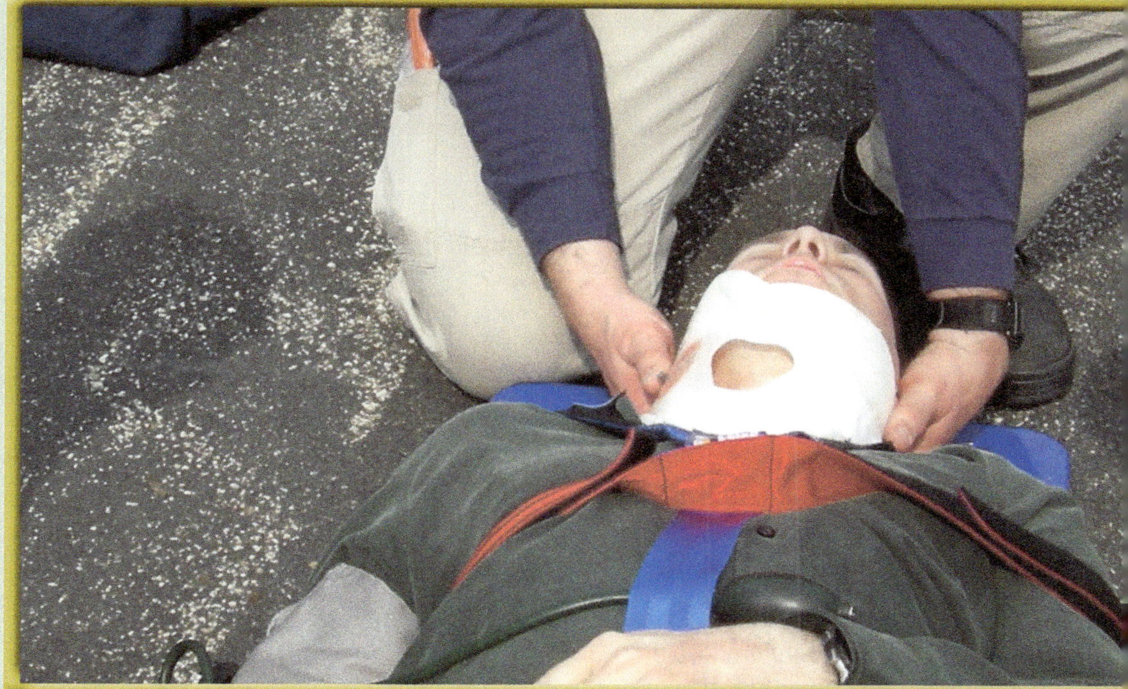

Section Contents

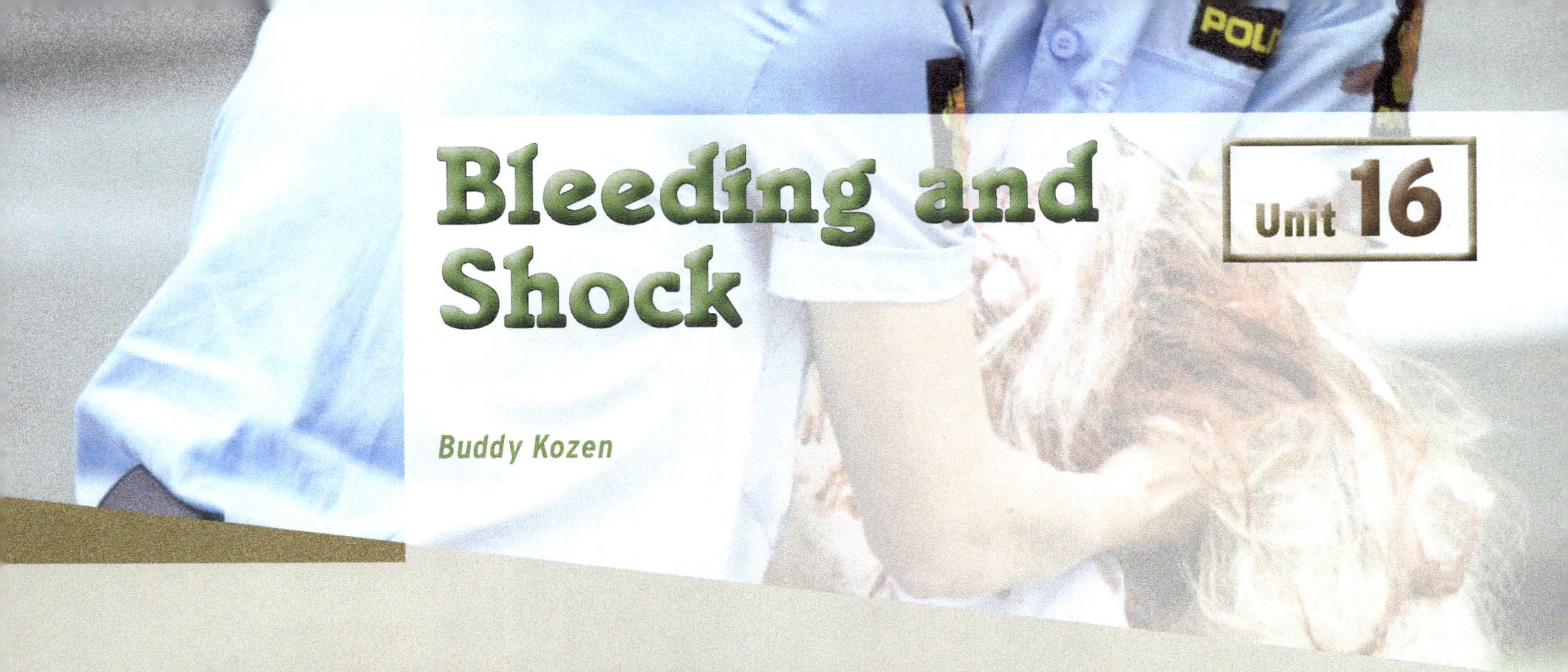

Bleeding and Shock

Unit 16

Buddy Kozen

Law Enforcement Responder Objectives

- Explain the basic anatomy and function of the human circulatory system. (pp 307–309)
- Discuss the different types of hemorrhage and the classification of shock. (pp 309–317)
- Describe means of assessing hemorrhagic soft-tissue injuries. (pp 309–311)
- Describe traditional and modern treatment modalities for hemorrhage and shock. (pp 311–315, 316–317)

National EMS Education Standard Competencies

Shock and Resuscitation

Uses assessment information to recognize shock, respiratory failure or arrest, and cardiac arrest based on assessment findings and manages the emergency while awaiting additional emergency response.

Trauma

Uses simple knowledge to recognize and manage life threats based on assessment findings for an acutely injured patient while awaiting additional emergency medical response.

Bleeding

Recognition and management of

- Bleeding (pp 309–315)

Multi-system Trauma

Recognition and management of

- Multi-system trauma (p 317)

INTRODUCTION

When considering a scenario that accurately represents a typical law enforcement medical response, many law enforcement responders (LERs) think of one thing: the bleeding patient, usually from some sort of penetrating trauma. Caring for an acutely bleeding patient is a vital component of the overall curriculum.

Most of the information regarding trauma in the tactical/combat setting arises from data collected during times of armed conflict. Studies of the US military experience have shown that approximately 50% of all preventable combat-related deaths can be attributed to uncontrolled hemorrhage. However, the extent of this type of injury is not simply confined to war. Severe hemorrhage and the resulting hypovolemic shock are a problem that overlaps both the civilian and military worlds. Studies of civilian trauma patients indicate that exsanguination accounts for up to 40% of deaths.

The purpose of this unit is to discuss some of the basic physiologic and management principles of bleeding and shock. One important point to keep in mind is that although there are actually several different causes of shock, this unit focuses on hemorrhagic (hypovolemic) shock, or shock due to blood loss. In addition, this unit focuses on soft-tissue, external sources of hemorrhage.

BLEEDING

For millennia, blood has been recognized as one of the—if not *the*—most important components of life. Putting the mystical qualities of blood aside for a moment, the scientific and physiologic importance of the human circulatory system is undeniable. Uncontrolled bleeding can, and likely will, lead to shock and death.

The human circulatory system is composed of three parts: the heart, blood vessels, and blood. Often the easiest way to visualize the circulatory system is to liken it to a mechanical system. The heart is akin to the pump that creates the pressure required to move the fluid through the system. The blood vessels are similar to the pipes or hoses that serve as a conduit to move fluid from the heart and lungs to the body and back again. Finally, the blood can be thought of as any fluid (fuel, lubricating oil, etc) that needs to be distributed to the system and aids in its overall function.

Starting with the pump, the heart is an organ whose primary function is to generate an adequate force to move blood through the blood vessels to the target organs and cells. Structurally, the heart is divided into four chambers: two **atria** and two **ventricles** primarily composed of cardiac muscle cells and separated by valves made of connective tissue. The heart is also thought of as being functionally organized into a right and left side based on the flow of blood through the organ. The right side of the heart receives deoxygenated blood from the body and pumps it to the lungs to pick up oxygen. The left side of the heart receives oxygenated blood from the lungs and pumps it around the body to the distal organs (**Figure 1**).

The heart is considered an involuntary organ, meaning a person cannot fully control its actions in a willful manner. Cardiac function is automatically controlled by electrical cells in the heart muscle that generate a coordinated rhythm to sequentially contract the atria and ventricles and move the blood through the body. Part of this system includes feedback sensors in the heart that can alter the electrical pathway and contractility of the heart in order to maintain an appropriate functional environment in response to external stressors, such as dehydration or fear. This means your body can change your heart rate and blood pressure as needed to respond to your environment. If either the electrical rhythm, the ability of the heart to mechanically contract, or the feedback mechanisms are disturbed, the overall function of the heart and the entire circulatory system may be compromised.

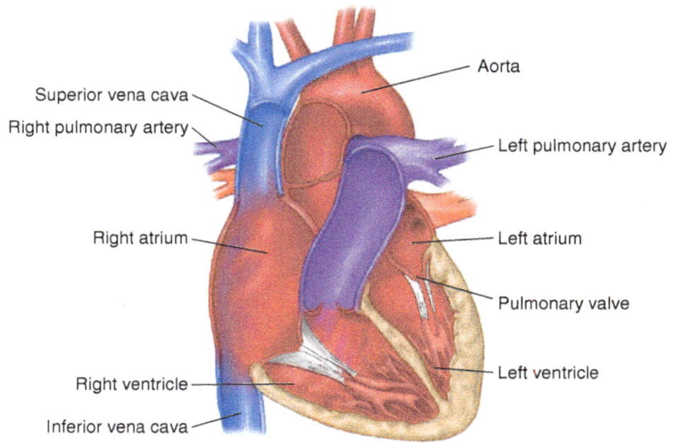

Figure 1 The human circulatory system is composed of three parts: the heart, blood vessels, and blood.

The purpose of the blood vessels is to direct blood in a closed circuit from the lungs to the end organs and cells and back. A closed system means that, in an ideal state, blood volume is not added or subtracted, at least in any significant amount. Blood vessels are most commonly thought of in three categories: arteries, veins, and capillaries. **Arteries** are thick-walled, muscular tubes that carry blood away from the heart to the tissue. The muscular nature of arteries is very important because it allows the body to maintain an adequate blood pressure to perfuse the brain and other organs by squeezing and relaxing the vessel walls.

The arterial system is often referred to as the high-pressure side of the system. When measuring a patient's blood pressure, you are actually measuring two arterial pressures. The first is the systolic pressure and is measured when the heart contracts, pushing blood through the blood vessels. The second is the diastolic pressure, the pressure in the artery when the heart is relaxed. Through feedback mechanisms, the heart and blood vessel walls can contract more or less to maintain an ideal and relatively constant mean arterial pressure. This process is termed **autoregulation**; if it malfunctions in either direction, it can lead to severe medical problems. As an example, in times of hemorrhage, when blood volume and pressure drop, the arteries can squeeze down in an attempt to elevate the blood pressure to a more normal range. The compression can also serve to clamp down on the bleeding vessels and slow or even stop the blood loss. If this response fails, bleeding may continue unabated, and the resulting low blood pressure may lead to a worsening of organ function.

Veins are thin-walled and less muscular tubes that return blood to the heart. This composition allows them to distend in response to an increase in blood volume without significantly elevating the internal pressure. A downside is that the lack of pressure means that flow through these vessels is largely dependent on gravity and the function of adjacent muscle groups. Veins are often referred to as the low-pressure side of the system. To assist flow through the venous system, veins have one-way valves located at intervals throughout the system. These valves assist in the prevention of backflow and pooling of deoxygenated blood in gravity-dependent areas.

An important caveat to remember about the nomenclature of arteries and veins is that they are defined by which direction they move blood in relation to the heart and not with regard to oxygenation. This difference becomes apparent when looking at the pulmonary artery, which moves deoxygenated blood away from the heart to the lungs, and the pulmonary vein, which moves oxygenated blood from the lungs to the heart.

Capillaries are the third category of blood vessels. They connect the arterial and venous systems (**Figure 2**). Arteries and veins branch more and get smaller as they move away from the heart. By the time they become capillaries, they are so small that only one red blood cell at a time can pass through them in single file. Capillaries are located at the target organs and cells of the body and serve as the means of transferring oxygen, nutrients, and waste both to and from target cells. By dramatically increasing the number of capillaries and maximizing the surface area of each cell in contact with the vessel wall, an efficient nutrient exchange mechanism is created.

The final component of the circulatory system is the blood itself. Blood is made up of many components, including red blood cells (oxygen carriers), white blood cells (immune mediators), platelets (clot formers), and plasma (water, enzymes, nutrients, and a host of other substances vital for function of the body). Although all of these components are vital to the function of the human body, for the purposes

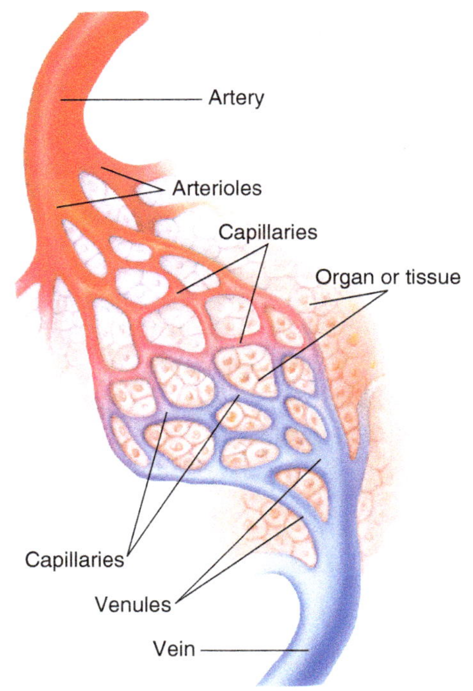

Figure 2 Blood enters an organ or tissue through the arteries and leaves through the veins.

of immediate prehospital care of bleeding and shock in the trauma patient, the most important component is the red blood cell. The inability to deliver oxygen at the cellular level can lead to shock, and this is dependent solely upon the red blood cell. Overall, the average circulating volume in an adult human is approximately 70 mL/kg, or 5 to 7 liters assuming average weight. Just over half, about 55%, of this volume is plasma. The rest is split between red blood cells and white blood cells.

TYPES OF ILLNESS OR INJURY

When assessing a type of injury associated with bleeding, the most important task is to address the underlying source of the bleeding (eg, lacerated liver, epidural brain hemorrhage, ruptured cardiac ventricle). Because these types of injuries are so varied, they are discussed in relevant anatomic units throughout this text. However, there are a few useful systems for generally categorizing bleeding injuries.

Arterial Bleeding

One important distinction to make is between arterial versus venous bleeding. This classification is based on a visual inspection of the source of bleeding. The primary indication of arterial bleeding is the pulsatile nature of the bleeding. The spurting correlates with the contraction of the heart. With each contraction, the arterial walls remain fairly stiff and there is a rapid increase and decrease in the internal blood pressure. As the pressure changes with each heartbeat, it creates a changing flow rate that is visualized by a pulsatile, or spurting, hemorrhage. Arterial injury can lead to rapid loss of a large volume of blood and rapid development of subsequent medical problems. As blood pressure drops, the pulsation may become less dramatic. Because of the high pressure, it can sometimes be difficult to control arterial bleeding.

Arterial blood is usually bright red. However, you may not always be able to rely on the color of blood to confirm whether it is arterial or venous. Sometimes the color of arterial blood in people with low oxygen levels, such as those with lung problems or people in cardiopulmonary arrest, among other medical conditions, may be darker than usual.

Venous Bleeding

Venous bleeding has different characteristics than arterial bleeding. As you may recall, vein walls are less rigid and can distend with changes in pressure and volume. The result is that there is no pulsatile nature to venous hemorrhage. Venous bleeding has more of a steady, oozing appearance. Although dependent on the caliber of the vessel, it most often takes a longer period of time to lose a similar volume of blood in a venous bleed compared with an arterial injury. Additionally, given that most veins carry deoxygenated blood, venous hemorrhage is usually much darker in appearance. Once again, however, you cannot solely rely on the dark color of blood to confirm whether it is venous. There are certain situations in which it might be bright red. For instance, patients with high levels of carbon monoxide exposure can demonstrate venous blood that is bright cherry-red. Although venous bleeding can be severe, it is often easier to control than arterial bleeding due to lower venous pressure.

Tip

Blood Color

In large complex wounds, both veins and arteries can be damaged. If this is the case, the bleeding may present with blood that is both dark red and bright red. Focus on treating the wound with immediate direct pressure regardless of the color of the wound.

Internal and External Hemorrhage

The other major method of classifying bleeding injuries is internal versus external. This categorization is also intuitive. An internal hemorrhage is defined as any bleeding that occurs within the confines of the body and is not directly visualized on routine exam. The most common places for internal hemorrhage are the head, chest, abdomen, and pelvis/thighs. Bleeding in these areas may be fatal through direct tissue injury or the development of shock. One of the biggest challenges of internal bleeding is the inability to see the bleeding source. Damage to internal organs may cause shock, as may long bone fractures. External hemorrhage is any bleeding that occurs outside the body. Although this type of bleeding may or may not be fatal, it occurs more commonly than internal injuries.

Assessment of Bleeding

Assessment of the bleeding patient can sometimes be daunting and even misleading. Bleeding can often be dramatic and have a significant psychological impact on the responder. The most important part of assessing a bleeding patient is to remain calm and not allow the drama of the situation to alter your usual approach to patient assessment.

The first step is always to assess the scene for safety. You need to make the tactical decision of whether or not it is important to address a threat before assessing the patient. The next step is to protect yourself with standard precautions, such as donning eye protection and gloves that are an adequate fluid barrier.

If you are treating a patient who has suffered a severely bleeding wound or you are involved in care under fire, some medical directors recommend that the primary assessment use the XABC mnemonic. As you approach the patient, you should evaluate for severe uncontrolled bleeding, or exsanguination (often abbreviated with an X in the system just recommended). First, look for external bleeding. If you see signs of external hemorrhage, such as blood on the ground or clothing, you must find and directly visualize the source. Expose the patient as much as possible near the site of the hemorrhage. Once the source is visualized, the type of bleeding (arterial versus venous) must be determined. If the bleeding is arterial and uncontrolled, it should be categorized as severe, and intervention should take place. There are not enough clues to ascertain internal hemorrhage at this point of the exam, and very little to do in terms of any intervention that can make a difference at this level.

Tip

Tactical Mnemonics

Many different tactical mnemonics are used in care under fire situations. Depending on your medical direction, you may utilize:

MARCH: Massive hemorrhage, Airway, Respirations, Circulation, and Head injuries

CBA: Circulation, Breathing, Airway

XABC: eXsanguination, Airway, Breathing, Circulation

Numerous studies have shown that visual estimation of blood loss by observers is grossly inaccurate, independent of the level of education, training, experience, or age. As such, do not rely on this method to judge severity of blood loss. As an experiment, test yourself by choosing various items of clothing and bandages, writing down how much fluid you think they can hold, and then actually soaking them with colored water to see the result. You can also have a colleague spray various fixed amounts of red-dyed water on the dirt, grass, pavement, and so forth, guess the volume, and then check the true amount. The results may surprise you. So, do not solely rely on a visual estimation regarding the amount of blood lost in order to treat bleeding at this stage. Rely on the type of bleeding that is occurring: arterial versus venous, and controlled versus uncontrolled.

To summarize, in the primary assessment, uncontrolled arterial hemorrhage warrants immediate intervention. Once that is complete, continue with the remainder of the ABC assessment.

The next most important point in assessing hemorrhage occurs in the secondary assessment. As the head-to-toe exam is performed, careful examination of the entire body surface is required. Any systematic method will suffice, so long as it is repeated the same way each and every time. One important point is that, as you sweep for hemorrhage, you should stop periodically to evaluate. This will ensure that you can more accurately localize the bleeding source to a particular area and reduce the opportunity for confusion. Let's use the example of an extremity hemorrhage to illustrate. Suppose you have circumferentially palpated the extremities looking for deformity and hemorrhage. You started at the right shoulder and went down the right arm, feeling no obvious fluid or instability. You then repeated the same maneuver on the left arm and both legs with the same results. It was only after you stopped and prepared to do some documentation that you noticed a small amount of blood on your left glove. Where did it come from? It is difficult to say for sure. One way to avoid this problem is to break your assessment into intervals. If you palpate the upper arm, look, feel/observe your gloves for blood, palpate the lower arm, look, feel your gloves, and so on, you're less likely to miss a source of bleeding on the first go around. This approach is especially useful in low-light situations.

The secondary assessment is also where you might find more subtle signs of internal bleeding that may require treatment. For example, you may encounter a tender, swollen thigh with a lower leg that rotates freely internally and externally. These findings may be associated with a femur fracture, which can secondarily create a shock state by significant hemorrhage into the thigh. Alternatively, you may find a rigid, exquisitely tender abdomen with or without some overlying bruising. This may indicate internal hemorrhage within the abdomen. The patient assessment may also reveal an increased respiratory rate; increased pulse rate; pale, cool skin; nausea and vomiting; thirst; and mental status changes. A more detailed description of the signs, symptoms, and treatment of specific injuries is found within other relevant sections of this text.

Finally, do not forget the reassessment phase of the encounter. After the bleeding is controlled, periodically check the site for any rebleeding. It is not uncommon for wounds to rebleed with movement or transport. You don't want to fall victim to this problem after getting the hemorrhage under control.

Patient Management

There are multiple interventions that can be used by a LER to control hemorrhage. Nevertheless, the response is tiered, with one treatment modality building upon the last. If one intervention fails, you should proceed to the next level of intervention. Treatment of a bleeding patient may be intuitive to many providers, at least in the setting of external hemorrhage. The first step to control mild bleeding or nonarterial bleeding is to expose the wound and administer direct pressure over the source of bleeding (**Figure 3**). The vast majority of simple wounds can be controlled with pressure from one or two fingers directly on the point of bleeding for several minutes. The flat part of the fingers should be used, and sterile gauze, if available, may be applied between the fingers and the source of bleeding. Larger wounds may require the entire hand to be used. Again, use the flat part of the hand to apply steady pressure for several minutes. Deep wounds may require more gauze to be applied. Most often the reason for this is that the gauze was, in actuality, not close to the source of bleeding with the first application, and blood may continue to escape around the dressing.

If bleeding still occurs around the gauze, reinforce the gauze with another layer. Do not remove the first gauze dressing. Removal may stimulate rebleeding by removing any clot that did form. Simply pack another layer and apply more pressure. This step may be repeated several times if oozing continues around the dressing. If you require the use of your hands, you may consider using your knee for pressure. You may also apply a pressure bandage over the site by wrapping another piece of stretch gauze over the site and tying it off. When applied properly, an overlying pressure bandage can be quite useful to control mild bleeding and free your hands for other activities. Again, it is very important to continually reassess for bleeding and move to the next intervention when necessary.

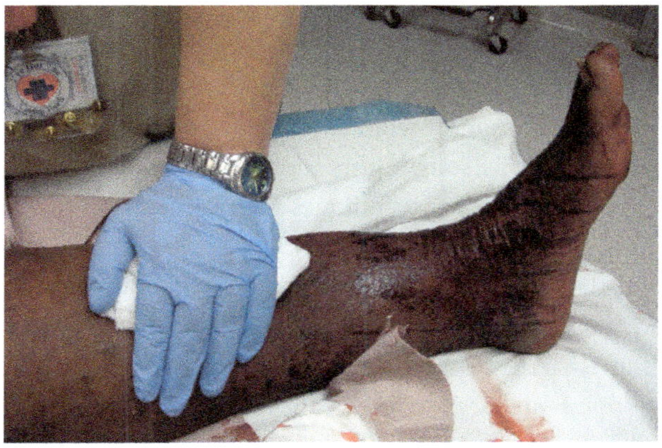

Figure 3 Applying direct pressure to a wound.

If direct pressure and a pressure dressing have not controlled this hemorrhage, the LER should move to the application of a tourniquet. Although the use of tourniquets have been debated, current methodology suggest that the aggressive control of the external extremity hemorrhage, to include the use of a tourniquet, is a sound approach. Tourniquets can be improvised using cravats and a windlass, a belt, a blood pressure cuff, or a ratchet strap. There are many types of commercial tourniquets. LERs must practice improvising tourniquets and operating the various types of commercial tourniquets that they may encounter. LERs should consult their medical protocols and confirm with their medical director regarding the preferred steps and methods. Follow the steps in **Skill Drill 1** to control bleeding with a tourniquet:

1. Apply direct pressure with a dry, sterile dressing STEP 1.
2. Apply a pressure dressing STEP 2.
3. If bleeding continues or recurs, apply a tourniquet above the level of bleeding STEP 3.

Despite some variations in protocols, there are a few universal tenets about the use of a tourniquet. When applied, the tourniquet should be tightened until a distal pulse is lost and bleeding stops or slows to the point at which it can be controlled by other means. After being applied, a tourniquet should never be covered with a dressing, clothing, or other apparatus. Whenever a tourniquet is applied, the time should be noted and permanently marked on the patient in a manner that cannot be separated from him or her. This may mean writing on the patient's forehead with a marker. Additionally, the LER should tell every health care provider further involved in the care of the patient about the tourniquet. The patient, if conscious, should also be encouraged to provide the same information. Although improvised tourniquets can

Skill Drill 1

Controlling Bleeding With a Tourniquet

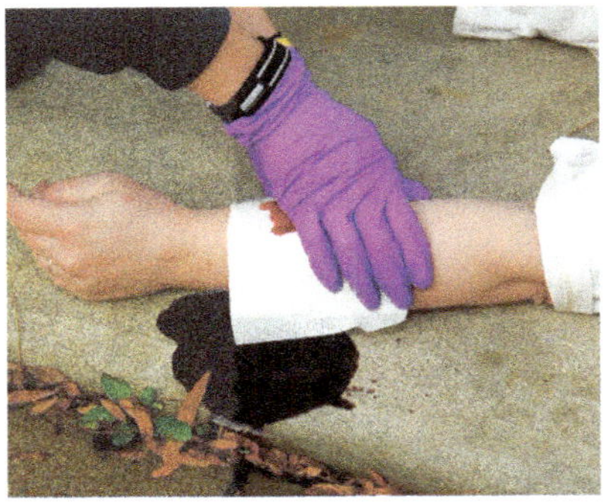

1. Apply direct pressure with a dry, sterile dressing.

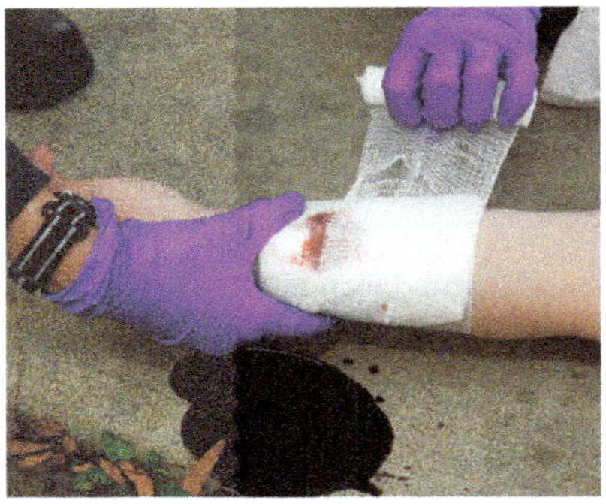

2. Apply a pressure dressing.

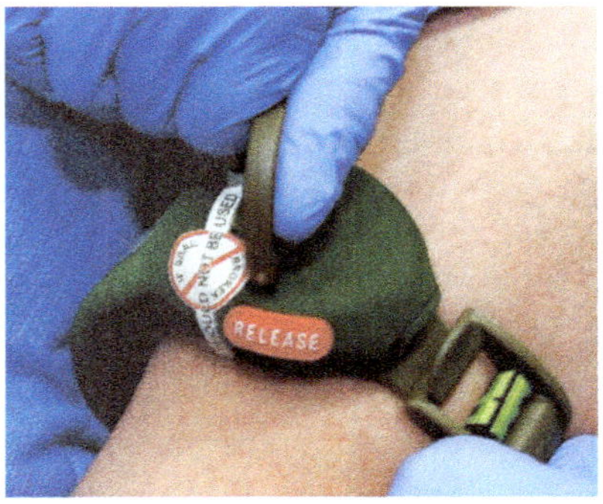

3. If bleeding continues or recurs, apply a tourniquet above the level of bleeding.

be effective, several commercial tourniquets that can improve speed and ease of application are available. Additionally, many are designed to be applied with one hand, facilitating self-application in a tactical environment. Consultation with local medical direction is recommended when choosing a uniform tourniquet within a department or agency.

Tactical combat casualty care (TCCC) guidelines recommend a tourniquet as the initial treatment of choice. This enables rapid control of hemorrhage to facilitate a quick evacuation from the hot zone. Once in the warm or cold zone, a transition to pressure dressings may be attempted. If rebleeding occurs with other treatment options, simply reapply the tourniquet.

Tourniquets are becoming more widespread in the non-military tactical medicine environment as well. If they are routinely issued within a department or agency, it is important to be familiar with local directives regarding use. Additionally, it is important to consider standardization in terms of tourniquet storage within gear configuration. This can facilitate rapid access and application.

The most traditional way to tie a tourniquet is to use a triangular bandage (cravat) or a sturdy strip of fabric and secure it above the uncontrolled bleed approximately 2 inches from the injury. Ensure that the tissue where the tourniquet is to be placed is rigid enough to allow the tourniquet to place preessure against the damaged arteries. If the tissue collapses, move the tourniquet up the extremity to more rigid tissue (**Figure 4**). Some styles of commercial tourniquets you may encounter include SOF-T (**Figure 5**), SOF-T wide (**Figure 6**), CAT (**Figure 7**), and MET (**Figure 8**).

Finally, a newer option for the treatment of bleeding is the use of topical hemostatic dressings. Hemostatic dressings were developed to control bleeding in noncompressible injuries that cannot be controlled by the placement of tourniquets or other direct-pressure dressings. Examples of these injuries include high femoral/groin, axillary, and neck wounds. There are many different types of hemostatic dressings (zeolite, chitosan, kaolin, etc) in many forms (powders, granules, gauze). Each of these agents has its own benefits and drawbacks. A detailed discussion of each agent is beyond the scope of this text. Current recommendations on the use of these agents are varied, and guidance on the use of these agents should be sought from local protocols.

Indirect bleeding techniques such as the use of pressure points, elevation, and splinting may be considered, especially when there is a lack of resources to apply pressure dressings and tourniquets. These measures should be considered as adjuncts to the normal hemorrhage control methods. Pressure points are locations where the arteries and veins lie close to the surface. Sites such as the radial, brachial, or femoral pulse can be utilized. Firm pressure, typically using the heel of the hand or a knee can reduce the pressure head at the site of the injury and help the creation of the clot.

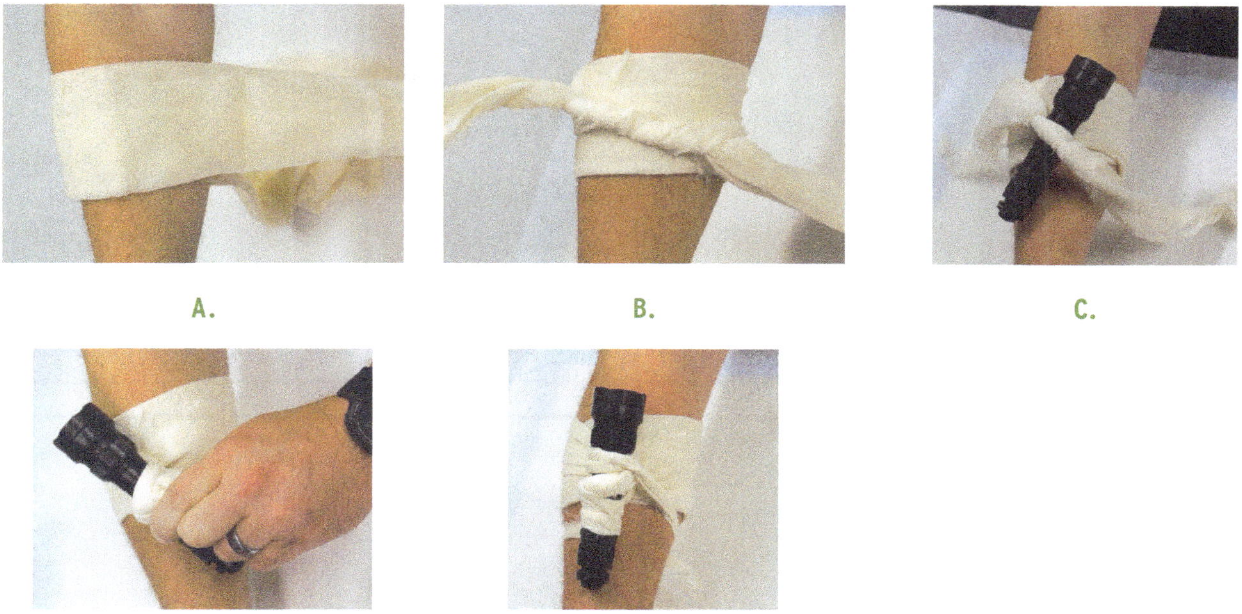

A. B. C. D. E.

Figure 4 Cravat tourniquet. **A.** Place the triangular bandage around the limb. **B.** Tie a surgeon's knot. **C.** Then place a sturdy object over the surgeon's knot and tie another surgeon's knot over the top sturdy object. This creates a loop that the sturdy object sits in. This object will need to stay in place and act as a windlass. **D.** Turn the windlass until you have stopped the bleeding. **E.** Finally, tie the windlass off using the excess fabric from the loop to prevent the windlass from unwinding.

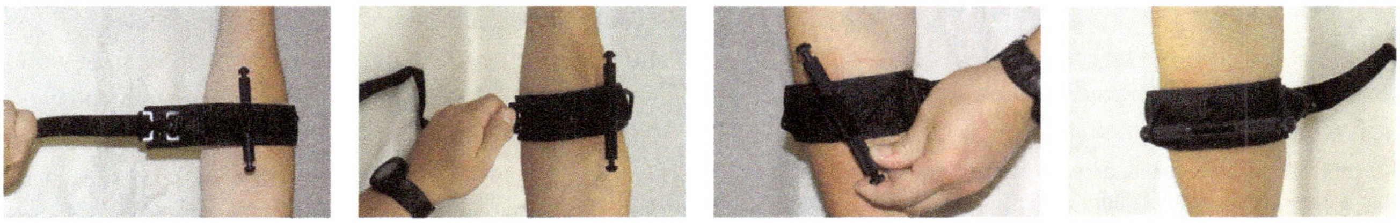

A. B. C. D.

Figure 5 SOF-T tourniquet. **A.** SOF-T tourniquet. Place the SOF-T tourniquet on the limb and pull it tight. **B.** Secure the safety screw to prevent the belt from slipping. **C.** Rotate the windlass until the bleeding stops. **D.** Finally, secure the windlass in the triangle-shaped catch.

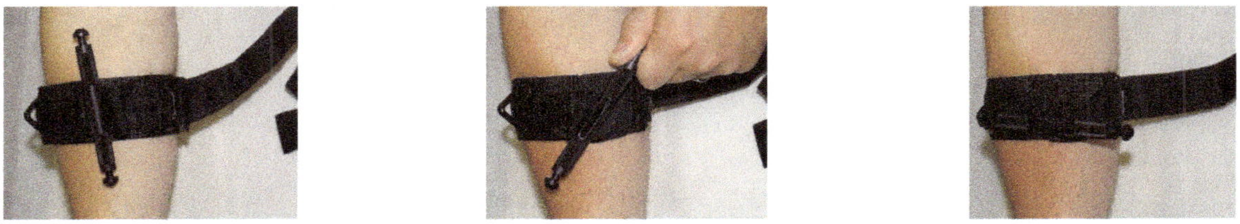

A. B. C.

Figure 6 SOF-T wide tourniquet. **A.** Place the SOF-T wide tourniquet on the limb and pull it tight. **B.** Rotate the windlass until the bleeding stops. **C.** Then secure the windlass to the triangle-shaped catch.

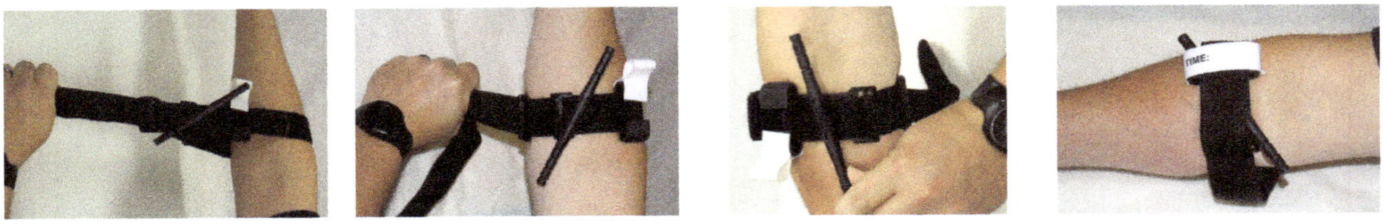

A. B. C. D.

Figure 7 CAT tourniquet. **A.** Place the CAT tourniquet on the limb. **B.** Pull it tight and secure the velcro strap. **C.** Then rotate the windlass until the bleeding stops. **D.** Finally secure the windlass to the U-shaped catch, and cover it with velcro.

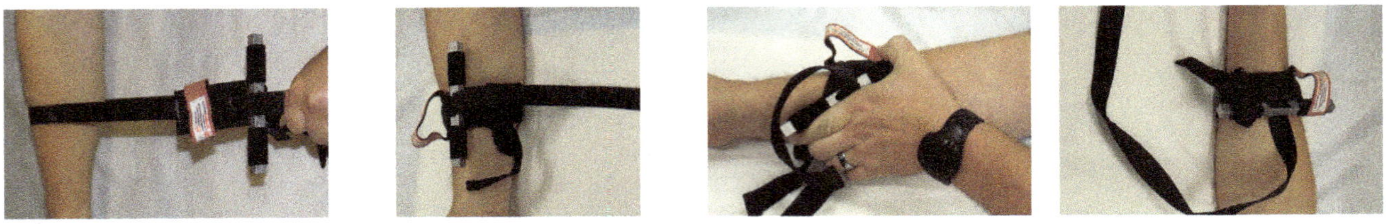

A. B. C. D.

Figure 8 MET tourniquet. **A.** MET tourniquet. Place the MET tourniquet on the limb. **B.** Pull it tight and secure the strap. **C.** Rotate the windlass until the bleeding stops. **D.** Then secure the windlass by using the velcro strap.

Tip

External Extremity Hemorrhage Control Guidelines

Always use your jurisdiction's protocols.

Uncontrolled severe bleed, arterial hemorrhage, or bleeding during a care-under-fire setting:

- Immediately apply direct pressure over the wound and a tourniquet to the extremity.
  - Tourniquets applied during care-under-fire settings should be reassessed for need and patency when the patient is safe.

Mild, nonarterial bleeding:

- Apply direct pressure.
- Apply a pressure dressing.
- If bleeding continues, apply a tourniquet.
  - Consider hemostatic agent or hemostatic gauze application.
  - Consider indirect bleeding control adjuncts such as pressure points, elevation, and splinting.

By elevating the wound above the level of the heart, the pressure requirement to reach the wound is also elevated. This forces the body to work harder to bleed. When used with the previous interventions, blood flow can slow enough to potentially stop. Additionally, splinting may provide a secondary means of hemostasis. The movement of soft tissue and bones at the site of injuries may reopen existing wounds by shearing off clots or creating new injuries to blood vessels. Simple stabilization may help minimize recurrent injury and rebleeding. These interventions do have some downsides. Elevation may be difficult, or even impossible, in some types of injury. Splinting may also be difficult with some wounds and may limit access for reassessment of the injury.

Once bleeding is controlled, a wound should be covered with a sterile dressing and bandaged securely with tape or roller gauze to prevent further contamination. The patient should be placed on his or her back or in a position of comfort, depending on the nature of the injury. The patient should also be kept warm and prevented from eating or drinking if shock is suspected or if surgery may be needed. Dressings should be reassessed periodically, especially after any movement of the patient. Finally, other illness or injuries should be treated. This last point cannot be overemphasized. Hemorrhagic wounds can be dramatic and distracting to a responder. It is easy to focus attention on the broken and bleeding femoral wound, so much so that the spinal injury, stroke, or heart attack may be missed. It is especially important to maintain vigilance regarding your systematic approach to your patient. If you maintain this standard, you are less likely to miss injuries.

SHOCK

Shock is a serious and potentially fatal medical condition defined as a state of inadequate tissue perfusion. Essentially this means that at the tissue and cellular level, the body is not receiving the oxygen and nutrients it requires to function. This condition can result in a cascading organ and cellular dysfunction that can ultimately lead to death. The causes of shock are many and revolve around the three major components of the cardiovascular system.

The first type of shock is **cardiogenic shock**. This form of shock occurs when the heart, or pump, fails to adequately move oxygenated, nutrient-rich blood to the end organs. This condition is caused by a variety of illnesses and injuries affecting the heart, such as heart failure, heart attack, cardiac tamponade, and tension pneumothorax. These last two causes are sometimes separated into the category of obstructive shock. With the exception of tension pneumothorax, shock resulting from pump failure can be extremely difficult to treat in the prehospital setting.

The second type of shock is **distributive shock**, which occurs when a problem arises with the blood vessels, or pipes, and fluid cannot get to its intended destination. In certain circumstances, the blood vessels can become "leaky" in response to inflammatory signals in the body. Oxygen and nutrient-rich blood seeps into a third space within the body (not in the blood vessels and not in the cells), lowering blood pressure and depriving tissues of needed resources. Two of the most common serious etiologies of this type of shock are anaphylactic shock, from a severe allergic reaction, and septic shock, from an overwhelming infection throughout the body. Prehospital treatment for these types of shock can be quite difficult as well, but some interventions, such as epinephrine pens and a large amount of intravenous fluid, can make a significant difference in patient outcome.

The third type of shock, hypovolemic shock, is related to the blood, or fluid. The major problem related to fluid is low volume. Sometimes an injured person is just not able to maintain enough blood volume in his or her body to adequately regulate blood pressure. When that happens, it can result in a lack of oxygen and other necessary substances making it to the tissues of the body. Two of the major causes of hypovolemic shock are dehydration and hemorrhage. This form of shock is most intuitive to people and is the focus of this section, specifically the problem of hemorrhagic shock.

Hypovolemic, or hemorrhagic, shock is often divided into four stages (**Table 1**). Stage 1 generally reflects a 15% or less loss of blood volume. This stage of shock is a fully compensated, mild form of shock. Patients can often recover on their own without significant intervention.

The second stage of shock is also a compensated shock because the body is able to maintain normal vital sign parameters, but it is considered progressive because the normal parameters are maintained through the use of every compensatory mechanism at the body's disposal. This stage tends to represent a 15% to 30% blood volume loss, and patients require intervention to prevent sliding into the next stage.

The third stage is decompensated shock, in which, despite all available fail-safes, the body can no longer maintain normal vital signs and perfusion. This stage represents a 30% to 40% blood volume loss and requires significant medical intervention. At this stage, the decompensation is still considered reversible.

The final stage of shock is considered irreversible decompensation and occurs when patients have a blood volume loss of greater than 40%. Patients in stage 4 shock exhibit significant derangement of their vital signs and, even with maximal medical intervention, have a high chance of developing secondary complications.

Table 1

Stages of Shock

Stage	Description
1	• Compensated • 15% blood volume loss
2	• Compensated • 15% to 30% blood volume loss
3	• Decompensated • 30% to 40% blood volume loss
4	• Irreversible decompensated • Greater than 40% blood volume loss

The signs and symptoms of shock are varied and require a responder to put together a complete picture of the patient. In mild forms of shock, the patient may appear completely normal. The earliest changes may include only behavioral changes. For example, a patient may complain of thirst, become slightly agitated or restless, or complain that he or she "just doesn't feel right." Additionally, skin changes may be seen early on in the form of a pale appearance, delayed capillary refill (greater than 2 seconds), and feeling cool and moist to the touch. As the shock state progresses, cardiopulmonary changes begin to reveal themselves in the form of tachypnea, tachycardia, elevated diastolic pressure, and narrow pulse pressure. Further progression of the shock state demonstrates worsening changes in these vital signs, eventually including the late sign of hypotension. Severely altered mental status and loss of consciousness are likely to follow. If untreated, this may lead to death.

A patient's overall morbidity and mortality from a shock state is directly related to the severity and length of time spent in that state. This is clearly seen in the problem of hemorrhagic shock resulting from acute trauma. Most people nowadays have heard of the Golden Hour, a concept promulgated by Dr. R Adams Cowley that stresses the dramatic improvement in survival from trauma when definitive care is rendered within the first hour after the injury. Within the past couple of decades, the concept of a Platinum 5, 10, or 15 Minutes (depending on the source) has highlighted an even greater survival in patients suffering from traumatic injuries whose initial problem was corrected in the first few minutes after injury. This is where field treatment of expeditious hemorrhage control and shock management can truly make a difference in whether a patient lives or dies. Recent studies from the US armed forces have demonstrated this trend in battlefield trauma. In tactical situations, standard emergency medical services resources may not be able to respond to these time-sensitive injuries. This is where the tactical LER has the potential to make a significant difference.

A final comment regarding shock is to pay particular attention to patients with extremes of age. The elderly may have comorbid conditions, such as heart failure, emphysema, and so on, that offer little reserve for the patient to compensate. Even a 15% blood volume loss that may be tolerated well by a healthy young adult can prove fatal to an elderly person with an inability to generate a required cardiovascular response, either because of disease or medications. Young children can also react differently to shock. Compensatory mechanisms are incredibly responsive in children and protect them from even serious shock states. However, when those compensatory mechanisms eventually fail, children can fall off the cliff and deteriorate very quickly, contrary to the slower progressive trend usually seen in adults. Additionally, it is important to remember that losing 500 mL of blood in a child is much more serious than losing the same amount in an adult.

Special Populations

Shock in Children

Compensatory mechanisms are incredibly responsive in children and protect them from even serious shock states. When those compensatory mechanisms eventually fail, however, children can deteriorate very quickly, contrary to the slower progressive trend usually seen in adults. Additionally, losing 500 mL of blood in a child is much more serious than losing the same amount in an adult.

Assessment of Shock

Assessment for shock is no different from the assessment for any other injury or illness, but ultimately, a provider looks to treat a specific cause of shock. Assessment starts with scene safety and universal precautions followed by the primary survey. There may be interventions at this stage appropriate for a shock patient. For example, you may need to stop uncontrolled hemorrhage or to treat a tension pneumothorax.

After the primary assessment is complete, a brief history and vital signs are obtained. At this point, a significant amount of information may be obtained to help classify a patient's type and degree of shock. A secondary assessment may or may not reveal further information in the case of shock.

The final and most important part of shock—and arguably any—assessment is the reassessment phase. Frequent reassessment is needed to establish the patient's trend and evaluate the success of an intervention.

Patient Management

Treatment of shock falls back to basic supportive care. As always, appropriate management starts with the XABCs. Initially, control any severe bleeding. Next, move on to opening the airway with airway adjuncts as necessary and stabilize the cervical spine as necessary. All patients in shock should receive high flow oxygen via a nonrebreathing mask. Ventilations should be assisted as necessary.

Other important treatment interventions for shock include the need to maintain a normal body temperature and prevent hypothermia. Shock in the setting of hypothermia can have worse outcomes. Additionally, attempt to keep patients calm and reassure them. This type of support not only treats the psychological impact of shock but also may reduce the physiologic stress on the cardiovascular system. Patients should be placed in an age-appropriate position for the illness or injury. It is also necessary to remember not to give food or drink to patients, because doing so may cause future complications when the patient heads to surgery. Most important, treatment must be directed at the underlying cause, and care must be taken not to overlook any other injuries.

MULTI-SYSTEM TRAUMA

A final concept worth discussing is **multi-system trauma**, or trauma that involves two or more organ systems (cardiovascular, respiratory, gastrointestinal, neurologic, musculoskeletal, soft tissue, etc). High levels of force, such as from a high-speed motor vehicle collision or a fall from a building, can produce injuries to more than one body system at the same time. Multi-system injuries can also contribute to the development of shock at a much faster rate. Often this is more easily identified in the field by the discovery of discrete anatomic regions of injury. For example, you might encounter a motor vehicle collision patient with a broken leg, briskly bleeding arm wound, rigid abdomen, head injury, and overall signs of shock. This could translate to trauma across four systems: musculoskeletal/soft tissue, cardiovascular (from the bleeding wound), gastrointestinal (from a liver or spleen injury), and neurologic (from the head injury). Clearly this patient is significantly ill and will require rapid assessment and expeditious treatment at a trauma center.

Multi-system trauma is of much higher concern than single-system trauma. The reason for this is simple. The risk of dying increases exponentially with each additional injured system. Recovering from a broken leg can be challenging enough for many people. But if the body is trying to do so in the setting of malfunctioning neurologic, cardiovascular, and gastrointestinal systems, it is that much harder.

To summarize, multi-system trauma patients have a very high risk of serious injury and death. Because of this, you should always maintain a high level of suspicion for multi-system injuries in all patients with a significant mechanism of injury. You should also be expeditious in transferring these patients to a higher level of care.

SPECIAL CONSIDERATIONS

Remember that protective glasses and gloves must always be used whenever dealing with bleeding patients. Protective gear significantly reduces the risk of infectious disease transmission. Additionally, if you have a high likelihood of performing in a medical role, make certain that your immunizations are up to date in accordance with your agency's occupational health guidelines.

The most important way in which you can help a trauma patient is to quickly and definitively control the bleeding. Most forms of bleeding can be successfully controlled with direct pressure.

Always remember that your agency's protocols dictate your possible treatment interventions. If you have questions about any of the options listed in this text, consult your protocols or medical director. Don't forget to use all of your resources (use tourniquet before knees or bystanders).

Always consider disarming patients if you suspect they may be suffering from shock. Oftentimes shock can lead to altered mental status and confusion. Depending on the situation, the last thing the patient may remember may be fighting for his or her life. As he or she responds to treatment, the patient may mistake you for an adversary.

Treatment guidelines change depending on the tactical environment. Incorporate TCCC into your training pathway.

Consider the effect of certain environmental restraints on the way in which you would treat a patient. For example, how would you assess for hemorrhage in a low-light environment? Blood may feel wet, but how do you distinguish that from water, urine, or other fluids? Think about using other senses, such as the warmer temperature of fresh blood, the stickiness that occurs when you repeatedly put your gloved hands together and pull them apart, the sweet, metallic odor, and so on.

CONCLUSION

Law enforcement is a profession in which exposure to injuries resulting in bleeding and shock can be high. The effective treatment of these injuries can make a significant difference in the overall survival of trauma patients. It is the responsibility of every law enforcement medical professional to know the most effective means of quickly and efficiently controlling hemorrhage.

Prep Kit

READY FOR REVIEW

- Blood has been recognized as one of the—if not *the*—most important components of what it is to be alive.
- The human circulatory system is composed of three parts: the heart, blood vessels, and blood.
- The purpose of the blood vessels is to direct blood in a closed circuit from the lungs to the end organs and cells and back.
- Arteries are thick-walled, muscular tubes that carry blood away from the heart to the tissue. The muscular nature of arteries is very important because it allows the body to maintain an adequate blood pressure to perfuse the brain and other organs by squeezing and relaxing the vessel walls.
- Veins are thin-walled and less muscular tubes that return blood to the heart. This composition allows them to distend in response to an increase in blood volume without significantly elevating the internal pressure.
- Capillaries are the third category of blood vessel. They connect the arterial and venous systems.
- When assessing the type of injury associated with bleeding, the most important task is to address the underlying source of the bleeding.
- Bleeding can often be dramatic and have a significant psychological impact on the responder. The most important part of assessing a bleeding patient is to remain calm and not allow the scenario to alter your usual approach to patient assessment.
- If one intervention fails, you should proceed to the next level of intervention. Treatment of a bleeding patient may be intuitive to many providers, at least in the setting of external hemorrhage.
- Tourniquets should be used on all severe bleeding from extremity injuries.
- Tactical combat casualty care (TCCC) guidelines recommend a tourniquet as the initial treatment of choice.
- Shock is a serious and potentially fatal medical condition defined as a state of inadequate tissue perfusion.
- The signs and symptoms of shock are varied and require a responder to put together a complete picture of the patient. In mild forms of shock, the patient may appear completely normal. The earliest changes may include only behavioral changes.
- As the shock state progresses, cardiopulmonary changes begin to reveal themselves in the form of tachypnea, tachycardia, elevated diastolic pressure, and narrow pulse pressure.
- A patient's overall morbidity and mortality from a shock state is directly related to the severity and length of time spent in that state.
- Compensatory mechanisms are incredibly responsive in children and protect them from even serious shock states. However, when those compensatory mechanisms eventually fail, children can fall off the cliff and deteriorate very quickly, contrary to a somewhat slower progressive trend usually seen in adults.
- Assessment for shock is no different from the assessment for any other injury or illness, but ultimately, a provider looks to treat a specific cause of shock.
- Treatment of shock falls back to basic supportive care. Appropriate management starts with the XABCs.
- Multi-system injuries can contribute to the development of shock at a much quicker rate.
- Multi-system trauma patients are of much higher concern than single-system patients. These patients' risk of dying increases substantially with each addition of another injured system.
- You should always maintain a high level of suspicion for multi-system injuries in all patients with a significant mechanism of injury.
- Treatment guidelines change depending on the tactical environment. Incorporate TCCC into your training pathway.

VITAL VOCABULARY

arteries Blood vessels that carry blood away from the heart.

atria The two upper chambers of the heart.

autoregulation The process in which the heart and blood vessel walls contract more or less to maintain an ideal and relatively constant mean arterial pressure.

capillaries The smallest blood vessels, which connect small arteries and small veins. Capillary walls serve as the membrane to exchange oxygen and carbon dioxide.

cardiogenic shock Shock resulting from inadequate functioning of the heart.

distributive shock Form of shock in which a problem arises with the blood vessels and fluid cannot get to its intended destination.

multi-system trauma Trauma that involves two or more organ systems.

shock A state of collapse of the cardiovascular system; the state of inadequate delivery of blood to the organs of the body.

veins Blood vessels that return blood from the capillaries to the heart.

ventricles The two lower chambers of the heart.

CHECK YOUR KNOWLEDGE

1. Which side of the heart receives deoxygenated blood from the body and pumps it to the lungs to pick up oxygen?
   - A. Right
   - B. Left
   - C. Top
   - D. Bottom
2. What are the thick-walled, muscular tubes that carry blood away from the heart to the tissue?
   - A. Arteries
   - B. Veins
   - C. Capillaries
   - D. Ventricles
3. Which type of bleeding is the most dangerous?
   - A. Capillary
   - B. Venous
   - C. Arterial
   - D. External
4. Tourniquet use can be a good tool to stop severe external bleeding.
   - A. True
   - B. False
5. Which is the first management technique to use when controlling mild to moderate bleeding in a nontactical environment?
   - A. Pressure points
   - B. Elevation
   - C. Tourniquet
   - D. Direct pressure

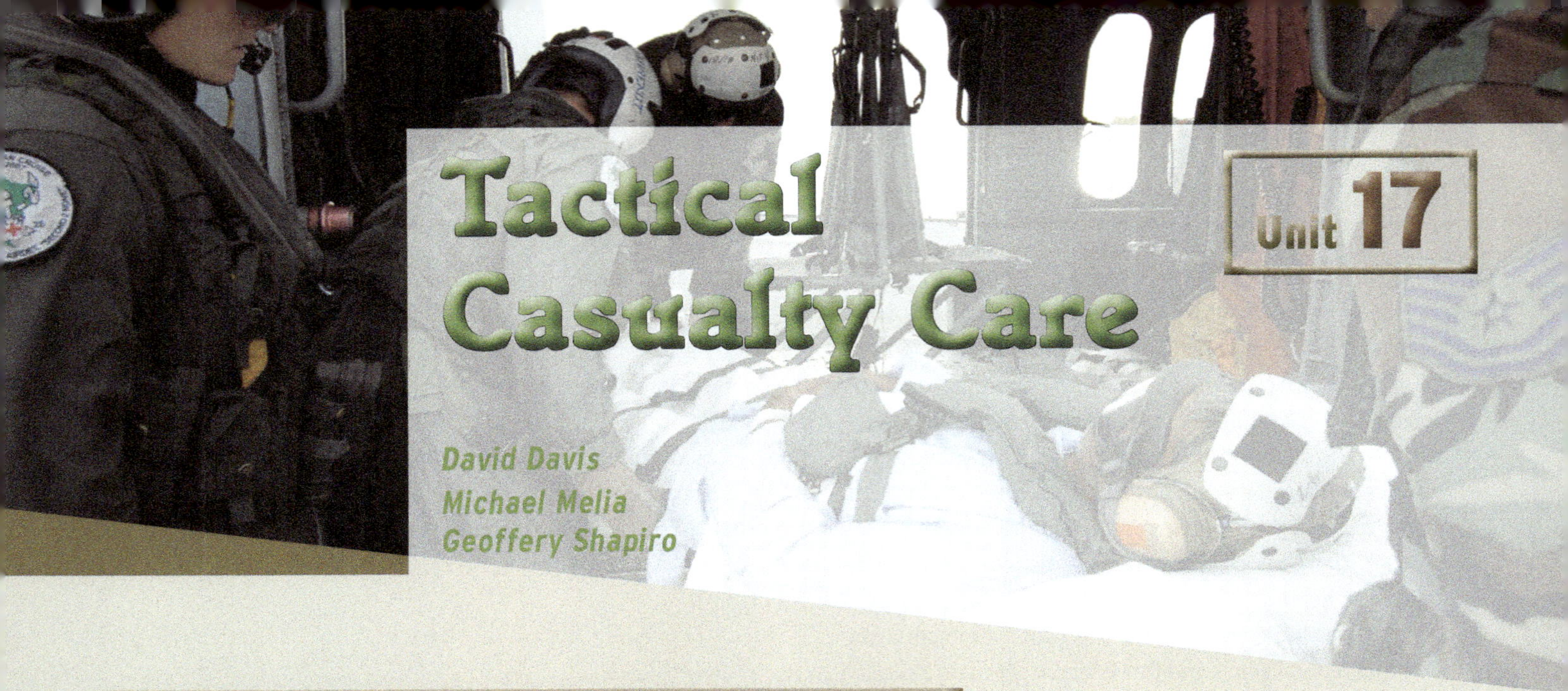

Tactical Casualty Care

Unit 17

David Davis
Michael Melia
Geoffery Shapiro

Law Enforcement Responder Objectives

- Explain the formation of tactical combat casualty care (TCCC). (p 321)
- List the three core tenets of TCCC. (p 322)
- Explain the purpose of tactical emergency casualty care (TECC). (p 322)
- Identify the phases of care in TECC. (p 322)
- Discuss the levels of training for military and civilian prehospital care providers. (pp 322–323)
- Explain the tiered system of military medicine. (pp 323–324)

National EMS Education Standard Competencies

There are no National EMS Education Standard Competencies for this unit.

INTRODUCTION

From the Carlisle bandage (invented during World War II) to the use of antibiotics, the impact of military medicine on civilian medical care has been undeniable. This influence continues today as proven combat medical techniques are used by civilian tactical medicine to save lives around the world.

Military emergency medicine made huge strides in improving patient survival during the Vietnam conflict. The advent of military medical evacuation (medevac) greatly shortened the time from the point of injury to definitive care. Medevac concepts were adopted by organizations across the United States and evolved into the modern aeromedical system. The principles of military emergency medicine saved countless lives by shortening the time interval to advanced medical treatment, but the preventable causes of death on the battlefield remained the same: hemorrhage, tension pneumothorax, and compromised airway.

TACTICAL COMBAT CASUALTY CARE

In the early 1990s, the US Special Operations Command (part of the Department of Defense) commissioned a study to evaluate battlefield treatments, and Captain Frank Butler, Lieutenant Colonel John Hagman, and Ensign George Butler published their results in the journal *Military Medicine* in 1996. The contents of the article, known as **tactical combat casualty care (TCCC)**, propelled battlefield casualty management to new levels of effectiveness, helping to lower the fatality rate to the lowest on record.

These tactical principles are directly relevant to civilian tactical emergency medical services (TEMS). The core tenets of TCCC are simultaneously to treat the casualty, prevent additional casualties, and complete the mission. TCCC is organized into three distinct phases, with a unique priority of care assigned to each phase. The three distinct phases of TCCC are:

1. Care under fire
2. Tactical field care
3. Tactical evacuation care

Care under fire is the period when the first responder and the patient are under effective hostile fire. Care is restricted to what can be done with resources carried on the person of the responder and victim. Tactical field care is the period where the first responder and the victim are no longer under effective hostile fire. During this phase, additional care can be rendered using supplies and equipment carried with the group. Depending on availability, medics and other advanced military medical personnel may be able to reach the victim. Tactical evacuation care, formally called casualty evacuation care (CASEVAC) prior to 2008, concentrates on the extraction of the victim from the site of the engagement. Whether by vehicle, boat, or aircraft, the patient will be moved toward more definitive care with tactical field care continuing during the transport. The phases of TCCC are designed to allow the priority of care to evolve as the security posture is improved, with each phase building on the one preceding to intervene regarding potential and actual life threats (**Figure 1**). The **Committee on Tactical Combat**

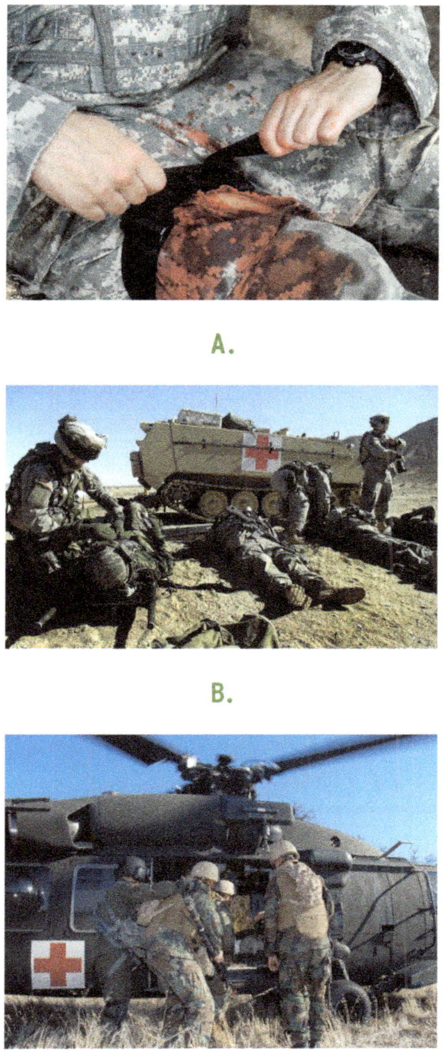

A.

B.

C.

Figure 1 **A.** Care under fire. **B.** Tactical field care. **C.** Tactical evacuation.

Casualty Care (CoTCCC) meets every four months to review the literature and real-world-tested practices and make recommendations. TCCC guidelines change frequently; the most current version of TCCC can be found at the Department of Defense's Military Health System web site (http://www.health.mil/Education_And_Training/TCCC.aspx).

> **Tip**
>
> **Tactical Versus Civilian**
>
> Although these practices are appropriate for combat operations, implementation may be inconsistent with civilian training and licensure. Responders should consult with their medical director before using the TCCC guidelines.

The treatment modalities of TCCC have been continually refined and proven in combat environments over the past decade; however, they are not without controversy in the civilian sector. Whereas the military is able to unify its training to one standard across services, civilian emergency medical services (EMS) are governed by each state's scope of practice and limits of certification and liability. This makes basic TCCC recommendations such as intravenous therapy, administration of drugs, and needle decompression of the chest beyond the scope of practice allowed for many EMS and TEMS providers. Fortunately, new organizations of combat-experienced physicians and medics are emerging to tackle these issues. To meet the challenges of implementing TCCC guidelines and practice for civilian use, the **Committee for Tactical Emergency Casualty Care (C-TECC)** was formed and is releasing parallel guidelines that take into account the differences between civilian and military medicine.

TACTICAL EMERGENCY CASUALTY CARE

The C-TECC was convened to expedite the appropriate transition of medical lessons learned from the battlefield to civilian crisis response. The goal of this transition was to reduce preventable causes of death in both first responders and the civilian population. The C-TECC is modeled after CoTCCC and comprises a broad range of interagency operational and academic leaders in the practice of high-threat medicine and fire rescue from across the nation, including members from emergency medicine, EMS, police, fire, and the military special operations community. The C-TECC remains an independent civilian entity but maintains a close relationship with CoTCCC for guidance and support.

The **tactical emergency casualty care (TECC)** guidelines are a set of best practice recommendations for casualty management during high-threat civilian tactical and rescue operations. The TECC guidelines are based on the principles of tactical combat casualty care but account for differences in the civilian environment, resources allocation, patient population, and scope of practice.

Some of the specific differences that the TECC guidelines address are provider levels of certification, age of patient population, general health and physical condition of patient population, availability of equipment, and proximity to definitive care. Further, the phases of care have been changed to better reflect the operating areas and terminology of civilian public safety entities. The phases of care are as follows:

- Direct threat care for care under fire
- Indirect threat care for tactical field care
- Evacuation care for tactical evacuation (TACEVAC)

Law enforcement departments should implement TCCC/TECC guidelines as a standard of care or as part of protocols only after careful consideration by leadership and the medical director. TCCC/TECC equipment should also be evaluated by departmental medical leadership because endorsements by TCCC are meant for equipment that has been proven to be effective on the majority of the military population, which may not be as effective on the civilian population. If used properly, TCCC/TECC guidelines will continue to reduce deaths from preventable causes during everyday and atypical emergency responses.

MILITARY PREHOSPITAL PROVIDERS

Service branches within the Department of Defense have a hierarchical approach to medical training similar to civilian fire and EMS systems. Although similarities exist, the roles and responsibilities of military medical personnel do not translate directly into civilian counterparts. **Table 1** delineates the levels of training for providers within each branch of service and correlates these "best fit" descriptions with civilian (prehospital) medical responders, including LERs. Some of the highest levels of training for prehospital care in the military are reserved for the special operations community.

Table 1

Emergency Medical Responder Training

Organization	Basic Prehospital Care		Advanced Prehospital Care	
EMS	CPR/first aid or emergency medical responder (EMR)	Emergency medical technician (EMT)/ advanced emergency medical technician (AEMT)	Paramedic	
US Army	Combat life saver, TCCC buddy aid/self aid	Combat medic (68W)	Combat medic (68W1) Special operations combat medic (SOCM)[a]	Special forces medical sergeant (SFMS) (18D)[b]
US Air Force	CPR	Medical technician		Pararescuemen (PJ) SOCM[a] SOF IDMT (4N071C)
US Navy	CPR/TCCC	Hospital corpsman (HM)	Dive med tech (8423) SEAL (5392) SOCM[a]	Independent duty corpsman: surface (8425) Deep sea diving (8429) Submarine (8402) SOIDC (5391)
US Marine Corps	Combat life saver, TCCC buddy aid/self aid (USMC)	Fleet marine forces corpsman (8404)[c]	Special amphibious reconnaissance corpsman (8427) SOCM[a]	SARC IDC[d] (8403)

[a]SOCM: Special operations combat medic; 36 weeks, Fort Bragg, North Carolina. These providers also complete the DoD Advanced Tactical Provider (ATP) exam. ATP certification needs to be maintained/recertified.

[b]SFMS/SOIDC: Special forces medical sergeant/Special operations independent duty corpsman. SOCM +22 weeks, Fort Bragg, North Carolina.

[c]Fleet marine forces: 7 weeks additional training at Camp Lejeune, North Carolina, or Camp Pendleton, California, following initial hospital corpsman qualification.

[d]SARC IDC: Special amphibious reconnaissance corpsman, independent duty corpsman.

SOF IDMT: Special Operations Forces Independent Duty Medical Technician

SOIDC: Special Operations Independent Duty Corpsman

SEAL: Naval Special Warfare Sea Air and Land Operator

68W (formerly 91B); 16 weeks at Ft. Sam Houston, San Antonio, TX

Data in parentheses indicate specialty nomenclature referred to Military Occupational Specialty (MOS) or Navy Enlisted Classification (NEC).

RECEIVING FACILITIES

Military medicine uses a tiered system not unlike the classification for civilian trauma centers. Each level is tasked with providing more definitive care than the level below and is often tasked to resupply and support the preceding level as needed. There is no requirement that a patient must pass through each level of care during treatment and evacuation. **Table 2** provides a brief overview of the progression of care between the military roles as well as the level stratification used by the American College of Surgeons (ACS).

Table 2

ACS Verification Review Committee Trauma Center Designations				
Level I	**Level II**	**Level III**	**Level IV**	**Level V**
24-hour in-house surgeons Emergency medicine and anesthesiology Full range of specialists and equipment available 24 hours a day (including orthopaedic surgery, neurosurgery, plastic surgery, radiology, internal medicine, oral and maxillofacial surgery, and critical care) Programs for research, trauma education, and injury prevention Referral resource for the local community	24-hour availability of all essential specialties, personnel, and equipment Not required to have an ongoing research or a surgical residency program	Resources for emergency resuscitation, surgery, and intensive care of most trauma patients Transfer agreements with level I or level II trauma centers	Where resources do not exist for a level III trauma center Initial evaluation, stabilization, diagnostic capabilities, and transfer to a higher level of care Trauma-trained nurse immediately available Physicians available upon patient arrival in the emergency department Transfer agreements with other trauma centers of higher levels	Initial evaluation, stabilization, diagnostic capabilities, and transfer to a higher level of care Trauma-trained nurse immediately available Physicians available upon patient arrival in the emergency department If not open 24 hours daily, must have an after-hours trauma-response protocol

Data Source: American College of Surgeons-Consultation Verification Program. (ACS-COT), http://www.facs.org/trauma/vcprogram.html

Trauma care for military personnel has become increasingly sophisticated. There are five levels of care, each progressively more advanced:

- **Level I:** Immediate first aid at the front line, often called buddy aid or self-aid, as it is frequently delivered by nonmedical personnel
- **Level II:** Surgical intervention by mobile surgical teams that directly support combatant units in the field
- **Level III:** Provided through combat support hospitals that offer more advanced medical, surgical, and trauma care, similar to a civilian trauma center
- **Level IV:** Definitive surgical management outside the combat zone; for current conflicts, the only Level IV facility is located in Landstuhl, Germany
- **Level V:** Final stage of evacuation to one of the major military centers in the continental United States, where definitive stabilization, reconstruction, or amputation of an injured extremity is performed

Communication

Military Terminology

Previously, the terms *level* and *echelon* were used interchangeably to represent the capabilities of a particular medical treatment facility. Present-day US military operations have adopted the term *level* as universal language throughout the North American Treaty Organization (NATO).

CONCLUSION

As medical advances continue in the military, civilian medicine will be able to incorporate changes that may improve care to the current system. One of the groundbreaking paradigm shifts, TCCC, has already reduced the number of deaths from preventable causes on the battlefield. Tenets of TCCC have application in the civilian world, especially in the tactical law enforcement arena, and guidelines and protocols to reflect that have been developed.

Prep Kit

READY FOR REVIEW

- Military emergency medicine made huge strides to improve patient survival during the Vietnam conflict.
- The advent of military medical evacuation (medevac) greatly shortened the time from the point of injury to definitive care.
- TCCC propelled battlefield casualty management to new levels of effectiveness, lowering the fatality rate to the lowest on record.
- The core tenets of TCCC are simultaneously to treat the casualty, prevent additional casualties, and complete the mission.
- The three distinct
  - Care under fire
  - Tactical field care
  - Tactical evacuation care
- Whereas the military is able to unify its training to one standard across services, civilian emergency medical services are governed by each state's scope of practice and limits of certification.
- The C-TECC was convened to expedite the appropriate transition of medical lessons learned from the battlefield to civilian crisis response. The goal of this transition was to reduce preventable causes of death in both first responders and the civilian population.
- The TECC guidelines are a set of best practice recommendations for casualty management during high-threat civilian tactical and rescue operations.
- Service branches within the Department of Defense have a hierarchical approach to medical training similar to civilian fire and EMS systems.
- Military medicine uses a tiered system not unlike the classification for civilian trauma centers. Each level is tasked with providing more definitive care than the level below and is often tasked to resupply and support the preceding level as needed.

VITAL VOCABULARY

Committee on Tactical Combat Casualty Care (CoTCCC) The CoTCCC was established in 2001 to monitor new developments in prehospital trauma care and use this information to periodically update the TCCC guidelines. This committee is now part of the Defense Health board and is hosted by the Military Health System at the Department of Defense. http://www.health.mil/Education_And_Training/TCCC.aspx

Committee for Tactical Emergency Casualty Care (C-TECC) The C-TECC was convened to expedite the appropriate transition of military medical lessons learned from the battlefield to civilian crisis response in order to reduce preventable causes of death in both our first responders and civilian population. The C-TECC is modeled after the Committee on Tactical Combat Casualty Care (CoTCCC) and is comprised of a broad range of interagency operational and academic leaders in the practice of high-threat medicine and fire/rescue from across the nation. http://c-tecc.org/

tactical combat casualty care (TCCC) Military medical paradigm that dictates care to be provided to a casualty based on the tactical scenario.

tactical emergency casualty care (TECC) Guidelines developed for high-threat civilian medical situations. Based on the concept of TCCC, takes into account differences in civilian populations and resources.

CHECK YOUR KNOWLEDGE

You are part of your department's special operations team. As part of your indoctrination training, you are taught Technical Combat Casualty Care (TCCC). During a high-threat warrant service operation in which you are participating, a suspect begins firing at the entry team. Two of the team members are injured. One of the officers has major bleeding from his arm, and the second officer appears to have difficulty catching his breath.

1. What should be your first priority?
   - **A.** Continue the tactical mission and secure the scene.
   - **B.** Immediately stop to assess the patients.
   - **C.** Drop medical supplies for the patients and notify EMS.
   - **D.** Withdraw from the structure and wait for instructions.
2. Which of the following would be the most significant injury to treat?
   - **A.** Airway obstructions
   - **B.** Sucking chest wound
   - **C.** Major bleeding
   - **D.** Broken femur
3. How would you treat major bleeding in this situation?
   - **A.** Trauma dressing
   - **B.** Tourniquet
   - **C.** Pressure bandage
   - **D.** Hemostatic agent
4. It is appropriate for you as a law enforcement officer with no additional medical certifications to perform needle chest decompression if needed.
   - **A.** True
   - **B.** False
5. If the suspect is injured, when should he receive medical care?
   - **A.** After both officers have been treated and transported.
   - **B.** Once local EMS arrives.
   - **C.** Once he is no longer a threat.
   - **D.** He should not receive medical care.

Law Enforcement Considerations

Unit 18

Liam Holtzman
Joshua Knapp
Matthew Sztajnkrycer

Law Enforcement Responder Objectives

Ordnance Ballistics

- Discuss ballistics and the associated terminology. (pp 329–330)
- Describe wounding patterns from gunshots. (pp 330–331)
- Discuss ballistic scene considerations. (pp 332–333)

Explosions and Blasts

- Identify scene safety considerations at a blast scene. (p 336)
- Describe the categories of blast injury. (pp 336–338)
- Explain management of blast injuries. (p 338)

Less Lethal Munitions

- Explain the properties and use of the following less lethal munitions:
    - Chemical munitions (p 339)
    - Specialty impact munitions (pp 339–340)
    - Conducted energy devices (p 341)
- Discuss assessment and management of injuries from less lethal munitions. (pp 341–344)

National EMS Education Standard Competencies

Trauma

Uses simple knowledge to recognize and manage life threats based on assessment findings for an acutely injured patient while awaiting additional emergency medical response.

Soft-Tissue Trauma

Recognition and management of

- Wounds (pp 329–345)

INTRODUCTION

As a law enforcement responder (LER), you likely will see a great number of extremity and soft-tissue injuries during your career. These are probably the most commonly seen injuries throughout all levels of law enforcement. There are many categories of extremity and soft-tissue injuries, ranging from minor to life threatening. LERs must take into account that they may see injuries in a hostile setting where care-under-fire techniques and tactical considerations will apply. It is appropriate practice for the LER to take the setting of the injury into account to determine the immediate care response. If your partner crushes his thumb in the door jamb of your cruiser at the end of your shift in the police yard, the standard medical response will apply. The approach to treatment would be different, however, if your partner were to crush his thumb in a door during a high-risk warrant service.

Ordnance Ballistics

The use of guns and resultant gunshot wounds constitute a significant percentage of violence in the United States. *All* confrontations involving the LER inherently involve the presence of a gun (at a minimum, that carried by the officer), making the risk of violence standard.

The evolution of small arms revolutionized warfare. The invention of gunpowder and the subsequent development of fired projectiles from artillery and small arms brought an ever-increasing lethality from hostile persons and small forces. Today, gunshot wounds are commonly seen in urban emergency centers. Furthermore, the use of special weapons and tactic (SWAT) teams for situations deemed too hostile for uniformed patrol response makes the likelihood of the LER encountering gunshot wounds even higher.

BALLISTICS

Ballistics is the science of mechanics that deals with the flight, behavior, and effects of projectiles. Certain terminology is used when discussing ballistics. A cartridge, or round, consists of several components, including a metal case containing a chemical primer and gunpowder capped by a bullet, which is propelled from a gun. When the primer is struck by the firing pin, it ignites the powder charge within the metallic cartridge case and expels the projectile down the rifled barrel toward a target.

The bullet (projectile) is constructed in a multitude of configurations, including various shapes and jacketing materials (**Figure 1**). A bullet consisting of a lead core encased in a copper jacket is termed a full metal jacket (FMJ). A bullet core having a hollow tip exposed through a metal jacket is termed a jacketed

A. B. C.

Figure 1 Bullets. **A.** Full metal jacket. **B.** Jacketed hollowpoint. **C.** Pointed soft point.

hollowpoint (JHP). A similarly clad bullet presenting a soft lead tip without the hollowed component is termed a pointed soft point (PSP). JHP and PSP bullets are specifically designed to expand in tissue, thereby increasing the cross-sectional area traveling through and disrupting tissue. Bullet weights are often expressed in grains (1 ounce = 437.5 grains).

Caliber refers to the diameter of a bullet. It is expressed as a decimal of an inch (eg, .357 magnum) or in metric measurements (eg, 9 mm Parabellum).

Rounds fired from handguns generally consist of calibers in the .22 to .45 range. Velocities of handgun cartridges range from subsonic to roughly 1,400 ft/s. Note that the distinction here between handgun and rifle rounds is for the purposes of describing low and high bullet velocities. There are, however, handguns that fire rifle-caliber rounds (eg, AR-15 style pistol) and shoulder-fired submachine guns and carbines that are chambered for pistol rounds (eg, HK MP5).

Generally, a high-velocity rifle round, such as those seen in hunting and tactical rifles, consists of a projectile driven to velocities several times the speed of sound (2,000–4,000 ft/s). Although the mass may be small (such as is seen in the 5.56 mm NATO round used in the US M4 platform), the high velocity projects a great deal of energy toward a target. The temporary wound cavity created is correspondingly larger and more devastating to tissue.

A shotgun is a large-bore weapon, traditionally fired from a smooth-bore barrel that is capable of firing a wide range of projectiles. Payloads consisting of multiple small pellets are characterized as birdshot (containing small lead projectiles en masse) or buckshot (containing fewer but larger spherical projectiles). OO buckshot (double aught), for instance, consists of nine 32-caliber (.32) balls, creating a concentrated area of energy at close range. The distribution of projectiles spreads as a function of the distance from the muzzle of the weapon, increasing the affected area but with a corresponding decrease in overall energy. Use of a choke concentrates the projectiles and reduces this spread increasing close range effectiveness via tight patterns and energy transmission.

Another common type of shotgun round is the rifled slug. Often consisting of a one ounce solid piece of lead, it is fired through a smooth-bore or rifled shotgun barrel. Its large mass, along with long range rifled accuracy, makes it a truly devastating round, having muzzle energies in the 3,000 foot-pound range.

Other shotgun rounds include specialty payloads such as flachettes, strung ball, pepper spray, and less lethal rounds (eg, rubber, baton, and beanbag).

Terminal Ballistics

Terminal ballistics, a subfield of ballistics, is the study of the behavior of a projectile when it hits its target. One often hears the term "knock-down" power as describing the terminal ballistics against a human subject. The literal notion of knock-down power is a fallacy. The third law of Newtonian physics—that for every force there is an equal and opposite force—dictates that a projectile that could actually knock down a person would likewise create a recoil that would knock down the shooter firing the round. This reaction is not feasible from small arms.

Generalizations based on velocity as a sole determinant in wounding do not take into account the multiple factors occurring at the projectile-tissue level. Factors include projectile mass (caliber), shape, construction, velocity, angle of incidence, and target tissue. Mass and velocity impart the potential, whereas the remaining factors result in actual injury. Intermediary materials such as wallboard, auto glass, wood doors, and heavy clothing also change the parameters of terminal ballistics and the resulting wound effect of the round. Finally, even psychology affects effectiveness. It is not unusual for a gunshot victim to continue to pose a threat despite multiple, even ultimately fatal, wounds due to the influence of "warrior mentality," preconceived notions of what should occur when sustaining a gunshot wound (conditioning), and use of mind/pain altering drugs. Only gunshot wounds that mechanically disrupt brain tissue or interrupt blood flow to the brain are predictably and reliably incapacitating.

WOUNDING PATTERNS

Injury suffered from ballistic trauma varies based on many factors, most notably the weight and velocity of the projectile and the anatomic location it traverses. As a bullet enters the body, it creates both a temporary wound cavity and a permanent wound channel. There is a third effect, a sonic wave (energy wave released from the explosion, traveling faster than the speed of sound), occurring with high-velocity projectiles. However, this has never been shown to exert any clinical wounding effects.

The first of these wounding effects, temporary cavitation, is a localized expansion of tissue resulting from the shock wave of the projectile. Temporary cavitation is most notable in high-velocity rifle rounds. (The term *high-velocity* is variably defined but tends to refer to velocities exceeding

2,000 ft/s, characteristic of many tactical and hunting rifles.) This temporary area of expansion causes the stretching and tearing of tissues. Forces follow the path of least resistance, separating tissue planes and tearing tissues at points of fixation where they cannot be displaced. Solid organs and hollow organs may fracture or rupture as a result of this temporary cavitation, causing serious internal injury. Elastic tissues that stretch, such as muscle and skin, may fare better during this temporary motion.

The permanent wound channel refers to the direct tissue injury caused by the projectile (or fragments of the projectile) as it passes through tissues. This penetration and crushing action internally results in permanent tissue injury along the wound track.

The NATO 5.56 mm FMJ round is classically a 55 grain FMJ projectile. It is spin stabilized along its long axis by rifling in the barrel of the weapon. As such, it travels and enters tissue pointed end first in stable, forward flight. As it penetrates, the projectile encounters tissue resistance and begins to yaw and rotate, presenting a larger cross-sectional area as it travels through the tissue. This results in a large temporary cavitation and permanent wound channel. Depending on several factors, the projectile may further break apart as it rotates, causing secondary internal projectiles and resulting in even larger tissue destruction.

A soft point projectile is designed to expand (mushroom) as it encounters resistance, thereby presenting a surface area at least twice that of the original entering projectile. This increase in surface area results in creation of a large temporary cavity and greater local permanent tissue destruction occurring at a more shallow tissue depth than the FMJ round. Fragmentation may also occur, resulting in multiple missiles.

Specific wounds vary widely with regard to underlying structures damaged and can be difficult to predict. There are numerous stories about gunshot wounds to the head miraculously tracking under the scalp and passing out of the victim without penetrating the skull. Conversely, there are numerous persons killed from what would be thought of as a possibly less dangerous small-caliber/low-velocity gunshot wound that struck a large vessel or caused some other mortal wound process. Ultimately, shot placement is often as important as the ballistics of the projectile.

The actual path a bullet travels within the body can be unpredictable. A projectile striking bones may change direction and come to lie in an area anatomically remote from entry, with resulting injury all along the extended path. For example, a gunshot wound to the thigh could deflect from the femur and enter the abdomen, resulting in a devastating peritoneal injury. All penetrating injuries from bullets are serious, and even an outwardly stable patient should be assumed to have critical internal injuries until proven otherwise.

The generally accepted rules as to how a gunshot wound appears are often inaccurate. The notion of the entrance wound always being small in size, and the exit wound large and destructive, depends on a myriad of circumstances. Factors such as distance, velocity, type of projectile, overlying garments, and whether the local tissue is supported by bone or outside materials determine the appearance of gunshot wounds on the skin. As such, a LER should not characterize a wound as "entrance" or "exit" during routine assessments. Responders should instead note objectively the location, size, and any surrounding characteristics of wounds and label them numerically.

ASSESSMENT OF GUNSHOT WOUNDS

Although varied in wounding patterns, all gunshot wounds are dangerous and must be approached with an appropriate sense of urgency. The primary assessment begins with the scene size-up, including noting the number of patients, the availability of cover and concealment, and always bearing in mind the potential for dangerous circumstances. As in any field victim encounter, the LER should ask several key questions when the circumstances of the call are not evident:

- Why is the victim down?
- Is the scene safe to enter?
- Is the victim armed (whether law enforcement or suspect)?
- Does the victim have munitions on his or her person that need to be secured in the case of the tactical operator?

In the case of an active shooter situation, the LER must also determine whether the victim is in an area that is reasonably safe to approach. A shrewd shooter may intentionally wound someone with the objective of drawing emergency responders into the open and creating further casualties. If the approach is deemed dangerous, initial interventions to access the victim may include the following:

- Directing a conscious victim who is able to self-extricate.
- Throwing a line for a victim to grab or securing the line onto the victim's gear or belt and dragging him or her to a position of cover.

- Using a tactical team with bunkers and a tactical blanket to extricate the victim.
- Using an armored vehicle interposed between victim and shooter, enabling the victim to be pulled into the vehicle and the team to be evacuated from the field of fire.

Exposing the rescuer to direct fire risks making the rescuer into another victim and requiring additional rescue efforts. LERs should evaluate the level of care they provide in a hostile environment. Advanced or elaborate care techniques may expose the victim and the rescuers to additional threats, creating more casualties.

Once the victim has been extricated to a position of relative safety (yellow zone) or evacuated from the active scene (green zone), it is time to examine and treat the victims as is appropriate to the tactical circumstances. Care for the gunshot victim proceeds in the usual fashion with attention to massive hemorrhage, airway control, breathing, and circulation, followed by a secondary assessment.

Ballistic Vest Removal

As much as body armor can help prevent ballistic trauma, the construction and configuration of the garment can likewise inhibit access to an injured officer. In particular, heavier "raid" armor vests worn by local tactical teams may be difficult to remove quickly. It is therefore important that an officer be familiar with the specific models of body armor worn by his or her and other local jurisdictions and practice opening or removing them to access the victim and provide emergency medical care.

SPECIAL ANATOMIC CONSIDERATIONS FOR GUNSHOT WOUNDS

Head and Neck Wounds

Studies suggest that the prevalence of cervical spine injury is very low in isolated gunshot wounds to the head. The use of a cervical collar therefore is unnecessary and may interfere with critical airway control. It is prudent, however, to use a cervical collar if available in the tactical environment when there is penetrating injury to the neck or an associated mechanism, such as a fall from height after being shot, unless its use interferes with airway control or impedes direct control of hemorrhage from the neck.

Chest Wounds

The chest presents a large target for gunshot wounds. As the center of mass, most civilian and tactical weapons training includes the use of the chest as point of aim. It contains essential anatomy including the heart, great vessels (aorta and venae cava), and lungs. Gunshot wounds to the chest area overlying the lungs almost always result in the penetration of the pleural cavity and collapse of the involved lung (pneumothorax). Air escaping from the collapsed lung may accumulate and become trapped in the pleural cavity, increasing pressures in the chest (tension pneumothorax), which compresses the heart, eventually causing cardiac arrest and death. The LER supporting a tactical mission should aggressively manage chest injuries. LERs should therefore have a low threshold to access advanced life support or, if trained and authorized, use needle thoracostomy to relieve this accumulated tension.

An open pneumothorax (sucking chest wound) may result from penetrating injury to the chest and should be rapidly stabilized using a commercial flutter chest dressing (chest seal) or other occlusive material to restore external integrity to the injured hemithorax.

Transmediastinal (crossing the midline of the chest, which contains the heart and large central blood vessels) gunshot wounds are imminently life threatening and require rapid transport to a trauma center. Emergency department thoracotomy (cracking the chest) performed in a trauma center may provide life-saving control of hemorrhage and temporarily stabilize the patient until definitive intervention.

Penetrating injury to the upper front sides of the chest can cause hemorrhage that is especially difficult to control. This area contains portions of the lung and the large blood vessels that supply each arm. These areas, lying behind the clavicles (collarbones), are difficult to manage by direct pressure while hemorrhaging. Mortality is high in these injuries.

Extremity Wounds

Penetrating injury to the extremities may result in fracture or acute blood loss. High-velocity gunshot wounds may create a highly unstable fracture and extensive soft-tissue injury with subsequent limb loss. Immediately control hemorrhage with direct pressure, pressure bandages, hemostatic agents, or tourniquets. The presence and quality of pulses in an involved extremity should be noted during the secondary assessment and periodically during prolonged casualty evacuation periods. In closed injury, hemorrhage may cause an increase in tissue pressure which compromises blood flow into the injured limb. If unaddressed, it will ultimately result in severe damage, infection, or amputation of the limb.

PRESERVING GUNSHOT EVIDENCE

Characteristics of a gunshot wound include surface features that may be useful in the reconstruction of a crime and trial. Because the care of a patient's wound will often necessitate the use of pressure dressings and other local manipulation, any surface features should be noted prior to or concurrently with treatment. The presence of soot, gun powder tattooing, a rim abrasion, or other features should be noted and recorded in the medical record (**Figure 2**). Likewise, clothing on a patient should be removed in a nondestructive fashion by cutting along seams and by avoiding cuts through bullet holes whenever possible. Removed clothing should be retained as evidence and placed in paper bags when the clinical situation permits.

BALLISTIC PROTECTION

Inherent to the concept of ballistics is protection from ballistic threats. At its most basic level, protection consists of the concept of concealment versus cover. **Concealment** refers to being visually shielded from a threat, whether or not physically protected from the ballistic threat posed. **Cover** refers to physical protection from a ballistic threat. Because the ballistic properties of projectiles vary, so do materials required to provide cover against a given threat. For example, common automobile door panels may provide concealment, but provide little protection against small arms fire. The engine block of the same automobile, however, provides protection against even the most substantial of small arms rounds.

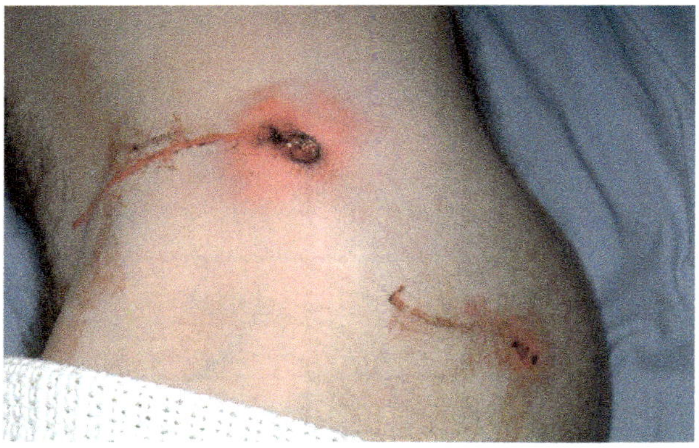

Figure 2 The presence of soot, gun powder tattooing, a rim abrasion, or other features should be noted and recorded in the medical record.

BODY ARMOR

Of all the equipment developed and evaluated in the 1970s by the National Institute of Justice (NIJ), one of its most significant achievements was the development of personally worn body armor that employed DuPont's Kevlar ballistic fabric, which was originally developed to replace steel belting in vehicle tires. Testing revealed that this material had properties suitable to providing ballistic protection and could be made into a garment. Kevlar 29, introduced in the early 1970s, was the first generation of bullet-resistant fibers developed by DuPont. Subsequent materials have been developed by various manufacturers and have brand names such as Kevlar 129, Kevlar Protera, Spectra, Aramid, Dyneema, and Zylon.

When a handgun bullet strikes body armor, it is caught in a meshwork of fibers. These fibers absorb and disperse the impact energy that is transmitted to the vest from the bullet. Kinetic energy is absorbed by each successive layer of material in the vest, slowing and stopping the projectile. These fibers work together both in the individual layer and with other layers of material in the ballistic garment such that a larger area of the garment becomes involved in resisting penetration. This dissipation helps to spread the now blunt force trauma of a nonpenetrating small mass projectile over a greater area, limiting "back-face deformation" and the resulting underlying injury. Regardless, the extent to which the ballistic material deforms inward as it slows and catches a projectile can impart significant injury to underlying structures, including contusions of the skin and fractured ribs. Cases of death due to this blunt mechanism have been reported.

Latest generations of concealable soft body armor can provide varying levels of protection to defeat most common low- and medium-energy handgun rounds. Body armor designed to defeat rifle fire is of either semi-rigid or rigid construction, typically incorporating hard materials such as ceramics and metals. Its weight and bulkiness make these higher threat armor solutions impractical for routine use by uniformed patrol officers and it is generally reserved for use in tactical situations, where it is worn externally when confronted with higher-level threats.

When someone is struck by a bullet, the extent of the injury sustained depends on where the bullet strikes the body and the trajectory of the bullet into or through the body. Injury to the vital organs is most often fatal. The primary and most obvious purpose of body armor is therefore to prevent a bullet from penetrating the torso.

Despite the popular term "bulletproof" armor, there is no such thing. Body armor provides protection against a significant number of types of handgun ammunition, but officers must bear in mind that armor protection from penetration is rated for different threat levels of ammunition. The National Institute of Justice Standard, *Ballistic Resistance of Personal Body Armor*, describes the minimum performance requirements and test methods for the ballistic resistance of body armor, categorizes the types of body armor available, and describes the various threat levels under which a specific level is rated (**Table 1**). At the time of this writing, the latest standard is *Ballistic Resistance of Body Armor NIJ Standard-0101.06*:

- **Type I (.22 LR; .380 ACP).** This armor protects against .22 long rifle (LR) lead round nose (LRN) bullets, with nominal masses of 40 gr, impacting at a minimum velocity of 1050 ft/s or less, and against .380 ACP FMJ round nose (RN), with nominal masses of 95 gr, impacting at a minimum velocity of 1025 ft/s or less. Type I body armor is light. However, because of increasing ballistic threats, this level is likely poorly suited to most patrol officers.

Table 1

Armor Type and Ballistic Resistance

Armor Type	Test Bullet	Bullet Weight/Grain	Reference Velocity (est)	Max Backface Deformation
I	.22 Caliber LR LRN	2.6 g/40 gr	1,050 ± 30 ft/s (329 ± 10 m/s)	1.73 in (44 mm)
	.380 ACP FMJ RN	6.2 g/95gr	1,025 ± 30 ft/s (322 ± 10 m/s)	1.73 in (44 mm)
II-A	9 mm FMJ RN	8.0 g/124 gr	1,190 ± 30 ft/s (341 ± 10 m/s)	1.73 in (44 mm)
	40 S&W FMJ	11.7 g/180 gr	1,025 ± 30 ft/s (322 ± 10 m/s)	1.73 in (44 mm)
II	9 mm FMJ RN	8.0 g/124 gr	1,175 ± 30 ft/s (367 ± 10 m/s)	1.73 in (44 mm)
	.357 Mag JSP	10.2 g/158 gr	1,400 ± 30 ft/s (436 ± 10 m/s)	1.73 in (44 mm)
III-A	9 mm FMJ RN	8.2 g/124 gr	1,400 ± 30 ft/s (436 ± 10 m/s)	1.73 in (44 mm)
	44 Mag SJHP	15.6 g/240 gr	1,400 ± 30 ft/s (436 ± 10 m/s)	1.73 in (44 mm)

- **Type II-A (9 mm; .40 S&W).** This armor protects against 9 mm FMJ round nose (RN) bullets, with nominal masses of 124 gr, impacting at a minimum velocity of 1090 ft/s or less, and .40 S&W caliber FMJ bullets, with nominal masses of 180 gr, impacting at a minimum velocity of 1025 ft/s or less. It also provides protection against Type I threats.
- **Type II (9 mm; .357 Magnum).** This armor protects against 9 mm FMJ round nose (RN) bullets, with nominal masses of 124 gr, impacting at a minimum velocity of 1175 ft/s or less, and .357 Magnum jacketed soft point (JSP) bullets, with nominal masses of 158 gr, impacting at a minimum velocity of 1400 ft/s or less. It also provides protection against Type I and Type II-A threats. Type II body armor is heavier and more bulky than either Types I or II-A.
- **Type III-A (High Velocity 9 mm; .44 Magnum).** This armor protects against 9 mm FMJ round nose (RN) bullets, with nominal masses of 124 gr, impacting at a minimum velocity of 1400 ft/s or less, and .44 Magnum jacketed hollow point (JHP) bullets, with nominal masses of 240 gr, impacting at a minimum velocity of 1400 ft/s or less. It also provides protection against most handgun threats, as well as the Type I, II-A, and II threats. Type III-A body armor provides the highest level of protection currently available from concealable body armor and, as with lower levels, may be used for routine wear by patrol officers.
- **Type III (Rifles).** This armor protects against 7.62 mm FMJ bullets (US military designation M80), with nominal masses of 148 gr, impacting at a minimum velocity of 2750 ft/s or less. It also provides protection against Type I through III-A threats. Type III body armor is intended for tactical situations when the threat warrants such protection.
- **Type IV (Armor Piercing Rifle).** This armor protects against .30 caliber armor piercing (AP) bullets (US military designation M2 AP), with nominal masses of 166 gr, impacting at a minimum velocity of 2850 ft/s or less. It also provides at least single-hit protection against the Type I through III threats (the ceramic material often employed is brittle and may not provide multi-hit capability as it breaks up on impact). Type IV body armor provides the highest level of protection currently available. As with Type III armor, Type IV armor is intended only for tactical situations when the threat warrants such protection.

As part of the Uniform Crime Reports, the Federal Bureau of Investigation (FBI) publishes its annual report *Law Enforcement Officers Killed and Assaulted* (LEOKA), which contains detailed analysis of the situations and circumstances surrounding assaults on law enforcement officers. The development of the NIJ body armor standards led to the introduction and increasingly common use of protective body armor by police officers. The first officer whose life was saved by the use of body armor was in 1973, and from then through the year 2000, a total of 2500 saves had been attributed to the use of body armor. Fifty-eight percent of these saves were connected with felonious assaults; forty percent of these felonious assaults involved firearms. Over the last decade, more than 500 more officers have been saved by body armor, bringing the total to more than 3000.

Explosions and Blasts

Explosives have been a source of injuries dating back to the ninth century, when the Chinese invented gunpowder. Since that time, the types of explosives, their acronyms, and their potency have changed and evolved with technology. Nevertheless, the primary management issues remain the same for LERs. Blast scenes present a hazardous operational environment. These scenes require LERs to focus all their cognitive abilities to give themselves the best chance to avoid becoming a casualty.

SCENE SAFETY

Unlike other types of emergency responses, LERs need to keep in mind that the explosion was a deliberate act. The perpetrator may have placed secondary explosive devices designed to initiate once emergency responders arrive. The perpetrator's goal in this case would be to maximize harm to civil authorities and turn a chaotic scene into one that will be unmanageable for some time. To maximize personal safety, LERs must begin their scene size-up well back from the approximate site of the explosion, regardless of the reactions from bystanders. LERs must closely scrutinize any onlookers, vehicle occupants, surrounding building window or door occupants, or other persons who look out of place. Any person who occupies one of these positions might be the "bomber" who initiated the first explosion and is now waiting to injure additional public safety personnel.

Once a LER is reasonably sure no additional perpetrators are present, it is necessary to look for any unusual or out-of-place items, such as packages, boxes, cars, wires, and leaking fluids. A secondary device may be disguised in this way and can be controlled by a simple timer. The bomber may have estimated how long it would take until the initial blast scene would be occupied with LERs and set a timer accordingly. If anything unusual is detected, LERs must hold their position and ensure this potential danger is communicated to all other responding units. Explosive specialists need to evaluate any potential explosive devices. LERs must always fall back on the emergency response question, "Is the scene safe?" You are of no use to patients if you are dead or injured.

When you are reasonably certain the scene is safe, you should proceed and begin to assess those injured by the explosion. In general, injuries follow a simple rule: those further away from a blast are less injured. LERs must rapidly triage all victims of an explosion but should expect to find those most severely injured closest to the site of the explosion.

The terrorist attacks of September 11, 2001, are foremost in the minds of emergency responders. This event offers tremendous opportunities for table top exercises and planning. Although planning for a large-scale event is helpful, all of the talk about possible use of weapons of mass destruction, dirty bombs, and biological weapons consumes hours of training and planning time of homeland security specialists. A more likely event LERs will encounter involves something much smaller in scale, such as a one- or two-device detonation. An example of this type of event is the abortion clinic bombing that occurred in Atlanta, Georgia, on January 16, 1997. In the Atlanta event, a secondary device was detonated with the intent to injure emergency responders on scene following an initial explosion. It is these types of smaller events that pose the greatest risk to LERs.

ASSESSMENT OF BLAST INJURIES

If the scene is free from any suspicious looking persons or items, LERs should venture closer to the seat of the explosion. If you suspect the presence of secondary devices, collect as many casualties as you can and withdraw to a safe area. Communicate to other responding units that you suspect the presence of secondary devices and that they should stop short of the incident area. You should request local explosive ordinance disposal personnel to respond immediately.

Although the need to determine scene safety and keep LERs safe is logical, the reality of assisting at such a scene is complicated by two major factors: casualties and bystanders. An explosion, whether criminal or accidental, often causes injuries. As a LER unit arrives, the walking wounded plus uninjured witnesses and bystanders will often gravitate toward emergency personnel. This crush of people complicates the scene size-up and safety assessment. In addition, responders often fail to initiate triage procedures because the emotion of seeing injured persons with graphic (but not necessarily life-threatening) wounds prompts responders to begin treating those they can see right away. This reaction results in delayed treatment for more severely injured persons lying close to the site of the blast who must therefore wait until additional resources arrive.

Once LERs have determined the scene is safe, the next step is to initiate triage. The easiest method to follow is the Simple Triage And Rapid Transport (START) (**Figure 3**). Each patient triage should be done in less than 1 minute.

When triage is completed, those victims classified as red get treated first (**Table 2**). When patient treatment resources are limited, LERs need to focus on doing the greatest good for the greatest number. LERs must avoid committing most of their resources to those who are likely to die if this commitment jeopardizes the lives of those who are potentially more salvagable. In other words, LERs should not do CPR on one victim while several others die from hemorrhage that could have been controlled.

CATEGORIES OF BLAST INJURIES

Blast injuries follow specific patterns that are categorized as primary, secondary, tertiary, and quaternary.

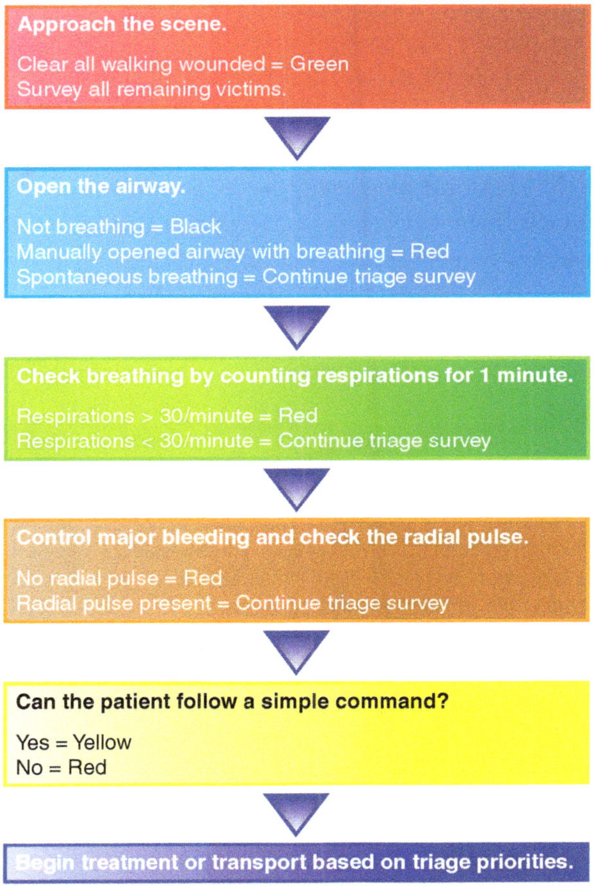

Figure 3 START triage.

Table 2

Examples of Triage

Category	Color	Examples
Category 1: Immediate	Red	Airway obstruction Flail chest Tension pneumothorax Hemorrhage
Category 2: Delayed	Yellow	Lonf bone fractures Soft-tissue injuries without active hemorrhage Head trauma Open abdominal wounds
Category 3: Minimal	Green	Minor abrasions, burns, and lacerations Moderate anxiety Open or closed fractures without complications
Category 4: Expectant	Black	Massive head or spine injury Third-degree burns over more than 70% of the body Injuries incompatible with life

Primary Blast Injury

Primary blast injuries are caused by the pressure wave from the explosive detonation passing through the human body. Hollow organs are especially susceptible to damage from this wave. Areas frequently injured include lungs, tympanic membrane, stomach, and small bowel. Of these, lung injury is most serious.

LERs should suspect a lung injury in any patient who is coughing, short of breath, or coughing up blood. LERs should keep these patients lying down. If no suction is available, these patients should lie on their side to allow any bloody mucus to drain out of the mouth without compromising the airway. Rapid transport to a hospital emergency department is the best treatment for these patients.

Suspect an abdominal injury in any patient who has abdominal pain, nausea, vomiting, and/or unexplained signs of shock (such as cool, clammy skin; prolonged capillary refill; and altered mental status).

Tympanic rupture should be suspected in any patient who has a hearing loss, bleeding or fluid from the ears, or dizziness following the blast.

Secondary Blast Injury

Secondary blast injuries are caused by debris picked up and thrown by the blast. In particular, the injuries are caused by projectiles from the blast and/or from collapsing buildings. The types of injuries include blunt injuries, penetrating injuries, abrasions, and contusions. In general, these victims will be further from the blast site than patients with primary blast injuries.

Tertiary Blast Injury

Tertiary blast injuries are caused by the victim being thrown physically by the blast. The objects the victim strikes and how the victim lands on the ground determine the types and extent of the injuries. These injuries include blunt injuries, penetrating injuries, and fractures.

Quaternary Blast Injury

Quaternary blast injures are any other injuries caused by the blast. Examples of quarternary blast injuries are topical burns, crushing wounds, psychological trauma, and respiratory tract damage. These injuries may take time to present and are seen only in patients surviving the acute phase of the explosion. LERs should focus on the first three categories, but treating and transporting all patients from an explosion will ensure no injuries are missed.

MANAGEMENT OF BLAST INJURIES

Like any other injury or illness response, LERs need to protect themselves with standard precautions. Because of the potential for large amounts of debris to be mixed in with blast patients, LERs should wear exam gloves under the gloves normally worn during arrest situations. Exam gloves alone will not adequately protect responders. The arrest-style or tactical gloves provide additional protection from debris.

If you are still involved in patient treatment prior to being relieved by EMS, you should focus on patients classified as red. Maintain the airways of patients who are breathing and control life-threatening hemorrhages. Be sure to keep triage principles in mind when choosing which patient to treat first. Treating a patient with no pulse or respirations while nearby patients have severe bleeding is incorrect. Focus on the most good for the most patients. Follow this rule until adequate medical resources are on scene.

Tip

Blast Site as Crime Scene

The blast site will be considered a crime scene until proven otherwise, which serves to complicate an already difficult response. Victims may have pieces of evidence lodged in their bodies. The law enforcement agency with jurisdiction must keep this in mind and balance the needs of patient treatment versus preserving evidence for the eventual prosecution of the perpetrator should the blast be proven to be a criminal act.

Less Lethal Munitions

The US military defines non-lethal weapons (NLWs) as weapons that are designed to disable personnel, weapons, supplies, or equipment in such a way that death or severe permanent disability to personnel are unlikely.

No physical action against another person can ever be completely without risk. This basic realization led civilian law enforcement authorities to abandon terms such as *nonlethal* or *less-than-lethal*, both of which suggest otherwise. Despite the name changes, few law enforcement terms have continued to cause so much controversy or remain as misunderstood as the term *less lethal*. It must be clearly understood that, regardless of terminology, less lethal does not imply lack of risk of permanent injury or death, simply an attempt to minimize these risks.

Once limited to civil unrest and large-scale disturbances, less-lethal munitions are increasingly being deployed as an integral part of the departmental use of force continuum at the patrol level (**Figure 4**). Medical outcome data on less-lethal deployments remain limited. The National Tactical Officers Association (NTOA) maintains a voluntary database on less-lethal munitions. This database provides some insight into weapon systems, deployment circumstances, and subsequent outcomes. Between 1995 and 2008, a total of 353 incidents were reported. A lack of injuries was specifically noted in 182 incidents. Twenty-six (7.4%) subjects died, although the cause of death was not always directly attributable to the less-lethal munition.

Less-lethal munitions may be divided into three broad categories:

1. Chemical munitions/riot control agents (RCA)
2. Specialty impact munitions (SIM)
3. Conducted energy devices (CED)

Each general category has specific tactical advantages, limitations, and health effects.

Figure 4 Less-lethal munitions are increasingly being deployed as an integral part of the departmental use of force continuum at the patrol level.

CHEMICAL MUNITIONS

The history of chemical munitions dates back to 2000 BCE and the use of a pepper-based agent in wars between India and China. In 423 BCE, allies of Sparta captured an Athenian fort during the Peloponnesian War through the use of directed coal, sulfur, and pitch smoke. Modern less-lethal chemical munitions can be classified as lacrimators (tear gas), inflammatory agents (pepper spray), and incapacitating/calmative agents.

The two most commonly encountered lacrimator agents are chloroacetophenone (CN), Mace (Color Code Red), and Orthochlorobenzalmalonitrile (CS) (Color Code Blue). Initially developed to manage civil unrest, and therefore called riot control agents (RCAs), these agents are also deployed during tactical operations, especially those involving barricaded suspects. Although both agents are commonly referred to as tear gas because of the intense tearing (**lacrimation**) they cause, neither is a gas. Both are actually heat stable, low volatility solids at room temperature and are dispersed either as fine solid particles or in solution, either through pyrotechnics (canisters, grenades) or through spray devices. When using canisters, the chemical agents are often disseminated with a pyrotechnic base. This allows the use of inert pyrotechnic smoke grenades to determine drift direction prior to deploying active munitions.

Oleoresin capsicum (OC, pepper spray, Color Code Orange) is the prototypical inflammatory agent. Originally developed as a RCA, OC is increasingly used by law enforcement agencies as an intermediate force option, typically positioned between empty hand techniques and deadly force on the use of force continuum. The active ingredient of OC is capsaicin, a naturally occurring compound found in hot pepper species, including *Capsicum annuum* and *Capsicum frutescenes*. Standard law enforcement OC formulations have a capsaicin concentration of 0.1% to 1.33%. This translates into a Scoville Heat Unit (SHU) value ranging from 500,000 to 2,000,000 SHU.

OC is typically deployed as a liquid preparation, in either an oil- or water/emulsifier-based formulation. The most common delivery system is the duty aerosol projector, although other systems (including high-volume units and paint-ball based platforms) are occasionally encountered.

Tip

Calmative Agent Case Study

Incapacitating/calmative agents are not currently in use by US law enforcement, although military organizations continue to investigate their use. A cautionary case study worth noting is the 2002 Nord-Ost (Moscow Theater) siege. On October 23, 2002, approximately 40 to 50 Chechen separatists seized 850 hostages at the House of Culture. On October 26, 2002, a calmative agent was introduced into the theater in an attempt to incapacitate the terrorists prior to a hostage rescue attempt. The identity of the calmative agent has never publicly been disclosed, but, based upon toxicologic studies of foreign nationals, is believed to have been a mixture of the ultra-potent narcotic carfentanyl and the anesthetic agent halothane [6]. 127 hostages died during the hostage rescue, the vast majority due to the effects of the calmative agent. Another 650 survivors required hospitalization. Nearly two weeks after the rescue, 67 hostages and 9 rescuers remained hospitalized, five of whom remained in critical condition.

SPECIALTY IMPACT MUNITIONS

As the name implies, **specialty impact munitions (SIMs)** are designed to incapacitate by direct impact against the intended target. The use of SIMs for civil unrest dates back to the 1960s and the development of plastic and rubber bullets. These older munitions have seen widespread use in Northern Ireland, the Arab-Israeli conflict, and South Africa. Although not intended to kill, these early agents are associated with significant potential for severe injury and occasionally death. In one study, a total of 151 patients suffered 201 injuries; two died as a direct result of the SIM. As a consequence, although considered an intermediate use of force option, these agents are often classified as a higher-level force option than other less-lethal munitions, and just below deadly force.

In modern US law enforcement, the most commonly deployed SIMs are rubber batons, foam batons, and bean-bag rounds (**Figure 5**). SIMs may be classified as either low-energy or high-energy. High-energy munitions are typically employed against a single subject, especially in high threat level incidents (eg, armed suspect, suicide by cop) where there is need to rapidly yet safely incapacitate the subject to effect an arrest. These munitions may also be classified in terms of targeting. Direct fire munitions are designed to be fired at the subject, whereas indirect fire munitions are not intended to be fired directly at the subject, but rather to strike the individual after skipping off another object (typically the ground) directly in front of the intended target.

In deploying SIMs, one critical element for both efficacy and safety is the location of shot placement. Modern specialty impact munition design has allowed for increased target accuracy over specified ranges. Target impact areas may be divided into three zones, based on anatomic location (**Figure 6**). It must be understood that, especially when firing at moving targets, sudden movements may result in unintended impact in a non-targeted zone.

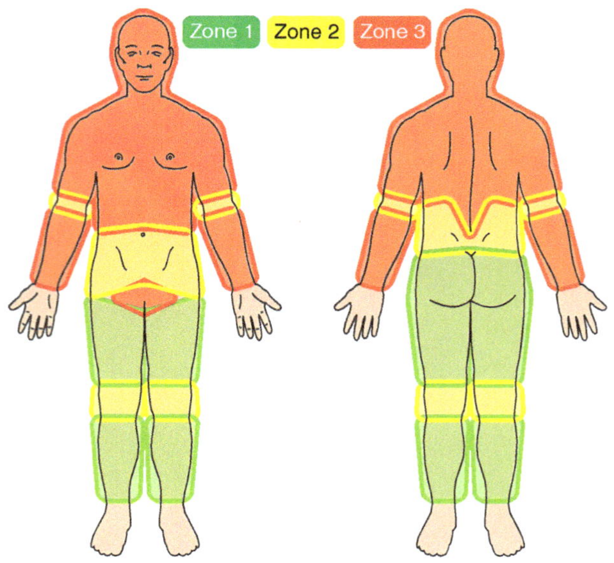

Figure 6 Target impact areas may be divided into three zones based on anatomic location.

Zone 1 (green) has the greatest amount of muscle mass (and therefore the greatest ability to absorb impact energy) and the least number of vital structures. Impacts in Zone 1 are least likely to result in serious or permanent damage; however, they should be capable of producing pain compliance. Zone 1 includes the buttocks, thigh, and calf, and specifically excludes the groin area. Zone 2 (yellow) has less muscle mass and therefore increased potential for injury when struck. Zone 2 includes the lower torso (abdomen, back) and joints (knees). Impacts in Zone 3 (red) have the greatest potential for death or serious injury, and therefore should be avoided whenever possible. Deliberate targeting of Zone 3 locations should be considered only when the threat level has escalated to a point where deadly force would be indicated. Zone 3 includes the head, chest, groin, and spine. The shoulders and arms are unique because they are predominantly skeletal structures (similar to Zone 1), and may be the only available target. However, they have relatively limited muscle density (like zone 2) and therefore have a higher injury potential. Due to anatomic location, arm and shoulder impacts are more likely to result in unintended Zone 3 strikes.

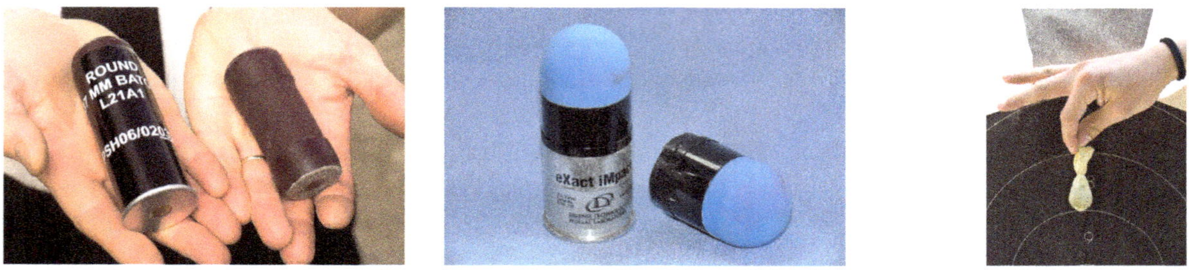

A. B. C.

Figure 5 Common SIMs used in US law enforcement. **A.** Rubber baton. **B.** Foam baton. **C.** Bean bag rounds.

CONDUCTED ENERGY DEVICES

Although credited with saving hundreds of lives, no piece of modern police technology has created so much controversy as the conducted energy device (CED). These devices have been shown to decrease both officer and suspect injuries by up to 80%. However, ongoing concern surrounds an increasing number of deaths temporally associated with CED use. A CED is designed to disrupt a person's central nervous system through electrical energy.

The most common devices currently in use by US law enforcement agencies are the Taser International M26 and X26 and the Stinger Systems S-200 and S-200 AT. Each uses a cartridge-based system to deploy two probes a predetermined maximal distance based on wire length. Contact of both probes into the subject allows completion of an electrical circuit and delivery of current to the target.

Taser (Thomas A. Swift's Electric Rifle) devices have been commercially available since 1974. First- and second-generation Taser systems affected only the sensory motor system and were designed to gain suspect compliance through painful stimuli. As such they were not technically CEDs. In contrast, newer generation systems affect both the sensory and motor nervous systems, through a process Taser International refers to as neuromuscular incapacitation (NMI), and are therefore true CEDs. Taser International reports more than 14,200 law enforcement agencies in more than 40 countries currently deploy Taser products, including 29 of the 33 largest US cities.

Both Taser and Stinger use proprietary waveform technologies to deliver their energy to the target. Much press has surrounded the fact that third- and fourth-generation Taser systems have a peak voltage of 50,000 volts. Both Taser and Stinger systems operate at relatively low amperage, however, and therefore low power output (**Table 3**).

ASSESSMENT OF LESS-LETHAL MUNITION INJURY

By definition, less lethal munitions were developed to incapacitate without a high likelihood of permanent disability or death. Despite this, individual subjects have been injured or killed. The primary assessment of any subject after less lethal deployment should follow a standard trauma approach, concentrating on airway, breathing, circulation, and disability (mental status and brief neurologic evaluation). After identifying and treating immediate life threats, assessment should focus on the management of obvious trauma and a search for hidden injury. In the setting of blunt trauma, c-spine immobilization should be performed as indicated.

Any direct subject contact should start with an evaluation of scene safety. Take appropriate steps to optimize the tactical environment for patient assessment and care. Because of the potential for loss of situational awareness, the LER should ideally not assess the subject in the absence of other personnel to provide immediate back-up. Responders should use standard precautions, including gloves and eye protection.

In many circumstances, people are subjected to less lethal munitions because they pose a threat to LERs or the general public. After less lethal deployment, they may remain violent and combative, possibly because of substance abuse or mental illness. These patients may continue to present a risk

Table 3

Comparison of Characteristics of Commonly Deployed Conducted Energy Devices

Device	Range (feet)	Voltage (peak)	Voltage (into load)	Pulse rate per second	Current	Energy per pulse	Energy at capacitor
Advanced TASER M26	15-35	50,000	N/A	15-20	3.6 mA	1.76 J	N/A
TASER X26	15-35	50,000	1200	19	2.1 mA	0.36 J	N/A
Stinger S-200AT	22	51,000	1000	13	1.5 mA	N/A	2.0 J

to the responders. Responders should also be aware of possible medical conditions that might cause abnormal behavior leading to the initial law enforcement contact (eg, diabetic hypoglycemia).

Special Populations

Less Lethal Munitions in Pregnancy

There is little medical information regarding the effects of less-lethal munitions on the pregnant subject. In a single published case, a 12-week pregnant woman miscarried 1 week after receiving a Taser deployment. It must be noted that this was reported in 1992, and therefore did not involve a CED. The risk of modern CEDs on pregnancy has yet to be determined. However, the simple act of falling as a consequence of less lethal deployment may increase risk to both the fetus and mother. As such, any pregnant subject who receives a less lethal deployment should be transported for definitive medical evaluation and fetal monitoring.

TYPES OF ILLNESS OR INJURY

Injury From Lacrimator Agents

The main clinical effects of lacrimator agents are pain, burning, and irritation of exposed mucous membranes and skin. The eye is most sensitive to the effects of these agents, resulting in profuse tearing (lacrimation), associated blepharospasm (blinking, involuntary eye closure), and irritation. Because these agents are actually fine particles, they may become embedded on the surface of the eye, resulting in corneal abrasions. Contact with the nose and mouth results in rhinorrhea (runny nose) and salivation. Respiratory effects include burning and irritation of the airways, with resultant bronchorrhea (mucous/phlegm production), coughing, and a sensation of chest tightness and difficulty breathing. Despite this sensation, studies have shown minimal changes in pulmonary function tests immediately after exposure.

Skin effects are typically limited to irritation and redness. Rarely, and usually in conditions of high temperature, high humidity, and high agent concentration, blisters similar to second-degree burns have been noted. The net effect of these agents is to cause discomfort, panic, disorientation, and confusion without long-term consequences.

Both CN and CS have high safety ratios, reflecting a large difference between the concentration of agent required to produce intolerable symptoms and the lethal agent concentration. CS is a more potent yet less toxic agent than CN. Despite the chemical designation CN, chloroacetophenone is not cyanide. Deaths have occurred from CN deployment, usually after deploying excessive concentrations in enclosed spaces. No deaths secondary to CS have been reported.

OC differs from CN and CS by causing actual tissue inflammation rather than simply irritation. As an inflammatory agent, it causes localized redness, swelling, heat, and pain. The two primary target organs of OC are the eye and the upper respiratory tract. Eye effects include pain, dryness, and blepharospasm, with resultant temporary visual impairment. Corneal abrasions have been reported. Subsequent evaluation suggests that the isopropanol vehicle, rather than the OC itself, was responsible. Inflammation of the respiratory system causes nose, mouth, and throat burning; rhinorrhea; and a sensation of shortness of breath or difficulty breathing, typically manifesting as coughing. These physical effects result in additional psychological effects, including anxiety and fear. Coupled with direct stimulation of nerve fibers and subsequent increased pain perception, the net result is improved suspect compliance.

It has been suggested that, especially in smokers and asthmatics, the inflammatory effects of OC may precipitate acute respiratory distress, and possibly death. More recent studies suggest that sudden in-custody deaths associated with OC are unrelated to the OC and likely reflect an underlying excited delirium state.

Injury From SIMs

Injuries related to SIMs can be divided into two categories: blunt or penetrating. Penetrating trauma is unintended, frequently catastrophic, and may be due to several factors. The design of the SIM may make it more likely to penetrate even if appropriately deployed. Many manufacturers have ceased production of square bag bean-bag rounds due to the potential for penetration if struck by a leading edge, switching instead to fin- or drag-stabilized rounds. Similarly, equipment failure may result in failure of sabot separation and subsequent penetration. Lastly, excessive kinetic energy, target distance, shot placement, and suspect clothing may all contribute to the type of penetration. Penetrating trauma should be managed like any other gunshot wound and requires emergent evaluation. Penetrating trauma to the head, neck, or torso has high potential for severe injury and/or death. Case reports describe eye impacts with subsequent penetration into the skull cavity, brain injury, and death.

More commonly, SIMs are associated with blunt trauma. The objective of SIM deployment is pain compliance, up to the point of incapacitation. This desired effect is by definition achieved through blunt trauma. In the majority of circumstances (especially involving the extremities), the blunt trauma is minimal and temporary. Most often, it involves contusions and abrasions. Lacerations and fractures can occur as well and may require operative interventions. Impact strikes in Zone 2 may result in blunt abdominal trauma, including solid and hollow organ injuries, and soft tissue injuries. Chest impact has resulted in pulmonary contusion. Although rare, commotio cordis (sudden cardiac death from blunt impact to the heart, resulting in ventricular fibrillation) has been reported with SIM use.

Eye trauma is the most frequently reported significant injury associated with SIM use. Although a potential problem with any SIM, particular concern exists for paintball-type munitions. The size of the paintball projectile is such that it is able to avoid the protection provided by the bones of the orbit and strike the eye directly. Specific injuries have ranged from hyphema to retinal detachment to ruptured globe. After treatment, 43% of patients had documented visual acuities of 20/200 or worse.

Injury From CEDs

The majority of CED deployments result in minimal and nonpermanent injuries, predominantly related to probe insertion. In one patient, probe penetration resulted in a pneumothorax. Penetration of a probe at sensitive sites (eg, eyes, groin, neck, female breast, or near a major blood vessel) may result in permanent injury. Intracranial penetration has resulted in seizures. In these circumstances, the probe should be secured in place and the subject transported for definitive medical evaluation.

Any subject receiving a CED deployment may stiffen and fall, sustaining injuries. Running subjects may fall with increased momentum and inability to protect themselves. Deaths have occurred when deploying CEDs on subjects standing on elevated platforms who have subsequently fallen. Any such person needs to be evaluated for blunt trauma. Because of the nature of energy delivery, CED use on subjects standing in water should not result in electrocution, but may result in drowning.

Animal studies have demonstrated metabolic abnormalities associated with CED use. In human subjects, respiratory and metabolic parameters (eg, serum pH, potassium) have been measured and do not appear significantly affected. However, these studies typically use single, 5-second deployments in healthy (ie, nonintoxicated, nonpsychotic) subjects, and may not reflect real-world deployment realities.

Although extremely rare, the primary medical concern surrounding CEDs involves the potential for the energy discharge to affect the heart and cause sudden cardiac death. CEDs are not biomedical devices, were never intended to treat a disease state, and therefore do not require FDA review. Data on cardiac safety are mixed, although the trend is toward safety. The National Institute of Justice has concluded that there are risks associated with CED use, but that there is no conclusive evidence that there is risk of serious injury or death.

The majority of animal studies have failed to demonstrate induction of lethal ventricular arrhythmia. However, some researchers have been able to generate fatal ventricular fibrillation in pig studies. No potentially fatal arrhythmia has been noted in human studies. A case report involving a 53-year-old subject with a permanent pacemaker who received two CED deployments demonstrated two episodes of ventricular myocardial capture related to CED discharges. Both were self-limited, and terminated at the end of the CED deployment cycle. No shock was delivered because the rapid heart rate was limited to the period of CED activation. In both of these high-risk cardiac patients, no sustained or delayed arrhythmia was noted.

If CEDs were responsible for inducing sudden cardiac death due to direct electrical stimulation of the heart, one would expect the effect to be immediate. However, sudden in-custody deaths temporally associated with CED deployment typically are delayed at least 5 minutes from the period of CED activation, suggesting a different etiology for the death. The majority of these deaths occur in subjects presenting with signs and symptoms of excited delirium syndrome.

MANAGEMENT OF MUNITION EXPOSURE

In most cases, symptoms of chemical munition exposure resolve between 15 and 60 minutes after removal from the source. As a consequence, treatment of exposed individuals is largely supportive, focusing on decontamination to prevent further exposure and management of eye and respiratory complaints. Less than 1% of exposed people have prolonged or severe symptoms directly related to the chemical agent, requiring formal medical evaluation. When necessary, such evaluation should focus on eye care and respiratory issues. Eyes should be carefully flushed with water or saline solution; ophthalmology consultation may be required. Pulmonary inflammation (especially with wheezing) should be managed similarly to an asthma exacerbation, with supplemental oxygen as needed and inhaled bronchodilators. The use of corticosteroids specifically for chemical agent-induced bronchospasm remains unstudied, but may be indicated, especially for inflammatory agents such as OC.

After deployment of chemical munitions, some form of decontamination is usually necessary. In the case of lacrimator agents, decontamination may simply involve removal from the source of exposure to fresh air, ideally with a slight breeze, to disperse remaining particulates. Copious amounts of water should be effective at removing non-oil–based products. If large supplies of water are not available, dry decontamination using paper towels and fans may suffice. For oil-based products, such as OC, anecdotal reports have suggested the use of diluted condensed milk or diluted mixtures of baby shampoo and sugar; these are believed to act as emulsifying agents, removing the oily base from the skin surface. LERs should always follow orders from medical direction. Failure to decontaminate has resulted in large-scale secondary contamination in hospital environments.

As a general rule, any subject struck by an SIM will require a medical screening examination to evaluate for the presence of significant trauma, including both obvious penetration and less obvious blunt trauma. SIM exposure frequently requires hospital evaluation and observation, especially in the setting of Zone 2 or 3 impact. LERs should plan to have an automated external defibrillator (AED) available or advanced life support standing by to deal with ventricular dysrhythmias that may occur after a patient has been stuck in the chest by an SIM. Ideally, prompt defibrillation capability should be available when deploying a specialty impact munition. However, this may not be tactically feasible in all settings, particularly those involving rapidly developing civil unrest.

CED darts should be treated as a biohazard, just as you would handle a contaminated needle. For the most part, probes may be removed on scene by approved personnel using standard techniques. Sites of probe penetration should be cleaned and dressed, and the probes examined to ensure that they remain intact.

The majority of deaths related to CED use occurred within 1 hour of deployment, typically within 5 minutes. In adult patients presenting to the emergency department with normal electrocardiogram, there is no need for further cardiac evaluation. Although controversy still surrounds the potential for induction of sudden cardiac death, current data do not support the routine deployment of an AED on every potential CED use call. Tactically, such a deployment may not be feasible.

SPECIAL CONSIDERATIONS FOR LAW ENFORCEMENT

From a tactical standpoint, the ability to deliver lethal force if necessary should always be available when deploying less-lethal munitions, especially during high threat-level incidents (eg, armed suspect). LERs should be prepared to deal with this eventuality.

By their very nature, less-lethal munitions have the potential to affect not only the intended target, but also those around the target, including law enforcement and medical personnel. This may occur through direct exposure (eg, from a misdirected deployment or from sudden unexpected changes in wind direction when using chemical munitions), from secondary-contamination through exposure to chemically contaminated individuals, or from failure of personal protective equipment (PPE). In one case, an officer suffered a seizure after being struck in the back of the head by his partner's CED while pursuing a suspect. LERs must also prepare for the possibility of multiple victims.

The primary decision regarding the need to deploy chemical munitions is tactical. A key medical question when performing a medical risk assessment involves who else might be exposed to such agents, especially in terms of high-risk groups (eg, very young, very old, chronically ill, developmentally disabled). For example, the deployment around or into an extended care facility containing elderly, oxygen-dependent people may be tactically necessary and appropriate. Prior to deployment, consider how multiple victims with the potential for significant cardiopulmonary disease will be managed.

An additional concern to LERs when deploying chemical munitions is the use of PPE, which limits sensory perception (particularly vision and hearing), increases the work of breathing, and increases the heat stress on LERs, all of which may decrease performance effectiveness. For LERs who do not regularly train in a PPE environment, the constricting effects of gas masks may also result in a sensation of claustrophobia.

Several national police organizations have developed guidelines for CED deployment, which include medical recommendations. Agencies should be aware of these guidelines in determining their own medical response to CED deployments. The Police Executive Research Forum CED guidelines state that anyone who has been exposed to a CED should be monitored regularly while in police custody. The International Association of Chiefs of Police recommends that departments provide medical attention and/or evaluation after CED use and suggested periods for monitoring in-custody subjects involved in CED incidents.

Similarly, many SIM product manuals recommend formal medical evaluation of all subjects after deployment. Departments should be aware of these printed requirements and develop appropriate policies to address these demands.

CONCLUSION

As a LER, you will have to respond to your needs and the needs of your partners or others during hostile scenarios ranging from brawls and riots to high-risk warrant service. Your personal safety, although frequently compromised, is of the utmost concern. LERs face threats not only from environmental conditions and the scene itself but also from exposure to infectious substances, including the patient's body fluids. Taking small steps to limit your exposure, such as wearing protective gloves and eye protection, will greatly benefit you.

As soon as LERs are free from law enforcement duties required to stabilize hostile or dangerous scenes they should use their agency's protocols for care under fire and tactical medicine.

Trauma is a common occurrence at incidents involving law enforcement. It is important for you to understand the special trauma situations of explosions and blasts, ballistics, and less-lethal munitions. LERs need a solid understanding of the specific traumatic injuries these mechanisms can inflict and the subsequent implications of these injuries. This information can then be relayed to healthcare providers to ensure appropriate continuity of care.

Prep Kit

READY FOR REVIEW

- Gunshot wounds comprise a substantial portion of trauma seen in urban emergency centers. Furthermore, the use of SWAT teams for situations deemed too hostile for uniformed patrol response makes it even more likely that the LER will encounter gunshot wounds.
- Injury suffered from ballistic trauma varies based on many factors, most notably the weight and velocity of the projectile and the anatomic location it traverses.
- Characteristics of a gunshot wound include surface features that may be useful in the reconstruction of a crime and trial.
- Inherent to the concept of ballistics is protection from ballistic threats. At its most basic level, protection consists of the concept of concealment versus cover.
- When a handgun bullet strikes body armor, it is caught in a meshwork of fibers. These fibers absorb and disperse the impact energy that is transmitted to the vest from the bullet.
- Blast scenes present a hazardous operational environment. These scenes require LERs to focus all their cognitive abilities to give themselves the best chance to avoid becoming a casualty.
- To maximize personal safety, LERs must begin their scene size-up well back from the approximate site of the explosion, regardless of the reactions from bystanders.
- Although the need to determine scene safety and keep LERs safe is logical, the reality of assisting at such a scene is complicated by two major factors: casualties and bystanders.
- Blast injuries follow specific patterns that are categorized as primary, secondary, tertiary, and quaternary.
- Once limited to civil unrest and large-scale disturbances, less-lethal munitions are increasingly being deployed as an integral part of the departmental use of force continuum at the patrol level.
- Less-lethal munitions may be divided into three broad categories:
  - Chemical munitions/riot control agents (RCA)
  - Specialty impact munitions (SIM)
  - Conducted energy devices (CED)
- By definition, less-lethal munitions were developed to incapacitate without a high likelihood of permanent disability or death. Despite this, individual subjects have been injured or killed.
- The main clinical effects of lacrimator agents are pain, burning, and irritation of exposed mucous membranes and skin.
- Injuries related to SIMs can be divided into two categories—blunt or penetrating—with blunt being more common.
- The majority of CED deployments result in minimal and nonpermanent injuries, predominantly related to probe insertion.
- From a tactical standpoint, the ability to deliver lethal force if necessary should always be available when deploying less-lethal munitions, especially during high threat-level incidents.

VITAL VOCABULARY

ballistics The science of mechanics that deals with the flight, behavior, and effects of projectiles.

concealment Visual shield from a threat, whether or not physically protected from the threat.

cover Physical protection from a threat.

lacrimation Tearing.

specialty impact munitions (SIMs) Munitions designed to incapacitate by direct force impact against the intended target.

terminal ballistics The study of the behavior of a projectile when it hits its target.

CHECK YOUR KNOWLEDGE

1. According to the START method of triage, which color represents a patient who is not breathing?
   - A. Red
   - B. Green
   - C. Yellow
   - D. Black
2. Which of the following is NOT an effect of ballistic trauma?
   - A. Temporary wound cavity
   - B. Permanent wound cavity
   - C. Mushroom expansion
   - D. Sonic wave
3. In the START method of triage, a patient who is able to answer questions is given the highest priority for treatment.
   - A. True
   - B. False
4. Which of the following is not considered a chemical munition?
   - A. CS
   - B. OC
   - C. SIM
   - D. CN
5. The term *terminal ballistics* refers to:
   - A. fatal gunshot wounds.
   - B. the interaction of a projectile with the lands and grooves of the barrel.
   - C. the infective properties of a bacteria-laden bullet.
   - D. the study of the behavior of a projectile when it hits its target.

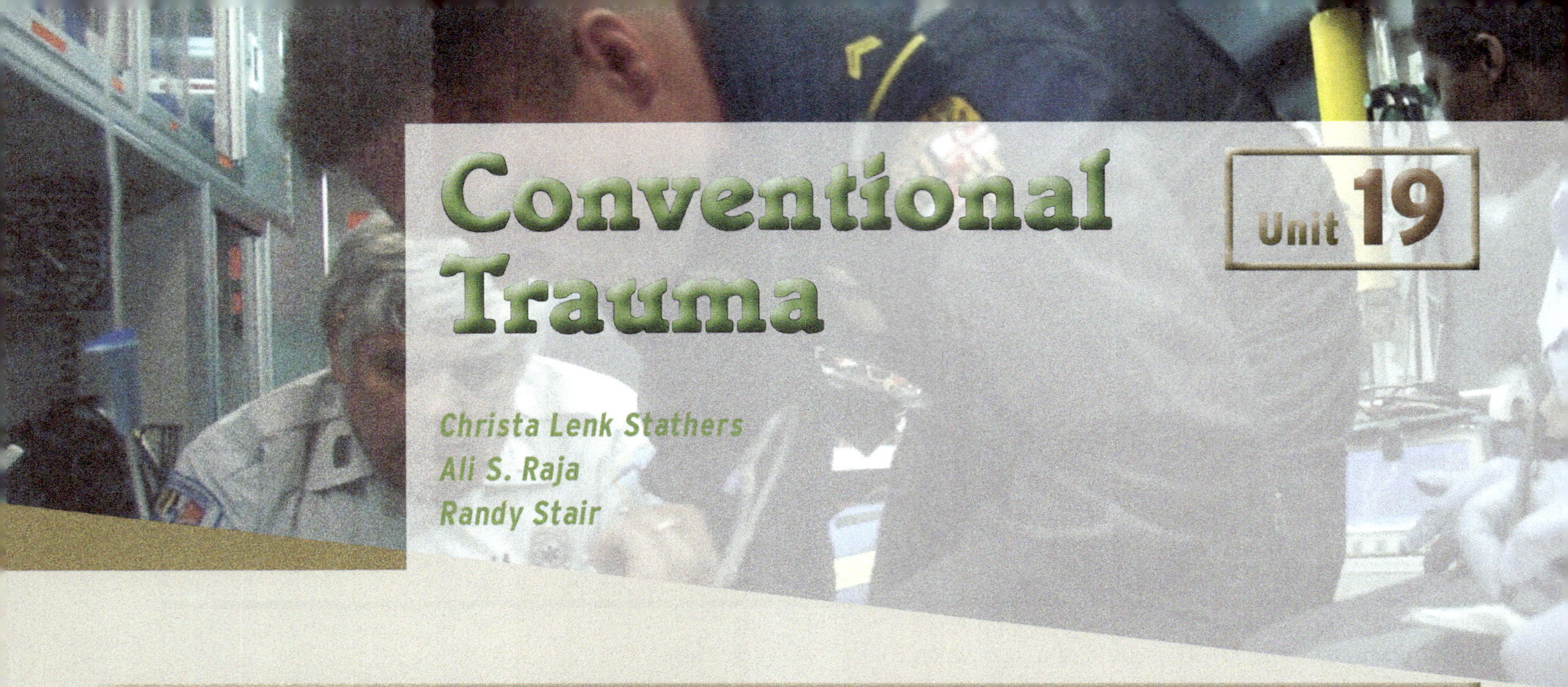

Conventional Trauma

Unit 19

Christa Lenk Stathers
Ali S. Raja
Randy Stair

Law Enforcement Responder Objectives

Injuries and Wounds

- Identify and provide the initial steps to stabilize and manage a patient with the following injuries:
  - Fracture (p 354)
  - Dislocation (p 354)
  - Sprain or strain (p 354)
  - Amputation (p 354)
  - Avulsion (p 356)
  - Abrasion (p 356)
  - Laceration (p 356)
  - Penetration or puncture wound (p 358)
  - Impaled object (pp 358–359)
  - Burn (pp 360–362)
- Differentiate between an open and a closed fracture. (p 354)
- List the distinguishing characteristics of a fracture and a dislocation. (p 354)
- Determine the severity of an injury and the need for additional medical assistance. (pp 351–362)
- Distinguish among superficial, partial-thickness, and full-thickness burns. (pp 360–361)
- Estimate the extent of a burn using the rule of nines. (pp 360–362)

Head, Neck, and Sensory Injuries

- Describe the anatomy of the head, face, and neck. (pp 362–364, 367–368)
- Recognize the signs and symptoms of head, face, and neck injuries. (pp 365–366, 368–369)
- Identify the major mechanisms of spinal injury. (p 364)
- Describe the emergency medical care of patients with head, neck, and sensory injuries. (pp 369–373)
- Demonstrate how to stabilize a possible spine injury. (pp 369–370)
- Manage an unresponsive patient with possible spinal injury until help arrives. (pp 369–370)
- Discuss special considerations for law enforcement responders during missions. (pp 373–374)
- Demonstrate how to remove a tactical helmet while maintaining spine stabilization. (pp 373–374, 375)

Chest and Abdominal Trauma

- Describe the anatomy and physiology of the normal chest and abdomen. (pp 374–376)
- Explain how to assess the chest and abdomen for injuries. (pp 377–379)
- Identify common chest and abdominal injuries. (p 377)
- Explain how to manage chest and abdominal injuries. (pp 377–381)
- Describe age-related variations and how they may affect chest and abdominal injuries. (p 379)

National EMS Education Standard Competencies

Trauma

Uses simple knowledge to recognize and manage life threats based on assessment findings for an acutely injured patient while awaiting additional emergency medical response.

Orthopaedic Trauma

Recognition and management of

- Open fractures (p 354)
- Closed fractures (p 354)
- Dislocations (p 354)
- Amputations (p 354)

Soft-Tissue Trauma

Recognition and management of

- Wounds (pp 356–360)
- Burns (pp 360–361)
  - Electrical (pp 361–362)
  - Chemical (pp 361–362)
  - Thermal (pp 361–362, 371–372)
- Chemicals in the eye and on the skin (pp 361–362, 371–372)

Head, Face, Neck, and Spine Trauma

Recognition and management of

- Life threats (pp 362–374)
- Spine trauma (pp 362–366)

Chest Trauma

Recognition and management of

- Blunt versus penetrating mechanisms (pp 377–381)
- Open chest wound (pp 377–381)
- Impaled object (pp 377–381)

Abdominal and Genitourinary Trauma

Recognition and management of

- Blunt versus penetrating mechanisms (pp 377–381)
- Evisceration (pp 377–381)
- Impaled object (pp 377–381)

Medicine

Recognizes and manages life threats based on assessment findings of a patient with a medical emergency while awaiting additional emergency response.

Diseases of the Eyes, Ears, Nose, and Throat

- Recognition and management of nosebleed (pp 372–373)

Injuries and Wounds

As an emergency responder, you likely will see a great number of extremity and soft-tissue injuries during your career. These are probably the most commonly seen injuries throughout all levels of law enforcement. There are many categories of trauma, ranging from mild to life threatening. Law enforcement responders (LERs) must take into account that they may see injuries in a hostile setting where care-under-fire techniques and tactical considerations will apply. The LER must make the distinction between the tactical environment and the conventional setting. It is appropriate practice for the LER to take the setting of the injury into account in relation to the immediate care response. If your partner crushes his thumb in the door jamb of your cruiser at the end of your shift in the police yard, the standard medical response will apply. The approach to treatment would be different, however, if your partner were to crush his thumb in a door during a high-risk warrant service.

Most open injuries require treatment. In some cases, simply cleaning and dressing a wound will suffice. In other cases, the situation will require the intervention of emergency medical services (EMS) and a surgeon in an operating room. It is important to be able to recognize the types of injuries, differentiate among the treatments, and know when to seek additional medical attention.

Regardless of the severity of the injury, you must minimize the risk of infection, control bleeding, and prevent further injury. Consider the patient's risk of losing consciousness; developing breathing issues; or going into cardiac arrest from blood loss, shock, or damage to internal organs. Often you will be required to assess the patient's mental status, breathing, and circulation continuously until EMS arrives. You must also practice standard precautions to protect yourself, your partners, your family, and your patients.

This unit introduces different types of soft-tissue and extremity injuries and assists you in handling these commonly seen emergencies. In many cases, seeking timely and appropriate medical treatment can save lives and preserve the healthy functioning of limbs.

ANATOMY AND PHYSIOLOGY

The skin protects the underlying bones, organs, and vessels by providing a barrier against infectious organisms and insulating against extremes in temperature. The three layers of the skin are as follows (**Figure 1**):

- The epidermal layer (**epidermis**), which is the outermost layer
- The dermal layer (**dermis**), the middle layer, is where skin cells grow and most of the structures (hair follicles, glands, blood vessels, nerves) in the skin exist.
- The subcutaneous layer (**hypodermis**), which is mostly fatty tissue

Any damage to the skin provides a possible entry point into the body for infection, which can be detrimental in and of itself, without major injury. Therefore, it is important to treat the injury and also to prevent contamination of any wounds. **Fractures** can disrupt skin integrity if the fractured bone ends protrude through the skin or tear nerves or blood vessels. It is important to take precautions to limit further injury to the surrounding tissues or structures.

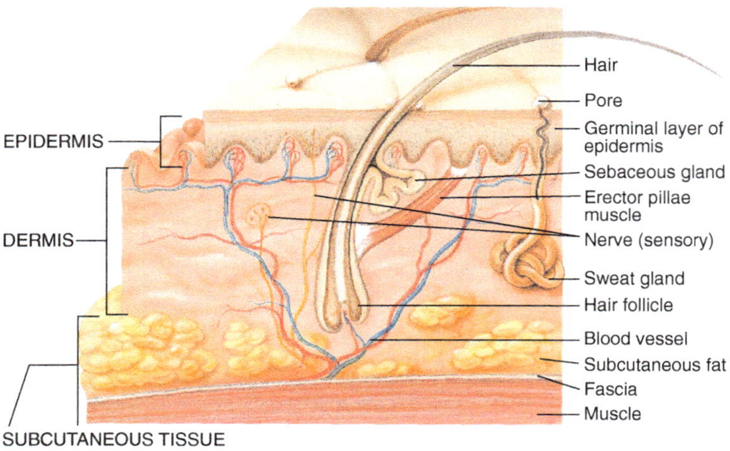

Figure 1 The skin.

Although many soft-tissue injuries appear grotesque or severe, they are often relatively minor or moderate. A common mistake at the scene of an incident is to become focused on the amount of blood, while failing to realize that the patient has an immediately life-threatening injury. Critical injuries with compromised airway, breathing, or circulation always take priority over non-life-threatening wounds and fractures.

Tip

Distracting Injuries

A common mistake at the scene of an incident is to become focused on the amount of blood, while failing to realize that the patient has an immediately life-threatening injury. Remember your ABCs during non-tactical emergencies. Compromised airway, breathing, or circulation always takes priority over non-life-threatening wounds and fractures. Many different tactical mnemonics are used when involved in a care-under-fire scenario. Depending on your medical direction, you may use one of the following:

- MARCH (**M**assive hemorrhage, **A**irway, **R**espirations, **C**irculation, and **H**ead injuries)
- CAB (**C**irculation, **A**irway, and **B**reathing)
- XABC (e**X**sanguination, **A**irway, **B**reathing, and **C**irculation)

MECHANISM OF INJURY

As an emergency medical responder (EMR) who is also a law enforcement officer, you will often find yourself in a variety of roles. When you are involved at the scene of a trauma incident, understanding the mechanism of injury (MOI) allows you to care for the patient better.

Mechanisms of injury are directly influenced by the laws of physics and the body's ability to respond to the absorption of energy during an event. Mechanisms of injury come in three forms: direct force, indirect force, and twisting force (**Figure 2**).

Direct force injuries occur when energy is directly absorbed by some part of the body. Examples include the entry and path of a bullet, a fist hitting someone's jaw, and a passenger in a car striking a knee on the dashboard.

Indirect force injuries result from what can be thought of as a secondary release of

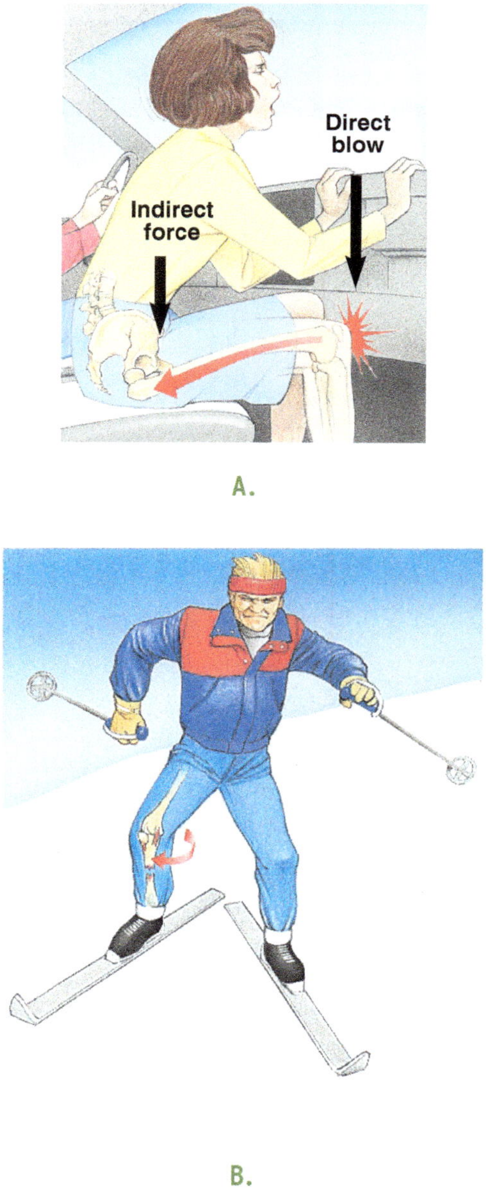

Figure 2 Three types of mechanisms of injury cause musculoskeletal injuries. **A.** Direct force and indirect force. **B.** Twisting force.

energy. The energy is transferred or transmitted along a path to the point of injury. An example is a person who falls and reaches out to brace the fall. The energy of the fall transfers up the arm and causes the clavicle to fracture. Another example is a fractured pelvis sustained when a car passenger strikes a knee on the dashboard. The knee sustains a direct force injury, but the energy of the impact is also transferred up the femur, causing an indirect force injury to the pelvis.

Twisting injuries are commonly seen in sports activities. Participating in activities where one's body is forced beyond its normal limits can result in stretching, tearing, or fracture—for example, runners or skiers who twist a knee when hitting a hole or trying to change directions suddenly.

GENERAL EXTREMITY AND SOFT-TISSUE INJURIES

Assessment

Scene safety is a priority with extremity and soft-tissue injuries. Securing any persons and weapons involved may supersede taking care of the patient. Regardless of the extent of an injury, situational awareness takes priority, as does your safety, which includes standard precautions. Once you are confident that the scene is secure and you are not at risk, your next priority should be the patient.

Once you are confident that there is no major external bleeding and the patient is breathing and able to maintain his or her own airway, then you can move on to thoroughly evaluate the injured area(s). A complete assessment requires you to check four things in an injured extremity: pulse, capillary refill, movement, and sensation.

Immediately verify that the patient has a pulse. Evaluate the pulse for presence, rate (normal, fast, or slow), rhythm (regular or irregular), and strength (strong or weak). Next, check the capillary refill of the tissue. Simply take your thumb and press on the tissue, fingernail bed, or toenail bed and look for signs that blood is still flowing to the tissue. The absence of such signs could indicate poor or absent circulation, which can quickly lead to shock.

An evaluation of movement and sensation can be done while you check for capillary refill. As you press with your thumb, ask the patient to identify where you have touched. If the patient identifies the location correctly, ask the patient to wiggle or move that area for you. You can also have the patient grip or push against your hand to demonstrate strength.

Follow the steps in **Skill Drill 1** to evaluate circulation, sensation, and movement in an injured extremity:

1. **Pulse.** Feel the pulse distal to the point of injury. If the patient has an upper extremity injury, check the radial (wrist) pulse STEP 1. If the patient has a lower extremity injury, check the posterior tibial (ankle)

Skill Drill 1

Checking Circulation, Sensation, and Movement in an Injured Extremity

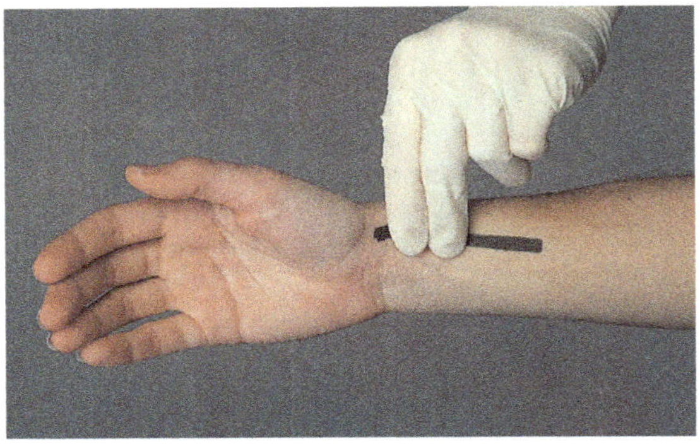

1. Check for circulation. If upper extremity injury, check radial pulse.

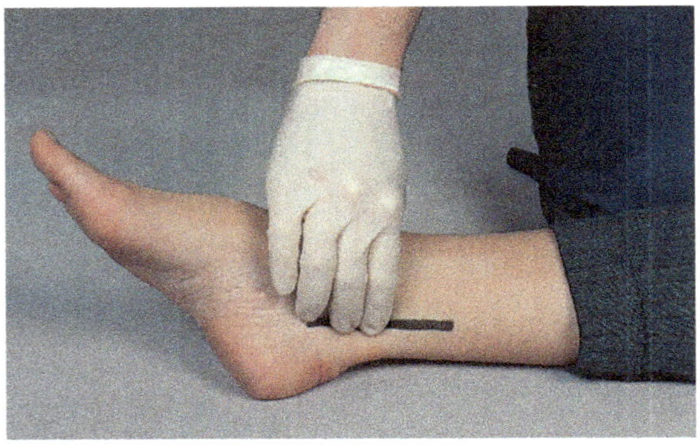

2. If lower extremity injury, check posterior tibial pulse.

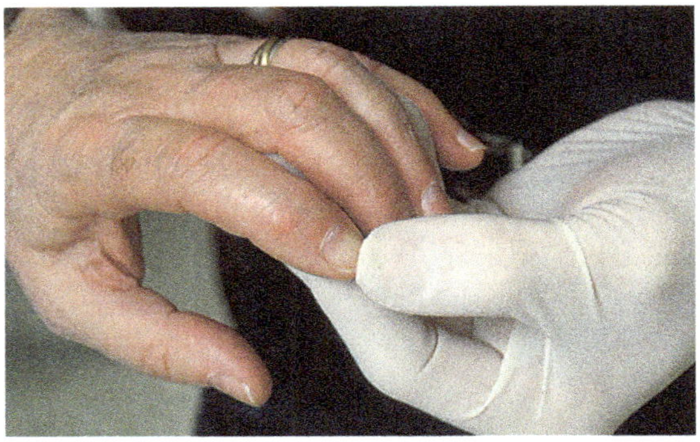

3. Test capillary refill on a finger or toe of injured limb.

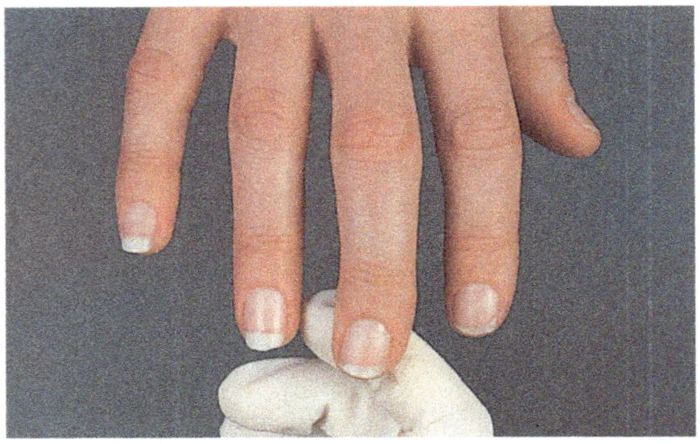

4. Release pressure, and the normal pink color should return by the time you say "capillary refill."

pulse, which can be found just behind the bony prominence on the inside of the ankle STEP 2.

2. **Capillary refill.** Test the capillary refill in a finger or toe of any injured limb. Firm pressure on the tip of the nail causes the nail bed to turn white STEP 3. Release the pressure, and the normal pink color should return by the time you can say "capillary refill" STEP 4. If the pink color does not return in this 2-second interval, capillary refill is considered to be delayed or absent and indicates a circulation problem in the limb. A cold environment will naturally delay capillary refill, so in that situation, do not use capillary refill to assess an injured limb. The absence of a pulse or capillary refill indicates that a limb is in immediate danger. Impaired circulation demands prompt transportation and prompt medical treatment at an appropriate medical facility.
3. **Sensation.** The patient's ability to feel your light touch on the fingers or toes is a good indication that the nerve supply is intact. In the hand, check sensation by touching lightly the tips of the index and little fingers STEP 5. In the foot, the tip of the big toe and the top of the foot should be checked for sensation STEP 6.
4. **Movement.** If the hand or foot is injured, do not have the patient perform this part of the test. When the injury is between the hand and the body or the foot and the body, have the patient open and close the fist STEP 7 or flex and extend the ankle of the injured limb STEP 8. These simple movements indicate that the

Skill Drill 1

Checking Circulation, Sensation, and Movement in an Injured Extremity *(continued)*

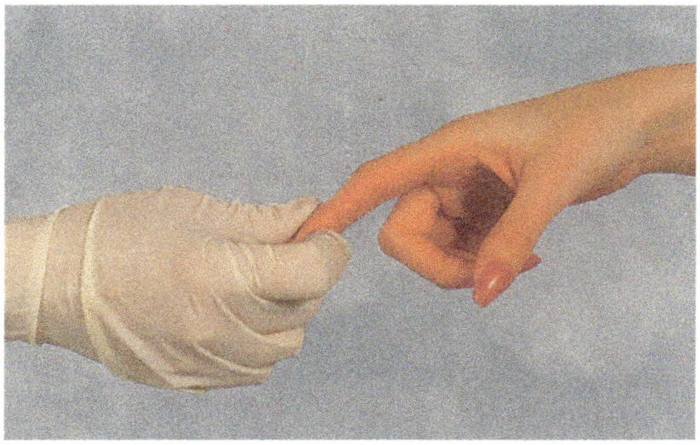

5. Check for sensation by touching the fingertips lightly.

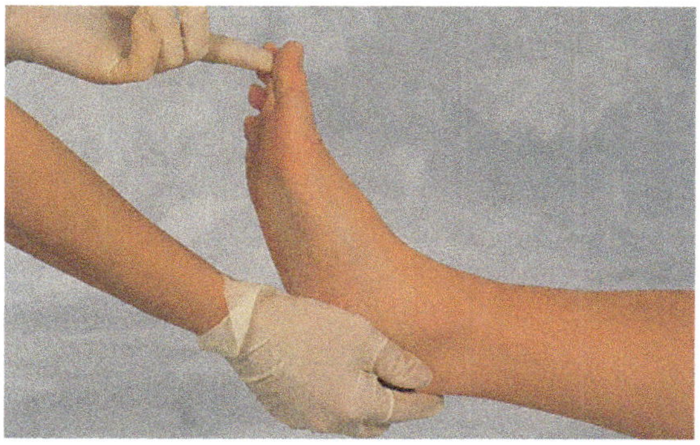

6. Check for sensation by touching the toes lightly.

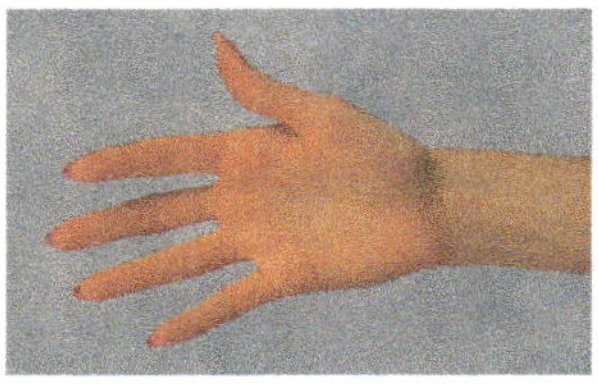

A.

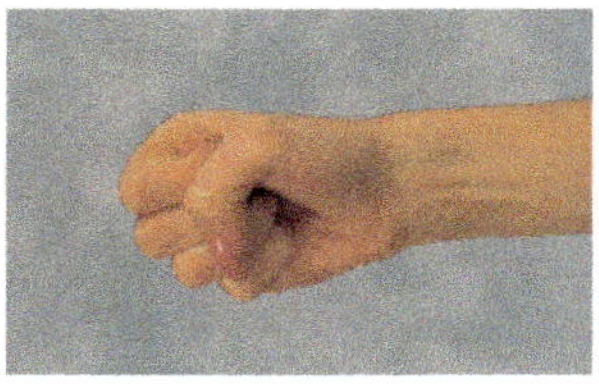

B.

7. Check for movement of the upper extremities by asking the patient to open (7A) and close (7B) the fist.

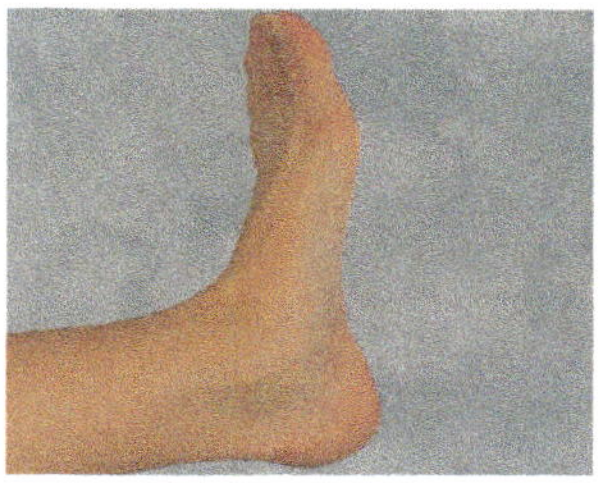

A.

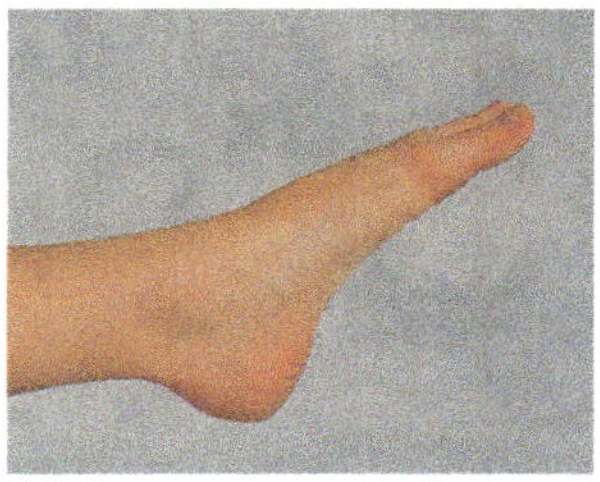

B.

8. Check for movement of the lower extremities by asking the patient to extend (8A) and flex (8B) the ankle.

nerves to these muscles are working. If any attempt at motion produces pain, do not ask the patient to move the limb any further. Any open wound, deformity, swelling, or bruising of a limb should be considered evidence of a possible limb injury and should be treated as such. Try to keep the extremity in a position of comfort for the patient.

Assess the patient using the head-to-toe method. When evaluating the extremities, it is best to check each one individually. Following this rapid scan, compare the left extremity to the right, especially when evaluating neurologic responses and muscle strength. Each assessment should include a quick evaluation for deformity and bleeding. Any obvious, uncontrolled bleeding that could be life threatening should be dealt with immediately. Any truly minor bleeding can be dealt with after more significant threats to life have been addressed.

In performing your assessment, obtain a patient medical history using SAMPLE (signs and symptoms, allergies, medications, past medical history, last oral intake, and events leading up to the incident). Patient injury should be evaluated using OPQRST (onset, provocation, quality, radiation, severity, and time of pain). Refer to the patient assessment unit for a detailed discussion of these methods.

Take note that tunnel vision can complicate matters. Large, grotesque wounds can attract your attention and delay your treatment of less dramatic, but more lethal, injuries. Your assessment is vital to locating life-threatening injuries. Some patients cannot properly determine a pain source, especially if the patient is under the influence of prescription or illicit drugs. A patient with multiple wounds can seem overwhelming, but systematically assessing and evaluating each wound will help you determine the proper steps and treatment techniques.

Orthopaedic Injuries

Bone injuries are very common in trauma patients. Different types of bone injuries can be confusing because they present with similar symptoms. Two types of injuries directly affect the bone itself: fractures and dislocations. Two additional types of injuries—sprains and strains—affect the supporting tissue near or attached to a bone.

Fractures

There are two categories of fractures: open and closed (**Figure 3**). **Open fractures** are associated with a break in the skin; **closed fractures** are not. Fractures can occur from a variety of MOIs and can have bleeding externally or internally depending on the type of fracture and the proximity of blood vessels to the fractured bone ends. Fractures do not always present with obvious deformities and pain. If the patient has pain, swelling, bruising, or lack of ability to move the affected area, it is best to err on the side of caution and to assume that the injury is a fracture.

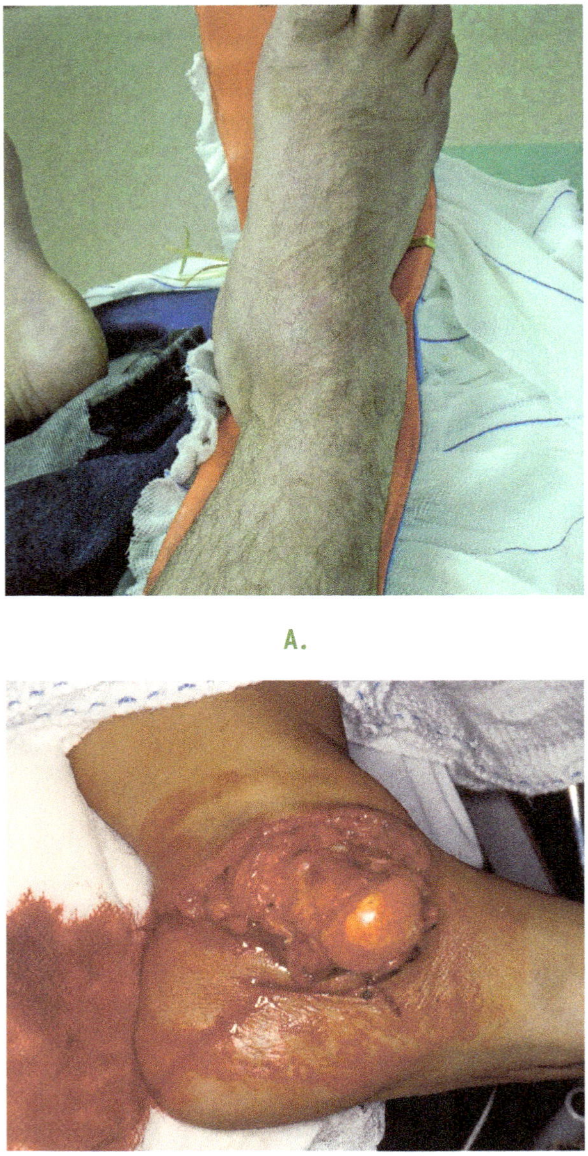

A.

B.

Figure 3 **A.** Closed fracture. **B.** Open fracture.

Dislocations

A **dislocation** is a separation between two bones at a **joint**. Dislocations can easily be mistaken for fractures because they often present with similar signs and symptoms. Dislocations can present with extreme pain or none at all and can result in a loss of ability to move the affected part. There may be obvious swelling and bruising to the area. A dislocation can be a serious emergency because the displaced bones can damage underlying nerves and blood vessels. If not managed promptly and properly, dislocations will result in permanent injury and dysfunction to the extremity.

Sprains and Strains

A **sprain** is a stretching injury that occurs to the supporting ligaments of an extremity at a joint. **Ligaments** are tough, elastic-like bands that attach two bones together. Muscles are attached to bones by **tendons**, and stretching or tearing injuries to muscles or tendons are known as **strains**. In the field, there is no way of knowing which type of injury has occurred, so patients should be stabilized and treated in the same manner.

Amputations

An **amputation** occurs when a body part or limb is severed (**Figure 4**). Hemorrhage from complete or incomplete amputations can be severe and life threatening. Control any bleeding to the stump. If bleeding cannot be controlled, you should quickly apply a tourniquet. Regardless of the size of the amputated part or the extent of the damage to it, the body part should be transported along with the patient to the hospital. If possible, place the severed part inside a sealed plastic bag, and place the bag in a bowl with ice and water. Some medical directors will recommend that you wrap the severed part in gauze dampened with normal saline or water. Do not allow the part to be submerged in water or to become saturated with water. Never place the body part directly on ice because of the potential for freezing the part.

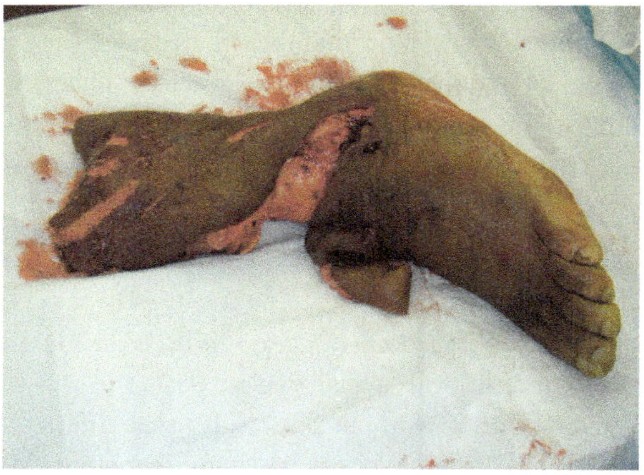

Figure 4 Amputated parts can often be reattached. Attempt to locate the amputated part and transport it to the hospital with the patient.

Management of Extremity Injuries

Treatment for injured extremities is generally the same whether the extremity is broken or not. Prior to stabilization, open wounds should first be covered with sterile **dressings** to prevent infection, and then with padding to prevent pressure on the injured area.

Most extremity injuries are treated with ice and stabilization after immediate life threats are controlled. The goal for both breaks and stresses is to reduce movement, thus preventing further injury to underlying structures and the bones and joints themselves. When stabilizing or splinting, you should always stabilize the body part both above and below the injury. For example, if a patient is suspected of having a knee injury, you should stabilize the thigh and lower leg because movement of either of these body parts affects the knee. If a patient is suspected of having a fractured lower arm, you should stabilize the elbow and hand because movement of either of these affects the lower arm.

Remember not to cause further injury with stabilization, such as blocking blood flow or damaging blood vessels. Regardless of whether you think the injury is a fracture or a dislocation, stabilize the area to reduce the risk of further injury prior to transportation to an emergency department for evaluation. The only definitive way to verify a fracture or dislocation is by radiography (X-ray).

Splinting

Splinting is a technique used to immobilize an extremity. The goal of splinting is to stabilize the limb, prevent further injury, and minimize pain. There are many splinting techniques and devices available. EMS carries many different types of devices, such as **rigid splints** and **traction splints**. In police work, however, carrying large quantities of equipment is simply not possible. You will have to use what is in your EMR kit, improvising as you can to control bleeding and stabilize the patient until EMS arrives. Use the steps in **Skill Drill 2** to splint a limb:

1. Follow standard precautions.
2. Cover all wounds with a dry, sterile dressing.
3. Supporting the injured limb, form the injured limb into a position of function. In the case of an injured arm, the position of function involves the wrist slightly bent down and all finger joints moderately flexed.

Skill Drill 2

Splinting the Hand and Wrist

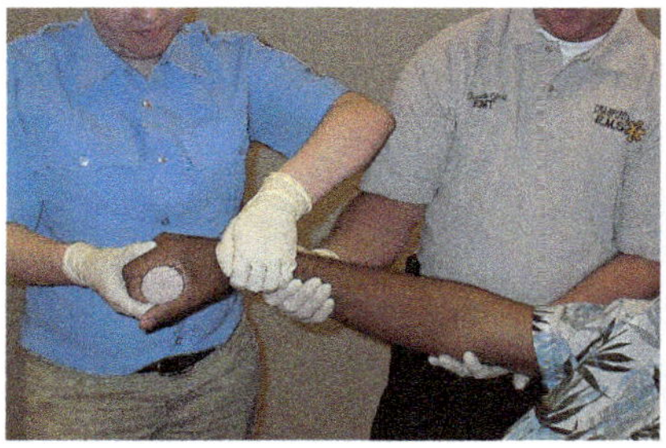

1. Support the injured limb and move the hand into the position of function. Place a soft roller bandage in the palm.

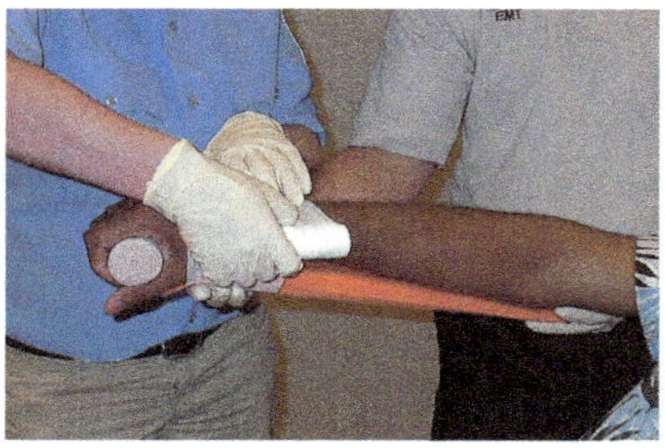

2. Apply a padded board splint on the palm side with fingers exposed.

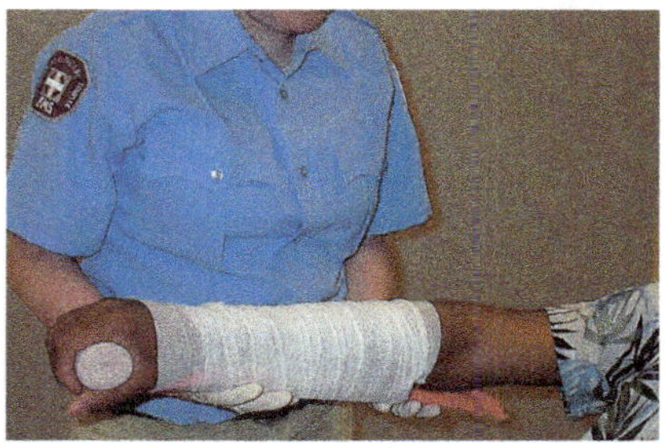

3. Secure the splint with a roller bandage.

4. When splinting the arm, place a soft roller bandage into the palm of the hand STEP 1.
5. Apply a padded board splint to the palm side of the wrist, leaving the fingers exposed STEP 2.
6. Secure the entire length of the splint with a soft roller bandage STEP 3.
7. Apply a sling and swathe, or prop the splinted hand and wrist on a pillow or on the patient's chest during transport to the hospital.

Table 1 summarizes different ways to immobilize a variety of injuries. Ultimately, it is up to you to manage the care of your patient using common sense and the emergency skills you have learned.

Soft-Tissue Wounds

Many incidents result in soft-tissue wounds. Because they can cause profuse bleeding, soft-tissue injuries can often look severe. As an emergency responder, you need to look past the superficial signs and symptoms and assess the patient's underlying condition. Your job is to evaluate the type and severity of the wound carefully and to manage the patient's potentially multiple conditions in the order of the threat they pose to the patient's life. This section presents the information and skills you need to recognize and manage four types of soft-tissue injuries: abrasions, lacerations, avulsions, and punctures.

Abrasions

Abrasions can occur from a variety of mechanisms and may be present with other soft-tissue injuries. Abrasions, commonly called a scrape or road rash, occur when the outermost layer of the skin is scraped off (Figure 5). Although this injury is superficial, it can be very painful. There may be minimal bleeding or oozing of blood from the injured area. The extent of the injury and the size of the area affected will determine treatment. It is important to prevent infection, so make sure to use clean dressings to bandage the wound and to control any bleeding. Verify that there is no underlying fracture and that no other injuries are present.

Lacerations

Lacerations are jagged cuts or tears in the skin caused by a forceful impact with a sharp object (Figure 6). They can be present with or without other soft-tissue injuries. For example, if a patient has been thrown from a motorcycle and landed on an arm, there may be an underlying fracture and a laceration with bleeding present. In this case, bleeding may be severe, and you must stabilize the fractured bones while also controlling the bleeding. Depending on the affected area, the size of the laceration, and the amount of bleeding, some lacerations may need sutures at the emergency department. Initial treatment includes bleeding control, treatment of other associated injuries, and bandaging the wounds.

Avulsions

Avulsions occur when a portion of the body is partially or fully torn off. In its most severe form, an entire part of the body is torn off; this is called a traumatic amputation. For example, an ear may be partially or completely torn from the body. The most common avulsions are to the skin as a result of trauma such as motor vehicle crashes, leaving the skin torn away to varying degrees of severity (Figure 7). These injuries are often jagged and dirty and can result in significant bleeding. Similar to other soft-tissue injuries, you should cover the wound

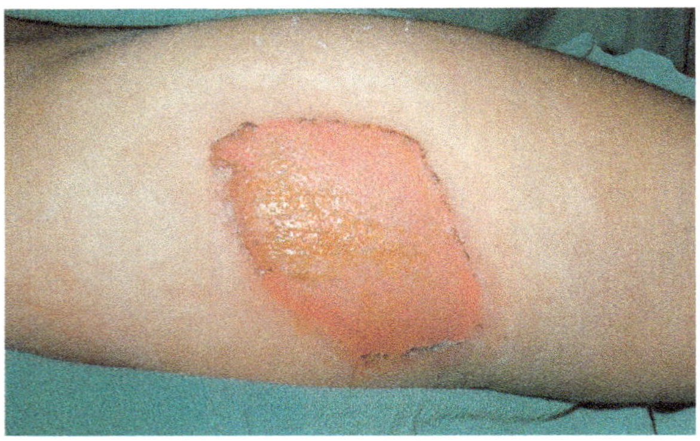

Figure 5 Abrasions involve variable depths of the skin; they are often called scrapes or road rash.

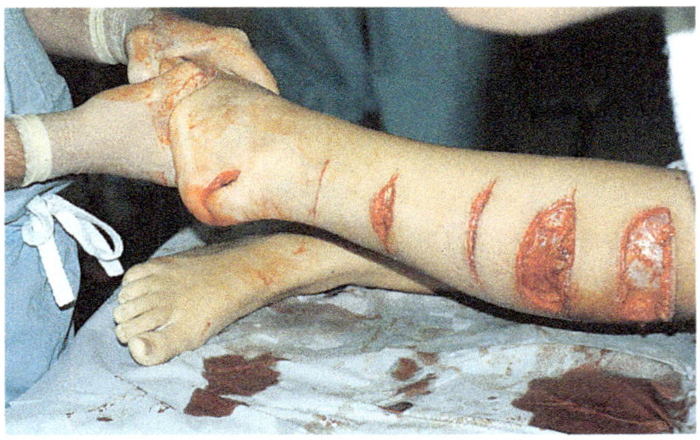

Figure 6 Lacerations are cuts produced by sharp objects.

Table 1

Injuries and Management Devices

Injury Location	Commercial Device	Improvised Device
Head	4″ × 4″ gauze, trauma pad, and cravats to control bleeding	Towel, washcloth, or piece of clothing to control bleeding.
Neck	Cervical collar for immobilization; 4″ × 4″ gauze and tape to control bleeding. Consider the use of an occlusive dressing if large blood vessels of the neck are involved.	Towel, washcloth, or piece of clothing to control bleeding. Plastic baggies, wrappers, plastic wrap, and duct tape can be used to make an occlusive dressing.
Back	Long backboard for immobilization; 4″ × 4″ gauze and tape to control bleeding	Requires commercial device for true immobilization. Do not move patient unless it is absolutely necessary to save life or if EMS delay will compromise survival. Towel, washcloth, or piece of clothing to control bleeding.
Chest	4″ × 4″ gauze, trauma pad, and cravats to control bleeding; chest seals to occlude penetrating wounds	Plastic wrap or aluminum foil to cover open wounds; a towel to keep the area sealed and clean.
Abdomen	4″ × 4″ gauze, occlusive trauma pad, and cravats to control bleeding	Plastic wrap or aluminum foil to cover open wounds; a towel to keep the area sealed and clean.
Pelvis	Long backboard for immobilization; 4″ × 4″ gauze, trauma pad, and cravats to control bleeding	Requires commercial device for immobilization. Towel, washcloth, or piece of clothing to control bleeding.
Shoulder	Cravats to make a sling and swathe	A belt, wide piece of clothes, or towel to create a sling and swathe. Towel, washcloth, or piece of clothing to control bleeding.
Humerus	Cravats to make a sling and swathe	A belt, wide piece of clothes, or towel to create a sling and swathe. Towel, washcloth, or piece of clothing to control bleeding.
Radius/Ulna	Rigid board splint, SAM splint, or air splint for immobilization; 4″ × 4″ gauze, trauma pad, and cravats to control bleeding	Anything rigid for immobilization, such as a ruler, magazine, or book. A pillow can also be used to splint. Towel, washcloth, or piece of clothing to control bleeding.
Wrist/Hand/Fingers	Rigid board splint, SAM splint, or air splint for immobilization; 4″ × 4″ gauze, and cravats to control bleeding	Anything rigid for immobilization, such as a ruler, magazine, or book. A pillow can also be used to splint. Towel, washcloth, or piece of clothing to control bleeding.
Femur	Traction splint for immobilization; 4″ × 4″ gauze, trauma pad, and cravats to control bleeding	Tie the patient's legs together and use the "good" leg to immobilize the fractured one. Towel, washcloth, or piece of clothing to control bleeding.
Tibia/Fibula	Rigid board splint, SAM splint, or air splint for immobilization; 4″ × 4″ gauze, trauma pad, and cravats to control bleeding	Anything rigid for immobilization, such as a ruler, magazine, or book. A pillow can also be used to splint. Towel, washcloth, or piece of clothing to control bleeding.
Ankle/Foot/Toes	Rigid board splint, SAM splint, or air splint for immobilization; 4″ × 4″ gauze, trauma pad, and cravats to control bleeding	Anything rigid for immobilization, such as a ruler, magazine, or book. A pillow can also be used to splint. Towel, washcloth, or piece of clothing to control bleeding.

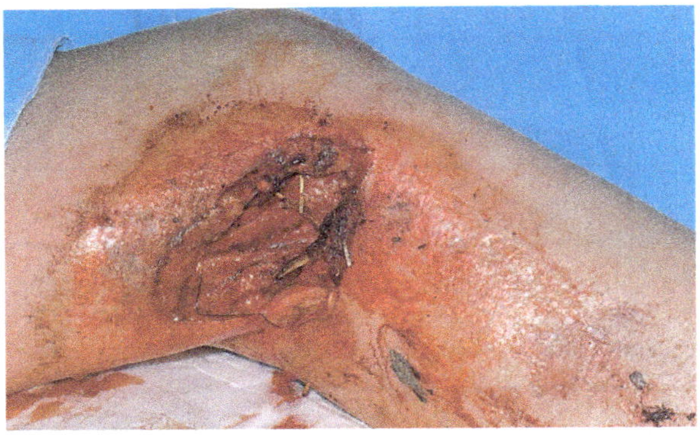

Figure 7 Avulsions raise flaps of tissue; significant bleeding is common.

with a sterile dressing and control bleeding. Patients should be transported to the emergency department, where relatively minor injuries will be cleaned and sutured. More severe skin avulsions may require skin grafts or reconstructive surgery.

Special Populations

Bleeding in Elderly Patients

Many older patients with heart conditions are prescribed blood thinners (anticoagulants) to keep blood clots from forming in their blood vessels. It may take longer to control bleeding from an open wound in such patients. As part of your SAMPLE history, ask patients—especially elderly patients—whether they are taking any blood thinners such as Coumadin (warfarin sodium), aspirin, heparin, plavix, or Lovenox.

Penetrations and Punctures

Penetration wounds, also called **puncture wounds**, are typically caused by sharp or pointed objects that penetrate the skin (**Figure 8**). Little to no external bleeding may be present, but internal bleeding may be severe and not initially evident. Gunshot and stab wounds are examples of serious puncture wounds. Depending on the mechanism and location of the injury, a puncture may have an exit wound, which would also require attention. Remember that underlying structures can be damaged by the path of a bullet, knife, or other object; a thorough assessment of the patient is paramount for identifying these injuries. Keep in mind that airway and breathing should be monitored and that the bleeding area should not make you lose focus of other potential life threats.

Impaled Objects

An **impaled object** is any object that creates a puncture wound but remains embedded. Examples of impaled objects could include shrapnel, debris, knives, utensils, and tools. Treatment

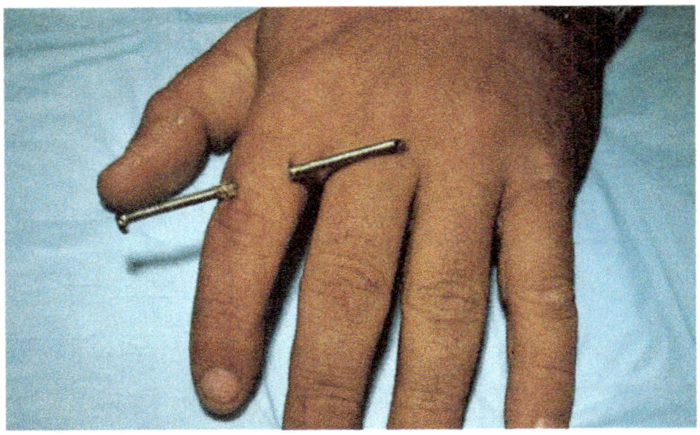

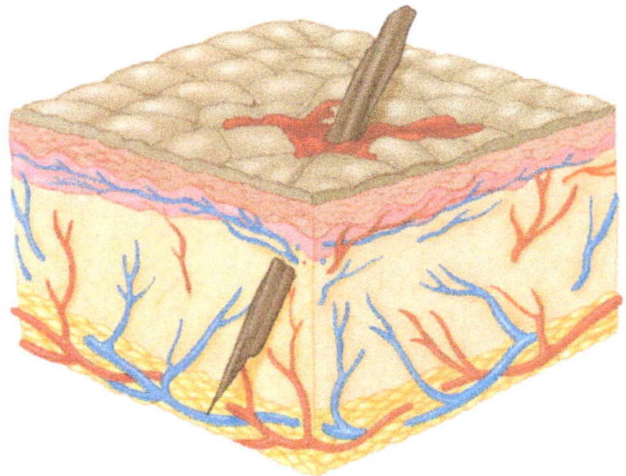

Figure 8 Puncture wounds may penetrate the skin to any depth.

involves bleeding control, monitoring airway and breathing, stabilizing the impaled object in place, and assessing for other underlying injuries. Do not remove the impaled object unless it is impairing the patient's breathing. You should stabilize the object to prevent movement and monitor the patient for complications. Follow the steps in **Skill Drill 3** to stabilize an impaled object.

1. Do not attempt to move or remove the object unless it is impaled through the cheek, causing airway obstruction, or if the object is in the chest and interferes with cardiopulmonary resuscitation (CPR) **STEP 1**. In most cases, a surgeon will have to remove the object; removing it in the field may cause more bleeding or may damage nerves, blood vessels, or muscles within the wound. Stabilize the impaled body part.
2. Remove any clothing covering the injury. Control bleeding, and apply a bulky dressing to stabilize the object. Some combination of soft dressings, gauze, and tape may be effective, depending on the location and

Skill Drill 3

Stabilizing an Impaled Object

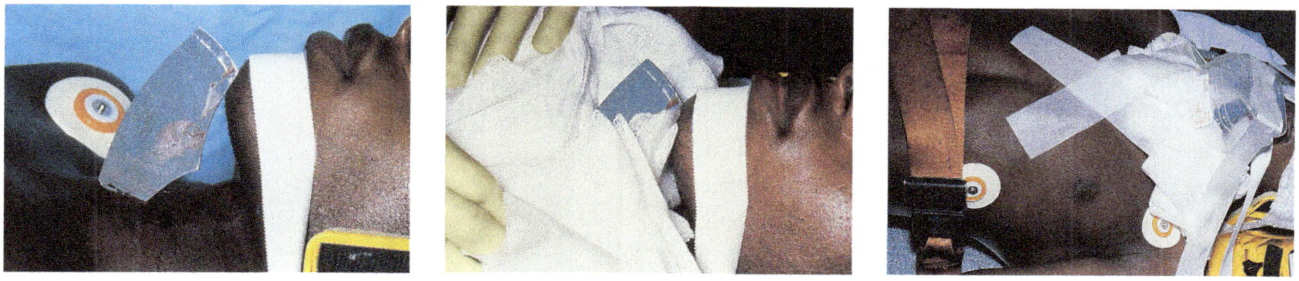

1. Do not attempt to move or remove the object.
2. Control bleeding and stabilize the object in place using soft dressings, gauze, and/or tape.
3. Tape a rigid item over the stabilized object to protect it from movement during transport.

size of the object. To prevent further injury, manually secure the object by incorporating it into the dressing STEP 2.

3. Protect the impaled object from being bumped or moved during transport by taping a rigid item such as a plastic cup, a section of plastic water bottle, or a supply container over the stabilized object and its bandaging STEP 3.

Management of Bleeding

The purpose of dressings and **bandages** is to control bleeding and decrease the risk of infection (**Figure 9**). Dressings are usually sterile and can be gauze pads, trauma dressings, or **occlusive dressings**. Bandages hold dressings in place and can be adhesive, roller gauze, cravats, or tape. If a sterile dressing is not available, then a clean, dry cloth should be used. If the dressing becomes soaked through with blood, it should not be removed unless it becomes difficult to maintain pressure. When trying to control bleeding, it is best to build on the initial dressing in place. Removing the dressing can result in a disruption of the clotting process and start the bleeding again. Once the bleeding has been controlled, the bandage should be applied. When bandaging, verify that the bandage is not restricting movement or circulation.

Communication

Reassuring Patients

Remember that patients who have injuries or are bleeding will likely be worried. It is your job to reassure them that you are doing everything you can to treat them. Do not forget to show your patients and their families that you care.

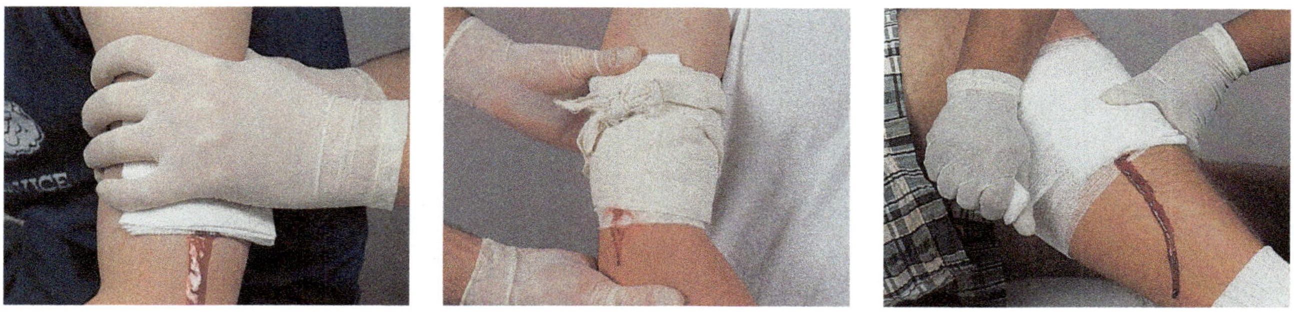

A. B. C.

Figure 9 Bandaging an extremity wound. **A.** Place a dressing over the wound. **B.** Secure the dressing with a cravat, or **C.** secure the dressing with a roller bandage.

In severe cases involving an extremity, sometimes bleeding cannot be controlled using a pressure dressing and elevation. Although these cases are rare, they can occur, especially in jagged or tearing injuries. In these situations, the use of a **tourniquet** must be considered. A tourniquet is a wide, constricting band that is tightened to the point at which all blood flow beyond the point of the tourniquet ceases. A tourniquet is used only when bleeding cannot be controlled by other techniques and there is a risk of severe hemorrhage or death. **Skill Drill 4** demonstrates the proper application of a tourniquet.

1. Apply direct pressure with a dry, sterile dressing **Step 1**.
2. Apply a pressure dressing **Step 2**.
3. Apply a tourniquet above the level of bleeding **Step 3**.

Burns

Burns can be caused by fire, steam, chemicals, or electricity, and they can range from mild to severe. Several factors determine the severity of burns, including the cause, depth, and extent of the burn; the part(s) of the body involved; and whether the respiratory system is involved.

The depth of the burn is related to the layers of the skin. **Superficial burns** (first-degree burns) involve only the outermost layer of the skin. One example of a superficial burn is a sunburn, which can be very painful, presenting with swelling and redness of the skin. Although painful, sunburns usually heal very quickly (**Figure 10**).

Partial-thickness burns (second-degree burns) involve the outer and middle layers of the skin (**Figure 11**). These burns present with extreme pain, redness, and blistering. **Full-thickness burns** (third-degree burns) extend through all three layers of the skin and may have exposed bone beneath the charred area (**Figure 12**). The skin may look white or yellow and feel leathery. The patient may have no tenderness in the severely affected area as a result of the nerves having been destroyed. It is common for severe burns to include all three types of burns based on the degree of exposure and the extent of the affected areas.

The extent of a burn depends on how much of the body surface is burned; other complications related to the burn, such as age or previous illness; other associated injuries; and whether the patient develops shock. The **rule of nines** is a tool you can use to estimate the extent of a burn. **Figure 13** shows how the rule of nines divides the body. In an adult, the head

Skill Drill 4

Controlling Bleeding With a Tourniquet

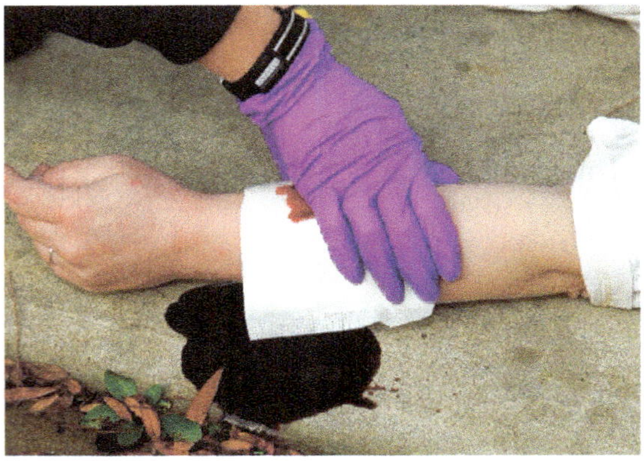

1. Apply direct pressure with a dry, sterile dressing.

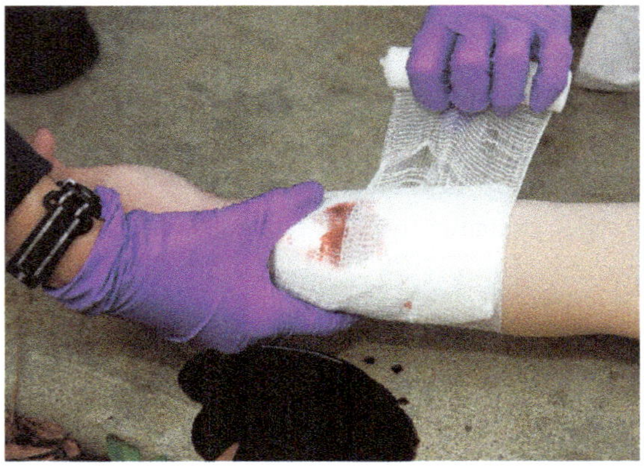

2. Apply a pressure dressing.

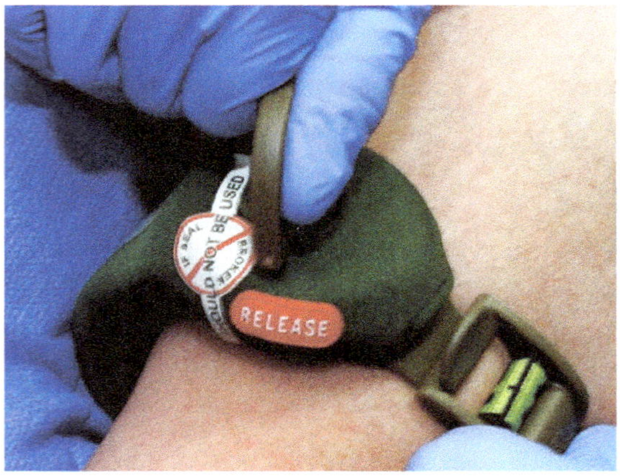

3. If bleeding continues or recurs, apply a tourniquet above the level of bleeding.

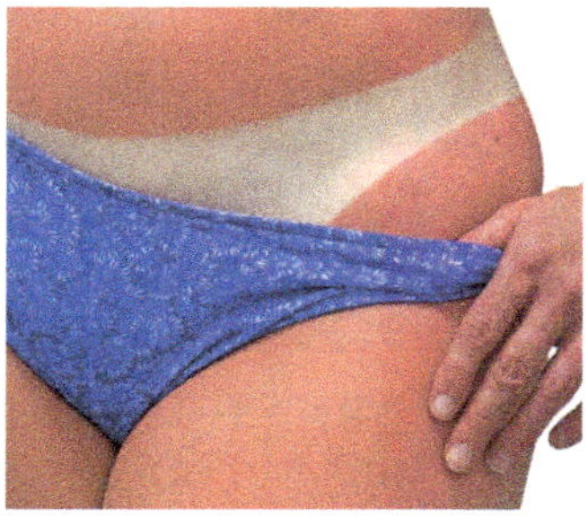

Figure 10 Superficial burn.

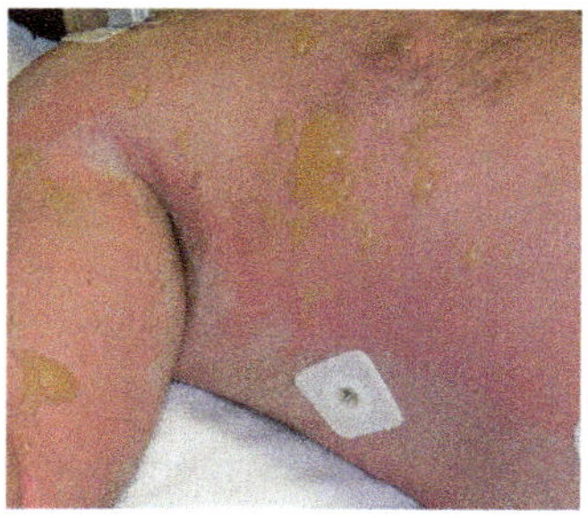

Figure 11 Partial-thickness burn.

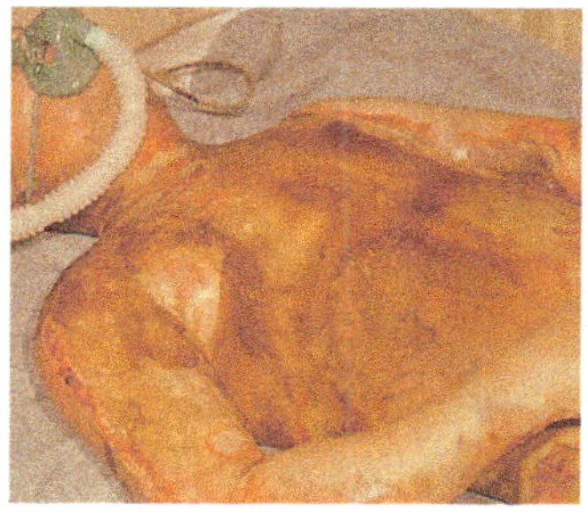

Figure 12 Full-thickness burn.

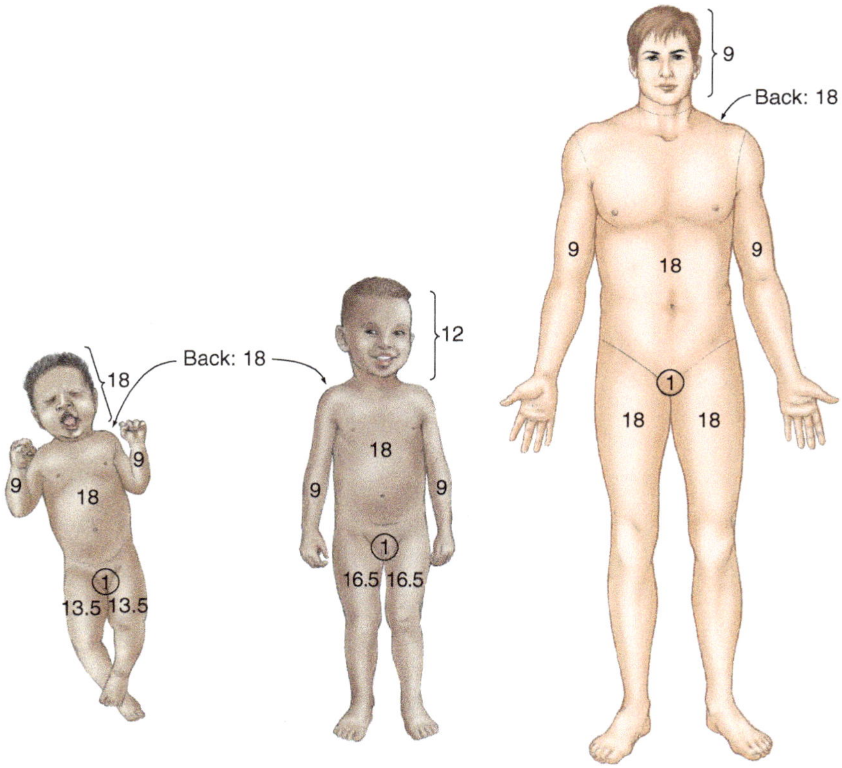

Figure 13 Use the rule of nines to determine the extent of burns.

and each arm represent 9% of the total body surface. The front and back of the trunk and the legs each equal 18% of the total body surface. For example, if one half of the back and the entire right arm of a patient are burned, the burn involves about 18% of the total body area. The rule of nines is slightly modified for young children, but the adult figure serves as an adequate guide.

Management of Burns

Management of burns depends on the severity and extent of the injury. Stopping the burning process is the first and most important step. To do this, remove the patient from the burn source, remove the patient's clothing if possible, brush any chemicals off the patient, and apply water if recommended. Keep in mind that the addition of water to some chemicals will cause further, more significant burning. Therefore, water should be applied only once the chemical is identified and you are sure that no negative reactions or further injuries will be caused.

Before you touch or treat a person whom you suspect may have sustained an electrical burn, be certain that the patient is not still in contact with the electrical power source that caused the burn or you may be burned as well.

After the burn process has been stopped, carefully monitor the patient's airway and breathing. The following signs or symptoms are indicative of exposure to smoke, heat, or toxic gases:

- Burns around the face
- Singed nose or facial hair

- Soot in mouth or nose
- Difficulty breathing
- Pain while breathing
- Changes in tone, pitch, or hoarseness of voice
- High-pitched sounds from airway during breathing
- Unconsciousness as a result of exposure to a fire, toxic gases, or smoke.

Regardless of whether the head or face is involved, the airway could have been burned by heat, inhalation of toxic substances, or splashing of chemicals. Although the percentage of body surface area burned is important, knowing whether a patient sustained an inhalation burn is the most reliable predictor of patient mortality. LERs should always administer oxygen according to their local protocols if they believe that the airway has been compromised by heat, smoke, or toxic gases.

Treatment includes covering the area with dry, sterile dressings. Do not break any blisters or apply any lotions, salves, or antiseptics. Keep the patient warm and calm while monitoring for shock. Bleeding control and other wound management may also be necessary if there was any other trauma associated with the burn. Once EMS has arrived, the patient may be given medication for pain.

Head, Neck, and Sensory Injuries

LERs can encounter many situations that may involve head, face, or neck injuries. Unfortunately, severe head or neck injuries can lead to brain damage, paralysis, or death. Improper handling of a patient with head or neck injuries can also result in severe injury or death. Serious spine injuries have been caused by well-intentioned citizens and by improperly trained law enforcement or EMS personnel. As an emergency responder, you must not only provide prompt treatment but also avoid any errors that may make the injury worse.

An injury as small as a grain of sand under the eyelid can immobilize and render anyone incapacitated due to the sudden and intense irritation. Sensory organs and the soft tissues of the head, face, and neck are filled with nerves and blood vessels. In our daily routine, these structures provide constant information flow to our brain about temperature, moisture, taste, smell, visual, and auditory cues. Most of these structures receive and send messages through nerves that are directly connected to the brain. LERs have to take immediate action when patients have injuries to sensory organs and other structures of the head, face, and neck. Damage to these sensitive and critical structures can result in permanent damage to sensory organs and possibly death.

HEAD AND NECK INJURY

To provide the best care for a patient with a head, face, or neck injury, the LER should become familiar with the anatomic structures that can be affected. In this region of the body, extremely important blood vessel, sensory, and airway structures are packed very close together and in some cases are exposed. The LER should also take time to develop simple tactics to deal with injuries to this area. Many basic life support functions can have a dramatic impact on the survival of the patient suffering head, face, or neck injuries. An important part of developing these care tactics is understanding your role relative to the law enforcement mission. Are you in a peaceful role where traditional stabilization methods can be used, or are you in a care-under-fire scenario where you may have to extract the patient from hostile surroundings and deal with the removal of helmets or body armor? LERs must train to manage head, face, neck, and spine injuries in various settings for a wide range of scenarios.

Anatomy of the Head, Neck, and Spine

There are three bony sections of the head and neck: the cranium, the facial bones, and the spine (**Figure 14**). The cranium is composed of a hard, four-bone shell that encases and protects the brain. The facial bones are thinner bones that protect the eyes and the airway. The spinal column primarily exists to provide protection to the spinal cord and nerves. The spinal column also is used as the central supporting column for the body, supporting the head, shoulders, and pelvis. The bony structures that wrap around the spinal cord are called vertebrae. **Vertebrae** are irregularly shaped bones that stack one upon the next (**Figure 15**). The bodies of the vertebrae are very thick, strong structures that provide the support to hold up the spine. Between each vertebrae body is a cushion-like

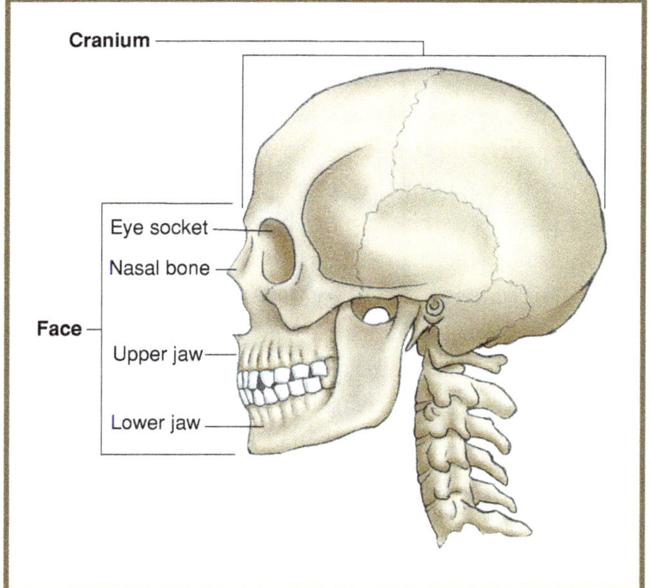

Figure 14 Bones of the head and neck.

structure called an **intervertebral disc**. The disc provides spacing that allows for some limited movement between individual vertebrae. Vertebrae are held together with ligaments. The spinal canal is the space created by the arches of bone that are posterior to the vertebral bodies. This canal exists throughout the entire spine, creating space for the spinal cord and the nerves traveling to and from the spinal cord. The spine is made up of 33 different vertebrae, divided into five different sections. These sections are the cervical, thoracic, lumbar, sacrum, and coccyx (**Figure 16**).

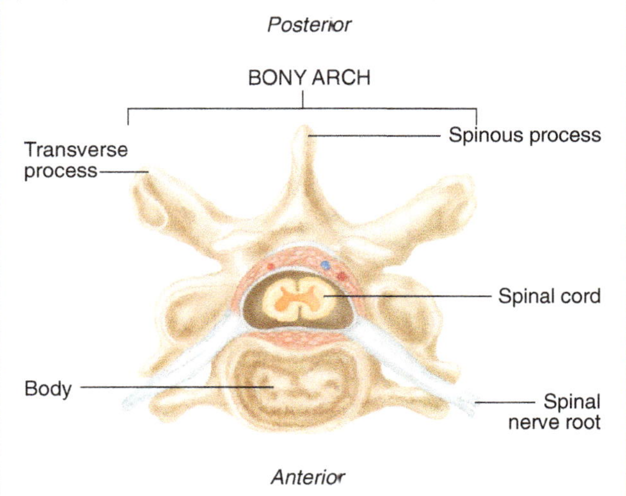

Figure 15 The spinal canal is formed by the vertebral body in the front and the bony arch in the back.

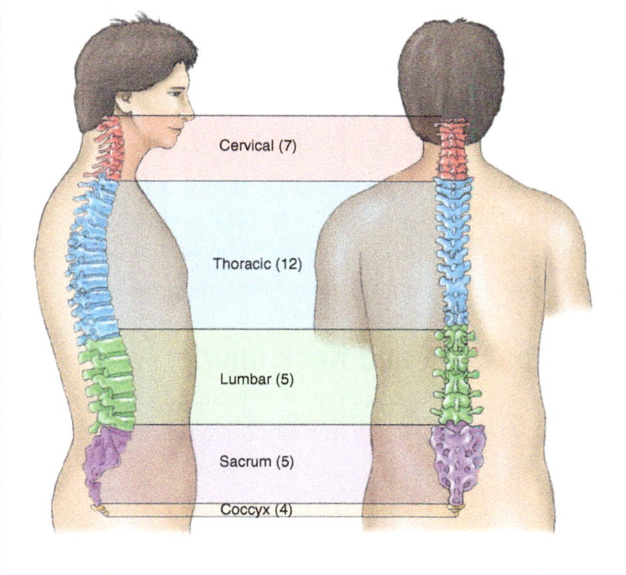

Figure 16 The spinal column is the body's central supporting system and consists of 33 bones divided into five sections. Injury to the vertebrae can cause paralysis.

The cervical spine is composed of seven vertebrae that protect the spinal cord as it carries signals from the brain to the body through the neck. The spinal cord continues to travel down the spine through the twelve thoracic and five lumbar vertebrae. The vertebrae continue down the back, to the pelvis with the five vertebrae of the sacrum and the four vertebrae of the coccyx. Peripheral nerves travel from the spinal cord throughout all the sections of the vertebral column. Behind the bony arches that make up the spinal canal are bony prominences. These structures are commonly felt when palpating the spine. The spine is wrapped with skeletal muscle.

Care should be taken to support all the structures of the spine when blunt or penetrating forces have affected this tissue. Depending on the injury, the patient may have a severe injury where the protective structures or foreign bodies have damaged the nervous tissue. In some injuries, only localized damage to the protective structures has occurred. Improper movement and poor handling can cause or increase the injury to the nervous tissue. Local protocols should guide your specific care.

The skull contains the brain as well as **cerebrospinal fluid (CSF)**, a fluid that cushions the brain in the event of a direct blow. CSF is a clear, watery, straw-colored fluid that fills the space between the brain, spinal cord, and their protective coverings. The skull and the CSF serve as the two major mechanisms of protection for the brain.

The soft tissue of the neck does not directly support any specific sensory organ. However, this tissue is full of nerves and major blood vessels that travel between the structures of the head and brain to the heart. Vital airway structures are also contained in the neck. Blunt force trauma can damage both the respiratory and the vascular structures. Penetrating wounds to the large vessels of the neck can result in intense bleeding and the potential for air to be pulled back into the blood vessels, creating the possibility of air emboli.

Types of Head and Neck Injury

Head injuries are considered either closed or open (**Figure 17**). In a **closed head injury**, the skull remains intact, although it may present with a depression of the skull bones. Bleeding or swelling inside the skull can cause increased pressure on the brain, which can lead to irreversible brain damage or even death if the pressure is not relieved. In an **open head injury**, there is either a hole or crack in the skull that allows some pressure to be relieved. Although severe open head injuries and lacerations to the scalp can bleed profusely, they are not always fatal. Note that any kind of head injury can also be associated with a spinal injury (**Figure 18**).

Spinal injuries should be suspected in patients with severe head, face, or neck trauma, as well as any patient involved in one of the common mechanisms of spinal injury:

- Motor vehicle crash
- Pedestrian–vehicle collision
- Fall
- Blunt trauma
- Penetrating trauma to head, neck, or torso
- Motorcycle crash
- Hanging
- Springboard or platform diving accident
- Unresponsive trauma patient

If one or more of the vertebrae are injured, the spinal cord they protect may also be damaged. A displaced vertebra, swelling, or bleeding may put pressure on the spinal cord and injure it (**Figure 19**). In severe cases, part or all of the spinal cord may be cut, leading to paralysis below the injury. If the injury is high enough in the spine, the paralysis may affect the diaphragm, resulting in death.

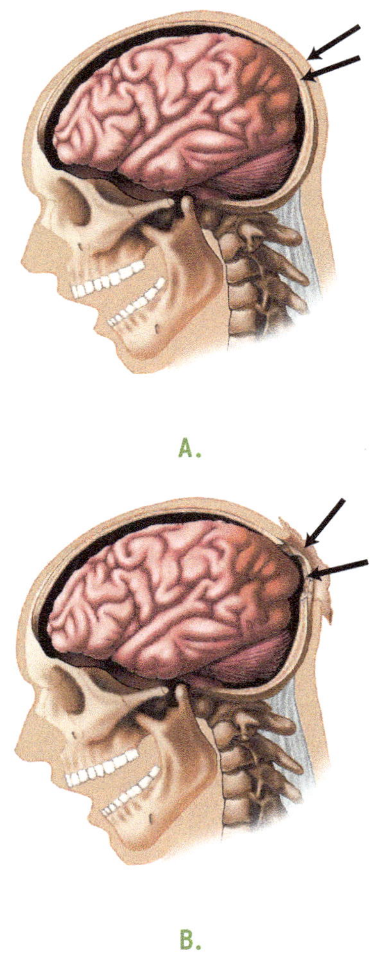

Figure 17 **A.** A closed head injury. **B.** An open head injury.

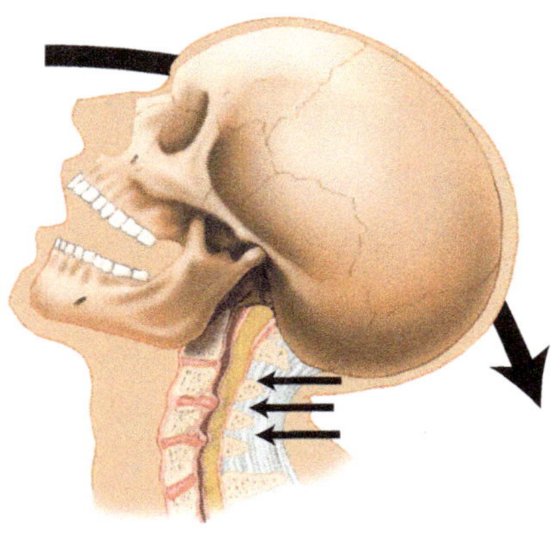

Figure 18 A head injury may occur in conjunction with a cervical spine injury.

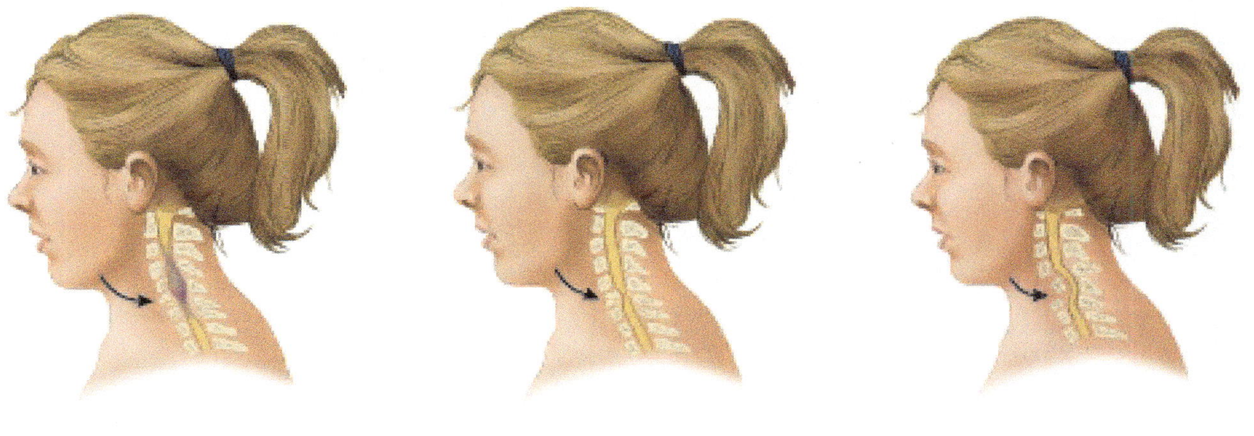

Figure 19 Types of spinal injuries. **A.** Pressure on the spinal cord from swelling or fracture. **B.** Bruising of the spinal cord by broken vertebrae. **C.** Injury by displacement and fractured vertebrae.

Assessment of Head, Neck, and Spine Injury

The assessment of a patient with a head, face, or neck injury begins by immobilizing the head in a neutral position. All patients with head or neck injuries, conscious or unconscious, should receive spinal immobilization until the responder can determine the extent and type of injuries that are present. If the patient is conscious, direct the patient to remain still. If the patient is in a hostile setting where safety threats exist, the LER may have to make a decision to move the patient to safety to avoid further injury. Assess the airway to ensure that the patient is able to breathe. If the airway is obstructed, perform the jaw-thrust technique to open it (**Figure 20**). Once the airway is open, support breathing if necessary. If there are any obvious sources of bleeding, apply firm pressure to them until the bleeding stops. Even a minor head wound can bleed significantly because of the large number of blood vessels in the scalp. Interrupt your assessment to treat life threats or to move to safety.

If your assessment reveals a potential head or face injury, examine the nose, eyes, and the wound itself to see if any blood or CSF is seeping out. In severe cases of open head injury, brain tissue or bone may be visible.

A serious head injury may also produce **raccoon eyes** (bruising around one or both eyes, similar to black eyes after a fight) and/or **Battle's sign** (a bruise behind one or both ears) (**Figure 21**).

Tip

Signs and Symptoms of Head Injury

Signs and symptoms of head injury include the following:

- Confusion
- Unusual behavior
- Unconsciousness
- Nausea or vomiting
- Blood coming from inside an ear
- Decreasing consciousness
- Seizures
- External head trauma: bleeding, bumps, and contusions

Presume that any patient with any sort of neck injury also has a spine injury. When the patient is conscious and presents with possible spine injuries, talk to the patient and determine the MOI, that is, the means by which traumatic injury occurred. Gently conduct a hands-on examination from head to toe to determine paralysis (by asking the patient to wiggle his or her fingers and toes) or weakness (by checking grip strength or foot extension). Ask patients to describe any points of tenderness or pain but do not let them move, aside from your examination of their extremities. If the patient is unconscious, you will have to rely on bystanders and others who witnessed the incident producing the injury to determine the MOI.

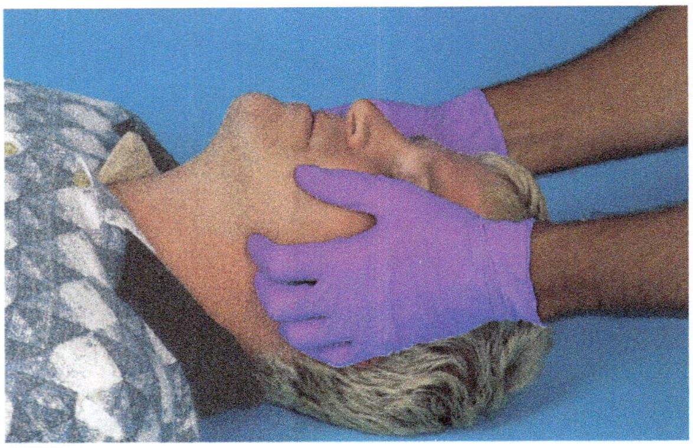

A.

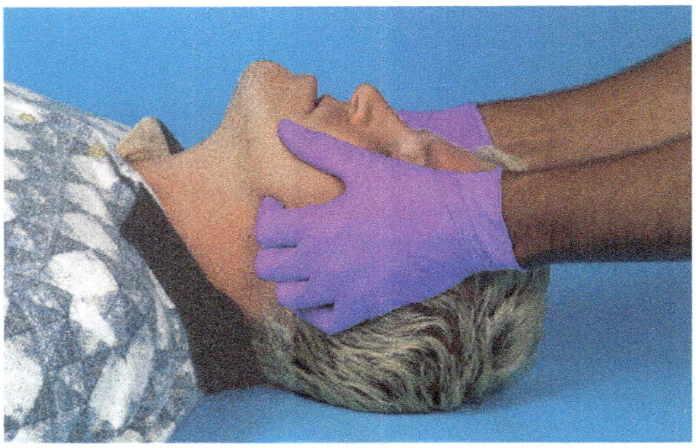

B.

Figure 20 The jaw-thrust technique for opening an airway. **A.** Stabilize the head and neck in a neutral position. **B.** With your fingers behind the angles of the lower jaw and your thumbs to help with positioning, move the jaw upward.

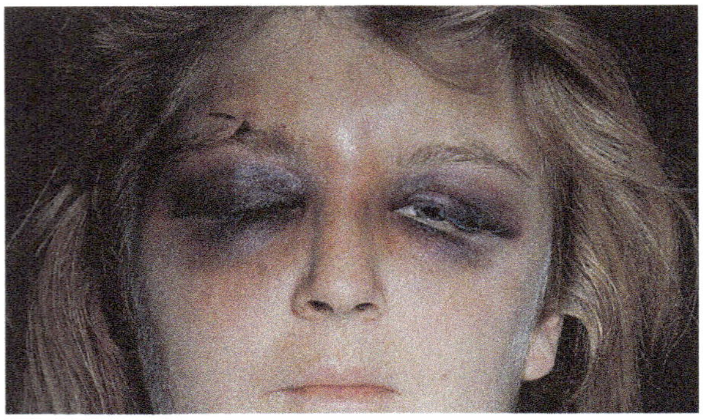

A.

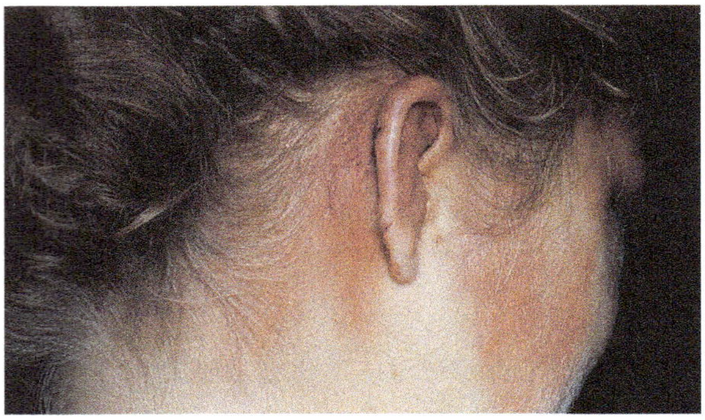

B.

Figure 21 Signs of head injury. **A.** Raccoon eyes. **B.** Battle's sign.

Tip

Signs and Symptoms of Spine Injury

The key signs and symptoms of spine injury are as follows:

- Laceration, bruise, or other sign of injury to the head, neck, or spine
- Tenderness over any point on the spine or neck
- Pain in the neck or spine or pain radiating to an extremity
- Extremity weakness, numbness, paralysis, or loss of movement
- Loss of sensation or movement, or a tingling/burning sensation in any part of the body below the neck
- Loss of bowel or bladder control

During your assessment, be extremely careful. Take your time, and emphasize to patients that they should not shake or nod their head when answering you. Position yourself so that they will not need to move their head to communicate with you, and, above all, do not transfer patients unless they are in a hazardous area. If patients must be transferred, be sure to keep the head and spine in alignment using the **log-roll technique** (**Figure 22**). The log-roll technique is the means by which a patient with a suspected spinal injury is turned without twisting or bending the spine. This procedure involves at least three people. If the patient is seated, you should wait for EMS to provide specific seated immobilization devices or rotate the patient onto a long backboard as directed by your local protocols.

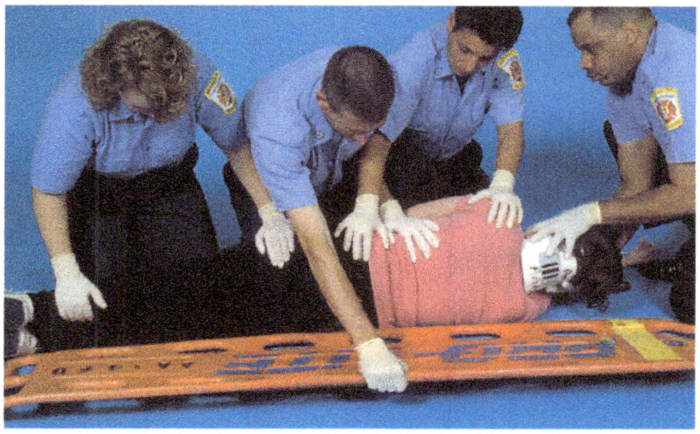

Figure 22 Keep the head and spine in alignment by using the log-roll technique when transferring the patient to a backboard.

FACIAL INJURY

Injuries to the face typically result in bleeding or collapse of the facial bones, which can, in serious cases, lead to airway obstruction. Although facial injuries can bleed considerably, as long as the airway is intact they are rarely life threatening.

Anatomy of the Face

The eyes are gelatinous globes that are set in a bony socket called the **orbit**. The orbit is created from several smaller bones that have grown in irregular shapes to accommodate the needs of this rounded structure. The eye continues back into the skull, where the rear of the eye connects to the optic nerve. The **optic nerve** takes the visual information from the eye to the part of the brain where visual cues are interpreted (**Figure 23**).

The functional unit of the eye contains an outer covering called the **conjunctiva**. This covering is very sensitive to dryness and foreign structures. It is lubricated by the tears created by the **lacrimal gland** and the eyelid. The **cornea** is a clear tissue that sits in front of the operational components of the eye. It provides a protective, supporting layer. Posterior to the cornea is the anterior chamber of the eye, which is filled with a small amount of clear fluid called the **aqueous humor**. The anterior chamber is supported on the sides by the **sclera**, the white tissue that makes up the outer covering of the eye. Inside the sclera is a second chamber that contains a clear, jellylike substance called the **vitreous humor**. The vitreous humor supports the structures of the eye and provides for uninterrupted transmission of the visual cues to the back of the eye.

The operational structures of the eye are contained directly behind the anterior chamber and are designed to shape reflected light and images toward the optic nerve in the back of the eye. The lens adjusts to allow the person to focus on objects. The **pupil** is the opening in the eye that allows light into the eye, aiding in the illumination of visual cues. Around the pupil is the **iris**, the colored portion of the eye. This tissue contains tiny structures that are used to receive information. The **retina** exists at the rear of the eye, where the image is received from the lens. The information from the retina is sent to the brain by the optic nerve, where the pattern is interpreted as a visual image.

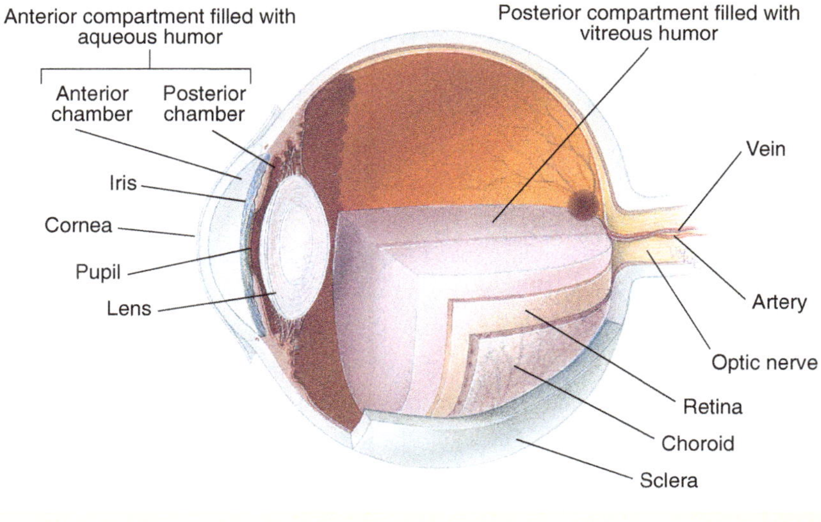

Figure 23 The major components of the eye.

The ear consists of external structures called the outer ear, or earlobe, and the ear canal (**Figure 24**). The middle structures start with the eardrum and three tiny bony structures called the hammer, anvil, and stirrup. The middle structures receive auditory cues from the external environment. The inner ear is called the **cochlea**. The cochlea is where sound is collected and processed, along with information regarding balance. The

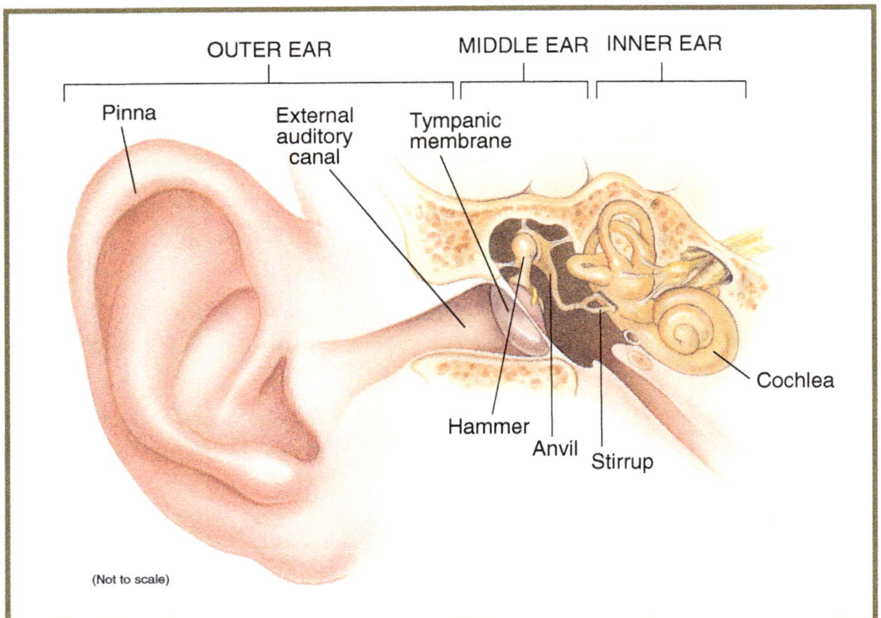

Figure 24 The major components of the ear.

cochlear structures send this information to the brain for processing.

The nose is lined with mucous membranes that exist to warm, humidify, and cleanse the air we breathe. Nerves inside the nose carry information about smells directly to the brain. This area is filled with blood vessels that can bleed severely when they are damaged.

The mouth is used to mechanically reduce food into particles we can digest and absorb for nutrients. The mouth, like the nose, is lined with mucous membranes that are very vascular. The mouth is full of nerves that are used in the chewing process as well as to deliver taste information to the brain. The mouth contains the tongue, teeth, and gums, which can be easily damaged. Even minor irritations to the mouth can be extremely painful.

Assessment of Facial Injury

Many sensory organ and facial wounds are obvious to the rescuer. Some injuries are so graphic and startling that they may draw the rescuers' attention away from their routine assessment. Assessing the patient for facial injuries should occur after the patient has been secured from a hostile environment, the airway has been managed, and spinal stabilization needs have been met. If the patient can communicate, get as much detail as you can about his or her symptoms and events prior to the injury. Assessment of soft tissue, muscle, and skeletal structures of the face should occur via inspection and palpation. Take care with palpation not to press too firmly. Otherwise, you may dislodge small facial bones or fractures of the thin layers of the skull.

The LER will benefit greatly from the use of a flashlight, which will help visualize the ears, mouth, and nose internal cavities. The focus should be on looking for blood, secretion, tissue abnormalities, and impaled objects. The mouth should be assessed for damage to the lips, gums, teeth, and tongue. The eyes should be assessed using the flashlight for pupil response, blood, secretions, deformity, and small foreign bodies.

Focused assessments of the eye should start with an inspection of the tissue and structures that make up the eye socket. With the eye shut, look for deformities or foreign objects (including loose eyelashes on the eyelid). Have the patient open the eyelids and observe the sclera, iris, and pupil for color changes, bleeding, swollen capillaries, deformities, and foreign objects. Determine whether the patient is wearing contact lenses; if so, and if permitted by your local policies, remove them. If the patient is complaining of a foreign body in the eye, gently pull open the eyelids using a gloved hand and ask the patient to look up, down, and from side to side to determine whether a foreign object is present. If you are concerned that the eyes are swollen shut, do not force them open.

If the eye can be opened and you believe that the foreign object has lodged under the top or bottom lid, a routine practice is to use a cotton-tipped applicator to pull the lid forward and back on the applicator (**Skill Drill 5**). Carefully look at the lid and on the sclera under the lid. Scan for objects or areas of irritation. If you do not immediately find an object and complaints persist, do not irritate the eye more by reassessing. Immediately transfer the patient to a higher level of care for more detailed assessment and management.

1. Tell the patient to look down while you grasp the lashes of the upper eyelid with your thumb and index finger. Gently pull the eyelid away from the eyeball **STEP 1**.

Skill Drill 5

Removing a Foreign Object From Under the Upper Eyelid

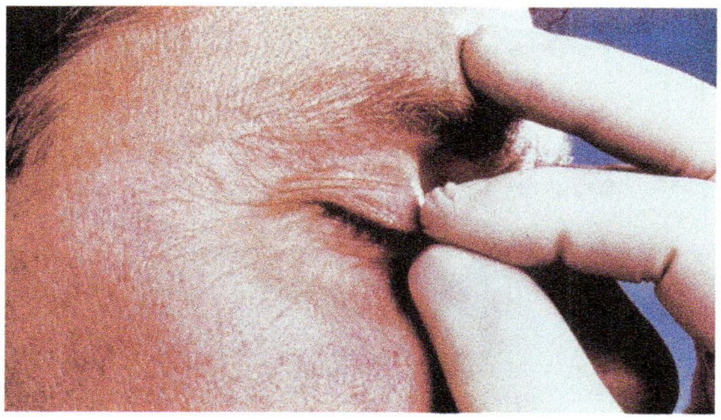

1. Have the patient look down, grasp the upper lashes, and gently pull the eyelid away from the eyeball.

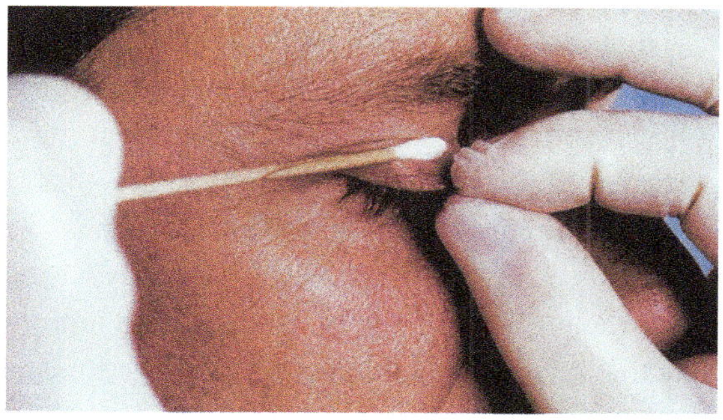

2. Place a cotton-tipped applicator horizontally along the center of the outer surface of the upper eyelid.

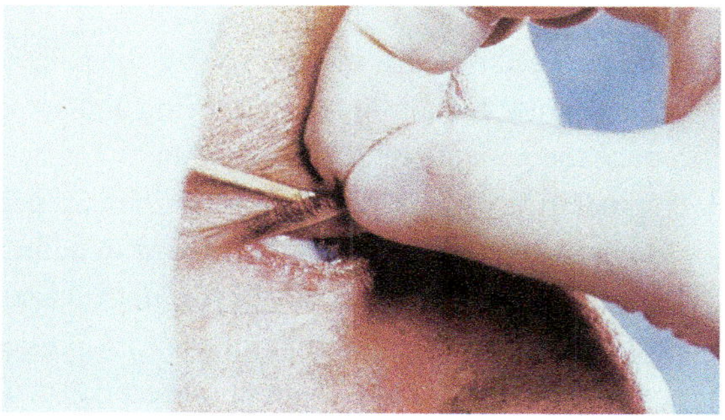

3. Pull the eyelid forward and up, folding it back over the applicator.

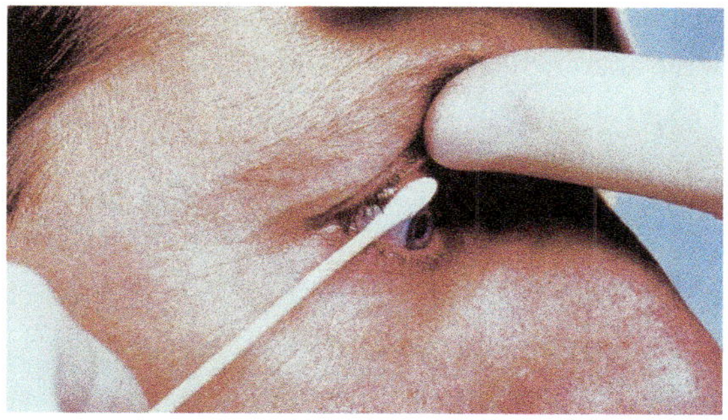

4. Gently remove the foreign object from the eyelid with a moistened, sterile, cotton-tipped applicator.

2. Gently place a cotton-tipped applicator horizontally along the center of the outer surface of the upper eyelid STEP 2.
3. Pull the eyelid forward and up, which causes it to roll or fold back over the applicator, exposing the undersurface of the eyelid STEP 3.
4. If you see a foreign object on the surface of the eyelid, gently remove it with a moistened, sterile, cotton-tipped applicator STEP 4.

The findings of the assessment should be passed on to the next level of care. LERs should take into account patient complaints of pain and never disregard a facial or sensory injury in the field. Too often, the responder cannot fully visualize sensory cavities, irritants, or tiny foreign objects that create overwhelming pain to sensory structures.

MANAGEMENT OF HEAD, FACE, AND NECK INJURY

Take the following steps when evaluating a patient with signs or symptoms of a head, face, or neck injury:

1. Immobilize the head in a neutral position. Stabilize the patient's neck to prevent any movement of the patient's head. If you encounter resistance when returning the head to a neutral position, leave it in the position found. If the patient is conscious, advise him or her of all treatments and attempt to gain important information about the MOI and symptoms.
2. Maintain an open airway using the jaw-thrust technique if the patient is unable to maintain his or her airway or if the patient is unresponsive. Clear any

blood or vomitus from the patient's mouth with your gloved fingers. Be prepared to suction or log roll the patient if vomiting occurs. Avoid the head tilt-chin lift technique taught for routine use for medical patients receiving cardiopulmonary resuscitation (CPR).

3. Be sure that the patient is breathing adequately on his or her own. If not, institute mouth-to-mask or mouth-to-barrier ventilation. As soon as oxygen becomes available, administer it to the patient. Oxygen is important to keep brain cells alive, especially when brain swelling is present after a serious head injury. Note that severe spinal injuries can paralyze some of the respiratory muscles, resulting in abnormal breathing patterns. In some cases, the diaphragm may be the only respiratory muscle working, resulting in **abdominal breathing**. Abdominal breathing occurs when a patient breathes using only the diaphragm, resulting in rising of the abdomen (and not the chest) with each breath.
4. If a spinal injury is suspected, ask the conscious patient the following questions:
   a. Does your neck or back hurt?
   b. Where does it hurt?
   c. What happened?
   d. Can you move your hands and feet?
   e. Can you feel me touching your fingers?
   f. Can you feel me touching your toes?
5. Assess pulse, movement, and sensation in the patient's hands and feet. Ask the patient not to move, aside from your examination.
6. Monitor the pulse and be prepared to support circulation by performing chest compressions if the patient's heart stops.
7. In patients with signs or symptoms of head injury, check to see if CSF or blood is seeping from a wound or from the nose and ears (**Figure 25**).
8. Do not try to stop leakage of CSF from a wound or other opening. Leakage from inside the skull relieves pressure.
9. Control bleeding from all head wounds with dry, sterile dressings. Use enough direct pressure to control the bleeding without disturbing the underlying tissue. Be sure to check for wounds inside the mouth. Try to prevent the patient from swallowing blood, because this can cause vomiting. Have suction ready for use and be ready to log roll the patient if bleeding from the mouth is severe.

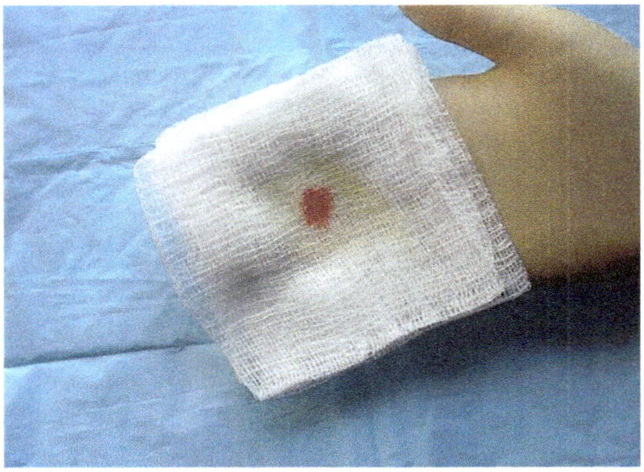

Figure 25 When CSF is present in blood or drainage, a stain in the shape of a target or halo will appear.

10. Bandage head or facial injuries so that the patient's eyes (if uninjured) remain uncovered. Being able to see will reduce the patient's tendency to panic.
11. If spinal injury is suspected, assist in immobilizing the patient using a short or long backboard in addition to a cervical collar and head blocks. Do not transfer the patient before immobilization unless it is necessary to perform CPR or because of an unsafe scene.
12. Arrange for prompt transport to an appropriate medical facility.

Management of Neck Injuries

Blunt trauma to the neck can result in crushing of the larynx or trachea (**Figure 26**). Blunt forces can also rupture blood vessels and damage the cervical spine. All direct blows to the neck should be managed with spinal immobilization and a call for EMS. LERs should observe the neck for swelling, bruising, and air trapped under the skin from airway damage. Air trapped under the skin will often result in crepitus when pressure is placed on the soft tissue. Stridor, loss of voice, and difficulty swallowing are also indications that the airway may be compromised. In some cases, these injuries may be so severe that the patient will require rapid transport to EMS or definitive care.

Penetrating injuries to the soft tissue of the neck can also result in airway damage or severe bleeding. Impaled objects in the neck should not be removed; they should be stabilized in place. Open wounds should be dressed with an occlusive dressing with direct hand pressure (**Figure 27**). Large blood

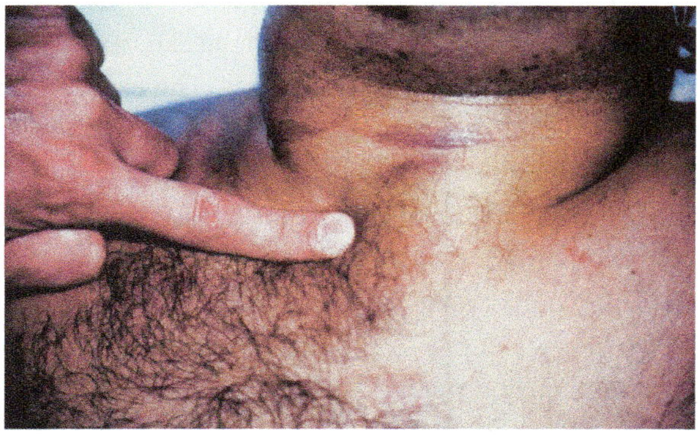

Figure 26 Fractures of the larynx or trachea can cause air to leak from the airway into the subcutaneous tissues.

vessels in the neck can suck in air that can cause air emboli and death.

Bandaging should take into account the need for cervical spine stabilization as well as providing pressure against the wound without compromising the airway. Using roller gauze, wrap in a figure-of-8 fashion going from the injured side of the neck to under the armpit and shoulder of the opposite arm. Responders should frequently assess for changes in status.

Management of Eye Injuries

Minor eye injuries often consist of irritants such as dirt, dust, eyelashes, or small foreign bodies. Do not let the patient rub the affected eye. Rubbing will cause abrasions to the outer structures of the eye. If the injury occurs near where metal fragments are present or during range exercises where brass or lead fragments are involved, a physician should inspect the eye. Immediate management of eye injuries includes a brief exam to look for larger objects. If larger foreign objects are observed freely floating in fluid behind the eyelid, they should be removed with irrigation. If no foreign bodies are visualized, consider the use of irrigation with water or eyewash (**Figure 28**).

Irrigation of the eye should always occur with copious amounts of water. If your program has access to eyewash, normal saline, or sterile water, use these fluids as directed by your protocols. If you have access to tap water only, apply the water under pressure but assess the injury and keep the water pressure to tolerable levels for the patient. Too much pressure may damage the sclera and lead to more complications. Some programs may use bulb syringes, intravenous tubing, or nasal cannulas to direct fluid into the eye. In lieu of these devices, shower heads, hoses, and faucets are more than adequate. Using basins of water should be considered a last resort. Static water does not add the benefit of washing away contaminants. If you are provided with basins of water, you would benefit from pouring the water from the basin directly on the injured eye.

Direct the selected fluid into the affected eye, flushing from the inner corner of the eye toward the outer corner. This method will protect an uninjured eye from the runoff. If both eyes are affected, rinse them both from the inside corners toward the outer corners of the eye. For burns and chemical exposures, most medical protocols suggest rinsing the eye for at least 20 minutes. After initial irrigation, you may need to irrigate the eye en route to the hospital. If further irrigation is not possible, cover the affected eye with a clean dry sterile dressing for transport. If the eyelids have suffered thermal or

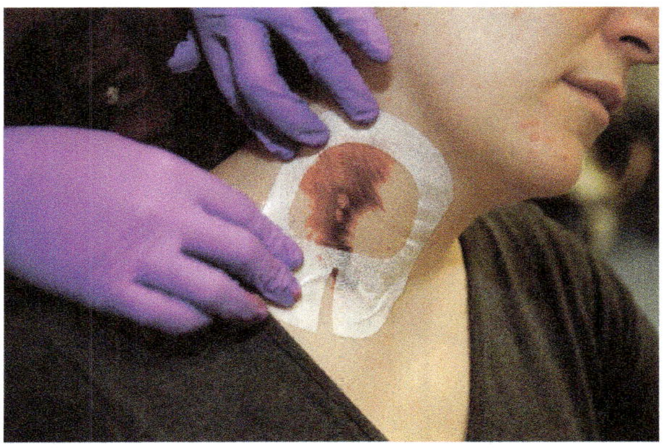

Figure 27 Apply a sterile occlusive dressing to open neck wounds.

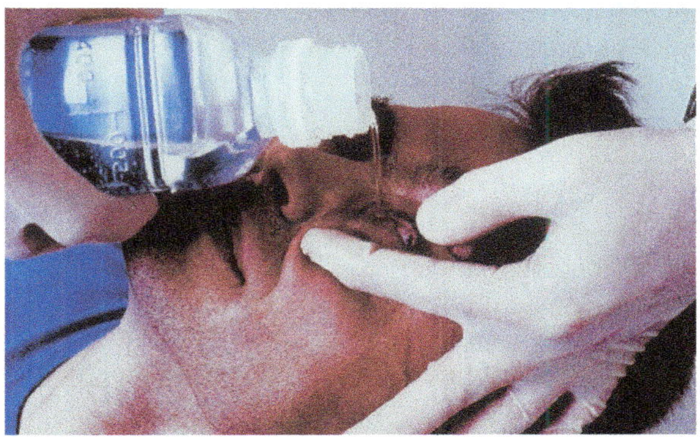

Figure 28 Eyes can be irrigated using a bottle (as shown here), shower, nasal cannula, or basin.

chemical burns, your medical direction may require you to moisten the dressings over the affected eyelid. If foreign bodies are observed and appear to be embedded in the eye, cover both eyes with dressings to prevent sympathetic movement of the injured eye and transport the patient to the emergency department.

When confronted with large, impaled objects in the eye, the LER should take care to stabilize the object and prevent it from being pulled out (Figure 29). The dressings should incorporate a paper cup or cone with a hole placed in the cup to support the impaled object. Again, both eyes should be dressed to prevent the sympathetic movement of the injured eye. If the orbit is crushed or blown out by a pressure-related injury, a gauze ring similar to a donut should be built and placed around the injured eye (Figure 30).

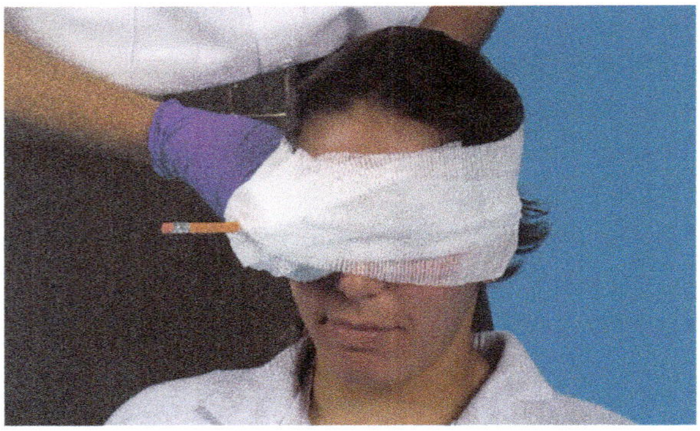

Figure 29 To bandage an eye impaled by an object, use a cup to stabilize the impaled object, then bandage both eyes to minimize eye movement.

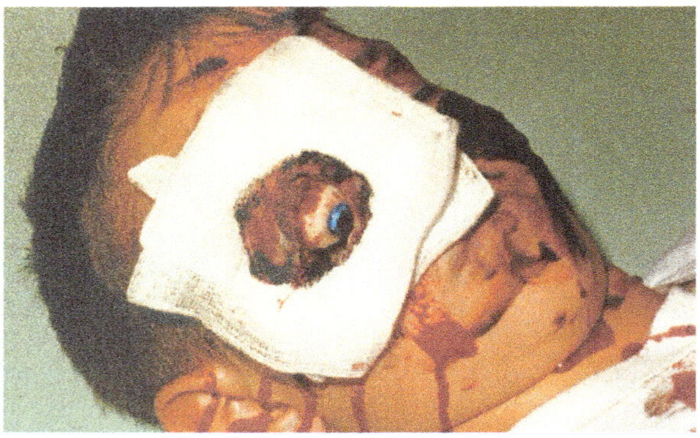

Figure 30 If the orbit is crushed or blown out, build a gauze ring similar to a donut and place it around the injured eye before applying the dressing.

Management of Ear Injuries

Ear injuries often consist of damage to the external ear or the placement of objects into the ear canal. The external ear is very vascular and can bleed freely. Direct pressure on these structures will reduce the bleeding. A dry dressing should be applied by wrapping roller gauze around the head to maintain pressure (Figure 31). If bleeding is coming from inside the ear after a head injury, take caution and do not pack a wound that may be a result of a skull fracture. Blood coming from a skull fracture may contain CSF. If you suspect that the bleeding from an ear is from a skull fracture, pack the external ear loosely with gauze and wrap with roller gauze, providing light pressure to keep the dressing in place.

Management of Nosebleeds

Signs of a nosebleed include pain or tenderness of the nose, deformity, swelling, and obvious bleeding. Symptoms include a sensation of drainage into the back of the mouth, a metallic taste, and nausea or vomiting as the result of swallowing blood. Always be on alert in these situations because blood is often swallowed into the stomach, which can cause a sudden onset of vomiting that results in the loss of the patient's airway, especially if the patient has an altered level of consciousness.

Nosebleeds can be a result of direct trauma; foreign bodies; high blood pressure; or drying of the tissue by cold, dry air. A patient with a sudden onset of a nontraumatic nosebleed should be asked about a history of nosebleeds, high blood pressure, sinus infections, and medication or drug use. Assess for facial fractures and treat per local protocols. Head and neck injury should be considered in patients with facial

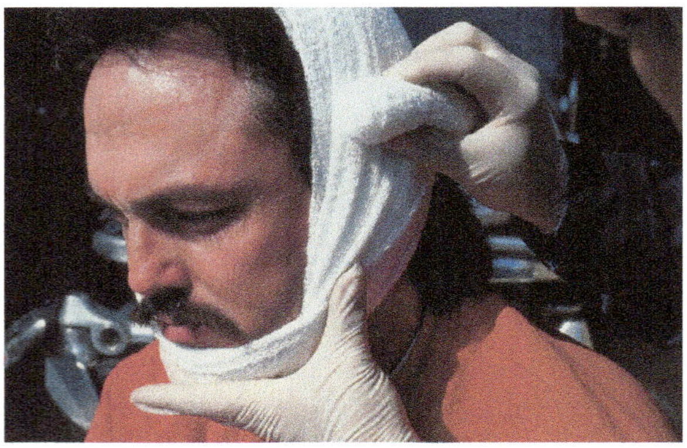

Figure 31 Apply a dry dressing around the head to maintain pressure on the ear after an ear injury.

fractures. If a skull fracture is suspected, check bloodied gauze for the halo effect.

Tip

Dangers of Nasal Trauma

The nose is often thought of as an organ of smell. However, it is also an integral part of the upper airway. Because of its prominent position on the face, the nose can be subject to blunt trauma, resulting in significant blood loss and airway compromise. The internal structures of the nose contain a large number of blood vessels necessary to carry out its many functions. Trauma to the nose generally results in profuse bleeding that is difficult to control. In addition to blood vessels, the shape of the nose is maintained by a flexible bony structure that is easily broken. The air passages of the nose lead directly to the back of the throat; therefore, any blood or bone matter forced through these passages may compromise the patient's airway.

If the nosebleed is determined to be a result of local tissue damage, drying, or high blood pressure, and the patient is capable of sitting upright, lean the patient forward and pinch the nostrils together (**Figure 32**). This technique helps the vessels in the anterior part of the nose clot and prevents blood from running down the back of the throat into the stomach. If bleeding is not controlled within a few minutes, call for EMS. Some nosebleeds are from blood vessels in the back of the nose that are not easily compressed by responders.

Because the nose is part of the upper airway, your primary concern is blockage of the airway by blood or bone fragments. Blood exposed to air can form clots large enough to block air passage to the lungs, especially in an unresponsive patient who cannot cough to clear the airway. With an unresponsive patient, it is important that you maintain an open airway, and if bleeding continues, place the patient in the recovery position to facilitate drainage.

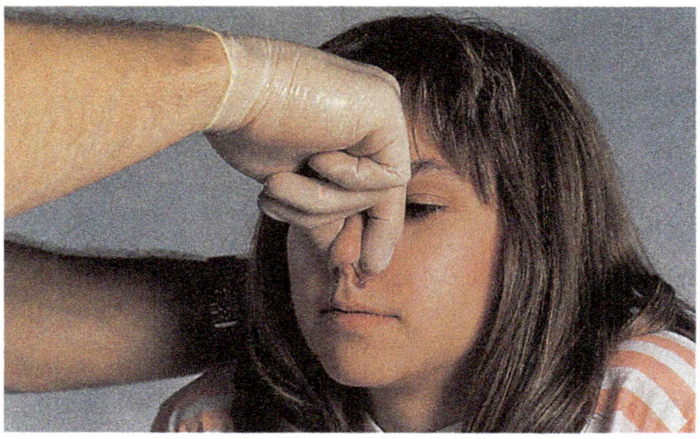

Figure 32 Control bleeding from the nose by pinching the nostrils together.

Special Populations

Nosebleeds in Pediatric and Geriatric Patients

In children, the air passages are narrow and even a small amount of blood may be sufficient to cause a blockage, thus making it important that you carefully monitor children for signs of airway compromise. Young children are also known to insert objects up their nostrils. If a child presents with a nosebleed, make sure there is no foreign object in the nose before applying pressure.

In older patients, nosebleeds may be spontaneous due to the weakening and rupture of small blood vessels due to high blood pressure. Nosebleeds may also be the result of trauma from a fall. Elderly patients may be hesitant to admit to a fall, but it is important that you determine the mechanism of injury that caused the bleed. If a fall is suspected, immediately consider the need for spinal immobilization and perform a complete trauma assessment of the patient.

It is common for the elderly or patients with a cardiac history to be taking a variety of medications for cardiac disease or clotting disorders. Be aware that people taking aspirin, Coumadin, or Plavix may have prolonged clotting times. Transport to the hospital is necessary in nearly all of these situations.

Management of Mouth Injuries

Mouth and dental wounds can be treated by placing direct pressure against the lacerated tissue with gauze. All of these wounds should be transferred to a physician for evaluation. If tissue is avulsed, it should be put back in place and held there with a gauze pad. Occasionally, teeth will be dislodged. Teeth should be handled by the crown and not the root. Immediately place dislodged teeth in normal saline, cool milk, or a commercial emergency dental solution. The tooth should be transported with the patient. If possible, make the receiving hospital aware of the dislodged tooth so personnel can be prepared to deal with a dental emergency.

SPECIAL CONSIDERATIONS FOR LAW ENFORCEMENT RESPONSE

There are two extra considerations specific to law enforcement during the evaluation of patients with possible head, face, or spine injuries: head and face protection, and care under fire.

Head and Face Protection

Although the armored helmets typically worn by tactical operators are very effective at preventing injuries to the skull, they may not protect against face or spine injuries. In most instances, the helmets can be left on the patient and secured directly to the spinal immobilization device. Other forms of head protection, including goggles and balaclavas, can be cut off using a pair of shears. Similarly, the chin strap of a helmet can be cut, if necessary, to perform a jaw thrust. The only time a helmet should be removed is when it is so loose that securing it to the spinal immobilization device will not provide adequate immobilization of the head. In this instance, two experienced people should perform the procedure outlined in **Skill Drill 6**.

1. Kneel down at the patient's head and stabilize the helmet by placing your hands on either side of it, ensuring that your fingers are on the patient's lower jaw to prevent movement of the head **STEP 1**.
2. If the patient is wearing goggles, cut the strap to remove them. Release the chin strap of the helmet or, if you cannot, cut it **STEP 2**.
3. Have your partner place one hand on the patient's lower jaw and the other behind the head to prevent the head from snapping back once the helmet is removed. Once your partner's hands are in position, remove the helmet and then stabilize the cervical spine **STEP 3**.
4. Apply a cervical collar, immobilize the head with head blocks, and secure the patient to a long backboard **STEP 4**.

Care Under Fire

Although the treatment strategies discussed in this unit apply to almost all patients with head, face, and neck injuries, they do not apply in tactical situations. The manpower and the time necessary to immobilize a patient properly are not feasible when providing care under fire. Moreover, there is little benefit to immobilizing the spine in cases of penetrating neck injury. Both of these factors lead to an unacceptable level of risk when under fire, so spinal immobilization should not be performed while in hostile environments. LERs should review their local protocols regarding head and spine trauma in the care-under-fire setting.

Chest and Abdominal Injuries

"Center mass" is the mantra of the firearms instructor because the center of the human body is large and packed full of vital organs. Placing a bullet in this area can quickly stop or eliminate a threat. As a LER, you must understand that energy from penetrating and blunt force injuries can severely injure patients. In the past, some of these injuries may have been considered minor, but that is not necessarily true. Law enforcement officers, agents, and members of the public have died from a lack of understanding regarding the seriousness of injuries to the chest and the abdomen.

ANATOMY

The human torso can be divided into the thorax and the abdomen. The thorax, also known as the chest, starts at the base of the neck and travels to the bottom of the rib cage. It is separated internally from the abdomen by the diaphragm, the large muscle that is used to help move air into the lungs. Inside the thorax, the chest and ribs are each covered by a thin lining known as the pleura. The space between these lining layers is called the **pleural space**, and the layers help to maintain a vacuum that adheres the surface of the lungs against the ribs. When the muscles between the ribs and the diaphragm contract, the chest expands, creating a negative pressure that causes the air to rush in. When the rib muscles and diaphragm relax, they push in against the lungs, creating a positive pressure that forces air out of the lungs (**Figure 33**). This process occurs 17,000 to 28,000 times a day in the average adult.

Inside the thorax, the lungs take up a large amount of the chest cavity. The lungs are located under the collarbone and ribs and extend from the top of the chest cavity down to the diaphragm. Air travels into the lungs through the trachea, which lies in the neck and behind the upper part of the sternum. The trachea then divides into the right and left mainstem bronchi behind the sternum, about a third of the way from the top. The mainstem bronchi continue into two smaller bronchial structures until the air enters the functional part of the lung, called the alveoli. The alveoli are the lung structures that are wrapped with capillaries where oxygen moves into the blood and carbon dioxide moves into the air.

Skill Drill 6

Helmet Removal With Spinal Stabilization

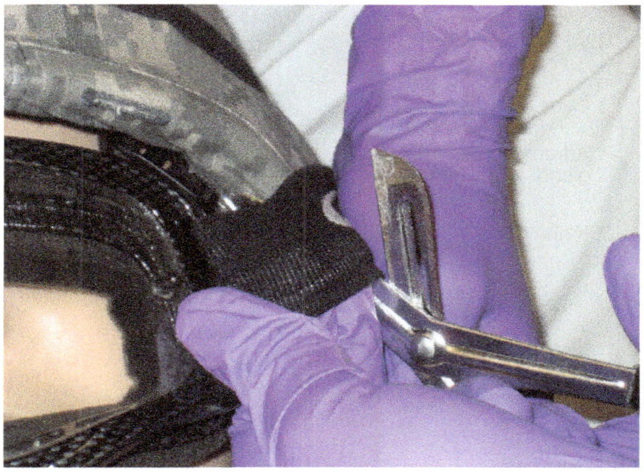

1. Kneel down at the patient's head and stabilize the helmet by placing your hands on either side of it, ensuring that your fingers are on the patient's lower jaw to prevent movement of the head. If the patient is wearing goggles, cut the strap to remove them.

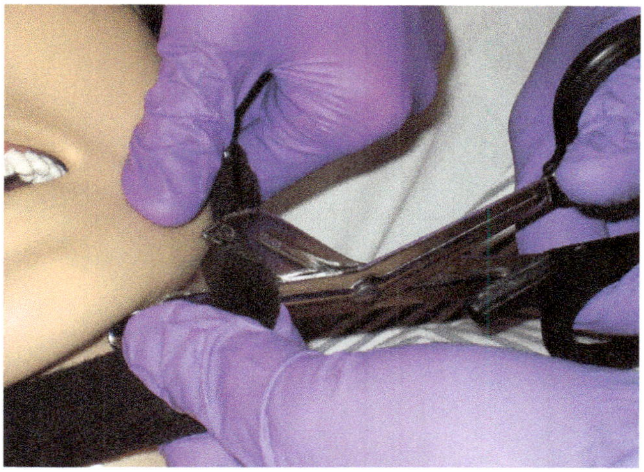

2. Release the chin strap of the helmet or, if you cannot, cut it.

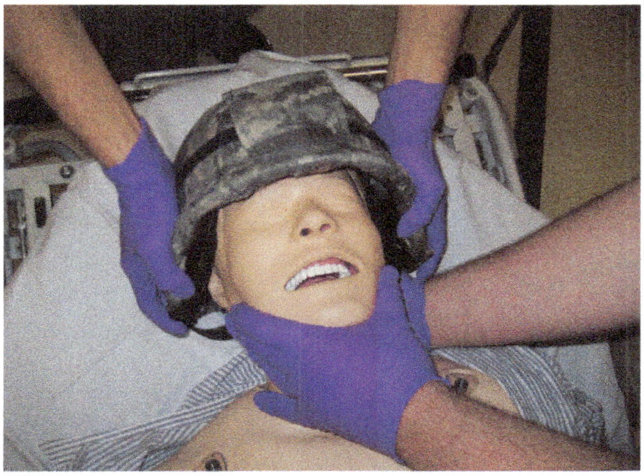

3. With your partner manually stabilizing the patient's head and neck, remove the helmet.

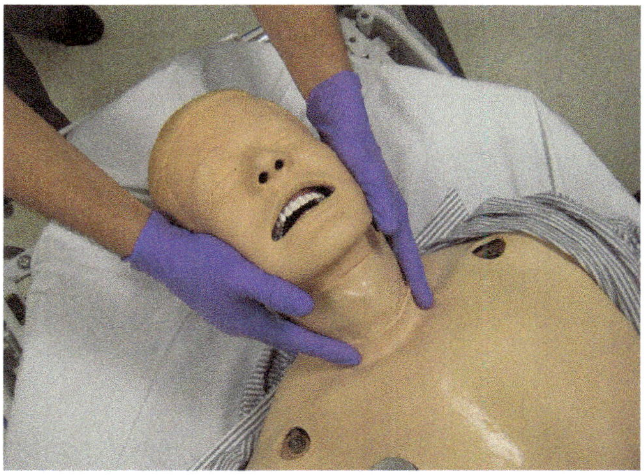

4. Apply a cervical collar, immobilize the head with head blocks, and secure the patient to a long backboard.

The heart sits behind the sternum, or breastbone, and to the left side of the chest. The heart sits inside a protective sac of very tough nonelastic tissue called the pericardium, or pericardial sac. Structures of the central circulation that travel through or near the center of the chest are the aorta, the vena cavae, and the major blood vessels of the lungs. The esophagus is a smooth muscular tube that travels from the back of the throat down through the center of the chest and into the upper left abdominal area. The esophagus is used to move food and water from the throat to the stomach (**Figure 34**).

The liver, stomach, and spleen are found inside the abdomen. They move up and down inside the bottom of the rib cage with the movement of the diaphragm. In addition to the many organs of digestion, large blood vessels run through the abdomen to support these organs and to take blood to the pelvis and legs.

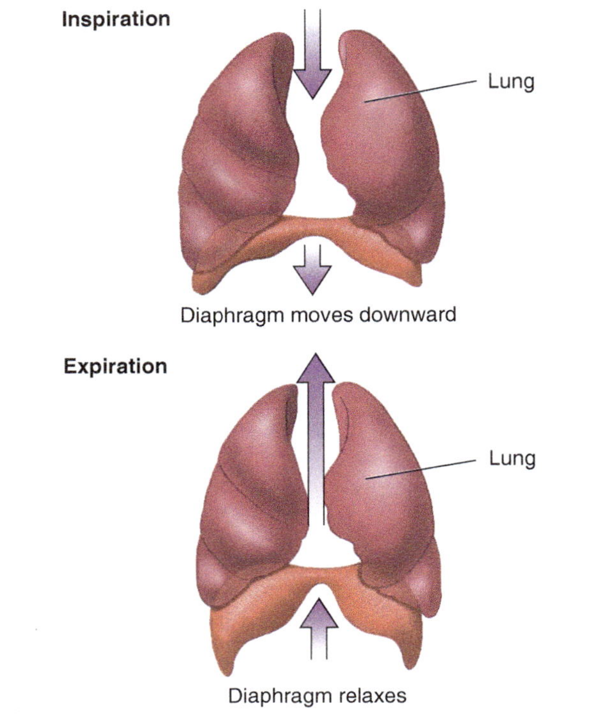

Figure 33 Mechanism of breathing.

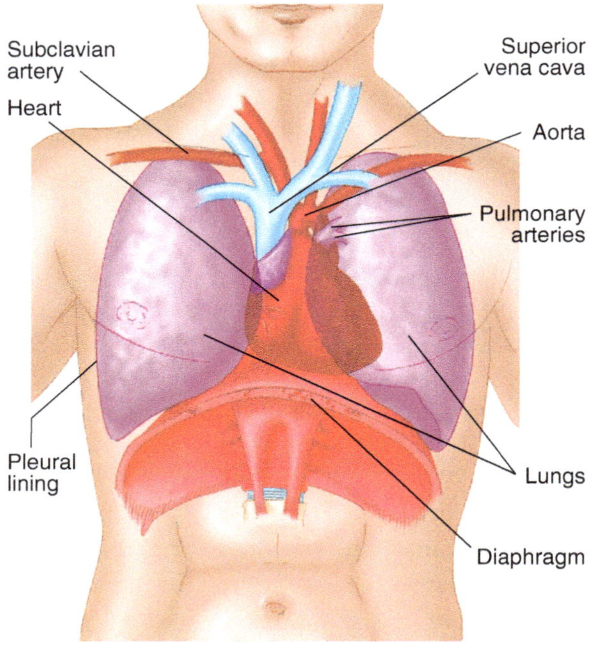

Figure 34 An anterior view of the chest shows the major organs beneath the surface.

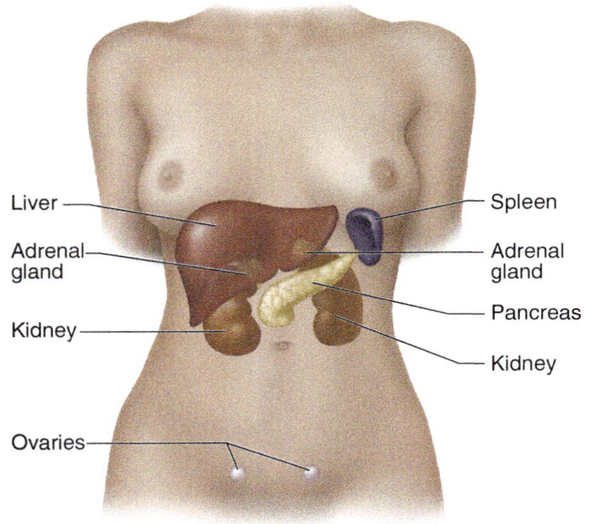

Figure 35 The solid organs are solid masses of tissue that do much of the chemical work in the body and receive a large, rich supply of blood.

The organs in the abdomen may be solid or hollow. Solid organs include the liver, spleen, kidneys, and pancreas (**Figure 35**). Hollow organs include the stomach, small intestine, large intestine, gallbladder, and urinary bladder (**Figure 36**).

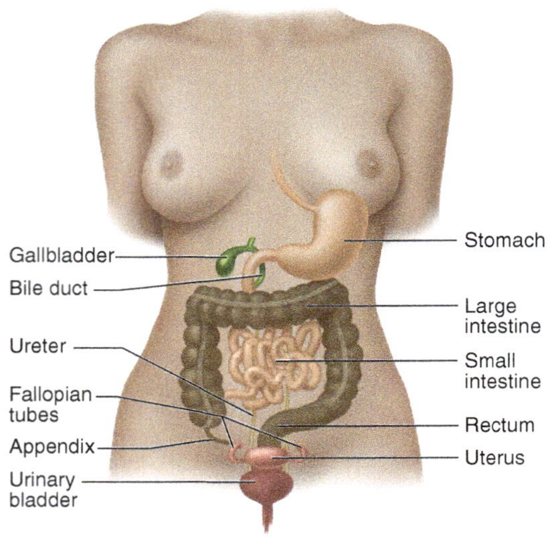

Figure 36 The hollow organs in the abdominal cavity are structures through which materials pass.

MECHANISM OF INJURY

Three types of force should be considered when determining the MOI for chest and abdominal wounds: blunt, penetrating, and blast. Damage to any part of the chest from penetrating or blunt forces can interrupt or reduce the effectiveness of the respiratory or circulatory process. These injuries immediately affect respiration and create respiratory compromise.

Blunt force involves a rapid deceleration of an object against the body or a rapid deceleration of the contents of the body against the body's coverings or support structures. Examples of mechanisms that may cause blunt force trauma are motor vehicle crashes, assault, an impact by a bullet on body armor, and a strike by a less-lethal munition. Blunt force can result in blood vessels and airways being sheared. Solid organs may crack or lacerate and bleed heavily. Hollow organs will often tear or burst, resulting in bleeding and leaking of digestive chemicals and particles into the sterile abdomen. Blunt force trauma generally results in bruising or swelling of the organs, drastically altering their function. Blunt force injuries are often referred to as closed injuries because they do not penetrate the skin.

Tip

Hollow Versus Solid Organs

When the body experiences blunt force trauma, solid organs may crack or lacerate and bleed heavily. Hollow organs will often tear or burst, resulting in bleeding and leaking of digestive chemicals and particles into the sterile abdomen.

Penetrating injuries result in the development of cavities perforating the structures (**Figure 37**). Examples of mechanisms that may cause penetrating injuries are gunshot wounds, stabbings, and shrapnel. Wounds generated by stabbing forces tend to create small temporary cavities. Wounds created by shrapnel or projectiles create larger temporary cavities directly related to the energy transferred at the time of impact of the projectile. Depending on the size of the projectile, permanent cavities about the size of the projectile may be created. These cavities can tear through blood vessels and through solid and hollow organs. Penetrating wounds that affect the chest cavity may bubble or make a sucking sound when the patient breathes in. These penetrating chest wounds are often called sucking chest wounds.

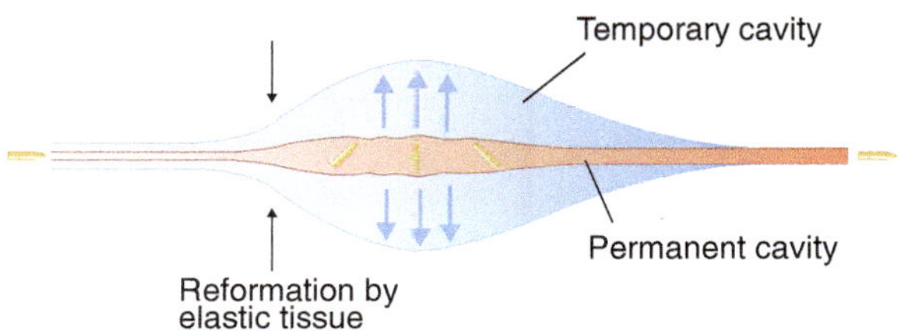

Figure 37 Shock waves from penetrating injuries result in cavitation.

Blast injuries can result in the rupture and swelling of tissue deep under the surface anatomy. Examples of mechanisms that can cause blast injuries include improvised explosive devices, military ordnance, and industrial accidents. Hollow organs can burst; airways and blood vessels can shear. The pressure wave of a blast can burst blood vessels in the lungs, creating a pathway for air embolisms.

The rib cage, pleural space, and pulmonary structures can be damaged by all three types of force. Blunt force trauma can fracture ribs, making it difficult for the patient to expand the chest. Rib fractures, lungs bursting under pressure, and penetrating wounds can all interrupt the vacuum created by the pleural space, reducing the ability of the patient to get air into the lungs.

ASSESSMENT AND MANAGEMENT

Chest and abdominal injuries can be very difficult for the LER to assess and manage. The best plan is to consider all chest and abdominal injuries as potentially dangerous. Do not take any wounds to the chest or abdomen lightly. Call EMS and let the EMS professionals make the final determination for care. During the immediate stabilization of the patient, focus your assessment on finding life threats.

Take the following steps in **Skill Drill 7** to assess the chest and abdomen:

1. Expose the chest and abdomen. Remove body armor and clothing.
2. Inspect the chest and abdomen for perforations and impacts (STEP 1). Thoroughly assess the entire chest and abdomen. Look at both the front and back and in the underarms. Do not discount areas that were covered by body armor. Look for bruises; open wounds; impaled objects; and problems with ventilation, such as rib fractures and swelling.

Skill Drill 7

Assessing the Chest and Abdomen

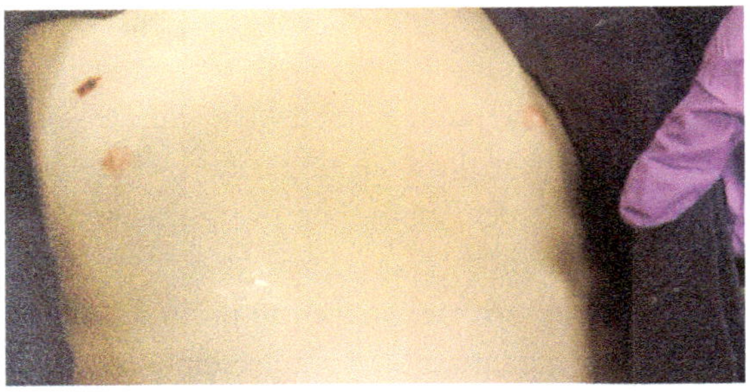

1. Expose the chest and abdomen and inspect them for perforations and impacts.

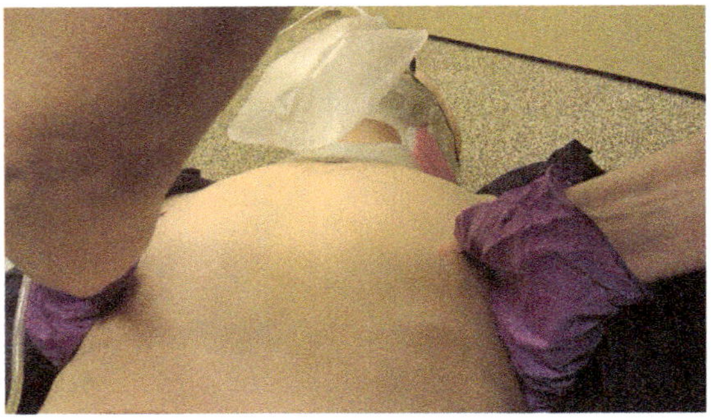

2. Feel for abnormalities, soft-tissue injuries, and pain or guarding upon palpation.

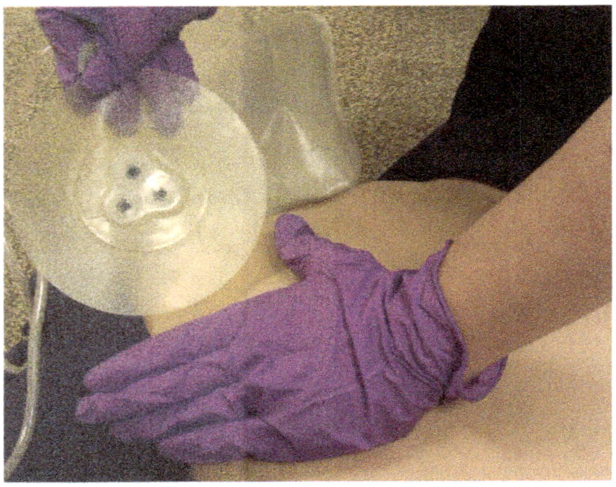

3A. Cover all open wounds to the chest and abdomen with an occlusive dressing made of plastic material.

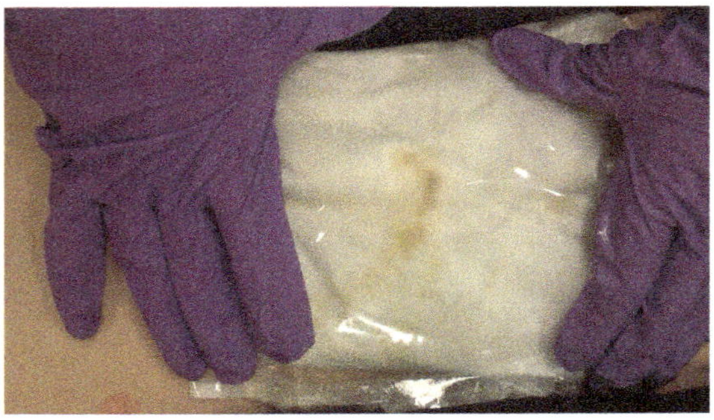

3B. If an abdominal wound presents with protruding abdominal organs, cover the organs with moist gauze and plastic.

3C. If there is active external bleeding, attempt to control the external bleeding by firmly placing gauze over the wound and applying direct pressure.

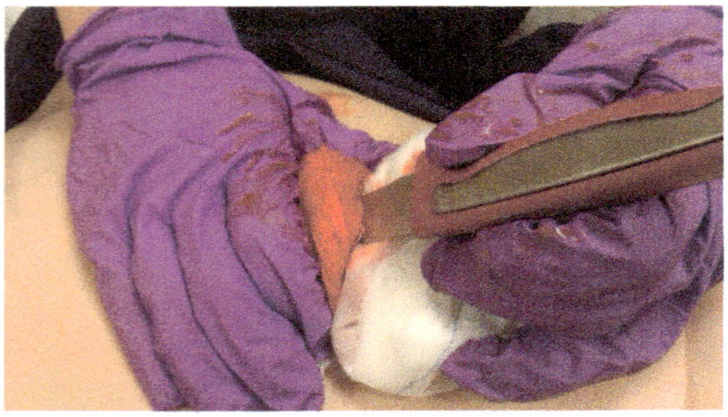

3D. Stabilize impaled objects with your hand until you are able to place gauze pads around the impaled objects for additional protection.

3. Feel for abnormalities, soft-tissue injuries, and pain or guarding upon palpation STEP 2. Note these findings, report them to other responders, and observe them for changes.
4. Cover all open wounds to the chest and abdomen with an occlusive dressing made of plastic material STEP 3A. Commercial seals are often used in care-under-fire scenarios to seal penetrating chest and abdominal wounds. They are often well packaged and easily applied. If a commercial dressing is not readily available, you may use clean plastic (such as sandwich bags), taping down three sides. Ensure that the plastic seals to the wound during inspiration and can vent during expiration. Refer to your medical direction for their preference of chest seals or dressing techniques.
5. If an abdominal wound presents with protruding abdominal organs, cover the organs with moist gauze and plastic STEP 3B. If you are unable to moisten gauze or dressings, cover directly with a plastic dressing. Rescuers should not attempt to return any protruding abdominal organs into the open abdomen unless specifically trained and authorized by the medical director.
6. If a wound to the chest or abdomen occurs with active external bleeding, attempt to control the external bleeding by firmly placing gauze over the wound and applying direct pressure STEP 3C. When possible, cover the wound with an occlusive dressing.
7. Stabilize rib fractures that are altering the patient's breathing with direct hand pressure and pressure dressings.
8. Stabilize impaled objects with your hand until you are able to place gauze pads around the impaled objects for additional protection STEP 3D. Never remove impaled objects without medical direction.

Although there are many complex chest wounds, such as **cardiac tamponade** (bleeding into the sac surrounding the heart) or **traumatic asphyxia** (crushing of the chest), the emergency responder can do little more for these patients than to call for EMS and provide general trauma care. **Table 2** provides a guide for the LER to use in preparing for the most common chest and abdominal injuries.

Special Populations

Respiratory Capacity in Elderly and Pregnant Patients

Elderly patients do not have good respiratory reserves. Damage to the thorax can cause immediate respiratory compromise. The rib cage becomes increasingly brittle with age. Muscle atrophy to the chest and abdomen allows for deeper penetration of energy into the body, creating a greater potential for significant trauma.

Pregnant patients have a reduced respiratory capacity because the pregnant uterus pushes up into the chest. The pregnant uterus also can precipitate severe abdominal hemorrhage. All efforts should be made to get pregnant patients experiencing chest or abdominal injuries to a medical facility.

Table 2

Chest and Abdominal Wounds

Assessment	Treatment*	Condition	Image
• Pain at site of chest injury • Penetrating wound to thorax • Trouble breathing	• Call for EMS. • Provide general trauma care. • Immediately cover open wound with a gloved hand. • Apply an occlusive dressing or a commercial chest seal. • Apply oxygen. • Monitor patient.	**Simple pneumothorax** • Air enters into a hole in the chest wall and travels in and out of the hole. • An occlusive dressing should prevent air entry into chest while allowing it to vent.	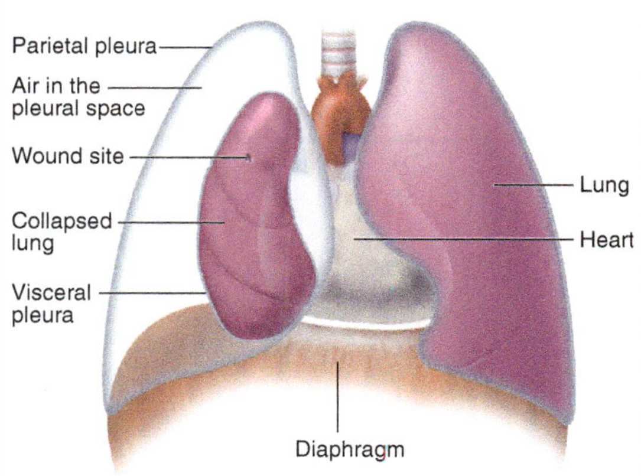

(Continues)

Table 2

Chest and Abdominal Wounds *(continued)*

<table>
<tr>
<td>
• Pain at site of chest injury
• Penetrating or closed wound to thorax
• Increasing trouble breathing
• Look for:
  ◦ Crepitus over injury site
  ◦ Jugular vein distension
  ◦ In very severe cases, trachea may move away from injured side
  ◦ Cyanosis
</td>
<td>
• Call for EMS.
• Provide general trauma care.
• Immediately cover open wound with a gloved hand.
• Apply an occlusive dressing or a commercial chest seal.
• For closed injuries, observe for a flail chest and treat as needed.
• Apply oxygen.
• Monitor patient.
</td>
<td>
<u>Tension pneumothorax</u>
• Air enters chest from outside through a penetrating wound or it leaks into the chest through damage to the lung or airways.
• Pressure builds up in the chest, collapsing the lungs. Death results from decreased blood flow to the heart as the pressure in the chest pinches off the vena cavae and reduces the effectiveness of the right side of the heart.
</td>
<td>
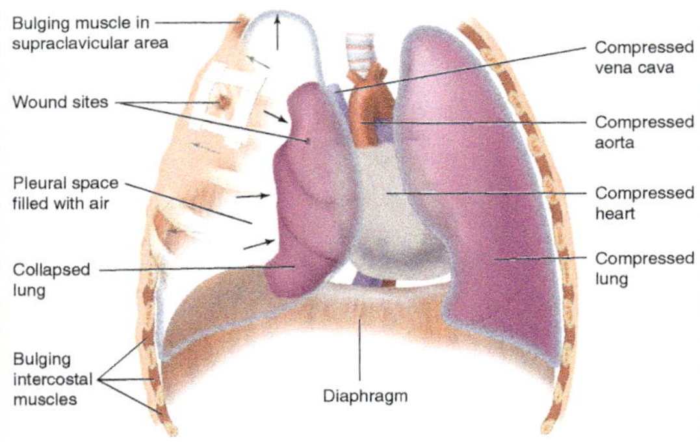

</td>
</tr>
<tr>
<td>
• Profound shock
• Pale, cool, clammy skin
• Penetrating or closed wound to thorax
</td>
<td>
• Call for EMS.
• Provide general trauma care.
• Immediately cover open wound with a gloved hand.
• Apply an occlusive dressing or a commercial chest seal.
• For closed injuries, observe for a flail chest and treat as needed.
• Apply oxygen.
• Monitor patient.
</td>
<td>
<u>Hemothorax</u>
• Massive bleeding into the chest. The chest can hold the patient's entire blood volume without external signs of bleeding.
</td>
<td>
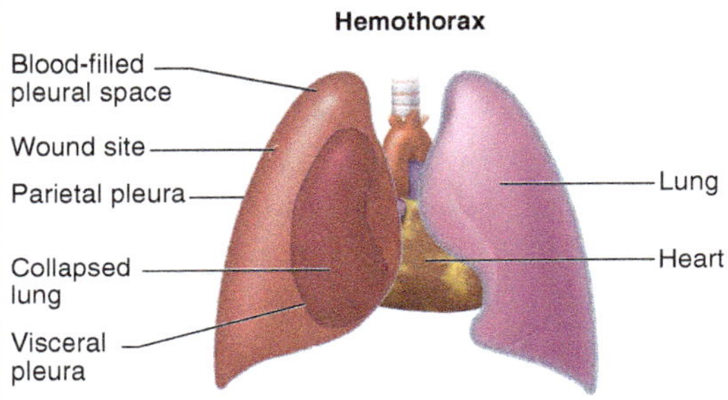

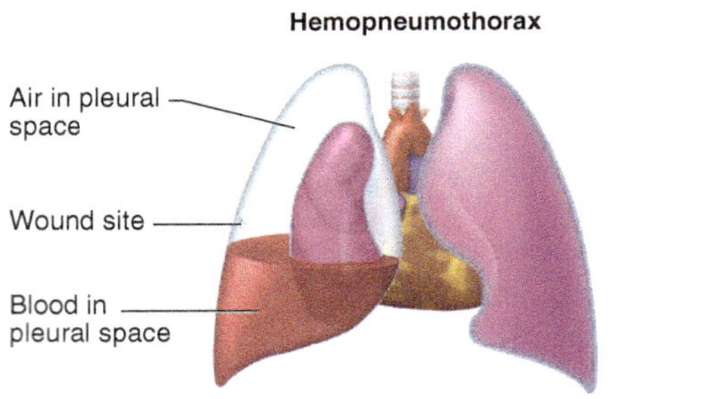

</td>
</tr>
</table>

Table 2

Chest and Abdominal Wounds *(continued)*

• Difficulty breathing • Deformity at the site of blunt force energy • Damaged ribs or sternum move in opposition to the surrounding chest wall • Look for crepitus over injury site	• Call for EMS. • Provide general trauma care. • Place firm hand pressure over flail segment. • Apply dressing material over area and splint with cravats. • Apply oxygen. • Monitor patient.	Flail chest • Ribs or sternum break off as a unit sheet and move against the normal expansion of the chest (paradoxical movement).	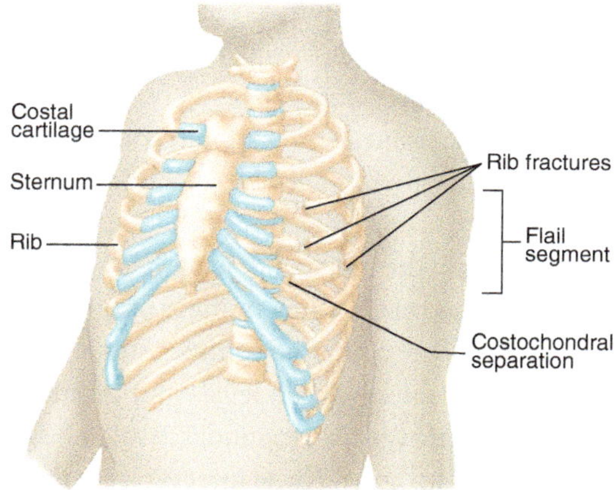
• Object, such as knife, tool, or shrapnel, passes through the body, chest, or abdominal wall. The object gets stuck in the tissue and remains visible to the exterior body, chest, or abdomen.	• Call for EMS. • Provide general trauma care. • **Do not remove the object unless it interferes with CPR.** • Place bulky dressing material around the object and splint with cravats. • Apply oxygen. • Monitor patient.	Impaled object	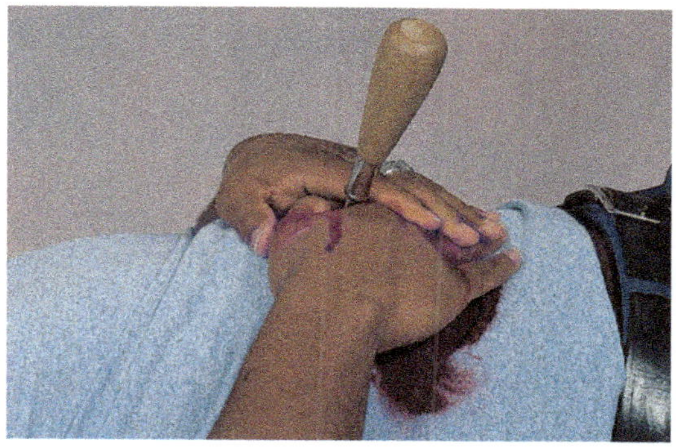
• Opening in abdominal wall with exposure or protrusion of abdominal organs to atmosphere	• Call for EMS. • Provide general trauma care. • **Do not repack organs into abdomen.** • Place occlusive dressing material over opening or abdominal organs. Cover occlusive dressing with bulky padding and splint with cravats or tape. • Apply oxygen. • Monitor patient.	Evisceration	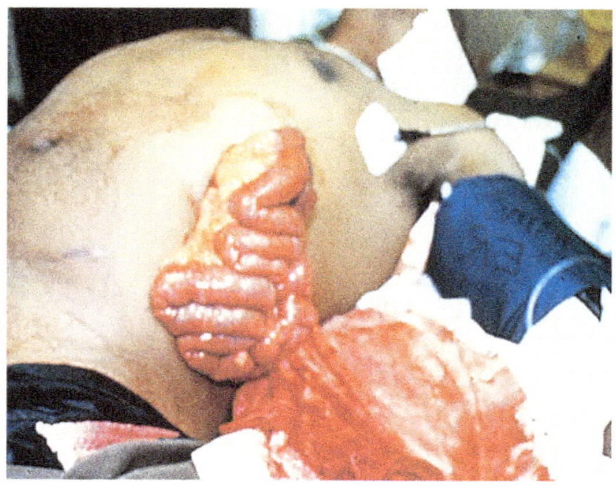

*Always follow local medical direction and protocols.

LAW ENFORCEMENT CONSIDERATIONS

Because of the diverse nature of law enforcement, LERs should have a plan and make resources available to treat any of the injuries identified. Falls, large animals, off-road vehicles, motor vehicles, assaults, and explosions are a few of the many encounters that can result in life-threatening chest and abdominal injuries. You should consider what you will need to do to provide self-help or buddy aid during care-under-fire situations. Focus on care that can be done quickly and falls within the scope of practice allowed by the medical director. Occasionally, some training programs and vendors do not take into account the complexities of emergency care provided at more advanced levels and promote these concepts at the emergency responder level. Ensure that your training program and medical director are fully involved and approve your approach to chest and abdominal care.

CONCLUSION

Conventional trauma occurs in all settings, all the time. LERs who are prepared and understand the importance of dealing with all injuries are assets to the public they serve and the force they protect. The tactical environment creates unique circumstances that place law enforcement officers and agents at high risk for a wide range of injuries. Some will assume that LERs need only to understand bleeding control and chest injuries. Although these injuries are lethal if left untreated, they cannot be the only goal of law enforcement trauma preparedness.

Soft tissue and extremity trauma are routinely encountered in police training and operations. Motor vehicle crashes, falls, explosions, and assaults are standard occurrences in today's society. These violent events lead to head, neck, spine, sensory, chest, and abdominal trauma without discrimination of age or duty status. LERs preparing for conventional trauma should focus on assessment and care techniques in the settings in which they may encounter these injuries. The swift action of the LER to trauma will provide the injured person the best chance for survival.

Prep Kit

READY FOR REVIEW

- Soft-tissue and extremity injuries can range from very mild to life threatening. A thorough assessment always needs to be performed.
- Although these injuries can be very dramatic or grotesque, a wound's appearance is secondary to the condition of the patient's airway and pulse.
- There are three layers of skin: epidermis, dermis, and subcutaneous.
- Mechanisms of injury are directly influenced by the laws of physics and the body's ability to respond to the release of energy during an event.
- There are three types of injury mechanism: direct force, indirect force, and twisting force.
- A fracture is another name for a broken bone.
- Fractures can be either open or closed, depending on whether the skin is broken.
- A dislocation is a separation between two bones at a joint.
- A sprain is a stretching injury to the supporting ligaments of an extremity that occurs at a joint.
- Stretching or tearing injuries to muscles or tendons are known as strains.
- Soft-tissue wounds can be classified as amputations, abrasions, lacerations, punctures, or avulsions.
- Sometimes foreign objects remain embedded in the tissue and are known as impaled objects. You should not remove an impaled object from a patient's body.
- Burns are classified by the depth and extent of the tissue involved. There are three types or degrees of burns: superficial, partial thickness, and full thickness.
- Use the rule of nines to estimate the extent of a burn.
- Whenever assessing an extremity, remember to check for pulse, capillary refill, movement, and sensation.
- Dressings are usually sterile and are placed directly over a wound. Bandages are used to hold dressings in place.
- Improper handling of a patient with significant head or neck injuries can cause brain damage, paralysis, or death.
- Injuries of the head are classified as open or closed. In a closed head injury, bleeding and swelling within the skull may increase pressure on the brain, leading to irreversible brain damage. An open head injury often bleeds profusely.
- When signs or symptoms of a head injury are present, immobilize the head and stabilize the neck; maintain an open airway; support breathing; monitor circulation; check to see if cerebrospinal fluid or blood is seeping; control bleeding with dry, sterile dressings; and arrange for prompt transport.
- Airway obstruction is the primary danger in severe facial injuries.
- When you suspect a spinal injury, do not move the patient during examination. Further, do not allow the patient to move.
- When a sign or symptom of neck injury is present, place the head and spine in a neutral position; immobilize the head and stabilize the spine; maintain an open airway; support breathing; monitor circulation; assess pulse, movement, and sensation; assist in immobilizing the patient using a long or short backboard; and arrange for prompt transport.
- Injuries to the face typically result in bleeding or collapse of the facial bones, which can, in serious cases, lead to airway obstruction. Although facial injuries can bleed considerably, as long as the airway is intact they are rarely life threatening.
- If a balaclava or goggles need to be removed, cut them off while stabilizing the patient's head. Helmets should stay on in most cases; if one must come off, however, use a partner and remove it while supporting and stabilizing the patient's head and neck.

- The chest (thorax) extends from the base of the neck and the collarbone down to the bottom of the rib cage. The organs and structures in the thorax are vital to survival.
- The abdomen starts under the diaphragm and travels down into the pelvis. The organs in the abdomen are susceptible to bleeding and damage that can release digestive fluids and material into the sterile abdomen.
- The components of the thorax that work together for respiration can be damaged from penetrating, blunt, or blast force trauma.
- Many chest injuries are difficult for the LER to assess and manage. Always call EMS and never discount injuries to the thorax or abdomen as minor.
- Do a thorough assessment of the chest. LERs should specifically inspect body armor for penetrations and impacts. Never discount areas covered by body armor as injury free.
- LERs should have resources approved by their training and medical direction to provide immediate care to thoracic and abdominal injuries.
- Elderly and pregnant patients are more compromised by thoracic and abdominal injuries than the typical adult population.

VITAL VOCABULARY

abdominal breathing Breathing using only the diaphragm, resulting in rising of the abdomen (not the chest) with each breath.

abrasions Injuries in which the outermost layer of skin, the epidermis, is scraped away. Commonly called road rash.

amputation An injury in which a body part or limb is completely severed.

aqueous humor A clear fluid that fills the anterior chamber of the eye.

avulsions Injuries in which a piece of skin is either torn completely loose from all of its attachments or is left hanging as a flap.

bandages Adhesive, roller gauze, cravats, or tape used to hold a clean, sterile dressing in place.

Battle's sign Bruising behind one or both ears. Caused by a particular type of skull fracture.

cardiac tamponade Caused by blood leaking into the sac that surrounds the heart. The bleeding will constrict the chambers of the heart and prevent the heart from pumping.

cerebrospinal fluid (CSF) A clear, watery, straw-colored fluid that fills the space between the brain and spinal cord and their protective coverings.

closed fractures Fractures in which the bone ends do not break the skin.

closed head injury Injury in which there is bleeding or swelling or both inside the skull.

cochlea The inner ear where sound is collected and processed, along with balance information.

conjunctiva The thin outer covering of the eye.

cornea Clear tissue that sits in front of the iris and pupil and provides protection and structural support to these structures.

dermis The middle layer of skin, which contains nerve endings, blood vessels, hair follicles, sweat glands, and oil glands.

direct force injuries Injuries resulting from energy released directly to a part of the body, such as being hit in the head with a baseball bat.

dislocation A separation between two bones at a joint.

dressings Sterile gauze or clean cloth placed directly over a wound.

epidermis The outermost layer of skin.

evisceration Open wound to the abdomen that exposes abdominal organs to the environment.

flail chest A portion of ribs or sternum that has broken free from the rest of the chest. It moves in the opposite direction of the normal chest structures, creating inadequate respiration.

fractures Broken bones.

full-thickness burns Burns involving all three layers of skin, possibly exposing muscle and bone beneath the charred area.

hemothorax Bleeding inside the chest cavity, which may fill the pleural space.

hypodermis The subcutaneous layer of skin, which is mostly fatty tissue.

impaled objects Objects, such as knives, tools, or shrapnel, that penetrate the body, become stuck in the tissue, and part may be visible outside the body.

indirect force injuries Injuries resulting from a secondary release of energy that is transferred or transmitted along a path to the site of the injury.

intervertebral disk A cushion-like structure between each vertebrae body.

iris The colored portion of the eye that contains structures that receive external information.

joint The location where two bones come together.

lacerations Jagged cuts or tears in the skin.

lacrimal gland The gland that creates tears and lubricates the space between the conjunctiva and the eyelid.

ligaments Tissues that connect bone to bone.

log-roll technique The means by which a patient with a suspected spinal injury is turned without twisting or bending the spine. This procedure involves at least three people.

occlusive dressings Dressings made of Vaseline-impregnated gauze, aluminum foil, or plastic that protects a wound from air and bacteria.

open fractures Fractures in which the bone ends break the skin.

open head injury Injury in which a hole or crack in the skull allows blood or cerebrospinal fluid to leak out, relieving the pressure on the brain.

optic nerve The nerve that takes the visual information from the eye to the brain for processing.

orbit The bony socket in the skull where the eyes are located.

partial-thickness burns Burns involving the outer and middle layers of skin, resulting in extreme pain, redness, and blisters.

pleural space The space that is created between the lining over the lungs and the lining of the ribs. Injuries to the chest that damage the pleural space can result in air, blood, or both air and blood in the space, compromising the vacuum.

puncture wounds Wounds caused by a sharp or pointed object.

pupil The dark open area inside the iris that controls the amount of light entering the eye.

raccoon eyes Bruising around one or both eyes. This occurs as a result of a certain type of skull fracture.

retina Located in the back of the eye, the structure that receives the visual cues from the lens, iris, and pupil. It collects the information for transfer to the brain.

rigid splints Splinting devices made of firm materials such as hard plastic, aluminum, or wood.

rule of nines A way to calculate the amount of body surface burned; the body is divided into sections, each of which constitutes approximately 9% or 18% of the total body surface area.

sclera The white structural portion of the eye.

simple pneumothorax An accumulation of air in the pleural space, it may decrease the effectiveness of ventilatory efforts.

sling and swathe Technique of using two cravats to secure the arm to the torso.

sprain A stretching injury that occurs to the supporting ligaments of a joint.

strains Stretching or tearing injuries that occur to muscles or tendons.

superficial burns Burns involving the outermost layer of skin, resulting in redness, pain, and swelling.

tendons Tissues that connect muscles to bones.

tension pneumothorax A life-threatening collection of air within the pleural space from a hole in the chest or from damage to the lung due to a blunt or blast injury.

tourniquet A wide, constricting band that is tightened to the point at which all blood flow beyond the point of the tourniquet ceases.

traction splints Commercial splints used to apply consistent force on the femur, hence restoring alignment and stabilization of a suspected fracture.

traumatic asphyxia Crushing of the chest that pushes the chest contents up into the top of the thorax and neck.

twisting injuries Injuries resulting when a part of the body is forced beyond its normal limit due to a spiral or spinning-type motion. Injuries commonly seen in sports in which a part of the body is forced beyond its normal limits due to a spiral or spinning-type motion.

vertebrae The 33 bones that make up the spinal column.

vitreous humor The clear, jelly-like fluid that fills the posterior chamber of the eye.

CHECK YOUR KNOWLEDGE

1. You are called to the scene of a domestic violence incident where your patient has been stabbed with a kitchen knife. The perpetrator has been secured, and you find that your patient has a severe laceration involving an artery in the arm. Following the application of gloves, you should immediately do the following:
   a. Administer oxygen.
   b. Grab a towel and apply firm, direct pressure.
   c. Apply a tourniquet above the laceration.
   d. Splint the arm in the hope that it will stop bleeding once immobilized.
2. A patient with a severe head injury is noted to have clear, straw-colored fluid coming from a cut on his forehead. Treatment for this wound should include:
   a. direct pressure over the source of the bleeding.
   b. a pressure dressing wrapped around the cut but not over the eyes.
   c. suction of the bleeding from the wound.
   d. none of the above.
3. Your buddy falls off a climbing wall while training in full tactical gear and lands on his back. You notice that his helmet is still on but that the strap has come loose, resulting in the helmet lying partially off his head. You should:
   a. ask him to take the helmet all the way off and get up.
   b. immobilize him to a backboard while taping the loose helmet in place.
   c. remove his helmet with a partner who is stabilizing his spine and then immobilize him on a backboard.
   d. call EMS and let him lie on the ground.
4. To treat a penetrating wound to the chest, you should:
   a. leave the wound uncovered.
   b. cover the wound with a dry, bulky dressing.
   c. place oxygen tubing directly into the wound.
   d. cover the wound with a gloved hand.
5. Impaled objects must be:
   a. stabilized in place.
   b. removed if loose.
   c. removed unless they are in the chest.
   d. stabilized in place only if they are in the abdomen.

Assessment in Action

SCENARIO

You respond to an incident involving a person shot in the right arm and right upper quadrant of the abdomen. Once the scene is secured you are tasked with aiding the victim until EMS arrives. As you approach the patient, it is obvious that there is significant bleeding from the arm and abdomen. The patient responds only when you talk loudly at him, and his skin is sweaty and pale.

ACTIONS

1. What is your first patient care priority?
   - **A.** Maintain cervical spine stabilization because the patient may have hurt his neck if he fell after being shot.
   - **B.** Stop the bleeding.
   - **C.** Open the airway.
   - **D.** Elevate the legs to treat for shock.
2. Which of the following methods would not be appropriate to use when controlling bleeding?
   - **A.** Tourniquet
   - **B.** Direct pressure
   - **C.** Pressure dressing
   - **D.** Large, absorbent dressing
3. Which type of shock is this patient exhibiting signs and symptoms of?
   - **A.** Hypovolemic
   - **B.** Distributive
   - **C.** Anaphylactic
   - **D.** Cardiogenic
4. What are other signs and symptoms that would indicate this patient is progressing through the stages of this kind of shock?
   - **A.** Becoming alert and oriented
   - **B.** Having strong radial pulses
   - **C.** Becoming cool to the touch
   - **D.** Having warm and dry skin
5. Which type of medical treatment facility should this patient be transported to?
   - **A.** Trauma center
   - **B.** Community hospital
   - **C.** Bariatric referral center
   - **D.** Closest walk-in clinic

SECTION 7

Special Populations

Section Contents

Pregnancy and Childbirth

Unit 20

Cathleen Vandenbraak

Law Enforcement Responder Objectives

- Understand the anatomy and physiology of the organs related to pregnancy. (p 391)
- Realize the seriousness of vaginal bleeding and know the steps for assessing and managing the condition. (pp 391–393)
- Realize the increased incidence of trauma in pregnant women and the role of the LER in reporting abuse. (p 393)
- Understand the three stages of labor and the factors in deciding whether to transport a woman to a medical facility for delivery or assist with an on-scene delivery. (pp 393–398)
- Assist a woman with the delivery of a baby. (pp 396–398)
- Know the contents of an obstetric kit and how to use them. (pp 396–398)
- Describe the unique positioning of a pregnant woman for transport and explain the reason for this positioning. (pp 394–396)
- Recognize abnormal childbirth situations and know the plan of care for each situation. (pp 399–400)
- Provide adequate care for a newborn and be able to resuscitate a newborn if necessary. Know the appropriate heart rate and respiratory rate for a newborn. (pp 398–399)

National EMS Education Standard Competencies

Special Patient Populations

Recognizes and manages life threats based on simple assessment findings for a patient with special needs while awaiting additional emergency response.

Obstetrics

Recognition and management of

- Normal delivery (pp 393–398)
- Vaginal bleeding in the pregnant patient (pp 391–393)

Neonatal care

- Newborn care (pp 398–399)
- Neonatal resuscitation (pp 398–399)

Trauma

Uses simple knowledge to recognize and manage life threats based on assessment findings for an acutely injured patient while awaiting additional emergency medical response.

Special Considerations in Trauma

Recognition and management of trauma in

- Pregnant patient (p 393)

INTRODUCTION

Calls to assist with female reproductive emergencies can be anxiety provoking because they don't happen very often. To alleviate any concerns you may have, remember several things. First, childbirth is a natural process. Women have been having babies for thousands of years. Even today, in many countries medical assistance during a birth is the exception, not the rule. The law enforcement responder's (LER's) role is to assist and reassure the mother in this natural process. Second, understanding basic medical information allows accurate assessment and support for the patient. Finally, remember to remain calm. Call for emergency medical services (EMS) support if needed. This unit discusses **obstetrics** and **gynecology** in terms of female reproductive anatomy and physiology, childbirth, and complications with pregnancy and childbirth.

BASIC ANATOMY AND PHYSIOLOGY

The primary purpose of the female reproductive anatomy is to accommodate pregnancy and carry out the childbirth process (**Figure 1**). **Ovaries** are small, almond-shaped organs located on each side of the lower abdomen. They release eggs that travel through the **fallopian tubes**. In normal reproduction, a sperm fertilizes the egg in the fallopian tube. The fertilized egg then travels down the fallopian tube to the **uterus**. The uterus, also known as the womb, is a vascular and muscular organ that expands to the size of a watermelon as the fetus grows. The fertilized egg attaches to the wall of the uterus and begins to develop into an **embryo**. The embryo grows into the **fetus** inside the **amniotic sac**. The amniotic sac, also known as the **bag of waters**, is full of amniotic fluid that serves to isolate and protect the fetus. The fetus exchanges oxygen, nutrients, and waste through the **umbilical cord**. The umbilical cord is attached to the **placenta**. The placenta is a fleshy, highly vascular organ that develops on the inner lining of the wall of the uterus. A full-term baby is delivered between 38 and 40 weeks of pregnancy.

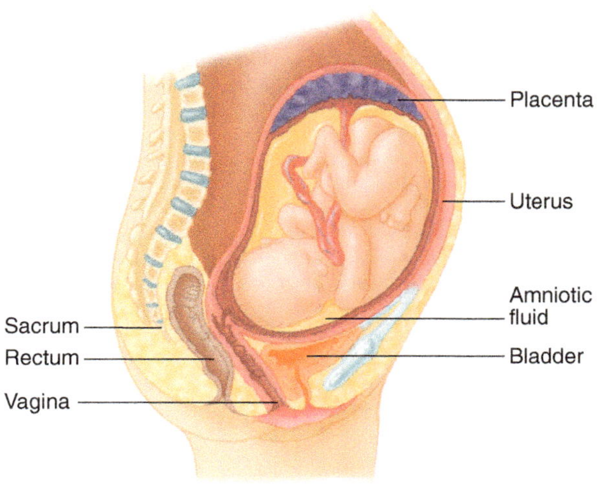

Figure 1 Anatomy of a pregnant woman.

This process is not seamless. Complications can arise at any stage in the reproductive process. If you remember when complication signs and symptoms arise in the pregnancy, you will have a good idea of what is going on and how to treat the patient.

PREGNANCY COMPLICATIONS

Early Complications

One early complication of pregnancy is an **ectopic pregnancy**. This occurs when the fertilized egg implants in the wrong place, usually the fallopian tube. As the fertilized egg grows into an embryo, it expands the fallopian tube, causing one-sided lower abdominal pain. Eventually, the tube ruptures, causing signs and symptoms of shock. A patient may not know she is pregnant when this occurs; therefore, all women of childbearing age presenting with one-sided lower abdominal pain should be transported immediately to an appropriate medical facility for an urgent evaluation.

Another complication that can occur during pregnancy is a **spontaneous abortion**, also known as a miscarriage. Although a spontaneous abortion can occur at any time in pregnancy, it is most common in the first 12 weeks. The patient may have vaginal bleeding and pass tissue. Sometimes this is accompanied by lower abdominal cramping. If a woman expels the fetus or any other tissues, collect them in a sterile bag and transport them with the patient to the hospital. Infection and bleeding are the greatest risks to the patient.

Tip

Signs and Symptoms of Shock

Signs and symptoms of shock include the following:

- Confusion, restlessness, or anxiety
- Cold, clammy, sweaty, pale skin
- Rapid breathing
- Rapid, weak pulse
- Increased capillary refill time
- Nausea and vomiting
- Weakness or fainting
- Thirst

Later Complications

In the second half of pregnancy, complications are likely to involve the placenta. Any injury to the placenta can affect the woman's health and the survival of the fetus. The placenta can separate from the uterine wall. This is called **abruptio placentae** (**Figure 2**). Abruptio placentae may be seen in trauma situations. Bleeding in the second half of pregnancy may be due to **placenta previa** (**Figure 3**). This condition occurs when the placenta does not attach high on the uterine wall and instead attaches partially or completely over the opening of the **cervix**. As the patient gets closer to the date of delivery, the opening of the cervix may widen, exposing the placenta and causing blood to flow into the **vagina**.

Assessment of Pregnancy Complications

If the patient consents, expose the genitalia to determine whether the patient is still bleeding and assess the amount and type of blood present. When evaluating vaginal bleeding in a pregnant woman, the same assessment principles for any medical emergency apply. It is important to remember that any vaginal bleeding in pregnancy is a serious sign until proven otherwise.

Management of Pregnancy Complications

When your assessment is completed, determine whether the patient is exhibiting shock symptoms and initiate oxygen therapy via a nonrebreathing mask at 15 liters per minute or according to your local protocol.

Do not pack the vagina with dressings to control the flow of blood. Cover the genitalia with bulky dressings to absorb the blood flow. Evaluate vital signs on a regular basis per agency protocol. Call for advanced life support (ALS) if you have any concern that the patient may be in shock. Attempt

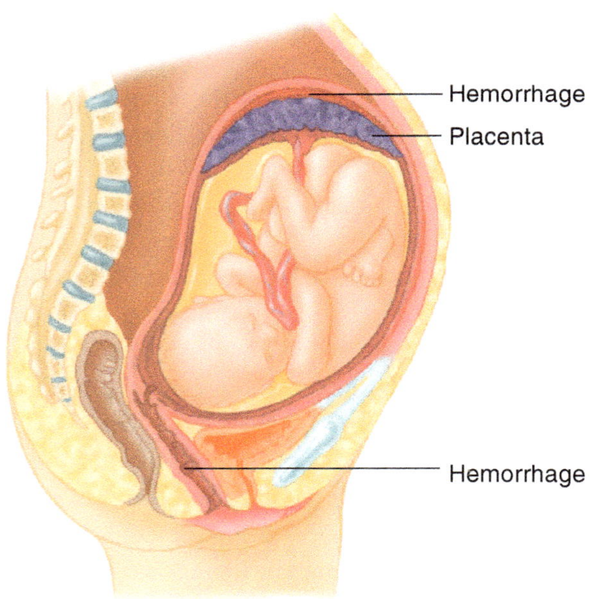

Figure 2 In abruptio placentae, the placenta separates prematurely from the walls of the uterus.

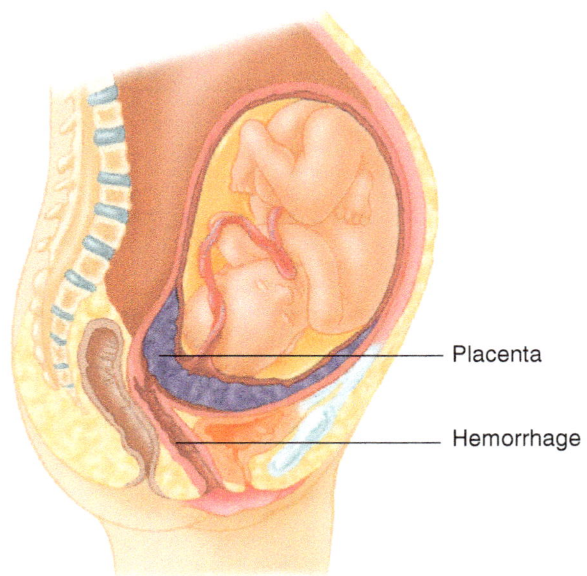

Figure 3 In placenta previa, the placenta develops over and covers the cervix.

to calm and reassure any patient with vaginal bleeding. Even minor bleeding may cause extreme anxiety and fear in the pregnant patient.

TRAUMA AND PREGNANCY

Traumas of all types and severity—from minor sprains to stab wounds—affect 7% of all pregnant women, and this percentage has risen steadily over recent years. As a LER, the majority of the trauma mechanisms you will see in pregnant patients is similar to what you would see in other patients—motor vehicle crashes, falls, etc. Keep in mind that the anatomy of a pregnant woman may make her prone to lose her balance, making falls more likely than for most nonpregnant patients.

Unfortunately, more women are victims of domestic domestic violence today than in the past. Maintain a high level of suspicion for domestic violence. Risk factors and signs of abuse include a woman being unmarried or lacking social support; delayed or no prenatal care; vague complaints; multiple uses of emergency services; and a possessive partner who answers for the woman or will not allow you to interview her alone.

Assessment of Trauma

The LER should use the standard trauma assessment techniques to assess a pregnant trauma patient. Pay special attention to the abdominal area. Bruising and tenderness to the abdominal area are important findings. Take note of the level of the **fundus**. A change in the fundal height while you are present may indicate rupture of the fetus into the abdomen or concealed bleeding.

The LER should determine whether the trauma is from blunt force or penetrating injuries. Blunt force accounts for most trauma in pregnancy. The most common causes of blunt trauma injury are the following:

- Motor vehicle crashes
- Domestic violence and assault
- Falls

Penetrating trauma also affects women during pregnancy. Mortality to the fetus is over 80% when the abdominal area is injured by penetrating wounds. Occasionally, the woman may be spared because the amniotic sac and fluid increase resistance to the penetrating object and decrease the energy transfer to other organs.

Management of Trauma

Management of trauma in the pregnant patient is similar to the management of trauma in others. Focus patient management as you would for any trauma patient. Assess the patient for spine stabilization and shock, and keep the patient warm until EMS arrives. If the patient meets your local protocol for spinal stabilization, provide for complete stabilization and tilt the patient on her left side to prevent excess pressure on the abdomen, which can limit blood return and decrease blood pressure. During stabilization, observe the patient for changes and watch for contractions or vaginal discharge or bleeding.

It is important to have the patient evaluated by an obstetrician as soon as possible. Aggressive assessment, care, and treatment of a pregnant trauma patient are the best hope for both maternal and fetal survival. If the woman does not survive, the fetus has no chance of survival. If physical abuse or an assault is suspected, follow your local jurisdiction protocols for mandatory reporting of abuse.

The safety of the LER is the priority. The pregnant trauma patient may have been a target of abuse, and the perpetrator may remain at the scene. Focus on patient management as you would for any trauma patient. During stabilization, observe the patient for changes and watch for contractions, premature rupture of membranes, and bulging membranes. If the patient meets your local protocol for spinal stabilization, provide for complete stabilization and tilt the patient to the left to prevent **supine hypotensive syndrome**.

> **Tip**
>
> **Supine Hypotensive Syndrome**
>
> Supine hypotensive syndrome occurs when the pregnant uterus compresses the inferior vena cava and prevents the return of blood to the heart.

NORMAL LABOR

Labor for first pregnancies averages 16 hours. The labor process is broken down into three stages. In stage 1, the cervix (the lower part of the uterus) dilates; in stage 2, the baby is pushed out; in stage 3, the placenta is delivered.

1. **Stage 1.** The first stage of labor is the longest. During this stage, labor contractions occur at regular intervals and the cervix dilates. When childbirth is ready to occur, the amniotic sac ruptures spontaneously.

Women often describe this stage by saying their "water broke." This marks the end of the first stage of labor.

2. **Stage 2.** The second stage of labor occurs when the baby's head advances in the birth canal. In a first-time mother, this stage usually takes 60 to 90 minutes. As labor progresses, the baby moves down the birth canal. **Crowning** occurs when the baby's head is visible at the vaginal opening during a contraction (**Figure 4**). When you see crowning, prepare for delivery. Stage 2 ends with delivery of the baby.
3. **Stage 3.** The third stage of labor is the delivery of the placenta. When the delivery of the placenta starts, the woman may experience contractions again. Be alert to the possibility that the mother may be delivering another baby. The placenta should be delivered within 20 to 30 minutes of the baby.

Tip

Placenta Care

Keep the placenta to take to the hospital. Transport the delivered placenta in a sterile bag.

Assessment of the Pregnant Patient

Approach this patient as you would any other. When arriving on scene, first determine safety. Next, perform the primary assessment. Ensure the patient has a patent airway and is breathing. Apply oxygen as authorized by your medical director and then assess circulation. Expect a rapid heart rate if the woman is in active labor. Obtain a SAMPLE history from the woman. When you are questioning the pertinent past medical history (including medical problems and surgeries), ask pregnancy-related questions. What symptoms does she have? When did the symptoms start? Did the woman notice a bloody discharge from the vagina? This bloody discharge (also called the mucus plug) indicates that labor is progressing. Did the amniotic sac rupture? If so, delivery is typically soon to follow. Does she feel like she is about to have a bowel movement? This sensation indicates that the baby's head is low in the birth canal and delivery is imminent. Find out whether the obstetrician identified the number of fetuses and their estimated date of confinement (due date). If the patient has had any other babies, were there any complications with those deliveries? To help you with your SAMPLE history, remember the seven Cs, listed in **Table 1**.

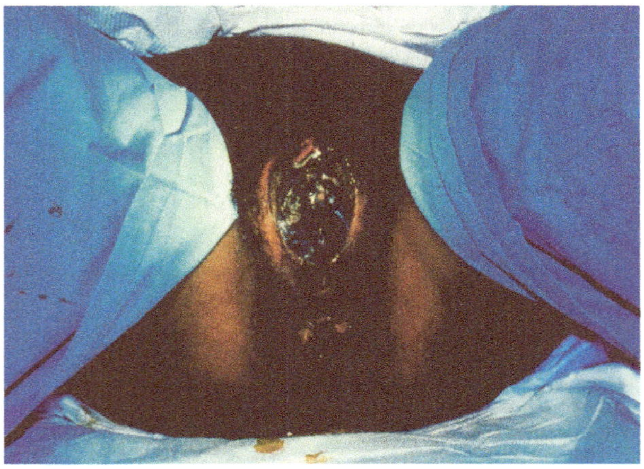

Figure 4 Crowning occurs when the infant's head appears at the vaginal opening.

A secondary assessment will help determine if you will need to deliver the baby on the scene. The physical examination of the woman in impending delivery is important. A good place to start is to take a good look at your patient. Does she appear uncomfortable and in pain? If so, she is most likely in active labor.

Although most patients should be kept lying down for assessment and transport, it is important to remember that after your primary assessment, a pregnant patient should be placed lying down on her left side for ongoing monitoring and transport to prevent supine hypotensive syndrome (**Figure 5**). Supine hypotensive syndrome occurs when a pregnant woman is lying on her back and the weight of the fetus compresses the large veins and aorta of the core circulation. Compressing these blood vessels may reduce the amount of

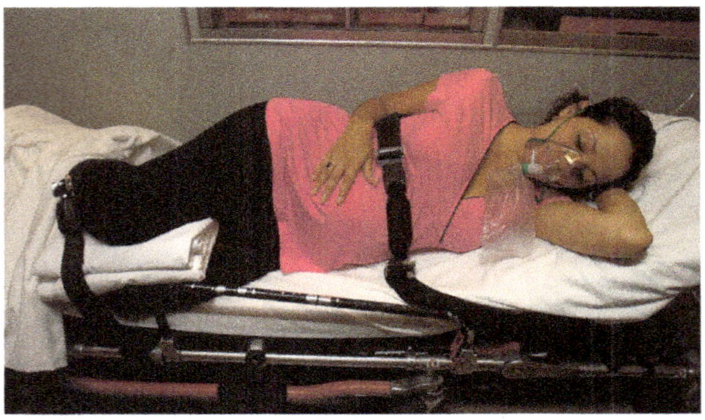

Figure 5 Pregnant woman in the correct left lateral recumbent position.

Table 1

Pertinent History Questions

Assess	Ask	Rationale
Prenatal **C**are	Did you have prenatal care? Were any concerns identified?	Being aware of any potential delivery problems identified by the obstetrician will alert the need to call for assistance and be prepared for delivery.
Estimated Date of **C**onfinement	What is your due date?	Knowing the gestational age of the baby will allow you to prepare for resuscitation.
Clock	What time did contractions or other symptoms start?	Knowing the time may help determine the stage of labor.
Count	How many other children have you delivered?	The labor time may decrease with each delivery.
Previous **C**omplications	Have you had problems with any previous deliveries?	The patient may be prone to delivery problems if she has experienced them before.
Crowning	Do you feel like you need to move your bowels?	The sensation to have a bowel movement indicates that the baby is in the birth canal and the delivery process is near. Check for crowning.
Color	Has there been vaginal discharge? If so, was it bloody, clear, green, yellow, or brown?	Bloody discharge can be normal with the mucus plug passing; a lot of blood can mean a greater emergency. Clear discharge is the draining of the amniotic sac. Green, yellow, or brown discharge can mean the baby had a bowel movement; be prepared with bulb syringe suction and consider calling for help.

blood returning to the heart, causing harm to the fetus and possibly the mother. Chest pain, shortness of breath, or dizziness may occur.

Warm-up contractions, known as **Braxton-Hicks contractions**, may start to occur as early as 20 weeks. These contractions have no regular pattern and may stop with change of position or rest. **Labor contractions** occur at regular intervals and will increase in intensity, frequency, and duration. A woman in labor usually looks very uncomfortable. Change in position does not affect the contractions. To time a contraction, start the clock at the beginning of a contraction to the beginning of the next (**Figure 6**). If the contractions are less than 2 minutes apart, you need to prepare for delivery. If they are more than 5 minutes apart, you usually have time to transport to the hospital. If contractions are 3 to 4 minutes apart, other factors should be considered to help with the decision:

1. Is this the woman's first pregnancy? A first pregnancy averages 16 hours of labor until delivery.
2. Has the woman had any vaginal discharge? A small amount of blood may be the mucus plug. This

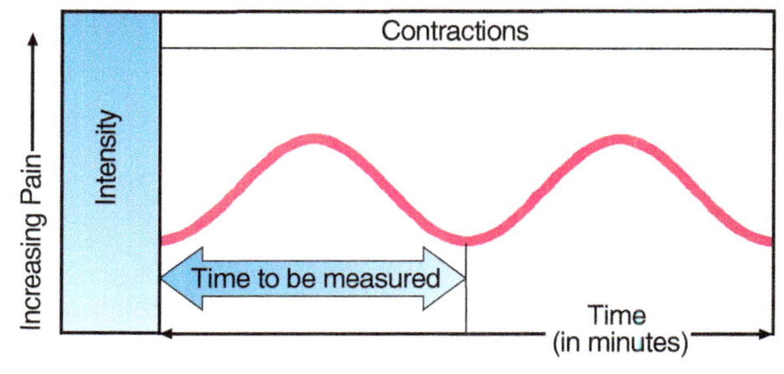

Figure 6 To time a contraction, start the clock at the beginning of a contraction to the beginning of the next.

indicates the start of the first stage of labor. A large amount of blood may indicate a medical emergency and the patient should be transported. A large amount of clear or colored fluid indicates that the amniotic sac has broken, which usually happens at the end of the first stage of labor.

3. Does the woman feel as if she needs to move her bowels? This sensation is the baby's head pressing on the rectum and means delivery is imminent. Do not allow the patient to go to the toilet.
4. Is the infant's head crowning? If you can see the top of the baby's head in the vaginal area with a contraction, birth will occur in the next few minutes.
5. Is transportation available? Is the scene safe for transport? What is the estimated time of arrival for an ambulance? What is the transport time to the hospital?

When the decision is made to deliver the baby outside of the hospital, it is important to ensure that you are prepared with enough resources, because you will have at least two patients after delivery. Your primary assessment is the priority. Maintaining a patent airway is no different from any other medical emergency. If available, administer oxygen to the mother. Rate and rhythm of pulse are important to note. Also, blood pressure may temporarily increase when a woman is in active labor.

If you decide the woman needs to deliver at the present location, remember to respect patient confidentiality and take the woman's wishes into account. Who does she want with her? Make sure the woman is in a comfortable position, often supine on the floor or bed with her knees up. Remember standard precautions for all individuals involved in the delivery, including strict eye protection and face shield, gown, and gloves.

Assisting With Delivery

To reduce your stress when the need to deliver arises, familiarize yourself with the obstetric kit you carry. Commercial obstetric kits are sold for delivering a baby outside of the hospital (**Figure 7**).

The typical obstetric kit contains:

- Drapes to place under the mother
- Towels to wrap up the baby
- A bulb syringe to clear the baby's airway
- Cord clamps to place on the umbilical cord after delivery
- Sterile scalpel or scissors to cut the cord
- A sanitary napkin to place over the mother's vaginal area after delivery of the placenta
- A plastic bag for wrapping up the placenta

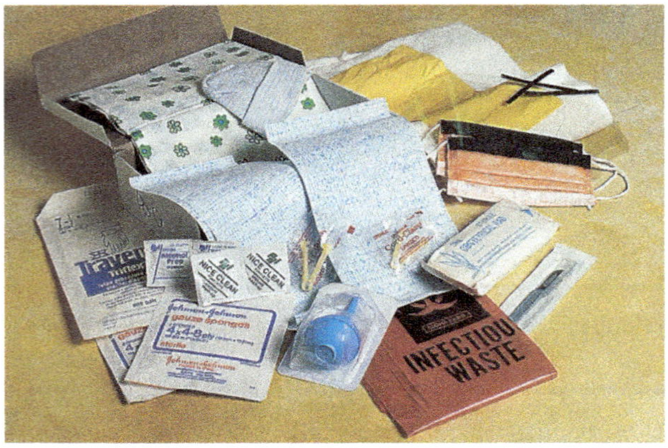

Figure 7 Commercial obstetric (OB) kit.

Emergency Delivery

If there is not enough time to get the patient to an appropriate facility for the birth, an emergency delivery will be necessary.

1. Conduct a primary assessment of the mother. Administer oxygen via face mask or nonrebreathing mask. Obtain the initial vital signs and on a regular basis thereafter.
2. Obtain a SAMPLE history, remembering the seven Cs (prenatal care, estimated date of confinement, clock, count, previous complications, crowning, and color).
3. Complete a secondary assessment. Determine whether the baby should be delivered on scene or transported.
4. If more than one responder is available, decide on your roles. The lead responder should communicate with the mother and take responsibility for her care. The second responder is responsible for the actual hands-on delivery and care of the infant.
5. When the head emerges, place a towel (if available) over your hands as you prepare to deliver the baby, rather than receiving the baby directly. Babies are slippery. If a bulb syringe is available, attempt to suction the baby's mouth and then nose before delivering the chest. Note whether the umbilical cord is wrapped around the baby. If it is around the baby's neck, try to slip it over the baby's head. If it is too tight, place two clamps on the umbilical cord and cut the cord between the clamps, preferably with a pair of scissors. If only a scalpel blade is available, cut away from the baby. This is a true emergency because a

tight umbilical cord (also known as a **nuchal cord**) can strangle the baby.

6. Continue to support the baby's head as the shoulders, torso, and lower extremities deliver (**Figure 8**). After the head is delivered, the remainder of the delivery is very fast.
7. Keep the baby's head low so fluids from the airway can drain.
8. With a bulb syringe, suction the baby's mouth several times, and then suction each nostril several times (**Figure 9**). Remember to compress the bulb syringe prior to inserting it into the mouth and nose. Expel the drainage each time into a nearby towel. Suctioning of the mouth and nose needs to be carried out numerous

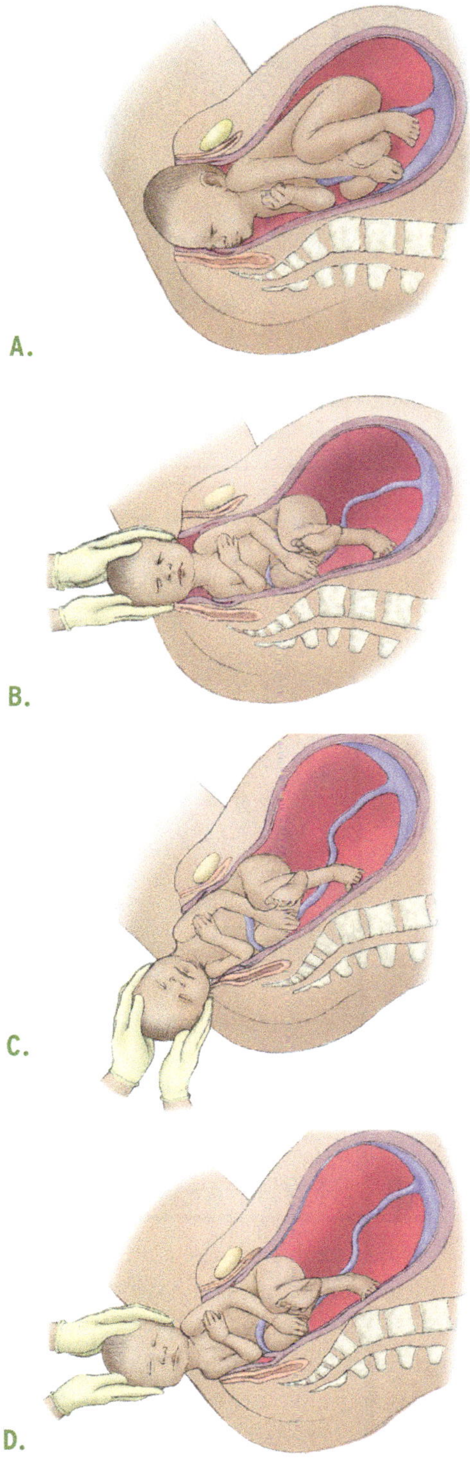

A.

B.

C.

D.

Figure 8 Phases of the second stage of labor. **A.** Head begins to deliver. **B.** Delivery of the head. **C.** Delivery of upper shoulder. **D.** Delivery of lower shoulder.

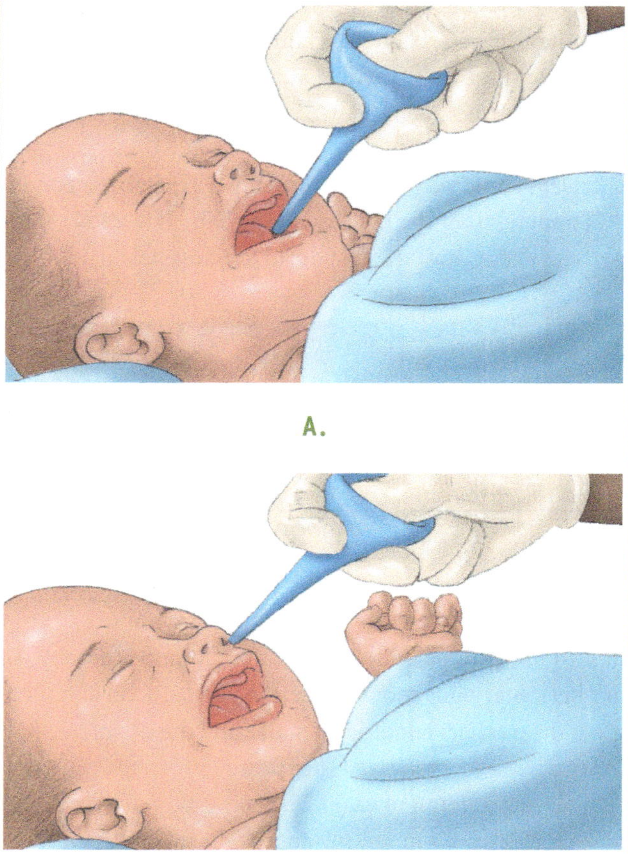

A.

B.

Figure 9 Suction the mouth and nose to clear the airway of mucus and amniotic fluid. **A.** Using a bulb syringe in a newborn's mouth. **B.** Using a bulb syringe in a newborn's nose.

times to ensure that the airway is clear. Note the color and consistency of the drainage from the baby. **Meconium** is the baby's first bowel movement, is often green, and may occur before delivery. If you notice that this has occurred, be sure to pass that information to the next level of care.

9. Use the towel to dry the infant. If the mother and the baby are both breathing adequately, place the baby on the mother's abdomen and cover them both carefully with a blanket to keep them warm. According to the World Health Organization, skin-to-skin contact between a mother and infant immediately after birth has many benefits, including reducing the infant's crying, improving mother-infant interaction, keeping the infant warm, and helping the mother breastfeed.
10. Note the time of delivery.
11. After delivery, clamp the cord 10 inches from the baby. Then place the second clamp 2 inches farther away. The area between the two clamps is where the cord should be cut.
12. Delivery of the placenta typically occurs about 20 to 30 minutes after the delivery of the baby (**Figure 10**). This can occur during transport to the hospital.

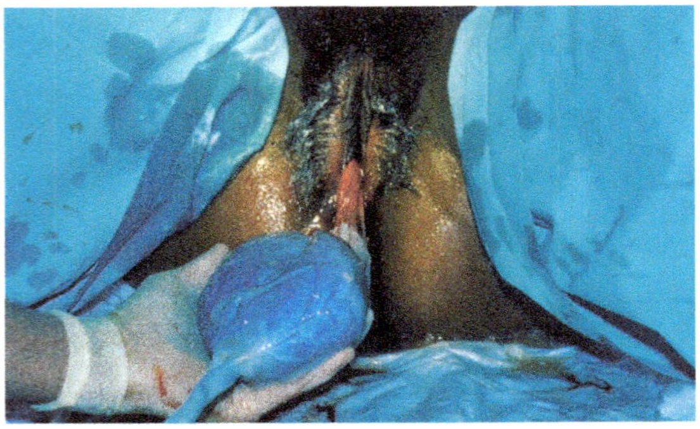

Figure 10 Allow the placenta to deliver itself. This usually happens 20 to 30 minutes after the infant is delivered.

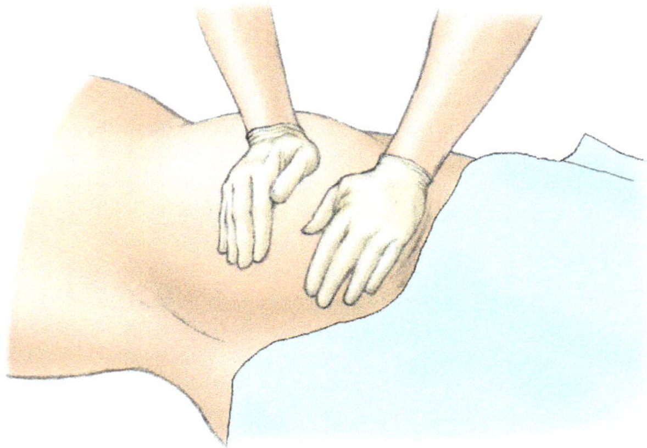

Figure 11 After delivery, massage the mother's abdomen in a firm, circular motion.

Special Populations

Newborn Body Heat

Newborns lose a large amount of heat if they are not kept warm. Dry the infant and keep the body and head covered to prevent loss of heat and hypothermia.

After Delivery

You should continue to observe the mother and infant carefully and keep them both warm. It is important to pay attention to the privacy and safety of the mother and baby. The mother's vital signs should return to normal soon after delivery. If the mother's condition is stable and the situation allows, the mother may breastfeed the baby.

A small amount of vaginal bleeding after delivery is normal. However, there are instances where too much bleeding occurs. It is important to assess the mother for potential hypovolemic shock. To check for excessive bleeding, place a sanitary napkin over the vaginal area and note whether the sanitary napkin becomes saturated. If there is a lot of blood in the sanitary napkin, you can massage the top of the uterus, known as the fundal area, with firm circular strokes (**Figure 11**). Do not massage too firmly.

INITIAL CARE OF THE NEWBORN

After the baby is delivered, complete a primary assessment. Next, assess the respiratory rate and heart rate. The respiratory rate of a newborn should be 40 to 60 breaths per minute. With newborns, assess the respiratory rate for a full minute. If the infant gasps or grunts after suctioning, the baby needs assistance with breathing. Assistance is also required if the respiratory rate is less than 40 breaths per minute. If properly trained, LERs should use a bag-mask device. If a bag-mask device is not available, the LER should provide rescue breathing using mouth-to-mask ventilations to provide puffs of air once every 3 seconds. After 30 seconds of assistance, re-

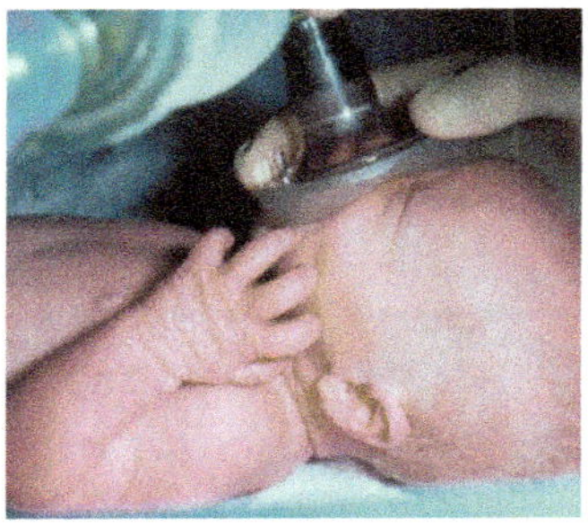

Figure 12 Use an infant bag and mask, and ensure that you cover the newborn's nose and mouth when providing ventilation.

evaluate the respiratory rate. If it is within normal limits, no further assistance is required. If the respiratory rate is still not within normal limits, continue with the rescue breathing or bag-mask device and reassess every 30 seconds.

Determine the newborn's heart rate through auscultation or palpation. If you are trained and comfortable with the use of a stethoscope, listen to the heart over the left side of the chest for 6 seconds and multiply by ten. To feel the pulse, place two fingers on the umbilical stump for 6 seconds and multiply by ten.

Chest compressions are rarely performed on a newborn. If the heart rate is less than 60 beats per minute, chest compressions are performed in conjunction with rescue breathing or bag-mask ventilation (**Figure 12**). The rate is three compressions to one ventilation for a total rate of 120 cycles per minute. LERs should reference and practice local protocols for neonatal resuscitation.

Special Populations

Signs of a Healthy Newborn

You should observe the following signs in a newborn:

- A respiratory rate of greater than 40 breaths per minute
- The infant should begin to cry right after birth
- A pulse rate of greater than 100 beats per minute (check the brachial pulse)

DELIVERY COMPLICATIONS

Although the majority of childbirths are uncomplicated, LERs should be familiar with the following complications.

Unruptured Amniotic Sac

Normally, the amniotic sac breaks on its own during labor. If this does not happen, you will notice the **unruptured amniotic sac** surrounding the baby as the baby begins to emerge from the birth canal. The baby cannot be delivered in this condition. You will need to tear the amniotic sac using your fingers. Use caution not to injure the baby. Suctioning of the mouth and nose after the sac breaks is imperative. Delivery of the baby can continue normally after this situation is corrected.

Breech Delivery

A **breech delivery** occurs when a baby enters the birth canal backwards and the legs or buttocks emerge from the vagina first instead of the head. This is not a normal delivery, and making prompt arrangements to transport the mother to a medical facility is important. Normally breech deliveries do not deliver vaginally. If labor is progressing, however, the LER cannot stop the delivery. Use your knowledge of the normal delivery process for this special situation. Support the infant and consider making a pathway for the child to breathe if the body delivers prior to head. Be alert for an umbilical cord wrapped around the neck of the infant, which can be a life-threatening situation.

Limb Presentation

Limb presentation is an emergency situation that occurs when a baby's arm or leg emerges from the birth canal first instead of the head. The mother cannot deliver vaginally and requires immediate transport to an appropriate medical facility so the baby can be delivered by cesarean section. Monitor the woman's vital signs, administer oxygen, and place the woman in a position so her pelvis is elevated. Do not pull or push the presenting limb at any time.

Prolapsed Cord

A **prolapsed cord** is an emergency situation that occurs when the umbilical cord emerges from the birth canal first instead of the baby's head. The danger of a prolapsed cord is that the baby will compress the cord, thereby cutting off the circulation between the mother and baby. The situation requires rapid intervention by the LER.

To treat a prolapsed cord, place the woman in the knee-chest position. Explain to her that the goal of repositioning her is to reduce the pressure of the baby on the cord. If this position is not optimal, attempt to elevate the pelvis. In some emergency systems, the local protocol requires the LER to insert a gloved hand into the vagina to elevate the fetal part off the cord. A cord that maintains circulation will typically be pulsating. When this procedure is used, the LER must stay in the assisting position and keep the fetal part elevated until he or she is relieved by trained personnel at the hospital. A patient with a prolapsed cord requires an emergency cesarean section.

Preterm Birth

The rate of **preterm births**, also called premature birth, is increasing in the United States. Any newborn weighing less than 5 pounds or delivered before 36 weeks of pregnancy is considered premature.

Prompt transport of the mother to an appropriate medical facility is important. There are measures that can be implemented to stop preterm labor and allow pregnancy to continue. If labor appears to be progressing, keep in mind that the normal birthing process can occur quickly and that resuscitation will likely be needed.

CONCLUSION

LERs need to have basic knowledge of pregnancy and childbirth. If a pregnancy or childbirth emergency occurs, responders must remain calm, use standard precautions, call for EMS, and provide supplemental oxygen. Carefully assess the patient, obtain a SAMPLE history, and encourage patients to get an immediate evaluation by a physician.

Prep Kit

READY FOR REVIEW

- A baby grows and develops in the uterus—supported by the placenta, the amniotic sac, and the umbilical cord—and is delivered through the cervix and the vagina, also called the birth canal.
- Vaginal bleeding is a potentially serious condition that may be symptomatic of a larger medical issue or a complication of pregnancy such as placenta abruptio or placenta previa. Any woman complaining of vaginal bleeding requires care by a physician.
- When assisting a pregnant woman, remember to practice standard precautions—including the use of eye protection, face shield, gown, and gloves—and ensure scene safety.
- Do not position a pregnant woman lying down on her back except for delivery. This can cause supine hypotensive syndrome. Position the woman on her left side.
- Trauma affects 7% of all pregnant women. Common causes of trauma are motor vehicle crashes, domestic violence, and falls. Aggressive assessment, care, and treatment are the best hope for both maternal and fetal survival in a trauma situation.
- Warm-up contractions, known as Braxton-Hicks contractions, have no regular pattern and the cervix does not dilate. They do not indicate labor.
- Labor contractions occur at regular intervals and will increase in intensity, frequency, and duration. Such contractions indicate that the process of childbirth has begun.
- The amniotic sac rupturing, also known as the woman's water breaking, is a sign that childbirth may be imminent. When the baby's head appears, also called crowning, the baby is about to be delivered.
- The placenta is normally delivered about 20 to 30 minutes after the baby.
- Do not pull any part of the baby during delivery, including the umbilical cord.
- The umbilical cord can strangle the baby if it is wrapped around the baby's neck. If this happens, clamp the cord in two places and cut the cord between the clamps with a pair of scissors or a scalpel, taking great care not to injure the baby.
- It is important to support the baby as he or she emerges from the birth canal. Place a towel over your hands to help hold the baby securely.
- When the baby emerges, suction the mouth and nose several times, check respiration and heart rate, and place the baby on the mother's abdomen covered with a blanket or wrap the baby to keep him or her warm.
- After delivery, observe the mother and infant carefully and keep them warm. Assess vital signs for both mother and child, and check the woman for vaginal bleeding and signs of shock. If the newborn does not cry and begin to breathe on its own within the first minute after birth, follow steps for suctioning, stimulating breathing, and resuscitation if necessary.
- A newborn should have a respiratory rate of greater than 40 breaths per minute and a pulse rate of greater than 100 beats per minute.
- The majority of childbirths are uncomplicated, but responders should be familiar with the following complications: unruptured amniotic sac, breech delivery, limb presentation, prolapsed umbilical cord, and preterm birth (also called premature birth).

VITAL VOCABULARY

abruptio placentae An emergency in the second half of pregnancy that occurs when the entire placenta, or a portion of it, detaches from the wall of the uterus prior to childbirth.

amniotic sac A thin, membranous sac that protects the growing fetus. The fetus is cushioned in this sac with amniotic fluid.

bag of waters *See amniotic sac.*

Braxton-Hicks contractions Irregular contractions, also called warm-up contractions, that produce no cervical change. They are not a sign of labor or imminent childbirth.

breech delivery Occurs when a baby enters the birth canal backwards and the buttocks emerge from the vagina first instead of the head.

cervix The lower part of the uterus.

crowning Appearance of the infant's head as it is pushed through the birth canal.

ectopic pregnancy A pregnancy that occurs outside the uterus, usually in a fallopian tube.

embryo The term for a developing baby during the first eight weeks after conception.

fallopian tubes Muscular tubes that connect the ovaries to the uterus. Eggs are fertilized in the fallopian tubes and travel down the tubes to the uterus.

fetus A developing baby from the eighth week of pregnancy to delivery.

fundus The top part of the uterus.

gynecology The area of medicine that deals with women's reproductive health.

labor contractions Regular and progressive contractions that produce cervical change.

limb presentation An emergency situation that occurs when a baby's arm or leg emerges from the birth canal first instead of the head. The mother cannot deliver vaginally and requires a cesarean section.

meconium A dark green material in amniotic fluid that can indicate distress or disease in the newborn.

nuchal cord When the umbilical cord is wrapped around the baby's neck.

obstetrics The area of medicine that deals with pregnancy, childbirth, and postpartum health.

ovaries Two small, almond-shaped organs that release eggs and female reproductive hormones.

placenta A fleshy, vascular organ that transports nutrients and oxygen from the mother to the fetus, transports waste from the fetus to the mother, and serves as a blood barrier for harmful substances. The placenta is connected to the fetus by the umbilical cord.

placenta previa An emergency in the second half of pregnancy that occurs when the placenta attaches partially or completely over the opening of the cervix. Placenta previa is usually diagnosed through prenatal care.

preterm birth Any newborn weighing less than 5 pounds or delivered before 36 weeks of pregnancy.

prolapsed cord An emergency situation that occurs when the umbilical cord emerges from the birth canal first instead of the baby's head. The mother cannot deliver vaginally and requires a cesarean section.

spontaneous abortion Delivery of the fetus before it is mature enough to survive outside the womb. Also called miscarriage.

supine hypotensive syndrome Occurs when a pregnant woman is lying on her back and the weight of the fetus compresses the woman's large veins and aorta. The condition can reduce the amount of blood returning to the heart, causing harm to the fetus and possibly the mother. Symptoms include chest pain and shortness of breath. Treat by rolling the mother onto her left side, out of the supine position.

umbilical cord The fleshy, off-white cord that connects the placenta to the fetus, transports oxygen and other nutrients to the fetus, and removes waste from the fetus.

unruptured amniotic sac Occurs when the amniotic sac does not rupture on its own before the baby crowns.

uterus The vascular organ where the fetus grows, also called the womb.

vagina The vascular and muscular organ through which a baby passes when it is born, also called the birth canal.

CHECK YOUR KNOWLEDGE

1. You encounter a 25-year-old pregnant woman complaining of abdominal pain after being assaulted. After assessing her abdomen, you find generalized tenderness only. There is no bruising or open wound. There is no further trauma, and vital signs are within normal limits. She does not wish to be transported to the hospital. Which explanation should the LER give to the patient?
   - A. "We do not know if there are injuries to your baby, and you need to be checked out."
   - B. "There is no bruising, so it is OK to stay home."
   - C. "If you want, we can call the doctor to see if he can see you tomorrow."
   - D. "You are required to be transported to the emergency department."
2. You arrive to find a 20-year-old woman who states, "I am going to have a baby now." She tells you that her contractions began 16 hours ago and are now occurring every 5 minutes and lasting for 90 seconds. She says her water just broke, and she describes the fluid as clear but tinged with blood. What do you do?
   - A. Explain to the woman that delivery will need to occur outside of the hospital and proceed with standard precautions and equipment setup.
   - B. Have the patient move to the stretcher for rapid transport.
   - C. Ask the patient what she wishes to do at this time.
   - D. Tell the patient to relax until an ambulance arrives.
3. You find a pregnant woman with profuse vaginal bleeding. You determined that she is in shock, and the emergency team is carrying out treatment. What is the one action you should not perform?
   - A. Administer high-flow oxygen via nonrebreathing mask.
   - B. Place the woman in the left lateral recumbent position.
   - C. Gently place a sanitary napkin over her vagina.
   - D. Offer the woman a cool beverage because she is complaining of thirst.
4. You are dispatched to a home only to find that it is dark and no one answers the doorbell. As you are preparing to enter the home, you hear a faint cry for help. While searching the home, you find a newborn wrapped in a blanket with the umbilical cord still attached to the mother. She states she delivered the newborn "very quickly" but managed to call for help. Which of these steps is not part of the newborn assessment?
   - A. Assess airway, breathing, and circulation.
   - B. Dry and warm the newborn and stimulate him or her to breathe.
   - C. Assess the umbilical cord for hemorrhaging.
   - D. Obtain a baseline blood pressure.
5. Continuing the scenario above, what steps are important for the mother?
   - A. Assess the ABCs.
   - B. Administer oxygen.
   - C. Evaluate vaginal bleeding and assist the mother with fundal massage.
   - D. All of the above.

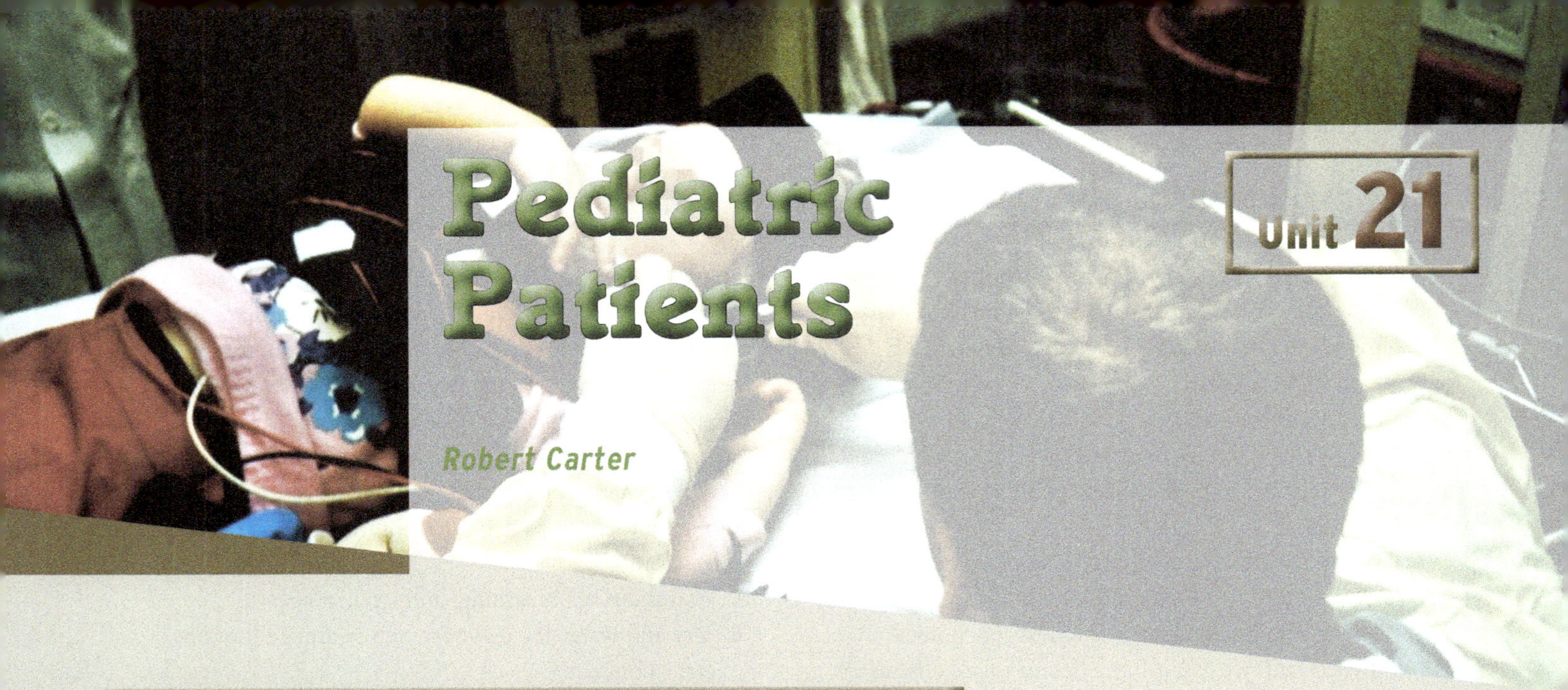

Pediatric Patients

Unit 21

Robert Carter

Law Enforcement Responder Objectives

- Describe the impact of parental involvement at the scene of a pediatric emergency. (p 405)
- Identify the anatomic and functional differences between children and adults. (pp 405–407)
- Discuss the assessment process for pediatric patients. (pp 407–410)
- Explain the components and use of the pediatric assessment triangle. (pp 407–408)
- Discuss respiratory issues in children and how to manage them. (pp 410–411)
- Discuss the potential causes and effects of shock in children. (pp 411–412)
- Discuss the assessment and management of a child experiencing a seizure. (p 412)
- Define sudden infant death syndrome and apparent life-threatening event. (p 412)
- Identify common mechanisms of injury in children. (pp 412–413)
- Identify indicators of abuse and neglect. (pp 413–414)

National EMS Education Standard Competencies

Special Patient Populations

Recognizes and manages life threats based on simple assessment findings for a patient with special needs while awaiting additional emergency response.

Pediatrics

Age-related assessment findings, and age-related assessment and treatment modifications for pediatric-specific major diseases and emergencies:

- Upper airway obstruction (p 411)
- Lower airway reactive disease (see Unit 13, *Medical Emergencies*)
- Respiratory distress, failure, and arrest (p 410)
- Shock (pp 411–412)
- Seizures (p 412)
- Sudden infant death syndrome (p 412)

Patients With Special Challenges

- Recognizing and reporting abuse and neglect (pp 413–414)

Trauma

Uses simple knowledge to recognize and manage life threats based on assessment findings for an acutely injured patient while awaiting additional emergency medical response.

Special Considerations in Trauma

- Recognition and management of trauma in the pediatric patient (pp 412–413)

Life Span Development

Uses simple knowledge of age-related differences to assess and care for patients.

INTRODUCTION

Pediatrics typically refers to the care and treatment of infants and children. This unit discusses the unique anatomic and physiologic considerations associated with pediatric patients, as well as special considerations related to the assessment process and common medical and trauma emergencies in pediatric patients.

Pediatric emergencies can be among the most stressful situations to manage. Many factors are involved, including the child's fear and anxiety, the parents' fear and anxiety, bystander involvement, possible communication difficulty, the overall atmosphere of the event, and the emotional aspects that arise from caring for a severely sick or injured child.

PARENTAL INVOLVEMENT

At the scene of a pediatric emergency, the parents of the ill or injured child present a unique challenge, either helping or hindering care. They are just as involved in the event as the child is, and they must be included in the management of the care.

Engage with the parents as much as possible and explain the care you are providing and the potential care yet to occur. The parents will be concerned about their child's condition, and a more thorough explanation will help alleviate their anxiety. However, with a critically ill or injured child, it is best to have one responder dedicated to explaining the situation to the parents and another responder focused solely on caring for the child. The parents should also be given information regarding the treatment facility where the child will be transported, if applicable.

Children often follow the example of their parents. Therefore, a calm parent usually helps to maintain a calm child, which assists responders in providing adequate care. It may be better to allow a parent to hold the child during the assessment and treatment process to maintain a calm environment. If the parents are present but not able to hold their child, be sure to allow a parent to touch the child and hold the child's hand, when safely possible or feasible.

The approach the responder uses with a child also affects the overall management of the emergency. Developing a good rapport with a child early on can be very helpful. Approach a child as gently as possible given the level of medical urgency. Approaching an alert child too fast may cause anxiety, which could interfere with assessment and worsen respiratory distress. Introduce yourself and ask the child his or her name. Use the child's name often during assessment and treatment and maintain as much eye contact as possible. Do not stand directly over the child. Instead, address the child at his or her eye level, either kneeling, squatting, or sitting.

Always be honest; do not misinform the child or the parents. For example, if treatment will be painful, tell the child and the parents that it will hurt and explain the steps that will happen before performing them, if possible. The child can also help in the treatment process if the situation allows. Let the child assist with holding a splint or a bandage. Young children often enjoy playing with penlights or stethoscopes as well. Maintaining honesty and allowing cooperation in care may help a child feel more comfortable with you and ease management of the emergency.

Communication

Parent Communication

Communication with parents is essential, because parents will be distraught over an ill or injured child. Calmly explain the child's condition and the care you are providing. A thorough explanation will help alleviate the parent's anxiety.

Clear communication with a pediatric patient's parents is also necessary from a legal standpoint. A parent's consent is required for any emergency care the child may receive.

PEDIATRIC ANATOMY AND FUNCTION

Children are not small adults. Many aspects of a child's anatomy and function differ from those of adults (**Table 1**).

Infancy (Birth to 1 Year)

In infants, the head is proportionately larger than in adults, which allows for more rapid heat loss when exposed. Maintaining warmth and covering the infant's head will help prevent hypothermia. Newborns and infants have "soft spots," or **fontanelles**, that allow the skull to flex so the head will pass more easily through the birth canal. There are two fontanelles; one is located on top of the infant's head (anterior fontanelle) and the other on the back of the head (posterior fontanelle). Sunken or depressed fontanelles may mean dehydration or fluid loss, whereas a bulging fontanelle may mean increased pressure within the skull. If a patient presents with either sunken or bulging fontanelles, more information

Table 1

Normal Vital Signs in Children at Rest

Age	Heart Rate (beats/min)	Respirations (breaths/min)
Newborn (0 to 1 month)	140-160	30-40
Infant (1 month to 1 year)	100-160	25-50
Toddler (1 to 3 years)	80-130	20-30
Preschool age (3 to 6 years)	80-120	20-30
School age (6 to 12 years)	70-110	20-30
Adolescent (13 to 18 years)	55-105	12-20

should be obtained. This may be an emergency requiring prompt management.

Infants' airways are easily obstructed as a result of their small size and the fact that a child's tongue is proportionately larger than an adult's (**Figure 1**). Infants are primarily nose breathers until age 4 weeks, so nasal inflammation and secretions may cause airway obstruction. The diaphragm is the chief muscle of respiration, so air in the stomach from cardiopulmonary resuscitation (CPR) can impair ventilation. The normal respiratory rate in infants is 25 to 50 breaths per minute. An irregular respiratory rate is common. Rapid respiratory rates lead to rapid heat and fluid loss from the infant. The average systolic blood pressure increases from 70 mm Hg at birth to 90 mm Hg at age 1 year.

Infants have a strong, coordinated suck and gag reflex. The gag reflex is an important reflex in that it helps protect the small airway from aspiration of food, liquid, and/or foreign objects when the back of the throat is stimulated.

The sweat glands in infants are not fully developed and therefore are inefficient to cool the body. This can lead to increased body temperature. Infants are also unable to shiver, which is a protective mechanism to help generate heat. Infants also have a greater body surface area relative to their mass, which allows for rapid heat loss if exposed. This is important to understand because an infant cannot self-regulate body temperature and therefore this requires care providers to provide warming or cooling measures.

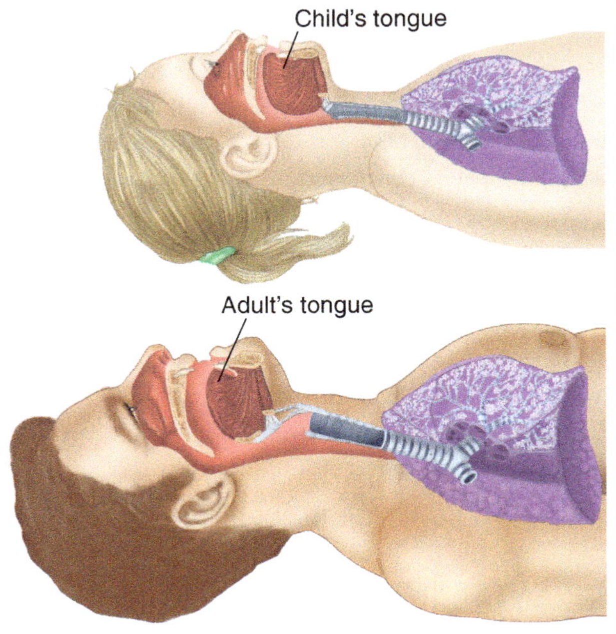

Figure 1 The anatomy of a child's airway differs from that of an adult. The tongue is proportionally larger and can more easily block the airway. Also, the back of the child's head is proportionally larger, so head positioning requires more care.

Special Populations

Nose Breathing

Research has demonstrated that infants prefer to breathe through their nose. This is extremely helpful when nursing. Infants can, however, breathe through their mouth when they have no alternative.

Toddler (1 to 3 Years) and Preschool Age (3 to 6 Years)

During the toddler and preschool years, there is much growth and development. The head is still proportionately larger in relation to the body; therefore, head injuries remain common. The tongue is also proportionately larger in the toddler, which can be a source of obstruction.

Vital signs in this age group include the following:

- Normal heart rate: 80 to 130 beats per minute in toddlers; 80 to 120 beats per minute in preschool-age children

- Normal respiratory rate: 20 to 30 breaths per minute in both toddlers and preschool-age children
- Normal systolic blood pressure: 70 to 100 mm Hg in toddlers; 80 to 110 mm Hg in preschool-age children
- Normal temperature: 96.8°F to 99.6°F (36°C to 37.6°C) in both toddlers and preschool-age children

School-Age Children (6 to 12 Years)

School-age children lose their primary teeth, which are then replaced with permanent teeth. At this age, children tend to be very active and are prone to injury.

Vital signs in this age group include the following:

- Normal heart rate: 70 to 110 beats per minute
- Normal respiratory rate: 20 to 30 breaths per minute
- Normal systolic blood pressure: 80 to 120 mm Hg
- Normal temperature: 98.6°F (37°C)

Adolescence (13 to 18 Years)

Adolescents tend to test the limits of authority. Because many adolescents feel invincible, they are more likely to engage in dangerous activities. This age group is especially prone to injury from motor vehicle crashes.

Vital signs for adolescents include the following:

- Normal heart rate: 55 to 105 beats per minute
- Normal respiratory rate: 12 to 20 breaths per minute
- Normal systolic blood pressure: 80 to 120 mm Hg
- Normal temperature: 98.6°F (37°C)

ASSESSMENT OF PEDIATRIC PATIENTS

Scene safety is paramount. Evaluate the scene for safety before managing the emergency and look for any clues related to the incident that can narrow your focus. For example, if you find empty pill bottles around the patient, an ingestion would be suspected. You should also evaluate the location and the position in which the patient is found. Compare caregivers' statements regarding the mechanism of injury to what you see. Also observe any interactions the child has with family members or others at the scene, because this may be a clue to potential fear or anxiety related to abuse or fear of punishment.

This information can all be obtained while approaching the incident and is valuable for both the medical team and law enforcement. For example, as you enter a room, you see a school-age child lying face down on the floor with obvious dark red blood around the child's nose. The child is crying vigorously and yelling "STOP!" to a violent-appearing adult in the room. From this, you can determine the scene may still be unsafe; the approximate age of the child; and that the child is conscious, the airway is open, the child is breathing, and trauma is highly suspected.

The initial evaluation of a sick or injured infant or child can be done by careful observation without touching the child and can provide critical information on the child's condition. As stated earlier, use the parent or guardian to help an infant or child become more comfortable with your examination and treatment. Assessment should continue until care is transferred.

Your evaluation of the child begins by using a simple tool called the **pediatric assessment triangle (PAT)**. From there, assess the ABCs and level of consciousness. Conclude your assessment by conducting a thorough secondary assessment of the child and taking a SAMPLE history. The following sections explain each of these steps in detail and tell you what to look for.

The Pediatric Assessment Triangle

The PAT is a quick assessment tool that allows the LER to assess the severity of a child's illness or injury in only 15 to 30 seconds. It does not require touching the patient, just looking and listening (**Figure 2**).

Appearance

A child's appearance is a good indicator of the overall status of the child's heart, lung, brain, and nervous system functions. If there is adequate oxygenation, ventilation, and blood flow, a child who is awake and able to interact and speak clearly is considered much more stable than a child who is unable to maintain eye contact, is flaccid, and has a weak cry. The less alert, more lethargic, or more ill-appearing child can be in this condition due to an alteration in oxygenation, poor ventilation, or impaired blood flow. In this case, a more in-depth assessment and prompt treatment would be required. Evaluate the child's appearance using the six characteristics and healthy or unhealthy reactions described in **Table 2**.

Work of Breathing

Work of breathing refers to the amount of effort one has to expend to breathe. Work of breathing is an important indicator of a child's status and is a more accurate assessment than the rate of breathing. Increased work of breathing reflects the child's attempt to compensate for deficiencies in oxygenation and ventilation. Evaluate the child's work of breathing using the four characteristics and accompanying features described

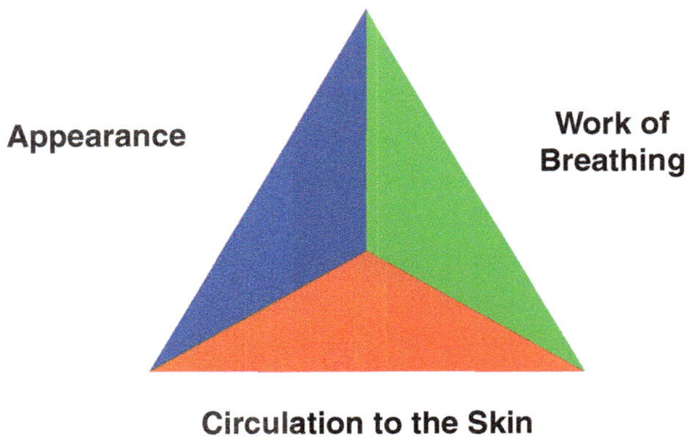

Figure 2 The three components of the Pediatric Assessment Triangle (PAT) are appearance, work of breathing, and circulation to the skin.

Source: Used with permission of the American Academy of Pediatrics, *Pediatric Education for Prehospital Professionals*, © American Academy of Pediatrics, 2000.

in Table 3. This evaluation can be performed by sight and does not require a hands-on assessment.

Circulation to the Skin

Circulation to the skin reflects the adequacy of the heart to pump blood to the brain, heart, and vital organs. Cold temperatures may cause false signs. For example, a child who has been outside in the cold may have normal circulation to the heart, brain, and lungs, but may have abnormal circulation to the skin and display a cold, pale, or **mottled** appearance. Inspect the skin, including the lips and mouth, for color. In dark-skinned children, the lips and mucous membranes are the best places to assess circulation to the skin. Evaluate circulation to the child's skin using the three characteristics and accompanying features described in Table 4.

Table 2

Characteristics of Appearance

Characteristic	Healthy Reaction	Unhealthy Reaction
Movement	Moving vigorously	Limp, listless, flaccid
Interaction	Reaches for a toy Reacts to a person or sound	Uninterested in playing or toys
Reassurance	Reassured by caregivers	Crying or agitated Unrelieved by gentle reassurance
Eye movement	Eyes follow movement of a person or toy	Glassy-eyed stare
Speech	Age-appropriate speech	Garbled or confused speech
Cry	Strong cry	Weak or high-pitched cry

Table 3

Characteristics of Work of Breathing

Characteristic	Features to Look For
Abnormal breath sounds	Noisy breathing, snoring, crowing, grunting, or wheezing
Abnormal positioning	Leaning forward while using the arms for support
Retractions	Retractions above the collarbone or between the ribs
Flaring	Flaring of the nostrils

Table 4

Characteristics of Circulation to the Skin

Characteristic	Features to Look For
Pallor	White or pale skin or mucous membranes
Mottling	Patchy skin discoloration caused by too much or too little blood flow to the skin
Cyanosis	Bluish discoloration of the skin and mucous membranes

Airway

After a brief assessment using the PAT, you must evaluate the child's airway. Asking the child's name and age is an easy way to determine whether the child's airway is clear and open. If the child is unable to speak or is having difficulty speaking, further attention should be given to evaluating the airway. If needed, suction the child to remove fluids, blood, or foreign objects.

See the unit on airway, breathing, and oxygenation for more information on suctioning. Refer to your local jurisdiction for the type of suction equipment available.

If a cervical spine injury is suspected, initiate spinal precautions before opening the airway Spinal precautions include keeping the patient flat and still and placing a cervical collar if available.

Ventilation and Oxygenation

After opening the airway, assess the child's breathing status. Look at the child's respiratory rate and work of breathing. The child should appear to be breathing comfortably at a regular rate. Because they are abdominal breathers, toddlers in particular should be assessed for work of breathing. The child should be able to speak several words without any increased work of breathing. If increased work of breathing is suspected, place the child on oxygen and assist breathing if necessary, using an appropriate sized bag mask device attached to oxygen. Refer to the unit on CPR for specific sizing and procedure. Often, the oxygen delivery device may cause anxiety in the child. Allowing the child to hold the device and administer the oxygen in a "blow-by" method can help alleviate anxiety while delivering the oxygen (**Figure 3**).

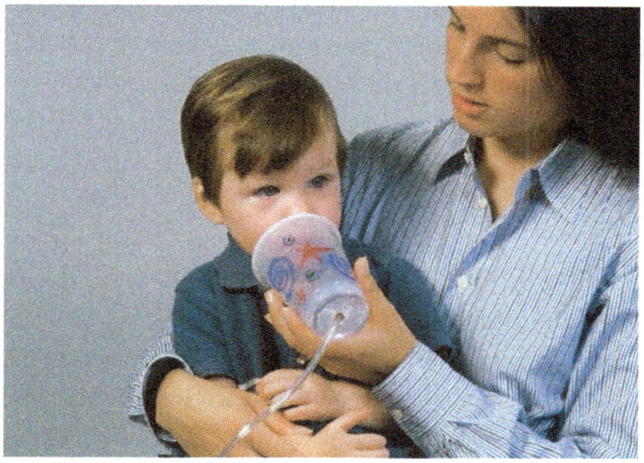

Figure 3 Blow-by techniques may be used when oxygen masks frighten children. One technique is to make a small hole in a small cup, then connect the cup to an oxygen source via tubing. Hold the cup about 1 inch to 2 inches from the child's face.

Circulation

Assess the child's heart rate by feeling for a pulse and looking for rate, rhythm, and quality. The brachial pulse, located on the inside of the upper arm, is the best place to feel the pulse in an infant up to 1 year of age. For children older than 1 year of age, check the radial pulse at the wrist. Carotid pulses can be used as alternative pulse sites in older children. An adequate blood pressure will produce a strong pulse and will be easily felt. Low or inadequate blood pressure will cause the pulse to be weak and can be a sign of impending **cardiorespiratory failure**.

Assessing circulation also includes assessing capillary refill time. This is assessed by pressing and releasing a nail bed, or the palm or heel, and watching the time it takes for normal skin color to return. Even individuals with different skin colors will show capillary refill times, though it is not as obvious as in light-skinned individuals. Normal capillary refill time is 2 to 3 seconds. However, cold temperatures can prolong capillary refill time by several seconds. Assess for any obvious bleeding and attempt to control it using direct pressure and dressing, or other bleeding control techniques if needed. Keep in mind that dark and thick clothing can conceal major bleeding and mask a major injury. Position the child flat to help maintain blood pressure and circulation and, if not already done, maintain warmth to prevent ongoing heat loss.

Determine Level of Consciousness

The AVPU scale is commonly used to determine level of consciousness. The mnemonic begins with the most awake and alert criteria and ends with unresponsiveness:

- **Alert:** The child is fully responsive and/or can answer your questions in an age-appropriate manner.
- **Verbal:** The child responds to your voice but may be drowsy and not able to keep eyes open.
- **Pain:** The child is not alert and does not respond to your voice but does respond to a painful stimulus like a gentle shake of the shoulders or pinch of the skin.
- **Unresponsive:** The child does not respond to voice or pain. The child is unconscious.

After determining the child's level of consciousness, assess the pupils. Open the child's eyelids (if the child cannot do this on his or her own) and look at the pupils. The pupils should be round and equal. Next shine a light source, commonly a penlight, into the child's eyes for 1 to 2 seconds. When light is directed at the pupil, the pupil should contract. If the pupils are not round, are unequal, or do not react to light, this is considered an abnormal finding and can indicate a head injury or brain-related emergency.

History Taking

It is important to take a history of recent events leading to or surrounding the emergency. As with all patient assessments, the SAMPLE mnemonic should be used to maintain consistency. This can be done before, during, or after the secondary assessment. Assess for any symptoms related to the emergency and make note of the duration of the symptoms:

- Fever
- Activity level
- Recent eating, drinking, and urine output history (diaper changes per day)
- History of vomiting, diarrhea, or abdominal pain
- Medications the patient is taking and medication allergies
- Past medical problems or chronic illnesses
- Key events leading to the injury or illness

Secondary Assessment

Once the ABCs have been assessed and managed, a secondary assessment should be performed on every child to assess for injuries not obvious to the child, parent, or emergency responder:

- **Head:** Bruising, swelling, deformity, condition of the fontanelles
- **Ears:** Drainage (suggestive of trauma or infection)
- **Mouth:** Loose teeth, identifiable odors, bleeding, foreign body
- **Neck:** Abnormal bruising, trachea deviated off center
- **Chest and back:** Bruises, injuries, or rashes
- **Extremities:** Deformities, swellings, or pain on movement

A toe-to-head approach can be used with an anxious child. A child's condition can change rapidly, so you need to repeat assessments every 5 to 10 minutes.

RESPIRATORY ISSUES

As stated earlier, a child's tongue is proportionately larger in comparison with the size of the oral cavity. In addition, a child's airway is smaller than an adult's in relation to the rest of the body. Both of these conditions make it easier for a child's airway to become obstructed by the tongue, secretions, or swelling. Remember that infants breathe only through their noses, so a nose that is congested or obstructed with mucus or secretions can cause respiratory distress. See the unit on CPR for specific foreign body aspiration removal techniques.

Respiratory Distress

Respiratory distress precedes respiratory failure and arrest and is indicated by the following:

- Respiratory rate greater than 60 breaths per minute in infants
- Respiratory rate greater than 30 to 40 breaths per minute in children
- Nasal flaring with each breath
- Retraction of the skin between the ribs, neck muscles, and below the margin of the ribs
- High-pitched sound as the child breathes in
- Cyanosis
- Altered mental status in which the child is combative, has a decreased mental status, or is unresponsive
- Grunting during respiration

If any of the above signs are present, attempt to determine the cause and support or assist the child's breathing with use of artificial airway adjuncts, oxygen, or assisted ventilations. Continue to monitor the child's vital signs and reassess frequently.

Respiratory Failure and Arrest

Respiratory failure and impending respiratory arrest are indicated by the following:

- A breathing rate of less than 10 breaths per minute in a child
- A breathing rate of less than 20 breaths per minute in an infant
- Limp muscle tone
- Unresponsiveness
- Slower, absent heart rate
- Weak or absent pulses of the arms and legs
- Cyanosis

Respiratory distress that worsens often leads to respiratory failure. A child in respiratory failure is on the verge of experiencing respiratory and cardiac arrest. Immediate intervention is critical to prevent brain damage or death. High-flow oxygen should always be administered and the use of artificial airway adjuncts or assisted ventilations may be necessary if the underlying cause is not corrected and oxygen is insufficient. Monitor the child's vital signs and reassess frequently.

Partial Airway Obstruction

With a partial airway obstruction, the infant or child is alert and responsive, but may exhibit abnormal breathing with a high-pitched sound, crowing, or noisy breathing. Retractions on inspiration can also be seen in conjunction with abnormal or increased work of breathing. The child may or may not have alterations in skin color related to deprived oxygenation from the obstruction. The child should also have a strong pulse and a capillary refill time of 2 to 3 seconds. Allow the child to choose a comfortable position, but do not let the child lie down because this could worsen the obstruction. The child may sit on a parent's lap. Do not agitate the child, because doing so could cause the obstruction to worsen, leading to a complete airway obstruction.

Complete Airway Obstruction

A complete airway obstruction is a serious emergency. A child with a complete airway obstruction is not able to cry or speak, and the skin looks bluish or purple. The child's cough is ineffective at dislodging the obstruction. The increased respiratory difficulty causes the child to lose responsiveness and display altered mental status or unconsciousness. You have only a few minutes to open the airway before permanent brain damage occurs.

If a complete airway obstruction is encountered, open the child's airway using the head tilt-chin lift maneuver in children over 1 year of age. If cervical spine injury is suspected, use a modified jaw-thrust maneuver to open the airway (**Figure 4**). In an infant or child younger than 1 year of age, you can open the airway using a tongue-jaw lift maneuver.

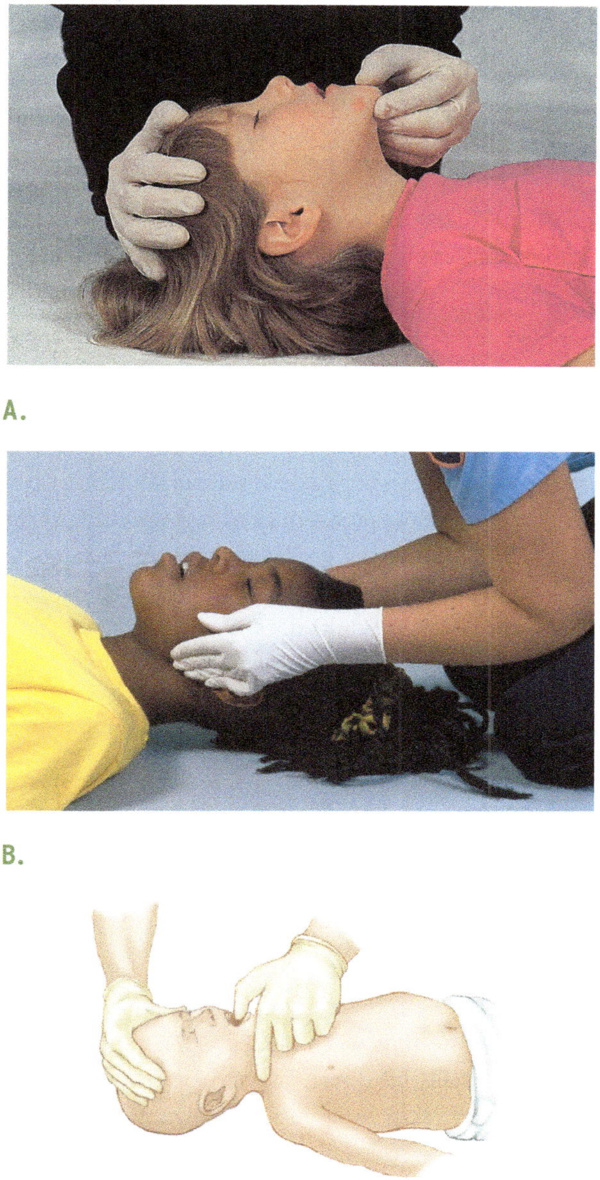

A.

B.

C.

Figure 4 **A.** Head tilt-chin lift maneuver. **B.** Modified jaw-thrust maneuver. **C.** Tongue-jaw lift maneuver.

Special Populations

Neck Overextension

In pediatric patients, you must be careful not to overextend the neck. In infants and some small children, overextension may actually obstruct the airway because of the flexibility of the child's neck. Smaller children may breathe more easily if the neck is held in a neutral position rather than overextended. To maintain the neutral position, you can use a towel to support the patient's shoulders.

Management includes clearing the airway using the age-appropriate foreign body removal procedures. Attempt artificial ventilations using the mouth-to-mask technique. If the obstruction is visible and easily removed, remove it, but do not blindly probe for the obstruction. Doing so could worsen the obstruction and lead to cardiac arrest secondary to complete blockage from oxygen entering the body and the inability to provide ventilations.

SHOCK

Shock is the body's inability to carry sufficient oxygenated blood to the organs. There are several potential causes of shock, including trauma, infection, vomiting, and diarrhea. Shock can lead to circulatory failure which, if left uncorrected, can cause cardiac arrest in infants and children. You can treat for shock by keeping the child flat to maintain blood pressure, keeping the child warm to improve circulation, applying high-concentration oxygen, and controlling bleeding.

Tip

Circulatory Failure

Signs and symptoms of circulatory failure include a pronounced rapid pulse or slow pulse, prolonged capillary refill time, weak to no peripheral pulses, cool to cold skin temperature, and mental status changes.

Management of shock includes maintaining an open airway and providing for adequate ventilation and respiratory support, including oxygen and assisted ventilation if needed. Perform chest compressions if the heart rate is less than 60 beats per minute for a child or less than 80 beats per minute for an infant. Control bleeding if needed and prevent heat loss.

A child's body does not exhibit signs of compensated shock as quickly as an adult's does. Once the signs and symptoms of shock appear, the child might be in a serious to critical condition. Stay attuned to the likelihood of shock and watch the pediatric patient carefully for signs of shock while he or she is under your care.

SEIZURES

Seizures can be caused by a high fever, infections, **epilepsy**, poisoning, low blood glucose levels, trauma, decreased levels of oxygen, or unknown factors. Seizures may be brief or prolonged and the convulsions can cause injuries. Although not usually dangerous when alone, seizures should be considered potentially life threatening if they are continuous and the child is unable to control his or her own airway. They have the potential to cause an airway obstruction due to secretions in the mouth entering the airway.

Assessment of a child with a seizure includes asking whether the child has had prior seizures or has a seizure disorder. If the child has a history of seizures, is this the child's normal seizure activity? How have past episodes been treated? Is the child taking any prescribed seizure medication? Could the child have ingested any other medications or poisons?

Observe the seizure activity if possible and be able to describe it. For example, does the child's whole body shake violently? Do just the arm and legs shake rhythmically? Do the eyes rhythmically deviate to one side or the other? Once the seizure has stopped, comfort and reassure the child while waiting for parents or additional resources. Protect the child from further injury by removing objects close to the child. Ensure patency of the child's airway by turning the child on his or her side once the seizure has stopped. Do not restrain the child or place anything into the child's mouth during or after the seizure because this could cause trauma and bleeding. Place the child in the recovery position if spinal injury is not suspected. Have suction available because seizures commonly produce significant oral secretions.

SUDDEN, UNEXPLAINED DEATH

Sudden Infant Death Syndrome

Sudden infant death syndrome (SIDS) is the death of an infant during the first year of life with no specific cause identified. The causes of SIDS have not yet been determined. The infant is most commonly discovered in his or her crib in the early morning.

Complete a scene size-up and primary assessment. Once it is discovered that the child is deceased, request additional resources (such as additional police, medical examiner, or others as defined by your jurisdiction) and attempt to comfort and calm the parents. Attempt resuscitation of the infant unless the baby is stiff or has other signs of obvious death. Avoid making comments that might suggest blame to the parents. Be aware of local legal guidelines for the management of SIDS.

Apparent Life-Threatening Event

An **apparent life-threatening event (ALTE)** refers to a sudden and unexplained occurrence of a breathing abnormality, such as apnea, and is usually associated with color changes in the skin or lips, choking, and listlessness. It commonly occurs with children younger than 1 year. Often, parents or caregivers will report an event like this occurring, but the child will not be examined by a medical professional. Like with SIDS, no specific cause of these events can be easily identified.

TRAUMA

The leading cause of death in infants and children are injuries. Motor vehicle crashes are the leading cause of these fatal injuries. Unrestrained passengers have a higher incidence of head and neck injuries, whereas restrained passengers have abdominal and lower spine injuries. Infant and booster safety seats are often improperly installed and secured which results in head and neck injuries in children using them.

Children who are struck by moving vehicles can present with injuries to the head, spinal, and abdominal areas, resulting in internal injuries, internal and external bleeding, and fractured bones. (**Figure 5**).

Figure 5 Look for these typical injuries when a child has been hit by a motor vehicle.

Falls from any height or diving into shallow water can result in head and neck injuries. Children have a proportionally larger head in relation to their body, as well as weak neck muscles, which makes them more prone to head and cervical spine injury. Children also have very soft, pliable ribs which can allow for significant internal injury without displaying any external signs such as fractures. The child's abdomen is commonly a source of hidden injury because force is transmitted to the internal organs.

Emergency care includes completing a proper scene size-up and performing primary and secondary assessments. Treat life-threatening injuries and bleeding first. Ensure that the airway is in the neutral position and that patency is maintained. Use the jaw-thrust maneuver if the airway needs to be opened. Place additional padding from the shoulders to the hips if needed during spinal immobilization to prevent flexion of the neck. Suction as necessary with a suction catheter appropriate for the child's age. Manually stabilize injuries to the extremities until proper splinting can be performed. Prevent hypothermia and maintain warmth during assessment and transport.

ABUSE AND NEGLECT

Child abuse and neglect do not have any socioeconomic boundaries. Abuse can be physical, emotional, or sexual. Some signs and symptoms of child abuse include multiple bruises in various stages of healing; injuries inconsistent with the description provided; and varying patterns of injury, including cigarette burns, fresh burns, or burns in various stages of healing, including scalding, submersion, or untreated burns (**Figure 6**).

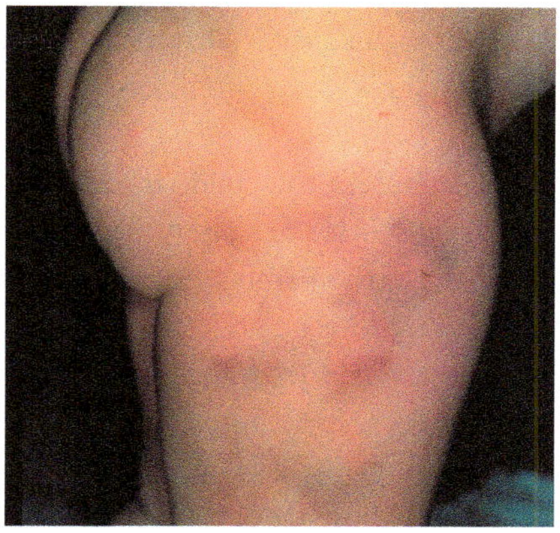

A.

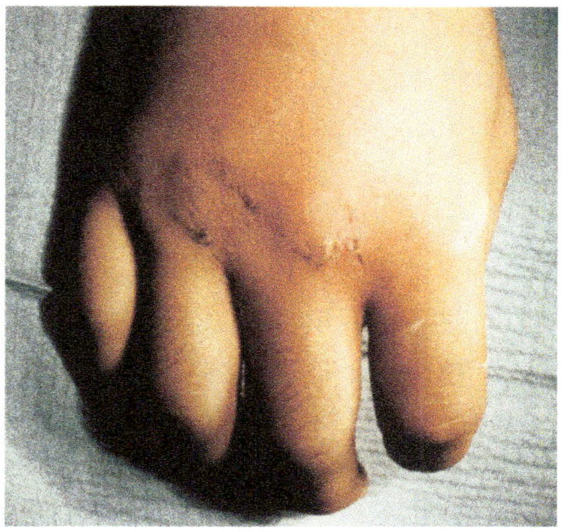

B.

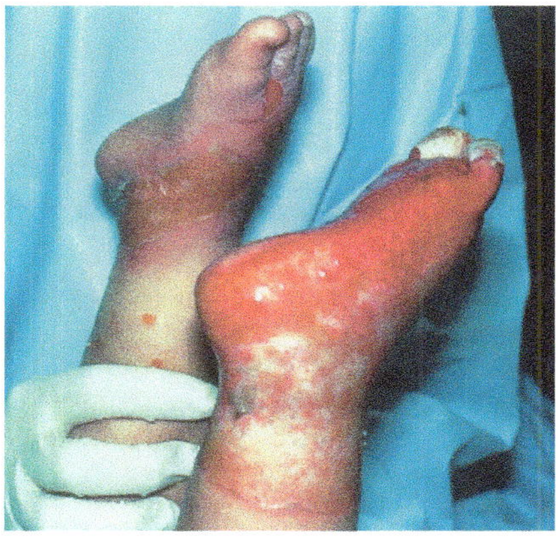

C.

Figure 6 **A.** Bruises of different ages suggest physical maltreatment. New bruises are red or pink; over time, bruises turn blue, green, yellow-brown, and faded.
B. A human bite wound has a characteristic appearance.
C. Stocking/glove burns of the hands and feet in the infant or toddler are almost always inflicted injuries.

Signs and symptoms of neglect include lack of adult supervision, malnourished or dirty appearance, or an untreated chronic illness (for example, a diabetic child with no insulin).

Suspect child abuse if the child's injuries do not match the story that parents or caregivers provide about how the injuries occurred or if the parents or caregivers seem inappropriately unconcerned. The child may also be hesitant to discuss how the injury occurred. In some cases, an emotionally abused child will exhibit fear, cower, aggressively defend a parent or guardian, or look sad and lack a normal affect. Be aware that sexual abuse can occur at any age. If you are treating an infant or child, assess for torn, blood-, or semen-stained clothing. Observe for abnormal patterns of blunt or penetrating trauma.

Shaken baby syndrome should be suspected if the infant or child is unresponsive or if severe internal injuries are found with no evidence of external injuries. Seizure activity may or may not be present.

Do not accuse anyone at the scene of abuse, regardless of your suspicions, because this only delays transport to a safer place and can induce violence. Reporting suspected child abuse or neglect is required by state law. Review and follow local laws and regulations. Remain objective and be certain to report your observations to EMS or to the receiving team at the hospital. Be certain to communicate your findings to appropriate child protective services personnel per your local protocol.

SPECIAL CONSIDERATIONS FOR LAW ENFORCEMENT RESPONSE

Emergency care of a sick or injured child may be one of the most stressful situations you will face in your career. As a LER, you must not only deal with the medical aspects of the situation, but also contend with possible criminal activity. Be aware that a child who appears sick or injured may be a diversion. A weapon could be hidden in an infant's crib. Proper preplanning of the mission should address all potential issues, and clear instructions should be given to the person(s) chosen to provide medical care in a given situation so as not to compromise the mission and the protection of all involved.

CONCLUSION

As a LER, you will come into contact with children and their illnesses and injuries. Being aware of the anatomy and physiology unique to infants and children, as well as the special considerations related to the assessment process, will assist you in determining the severity of an illness or injury, allowing you to provide safe and efficient emergency care.

Prep Kit

READY FOR REVIEW

- Pediatric emergencies can be among the most stressful situations to manage. Many factors are involved, including fear and anxiety from the child, parents, and bystanders.
- At the scene of a pediatric emergency, the parents of the ill or injured child present a unique challenge, either helping or hindering care.
- Talk to the parents as much as possible and explain the care you are providing and the potential care yet to occur.
- Approach a child as gently as possible given the level of medical urgency.
- Children are not small adults. Many aspects of a child's anatomy and function differ from those of adults.
- The initial evaluation of a sick or injured infant or child can be done by careful observation without touching the child and can provide critical information about the child's condition.
- Your evaluation of the child begins using a simple tool called the pediatric assessment triangle (PAT). The three components of the PAT are appearance, work of breathing, and circulation to the skin.
- Once the ABCs have been assessed and managed, a secondary assessment should be performed on every child to assess for injuries not obvious to the child, parent, or emergency responder.
- Because of their anatomy, children's airways are more easily obstructed by the tongue, secretions, or swelling than adults'.
- There are several potential causes of shock, including trauma, infection, vomiting, and diarrhea. Shock can lead to circulatory failure which, if left uncorrected, can cause cardiac arrest in infants and children.
- A child's body does not exhibit signs of compensated shock as quickly as an adult's does. Once the signs and symptoms of shock appear, the child might be in very poor condition.
- Seizures can be caused by a high fever, infections, epilepsy, poisoning, low blood glucose levels, trauma, decreased levels of oxygen, or unknown factors. Seizures may be brief or prolonged, and the convulsions can cause injuries.
- Sudden infant death syndrome (SIDS) is the death of an infant during the first year of life with no specific cause identified. The causes of SIDS have not yet been determined.
- An apparent life-threatening event (ALTE) refers to a sudden and unexplained occurrence of a breathing abnormality, such as apnea, and is usually associated with color changes in the skin or lips, choking, and listlessness.
- Injuries are the leading cause of death in infants and children. Motor vehicle crashes are a leading cause of injuries to children.
- When treating an injured child, consider placing additional padding from the shoulders to the hips during spinal immobilization to prevent flexion of the neck.
- Child abuse and neglect do not have any socioeconomic boundaries. Abuse can be physical, emotional, or sexual.
- Signs and symptoms of neglect include lack of adult supervision, malnourished or dirty appearance, or an untreated chronic illness.
- Do not accuse anyone at the scene of abuse, regardless of your suspicions, because this only delays transport to a safer place and can induce violence.
- Reporting suspected child abuse or neglect is required by state law. Review and follow local laws and regulations.

VITAL VOCABULARY

apparent life-threatening event (ALTE) A sudden and unexplained occurrence of a breathing abnormality in an infant.

cardiorespiratory failure A condition in which the heart and lungs stop functioning.

epilepsy A disease manifested by seizures, caused by an abnormal focus of electrical activity in the brain.

fontanelles Areas where the infant's skull has not fused together; usually disappear at approximately 18 months of age.

mottled A patchy skin discoloration caused by too little or too much circulation.

pediatric assessment triangle (PAT) A 15- to 30-second assessment tool used to assess the severity of the child's illness or injury.

sudden infant death syndrome (SIDS) The death of an infant during the first year of life, with no specific cause identified.

work of breathing The amount of energy one has to expend in order to breathe.

CHECK YOUR KNOWLEDGE

1. The three elements of the pediatric assessment triangle (PAT) are:
   A. airway, breathing, and circulation.
   B. appearance, work of breathing, and circulation.
   C. appearance, circulation, and level of consciousness.
   D. appearance, level of consciousness, and capillary refill.
2. Signs and symptoms of circulatory failure include all of the following, except:
   A. increased heart rate.
   B. difficulty breathing.
   C. prolonged capillary refill time.
   D. mental status changes.
3. A child's body does not exhibit signs of compensated shock as quickly as an adult's does.
   A. True
   B. False
4. Which of the following is the best way to ensure airway patency of a child experiencing a seizure?
   A. Gently insert a tongue depressor or similar item into the child's mouth to keep the teeth from clenching.
   B. With the assistance of other rescuers or bystanders, restrain the patient and provide oxygen via bag-mask device.
   C. Turn the child on his or her side once the seizure has stopped.
   D. Nothing. The airway is not a concern with seizure patients.
5. Which of the following is a potential indicator of child abuse?
   A. Burns of the hands or feet.
   B. Many bruises of different ages.
   C. A child afraid to discuss how he or she was injured.
   D. All of the above

Elderly Patients

Unit 22

David Callaway

Law Enforcement Responder Objectives

- Discuss age-associated changes specific to anatomy and physiology. (p 419)
- Discuss assessment and patient care considerations specific to elderly patients. (pp 419–420)
- Discuss common types of sensory changes in geriatric patients and strategies for dealing effectively with these limitations. (pp 420–421)
- Identify medical issues commonly seen in the elderly population, including cardiovascular disease and respiratory disease, and the approach law enforcement responders should take if these issues are suspected. (pp 421–422)
- Identify conditions that could lead to altered mental status in elderly patients. (p 422)
- Discuss risk factors for and effects of trauma in elderly patients and identify responder considerations. (pp 422–423)
- Discuss psychiatric issues common in the elderly population and identify responder considerations. (pp 423–424)
- Describe common signs of elder abuse. (pp 424–425)
- Discuss issues related to the extraction and evacuation of geriatric patients. (pp 425)
- Discuss age-related concerns in hostage situations. (pp 425–426)
- Discuss the implications of using less lethal technologies with the elderly population. (p 426)

National EMS Education Standard Competencies

Special Patient Populations

Recognizes and manages life threats based on simple assessment findings for a patient with special needs while awaiting additional emergency response.

Geriatrics

- Impact of age-related changes on assessment and care (pp 419–420)

Patients With Special Challenges

- Recognizing and reporting abuse and neglect (pp 424–425)

Trauma

Uses simple knowledge to recognize and manage life threats based on assessment findings for an acutely injured patient while awaiting additional emergency medical response.

Special Considerations in Trauma

Recognition and management of trauma in

- Geriatric patients (pp 422–423)

Life Span Development

Uses simple knowledge of age-related differences to assess and care for patients.

INTRODUCTION

The elderly are generally considered to be persons who are older than 65 years, which accounts for one in every 8 persons (approximately 36 million people). This age demographic is the most rapidly growing segment of our population and is expected to double in the next 30 years (**Figure 1**). As the population ages, law enforcement responders (LERs) are interacting more frequently with elderly patients, also known as **geriatric** patients. The geriatric population is increasingly active, resulting in more frequent injuries. In addition, as life span increases, more patients with chronic medical, physical, and psychiatric conditions are living in our communities.

The natural aging process results in a decline in the functioning of all body systems. This gradual decline is affected by heredity and by lifestyle choices such as diet, stress, exercise, and community engagement. The LER must have a basic understanding of these changes to manage emergencies involving elderly people effectively. It is important that responders not prejudge the physical or mental condition of older patients (**Figure 2**). Some elderly people are vibrant and healthy at age 80 years, whereas others suffer from chronic, debilitating disease at age 65 years. The same is true of mental capacity.

For LERs, the elderly present several unique challenges because they are at particular risk and require tailored response protocols. This unit outlines some of the physical, emotional, medical, and psychiatric challenges that LERs may encounter when interacting with or caring for elderly patients. It also gives responders a basic understanding of the physiology of aging and strategies for communicating effectively with the elderly.

ASSESSMENT

Because other health care providers rely on the LER's observations, primary and secondary assessments are particularly important when responding to elderly patients. The primary assessment should begin with a scene size-up to ensure safety within the parameters of your response protocols. The primary assessment should generally proceed through the traditional algorithm of airway, breathing, and circulation. Several age-related anatomic and physiologic changes make assessing the elderly patient challenging. For example, the elderly airway may be compromised by neck masses or tumors, dentures, and limited mobility from arthritis. While assessing breathing, it is important to note that the elderly have decreased functional residual capacity, making them more susceptible to respiratory compromise with minimal insult such as pneumonia, rib fractures, or pulmonary contusions.

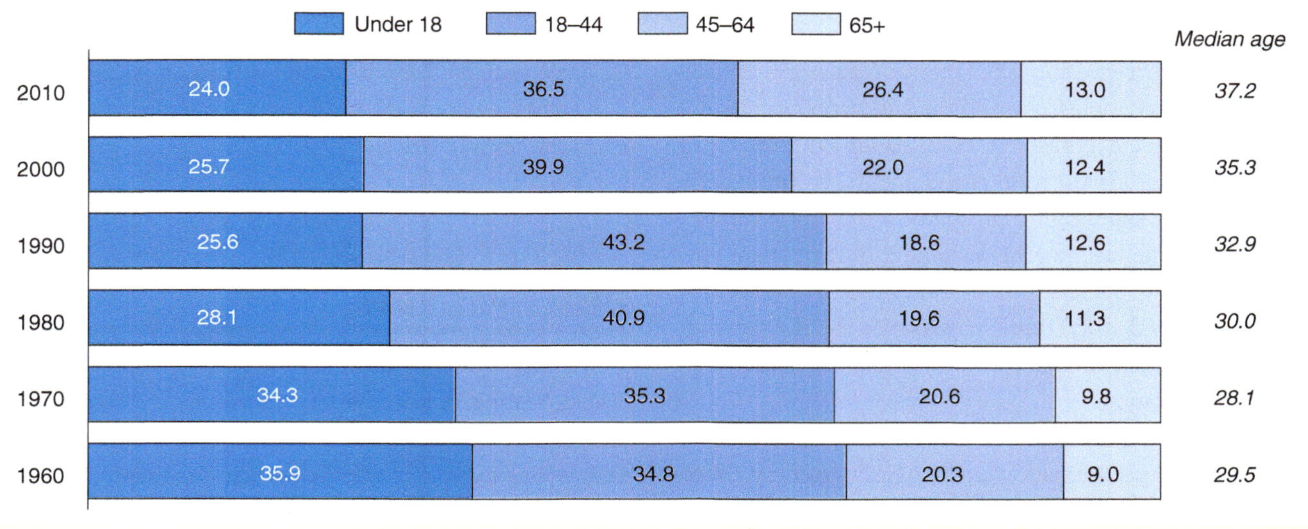

Figure 1 Population distribution, 1960 to 2010. The elderly population is expected to continue to grow over the coming years.

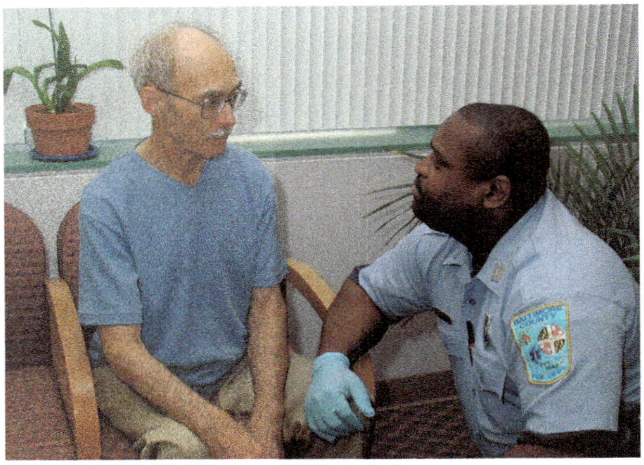

Figure 2 The LER must understand the natural changes that occur as people age and take those changes into consideration without judgment.

The circulatory exam in the elderly is particularly challenging. First, the elderly often have baseline hypertension; therefore, a normal systolic blood pressure of 120 mm Hg may actually represent significant hypotension. Likewise, the incidence of arrhythmias such as **atrial fibrillation** can make radial pulse assessment challenging in the prehospital setting. Finally, polypharmacy (taking several medications) and medication reactions can cause significant cardiovascular compromise. In the hypotensive elderly patient, it is important to conduct a brief survey for any transdermal patches (eg, Imdur, nitroglycerin) that could be precipitating the shock state.

The elderly have diminished thermoregulatory capabilities and are susceptible to heat stroke and hypothermia. It is critical to complete a thorough examination while ensuring the patient is protected from the elements. In the elderly, this may mean exposing certain body regions in a sequential fashion while keeping the remainder of the patient covered. **Osteopenia** (decreased bone volume) and **osteoporosis** (decreased bone density) result in weakened skeletal structure in the elderly. Even apparently minor mechanisms can result in significant trauma.

The secondary assessment is a more thorough evaluation that provides vital information on the patient's medical condition (eg, collecting medication bottles), physical impairments (eg, crutches, walker, or hearing aids), and psychiatric and physical well-being (eg, empty liquor bottles or disheveled appearance), as well as alerting the responder to signs of neglect or abuse. Use all of your senses: visual clues (eg, clutter), smells (eg, urine or feces), and hearing (listen to the patient and the family). This information can be vital for the physician and other health care providers (Table 1).

Table 1

Vital Information to Collect About a Patient

Medical Information	Physical Impairments	Psychiatric and Physical Well-Being
Complete medical history	Crutches, walker, cane, wheelchair	Empty liquor bottles
Results of patient assessment	Hearing aids	Disheveled manner, dirty, or soiled with urine or feces
Information collected from family members, friends, or caregivers	Glasses	Clutter, signs of hoarding, dirty or unsafe living conditions
Any medication bottles, inhaler, diabetes kit	Home oxygen tank or dialysis machine	Signs of abuse or neglect

A physical assessment of the geriatric patient can be challenging. Elderly people often wear more clothing than younger people, even during warmer months. The LER must be particularly vigilant. Even in stable patients, it is essential that you conduct a complete head-to-toe examination; do not let extra clothes interfere.

SENSORY CHANGES IN OLDER PATIENTS

Communication difficulties may impede patient assessment. Visual, hearing, or language barriers can make communicating with elderly patients more challenging. Two of the most socializing senses are hearing and sight. These important senses begin to decline in many people as they age. For some elderly people, this change means using eyeglasses, hearing aids, contact lenses, or basic sign language.

Communication

Communicating With Older Patients

Techniques for communicating with older patients include the following:

- Identify yourself.
- Look directly at the patient.
- Speak slowly and articulate your words.
- Explain what you are going to do in clear, simple language.
- Listen to the patient.
- Show the patient respect.
- Do not talk about the patient to others in front of the patient.
- Be patient and remain calm.
- Remember to get the patient's belongings.

Hearing

Hearing loss may be related to repeated exposures to loud noises or to congenital degeneration. Hearing loss is often most pronounced at higher frequencies. As a result, a patient may be able to hear a low-pitched voice but not hear a higher-pitched voice. You should ensure that the elderly patient can hear and understand instructions. Identify yourself, speak at a reasonable pace, and articulate your words. If you think a patient is having difficulty hearing you, ask, "Can you hear me?" You can attempt to speak directly into the patient's ear while maintaining eye contact. You may also consider placing a stethoscope to the patient's ears and speaking into it. Many elderly patients with hearing difficulties have adapted to their deficit and can read lips to some degree. If these techniques are not effective, write down your questions and offer pen and paper to the patient for response.

Communication

Avoid Handcuffs

Every effort should be made not to handcuff a person who is deaf. Doing so will limit the patient's ability to communicate with his or her hands.

Vision

During your primary assessment, look for signs that the patient may be visually impaired. These signs may include eyeglasses, a white cane, or a service dog. As you approach, introduce yourself. If you think the patient is blind, ask, "Can you see?" You should recognize that a visually impaired patient may feel especially vulnerable during the chaos of an emergency. Tell the patient what is happening, identify noises, describe the surroundings as much as possible, and explain your actions. Use the patient's name throughout the assessment, treatment, and extraction phases. If an elderly patient wears eyeglasses, attempt to keep them with the patient. If the glasses are lost and the situation permits, you should attempt a brief search. The patient may be severely handicapped and anxious without his or her glasses. Please follow your agency's or department's policy when dealing with service dogs. These animals are vital to the impaired patient's daily activities.

Even if the patient does not consider himself or herself visually impaired, vision changes are common as people age and include decreased night vision and depth perception, farsightedness, and difficulty differentiating colors.

MEDICAL ISSUES

Cardiovascular Disease

Cardiovascular disease is widespread in elderly patients. Conditions such as coronary artery disease, heart attack, congestive heart failure, hypertension, angina, and strokes are significant illnesses in the elderly population. These conditions frequently result in chronic debilitation. As people age, their blood vessels harden and narrow from plaque accumulation. They suffer higher rates of hypertension and demonstrate decreased ability to mount appropriate cardiac responses to shock states. In addition, traditional pain sensors frequently become less sensitive. As a result, geriatric patients may present with vague and often misleading symptoms. For example, a geriatric patient having a heart attack may not report chest pain or difficulty breathing, instead only complaining of fatigue or shortness of breath. Likewise, some patients who are having a stroke may be unaware of the symptoms they are experiencing. It is critical that the responder obtain a proper medical history and understand the unique pathophysiology of geriatric patients. Treat all geriatric patients with a high degree of concern and caution. It is better to "err on the side of caution" and treat than to fail to recognize a life-threatening condition.

Respiratory Disease

Respiratory disease frequently affects the geriatric population and can be categorized as chronic or acute. Generally, as people age, they have decreased functional residual capacity (FRC), decreased lung compliance, and weakened muscles of respiration. Patients with chronic obstructive pulmonary disease (COPD) may live with the disease for years, managed by medication and home oxygen. However, infection, stress, medication noncompliance, malfunctioning oxygen tanks, or various chemical or environmental factors can worsen COPD and trigger a life-threatening, acute condition. The LER should note the presence of home oxygen and collect a standard history. If the patient is **hypoxic** or demonstrating signs of respiratory distress, oxygen should be applied immediately.

Acute respiratory disease can be infectious—for example, pneumonia, which is a common and frequently fatal infectious disease in the elderly—or it can be a manifestation of a chronic disease, such as congestive heart failure or COPD, that has become significantly worse. In the elderly, respiratory infections can rapidly progress and threaten the patient's life, even if they do not carry the same signs and symptoms they would in a younger patient. You should perform a careful assessment, examine the patient, provide treatment according to local protocols, and arrange for immediate transport to an appropriate medical facility when indicated.

It is important to note that hypoxia and infections can result in significant mental status changes, including agitation. Providing ample reassurance and explanation to an agitated patient can help keep him or her calm and enable you to focus more effectively on patient assessment and care. During support for law enforcement operations, the oxygen used in the homes of patients with COPD may represent a significant fire or explosive hazard during the use of standard diversionary devices and less-lethal weapons. This should be a consideration during the medical threat assessment and planning stages of a mission.

Altered Mental Status

There are myriad reasons for **altered mental status** in the elderly, including medication reactions, infection, stroke, low blood glucose levels, **dementia**, and psychiatric disease. An accurate assessment of the patient's mental status is critical for determining the proper level of medical or law enforcement response. Altered mental status can result in acts of violence, confusion, and self-injurious behavior. Conduct a rapid mental status examination during the primary assessment that includes the Glasgow Coma Scale (GCS) as well as orientation to person, place, and time (**Figure 3**). You can also have the patient write an answer to a simple question on a pad of paper to assess comprehension, expression, and motor skills.

GLASGOW COMA SCALE

Eye Opening		
Spontaneous	4	
To Voice	3	
To Pain	2	
None	1	
Verbal Response		
Oriented	5	
Confused	4	
Inappropriate Words	3	
Incomprehensible Words	2	
None	1	
Motor Response		
Obeys Command	6	
Localizes Pain	5	
Withdraws (pain)	4	
Flexion (pain)	3	
Extension (pain)	2	
None	1	
Glasgow Coma Score Maximum Total	**15**	

Figure 3 The Glascow Coma Scale can be used to evaluate level of consciousness. The lower the score, the more severe the brain injury.

MUSCULOSKELETAL AND MOBILITY ISSUES

Geriatric patients frequently suffer from decreased mobility. As people age, their muscles lose strength and they are less able to carry out routine activities. In addition, diminished vision and age-related changes in the brain can result in difficulty with balance and an increased risk of falls. When examining an older patient, be aware of these changes and offer assistance. Always provide extra support to an elderly patient. Lend a helping hand or a supporting arm. Most elderly patients are afraid of falling; your support will help them overcome this fear. Allow enough time for patients to move safely rather than trying to rush them. In situations requiring emergent evacuation, be aware of the geriatric patient's limitations and plan accordingly.

Special Populations

Support for Elderly Patients

Diminished vision and other age-related changes in the elderly can result in difficulty with balance and an increased risk of falls. Most elderly patients are afraid of falling, and your support will help them overcome this fear. Remember the following points when assisting older patients:

- Always provide extra support and encouragement.
- Lend a helping hand or supporting arm.
- Allow enough time for patients to move safely.
- Don't rush them.

Geriatric patients are at high risk for fractures from seemingly minor trauma. As people age, their bones lose calcium and become more brittle. This process is especially pronounced in **postmenopausal** women and can result in osteoporosis. Simple falls from a standing position can result in hip, wrist, spine, and neck fractures. (In fact, sometimes a fall is actually caused by a fracture.) Age-related loss of pain sensors may also mask the severity of the patient's trauma. With hip fractures, the affected leg is generally shortened and externally rotated (toes facing outward) (**Figure 4**). In general, the LER should attempt to discover the reason for the fall. As you conduct your primary assessment, remember that many conditions—including strokes, heart attacks, **sepsis**, and medication reactions—can make patients unsteady and cause them to fall.

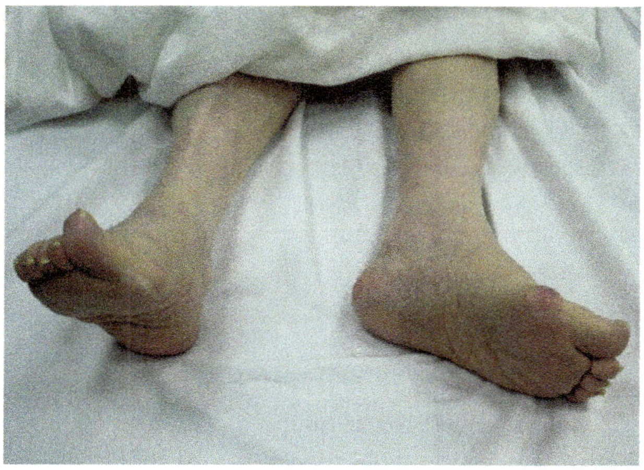

Figure 4 Signs of a hip fracture may include external rotation and shortening of the injured leg.

After the secondary assessment, you should splint the patient as described in the extremity and soft-tissue injury unit, and arrange for prompt transport to a medical facility.

PSYCHIATRIC ISSUES

Geriatric patients may experience a wide range of mental problems, ranging from chronic dementia to acute delirium. Four of the most commonly encountered and challenging conditions are **depression**, anxiety, suicidal thoughts, and dementia. These conditions are particularly relevant for the LER supporting a mission.

Depression is the most common psychiatric condition experienced by elderly adults, affecting over 2 million Americans older than 65 years. Depression is more common in women than in men and is particularly pronounced in nursing homes, assisted-living facilities, and in elderly people living alone. Important triggers are loss of a spouse, declining mental or physical functions, recent diagnosis of terminal illness, or recent placement in a long-term care facility.

Progressing depression or dramatic life-altering events can prompt suicidal thoughts and attempts in the elderly. Nineteen percent of suicides in the United States occur in people older than 65 years. The elderly population also has a higher rate of violent **suicide** (eg, guns, hanging). Despite lower rates of depression, older men have higher rates of suicide. Risk factors for suicide include physical illness, loss of loved ones, a solitary living situation, alcohol abuse, and certain medical conditions.

Most elderly people who commit suicide have seen a primary care physician during the month prior to their death, underscoring the importance of close observation by all medical personnel. If you think a patient may be considering suicide, arrange for transport to an appropriate medical facility (**Figure 5**). Depression and suicidal thoughts may prompt individuals to strike out violently at caregivers or family members, and weapons may be involved, so it is important to remain alert for your safety and that of others nearby. LERs need to understand the unique aspects of depression and altered mental status in the elderly. This understanding can facilitate peaceful resolution to potentially complex and chaotic incidents involving elderly patients.

Dementia is a progressive and irreversible decline in mental function that affects many elderly patients. Dementia is marked by impaired memory and a decreased capacity for

Figure 5 If you think a patient may be considering suicide, arrange for transport to an appropriate medical facility.

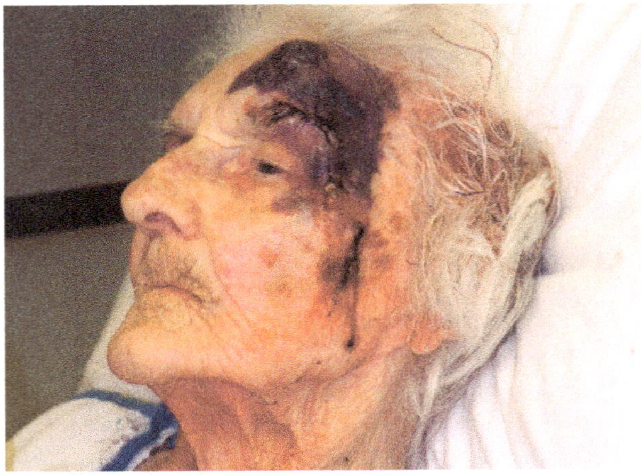

Figure 6 Physical abuse is one form of elder abuse.

reasoning, judgment, comprehension, and verbal communication. (One example of dementia is **Alzheimer disease**.) In addition, patients with dementia often experience dramatic fluctuations in mood. Dementia tends to be chronic and progressive. **Delirium**, on the other hand, tends to be acute, present with significant visual or auditory hallucinations, and have an underlying physiologic cause such as infection, medication reaction, or trauma.

Special Populations

Be Alert for Responder Safety

The elderly have higher rates of violent suicide and may strike out aggressively at caregivers, family members, or responders if they are depressed, suicidal, or mentally impaired. It is important to remain alert for your safety and that of others nearby.

ELDER ABUSE

Elder abuse is a frequently under-recognized problem that encompasses physical, emotional, financial, or sexual abuse or neglect of individuals older than 65 years (**Figure 6**). Elderly people with physical or mental deterioration are the most susceptible to abuse by spouses, family members, friends, caregivers, or unrelated persons. Elder abuse is often hard to detect because those at highest risk are often isolated from public view, frequently confined to their home or assisted care facilities. In addition, patients with dementia may be unable to report abuse to the authorities.

Tip

Signs and Symptoms of Abuse

Elder abuse is often hard to detect because those at highest risk are often isolated from public view or may be unable to report abuse to the authorities due to dementia. To protect the elderly, familiarize yourself with these signs and symptoms of abuse:

- Bruises, burns, or trauma, particularly on the following areas:
  - Buttocks
  - Lower back
  - Genitals
  - Cheeks
  - Neck
  - Wrists
  - Earlobes
- Bruises shaped like objects or hands
- Multiple bruises in various stages of healing
- Signs of neglect, including malnourishment

Emergency medical services (EMS) and LERs may be in a unique position to detect unreported elder abuse. To protect the elderly, you must be familiar with the signs and symptoms of abuse. Bruising is an important sign of potential abuse. In particular, bruises on the buttocks, lower back, genitals, cheeks, neck, wrists, and earlobes, as well as bruises shaped like objects or hands, can be suggestive of abuse. Frequently, victims of abuse have multiple bruises in various stages of healing. Burns, trauma to the genital area, malnourishment, and signs of neglect should also be noted and reported per agency protocols to the Department of Protective Services (DPS), Department of Public Health (DPH), or local law enforcement. Learn the local requirements for reporting elder abuse and contact medical control if there is any suspicion of abuse.

MANAGEMENT

Most EMS agencies have standard protocols for on-scene management of physical, medical, and psychological conditions. It is important to familiarize yourself with these protocols. In general, if the situation is emergent or related to a law enforcement mission, the EMS personnel should limit treatments to life- and limb-saving interventions. The exception to this rule is prompt pain control with splinting of fractures as the situation allows.

Extraction and Evacuation

The elderly present several unique challenges for extraction and evacuation. Physical threats, impaired vision, or loss of hearing may limit the geriatric patient's ability to follow commands. In addition, diminished strength and balance may make rapid self-evacuation dangerous or impossible. Finally, osteoporosis and degenerative joint disease may limit the rescuer's ability to implement standard extraction techniques such as harness rescues, drags, and casualty carries. These considerations should be acknowledged, and training programs should be implemented to address the potential limitations of geriatric extraction.

Tip

Reluctance to Leave

It may be difficult to get an elderly patient to agree to go to the hospital for emergency care. They may fear that leaving their home will result in them being placed in a nursing facility.

Transport considerations for geriatric patients frequently include the need for more advanced monitoring. There is a significant risk of skin breakdown and pressure ulcers when placing and transporting elderly patients on long boards (Figure 7). In addressing this challenge and others, preplanning and drilling can identify weaknesses in extraction strategies and allow for more targeted techniques in geriatric rescue. Remember to communicate with the patient. Offering simple words of comfort and reassurance can significantly reduce the anxiety of patients and facilitate all stages of care.

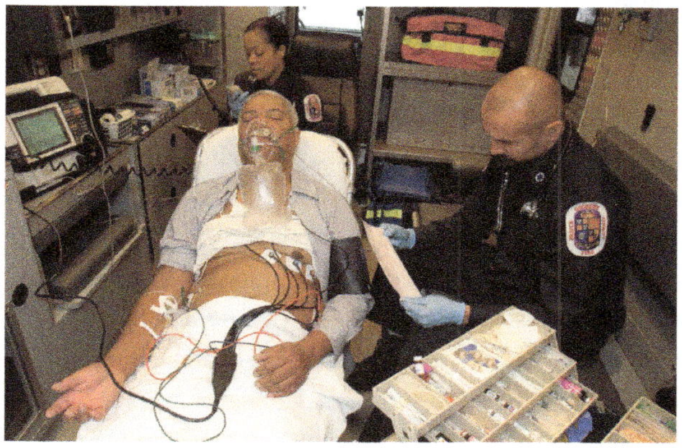

Figure 7 Extra care must be taken when transporting geriatric patients.

HOSTAGE CONSIDERATIONS

Elderly Individuals as Hostages

All hostage situations are stressful for both the victims and the responders. Medical intelligence becomes particularly important when dealing with elderly hostages. A hostage's medical conditions (eg, angina) could make him or her susceptible to negative consequences from extreme stress. Medical information can also help the responding agency. For example, if the hostage has a condition requiring medication or advanced care, the negotiator can potentially use this information to de-escalate the scenario.

Medical intelligence should also be used in tactical decisions that may affect elderly hostages. Traditional acoustic distraction devices result in **hyperadrenergic surge**. In the elderly, the shock may provoke cardiac or neurologic events. Irritant gases or obfuscation smoke may have implications for victims suffering from pulmonary disease. The use of flash bangs or incendiary devices may result in fires or explosions in homes with patients using medical gas such as oxygen.

Elderly Individuals as Hostage Takers and Elderly Emotionally Deranged Persons

In situations where an elderly person is a hostage taker, the responding team must seriously consider medical or psychiatric causes and understand the basic differential diagnosis of mental status change in the geriatric population. Effective response can rely heavily on being aware of triggers that can result in agitation, delirium, or suicidal thoughts in the elderly. Understanding the underlying pathology of the elderly hostage taker can help shape negotiation strategies, affect duration of negotiations, and determine the use of appropriate medical and psychiatric resources. The responding team should remember that there are higher rates of both suicide attempts and suicide success in the elderly, often by violent means. This should raise the suspicion of "suicide by cop." Communication with an elderly hostage taker may be limited by the previously mentioned physical and mental constraints. As a result, traditional visual and voice strategies may fail if the perpetrator suffers from diminished senses. Listen for clues and adjust your techniques accordingly.

Implications of Less-Lethal Technology

Decreased muscle mass and the likelihood of multiple medical conditions make the elderly a high-risk population for the use of less-than-lethal technology. No studies have specifically examined the effects of Tasers, bean bags, or other devices on the elderly. However, Tasers have been shown to alter cardiac conductivity and heart rate and may adversely affect patients with pacemakers or implanted defibrillators. Because the LER will not likely know whether a perpetrator has a pacemaker, caution should be exercised when deploying such means against the elderly. Elderly patients may also be at higher risk for spine fractures, traumatic head injuries, or long bone injuries after Taser deployment. Therefore, when deploying less-lethal devices against elderly suspects or perpetrators, LERs should expect a higher risk of rib fractures, pulmonary contusions, and cardiac contusions, and should be prepared to care for those injuries.

CONCLUSION

The elderly patient presents common and complex challenges for LERs. The basic principles of the primary assessment and secondary assessment remain an important framework for the examination and treatment of this expanding population. The unique aspects of elder care warrant special attention during the planning, training, and execution phases of emergency operations.

Prep Kit

READY FOR REVIEW

- The natural aging process results in a decline in the functioning of all body systems.
- Elderly patients have decreased sensory functions, including hearing and sight, which can make communication, evaluation, and extraction more difficult.
- Elderly patients are more susceptible to significant traumatic injuries after apparently minor trauma.
- Common medical concerns for geriatric patients include cardiovascular, respiratory, and infectious diseases.
- Altered mental status is common in the elderly population. Effective care at the hospital relies heavily on responders collecting information about the living situation, gathering available medication bottles, and obtaining additional history from family, friends, and caregivers.
- Geriatric patients frequently suffer from decreased mobility and are at increased risk of falling. Always provide extra support to an elderly patient.
- Be alert to signs of depression, dementia, and suicidal thoughts in elderly patients.
- Abuse and neglect of elderly people is frequently under-recognized and often hard to detect. Watch for signs of abuse such as bruising, burns, trauma to the genital area, malnourishment, and signs of neglect.
- During law enforcement operations involving geriatric patients, attention should be paid to chronic medical conditions, specific medical needs (eg, supplemental oxygen), and potential medical issues such as dementia that could influence response strategies.
- Use caution when deploying less-lethal technologies with the elderly because they are at increased risk of harm from such interventions.

VITAL VOCABULARY

altered mental status A change in one's mental activity or responsiveness.

Alzheimer disease A chronic, progressive dementia that accounts for 60% of all cases of dementia in the United States.

atrial fibrillation A cardiac dysrhythmia common in the elderly that results in an irregular pulse.

delirium An acute change in mental status that can be caused by medications, physical or psychiatric illness, neurologic insults, trauma, or acute changes in an elderly person's environment.

dementia A progressive, irreversible decline in mental functioning marked by impairments in memory and reasoning.

depression A psychiatric disorder marked by persistent feelings of sadness, hopelessness, and loss of interest in daily activities. At extremes, depression can lead to thoughts of suicide or attempts to harm one's self.

elder abuse An action taken by a family member or caregiver that results in physical, emotional, or sexual harm to a person older than 65 years.

geriatric Older than 65 years.

hyperadrenergic surge The body's release of adrenaline and the subsequent physiologic responses including tachycardia, hypertension, hyperthermia, and potentially agitation.

hypoxic Experiencing a dangerous and potentially life-threatening condition in which the cells and tissues of the body do not have enough oxygen to survive.

osteopenia A bone condition characterized by reduced bone volume.

osteoporosis An abnormal brittleness of the bones caused by a loss of calcium. Affected bones are more susceptible to fractures.

postmenopausal The stage of life when a woman has stopped having her monthly menstrual cycle. It is marked by a decrease in estrogen, which can contribute to changes in a woman's health.

sepsis A condition of generalized infection that has spread throughout the body.

suicide The intentional taking of one's own life. Suicide is more commonly attempted and more commonly successful in elderly patients.

CHECK YOUR KNOWLEDGE

1. Which of the following would not account for a mental status change in an elderly patient?
   - A. Infection
   - B. Stroke
   - C. Attending a celebration
   - D. Low blood glucose level
2. You are confronted with an elderly patient who has a severe hearing deficit. The patient is awake, alert, and can see. Which of the following strategies is least appropriate to aid in communications?
   - A. Write down questions and information legibly on a pad.
   - B. Speak loudly and clearly, look directly at the patient, and use hand gestures.
   - C. Do not attempt to communicate with the patient because doing so will likely lead to confusion. Simply arrange for immediate transport to the nearest hospital.
   - D. Lower the pitch of your voice and talk more slowly.
3. You have been called to an apartment for excessive noise. Upon arriving, you find an elderly woman lying on the ground just inside the doorway. She advises you that she fell and has been unable to get up. You should:
   - A. Reach down, help her up, and gently set her in a chair.
   - B. Remain at the doorway and politely ask her if she is able to stand.
   - C. Ensure scene safety and assess the patient for injuries, specifically fractures.
   - D. Reassure the woman and call a family member or caregiver to assist her.
4. A patient suffering from feelings of hopelessness and despair is experiencing which emotional condition?
   - A. Dementia
   - B. Depression
   - C. Atherosclerosis
   - D. Osteoporosis
5. Which of the following statements regarding suicide in the elderly population is true?
   - A. The elderly typically commit suicide using passive means such as ingesting poison.
   - B. Women are more prone than men to commit suicide.
   - C. Elderly suicide victims have often seen their physician during the month before their death.
   - D. Most suicides in the elderly population occur before the person reaches 65 years.

Behavioral Emergencies

Unit 23

Matthew Levy

Law Enforcement Responder Objectives

- Define the term *behavioral emergency*. (p 431)
- Identify the signs and symptoms of an individual experiencing a behavioral emergency. (p 431)
- Identify medical conditions that may cause, or be misinterpreted as, a behavioral emergency. (pp 432–433)
- Identify techniques for approaching a patient and maintaining officer safety when responding to a possible behavioral emergency. (pp 431–432)
- List the components of the SEA-3 evaluation tool and the SAFER-R model. (pp 433–435)
- Discuss techniques for managing behavioral emergencies. (pp 434–435)
- Recall techniques for medically restraining patients who are a danger to themselves or others. (pp 435–437)
- Identify times when an officer might use a conducted electrical weapon or electronic control device. (p 437)
- Identify signs and symptoms of excited delirium and understand what you should do if you suspect a patient has this condition. (p 437)
- Identify factors that may place an individual at heightened risk for suicide. (pp 437–438)

National EMS Education Standard Competencies

Medicine

Recognizes and manages life threats based on assessment findings of a patient with a medical emergency while awaiting additional emergency response.

Psychiatric

Recognition of

- Behaviors that pose a risk to the emergency medical responder, patient, or others (p 431)

INTRODUCTION

Behavioral emergencies may be the result of situational stress, physical trauma, medical conditions, substance abuse, or an underlying mental illness. These situations can sometimes cause an individual to behave in an unexpected and possibly dangerous manner. Remember that your safety is paramount; when needed, you should request appropriate law enforcement resources, such as additional personnel. This unit provides the law enforcement responder (LER) with an introduction to behavioral emergencies, their causes, and general management principles.

BEHAVIORAL EMERGENCIES

Behavior is the manner in which people act or conduct themselves. This activity may be physical (such as running) or mental (such as hallucinating). Some behaviors are the physical manifestations of emotions, such as yelling, laughing, or crying. As both a law enforcement officer and a provider of emergency medical care, you will encounter individuals exhibiting behaviors that may be considered abnormal. Sometimes these behaviors are the result of the physical stresses experienced by a patient having an acute medical emergency or traumatic injury. Other times the behavioral condition itself may result from a mental illness and be the primary issue prompting a request for help or emergency response. Regardless of the reason, it is important for you to recognize behavioral emergencies and be suspicious of causes of abnormal behavior.

A behavioral emergency can be thought of as a situation in which an individual's behavior is not typical for a given set of circumstances. This abnormal behavior is often unacceptable, intolerable, or dangerous to the patient or others around the patient. There are also situations in which patients themselves may recognize that they are having a behavioral emergency, such as being suicidal. A key concept in this definition is that the behavior is abnormal within the context of a given situation. For example, the mother of a missing child might be yelling, crying, or displaying other emotional outbursts. In the context of this situation, such behavior would not be considered unusual. However, a display of the same behaviors without any apparent cause might indicate a behavioral emergency. Because you are exposed to people from different cultural backgrounds and lifestyles, remember that some behaviors may seem unusual or abnormal to you but can be normal to the person displaying them.

Figure 1 When someone has lost control of the balance between thoughts and emotions, he or she is considered to be in a behavioral crisis.

People live in a state of balance between emotions and thoughts. Crisis develops when this balance is disrupted. A **behavioral crisis** is a state of emotional turmoil in which someone has lost control of the balance between thoughts and emotions (**Figure 1**). One might say that emotions overcome thoughts in a behavioral crisis. Normal coping mechanisms fail, and the person loses control of the situation. Most people in a behavioral crisis are not severely mentally ill but are simply normal people responding to an abnormal situation. Many are able to help themselves with simple redirection. Recognizing that someone is in a behavioral crisis is key to providing the help and support that is needed. The most important tool in behavioral crisis intervention is your ability to communicate with words and body language.

SCENE SAFETY AND PATIENT APPROACH

As with any emergency response, maintaining the safety of yourself and responding emergency services personnel is paramount. Identification of behavioral emergencies is important to avoid placing yourself, the patient, and others around you in danger. Individuals experiencing behavioral emergencies can become unreasonable or violent. Always follow your instincts. If something doesn't feel right, it probably isn't right. In these circumstances, good judgment must be exercised. If the scene becomes unsafe for you or others providing aid, assume that the patient could be dangerous and act accordingly.

When speaking to a patient in distress, attempt to be at eye level. Speak in a soft but firm voice. Avoid yelling or raising your voice, even if the patient raises his or her voice. Maintain a comfortable and safe distance from the patient, ideally at least 3 feet away, or beyond arm's length, and be aware of your closest exit.

Tip

Time for Calm

Most violent patients calm down as time passes. The longer you can keep the patient talking, the better your chances are of resolving the situation without violence. Time is on your side.

Be aware that static and loud interruptions from police radios can sometimes agitate emotionally disturbed individuals. Some individuals with paranoia or schizophrenia may believe that they are being watched or monitored by your radio. The delusion of radio frequencies invading the body is very real to them. It is not uncommon to see patients with paranoid schizophrenia wrapped in aluminum foil or wearing a foil hat to stop the bombardment of radio waves. Likewise, their windows may be completely covered in aluminum foil.

Tip

Crisis Intervention

The following crisis intervention tips may help you at the scene of a behavioral emergency:

- Take your time.
- Remain calm.
- Reassure the patient.
- Use eye contact.
- Speak in a calm, steady voice.
- Demonstrate confidence.
- Do not take the patient's comments personally. Keep your sense of humor.

MEDICAL CAUSES OF BEHAVIORAL EMERGENCIES

When responding to a behavioral emergency, it is important first to consider that abnormal behavior may be the result of a medical condition or emergency. If there is any concern about an emergency medical cause of the patient's condition, the patient should receive a medical evaluation at the emergency department. This section contains a brief review of these causes. For further information on these medical conditions, please see the unit on medical emergencies.

Shock and Trauma

Shock results when not enough blood and oxygen reach vital organs, including the brain. This condition may be the result of a variety of causes, including a traumatic injury with blood loss, dehydration from exertion, insufficient pumping of blood by the heart, or the inability to get oxygen into the lungs due to illness or injury. Assess vital signs for fast breathing (greater than 20 breaths per minute) and fast heart rate (greater than 100 beats per minute), and look for cyanosis (blue-gray tinting of the skin) as an indicator of inadequate oxygenation. Shock may cause loss of consciousness, seizures, or agitation.

A traumatic head injury can cause confusion, agitation, and personality changes that may include irritability, irrational behavior, or verbal outbursts. Such an injury may also be accompanied by changes in vital signs, including slow pulse, high blood pressure, and irregular respirations.

Medical Emergencies

Many medical conditions can cause behavioral changes, including low blood glucose levels and altered electrolyte balances. Patients with hypoglycemia (low blood glucose level) often present with erratic or even hostile behavior. The person may appear to be under the influence of alcohol or a controlled substance. The patient is often sweating profusely, may have a rapid pulse, and may become unconscious or have a seizure. Strokes are medical emergencies that can present as abnormal behavior similar to that seen with a traumatic brain injury. Be sure to look for the loss of function or paralysis of one side of the body.

Environmental Exposures

As the body's metabolism changes in response to the extremes in temperatures, so does the patient's mental status, and therefore his or her behavior. Hypothermia (excessively cold body temperature) may cause shivering, numbness in the extremities, drowsiness, slow respirations, and slow pulse. For example, someone who is hypothermic, or very cold, will appear to be very sleepy, or lethargic, and may look intoxicated.

Hyperthermia (excessive body heat) may cause a decreased level of consciousness and result in agitated behavior. Someone who has a very high body temperature will appear to be agitated or aggressive and may look as though he or she has taken a stimulant such as cocaine or amphetamines.

Drugs and Alcohol

Ingestion of mind-altering substances, drugs, and alcohol can cause a variety of signs and symptoms related to an altered level of consciousness, agitation, and hallucinations. Also, withdrawal from these same substances of abuse may also result in a behavioral emergency. If you believe that the patient may have overdosed on pills or a poison, attempt to gather as much information as possible, including the name of the substance(s) ingested, the dose (strength) and quantity ingested, and the time that ingestion occurred. This information should be given to emergency medical services (EMS) personnel to pass to the receiving physician at the emergency department.

Tip

Common Medical Causes of Behavioral Alteration

Common medical causes of behavioral changes include the following:

- Lack of oxygen to the brain (hypoxia)
- Very low blood pressure
- Low blood glucose level (hypoglycemia)
- Illnesses such as a seizure disorder, Alzheimer disease, or brain infection
- Dehydration
- Abnormal electrolyte levels
- Situational stress (eg, witnessing the death of a loved one)
- Head trauma
- Environmental exposures (hypothermia or hyperthermia)
- Accidental ingestion of mind-altering substances such as wild herbs, berries, or mushrooms
- Drugs and alcohol
- Psychiatric conditions or noncompliance with psychiatric medications

Psychiatric Conditions

Psychiatric conditions, also known as mental illness, are very common and range in their complexity and seriousness. Occasionally a patient not known to have a psychiatric illness will initially present as a behavioral emergency. Noncompliance (not taking the medication regularly as prescribed) or mixing psychiatric medications with drugs of abuse may result in a behavioral emergency.

ASSESSMENT OF PATIENTS WITH BEHAVIORAL EMERGENCIES

Patients with behavioral problems may exhibit a range of mannerisms, from being withdrawn and quiet to overly talkative or threatening. LERs often find themselves called into situations in which people are reported to be acting bizarrely or to be "not acting right." These changes in behavior may be acute (occurring over a short period of time) or chronic (occurring over a prolonged period of time). It may not always be obvious that someone is experiencing a behavioral emergency. Behavioral emergencies can be dangerous to the responder, the patient, or others. It is therefore important to recognize the signs and symptoms of behavioral emergencies.

Always assume that there is a medical cause for the behavioral situation. Complete a thorough assessment as you would for any patient. Some patients might be confused or agitated, which might prohibit a full assessment. On general appearance, you should observe the patient for signs of threatening behavior such as tense muscles, tense posture, clenched fists, or pacing back and forth (**Figure 2**). Listen to the patient's

Figure 2 Observe the patient for signs of threatening behavior such as tense muscles, clenched fists, or pacing back and forth.

tone of voice. Is the patient yelling? Is the speech pressured, as if the patient can't get the words out fast enough? Notice the patient's skin; is the patient sweating heavily? Is the skin dry?

Check with bystanders or family to determine whether the patient has a known history of combativeness, violence, or aggression. Also ask about past medical history (such as thyroid disorder, electrolyte disorder, low blood glucose levels, head injury), psychiatric history (known mental illness, violence, suicide attempts), and substance abuse history (drugs and alcohol). This history should be obtained through the SAMPLE and OPQRST questions, covered in the assessment unit. Be sure to inquire about environmental history (prolonged environmental exposure to heat [hyperthermia] or cold [hypothermia], ingestion of wild vegetation, dehydration).

Tip

Signs and Symptoms of Behavioral Emergencies

Signs and symptoms of behavioral emergencies may include any of the following:

- **Agitation:** Repetitive motions, threatening actions, withdrawn stance, anger, hostility, rage
- **Paranoia:** Anxiety and fearfulness, thinking that someone or something is going to harm them
- **Pressured speech:** Speech pattern that is very rapid and difficult to understand, which can be seen with patients on stimulants such as cocaine or methamphetamine
- **Bizarre thinking or actions:** May be the reason the initial call for help was made
- **Self-destructive behavior or attempted suicide:** Physical actions or verbal statements implying that the patient is trying or did try to hurt himself or herself
- **Danger to others:** Making threatening comments or homicidal statements, violence toward others, access to weapons
- **Mental confusion:** Disorganized words or thoughts that are difficult to follow during a conversation
- **Unusual appearance:** Clothing in the wrong order, poor personal hygiene, multiple layers of clothes (especially in the summer)

Assessing a person with a behavioral emergency can be a very complicated task. A common tool used by physicians or counselors is the **mental status examination (MSE)**. There are many types of MSE tools, ranging from very brief to quite time consuming. One of the simplest and most efficient MSEs for field use is the **SEA-3 assessment tool** (which stands for **S**peech, **E**motion, **A**ppearance, **A**lertness, and **A**ctivity) (**Table 1**). SEA-3 is a short, five-component evaluation of a person in crisis. It can be used quickly in any field setting

Table 1

The SEA-3 Assessment Tool

SEA-3 Factor	Questions to Ask or Observations to Make
Speech	Quantity and quality of speech, as well as the flow and the organization of content of the speech
Emotion	Dominant mood, appropriateness of mood, absence of emotion, euphoria, depression, anger, hostility, fear, anxiety, apprehension
Appearance	Unkempt; unclean; clothing disheveled, dirty, atypical, unusual, or bizarre; unusual physical characteristics
Alertness	Oriented to person, place, and time; has insight into internal psychological reactions; can judge personal behavior as appropriate or not; memory and intellectual functions appear intact; stream and content of thought appear appropriate; hallucinations; delusions; thought disorders
Activity	Appropriateness of facial expressions, posture, movement, and interaction with helper

and provides a good primary assessment of an individual's mental status or level of consciousness. The SEA-3 is in no way a full mental status evaluation, but it will help you to understand the general mental stability of the person in crisis at that point in time.

MANAGEMENT OF PATIENTS WITH BEHAVIORAL EMERGENCIES

Patients experiencing behavioral emergencies should be handled carefully. Calming the patient and gaining his or her trust is one of the most important initial components of managing someone experiencing a behavioral emergency. In simple terms, explain to the patient what you are doing. Ask your questions in a calm, reassuring voice. Validate and acknowledge that the patient seems upset, and reinforce that you are there to help while maintaining a comfortable distance from the patient. Encourage the patient to discuss what is troubling him or her. Listen to what the patient is saying, and from time to time repeat or paraphrase what the patient has said to show that you are listening.

It is important to be honest with patients, but you must avoid being judgmental or accusatory. Also remember that a patient who is hallucinating—seeing or hearing things that others do not—is truly experiencing what he or she is seeing or hearing. If your patient shows signs of hallucinating, do not reinforce the patient's perceptions by saying that you see and hear the same things. Rather, redirect the patient to focus on you and what you are asking.

Tip

Approaching a Patient with a Behavioral Emergency

Consider the following guidelines when approaching a patient experiencing a behavioral emergency:

- Maintain your safety at all times. Always have an escape route.
- Treat any life-threatening problems you encounter.
- Remember that medical conditions may appear to be a behavioral emergency.
- Patients with complicated or questionable medical conditions should have a medical evaluation by EMS or at an emergency department.
- Approach the patient where he or she can see you; do not make any quick movements.
- Attempt to maintain eye contact so the patient can focus on you.
- These situations often take extra time to work through on scene. Be prepared for a long scene time.
- Never lose sight of the patient.
- Take time to talk to the patient and listen to his or her responses. Reinforce that you are listening by using body language such as nodding your head, or stating, "please go on."
- Avoid statements such as "I know what you are going through."
- Be supportive and empathetic.
- Validate the patient's emotions by using phrases such as, "I understand that made you angry, sad, upset, etc."
- Limit interruptions.
- Avoid unnecessary postures and unnecessary physical contact with the patient.
- Try to calm the patient.
- Never go along with any auditory or visual hallucinations.
- Never lie to the patient.
- Be honest and open about the patient's need for emergent medical or psychiatric evaluation.
- Do not threaten, challenge, or argue with disturbed patients.
- Monitor the patient for signs of agitation or worsening of his or her condition.

The SAFER-R Model

There are many things to be addressed when dealing with a patient experiencing a behavioral emergency. You learned many of these things in the academy when you were a new law enforcement officer. The **SAFER-R model** for crisis intervention allows the LER to establish a conversation with a person in distress while gaining time, information, and trust. The components of the SAFER-R model are stabilize, acknowledge, facilitate, encourage, recovery, and referral (**Table 2**).

RESTRAINING PATIENTS

If a behavioral emergency escalates to the point where verbal calming skills are no longer effective, a patient may need to be restrained to protect the safety of the patient or the public. A **physical restraint** is any method or device, physical or mechanical, that restricts a patient's movement or the LER's normal access to the patient. A physical restraint limits full access to the patient and reduces the responder's ability to perform an ongoing patient assessment. From a medical perspective, only patients who are clearly demonstrating an imminent danger to themselves or others should be restrained. When restraining patients, it is important to employ **reasonable force**—that is, only the force or strength needed to keep patients from hurting themselves or others, but no more. Many factors contribute to determining this level of force, such as the patient's size and strength, the degree of agitation, the type of abnormal behavior, the patient's mental status, and the methods available for restraint.

If an emotionally disturbed patient refuses to consent to a critical, safety-based request, consent is implied and patient restraint may be necessary to protect the patient from further harm to himself, herself, or others. For the purposes of this unit, restraint is considered a medical treatment. For the LER to restrain a patient, reasonable belief must exist that the patient will harm himself or herself or others. A minimum of four personnel is usually required to restrain a combative patient. Restraining a patient with insufficient personnel will likely result in physical harm to the patient and the officers.

Establish a plan and brief all personnel on their roles. Often just a show of force will cause a patient to submit. Once the patient is physically restrained, only the minimum force necessary to keep the patient submissive should be used; any additional force is excessive.

Table 2

Using the SAFER-R Model in a Crisis

S	Stabilize the situation.	Create a scene that is likely to feel stable and safe to the patient. This might include removing various stimuli or family members, turning off televisions, or moving the person to a quiet setting.
A	Acknowledge that something distressing has occurred.	Discuss and acknowledge the emotional situation that the individual is in at that moment. Comments such as "I can see that you're distressed" or "I can see how you would be upset by this" can be useful and show the person in crisis that you are empathetic and making an effort to assist him or her.
F	Facilitate the person's understanding of the situation.	Discuss the situation with the patient to the best of your ability. Remember that information can be powerful. Provide answers in a calm manner and help the person grasp the situation.
E	Encourage the person to make an acceptable plan of action.	At this point, the power of positive persuasion can help you greatly with the patient. Every effort to gain trust and help should be made.
R	Recovery is evident.	If all goes well, it is common to see the person in crisis go from a state of escalation to one of calm and cooperation. When patients are in an acute recovery phase, meaning that the crisis situation or irrational behavior is resolving, you can gain the support of friends, family members, or clergy to assist you with the patient.
R	Refer the patient to additional sources of help.	Once you have stabilized the situation, your goal is to get additional help for the patient. If the patient is psychologically unstable, transportation via police vehicle or ambulance is appropriate. If the patient is stable, you can refer him or her to community services such as police chaplains, mental health organizations, support groups, or need-based groups.

Ideally, the patient should be placed on a backboard and secured to the board, face up, with the right arm above the head (**Figure 3**). This method prevents the patient from sitting up. It also allows for safe transportation of the patient and careful monitoring of vital signs. Never "hog-tie" a patient or place a patient prone or facedown. Doing so has resulted in in-custody deaths from **positional asphyxia**, a condition in which the patient's own body weight impairs the ability to breathe and suffocates the patient.

Continuous monitoring of the restrained patient is imperative. Until medical care is transitioned to EMS or hospital personnel, the LER must monitor and document distal pulses in every restrained extremity every 5 to 10 minutes.

Patients will often try to reason with responders to remove the restraints. However, once initiated, the restraints should remain until patient care is turned over to the nearest emergency medical care facility. Remember to wear proper personal protective equipment, including masks and gloves, because angry or violent patients may spit at you.

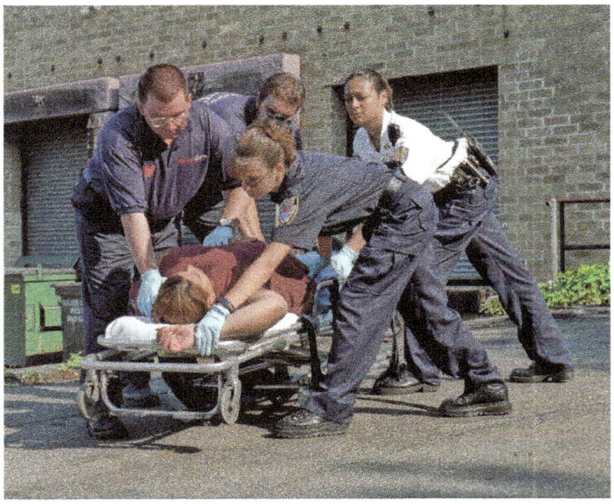

Figure 3 When restraining a patient, place the patient on a backboard and secure him or her to the board, face up, with the right arm above the head.

Restraint of a patient experiencing a behavioral emergency is considered a last resort. LERs should ensure protection against false accusations. Angry bystanders and family members, who perhaps don't fully understand the severity of the situation, may not agree with your decision to restrain the patient. If possible, the reason for restraining a patient should be explained to family and bystanders. This explanation should be tactful because it is emotionally upsetting to witness the application of force to a loved one, which is what will likely be perceived. You must make efforts to preserve the patient's privacy. Your explanation should *not* include specifics about the patient's medical condition; rather it should emphasize the need to stabilize an unstable and unsafe scene. However, you should not delay restraint of a patient by taking time to explain your actions if doing so will sacrifice patient care or safety.

Allegations of misconduct against medical personnel by patients who have been restrained are common. Be sure to provide thorough documentation of the patient's abnormal behavior and the reason for the restraint. Documentation should also include the method of restraint, total time restrained, and what efforts were taken to avoid restraining the patient.

CONDUCTED ELECTRICAL WEAPONS

Certain circumstances may necessitate the use of a **conducted energy device (CED)** to obtain initial control of a hostile or violent individual (**Figure 4**). A CED is also known as an **electronic control device (ECD)**. CEDs deliver an electric current that causes uncontrollable muscle contractions and severe pain in order to incapacitate a subject.

Figure 4 The Taser is an example of a conducted electrical weapon.

Excited Delirium

A subgroup of patients continues to remain agitated and combative after being subjected to a CED discharge. These individuals must be carefully assessed for **excited delirium**, a life-threatening condition associated with in-custody deaths following CED use. This condition is seen frequently in association with cocaine and stimulant use. Other factors associated with excited delirium include a history of schizophrenia, psychosis, or mania; previous similar presentation(s); or a history of illicit drug or alcohol use. Physical findings in excited delirium include superhuman strength, imperviousness to pain, bizarre and/or violent behavior, hyperactivity, paranoia, tachycardia (elevated heart rate), very hot skin, profuse sweating, or extremely dry skin for the level of exertion. Excited delirium is considered a medical emergency, not a psychiatric one, and can lead to sudden death. EMS should transport these patients to the hospital for evaluation.

Tip

Common Findings in Excited Delirium

Common findings in excited delirium include the following:

- History of schizophrenia
- Psychosis or mania
- Previous similar presentation(s)
- A history of illicit drug or alcohol use
- Superhuman strength
- Imperviousness to pain
- Bizarre, purposeless, and violent behavior
- Hyperactivity
- Paranoia
- Tachycardia
- Very hot skin
- Profuse sweating or skin extremely dry for level of exertion

THE SUICIDAL PATIENT

A variety of factors may place a person at heightened risk for suicide, including depression, prior suicide attempts, high stress levels, recent emotional trauma, age, and substance abuse.

Special Populations

Suicide Risk

One of the main causes of suicide in older people is terminal disease. A person who knows that he or she is going to die of an incurable condition may choose to commit suicide to avoid the final disability and suffering associated with that disease. In these cases, the family will be dealing with the grief from the diagnosis of the terminal disease as well as the patient's suicide. This is a time when they need your comfort and understanding.

A second age group at high risk for attempted suicide is teenagers. For many people, the teenage years are a difficult time of adjustment to growth and change. Stressors in this age group include school, interpersonal relationships, sexual identity issues, cultural and societal expectations, problems at home, and experimentation with drugs and alcohol. The rate of suicide among teenagers is high. Be especially alert for signs of depression and attempted suicide in teenage patients.

There are many means of suicide, such as hanging, drug overdose, jumping from heights, or the use of weapons. When responding to an attempted suicide, you must first and foremost be concerned with your safety. A suicidal patient may intentionally or accidentally harm you. Once any safety issues have been addressed, care for a suicidal patient in the same manner as you would any behavioral emergency patient.

When assessing the suicidal patient, attempt to obtain information, including whether there was an actual attempt. If so, determine the type of attempt, and whether a medical emergency or traumatic injury has resulted. Has the patient been searched? Does the patient have easy access to a weapon? If the patient attempted an overdose, find out (what) was taken, how much, and when. It is also helpful to know whether the patient has previously attempted suicide.

Tip

Homicidal Danger

A suicidal patient must always be considered homicidal until the scene is secure.

CONCLUSION

In law enforcement, you will often come across behavioral emergencies. However, no two calls involving a person in crisis are ever the same. Whether the situation is a true psychiatric emergency or a person reacting to the sudden death of a loved one, LERs must always be prepared to respond to a person in need carefully, safely, and empathetically. It is important to remember that many medical conditions mimic psychiatric events. When in doubt, the person should always be transported to an emergency department for medical evaluation.

Prep Kit

READY FOR REVIEW

- Your safety and the safety of fellow responders is your top priority. Remain at least 3 feet away from the patient and be aware of your closest exit.
- Behavioral emergencies are situations in which a person's behavior is not typical for a given set of circumstances and is often unacceptable, intolerable, or dangerous.
- Behavioral emergencies may be the result of situational stress, physical trauma, medical conditions, substance abuse, or an underlying mental illness.
- A variety of medical emergencies may initially appear to be behavioral emergencies, including shock, low blood glucose levels, and head injuries.
- An acute change in a person's behavior may indicate that he or she is experiencing a behavioral emergency.
- Signs of a behavioral emergency include panic, agitation, irrational thoughts, violence, and self-destructive behavior.
- The most important tool in behavioral crisis intervention is your ability to communicate with words and body language. When speaking to a patient in distress, be at eye level, speak in a soft but firm voice, and try to calm the patient.
- Use of the SEA-3 assessment tool provides a quick and easy way to evaluate the mental status of an individual in crisis. The components of SEA-3 are speech, emotion, appearance, alertness, and activity.
- The SAFER-R model helps a LER establish a conversation with an individual in distress while gaining time, information, and trust. The components of SAFER-R are stabilize, acknowledge, facilitate, encourage, recovery, and referral.
- Whenever possible, patients in crisis should always be talked down. The use of physical restraints is a last resort, used only when patients appear to be at risk of harming themselves or others.
- Conducted electrical weapons or electronic control devices, such as the Taser, are used when all other means of patient management have failed.
- Excited delirium is a syndrome that presents with agitation, tachycardia (elevated heart rate), hyperthermia (elevated body temperature), and other symptoms and can result in sudden death. Excited delirium is seen in a subgroup of patients after being subjected to a conducted electrical weapon discharge.
- Factors that may place a person at heightened risk for suicide include depression, prior suicide attempts, high stress levels, recent emotional trauma, age, and substance abuse.
- A suicidal patient must always be considered homicidal until the scene is secure.

VITAL VOCABULARY

behavior The manner in which people act or conduct themselves.

behavioral crisis A state of emotional turmoil in which a person has lost control of the balance between thoughts and emotions.

behavioral emergencies Situations in which a person acts in a way that is not acceptable or tolerable to those around them, often posing a danger to themselves or others.

conducted energy device (CED) A device that delivers an electric current that causes uncontrollable muscle contractions and severe pain in order to incapacitate a subject.

electronic control device (ECD) See *conducted electrical weapon*.

excited delirium A syndrome that presents with agitation, tachycardia (elevated heart rate), hyperthermia (elevated body temperature), and other symptoms and can result in sudden death.

mental status examination (MSE) A common tool used by physicians or counselors to assess a person with a mental illness or behavioral emergency.

physical restraint Any method or device, physical or mechanical, that restricts movement or normal access to the patient.

positional asphyxia A condition in which the patient's own body weight impairs the ability to breathe and suffocates the patient.

reasonable force The minimum strength needed to keep patients from hurting themselves or others, but no more.

SAFER-R model A tool used in crisis intervention to allow the LER to establish a conversation while gaining time, information, and trust with the patient.

SEA-3 assessment tool A short, five-component mental status examination tool used to evaluate a patient's speech, emotion, appearance, alertness, and activity.

CHECK YOUR KNOWLEDGE

1. You are dispatched to a local fast-food restaurant to assess an elderly gentleman who is acting strangely. Customers report that he has been talking to himself and acting in a bizarre manner. Witnesses report that he seems confused and doesn't seem to know where he is. You suspect which of the following?
   A. Diabetes
   B. Psychosis or schizophrenia
   C. Medication reaction
   D. All of the above
2. The SEA-3 assessment tool is a quick and easy way to evaluate which of the following?
   A. Distance between the officer and a patient experiencing a behavioral emergency
   B. A patient's mental status
   C. Whether to restrain a patient
   D. Whether a conducted electrical weapon should be used
3. The SAFER-R tool provides an opportunity for an officer to gain all of the following when managing an individual in a behavioral crisis except:
   A. Time
   B. Information
   C. Blood alcohol level
   D. Trust
4. Patients who are restrained and transported in a face-down or prone position may die due to respiratory compromise. This condition is known as:
   A. Traumatic suffocation
   B. Positional asphyxia
   C. Respiratory distress
   D. Diaphragm rupture
5. In the case of excited delirium, an individual would most commonly present with any of the following conditions except:
   A. Superhuman strength
   B. Tachycardia
   C. Passivity or withdrawn behavior
   D. Violent outbursts

K-9 First Aid

Unit 24

Dawn Ruben

Law Enforcement Responder Objectives

- Discuss key differences between canine and human anatomy and physiology. (pp 443–444)
- Describe canine behavior and body language and its significance. (p 444)
- Explain how to approach an injured dog. (p 444)
- Demonstrate how to restrain an injured dog. (pp 444–446)
- Identify common canine injuries and illnesses and their treatments. (pp 446–452)
- Discuss transport options for injured dogs. (p 452)

National EMS Education Standard Competencies

There are no National EMS Education Standard Competencies for this unit.

INTRODUCTION

Law enforcement responders (LERs) are often called to provide first aid to victims at scenes. At some scenes, dogs will also be injured. First aid skills can readily be adapted to canines, and, as in people, first aid can significantly increase a dog's chance of survival. This is particularly important in the case of working dogs. These dogs are valuable members of the law enforcement team, have years of training, are loyal partners, and deserve the best medical care, even in the field.

Before learning first aid techniques, a basic knowledge of canine anatomy, physiology, and behavior is crucial. Understanding the similarities and differences between humans and dogs will allow LERs to evaluate the situation quickly and to provide the most appropriate and effective care.

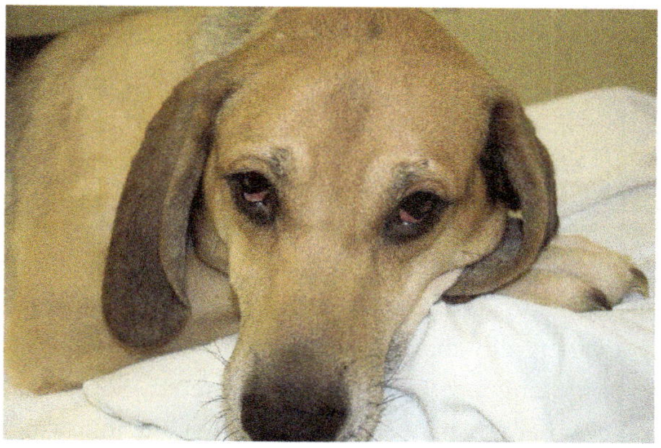

Figure 1 Dogs have a third eyelid that helps in tear production and cornea protection.

ANATOMY AND PHYSIOLOGY

The internal structures of a dog's anatomy are the same as those of a human's, with some exceptions:

- **Appendix.** Dogs do not have an appendix.
- **Sweat glands.** The majority of sweat glands in dogs are located around the pads of the feet. Dogs use panting as a primary method of cooling.
- **Clavicles (collarbones).** Dogs do not have clavicles.
- **Third eyelid.** In the inside corner of each eye is a **nictitating membrane**, also called a third eyelid (**Figure 1**). It is important in tear production and protection of the cornea. The third eyelid may elevate when there is damage to the eye, when the dog is generally ill, or when the dog has been sedated. On first glance it may appear that the eyes are rolled back.

Canine organs also function very similar to human organs. When injured, dogs can have the same signs and symptoms as people, but the treatments are altered to conform to canine anatomy. Some major differences are that dogs do not have heart attacks (myocardial infarctions) and rarely have true strokes.

Vital signs of dogs include body temperature, heart rate, respiratory rate, and capillary refill time (**Table 1**). Blood pressure is more difficult to obtain than for people, and the standard methods used in people do not give accurate readings. The heart rate can be determined by placing a hand on the left side of the chest or by feeling for the femoral pulse (**Figure 2**).

Table 1

Normal Vital Signs of Dogs

Vital Sign	Normal Value
Temperature	100°F–102.5°F [37.8°C–39.2°C] (taken rectally)
Heart rate	60–100 beats/min
Respiratory rate	15–30 breaths/min, but often panting
Capillary refill time	Pink gums, with refill time of 1 second

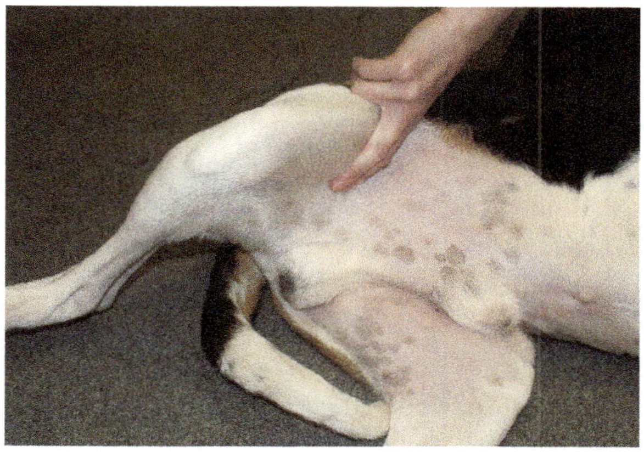

Figure 2 Check a dog's heart rate by feeling for the femoral pulse.

Gum color should be pink; when pressed, the gum should blanch and return to pink in about 1 second.

BEHAVIOR

Before approaching any dog, a basic understanding of canine behavior is crucial. Dogs who are hurt or frightened may display a variety of behaviors. Be knowledgeable of how your own body language can be misinterpreted. Some Canine behaviors that you may encounter include the following:

- **Staring.** Staring is most often a sign of aggression. Do not stare back at the dog.
- **Flattened ears.** Depending on other behaviors, this can mean aggression, fear, or submission.
- **Lip curling.** A snarl indicates fear or aggression. Some dogs will curl their lips in submission, and some dogs can actually smile.
- **Rolling on back.** Exposing the abdomen is a sign of submission.
- **Urinating.** Dribbling urine or urinating is a sign of submission.
- **Tail wagging.** Tail wagging is often misleading. A quick, full wag usually means the dog trusts you. A short, slow wag can mean aggression, especially when combined with staring. It is not recommended to use tail wagging as a definitive way to determine whether a dog is safe to approach or not.

It is best to evaluate all these signs together. Fearful dogs are not always submissive. Some respond by biting.

Some human behaviors that can be misinterpreted by a dog include the following:

- **Standing and leaning over a dog.** This can be interpreted as threatening and dominating.
- **Patting on the head.** This can also be interpreted as a threat. Avoid reaching over the top of the dog in any way. Approach from the side.
- **Staring.** Staring is a sign of dominance and a threat to dogs that are already aggressive or fearful.
- **Quick movements.** This can induce a fear response that may include biting and trying to escape.
- **Voice.** Using a loud voice is threatening behavior.
- **Impatience.** It is very difficult to remember to go slowly. Take a deep breath and try not to show any signs of frustration or impatience.

APPROACHING AN INJURED DOG

Personal safety is always a priority. After the scene has been surveyed and secured, attempt to approach the dog. The goal is to gain the dog's trust quickly. Be patient. Walk slowly and speak in a calm, soothing voice. Don't make any quick movements or have multiple people walking toward the dog. When close to the dog, get to its level. Kneel, squat, or sit on the ground and continue to speak encouragingly, slowly moving closer. Avoid bending over the dog or patting its head. These actions can be threatening and misinterpreted as signs of aggression and dominance. Do not attempt further restraint if the dog growls or tries to bite.

Communication

Communicating With an Injured Dog

When close to the dog, get to its level. Kneel, squat, or sit on the ground and continue to speak encouragingly, slowly moving closer. Avoid bending over the dog or patting its head. These actions can be threatening and misinterpreted as signs of aggression and dominance.

RESTRAINT

All injured dogs should be muzzled prior to any examination, unless the dog is unconscious. Even dogs that seem too weak may have just enough strength to bite, especially when in pain. However, few dogs willingly allow a muzzle to be placed. If no premade muzzle is available, temporary muzzles can be made of gauze, leashes, rope, belts, cut-up IV tubing, or even folded duct tape. Muzzling typically requires two people. One person restrains the dog while the other person places the muzzle. To restrain the dog, place one arm around the underside of the neck and the other over the top of the chest and hold the dog close to your body (**Figure 3**).

If the dog cannot be restrained or muzzled, confine it to a secure area and wait for further assistance. Do not muzzle any dog that is seizing, vomiting, or excessively panting. If a muzzled dog starts to vomit, remove the muzzle immediately.

After the dog is restrained, the second responder should stand on the other side of the dog. Do not approach from the front. Make a loop out of the muzzle material and place it over the dog's muzzle. Tighten and cross the ends under-

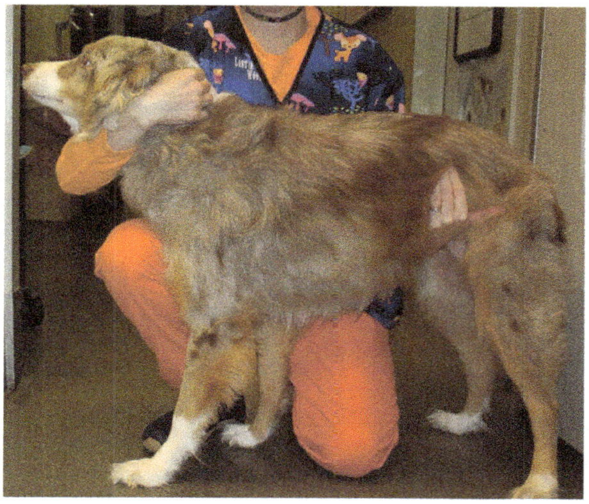

Figure 3 To restrain an injured dog, place one arm around the underside of the neck and the other over the top of the chest and hold the dog close to your body.

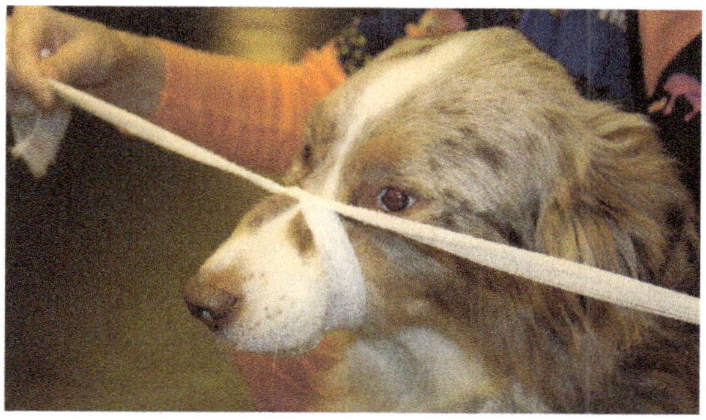

A.

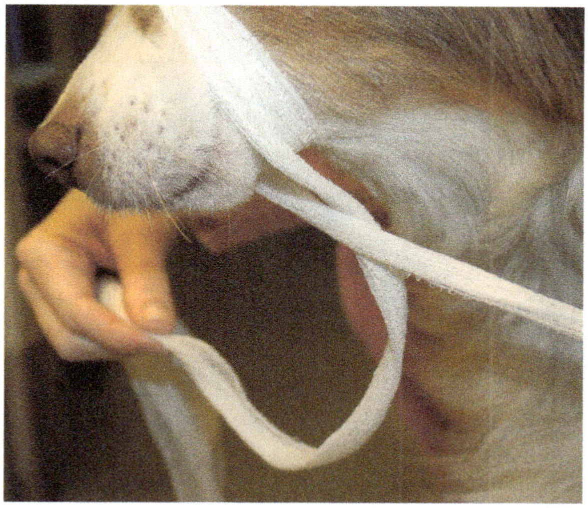

B.

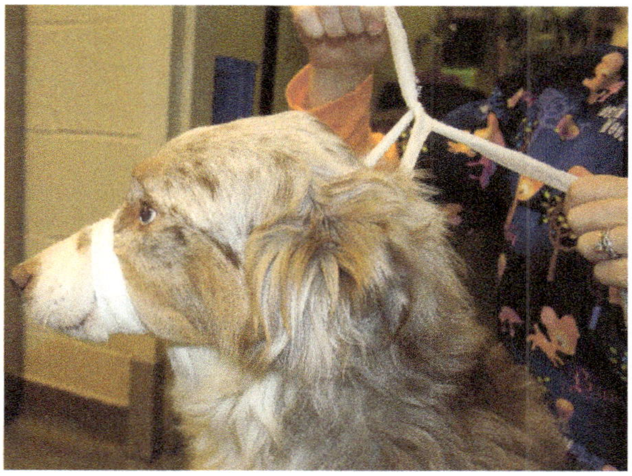

C.

Figure 4 Making a muzzle for a dog. **A.** Make a loop and place it over the dog's muzzle. **B.** Tighten and cross the ends underneath. **C.** Knot the ends behind the ears.

neath the dog. The ends are then placed behind the ears and a knot tied (**Figure 4**).

It is very important to tie the muzzle behind the ears. Without this extra precaution, the dog will simply reach up and pull off the muzzle. Muzzling needs to be done quickly to reduce the stress on the dog.

After the muzzle has been placed, there are two ways to restrain the dog for examination, which is also best done with two people. One way is to continue to hold the animal in the same position after the muzzle has been placed. This method can be used only for a cursory examination and minimal treatment.

For a better examination and to make treatment easier, one LER restrains the dog on its side, and the second LER does the exam and treatment (**Figure 5**). Kneel on the side of the dog. Reach over and grab the legs nearest your body. (For example, if you are on the left side of the dog, reach over and grab the left legs at the wrist and ankles.) Pull the legs up, allowing the dog to slide slowly down your body.

This will force the dog to lie on its side. Do not let go of the dog. Use your elbow to lie over the neck to prevent the dog from trying to get up. It is important to place the arm grabbing the front leg in front of the other front leg and to

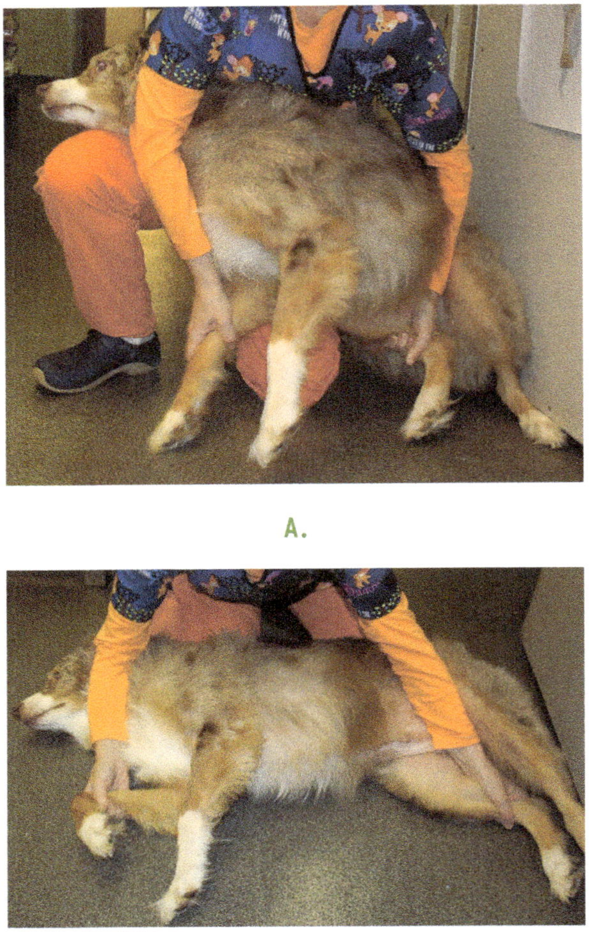

A.

B.

Figure 5 Restraining a dog for examination. **A.** Grab the legs nearest your body. **B.** Pull the legs up.

place the other arm over the abdomen and in front of the other rear leg.

EVALUATION

After the dog has been restrained, do a quick visual survey to determine the location and severity of any injuries. Active hemorrhage must be controlled immediately. If no active bleeding is noticed, examine the dog for lacerations, wounds, or other traumatic injuries. Observe the dog's behavior and response to stimuli.

Tip

Basic Canine First Aid Kit

A small first aid kit for canines is easy to make. The following items are recommended:

- Alcohol prep pads
- Bandage material (such as Co-Flex)
- Dosing syringe (60 mL)
- Eyewash or artificial tears
- 4 × 4 gauze
- Hydrogen peroxide
- Iodine solution
- Leash
- Roll gauze for muzzle
- Scissors
- Superglue
- Tape
- Thermometer
- Triple antibiotic ointment
- Tweezers

INJURIES, ILLNESSES, AND TREATMENTS

Numerous injuries and illnesses can afflict dogs. Some of the more common ones are described in this section, along with first aid treatments. All dogs should be examined by a veterinarian as soon as possible after treatment at the scene.

Hemorrhage

Acute bleeding—arterial or venous—can quickly lead to death and must be addressed immediately. After restraining the dog, isolate the source of the bleeding and apply direct pressure. A towel, piece of clothing, or a person's hand can be used to stop the bleeding temporarily. Continue to hold direct pressure for at least 5 minutes and then check to see whether the bleeding has stopped. If not, continue to hold direct pressure and place a temporary pressure bandage.

If there is bleeding through the bandage, do not replace it. Simply add more gauze and tape. Dogs with these injuries must have direct pressure applied and be taken to a veterinary hospital immediately. Avoid using a tourniquet. This will stop all blood flow to the leg, resulting in serious injury that may lead to amputation. An inflated blood pressure cuff can be used instead. Follow your local protocols regarding tourniquet use for canines. Another option is to use a wide band of material as a makeshift tourniquet. Do not use anything thin (such as rope).

Tip

Do Not Use Commercial Tourniquets

Using a commercial tourniquet can stop all blood flow to the leg, resulting in serious injury that may lead to amputation. An inflated blood pressure cuff can be used instead. Another option is to use a wide band of material as a makeshift tourniquet. Do not use anything thin (such as rope).

Lacerations

Lacerations can occur anywhere on the body and may be due to impalements, stabbings, or contact with sharp objects. Lacerations may appear small, but depending on the cause and depth, may have a tremendous amount of damage underneath (**Figure 6**). All lacerations should be considered potentially serious. Internal organ damage may have occurred if a laceration is found on the abdomen or chest. Even lacerations on the legs may be covering significant muscle or tendon damage. For working dogs, even a small cut of a tendon can end their career if appropriate treatment is not administered.

The goal of laceration treatment is to stop the hemorrhage and to remove as much debris as possible. Treat hemorrhage as described earlier. If there is significant contamination, use hydrogen peroxide, iodine solution, sterile saline, or even tap water to remove as much debris as possible. Simple, clean lacerations can be closed using staples, suture, or glue, if available. If not available, place a temporary bandage over the wound to prevent further contamination. If a laceration over the chest has air coming out of it with each exhalation, cover the wound immediately with some type of plastic wrap or duct tape to prevent additional leakage of air.

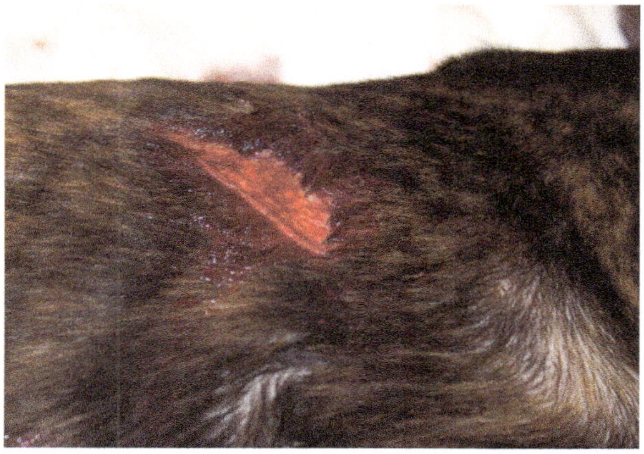

Figure 6 Lacerations may be more serious than they first appear.

Torn Toenail

Torn toenails are very common in dogs. The nail becomes snagged as the dog is walking, running, or searching. Often, the nail breaks at the base but is not completely removed. There can be bleeding, pain, and irritation from the torn nail (**Figure 7**). Ideally, the remainder of the nail is removed and a temporary bandage is placed (gauze and tape). In some situations, the remaining nail can be pulled off. Sometimes it will need to be cut off with canine nail trimmers or a similar device. This will hurt briefly, but the nail will be gone. If the nail cannot be removed, apply a pressure bandage until the bleeding stops (usually 10–15 minutes). If the dog will allow it, leave the bandage on until the nail can be removed by a veterinarian. Superglue can also be used to cover the torn nail temporarily if the nail cannot be removed.

Foot Pad Injuries

Dogs have six pads on the front paws and five on each of the rear paws. There are pads associated with each toe (digital pads), one large central pad (metacarpal or metatarsal pad), and a carpal (wrist) pad located further up on the front leg that does not come in contact with the ground. The foot pad of the dog is the part of the body most at risk for lacerations, impalements, and abrasions (**Figure 8**). This is particularly true for working dogs that do a lot of their work in the field. Pad lacerations can bleed and are painful for the dog. A temporary bandage should be placed if there is active bleeding. If there is no bleeding or after the bleeding has stopped, use

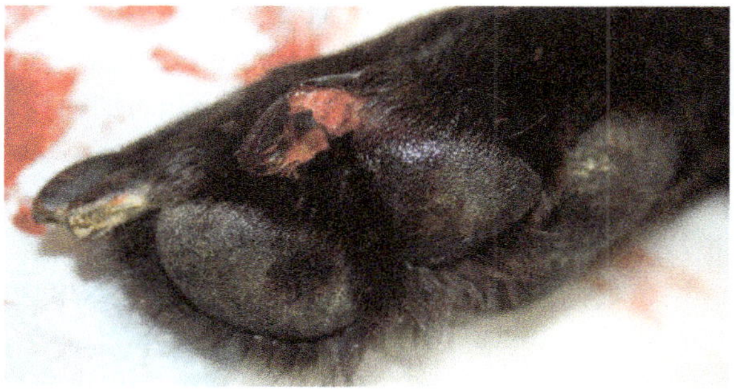

Figure 7 A torn toenail can cause bleeding, pain, and irritation.

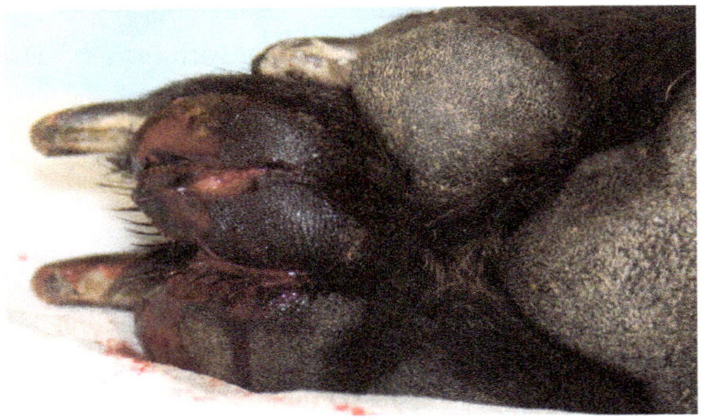

Figure 8 The foot pad is the part of a dog's body most at risk for lacerations, impalements, and abrasions.

approved cyanoacrylate glue to keep the laceration closed and to prevent further contamination. These injuries will usually heal without further treatment. Severe lacerations may need to be sutured.

Various objects can become impaled in a foot pad: thorns, broken glass, grass awns, fishhooks, foxtails, or anything small and sharp. The dog will usually be limping. On inspection of the foot, a foreign object may be found. If possible, try to remove the object. Some objects, such as fishhooks, are difficult to remove (**Figure 9**). The hook has a barb on the end that makes it difficult to pull out. The hook needs to be pushed further into the pad until the tip is exposed. The barb is then cut off with a pair of pliers and the hook removed from the initial wound.

Fractures

Fractures are most often suspected when a leg is in an unnatural position or bone is exposed through the skin. Dogs with fractures of the long bones (radius, ulna, humerus, tibia, and femur) are unable to bear weight on the leg and will be using only three legs to walk. Fractures can be associated with falls, blunt force trauma such as getting hit by a car, gunshot wounds, or other significant trauma. Stabilizing fractures is the key to reducing pain and future complications. The best way to stabilize a fracture is to place a splint or keep the dog immobilized **(Figure 10)**.

To prevent a fracture from moving, the joint above and below the fracture must be stabilized. Because the shoulder and hip cannot be stabilized, fractures of the upper arm (humerus) and thigh (femur) are best left not bandaged. Keep the dog quiet and confined and do not let it attempt to walk. Fractures of the lower legs can be successfully bandaged and splinted. If there is any doubt, it is best not to place a splint.

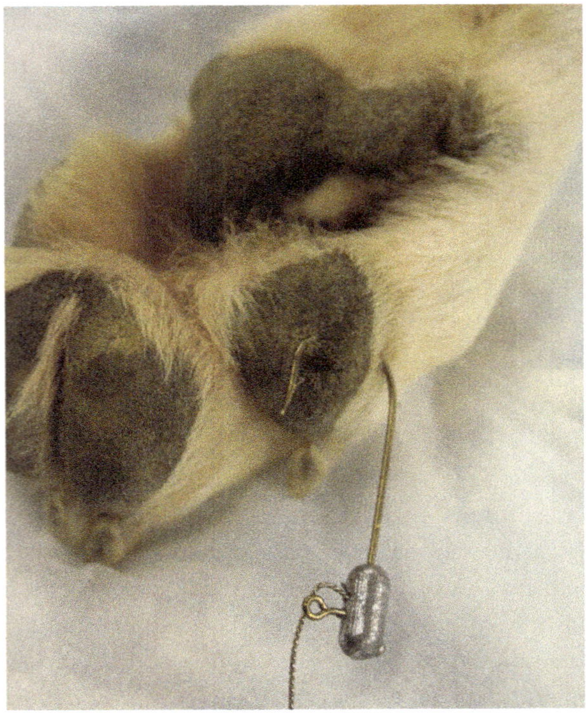

Figure 9 Fishhooks can be removed by pushing the tip through, cutting off the barb, then removing the hook from the initial wound.

Do not give any pain medication. Dogs do not metabolize ibuprofen, naproxen, and other drugs in the same way that people do, and even a small dose has the potential to cause serious organ damage.

The goal of placing a splint is to stabilize the joint above and below the suspected fracture and to keep the splint on until the dog is examined by a veterinarian. To begin splinting, place two tape stirrups on the leg to help prevent the splint from slipping. The stirrups extend past the foot.

The next layer is some kind of padding that will extend from the toes to the joint above the fracture. Ideally, roll cotton would be used, but other options include a piece of blanket,

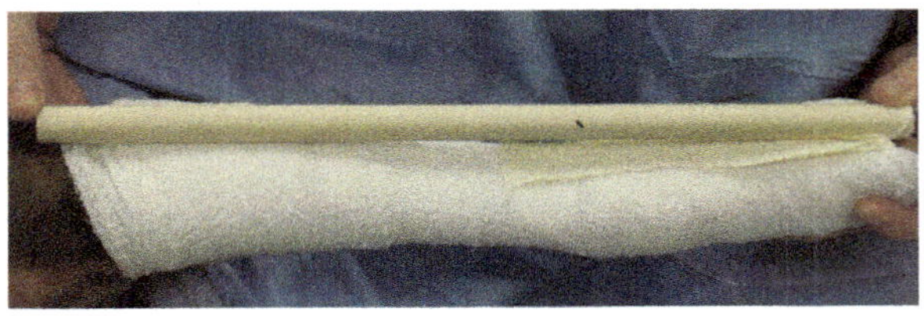

Figure 10 The best way to stabilize a fracture is to place a splint or keep the dog immobilized.

towel, clothing, or similar material. This is used to cushion the splint so it doesn't damage the underlying skin. After the padding has been placed, the ends of the stirrups are taped to the bandage.

The splint material is then placed along the back or side of the leg. Splints can be made using a variety of materials, such as sticks, folded newspaper, a broom handle, or PVC tubing. It is important that the splint material starts at the foot and goes past the joint above the fracture.

The top layer is bandage or tape. This layer should be tight enough to prevent any movement of the fracture site, but not so tight that it cuts off circulation to the leg.

Due to conformation, it is much more difficult to splint the rear legs.

Impalement

Dogs can be impaled with just as many objects as people can: branches, pipes, metal bars, arrows, and so forth. An impaled object in a dog should not be removed. Bandage the object in place to prevent movement and further internal injuries. If possible, tape the dog to a board or stretcher to keep it from moving and transport it to a veterinary clinic immediately.

Evisceration

Evisceration is an injury that results in exposure of internal organ(s) (**Figure 11**). This can occur from gunshot wounds, stabbing, or lacerations. After stopping any acute hemorrhage, attempt to clean the exposed organ(s) with sterile saline or water. If possible, try to replace the organ(s) into the body cavity. Cover the exposed organ(s) or the wound with a nonporous material such as plastic or duct tape. Immediately take the dog to a veterinarian.

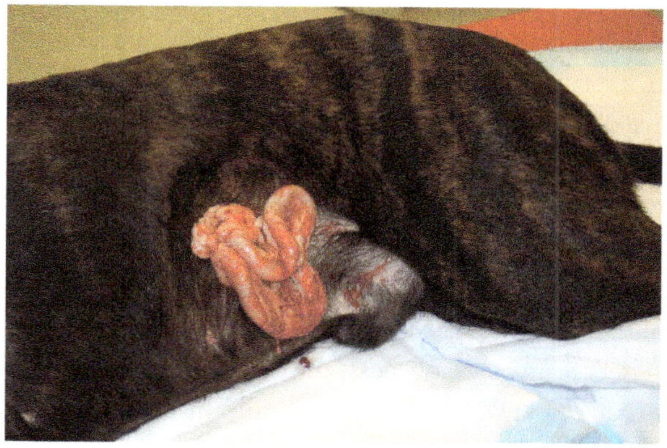

Figure 11 Evisceration.

Poisoning

Dogs are exposed to numerous toxic substances and foreign objects. Depending on the item or substance ingested, inducing vomiting may be recommended. Dogs that have ingested an object but appear normal can be taken to the veterinarian for examination, possible radiography (X-ray), and object removal.

Chemical ingestion can be very serious. For example, ingestion of antifreeze, rat poison, insecticides, and similar substances can be life threatening. If a dog was seen ingesting a chemical that is not caustic, induce vomiting with 3% hydrogen peroxide. Give 1 tablespoon per 20 pounds of body weight. Wait about 15 minutes. If there is no response, repeat a second time. If there is still no response, do not repeat. Do not use saltwater, soap, ipecac, or mustard water because these can cause illness if vomiting does not occur. If the chemical is caustic, such as bleach or disinfectants, do not induce vomiting. If the type of chemical or liquid is unknown, it is safer not to induce vomiting and to take the dog to a veterinarian. If possible, bring the container with you to help the veterinarian determine the appropriate treatment.

Tip

Ingestion of Caustic Chemicals

If a canine ingests a caustic substance, such as bleach or disinfectant, or an unknown substance, do not induce vomiting.

Gunshot Wound

Many injuries can be caused by gunshot. The severity of damage depends on the part of the body and the type of ammunition. Initial treatment is to use direct pressure to stop the bleeding, splint any possible fractures, and treat any wounds as described previously in the section on lacerations. Significant internal damage may occur from a gunshot wound. Transport the dog to a veterinary clinic immediately.

Choking

Before administering any aid, make certain that the dog is choking on an object. Coughing is often misinterpreted as choking. A choking dog will usually paw at the mouth and have difficulty breathing. Do not muzzle a choking dog. If safe to do so, open the mouth and look for an object. If one is seen, try to remove it with your hand. If an object is firmly lodged in the back of the mouth, perform the Heimlich maneuver. Kneel behind the dog, wrap your arms around the dog's abdomen just behind the ribs, and stand up quickly.

Seizure

Following trauma, especially to the head, some dogs may have a seizure. Unfortunately, there is no first aid treatment to stop an active seizure. Watch the dog closely so that it doesn't injure itself during the seizure. Do not place a muzzle and do not place your hands in the dog's mouth. It will not swallow its tongue.

After the seizure, the majority of dogs behave abnormally. Some will become aggressive, fearful, lethargic, or weak. Some may not regain consciousness, and some may continue to have multiple seizures. Extreme care should be used when transporting a dog that is actively seizing or is recovering from a seizure because its behavior can be unpredictable.

Blunt Force Trauma

Dogs that have experienced blunt force trauma may not have any external injuries but have serious internal damage. Ruptured spleen or liver, internal hemorrhage, head trauma, fractures, and bruising of the lungs can all occur. Blunt force trauma injuries should be expected if a dog has been hit by a car, fallen from a height, been exposed to a blast or explosion, or even found trapped under rubble. There is little that can be done at the scene. Supplemental oxygen can be supplied if available. Nose prongs work well in dogs if they are sedate enough to tolerate them. A cervical spine collar is not necessary. Dogs will more likely have a fracture in the mid to lower back than the neck.

Eye Injuries

Dogs, particularly working dogs, can easily sustain damage to their eyes while searching wooded areas or rubble piles. Dogs in need of treatment may have red eyes, elevated third eyelids, and be pawing or rubbing the eyes. Use eye flush, artificial tears, or contact lens solution. Do not use Visine or similar products. To prevent further damage, do not allow the dog to continue to paw or rub at the eyes.

Allergic Reaction

As with people, dogs can develop allergic reactions, primarily to insect stings. The face will begin to swell, and the dog may develop hives all over its body. The swelling rarely extends to the throat, so suffocation is very unlikely. The facial swelling can be itchy, and dogs will rub and paw at their faces. Dogs can be given diphenhydramine (eg, Benadryl) to help with some of the symptoms. The dose is one 25-mg tablet per 25 pounds of body weight. In some instances, this will not be effective. If the swelling does not go down in 1 to 2 hours, or if the dog develops any breathing difficulty, a veterinarian should be consulted.

Overheating

Dogs working in hot, humid environments or left in a car can easily overheat. Panting is the primary method of dissipating heat. Preventing overheating is crucial for the health of the dog and its ability to work.

When the outside temperature exceeds what the dog is able to handle, heat damage occurs to the body. When the outside temperature is 80°F (26.7°C), the inside of a car can reach over 110°F (43.4°C) within 30 minutes. If the outside temperature is 100°F (37.8°C), the interior of a car can reach over 150°F (65.6°C) within 30 minutes.

There are different levels of heat illness. Heat exhaustion can occur when the dog's body temperature is over 104°F (40°C). These dogs may appear frantic, excessively panting, or may be weak. Heatstroke (organs affected) can occur when the dog's body temperature is over 106°F (41.1°C). These dogs may be stumbling, exhausted, incoherent, seizing, or panting. Some may no longer be panting due to exhaustion of the respiratory muscles. When the dog's temperature rises over 109°F (42.8°C), the body begins to decompensate and death may be imminent. Heatstroke is a true emergency that must be treated immediately.

The first step in treating overheating is to remove the dog from the area if possible. Drench the dog in lukewarm water. Do not use cold water; this can bring the body temperature down too quickly. Make sure the water has soaked through the hair. Place the dog in a car with the windows down and the air conditioner on high and have the dog examined by a veterinarian as soon as possible.

Hypothermia

Dogs can also suffer from hypothermia. This is most often associated with falling into a body of water in a cold environment. When the coat is wet, it can no longer provide the insulation that keeps the dog warm. Mild hypothermia occurs when the body temperature is less than 98°F (36.7°C). Dry the dog and keep it in a warm place. With minimal treatment, most dogs can correct mild hypothermia.

Moderate hypothermia occurs when the body temperature is less than 90°F (32.2°C). Metabolism slows, there is no shivering, and the dog becomes weak. Dry the dog, place it in a warm environment, and get it to a veterinarian as soon as possible.

Severe hypothermia occurs when the body temperature is less than 85°F (29.4°C). These dogs will likely be comatose and may appear dead. Despite appearing dead, start rewarming the dog. Dry the dog as thoroughly as possible. Use space heaters (at least 2 feet away), heating pads, warm water bottles, blankets, or heat lamps. The heater in a car is another option. If the heat sources are limited, concentrate on warming the neck, body, and thorax. Take the dog to the nearest veterinarian as soon as possible.

Snake Bite

There are many different species of venomous snakes in the world. In the United States, the primary venomous snakes are rattlesnakes, copperheads, and water moccasins. If a snake bite is witnessed, confine the dog and try to keep it as quiet as possible. The best treatment is not to do anything that will worsen the situation and to get to a veterinarian as soon as possible.

- Do not allow the dog to walk. Snake bites are painful, and walking on the leg can cause the heart rate and blood pressure to rise, circulating the venom quicker.
- Do not attempt to suck out the venom. This is not effective and can increase the risk of an infection.
- Do not cut the bite wound area. This does not slow down the absorption of the venom.
- Do not place ice on the wound. The ice can damage the skin.
- Do not use electric shock from a car battery, sparkplugs, or stun gun to try to neutralize the venom. This has been suggested in some older literature and other sources for people and dogs. It has been proven to be ineffective and dangerous.
- Do not place a tourniquet. This will prevent all blood flow to the area, possibly resulting in serious injury or amputation. A blood pressure cuff can be inflated to reduce (but not stop) blood flow from the area, but it is not necessary.

Bloat

Gastric dilatation-volvulus, also called **bloat**, is a life-threatening medical emergency that can occur rapidly. Large, deep-chested dogs have a higher risk of developing bloat, but it can occur in any size dog. The cause of bloat is unknown, and there are disagreements among the veterinary community on ways to prevent it.

Bloat occurs when the stomach twists. This allows air to get in but not out. More air fills the stomach, and the dog begins pacing and tries to vomit. The abdomen becomes distended and tight. Dogs that are aggressively treated within 6 hours after the onset of signs have up to a 90% chance of survival. After 6 hours, survival rates rapidly decline.

The best treatment is to get the dog to a veterinary clinic as soon as possible. If there will be a significant delay in treatment (over an hour) and the dog is in significant distress, a large-bore needle can be passed into the air-filled stomach. To find the safest area to insert the needle, "thump" or "ping" the abdomen on the left side, in the upper middle, until you find an area that sounds most hollow. Insert the needle; air should immediately start rushing out. The left side is preferred because the spleen has likely shifted to the right side when the stomach twisted. If there is no needle available, a small, narrow knife can be used to stab a small hole through the skin and into the abdomen. This should be done only if there are no other options and the dog is in severe distress and near death. Although drastic, this may be the only option to attempt to save the dog's life.

Cardiopulmonary Resuscitation

Canine cardiopulmonary resuscitation (CPR) can be performed; however, the success rate when associated with trauma is dismal. Automated external defibrillators (AEDs) unfortunately cannot be used successfully in dogs. The AED must be in contact with the skin to be effective, so the dog's fur prevents its use.

To perform CPR, place the dog on its side on the ground or other hard surface. Check for an open airway by opening the mouth and pulling the tongue forward. Unlike in people, performing only chest compressions (as promoted in hands-only CPR) does not provide sufficient filling of the lungs. Rescue breaths are required. Begin rescue breathing by grasping the muzzle, keeping the mouth closed, and forcefully blowing air into the dog's nose. This is best done by covering the dog's nose with your mouth. Do this twice and then begin chest compressions at the highest point of the chest. Kneeling behind the dog and using two hands, push down until the chest is compressed about 2 to 3 inches for a large dog. Do this as fast as you can. After 30 chest compressions, give two more rescue breaths. Continue until the heartbeat returns, help arrives, or you are too exhausted to continue.

Electrocardiograms (ECGs) can be used in dogs. Stick the ECG pads onto the dog's paws, tape them in place, and attach the leads as in people. A normal heart rhythm in a dog has the same appearance as in people.

TRANSPORT

After providing first aid, the dog should be seen by a veterinarian. Methods of transport will depend on the severity of the illness. For most situations, the dog can be transported in the back seat of a car. If it must be transported in the back of a truck, another person must ride in the back to hold the dog and prevent it from jumping out. For more severe cases, the dog can be placed on its side on a board or stretcher and taped down. Before lifting the animal, make sure a muzzle has been placed.

CONCLUSION

Canines are an important part of law enforcement and security operations. Canines are used widely, at various settings, and in all environments. Canine handlers and others should have a good understanding of canine behavior, anatomy, physiology, and common diseases. LERs or medical support providers working around canine teams may be called to assist with the animal's health or to take care of the animal in an emergency. Many of the same care techniques and protocols designed for humans work for canines as well. LERs should make an effort to interact with canine handlers and the canines, so they can optimize caring for the animals in an emergency.

Prep Kit

READY FOR REVIEW

- First aid skills can readily be adapted to canines and can significantly increase a dog's chance of survival. This is particularly important in working dogs, who are valuable members of the law enforcement team, have years of training, and are loyal partners.
- There are several notable differences in anatomy and physiology between canines and humans.
- Before approaching a dog, whether the animal is injured or not, a basic understanding of canine behavior is crucial.
- When approaching an injured dog, the goal is to gain the dog's trust quickly. Be patient; walk slowly; and speak in a calm, soothing voice. Don't make any quick movements or have multiple people walking toward the dog.
- All injured dogs should be muzzled prior to any examination, unless the dog is unconscious.
- All dogs should be examined by a veterinarian as soon as possible after treatment at the scene.
- Common illnesses and injuries to dogs include hemorrhage, lacerations, torn toenail, foot pad injuries, fractures, impalement, evisceration, ingestion, gunshot wound, choking, seizure, blunt force trauma, eye injuries, allergic reaction, overheating, hypothermia, snake bite, and bloat.
- Canine cardiopulmonary resuscitation can be performed; however, the success rate when associated with trauma is dismal.

VITAL VOCABULARY

bloat Twisting of the stomach that allows air to get in, but not out; also called gastric dilatation-volvulus.

nictitating membrane Located in the inside corner of each eye, this membrane is important in tear production and protection of the cornea. Also called the third eyelid.

CHECK YOUR KNOWLEDGE

1. AEDs are effective when used on canines.
   - A. True
   - B. False
2. Where are the majority of a dog's sweat glands located?
   - A. In the eyelids
   - B. On the tongue
   - C. Around the pads of the feet
   - D. On the abdomen
3. Which of the following may be a sign of canine aggression?
   - A. Flattened ears
   - B. Lip curling
   - C. Tail wagging
   - D. All of the above
4. Which of the following is a recommended treatment for a dog that has ingested a chemical?
   - A. 3% hydrogen peroxide
   - B. 25 mg diphenhydramine
   - C. Ipecac
   - D. Activated charcoal
5. A dog experiencing heatstroke may not be panting.
   - A. True
   - B. False

Incarceration and Prisoner Care

Unit 25

Andrew Smith

Law Enforcement Responder Objectives

- Identify the six categories of detainee conduct. (p 455)
- Identify common medical conditions known to affect mental status. (pp 456–459)
- Discuss the effects of alcohol on mental status. (p 456)
- Discuss the effects of diabetes on mental status. (pp 456–457)
- Discuss the effects of seizure on mental status. (p 457)
- Discuss the effects of trauma on mental status. (p 457–458)
- Discuss the effects of psychosis on mental status. (p 458)
- Discuss the effects of drug abuse on mental status. (pp 458–459)
- Explain how to clear a person for incarceration. (p 459)
- Explain how to refer a detainee to the emergency department. (pp 459–460)

National EMS Education Standard Competencies

There are no National EMS Education Standard Competencies for this unit.

INTRODUCTION

The Fourth Amendment of the US Constitution states: "The right of the people to be secure in their persons, houses, papers, and effects, against unreasonable searches and seizures, shall not be violated, and no Warrants shall issue, but upon probable cause, supported by Oath or affirmation, and particularly describing the place to be searched, and the persons or things to be seized." This amendment has been interpreted by courts many times over the past 200 years. Essentially, it has been interpreted to provide for the rights of people as they pertain to criminal law.

The Fourth Amendment initially was applied to only the federal government; however, the US Supreme Court ruled in 1961 that the provisions of the Fourth Amendment were applicable to state governments under the due process clause of the Fourteenth Amendment. Federal and state laws provide authority for law enforcement to enforce the standards of society as codified by federal and state legislatures. Law enforcement officers are granted the authority to deprive a person of his or her liberty when they have probable cause to believe a violation of law has been committed. Once a person's liberty has been abridged, that person no longer has the ability to provide for his or her own safety and security. This has been established in legal decisions that have held that once a person has been taken into custody, the government assumes the responsibility for the person's safety and security (**Figure 1**).

Figure 1 Once a person has been taken into custody, the government assumes the responsibility for the person's safety and security.

Safety and security have been found to include the responsibility for detainee medical care. This unit is intended to provide a brief overview of medical conditions, as well as information useful in decision making as it pertains to detainee medical care.

In 2007, the Bureau of Justice Assistance of the United States Department of Justice released its report on arrest-related deaths in the United States from 2003 to 2005. This report entailed an analysis of all in-custody deaths during the referenced time period as reported per the Death in Custody Reporting Act. This study indicated that of the 2,002 deaths that occurred in custody, 25.8% of the deaths occurred from causes listed as intoxication, accidental injury, and natural causes.

This study also addressed the conduct of persons prior to arrest. The study categorized detainee conduct in six different categories:

- Appeared intoxicated
- Threatened officers
- Resisted arrest
- Tried to flee or escape arrest
- Grabbed, hit, or fought with officers
- Used weapon to threaten or assault officers

In 97% of the in-custody deaths, the decedent exhibited one of these types of behavior. In 75% of the cases, two or more of the listed types of behavior were demonstrated. It is possible that enhanced medical education of LERs could potentially decrease the number of in-custody deaths while maintaining the integrity of the judicial system.

ALTERED MENTAL STATUS

As demonstrated in the Bureau of Justice Assistance study, LERs often interact with people who demonstrate erratic, potentially violent behavior. These persons often have an altered **sensorium**, that is, an altered mental awareness of their surroundings. These types of behavior are often dismissed as alcohol intoxication or pure psychotic episodes. Unfortunately, this behavior may be attributable to a medical illness or adverse reaction to a traumatic event. Delay in medical care for these conditions often results in markedly more severe illness and, potentially, death.

Several different types of medical conditions are known to cause altered mental status. Typical causes of clinical altered mental status are represented in the mnemonic AEIOU TIPS and are discussed in the medical emergencies unit.

Many of the medical causes will produce a depressed level of consciousness, not the combative behavior that would cause an issue for law enforcement. Some of the more common emergencies seen by LERs include alcoholism, diabetic emergencies, seizures, trauma, psychiatric episodes, and drug overdose.

Alcoholism

The beer, wine, and liquor industry has an annual revenue of roughly $30 billion. According to the National Institute on Alcohol Abuse and Alcoholism, approximately 4.65% of the population of the United States have been diagnosed with alcoholism. Alcohol is widely available and has been found to be a factor in approximately 40% of crimes. In addition to a myriad of effects at low doses, higher doses of alcohol cause a depression of central nervous system activity. This results in fatigue, disorientation, and unconsciousness.

At extremes, alcohol may affect a person's ability to maintain or protect an open airway, resulting in an immediate life-threatening emergency. This is significant to LERs because many intoxicated people are detained while they sober up. Many of these subjects are left to sleep off their intoxicated state, particularly because they are often combative, vomiting, and generally unpleasant. These detainees require frequent monitoring to ensure their medical status is not deteriorating. Security personnel should also take suicide precautions and ensure that the detainee does not have access to potential weapons or harmful objects. Those who are unresponsive to attempts to wake them, particularly in light of alcohol consumption, will require evaluation by medical personnel.

Diabetes

Diabetes (or diabetes mellitus) is a long-term medical condition that is tremendously debilitating and affects the entire body. Diabetes is characterized by high levels of glucose in the blood, which occur as the body's organs become unable to metabolize or break down the glucose in the bloodstream. The glucose begins to affect the small blood vessels in the body, most commonly in the hands and feet and in the retinas in the eye. Most commonly diabetes is discovered during treatment for another condition or injury. If untreated, the disease can cause conditions such as diabetic retinopathy (which causes blindness) and decreases circulation in the extremities that lead to infections and skin breakdown that may result in surgical amputations.

Potential treatments of diabetes are long term and require very close monitoring of food and beverage intake and physical activity by the patient. This is particularly true for those who require insulin injections or an insulin pump for treatment. Persons with blood glucose levels that vary widely are often referred to as "brittle" diabetics.

Blood glucose levels that are too low result in a condition known as insulin shock, or hypoglycemia. To untrained personnel, a diabetic person in insulin shock often appears to be drunk. He or she is typically slow to respond to any stimuli, possibly slurs words, and is often disoriented. This condition occurs rapidly and is extremely dangerous. These persons need to raise their blood glucose level, typically through eating something sweet. Orange juice and other high-sugar foods are used for this purpose with good results. However, do not attempt to force-feed someone who is unconscious or unresponsive.

The opposite of insulin shock is a condition known as hyperglycemia, or diabetic coma. This condition has an onset over a few days and is characterized by extremely high blood glucose levels. These individuals begin to use all available metabolic processes to break down the glucose in the blood. One of these pathways results in sweet-smelling breath, which is sometimes mistaken for the by-products of alcohol intoxication. Similar to those in insulin shock, these persons are potentially disoriented. Again, they require immediate emergency medical attention.

Because proper management of diabetes typically requires a stable living environment, the more severe effects of diabetes are often seen in the lower socioeconomic groups. This is particularly true because supplies for proper diabetic care

are often expensive and proper nutrition is challenging for those on fixed incomes. Furthermore, diabetes combined with alcoholism results in extremely difficult management conditions.

Insulin shock and diabetic coma both cause disorientation, potentially slurred speech, and other behavioral irregularities. Because the effects of these conditions are more prominent in the less privileged, LERs have ample opportunity to interact with people experiencing one of these conditions. In these cases, information elicited from family or bystanders can be extremely useful in making the determination between a legal or medical issue. Consider that diabetic patients can become combative and that emergency medical services (EMS) may require police intervention for transport of the individual to the hospital.

Special Populations

Diabetes and Insulin

Potential treatments of diabetes are long term and require very close monitoring of food and beverage intake and physical activity by the patient, especially for those who require insulin injections or an insulin pump for treatment. Insulin is a naturally occurring hormone that facilitates the metabolism of sugar. Insulin-dependent diabetic individuals typically inject themselves with insulin to lower their blood glucose levels.

Additionally, once in police custody, persons with diabetes may need scheduled nutrition and access to medical care for purposes of insulin administration. Nearly all detention centers have established policies on management of detainees with special medical requirements. For purposes of care by LERs, provision of oral glucose (often supplied in emergency medical kits) will yield more benefit than potential detriment.

Seizures

Seizures are defined as events in which the electrical system in the brain malfunctions. If only part of the brain is affected, it may cloud awareness, block normal communication, and produce a variety of undirected, uncontrolled, unorganized movements. These seizures can be focal, meaning isolated to a certain part of the body, or generalized, in which the entire body is involved.

Many times, during generalized seizures, persons will lose control of their bladder or bowels. Seizures involving uncontrolled muscle contractions are very disturbing to watch for the layperson. Seizures can last for seconds or, in some persons, for minutes. A known seizure patient having seizures that last longer than 5 minutes requires immediate emergency medical care. During the seizure, the patient will not be able to comply with any instruction provided by the LER. This is the case whether the person has had an absence seizure (a period of unresponsiveness, but with eyes open) or the classic full-body shaking. The actual act of seizing consumes much of the available energy of the body, which results in a postictal state after the seizure. During this state, patients are typically unresponsive to verbal stimuli and appear to be under the effects of alcohol or other drugs.

Seizures themselves are caused by many different disorders, including brain injury, cancer, epilepsy, and metabolic imbalances, among others. Individuals with previously diagnosed seizure disorders are commonly prescribed oral medication, taken daily, that is intended to prevent them from experiencing future seizures. These medications often are referred to by creative names, such as "peanut butter balls" for phenobarbital. They require compliance with dosing instructions so as to prevent future seizures.

Emergency medical care by LERs for someone experiencing a seizure is relatively straightforward, no matter the cause of the seizure. Activate EMS. During the seizure, it is important to keep such patients from injuring themselves further. After the seizure has ended, it is best to roll the person onto his or her side, into the recovery position. This allows the airway to remain open, as well as any secretions or vomit to drain from the mouth as opposed to entering the airway. As someone recovers from a seizure (between 5 to 30 minutes), he or she may be disoriented; amnesia is often seen. Tell the person he or she has had a seizure. Most patients have had seizures before, and this information will assist in their recovery.

Never insert anything into the mouth of someone who is actively seizing. Many people were once taught to insert a bite block or tongue depressor into the mouth of a seizing patient to prevent him or her from swallowing his tongue. This is neither effective nor necessary, as swallowing his or her own tongue is not possible. Furthermore, the patient could aspirate a part of something he bites off or gag and vomit.

Trauma

Law enforcement observes the aftereffects of traumatic injury on a daily basis, no matter whether it is the victims of a high-speed motor vehicle crash or an aggravated assault victim who has been attacked by multiple subjects with blunt weapons.

Trauma to the central nervous system, which includes the brain and spinal cord, can create injuries that will alter a person's level of consciousness. The most prominent injury to the central nervous system is traumatic brain injury (TBI).

When children are born, the skull is very flexible, which allows for growth. Over time, the skull begins to become more rigid. In adults, the bones of the skull are completely fused together, providing a very effective barrier to protect the brain. However, this is somewhat of a double-edged sword.

If the brain does become significantly injured from a traumatic event, it begins to bleed (cerebral hemorrhage). Because this bleeding occurs internally, it is not visible. As the brain continues to bleed, it builds up pressure inside the skull. This pressure, referred to as intracranial pressure (ICP), begins to compress the brain and the brain stem, which controls vital functions such as heartbeat and breathing. Unaddressed cerebral bleeding and associated pressure can be fatal.

Persons with a traumatic brain injury may exhibit many different signs or symptoms. Persons who are behaving inappropriately after a head injury, or potentially disoriented in the setting of a traumatic event, require medical evaluation. Furthermore, certain medical conditions should raise the level of suspicion for potential TBI. The elderly, persons on blood-thinning medication, and chronic alcoholics are all at greater risk of cerebral hemorrhage, even from simple falls from a standing position (**Figure 2**). These persons should be referred to EMS, whose personnel will most likely transport them to a hospital capable of addressing traumatic injuries.

Figure 2 The elderly are at greater risk for cerebral hemorrhage.

Psychotic Episodes

Psychosis is a loss of contact with reality, usually including false beliefs about what is taking place or who one is (delusions) and seeing or hearing things that are not there (hallucinations). These persons will exhibit erratic, unpredictable, and seemingly irrational behavior. Despite public opinion, research indicates that the majority of these individuals do not exhibit violent behavior. However, history demonstrates that a lack of attachment with reality may result in levels of violence not typically seen in other violent offenders.

Individuals suffering from psychotic episodes need to be treated by mental health professionals as soon as possible. Often this treatment is against their wishes. LERs must take all precautions to take these individuals into custody safely. The concern in these cases is for the safety of both the LERs as well as the psychotic individual. The advent of less lethal weapons systems, for instance electrical-mechanical disruption weapons such as the Taser, has greatly expanded the available options of LERs to care for these persons safely.

Psychiatric care is often long term. There may be individuals in custody who are currently under a physician's care for any number of psychiatric disorders. If possible, these persons should be segregated from other detainees. Additionally, particular care should be exercised to ensure that they are constantly monitored and not able to harm themselves. These individuals are often creative in using mundane objects to harm themselves; for instance, a small metal insert on an identification bracelet can be used to cut the wrists in a suicide attempt. If detainees require medication for treatment of their disorder, consult with medical staff.

Drug Abuse

All types of drugs are abused. These drugs are abused because they make the user feel a certain way. However, most drugs do not have only one effect. For instance, cocaine, which is a stimulant, provides a feeling of euphoria, but also accelerates the heart to dangerous levels. It would be futile to attempt to discuss the effects of all of the different classes of drugs here, particularly because street drugs are mixed with other drugs, cutting agents, and such.

Of critical importance is that the LER recognizes when someone may be under the influence of a drug. Most narcotics officers can make this decision from many feet away from an offender. Most drugs of abuse cause an effect on the central nervous system. A very easy field test is to examine the pupils of an individual. The pupils routinely expand and contract to adjust for available light. In bright light, the pupils should contract to limit the amount of light entering the eye. In darkness, they expand to allow more light to enter the eye. A subject outside in bright light should not have large pupils without adequate explanation. Detection of drug intoxication is essential for the safety of law enforcement officers and the individual.

Cocaine has recently been to blame in many episodes of what has been termed by medical professionals as excited delirium. Excited delirium is characterized by a relatively rapid onset of disorganized thought characterized by inattention, memory impairment, disorientation, confusion, and/or visual hallucinations (see the behavioral emergencies unit for more information).

Once placed in custody, many of these subjects require additional restraining devices to curtail their violent behavior. Phencyclidine (PCP) is one example of a drug known for causing violent behavior. Previously, these subjects were placed face down in the back of police cars while wearing handcuffs behind their backs, attached to leg irons (often referred to as hog-tied). This position results in greater effort being required to breathe. As these individuals became fatigued, they would stop breathing. This phenomenon is termed *positional asphyxia*.

Respiratory arrest lasting longer than several minutes typically has a very low survivability. Positional asphyxia can be avoided by placing these subjects in any other position that allows their chest to expand fully. Many law enforcement agencies now have policies that strictly regulate enhanced restraint application so as to greatly reduce the occurrence of positional asphyxia.

CLEARANCE FOR INCARCERATION

Many causes of altered mental status and combative behavior have been addressed in this unit, the majority of which require medical attention by hospital personnel. However, some detainees will complain of medical problems that are minor or even contrived. Many large police departments and correctional institutions require that a prisoner complaining of an injury be seen by a doctor. Given the ongoing problem of overcrowding in emergency departments (EDs), this requirement could result in a prisoner and law enforcement officers spending on average a minimum of 4 hours in an ED. Additionally, the cost of the medical evaluation, potential overtime for the officers, and lost productivity are all borne by the law enforcement agency.

There are a number of creative solutions to these issues. Some law enforcement agencies have taken to training their personnel as emergency medical technicians (EMTs) or paramedics. In these cases, a close collaborative relationship with the medical community has resulted in these personnel being able to perform specific field medical tests on a detainee to medically clear him or her for incarceration. For instance, a detainee who complains of having asthma is examined by a LER in accordance with previously written instructions (protocols) from the physician. Law enforcement departments should partner with a physician medical director to set a policy that both meets the needs of the department and provides safe, quality care to the patient. This protocol could satisfy the department requirement or that of the detention center for medical evaluation. It is imperative in these cases that the evaluating EMT or paramedic document his or her findings and maintain the medical record in accordance with department policy.

REFERRAL TO THE EMERGENCY DEPARTMENT

In some cases it will be impossible to avoid a visit to the ED. Depending on the security requirements for the detainee, as well as the medical situation, it may be advisable to send a law enforcement officer in advance to meet with the ED staff, identify the treatment room, discuss security precautions, and so forth (**Figure 3**). Some EDs have preestablished lockdown procedures in cases of gang violence where retaliation is a serious concern.

These procedures will be familiar to all ED staff and can be enacted to enhance security. Hospital security staff may also be helpful in assisting with access control and other tasks. In cases involving the highest security, a separate identification system may be required to limit access to the detainee to only essential personnel. Additionally, the inclusion of a physician sensitive to the law enforcement mission may be helpful in the planning process. Once inside the hospital, law enforcement must recognize that the primary focus of the ED is medical care, which will sometimes cause conflict between the medical staff and law enforcement. In such circumstances, a pleasant personal demeanor combined with professionalism can ensure that the patient receives timely care.

Figure 3 A law enforcement officer may meet with the ED staff, identify the treatment room, and discuss security precautions prior to admitting a detainee.

CONCLUSION

Society trusts law enforcement officers and agents to protect and care for those in their custody. Limited resources and physical danger from violent detainees will complicate the LER's position. As soon as the patient is subdued and the threat from the detainee is manageable, you must evaluate your prisoner's well being. Officers and agents with a good working knowledge of the medical threats that face the incarcerated patient will move swiftly to seek additional, qualified help to limit the effects of some medical emergencies.

Prep Kit

READY FOR REVIEW

- The Fourth Amendment has been interpreted to provide for the rights of people as they pertain to criminal law.
- Conduct of persons prior to arrest that indicates they may be at risk for in-custody death falls into six different categories:
  - Appeared intoxicated
  - Threatened officers
  - Resisted arrest
  - Tried to flee or escape arrest
  - Grabbed, hit, or fought with officers
  - Used weapon to threaten or assault officers
- LERs often interact with individuals who demonstrate erratic, potentially violent behavior.
- At extremes, alcohol may affect the body's ability to maintain or protect an open airway, resulting in an immediate life-threatening emergency. Many of these subjects are left to sleep off their intoxicated state, particularly because they are often combative, vomiting, and generally unpleasant. These detainees require frequent monitoring to ensure their medical status is not deteriorating.
- Insulin shock and diabetic coma both cause disorientation, potentially slurred speech, and other behavioral irregularities. Because the effects of these conditions are more prominent in the less privileged, LERs have ample opportunity to interact with people experiencing one of these conditions.
- During a seizure, the individual will not be able to comply with any instruction provided by a LER. This is the case whether the person has had an absence seizure or the classic full-body shaking.
- Trauma to the central nervous system, which includes the brain and spinal cord, can create injuries that will alter an individual's level of consciousness.
- Psychotic persons may demonstrate erratic, unpredictable, and seemingly irrational behavior. Despite public opinion, research indicates that the majority of these individuals do not exhibit violent behavior.
- Of critical importance is that the LER recognizes when someone may be under the influence of a drug. Most narcotics officers can make this decision from many feet away from an offender.
- Some detainees will complain of medical problems that are minor or even contrived. Many large police departments and correctional institutions require that a prisoner complaining of an injury be seen by a doctor.
- In some cases it will be impossible to avoid a visit to the emergency department. Depending on the security requirements for the detainee, as well as the medical situation, it may be advisable to send a law enforcement officer in advance to meet with the emergency department staff, identify the treatment room, discuss security precautions, and so forth.

VITAL VOCABULARY

psychosis A loss of contact with reality, usually including false beliefs about what is taking place or who one is (delusions) and seeing or hearing things that are not real (hallucinations).

sensorium Mental awareness.

CHECK YOUR KNOWLEDGE

1. Which constitutional amendment ensures a person's right "to be secure in their persons, houses, papers, and effects, against unreasonable searches and seizures?"
   - A. The First Amendment
   - B. The Fourth Amendment
   - C. The Fifth Amendment
   - D. The Sixth Amendment
2. High doses of alcohol cause a depression of central nervous system activity.
   - A. True
   - B. False
3. Insulin shock and diabetic coma cause which of the following signs?
   - A. Disorientation
   - B. Slurred speech
   - C. Behavioral irregularities
   - D. All of the above
4. Disorders such as brain injury, cancer, epilepsy, and metabolic imbalances can all cause which of the following conditions?
   - A. Diabetes
   - B. Psychosis
   - C. Alcoholism
   - D. Seizure
5. All police departments and correctional institutions require that a prisoner complaining of an injury be seen by a doctor.
   - A. True
   - B. False

Assessment in Action

SCENARIO

You are dispatched to a local gas station for a report of a female patient in labor. As you arrive on scene, you are approached by the patient's husband, who is visibly shaken and tells you his wife is about to deliver their baby. Assessment of the mother reveals that the baby's head is protruding from the birth canal.

ACTIONS

1. Which stage of labor is this?
   A. Stage 1
   B. Stage 2
   C. Stage 3
   D. Stage 4
2. The best course of action at this point is:
   A. to tell the mother to close her legs, not push, and wait for EMS.
   B. to instruct the father to find clean rags and to boil water.
   C. to prepare for delivery of the baby.
   D. to look for a better place to deliver the baby.
3. Once the baby delivers, priority should be placed on all of the following except:
   A. cutting the umbilical cord.
   B. warming the baby.
   C. ensuring a clear airway.
   D. ensuring the baby is breathing adequately.

The father watches the baby being delivered and becomes distraught and agitated. He begins threatening you if you don't stop. He is upset that his child is being born in a gas station.

4. This activity can be described as:
   A. normal behavior.
   B. psychiatric behavior.
   C. bipolar emergency.
   D. behavioral emergency.
5. Which management model should be employed with this patient?
   A. Emergency restraint
   B. Conducted electrical weapon
   C. SAFER-R
   D. Psychological support

SECTION

8

Operational Considerations

Section Contents

Deployment Preparation

Unit 26

Lisa Steiner
William Northington
Geoffrey Shapiro

Law Enforcement Responder Objectives

Travel and Foreign Missions

- Explain the importance of preventive measures in preparing for travel or foreign missions. (pp 467–471)
- Develop a comprehensive medical risk assessment and travel plan for foreign missions. (pp 467–468)
- List and describe the preventive measures for avoiding illness during foreign missions. (pp 468–470)

In-Flight Emergencies

- Identify the most common types of medical emergencies encountered on commercial airline flights and what treatment can and should be rendered. (pp 473–475)
- Identify the medical equipment that is required to be carried on commercial flights. (p 472)
- Discuss the limitations of providing medical care on a commercial flight. (pp 471–472)

Maritime Deployments

- Describe various types of maritime medical operations. (pp 476–477)
- Identify additional medical equipment and training that may be needed while working in a maritime environment. (pp 476–477)

National EMS Education Standard Competencies

There are no National EMS Education Standard Competencies for this unit.

INTRODUCTION

Law enforcement responders (LERs) frequently encounter environments and conditions that are not routine. All experienced officers and agents can relate stories of traveling in aircraft, watercraft, or abroad. Inhospitable travel conditions and the stress associated with traveling can lead to exposure to allergens, infections, and poor sanitary conditions. Law enforcement officers and agents traveling for security or enforcement purposes may be part of a small team and not easily replaced during a mission. A poor decision to handle an exotic animal or eat the local delicacies can result in the early termination of a mission.

Travel and Foreign Missions

The increased risk of illness and injury during travel is well documented. Injury data from the State Department and reported by the Centers for Disease Control and Prevention (CDC) list motor vehicle, aquatic, aviation, and drug-related injuries as the leading causes of non-violence-related US deaths overseas. When missions involve travel, either foreign or domestic, there is significant potential for increased risk. Travel medicine is an emerging field that helps identify and eliminate as many risks as possible encountered during travel.

The success of a foreign mission will largely depend on the effectiveness of the operators. Ensuring that operators are functioning at their highest level will contribute to the success of that mission and the safety of team members. The importance of medical preplanning and providing medical support during travel and foreign missions should not be overlooked. Medical staff should be involved from the preplanning stages of foreign missions and for several weeks after the return of the mission team. Involvement of the medical team through all stages will ensure the development of a comprehensive plan for the entire team. Although being prepared is necessary, remember that flexibility and adjustment to changes in plans are equally important.

The responsibilities of the medical staff during travel are the same as for missions that are local, including conducting a medical risk assessment, ensuring team preparedness, monitoring the team during and after the mission, and medical treatment of the team as needed. Missions involving foreign travel will require quite a bit more planning, will use more resources, and will involve more premission training of operators than local operations.

MEDICAL RISK ASSESSMENT

Conducting a medical risk assessment must be done for foreign missions as well. The medical risk assessment for foreign travel will need to include additional information not generally collected for domestic missions. Additional information should include the following:

- Type of in-country travel. Travel within a country could be hazardous and may require much more planning than local operations do. Logistic members of the team may be making these decisions, but the medical personnel should be aware of potential changes of route as well as method of travel. Transport by personal vehicle that changes to transport by boat can affect a mission if the possibility of motion sickness has not been addressed or prepared for. No matter what the plan, backup transportation and alternative routes should be considered.
- Safety of in-country travel. Awareness of foreign driving laws (eg, who to notify in the event of a crash), driving patterns, and usual customs can assist in providing team safety while traveling to and from a mission. Realize that formal emergency transport may or may not exist.
- Knowledge of communicable disease outbreaks within the country.
- Potential for civil unrest.
- Potential for natural disaster (eg, hurricane season, avalanche if at altitude).
- Communication plan with backup options, including meeting location and time if separated or during communication failure.

- Local medical resources. In some instances local medical resources may be very sparse. Include in the survey what types of emergency medical services are available (**Figure 1**).
- Need for vaccinations required for travel to specific countries.
- Need for interpreter services, especially if there is potential need for securing in-country health care.

A number of resources are available to assist in gathering the information needed in preparation for foreign travel. The majority of these resources are available online. The CDC provides information on a variety of topics, from packing a personal medical kit to vaccination recommendations. The Yellow Book, also known as CDC Health Information for the International Traveler, covers such topics as travel preplanning, disease prevention, disease treatment, and post-travel evaluations. Other valuable resources are the country-specific fact sheets available from the US Department of State web site. The web site includes the following information for each country:

- Country description
- Smart Traveler Enrollment Program (STEP) and embassy location
- Entry and exit requirements for US citizens
- Threats to safety and security
- Crime and victims of crime
- Criminal penalties
- Special circumstances
- Medical facilities and health information
- Medical insurance
- Traffic safety and road conditions
- Aviation safety
- Children's issues

Figure 1 In planning for a foreign mission, determine what types of medical services are available.

The US Department of State web site also contains embassy and consular information, emergency services, and information about how to register with an embassy or consulate. Another potential resource may be embassy medical staff. They may be the best source of information regarding current local medical care, including the reliability of emergency services, level of care (eg, whether there are intensive care unit capabilities), and the location of the nearest operating room or computed tomographic scanner. The embassy medical staff may also be able to offer assistance with evacuation if necessary.

PREPARING THE TEAM FOR TRAVEL

Preparing for travel or foreign missions requires not only knowledge of the location but also a certain level of knowledge of the operators' health status. Each member of the team should have an emergency card that includes basic medical and surgical information, current medications, and allergies. In addition to medical history, this card may provide a means of documenting care given. Preplanning should include pre-travel physicals and physician clearance depending on the type, duration, and location of the mission. As mentioned previously, information about vaccinations can either be found on the CDC web site or by seeing a travel medicine physician. There may be some benefit in using a travel medicine clinic; personnel there can not only assist in obtaining necessary country-specific vaccinations but also ensure that all vaccinations are up to date and provide **prophylaxis** and treatment medications. Examples include prophylaxis for malaria and prescriptions that may be needed for respiratory infections, **traveler's diarrhea**, or nausea.

These preparations will need to take place as soon as possible. For an individual without recent travel, the current recommendation is to begin this process 4 to 6 weeks prior to travel. This time frame may not be realistic for missions that require swift response. Being as comprehensive as possible in preplanning can eliminate potential complications for the entire team.

Ensuring Team Preparedness

Completing an assessment of the persons in the group will help avoid being caught off guard by health conditions. It is also good to identify those members of the team with previous first aid, first responder, or formal medical training.

These members could be an additional resource if needed. In addition to the team preparations that usually occur prior to a mission, foreign travel and country-specific information will need to be disseminated to the team members.

Team members should be briefed on the following topics:

- **Preventive care.** Discuss the importance of keeping as close to a normal routine as possible. Significant changes to diet and exercise can alter operators' ability to perform at the same level. Instruct team members to continue their daily vitamins and supplements and usual exercise activities.
- **Preexisting conditions.** It is important that preexisting conditions be known to medical staff and that treatment be optimized prior to travel.
- **Injury prevention.** Discuss the importance of seat belt use, traffic safety, and the use of ear and eye protection.
- **Sun exposure.** Apply waterproof sunscreen and stay in the shade as much as possible.
- **Insect repellents.** Proper use of insect repellants is vital to those traveling in countries with conditions caused by contact with mosquitoes or other insects. Repellants can be applied directly to skin or clothing, and fabrics can be pretreated.
- **Water safety.** Caution members regarding diving and water safety, avoiding alcohol while swimming, and avoiding freshwater swimming and drinking in certain countries where waterborne parasitic and protozoal infections are common.
- **Infectious disease prevention.** In addition to food- and waterborne illnesses, communicable disease prevention, including influenza, tuberculosis, hepatitis, and sexually transmitted diseases, should be discussed.
- **Travel considerations.** Jet lag can significantly affect an operator, and attempts should be made to adjust ahead of time. Medications to induce sleep and the use of acclimating to the time zone upon arrival can assist in resolving the issue of jet lag. It is recommended that for every time zone crossed, one half to one day be added after arrival before the operation is to begin. If travel is extended, instructing the team to stand up, stretch, or walk each hour will assist in preventing both fatigue and **thrombosis**. Staying well hydrated during travel will also lessen the effects of jet lag. When traveling in another country, it is very important to be aware of driving laws, typical customs, and motor vehicle safety, because motor vehicle accidents are the most common cause of injury to those who travel overseas.
- **Hydration and nutrition.** Drinking water should either be bottled or treated before drinking in certain countries. In some cases, this may make it difficult to prevent dehydration. Best efforts, especially in a warm or dry climate, to stay well hydrated are imperative. The most common mantra regarding food safety is "Boil it, cook it, peel it, or forget it." This guideline should be strictly followed in those countries in which the water is unsafe to drink. Remind operators that items such as salsa, lettuce, and fruit salads do not meet these standards and should be avoided.
- **Climate and environments.** It is important to discuss differences in medical equipment, clothing, and preventive measures with all team members prior to travel. Some of these environments include tropical or marine, diving, wilderness, hot or cold, and high altitude.
- **Self-treatment and self-aid.** Each operator should have training in critical self-care prior to travel. For instance, if the medical staff is in another location, unavailable, or injured, the operator should be able to begin critical lifesaving techniques. Each operator should have a basic medical kit and should be proficient in how to use the items contained in it.

Tip

Adaptability

Providing medical support to a law enforcement mission requiring travel, especially if that travel is international, adds a multitude of additional considerations. When a mission is in a location that requires water purification, where there is no option to restock supplies, or where there are no reliable emergency medical services, it falls on the medical team to ensure comprehensive planning and attention to detail. Adapting to unexpected changes in plan and being prepared to adjust to different circumstances are essential capabilities for the success of any mission.

MEDICAL SUPPLIES

When it comes to medical gear and supplies, there is one goal: carry as little as possible that includes everything you need. In most cases, the medical supplies will need to be altered for differences of environment and length of mission. In addition to the country of travel and the duration of travel, it is important that the medical provider know the number of team members and whether there will be additional team members added upon arrival in the country. All of this information will be essential in determining the type of medical kit to pack as well as the quantity of items. It is essential to have a resource book related to field medicine for specific and in-depth assessment and treatment information. There are many options, and which one you choose depends on your level of medical training, location of travel, and recommendations from the team's medical direction.

PATIENT MANAGEMENT

During the preplanning stages for travel or foreign missions, a discussion should be held about who will provide medical support to the team if consultation or evacuation is to occur. The majority of illnesses and injuries are covered in other locations in this book. Most commonly a team member will present with a symptom or constellation of symptoms, such as fever, chills, diarrhea, ear pain, nausea, and vomiting. It will be necessary to obtain specific details to determine treatment options and level of care. As with any complaint of illness or injury, standard evaluation should occur followed by special considerations regarding travel or foreign missions. The on-site medical team will need to incorporate time and distance to definitive care, stabilize the patient, and make a determination regarding evacuation.

Common Travel Illnesses

Some of the most common travel illnesses include traveler's diarrhea, malaria, parasitic infections, and animal bites. Because of their frequency and the fact that there are a number of preventive measures, these illnesses and injuries are covered more in depth here.

Communication

Disclosing Small Complaints

Assessment and reassessment of team members throughout travel will ensure that the team is well and functional for the duration of the mission. Discussing the importance of disclosing small complaints before they develop into something that is difficult or impossible to manage in the field is essential.

Traveler's Diarrhea

Traveler's diarrhea is by far the most common medical condition encountered during travel and upon return. Preventive measures are crucial. Drink only bottled or treated water, do not use ice, and consume only safe foods, using the reminder "Boil it, cook it, peel it, or forget it." Symptoms of traveler's diarrhea vary from mild and brief with spontaneous resolution to lengthy bouts that can become longstanding and life threatening. Symptoms begin as frequent loose bowel movements with or without fever; the bowel movements are associated with cramping abdominal pain and may or may not contain blood.

Treatment of traveler's diarrhea begins with supportive care. Oral rehydration is the mainstay of treatment, and agents that replace electrolytes should be used. Antimotility agents (such as Imodium) are available over the counter and can be useful in keeping a team member active on the mission. These agents should be avoided if there is significant duration of symptoms and there is blood present in the stool. Antibiotics are typically prescribed along with other prophylactic medications during a travel medicine appointment. Early use of antibiotics starting immediately after onset of symptoms such as cramping or loose stool can markedly decrease the severity of certain types of diarrheal illness encountered.

Malaria

Malaria is a bloodborne disease that is transmitted by certain species of mosquitoes. Signs and symptoms include high fever, chills, and headache. For travel into a country where malaria is prevalent, many levels of prevention exist, all of which should be employed simultaneously. The first level of protection is the use of prophylactic medications. There are many different varieties of malaria, with varied distribution patterns. In addition, there are a variety of medications used to prevent malaria. Given the many variables, determining which medication should be taken should either be left to a travel physician or researched using sites discussed earlier in this unit. Taking these medications before, during, and after return from deployment will decrease the chance of dying from this disease.

Malaria is transmitted by mosquitoes; therefore, limiting exposure is the mainstay of prevention. Long-sleeved shirts, long pants, and mosquito nets will decrease exposure. Treating exposed skin with a DEET-containing product as well as using insecticides to treat clothing and mosquito nets can also offer assistance. These products can be obtained at a variety of different stores. Treatment of malaria is a matter of taking the proper antimalarial medications.

Parasitic Infection

There are a large variety of **parasitic infections** commonly acquired during travel. These infections can affect one or more body systems, including the skin, blood, gastrointestinal tract, muscle, brain, or lungs. It is important that risks be identified and precautions taken. Obtaining information about parasitic infections that are endemic to the region of travel can be accomplished through your travel physician or via the CDC web site. Initial signs and symptoms can occur during travel but can also present weeks or months later.

Animal Bites

Of special concern during travel are animal bites or scratches. If there is any concern that an animal may carry or be infected with rabies, or if the identity or location of the animal is unknown, treatment should begin as soon as possible.

All bites and scratches should be evaluated at a hospital and thoroughly cleaned. Many animal-borne diseases are indigenous to a particular region. Immediately seek qualified local physicians for detailed information on local diseases.

LERs should always advise all travelers in their party never to touch animals in foreign countries. Frequently exotic animals will be offered for entertainment purposes. Primates, felines, canines, reptiles, and exotic waterborne animals all have been documented as having bitten or scratched travelers.

In-Flight Emergencies

As the number of air travelers continues to increase, so does the number of in-flight medical emergencies. Because of the aging of the population as a whole (including air travelers) and the increasing mobility of individuals afflicted with acute and chronic diseases, the rate of in-flight emergencies is increasing as well. As a LER, it is quite possible that you may at some point find yourself on board a flight when a medical emergency occurs. Providing medical care to a patient while in flight poses unique challenges (**Figure 2**). There are no universal guidelines for managing in-flight medical emergencies, but there are certain considerations to keep in mind.

It is estimated that there are at least 20 to 100 in-flight medical emergencies per million passengers. The true rate, however, is likely much higher because there is no standardized system of reporting such events and the number just cited reflects only those cases that require ground medical support, not the minor medical incidents that are treated during flight and require no further outside intervention. The death rate on commercial flights is estimated at 0.1 to 0.3 death per million passengers (that is, roughly 1 person will die during flight for every 3 to 10 million passengers who travel on commercial airlines). However, severe emergencies have been substantially increasing over the last decade and are projected to continue to do so as the general population (and air-traveling population) continues to age and those with acute and chronic illnesses have access to the increased mobility of air travel.

LIABILITY OF PROVIDING CARE

The question often arises as to what legal protection a medical provider has when rendering care for an in-flight medical emergency. The Aviation Medical Assistance Act of 1998

Figure 2 Providing medical care on an aircraft in flight poses unique challenges.

established that a provider is protected against malpractice litigation if the following five conditions are met:

1. The provider is medically qualified to perform the service.
2. The provider acts voluntarily.
3. The provider acts in good faith.
4. The provider does not engage in gross negligence or willful misconduct.
5. The provider receives no monetary compensation. (Seat upgrades and travel vouchers do not count as compensation if offered freely by the airline and not requested by the provider.)

The key for those who are prehospital providers serving as medical providers in flight is not to do anything unfamiliar or outside the individual's accepted scope of practice.

ASSESSMENT OF IN-FLIGHT EMERGENCIES

Tip

Law Enforcement Considerations for In-Flight Emergencies

- If flight attendants are onboard, immediately confirm with them that they want your help.
- The size and type of the aircraft will dictate where you can work.
- If possible, place the patient in or near a lavatory facility.
- If the patient needs to lie down, consider using the rear of the aircraft to prevent compromising cockpit security.
- If you are concerned about secretions and exposure to other passengers, ask the flight crew to intervene and use plastic bags as barriers or relocate the passengers.
- Manage injuries as you would anywhere else. Notify receiving EMS units of your situation and possible needs.
- If the patient is an armed law enforcement officer or agent, secure his or her weapon in accordance with your agency's policies.
- If you are traveling in a covert manner, you may need to weigh your decision to act based on your agency's policies.

The assessment of an airline passenger with a medical complaint should be no different from that of a patient being evaluated in a different setting. The key history elements covered by the SAMPLE mnemonic should be gathered. The medical assessment should focus on the overall general appearance and impression of the passenger, as well as on the chief complaint, and should always include a complete set of vital signs. During in-flight medical emergencies, ground-based medical control will likely become involved. These physicians and trained providers depend on the information that the emergency responder on the flight relays to make important decisions, in conjunction with the captain, as to whether the flight needs to be diverted so the passenger can receive expedited medical care. A large portion of this decision is often based on the vital signs and overall appearance of the passenger. If the on-ground medical control provider needs more detailed information or further history and a secondary assessment, he or she will request them from the in-flight emergency responder.

MEDICAL EQUIPMENT ONBOARD AN AIRCRAFT

The Federal Aviation Administration (FAA) requires every commercial flight with flight attendants to carry an emergency medical kit (EMK) that consists of a first aid kit, oxygen tank, automated external defibrillator (AED), and intravenous (IV) start kit with normal saline and basic medications. **Table 1** outlines the required components of each EMK.

The list in Table 1 represents only what the FAA requires commercial airlines to carry. Some US carriers have kits that include more supplies and more medications. However, many airlines carry only what is required, and medical providers should expect to have access to only these medications and equipment. On large commercial flights, other materials may be available to use as makeshift splints and dressings. Occasionally other passengers may have items that could help. Be aware of what is commonly available and ask flight attendants and others whether they have resources not routinely available in the EMK.

DIVERSION OF AIRCRAFT

Certain medical emergencies require immediate care in a hospital to diagnose and treat life-threatening conditions effectively. In such cases, the captain of the aircraft may decide to divert the flight from the original course to land at a closer airport so the passenger can receive medical care sooner. This is a decision that is not taken lightly. Diverting a commercial flight is very expensive, usually over $100,000, and causes disruptions in the travel plans of the other passengers on the flight as well as the flights scheduled to arrive and depart from the airport to which the plane is being diverted. Furthermore, once the decision to divert is made, it will take at

Table 1

Components of a Commercial Flight Emergency Medical Kit

Type of Equipment	Required Items
Airway equipment	• Self-inflating resuscitation bag with three sizes of masks • Three sizes of oropharyngeal airways
Wound equipment	• Bandages, gauze pads • Antiseptic wipes • Nonlatex gloves • Wound closure strips • Trauma shears • Burn dressing • Arm and leg splints (one of each)
Injectable medications	• Atropine 0.5 mg • Dextrose 50%/50 mL • Diphenhydramine 50 mg • Epinephrine 1:1,000 (for intramuscular injection) • Epinephrine 1:10,000 • Lidocaine 2%
Oral medications	• Aspirin 325 mg tablets • Inhaled bronchodilator (eg, albuterol metered-dose inhaler) • Non-narcotic analgesic (eg, acetaminophen 325 mg tablets) • Antihistamine tablets (eg, diphenhydramine 25 mg tablets) • Nitroglycerin 0.4 mg sublingual tablets
IV equipment	• 0.9% saline solution, 500 mL • IV catheters (two each): 18 g, 20 g, 22 g • IV set tubing with Y connectors • IV start kit
Needles/syringes	• One 5 mL and two 10 mL syringes • Needles (two each): 18 g, 20 g, 22 g
Miscellaneous	• Large trauma dressing • Contents/instruction card • Blood pressure cuff • Stethoscope • Nonpermeable gloves (one pair) • Approved AED

least 20 minutes (but usually more than 30) for the flight to actually descend and land because of the logistics involved.

The decision to divert an aircraft is usually made after discussion between the captain and on-ground medical control. Ultimately, the captain always has the final decision-making authority. Several other factors are taken into account when deciding whether and where to divert: the distance from the airport to appropriate medical facilities, how much quicker diverting would allow a passenger to receive definitive medical care, and what the risk of delaying medical care until landing at the planned destination would be to the passenger.

MEDICAL CONTROL

All major commercial airlines have an established ground-based medical control system. This system allows airlines to have access to a physician and any applicable medical advice and orders. These physicians and associated medical personnel have specific experience with aviation medicine and are familiar with the resources on board the aircraft. They can advise the flight crew or on-board medical personnel on treatment options and discuss with the captain possible considerations for diversion of the aircraft. It is important to note that the final decision regarding aircraft diversion always lies with the captain of the aircraft, not the medical control physician.

COMMON IN-FLIGHT MEDICAL COMPLAINTS

The most common in-flight medical complaints are cardiac, neurologic, and respiratory, although gastrointestinal and traumatic complaints are also common.

Cardiac Complaints

The most common cardiac complaint is chest pain or angina. These complaints comprise roughly 20% of in-flight medical emergencies and are the most common cause of diversion and passenger death. The decreased cabin oxygen pressure can lead to decreased oxygen saturation levels in the blood and cause angina when the heart is not delivered the full amount of oxygen it requires. The added stress and exertion of travel may also cause episodes of angina.

Any passenger experiencing chest pain must be taken seriously. A detailed history and vital signs must be obtained.

There should be a low threshold to suspect that the passenger is having a myocardial infarction (heart attack), and the airline's ground-based medical control should be contacted to help decide whether the aircraft needs to divert instead of continuing on the planned course.

On-board items included in the EMK that may be used for passengers suffering from chest pain include a stethoscope and blood pressure cuff to assess vital signs, oxygen, aspirin, nitroglycerin, atropine, and epinephrine. If there is the possibility of a cardiac arrhythmia or if the patient is seen to lose consciousness suddenly, the AED should be attached immediately and its directed prompts should be followed.

Tip

Medication Administration

Medications, including those listed here, should be administered only within the medical provider's scope of practice and often only with direct guidance from ground-based medical control.

Neurologic Complaints

Common neurologic complaints encountered on commercial flights include syncope, seizure, light-headedness, and vertigo.

Syncope, also referred to as fainting or passing out, can have many different causes, some of which may be serious. Any passenger who loses consciousness should initially be treated as if suffering a life-threatening cardiac arrhythmia and have an AED immediately applied. Several other factors encountered in air travel might precipitate a brief episode of loss of consciousness, such as quickly standing after prolonged sitting, relative dehydration caused by a limited fluid intake and the dry cabin air, or excess alcohol consumption. The cause may also be a **vasovagal episode**, in which blood vessels dilate and the heart may momentarily slow down, decreasing the blood flow to the brain and causing loss of consciousness.

It is important to attempt to determine why the patient suffered a loss of consciousness through a careful history and assessment, paying special attention to the vital signs. If the patient quickly regains consciousness, the treatment will likely be supportive and include laying down the passenger and elevating the feet, providing low-flow oxygen, and possibly beginning an IV and administering normal saline. If the patient is fully conscious—without nausea or vomiting—and advises that he or she is able to drink, fluids by mouth are often just as effective as IV fluids. Use caution if you are unsure about the patient's level of consciousness. If you feel the patient may pass out again, withhold fluids until you have consulted with a physician.

Seizures often appear much more dramatic, frightening, and serious than they are. If a passenger begins seizing, it is important to move the passenger to an area where he or she will not strike his or her head or sustain any trauma. Once moved, supplemental oxygen should be given to the patient. Seizures are often self-limiting, and the erratic shaking behavior usually lasts only a minute or two. Should a passenger begin seizing, it is important to identify any travel companions who can provide any medical history or events leading up to the seizure. Unfortunately, the FAA does not require airlines to carry any medications to treat seizures; however, if the patient has a history of frequent seizures, he or she may have an appropriate seizure medication available. Remember not to give any oral medications to a patient who is actively seizing or has not returned to a normal baseline mental state.

If the patient has a history of diabetes, it is possible that the seizure was caused by a low blood glucose level. The blood glucose level can be checked if anyone on the aircraft has a glucometer available. If the patient's blood glucose level is found to be low or the patient has a history of diabetes and no glucometer is available, IV dextrose can be given. If you are unable to administer IV dextrose as part of your scope of practice, you may want to consider the use of oral glucose paste or sugar based on the availability of these items, the patient's airway status, and the authorization of the in-flight medical direction.

Once seizure activity stops, the patient should not be expected to return to a completely normal state immediately. After a seizure, a person usually remains drowsy and slightly confused for several minutes. Place the patient in the recovery position and monitor his or her airway.

Respiratory Complaints

The most common respiratory events encountered during commercial flights are shortness of breath and wheezing as a result of exacerbations of asthma or chronic obstructive pulmonary disease (COPD). Shortness of breath can have many underlying causes. It is important to obtain a thorough history, including other symptoms such as chest pain, to determine more serious causes of shortness of breath. Asthma and COPD exacerbations can be triggered by environmental changes encountered during travel or the dry air found in the plane's cabin. Often patients with a history of asthma or COPD will have medication with them to treat their condition; if not, a bronchodilator such as albuterol is available in the EMK. Any patient suffering from continued shortness of breath can also be given low-flow oxygen.

Gastrointestinal Complaints

Abdominal pain, nausea, vomiting, and diarrhea are all commonly encountered in-flight complaints. These symptoms may be the result of something as simple as motion sickness or a transient viral illness but could also signal a developing abdominal infection (such as appendicitis) that, left unrecognized and untreated, could become quite serious. It is important to elicit a detailed history and exam in regard to gastrointestinal symptoms, including recent meals, foreign travel, and presence of a fever.

Allergic Reactions

Minor allergic reactions can usually be treated easily with an antihistamine found in the EMK. For more serious responses in which the airway is involved and there is a sensation of throat tightening or closing and wheezing, or if the passenger appears to be suffering from anaphylaxis with a drop in blood pressure, epinephrine from the EMK may need to be administered intramuscularly. Oxygen and the bronchodilator medication in the EMK may also be given to help with any difficulty breathing. If the passenger is found to have a low blood pressure, an IV may be started and normal saline given.

Diabetic Complaints

Diabetes is becoming a much more commonplace disease in the United States. Subsequently, a greater number of air travelers are on medications to treat high blood glucose levels. The stress of traveling and the break from a regular schedule may cause a passenger to miss meals and have difficulty adequately monitoring glucose levels and adjusting medication doses. This may ultimately lead to a passenger suffering a hypoglycemic episode. Mild episodes of hypoglycemia are usually marked by generalized weakness or fatigue and an overall ill feeling. In these situations, the passenger is still conscious and can often be treated with a glass of juice or a snack to increase the blood glucose level. In more severe cases, the passenger may appear in distress, with profuse sweating, paleness, nausea, and vomiting, and may ultimately suffer a seizure or loss of consciousness. In cases such as this, it is important to identify that the patient is diabetic and likely suffering from low blood glucose levels. An IV should be started, and dextrose from the EMK can be given. Again, if you are unable to administer IV dextrose as part of your scope of practice, and based on the availability of these items, the patient's airway status, and the authorization of the in-flight medical direction, consider the use of oral glucose paste or sugar. Do not attempt to give a diabetic passenger who is unconscious or has an altered mental status any juice to drink or anything else by mouth; he or she may choke on the fluids.

Trauma Complaints

Minor scrapes, bumps, or bruises are not uncommon during air travel. Most of these cases can be managed with basic first aid principles and the gauze and bandages found in the EMK. Given the placement of the overhead storage bins above passengers, it is possible that an item may fall and strike a passenger in the head when a bin is opened. This could cause a head injury such as a concussion or rarely a cervical spine injury. In these cases, it is important to monitor the patient's mental status and assess for any weakness, numbness, tingling, or other neurologic deficits. If appropriate, the cervical spine should be immobilized and ground-based medical control should be contacted.

Behavioral Complaints

Passengers displaying unacceptable behavior in flight are often difficult to treat because of the wide array of possible underlying causes and the unpredictable responses that a passenger may display to those trying to intervene. A passenger displaying aggressive or violent behavior places the crew and other passengers at risk for serious injury. The primary cause of a behavioral disturbance can vary greatly—from an underlying psychiatric disorder to the unintentional overdose of prescribed medications (eg, medications to help with motion sickness or ease the anxiety of air travel), or even to medical disorders such as hypoglycemia or low oxygen levels or to use of alcohol or drugs. With in-flight behavioral issues, it is important to attempt to calm the passenger and to keep him or her from harming himself, herself, or others. A medical provider should attempt to gather a thorough history (including past medical history and any medications) from the passenger or companion travelers and address any possible medical causes for the behavioral disturbance. If the passenger continues to display behavior that places others at risk, the captain and crew should address the overall risk to the safety of the flight and the possible need to divert.

Maritime Deployments

While working in a maritime setting, mariners often face a wide variety of medical emergencies and traumatic injuries without the benefit of a dedicated medical care provider or readily available definitive care. In many circumstances, the best chance to reduce morbidity and/or mortality on board the vessel is to have personnel available who are able to stabilize a patient and/or arrange and prepare for evacuation. These personnel, who receive additional training to the standard emergency medical responder (EMR) curriculum, also reduce lost productivity and improper use of medical resources by remedying minor ailments and injuries.

The need for medical care potentially exists everywhere, even at sea. Training and technology have assisted mariners in coping with emergencies and routine illness and injuries while at sea. With the implementation and enforcement of the Standards of Training, Certification, and Watchkeeping for Seafarers 1995 amendments, all seafarers are required to receive basic safety and first aid training. The United States Coast Guard also states that officers may also be required to successfully complete a first aid certification course, and/or a Person in Charge of Medical Care course.

In addition to the standard topics included in the EMR curriculum, mariners may also be required by their employer to learn IV line insertion and management; intramuscular, subcutaneous, oral, transdermal/topical, and sublingual medication administration; and advanced wound management (suturing and other forms of closure). Other topics such as patient packaging, health and wellness, and injury prevention are also included in the program. Perhaps one of the most important skills included in the training is communication with a medical advice provider.

Typically, proper and successful treatment of a patient cannot be accomplished by a mariner acting alone on board a vessel. Even if a patient does not require evacuation, consultation with a medical advice provider allows an experienced medical provider to review the case and offer insight to treatment and patient disposition. Various technologies are available for medical consultation, including radio, cellular phone, satellite phone, internet/email, and digital imaging. More information on this topic appears in the rescue unit.

THE MARITIME ENVIRONMENT

Law enforcement maritime operations are greatly varied, and may range from near-shore patrols to deep sea operations (**Figure 3**). Encountering a medical emergency in the maritime environment can be challenging because you may not have the same equipment or personnel as would be available to mitigate the emergency shore-side.

If a maritime unit is called to assist with a medical situation on a ship or structure that is located near the shore, it may not be necessary for those caring for the patient to perform any interventions other than what would be done on land. However, if operations are such that a patient cannot be evacuated to shore immediately, additional skills, medications, and procedures may be needed. It is important to note that additional high-level interventions should not be performed unless directed to do so by medical control.

Carrying additional medical supplies may also be challenging in a maritime environment. Making sure that medications and equipment are accounted for, in working order, and secure must be part of the operation (**Table 2**). Most importantly, it is imperative to ensure that all personnel who may be called to use these additional skills are properly trained to do so and are doing so under direct medical supervision.

Figure 3 Law enforcement maritime operations are greatly varied and may range from near-shore patrols to deep sea operations.

Table 2

Examples of Medications for a Maritime Medical Kit

Medication Types	Examples
Over-the-counter	• Acetaminophen • Ibuprofen • Diphenhydramine • Pseudoephedrine • Aspirin • Hand sanitizer • Triple antibiotic ointment • Eyewash • Antacid • Glucose gel
Nausea/vomiting/diarrhea	• Zofran • Loperamide
Prescription pain	• Morphine sulfate • Diazepam • Oxycodone
Emergency prescription	• IV fluids • Dextrose 50% • Nitrogylcerin • Epinephrine • Albuterol • Naloxone • Prednisone
Antibiotics (injectable and oral)	• Ancef • Azithromycin • Ciprofloxacin • Doxycycline • Penicillin

CONCLUSION

Law enforcement officers and agents travel. Many specialized federal agencies place large numbers of security forces and task forces in third world locations to apprehend terrorists or drug cartel members, or to extradite fugitives apprehended by local police. Traveling to a third world country without prior preparation can quickly result in illness from food and water-borne pathogens. LERs are always facing the potential for injured personnel as a result of vehicle crashes or assaults. The LER must have a good assessment of the local advanced medical care and a plan for when to leave the area for definitive care. LERs should understand that travel by plane or boat can also occur in the practice of their duties. These expeditions raise the physical and emotional stress placed on law enforcement personnel. During a flight or cruise, the LER must plan to be isolated from traditional EMS for at least 30 minutes, and in some cases days. Realizing that many aircraft and ships have onboard medical supplies and equipment can place the LER at an advantage when handling a patient under these conditions.

Prep Kit

READY FOR REVIEW

- As the number of air travelers continues to increase, so does the number of in-flight medical emergencies.
- The Aviation Medical Assistance Act of 1998 was designed to protect medical providers volunteering to provide care on a US commercial flight. It is important that the medical provider practice only within his or her accepted scope of practice to be protected by this act.
- During in-flight medical emergencies, ground-based medical control will likely become involved.
- Limited medical resources are available on commercial flights. These can be found in the EMK.
- Diverting an aircraft is a costly and time-consuming decision that might become necessary if an ill passenger needs immediate medical care. The captain has the ultimate decision-making authority.
- All major commercial airlines have an established ground-based medical control system that allows airlines to have access to a physician and any applicable medical advice and orders.
- When missions involve travel, either foreign or domestic, there is significant potential for increased risk.
- Medical staff should be involved from the preplanning stages of foreign missions and for several weeks after the return of the mission team.
- A medical risk assessment for foreign travel needs to include additional information not generally collected for domestic missions.
- Preparing for travel or foreign missions requires not only knowledge of the location but also a certain level of knowledge of the operators' health status. Each member of the team should have an emergency card that includes basic medical and surgical information, current medications, and allergies.
- When it comes to medical gear and supplies for a foreign mission, there is one goal: carry as little as possible that includes everything you need.
- Adapting to unexpected changes in plans and being prepared to adjust to different circumstances are essential for the success of any mission.
- In addition to the standard topics included in the EMR curriculum, mariners may also be required by their employer to learn intravenous (IV) line insertion and management; intramuscular, subcutaneous, oral, transdermal/topical, and sublingual medication administration; and advanced wound management (suturing and other forms of closure).
- Carrying additional medical supplies may also be challenging in a maritime environment. Making sure that medications and equipment are accounted for, in working order, and secure must be part of the operation.

VITAL VOCABULARY

malaria A bloodborne disease that is transmitted by certain species of mosquitoes.

parasitic infections Infectious diseases caused or transmitted by a parasite. Examples include yellow fever, malaria, and tapeworm.

prophylaxis Measure(s) taken to prevent a condition or disease.

thrombosis Formation of a blood clot within the vascular system; of concern during travel because of prolonged immobility.

traveler's diarrhea Increased frequency of unformed, watery stool during travel.

vasovagal episode A reflex of the involuntary nervous system that causes the heart to slow down, affecting the nerves to the blood vessels in the legs and permitting those vessels to dilate (widen). As a result, the heart puts out less blood, blood pressure drops, and what blood is circulating tends to go into the legs rather than to the head.

CHECK YOUR KNOWLEDGE

1. A law enforcement responder can perform advanced procedures without completing additional training if told to do so by medical control.
   A. True
   B. False
2. The __________ has the authority to determine if the plane will divert for a medical emergency.
   A. chief flight attendant
   B. medical control physician
   C. pilot
   D. tower
3. The most common mechanism of serious injury occurring during international travel is a:
   A. fall.
   B. gun shot wound.
   C. motor vehicle crash.
   D. blast injury.
4. Which of the following is not an acceptable food product when trying to prevent traveler's diarrhea?
   A. Banana
   B. Hard-boiled egg
   C. Salsa
   D. Pineapple
5. All seafarers are required to receive basic safety and first aid training.
   A. True
   B. False

Special Missions and Responses

Unit 27

Scott Kimball
Frank Larkin
Nelson Tang
David Stair

Law Enforcement Responder Objectives

Special Operations and Tactics

- Discuss the law enforcement responder's role in special operations and tactics. (pp 481–482)
- Identify the minimum skills for a Special Weapons and Tactics (SWAT) team. (pp 481–482)
- Explain the SWAT team role in casualty care. (p 483)

Executive Protection

- Identify methods of executive protection. (p 484)
- Discuss the role of the law enforcement responder in executive protection. (p 484)
- Identify the factors influencing protective planning. (pp 484–485)
- Explain protective medical support and how it can be implemented. (pp 485–486)
- Discuss the creation of executive protection-specific protocols. (p 486)
- Discuss the use and accessibility of protection-based supplies and equipment. (p 486)

Active Shooter Scenarios

- Discuss medical response in active shooter scenarios. (pp 487–488)
- Describe the law enforcement responder's role in casualty care in active shooter scenarios. (pp 486–487)

Animal Threats and Control

- Explain the role of animal control officers during an emergency response. (p 488)
- Identify the potential threats raised by domestic pets, exotic pets, livestock, and wildlife. (pp 488–491)
- Identify the components of canine aggression. (pp 489–490)

National EMS Education Standard Competencies

There are no National EMS Education Standard Competencies for this unit.

Special Operations and Tactics

In police special operations and tactics, mission-specific considerations such as the selection of medical equipment, supplies, and load-out are more scrutinized, and the application of tactical medicine is very closely followed. The equipment selected and the tactics, techniques, and procedures currently being deployed have been developed as a direct result of actual tactical team missions conducted worldwide. Additionally, the approach has been shaped by rapid domestic deployments and international missions, including robust combat experience in Iraq and Afghanistan in support of the global war on terror. The practice of tactical medicine continues to evolve as threat assessments are conducted and after-action reports are reviewed. Lessons learned may be translated to the individual law enforcement responder (LER) as well as those charged with developing or enhancing tactical medical programs.

Although each agency favors a different acronym for special operations (eg, Special Response Team [SRT], Special Operations and Reaction Team [SORT], Special Tactics and Response [STAR], Emergency Services Unit [ESU]), a police tactical team, for the purpose of this unit, will be referred to as Special Weapons and Tactics (SWAT). The National Tactical Officers Association (NTOA) defines a SWAT team as "a designated law enforcement team, whose members are recruited, selected, trained, equipped, and assigned to resolve critical incidents involving a threat to public safety which would otherwise exceed the capabilities of traditional law enforcement first responders and/or investigative units."

In accordance with NTOA standards, a SWAT team should, at a minimum, be able to engage in the following:

- Tactical command
- Containment
- Emergency action
- Deliberate action
- Precision long rifle use

Historically, the public has been able to differentiate between traditional law enforcement officers and SWAT team operators by their weapons. With the proliferation of patrol rifle programs and less-lethal delivery systems such as conducted electrical weapons and bean-bag shotguns, the prior lines between conventional law enforcement and SWAT have blurred. Threat-based preparedness made necessary by active shooter incidents and preparedness for domestic terrorism have resulted in training that was formerly typically reserved for SWAT teams now often being taught at the academy level. To face these emerging threats, equipment lines are being similarly blurred as patrol officers are increasingly being equipped with helmets and load-bearing vests (LBVs) fitted with plates capable of defeating rifle rounds.

Recognizing the capabilities of agencies with specially trained units but without SWAT teams, the NTOA acknowledges that these units may engage in the following operations until the arrival of SWAT:

- Tactical command
- Containment
- Emergency action

By these delineations, deliberate action and precision long rifle use remain firmly in the hands of SWAT. Although it could be argued that the use of a sniper is a deliberate action, NTOA states that the primary distinguishing characteristic of SWAT is the focus on resolving a critical incident with tactical solutions.

Modern SWAT missions or critical incidents typically include the following:

- Hostage rescue
- High-risk entry, such as search warrant, dangerous felon, or fugitive
- Barricaded gunman
- Vehicle assault
- Personnel security and protection details
- Sniper

This list does not address the seemingly endless number of SWAT responsibilities, dependent on an individual agency's area of operation and threat review, which may include everything from crowd and riot control to tactical tracking operations.

An essential specialty assignment within the SWAT team is a member who is also trained as a tactical medic (often shortened to medic). In traditional settings, an emergency medical responder (EMR) faced with a medical situation is trained to activate the emergency medical services (EMS) system immediately, then to initiate patient assessment and first aid. This call typically results in an EMS professional responding and transporting the patient to a higher level of care. Within SWAT, the call for a medic does not ensure immediate medical assistance. The medic focuses first on the threat and then turns to assist injured SWAT members.

CASUALTY CARE AND SWAT

Tactical combat casualty care (TCCC) has become the widely referenced military model for tactical medicine and has resulted in both the development of an approach and streamlining of equipment to address predictable causes of preventable death. Medical equipment for the individual operator, medic, and entire SWAT team (as well as specific training for casualty care) is emphasized for the tactical arena.

Individual First Aid Kit

The individual first aid kit (IFAK) is supplied to the SWAT operator to save his or her own life and specifically to address hemorrhage, tension pneumothorax, and airway obstruction. **Figure 1** shows typical contents of the IFAK. Every SWAT operator should have an approved tourniquet secured to the front of his or her LBV so it is accessible by either hand (**Figure 2**).

Several manufacturers produce pouches designed to contain a tourniquet and an accompanying indelible marker. Not only are they visually indistinguishable from the assortment of pouches that operators may opt to carry, but be forewarned—a 2-by-6-inch pouch provided to a SWAT operator will soon contain a multi-tool, flashlight, or energy bar.

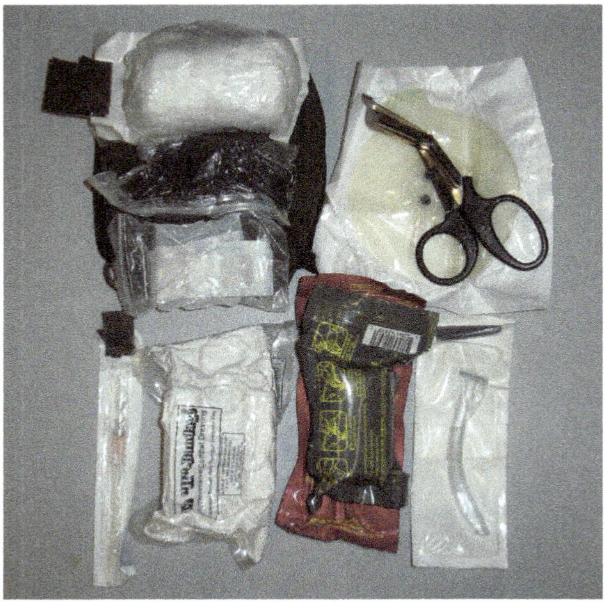

Figure 1 Typical contents of a SWAT member's individual first aid kit.

Figure 2 Every SWAT operator should have an approved tourniquet secured to the front of his or her load-bearing vest so it is accessible by either hand.

Commercially sealed or vacuum-packaged supplies may or may not come with small precut notches to aid in opening. Regardless, they are generally inadequate for use by the SWAT operator who is wearing gloves and functioning under stress. Loose ends of sealed bags should be tagged with two different lengths of adhesive tape to act as pull tabs. If a packet is completely sealed, a small cut can be made in the top corner of a packet and tape placed above and below the notch to serve as pull tabs.

A small assortment of simple adhesive bandages should be included within each IFAK. It can be frustrating for a SWAT operator with a small laceration to find only a roll of gauze or hemostatic dressing in his or her individual kit.

Tactical Medic Bag

The medic's bag must be low profile and maneuverable enough to address the deliberate action missions of the team and to support the priorities of combat casualty care. The low profile allows the medic to sit in a vehicle or aircraft and move freely, and still allows for tolerable spacing between SWAT operators in entry formation or confined spaces. Medical emergencies beyond those encompassed by TCCC remain a common concern for medics, and additional load-out (including pharmacology) must be deployed to address these.

All the items required to perform a specific procedure should be packaged together in a single water-resistant pouch. These pouches, as with items in the IFAK, should be tabbed for easy opening. If medications are included within the kit, ensure that the names and expiration dates are clearly visible. Reference cards or notes should be included in the kits to provide backup visual cues to aid the medic.

Team Medical Kit

The team medical kit (TMK) is specifically designed to support the evacuation phase of care and also to address the potential need for additional supplies in the event of a mass casualty. Typically prepositioned within a SWAT vehicle and retrieved or accessed as necessary, the TMK includes an automated external defibrillator (AED), collapsible litter, and oxygen. Additional equipment to support this phase of care may include airway adjuncts, a traction splint, malleable splints and cravats, cervical collars, burn sheets, and a hypothermia system. To address mass-casualty events, the TMK should be well stocked with redundant supplies contained in the IFAK, with contents readily identifiable by LERs.

SWAT TEAMS AND MEDICAL TRAINING

Once the techniques and procedures are taught in the classroom, practical medical training is typically delivered in a dedicated block. Medical scenarios should be incorporated into every SWAT training evolution. During team rappelling, fast-rope, or obstacle course training, incorporate patient packaging and transport with immobilization and cervical spine precautions. Practice glass breaking and vehicle extrications during motorcade operations. Teach improvised splinting during rural motorcycle and all-terrain vehicle (ATV) operations.

A common adage within the Special Operations Forces (SOF)/SWAT community is that people will not rise to the occasion, but default to their level of training. It is important to ensure that the training scenarios presented are threat-based, dynamic, and address all three phases of care under TCCC.

To illustrate the fundamentals of care under fire, tourniquet drills are simple and highly effective. One example is a training scenario in which a SWAT operator in full kit sustains a simulated gunshot wound in an extremity and is then faced with several threat or shoot targets that must be immediately engaged with the SWAT operator's primary weapon. The operator can then move to cover, announcing the injury. Once behind cover, a tourniquet is self-applied. To complete the drill, the operator readies his or her primary weapon and moves back to the starting position, at which point the tourniquet is checked for proper placement and application. This drill reinforces that even if shot, SWAT operators can still shoot, move, and communicate while saving their own lives.

Equally simple and effective tactical field care scenarios can be inserted into tactical entry training. As an example, the SWAT team can be made to encounter an occupant with a gunshot wound with gross bleeding during room entry. Members enter, search, and clear their areas of responsibility. They announce the occupant and, upon seeing the injury, request a medic. While next threats are covered, the injured person is searched and the life-threatening hemorrhage is addressed. An entry team member applies a tourniquet as the team advances. The responding medic, after being relieved from any direct threat responsibilities, can assume care and relieve the entry member.

The options available in training for casualty evacuation are endless. EMS staged at the perimeter could be directed to assume care; a team armored vehicle may be driven directly to the casualty collection point to move patients to a staging area on the perimeter; or helicopter services may be activated, requiring transport of casualties to a landing zone. Although EMS and air medevac are often staged assets for real operations, they are not always available for training. These are opportunities to test procedures such as communications with incident command, notification of perimeter security and sniper/observer teams, retrieval of the TMK from a vehicle, and entry team departure with a casualty. Potential training concentrations include hypothermia prevention management, securing a tactical litter for transport, placement into the designated vehicle (and transport), and medic reassessment and treatment during evacuation.

The need and impact of adding realism to tactical medical scenarios cannot be overstated. A SWAT team member who is repeatedly asked to bring his or her tourniquet to class, apply it, and then check his or her radial pulse is not being adequately trained; a team member who stacks on a door, deploys a flash bang, makes entry, and discovers a screaming role player with a pulsatile femoral bleed is being adequately trained. SWAT operators exposed to an active hemorrhage often report experiencing tunnel vision and auditory exclusion. Realism in trauma scenarios has proven to reduce hesitancy and indecision in both medics and EMS responders. Exposing all team members to this realism in training is critical.

Executive Protection

Today's complex relationships among nations, governments, corporations, and ideologies have led to an increased need for protection of people and places. Although the incidence of hostile incidents may be low in comparison with high-risk warrant service, the protective assignment should not be considered a routine, low-risk detail. Law enforcement, private security, and government agencies have all found that the protective service is itself a tactical environment. The political rally, corporate meeting, and public gathering can each place a very important person (VIP), or protectee, in a position of vulnerability (**Figure 3**). Longitudinal experience has demonstrated that terrorists and other assailants monitor the security approach to these venues for mistakes that afford an opportunity for ambush. **Executive protection** is defined as the use of protective methodologies to reduce the opportunity for hostile forces to impair or eliminate a VIP or protectee.

The most common way to provide protection is to use a bodyguard approach. The bodyguard approach simply provides a strong personal security presence in and around a VIP in an attempt to prevent up-close and clear access to the protectee. This approach is easily defeated and has resulted in the development of dynamic protective methodologies. Major protective services develop elaborate security plans that are based on in-depth assessments of the protective threat. These large, complex plans may vary greatly and attempt to address as many variables in the protective environment as possible.

Figure 3 The political rally, corporate meeting, and public gathering can each place a protectee in a position of vulnerability.

All protective plans immediately face compromise if an injury or medical emergency occurs. Such emergencies require the introduction of a variable response element into the protective environment. If a protective detail has not planned for this diversion, medical responses may be delayed or otherwise hindered, resulting in potential compromise of the patient. Medical emergencies can affect the protectee, a member of his or her staff or family, or even protective detail personnel. An inability of the protective detail to respond, and to respond properly, may have a critical impact on the confidence of the public as well as that of the protectees using the protective service. The most proactive approach to preventing this consequence is to incorporate LER capabilities into the overall protective plan. Whether the LER within a protective service is standing a post, driving in a motorcade, or providing up-close security, his or her expertise in response to a crisis may make the difference between life and death after a hostile threat is encountered. Training, protocols, and resources must be dedicated to ensuring that responders are prepared to manage all medical emergencies, not just penetrating injuries and physical assaults.

The most important consideration of the LER on a protective detail is the understanding that the protective responsibility takes precedence over his or her medical role. Pulling LERs away from their primary role can quickly damage the protective envelope and allow threats to affect the protective detail. LERs assigned to protection must plan to manage medical situations not directly related to the protective assignment with local resources or other dedicated medical personnel. Historical analysis has shown that preventing or eliminating threats is the best way to keep protectees safe. Similarly, preventive health measures and proactive interventions have a significant impact on the health and wellness of protectees and the entire protective detail.

FACTORS INFLUENCING PROTECTIVE PLANNING

A multitude of factors affect the overall security plan. A key factor that the LER should consider is the VIP's own approach to protection, travel, and required exposure. All protective detail leaders and planners would be most comfortable if their protectees were secured in a bunker surrounded by layers of security teams and countermeasures. Unfortunately, this is not feasible, because protectees must generally be interactive and accessible.

A major concern for protective details is the protectee who does not want protection. Whenever possible, the protective detail should include the protectee and his or her staff and families in security planning to prevent confusion and conflict. Frequently, a thorough explanation of the threats and need for resources will reduce the protectee's apprehension. Depending on a specific VIP's attitude about protection, the protective detail may need to provide security interventions covertly. Similarly, medical assets, equipment, and supplies may need to be deployed in nontraditional manners, such as in standard luggage bags. Dedicated medical personnel and resources can be staged discretely in remote locations.

Communication

Include the Protectee in Planning

If possible, the protectee and his or her staff and families should be included in security planning. This allows the protective detail the opportunity to explain the potential threats and resources involved, thus preventing confusion and conflict. Including the protectee in planning is especially helpful when the protectee does not believe protection is needed.

Public gatherings and venues are an inherent obligation for many protectees, and these locations pose threats to protection by creating exposure. LERs should have intimate knowledge of these locations to anticipate threats and to plan for emergencies. Equipment, supplies, and personnel should be staged for secure and immediate access. LERs dedicated to emergency response should have an aperture view of the protectee and his or her surroundings during the entire exposure. The ongoing monitoring should include assessments of the immediate environment for air integrity, radiation, and other physical threats. The LER should also observe the people interacting with the protectee, focusing on movement or conditions that might pose a threat. Should a threat occur, the LER should remain in a position to deploy immediately to the threat or the protectee as needed.

Protectee travel eliminates the safety of a fixed position and creates multiple scenarios that may compromise the protective environment. Even if travel simply uses automotive transportation, LERs must ensure that they are intimately familiar with the routes of travel. Additionally, they should plan for motorcade egress points, potential safe houses, and receiving hospitals that may be necessary should an emergency occur. Medical equipment and personnel should be included in the primary vehicle or motorcade to allow immediate access in the event of life threats. If the travel includes aircraft, both the threat level and logistics of protection planning are increased exponentially. This is further complicated by international itineraries because of the distances involved, the exposure to potential threats, and the inherent medical risks of traveling overseas.

PROTECTIVE MEDICAL SUPPORT

Protective medical support encompasses the plans and protocols that are set in place by a protective detail to respond to a broad range of medical emergencies. The three major categories of medical support models are local resource–dependent, hybrid, and dedicated resource–dependent. Protective details are responsible for determining the best approach to their specific protective environment or threats.

Local Resource–Dependent Model

The local resource–dependent model is often used when a protective detail does not have sufficient resources to allocate to medical response. Using local emergency medical resources has the distinct advantage of reducing costs, interacting well with the local health system, and using nonprotection resources. A major drawback of using local resources is that people outside the protective service may need to be brought into secure areas or have access to protective plans. Further, local resources by definition do not have intrinsic familiarity with fundamental protection logistics and operational principles. For the local resource–dependent model to be successful, the protective details must still receive at least LER training with regular practice and evaluations to allow an effective bridge to the local assets.

Hybrid Model

The hybrid model incorporates dedicated protective detail LERs, emergency medical technicians (EMTs), paramedics, and/or physicians with specific local resources to back up the protective responders. These programs typically work well and are easily replicated by local, state, or federal programs that have emergency medical response assets. This type of program incurs moderate costs but controls the need for local medical access to the immediate protective environment.

Dedicated Resource-Dependent Model

The dedicated resource approach is an elaborate program incorporating medical response teams, vehicles, preplanning, and scenario-based threat countermeasure training. This type of program is necessary in the highest threat environments. Additionally, this type of program most comprehensively maintains operational security needs. Local resources may still often be used to serve backup functions or as remote extensions of the dedicated assets. The major drawbacks of this model are cost and management complexity.

Tip

Medical Support Models

The three major categories of medical support models are as follows:

1. Local resource-dependent
2. Hybrid
3. Dedicated resource-dependent

EXECUTIVE PROTECTION-SPECIFIC PROTOCOLS

Protection-specific medical protocols should be formulated under the direction of the agency's or program's physician medical direction. The medical direction must prioritize the LER's approach to the medical incident, again within the unique context of the protective mission. Conventional EMS protocols typically are driven by responder safety and incremental responses based on threats. Protective medical protocols must adopt the tactical approach that the safety of the protectee is the sole priority, taking precedence over that of the LERs. Using immediate response tactics to provide care under fire and unconventional threats is the priority. LERs may be required to engage ongoing threats or evacuate protectees prior to initiating detailed medical interventions. Medical providers being newly introduced into this environment generally require extensive retraining and conditioning to ensure that the protective mission is not compromised for medical considerations.

Protective protocols should specifically delineate the responsibilities of the LERs, prioritize treatment modalities, provide guidance for patient transfer, and establish transport and hospital designations. Protective detail supervisors should consider these protocols as law enforcement-sensitive and routinely support responder training. Medical training based on these protocols should be mission-specific and, if time and resources permit, include all tiers of dedicated resources.

PROTECTION-BASED SUPPLIES AND EQUIPMENT

The potential need to deploy medical supplies in a covert, nonconventional bag, such as a suitcase or attaché case, has already been described. Additionally, the logistics of executive protection typically preclude the amount of individual and protective detail supplies and equipment, both security and medical, that is deployable as compared with a SWAT operation. This limited depth of supply availability is evidenced by the fact that heavy body armor under LBVs is not routinely worn by protection personnel, and bulky IFAKs are either impractical or unsuitable. In such instances, the protective detail LER may vacuum-seal and distribute personal trauma kits to be paired with tourniquets and carried in a suit pocket. The tactical medical bag may be prepositioned out of view or in a nearby vehicle. Whatever the specifics, these barriers emphasize the need for highly specific training on a routine basis to prevent delays or lack of effectiveness in the event of an emergency.

Active Shooter Scenarios

The proliferation of active shooter incidents is an unfortunate reality both nationally and internationally. Although a root cause analysis remains the subject of intense scrutiny by public health experts and public safety officials alike, law enforcement agencies and EMS systems have worked to develop increasingly effective strategies to respond to such incidents.

What has become clearer as more incidents of this type unfold is that law enforcement and EMS must work closely to plan, train, and ultimately intervene in active shooter scenarios. The LER is uniquely positioned in active shooter scenarios because of the LER's response priorities.

Mass shootings in a civilian setting are not a new phenomenon. The University of Texas shooting event in 1966 was critical in demonstrating that certain hostile situations require a police response beyond the capability of the patrol officer. This event is often cited as a key impetus to the development of the SWAT concept within modern law enforcement. It is perhaps historically ironic, then, that more recent active shooter events in our history have led to the evolving consensus that an effective law enforcement response must go beyond that of a tactical team. Following the high-profile incident at Columbine High School in 1999, among others, law enforcement has specifically reevaluated priorities in response to active shooter scenarios (**Figure 4**).

An active shooter incident occurs when "one or more individuals use deadly force against others and continue to do so while having unrestricted access to additional victims." Since the advent of SWAT, the conventional law enforcement response to an ongoing shooting incident has involved responding patrol officers cordoning off the perimeter and awaiting the arrival of a tactical element. This approach typically costs time. When balanced against the recognition that time is the enemy in traumatic injuries and that delays add to the predicted morbidity and mortality of casualties in an active shooter scenario, alternate strategies have been developed.

Figure 4 Following the high-profile incident at Columbine High School in 1999, among others, law enforcement has specifically reevaluated priorities in response to active shooter scenarios.

MEDICAL RESPONSE IN ACTIVE SHOOTER SCENARIOS

The current paradigm in active shooter response by law enforcement prioritizes speed. Along these lines, the model adopted by many agencies involves hastily organized teams of typically four responding officers, deploying forward in a diamond formation. This team moves through unsecured areas, in the direction of ongoing shooting, bypassing casualties. Its singular mission is to seek, engage, and neutralize the shooter or shooters.

Conventional EMS protocols hold as a fundamental tenet of scene and provider safety. This presents a challenge in active shooter scenarios because often the time required to declare an entire scene fully secured can be prolonged. This can be true despite the successful efforts of an impromptu law enforcement response team in neutralizing the threat. In such instances, the initial medical care of casualties may still be delayed until EMS providers are allowed to enter a scene or casualties are evacuated by law enforcement to a collection point.

LERs can be a tremendous asset, filling a critical void in these situations. The initial response priority would remain the law enforcement mission; however, once threats are neutralized, the LER would immediately be able to backtrack and render casualty care to the critically wounded. Because the composition of active shooter response teams is expected to be heterogeneous, potentially composed of both on- and off-duty officers drawn from different agencies, the availability of LERs in specific incidents cannot be reliably predicted. However, widespread LER training would ultimately mitigate such inconsistencies. This further justifies the wide distribution of IFAKs at the patrol officer level, as well as dedicated LER kits if applicable.

There are evolving models of EMS care in response to active shooter incidents. Certain modified approaches shift EMS personnel into more forward elements of initial responses, whether incorporated into the actual law enforcement response team or paired with tactical officers for direct cover. Regardless of specifics, all such approaches present greater risk to EMS providers and mandate prospective planning, aggressive training, and close working relationships among law enforcement and EMS agency personnel.

The staging and deployment of EMS equipment and supplies for the active shooter incident is also subject to reevaluation. EMS providers typically work in pairs or teams, working out of one or more large shared supply bags that are typically staged in vehicles. As alternative EMS approaches to active shooter scenarios develop, it is likely that individual providers will work singly, or partnered with law enforcement personnel. The need to deploy with smaller, individualized medical bags is likely to become increasingly apparent.

Animal Threats and Control

People view animals as family, friends, property, a form of recreation, and an interesting diversion. Love them, like them, or hate them, animals are a part of all our lives. Animals, like people, have their own opinion about their place in the world. Many of their behaviors are consistent with how they have been treated, trained, and socialized. All animals have the potential to respond with aggression when they perceive danger. No one has a better understanding of these threats than the animal control officer. Routinely, these officers are called to deal with frightened, sick, injured, or abandoned animals. Many animal control officers deal with domestic livestock and wildlife as well. All LERs should have some general understanding about types of animals, their risks, and techniques to prevent personal harm. Most responders should be especially familiar with dogs as a potential personal safety concern.

Animal Control Officers

If you are conducting a mission and anticipate encountering a wild or domestic animal, interview the animal control resources that are available in that area. Animal control programs are typically local or state programs. They can range from unarmed volunteers to sworn law enforcement officers. All of these programs have regular experience in handling, managing, and caring for the animals typically found in their region. Many programs also have access to specialists who are capable of helping you with exotic pets or livestock.

During an emergency response, the typical animal control program should be able to gain control over routine domestic pets such as dogs and cats, as well as exotic pets such as birds and reptiles. Some programs have the ability to handle large livestock and may also have access to a specialist who can provide sedation to troubled herd animals.

Occasionally, an animal control program may have wildlife responsibilities. If wildlife is a concern and your local animal control program does not have wildlife responsibilities, contact local or state departments of natural resources, park police, or park rangers for guidance.

Animal control officers are an asset in educating you about or assisting you with an animal you encounter during a warrant service or investigation. To possess certain livestock or kennels, a jurisdiction may require an inspection of the property for licensing. Locations with watchdogs may have a history of the dogs making noise or threatening people. It is likely that the animal control officer has been to the location of your mission in the recent past. This site knowledge can be a great resource when assessing threats, floor plans, work schedules, and occupants of a home or neighborhood.

Animal control officers are busy responding to their normal assignments. If your need is not an emergency, you should schedule a briefing, show them surveillance footage of any animals you are unclear about, and, if possible, have them stand by at a staging area prior to the mission. If you take the owner of an animal into custody, you must consider the care and handling of any pets or livestock left behind. Planning this in advance will allow the movement of logistics and resources to reduce injury or suffering to you and the animals.

Animal Threat Tactics

LERs should immediately assess for danger associated with domestic or wild animals at the location of a mission. Although you may encounter exotic pets or livestock, domestic dogs are overwhelmingly the primary threat when responding to an emergency.

Threats From Canines

Domestic dogs are credited with 800,000 bites each year. The primary victims of these bites are children, the elderly, and US postal workers. The LER entering a location with dogs should assess the scene for the following:

- Beware of Dog signs
- Food or water bowls
- Pet toys
- Dog chains, runs, feces, or houses
- Scratches on doors

Dogs exhibit a wide range of behaviors; even the most adorable dog can and will display **aggression** in certain circumstances (**Figure 5**). For dogs, aggression is best defined as a range of behaviors that may result in a sequence of increasing hostility or may occur at random with little or no warning. Aggressive behaviors may include a quiet, rigid stance; guttural barks; growling; lunging; showing teeth; snarling; snapping; mouthing; nipping; biting; and shaking. Aggressive behavior can occur as a result of training, breeding, or circumstances. Responders should consider different types of aggression and how their actions may stimulate a hostile response (**Table 1**).

Figure 5 Even the most adorable dog can become aggressive in certain circumstances.

All breeds can respond with aggression. Dogs that are bred to provide security or to protect against predators are more

Table 1

Aggressive Canine Behaviors

Behavior	Description
Territorial	Guarding area or property from intruders.
Protective	Defending perceived threats to the pack or a pack member.
Possessive	Protecting others from access to objects or places associated with the pack.
Fearful	Unable to escape a threat, the dog will prepare to fight.
Defensive	No attempt to retreat; the dog chooses to put up a fight to fend off the threat.
Social	Responding with aggressive behavior to a member of the pack.
Frustrated	Held back from achieving a goal, the dog strikes at the restraint or obstacle.
Redirected	A nonrelated person or object gets in the way of the dog's aggressive response.
Pain	An injured or ill dog strikes out as a result of potential or realized pain.
Sex-related	Competing for access to the opposite sex.
Predatory	Classic canine hunting urge; the dog attacks fast-moving or running objects with no warning.

Source: American Society for the Protection of Animals.

likely to move quickly into an aggressive stance. If these animals are further conditioned by humans to alert and respond to perceived intruders, the response can be devastating. If you are confronted by a dog and you have time, assess the dog's posture. Dogs staring directly at you or out of the corner of their eyes can indicate a pending aggressive outburst. Do not stare directly at the dog's eyes; doing so is considered a threat and will precipitate an aggressive response. Dogs will retract their lips and expose their teeth to signal they are prepared to respond forcibly to your presence. Some breeds will extend their lips over the front of their gums and blow up their mouths to look larger. A wrinkled brow, laid-back ears, an extended muzzle, and exposed teeth are visual evidence a dog has turned aggressive and that an attack may occur if the dog is further provoked.

If you are confronted by a dog that displays aggressive behavior, stop, do not make eye contact, and keep your hands or arms at your side. If possible, do not stand facing the dog; attempt to stand with the side of your body facing the dog. If you have to move a hand or arm, move slowly. Do not turn and run. When the dog loses interest, back away slowly. If the dog does attack, present to the dog's mouth some item like a jacket, purse, backpack, or flashlight and continue to back away, protecting your arms and body from bites. If you get knocked down, cover your ears and roll into a ball, protecting your face and throat (**Figure 6**). If you have a fire extinguisher or defensive spray canister and are confident in its use, you may be able to scare off many breeds of dogs. Dog sprays, mace, pepper sprays, and tear gas do not work on all dogs. Lethal force should be used based on your agency's policies.

Figure 6 If you get knocked down by an animal, cover your ears and roll into a ball, protecting your face and throat.

If you are bitten by a dog, don't panic. As soon as you are free from the dog, call for assistance and secure yourself in a protective location such as a vehicle or building. The dog may be excited to the point that it will attack others. Treat all wounds as you would any other wounds. If the wounds are minor in nature, wash, clean, and bandage the wounds. If the dog bites a body part such as a finger, arm, or leg, it is possible that tissue will be damaged and bones will be broken. Do not disregard the seriousness of a dog bite.

After you have ensured your safety, secure the dog and owners based on your agency's policies and seek physician evaluation. If the dog is wounded, do not approach it. Wounded animals will be quickly provoked into a defensive response. The animal's immunization records will be required. If the animal does not have records, it may be detained or examined for disease.

Threats From Exotic Pets

An exotic pet is any animal that is not indigenous to the environment. Domestic dogs and cats are considered indigenous to American society. Examples of exotic pets include reptiles, primates, hedgehogs, predatory cats, spiders, zebras, pigs, camels, scorpions, wolves, wolf hybrids, dingoes, dingo hybrids, coyotes, birds of prey, and parrots. Many of these animals can be possessed legally. Exotic pets that have a history of aggressive activity may require local, state, or federal permits.

When dealing with exotic species, the LER should always be on the alert for aggressive behavior. There are cases in which exotic pets such as poisonous reptiles, aggressive lizards, and predatory cats and dogs are kept illegally and discretely by the pet owner. When apprehended, pet owners keeping illegal, aggressive exotic animals often say they kept them as status symbols or as defensive measures against trespassers or law enforcement.

When dealing with a scene that may contain exotic pets, you should always have animal control officers (and, in certain cases, specialty veterinarians) available near or at the site to identify the animal and advise on how to work with or around the animal. A good practice when issuing a warrant is to secure the humans and then have the animal control officers locate the exotic pets and house them until after the property search is completed. If you face the threat of injury from a predatory exotic animal, EMS should also be staged near or at the site. Wounds from exotic animals can range from simple bites and scratches to mauling, crushing injuries, and lethal envenomations.

Threats From Livestock

If your assignment puts you in close proximity to livestock, take a good look at the animal housing areas. Assess pens and housing, ensuring that the animals are well contained. A pursuit in or around livestock can lead to encounters with heavy animals that can cause severe injury or death. Horses, swine, and cattle will defend themselves by flight. They will turn and run until they feel cornered. Horses can defend themselves with kicking, biting, or crushing. Cattle can kick, bite, stampede, or gore when threatened. Swine will attack when threatened and can bite or gore their intended target. Domestic swine typically have short tusks, which can cause serious injury (**Figure 7**). When a domestic swine flees captivity, it can quickly adapt to survive in the wild. A domestic swine that turns wild is called a **feral pig**. Feral pigs do not change drastically in appearance from the domestic pig, but the feral pig's tusks will lengthen, sharpen, and be capable of producing lethal injuries.

Figure 7 Domestic swine typically have short tusks, which can cause serious injury. When a domestic swine flees captivity, it can quickly adapt to survive in the wild.

Livestock involved in transportation accidents or loose in public can create an extreme hazard. Responding vehicle lights and sirens can spook large animals, resulting in unwanted movements or stampedes. Immediately, LERs should clear all people away from the area and call in animal control officers to manage the herd. Novice attempts to control, exterminate, or herd livestock can quickly result in stampedes that result in property damage and loss of life. LERs should consider a few hours' training from a local source to address how to respond to livestock-related emergencies. Agencies that may encounter livestock should develop use of force policies and shooting instructions that can result in the swift termination of a livestock threat.

Agencies should keep a list and contact information of area veterinarians who are capable of responding to motor vehicle crashes involving livestock to help manage wounded animals or advise on the need to humanely euthanize an animal.

Threats From Wildlife

Animals that live on their own without domestic support are considered **wildlife**. LERs must become familiar with the types and habits of wildlife found in their response area (**Figure 8**). Behaviorally, a good rule of thumb is to sort these animals into classes such as herd animals (deer, sheep, antelope, feral pigs), predators (cats, canines, bears, birds of prey, wolverines, badgers), and varmints (groundhogs, squirrels, raccoons).

It is common for wildlife to enter suburban or urban settings, creating panic and injury. A well-founded understanding of these animals' traits can help the LER reduce injury and damage. Any bite or scratch from a wild animal requires medical attention. All of these animals potentially carry diseases such as rabies and distemper. Saliva from a rabid animal can enter the human body from any skin opening or contact with a mucous membrane.

Agencies available to help the LER include local animal control, state departments of natural resources and wildlife, local or state wildlife biologists, park police, and park rangers.

CONCLUSION

LERs are a vital part of special missions and responses. In many special weapons and tactics programs, members routinely practice for care under fire and tactical field care. Tactical

Figure 8 LERs must become familiar with the types of wildlife found in their response area.

medical personnel are frequently part of these teams. Local EMS programs are not routinely aware of the capabilities of the LER or tactical medics. In some cases, special teams do not have routine training with traditional police forces. LERs as members of special teams and LERs from traditional police services should consider joint training exercises to ensure the best possible results when an operational emergency occurs. Special teams should also establish relationships with local EMS programs to prevent complications that can occur with patient hand-off and tactical evacuation care. Special teams and security programs that specialize in executive protection face unique challenges associated with operating inside the protective environment. Security can result in a delay for traditional EMS resources. Understanding the resources you have available and implementing a protective medical program will provide life-saving interventions should an accident or attack occur.

Animals are frequently and routinely encountered by police, security, and special teams. Animal control officers and park rangers are specialized law enforcement programs that are well versed in handling domestic animals and wildlife. LERs should be aware of the resources they have available to assist them when they encounter animals that can threaten their personnel. Law enforcement agencies should recognize the significance of these animals as threats and practice methods to prevent or survive an attack from a canine.

Prep Kit

READY FOR REVIEW

- In police special operations and tactics, mission-specific considerations such as the selection of medical equipment, supplies, and load-out are more scrutinized, and the application of tactical medicine is very closely followed.
- An essential specialty assignment within the SWAT team is a member who is also trained as a tactical medic.
- Tactical combat casualty care (TCCC) has become the widely referenced military model for tactical medicine and has resulted in both the development of an approach and streamlining of equipment to address predictable causes of preventable death.
- Medical scenarios should be incorporated into every SWAT training evolution.
- Realism in trauma scenarios has proven to reduce the hesitancy and indecision in both medics and EMS responders. Exposing all team members to this realism in training is critical.
- The most common way to provide executive protection is to use a bodyguard approach, providing a strong personal security presence in and around a VIP in an attempt to prevent up-close and clear access to the protectee.
- The most important consideration of the LER on a protective detail is the understanding that the protective responsibility takes precedence over his or her medical role.
- A major concern for protective details is the protectee who does not want protection. Whenever possible, the protective detail should include the protectee and his or her staff and families in security planning to prevent confusion and conflict.
- The three major categories of medical support models are local resource–dependent, hybrid, and dedicated resource–dependent. Protective details are responsible for determining the best approach to their specific protective environment or threats.
- Protection-specific medical protocols should specifically delineate the responsibilities of the LERs, prioritize treatment modalities, provide guidance for patient transfer, and establish transport and hospital designations.
- The current paradigm in active shooter response by law enforcement prioritizes speed.
- Conventional EMS protocols hold as a fundamental tenet scene and provider safety. This presents a challenge in active shooter scenarios because often the time required to declare an entire scene fully secured can be prolonged.
- Many animal behaviors are consistent with how the animal has been treated, trained, and socialized.
- All law enforcement responders should have some general understanding about types of animals, their risks, and techniques to prevent personal harm.
- If you are conducting a mission and you anticipate encountering a wild or domestic animal, interview the animal control resources that are available in that area.
- Law enforcement responders should immediately assess for danger associated with domestic or wild animals at the location of a mission. Although you may encounter exotic pets or livestock, domestic dogs are overwhelmingly the primary threat when responding to an emergency.

VITAL VOCABULARY

aggression A range of behaviors that may result in a sequence of increasing hostility or may occur at random with little or no warning.

executive protection The use of protective methodologies to reduce the opportunity for hostile forces to impair or eliminate a VIP or protectee.

feral pig A domestic swine that turns wild.

protective medical support The plans and protocols that are set in place by a protective detail to respond to a broad range of medical emergencies.

wildlife Animals that live on their own without domestic support.

CHECK YOUR KNOWLEDGE

You are going to serve a warrant on a potentially violent criminal who owns three attack dogs. Surveillance has indicated that the dogs are very aggressive and bark regularly. Animal control has made visits to deal with neighborhood complaints.

1. Animal control should be contacted prior to the raid to gain intelligence on the residence and to stand by to handle dogs after the warrant is served.
   - A. True
   - B. False
2. Which of the following occupations are most frequently injured by dogs annually?
   - A. Farm workers
   - B. Veterinarians
   - C. Postal workers
   - D. Teachers
3. Which of the following clues would indicate that a dog resides at a residence you have responded to?
   - A. Children
   - B. Food and water bowls
   - C. "No trespassing" signs
   - D. Loud music
4. You open your cruiser door and you see a golden retriever barking loudly and showing his teeth, inside a chain-link fence that surrounds the residence. What kind of behavior is this dog showing?
   - A. Territorial
   - B. Fearful
   - C. Social
   - D. Frustrated
5. Which of the following fluids can transmit rabies from an animal to a human?
   - A. Urine
   - B. Blood
   - C. Saliva
   - D. All of the above

Assessment in **Action**

SCENARIO

You are preparing to travel to an international law enforcement symposium and will be away from home for 10 days. The country to which you are traveling is known to have problems with its drinking water supply. Flying to your destination will take approximately 12 hours.

ACTIONS

1. Which of the following would be acceptable while visiting the country?
   A. Eating local produce
   B. Using a water purification device
   C. Swimming in a lake near your hotel
   D. Self-medicating with prescription antibiotics
2. Additional information regarding health care and common travel illnesses in the country you are visiting should be obtained from all of the following, EXCEPT:
   A. A travel magazine
   B. US State Department
   C. Your department's medical director
   D. A travel clinic

During flight, the crew announces there is a medical emergency onboard and is soliciting help from anyone who has medical training. You identify yourself as being able to help, so the crew takes you to the patient. The patient is complaining of being nauseated and weak. He has vomited several times and appears pale.

3. Who will provide on-line medical direction for care of this patient?
   A. The airline's medical service
   B. Your agency's medical director
   C. The State Department
   D. You don't need medical direction when in-flight.
4. Performing skills that are not part of your regular scope of practice is acceptable when traveling.
   A. True
   B. False
5. The decision to divert the plane and land before reaching the final destination will be made by:
   A. the medical care provider.
   B. flight attendants.
   C. medical direction.
   D. the captain.

Answer Key

ASSESSMENT IN ACTION

Section 1
1. C
2. B
3. B
4. B
5. D

Section 2
1. C
2. D
3. A
4. B
5. C

Section 3
1. A
2. B
3. C
4. A
5. C

Section 4
1. B
2. A
3. A
4. B
5. D

Section 5
1. A
2. A
3. D
4. C
5. D

Section 6
1. B
2. D
3. A
4. C
5. A

Section 7
1. B
2. C
3. A
4. D
5. D

Section 8
1. B
2. A
3. A
4. B
5. D

CHECK YOUR KNOWLEDGE

Unit 1
1. A
2. C
3. B
4. B
5. B

Unit 2
1. A
2. C
3. C
4. D
5. B

Unit 3
1. A
2. D
3. C
4. B
5. A

Unit 4
1. C
2. A
3. A
4. D
5. D

Unit 5
1. C
2. B
3. B
4. D
5. D

Unit 6
1. C
2. D
3. B
4. B
5. A

Unit 7
1. C
2. D
3. D
4. D
5. C

Unit 8
1. C
2. B
3. C
4. A
5. B

Unit 9
1. A
2. D
3. A
4. C
5. B

Unit 10
1. C
2. D
3. A
4. A
5. B

Unit 11
1. B
2. A
3. C
4. D
5. A

Unit 12
1. A
2. A
3. C
4. D
5. B

Unit 13
1. C
2. B
3. C
4. A
5. C

Unit 14
1. A
2. B
3. B
4. B
5. A

Unit 15
1. C
2. B
3. B
4. B
5. D

Unit 16
1. A
2. A
3. C
4. A
5. D

Unit 17
1. A
2. A
3. B
4. B
5. C

Unit 18
1. A
2. C
3. A
4. C
5. D

Unit 19
1. B
2. D
3. C
4. B
5. A

Unit 20
1. A
2. A
3. D
4. D
5. D

Unit 21
1. B
2. B
3. A
4. C
5. D

Unit 22
1. C
2. A
3. C
4. B
5. C

Unit 23
1. D
2. B
3. C
4. B
5. C

Unit 24
1. B
2. C
3. D
4. A
5. A

Unit 25
1. B
2. A
3. D
4. D
5. A

Unit 26
1. B
2. C
3. C
4. C
5. A

Unit 27
1. A
2. C
3. B
4. A
5. D

References

Jones and Bartlett Internal References are on file and available upon request.

EMERGENCY MEDICAL SERVICES SYSTEMS

National Highway Traffic Safety Administration (NHTSA), EMS [homepage]. Washington, DC. http://www.ems.gov. Accessed October 9, 2009.

MISSION PREPLANNING

North Carolina Tactical Medical Association, Medical Threat Assessment/Preplanning Template. http://www.tacmedics.com/sections/resources/med_threat_assess/mta_template_draft%20_v2_1.pdf

Planning and Managing Security for Major Special Events: Training and Curricula. Medical Threat Assessment.

DOCUMENTATION

Commonwealth of Pennsylvania: *The Pennsylvania Code.* http://www.pacode.com/secure/data/028/chapter1001/subchapCtoc.html. Accessed May 8, 2010.

ETHICAL AND LEGAL CONSIDERATIONS

Scholendorff v. Society of New York Hospital, 211 N.Y. 125, 105 N.E. 92 (1914).

FORENSICS

US Department of Justice: *Death Investigation: a Guide for the Scene Investigators.* http://www.ncjrs.gov

US Department of Justice: *Crime Scene Investigation: a Guide for Law Enforcement.* http://www.ojp.usdoj.gov/nij/pubs-sum/178280.htm

MENTAL AND PHYSICAL WELLNESS

Chaplain Fellowship Ministries, a national Law Enforcement Organization. http://www.chaplain-ministries.com/. Accessed June 12, 2010.

Goldfarb, D: *The Effects of Stress on Police Officers.* http://www.heavybadge.com/efstress.htm. Accessed June 10, 2010.

Goldfarb, D: *Police Stress.* http://www.soc.umn.edu/~samaha/cases/police_stress.htm. Accessed June 10, 2010.

Huda, MN. (July 3, 2003). The Daily Star. *The Stress Factor in Policing.* http://www.thedailystar.net/2003/07/03/d30703150278.htm. Accessed June 10, 2010.

Institute of Hazardous Materials Management. http://www.ihmm.org/dspwhatishazmat.cfm. Accessed June 12, 2010.

Twersky-Glasner, A: Police Personality: What is it and why are they like that? *J Police & Criminal Psychol* 2005; 20(1).

LINE OF DUTY DEATH

McGuire, DJ: CISM Perspectives, 2002. CISM Perspectives. www.cismperspectives.com. Accessed September 18, 2009.

Kates, AR: *Cop Shock.* Tucson, AZ, Holbrook Street Press, 1999.

National Law Enforcement Memorial Foundation, Annual Report, 2008.

SCENE MANAGEMENT

Federal Emergency Management Agency (FEMA) website: http://www.fema.gov

HAZARDOUS MATERIALS ACCIDENTS AND WEAPONS

US Fire Administration (USFA): *Information for emergency responders.* 2003(July 17).

NARCOTICS AND CLANDESTINE LABS

National Drug Intelligence Center [Homepage], 319 Washington Street, 5th Floor, Johnstown, PA 15901-1622, July 31, 2009. http://www.usdoj.gov/ndic/index.htm#Top. Accessed October 5, 2009.

National Drug Intelligence Center [Homepage], 319 Washington Street, 5th Floor, Johnstown, PA 15901-1622, July 31, 2009. http://www.usdoj.gov/ndic/pubs37/37035/indoor.htm#Top. Accessed October 5, 2009.

Oregon Department of Human Resources Drug Lab Cleanup Program [Homepage], 800 NE Oregon St., Suite 640, Portland, OR 97232, June 25, 2005. http://www.oregon.gov/DHS/ph/druglab/docs/methlab.pdf. Accessed October 12, 2009.

Partnership for a Drug-Free America, [Homepage], 405 Lexington Avenue, Suite 1601, New York, NY 10174. http://www.drugfree.org/Portal/DrugIssue/MethResources/meth_faq.html. Accessed October 12, 2009.

National Drug Intelligence Center [Homepage], 319 Washington Street, 5th Floor, Johnstown, PA 15901-1622, July 31, 2009, archived January 1, 2006. http://www.usdoj.gov/ndic/pubs7/7341/index.htm. Accessed October 6, 2009.

Mallinckrodt Inc. [Homepage], 675 McDonnell Blvd., St. Louis, MO 63042, April 9, 2008. http://bulkpharm.mallinckrodt.com/_attachments/msds/COCAI.htm. Accessed October 2, 2009.

WATER RESCUE

DuBois David: Stingray Injury. http://www.emedicinehealth.com/stingray_injury/page6_em.htm. Accessed February 27, 2012.

MedlinePlus: Scorpion Fish Sting. http://www.nlm.nih.gov/medlineplus/ency/article/002849.htm. Accessed February 28, 2012.

Stöppler Melissa Conrad: Motion Sickness. http://www.emedicinehealth.com/motion_sickness/article_em.htm. Accessed February 27, 2012.

Mayo Clinic staff: Motion sickness: First aid. http://www.mayoclinic.com/health/first-aid-motion-sickness/HQ01099. Accessed February 27, 2012.

Plantz Scott H: Coral Cuts. http://www.emedicinehealth.com/wilderness_coral_cuts/page2_em.htm. Accessed February 27, 2012.

Centers for Disease Control and Prevention: Unintentional Drowning: Fact Sheet. http://www.cdc.gov/HomeandRecreationalSafety/Water-Safety/waterinjuries-factsheet.html. Accessed February 27, 2012.

Website: Cold Water Boot Camp. http://www.coldwaterbootcamp.com/pages/home.html. Accessed February 27, 2012.

US Department of Commerce, NOAA: A Mariner's Guide to Marine Weather Services: Coastal, Offshore and High Seas. http://www.nws.noaa.gov/om/brochures/mw_coastal.pdf. Accessed February 27, 2012.

Pearn JH: Secondary drowning in children. *BMJ* 1980; 281(6248):1103-1105. http://www.ncbi.nlm.nih.gov/pmc/articles/PMC1714551/. Accessed February 27, 2012.

TOXICOLOGY

Nelson LS, Lewin NA, Howland MA, Hoffman RS, Goldfrank LR, Flomenbaum NE: *Goldfrank's Toxicologic Emergencies*, ed 9. New York, McGraw-Hill, 2011.

Choi IS: Delayed neurological sequelae in carbon monoxide intoxication. *Arch Neurol* 1983;40:433-435.

Weaver LK, Hopkins RO, Chan KJ, et al: Hyperbaric oxygen for acute carbon monoxide poisoning. *N Engl J Med* 2002;347:1057-1067.

Holstege CP, Kirk M, Sidell FR: Chemical warfare nerve agent poisoning. *Crit Care Clin* 1997;13:923-942.

Duodote Auto-Injector [package insert]. Columbia, MD, Meridian Medical Technologies Inc., 2007.

EROWID website: Documenting the Complex Relationship Between Humans & Psychoactives. http://www.erowid.org. Accessed February 27, 2012.

Duberstein JL, Kaufman DM: A clinical study of an epidemic of heroin intoxication and heroin-induced pulmonary edema. *Am J Med* 1971;51:704-714.

Marzuk PM, Tardiff K, Leon AC, et al: Ambient temperature and mortality from unintentional cocaine overdose. *JAMA* 1998;279:1795-1800.

Goldfrank LR, Hoffman RS. The cardiovascular effects of cocaine. *Ann Emerg Med* 1991;20:165-175.

Ajaelo I, Koenig K, Snoey E: Severe hyponatremia and inappropriate antidiuretic hormone secretion following ecstasy use. *Acad Emerg Med* 1998;5:839-840.

McCarron M, Schulze BW, Thompson GA, et al: Acute phencyclidine intoxication: Incidence of clinical findings in 1000 cases. *Ann Emerg Med* 1981;10:237-242.

Mills CA, Flacke JW, Flacke WE, et al: Narcotic reversal in hypercapneic dogs: Comparison of naloxone and nalbuphine. *Can J Anaesth* 1990;37:238-244.

Chin MY, Kreutzer RA, Dyer JE. Acute poisoning from gamma-hydroxybutyrate in California. *West J Med* 1992;156: 380-384.

Chan TC, Vilke GM, Neuman T: Reexamination of custody restraint position and positional asphyxia. *Am J Forensic Med Pathol* 1998;19:201-205.

Hurblut KM, Dart RC, Spaite D: Reliability of clinical presentation for predicting significant pit viper envenomation. *Ann Emerg Med* 1988;12:438.

Simon TL, Grace TG: Envenomation coagulopathy in wounds from pit vipers. *N Engl J Med* 1981;305:443-447.

Kitchens CS, Van Mierop LHS. Envenomation by the eastern coral snake (*Micurus fulvius fulvius*). *JAMA* 1987;258: 1615-1618.

Maretic Z. Latrodectism: Variations in clinical manifestations provoked by *Latrodectus* species of spiders. *Toxicon* 1983;21:457-466.

Gueron M, Ilia R, Sofer S: The cardiovascular system after scorpion envenomation. A review. *J Toxicol Clin Toxicol* 1992;30:245-258.

HEAT AND COLD EXPOSURE

Bouchama A, Knochel JP: Heat stroke. *N Engl J Med.* 2002;346:1978-1988.

Kilbourne EM, Choi K, Jones TS, Thacker SB: Risk factors for heatstroke. *JAMA.* 1982;247:3332-3336.

Danzl DF, Pozos RS: Accidental hypothermia. *N Engl J Med.* 1994;331:1756-1760.

Lazar HL: The treatment of hypothermia. *N Engl J Med.* 1997;337:1545.

HIGH ALTITUDE SICKNESS

Auerbach PS, Donner HJ, Weiss EA. *Field Guide to Wilderness Medicine*, ed 3. Philadelphia, PA, Mosby Elsevier, 2008.

Basnyat B, Murdoch DR: High-altitude illness. *Lancet* 2003;361:1967-1974.

Hackett PH, Roach RC: High altitude cerebral edema. *High Altitude Med Biol* 2004;5(2):136-146.

Hackett PH, Roach RC: High altitude illness. *N Engl J Med* 2001;345(2):107-114.

Wedmore, Laselle BT: Altitude illness: Strategies in prevention, identification, and treatment. *Emergency Medicine Practice* 2007;9(3):1-24.

West JB: The physiologic basis of high altitude diseases. *Ann Intern Med* 2004;141:789-800.

TACTICAL CASUALTY CARE

Butler FK, Hagmann J, Butler EG: Tactical combat casualty care in special operations. *Mil Med* 1996;161(suppl): 3-16.

American College of Surgeons-Consultation Verification Program. (ACS-COT). http://www.facs.org/trauma/vcprogram.html

NATO Logistic Handbook, October 1997, Chapter 16.

CoTCCC, Tactical Combat Casualty Care guidelines, update 2010. Current TCCC Guidelines can be found at: http://www.health.mil/Education_And_Training/TCCC.aspx

Co TECC, Committee for Tactical Emergency Care, 2012. Information found at: http://c-tecc.org/?doing_wp_cron

ORDNANCE BALLISTICS

Apfelbaum JD, Shockley LW, Wahe JW, Moore EE: Entrance and exit gunshot wounds: Incorrect terms for the emergency department? *J Emerg Med* 16:741-745.

Fackler ML: Ballistic injury. *Ann Emerg Med* 15:110-114.

Fackler ML: Gunshot wound review. *Ann Emerg Med* 1996;28(2):194-203.

Greenberg MJ, Wipfler EJ: Medical ballistics. *The Tactical Edge* 2006;Fall.

The forensic aspects of gunshot wounds in Marx J, Hockberger R, Walls R (eds): *Marx: Rosen's Emergency Medicine*, ed. 7. Philadelphia, PA, Mosby Elsevier, 2009.

US Department of Justice: Ballistic Resistance of Body Armor NIJ Standard-0101.06. *NIJ Standards* 2008;July.

Beekley AC, Starnes BW, Sebesta JA: Lessons learned from modern military surgery. *Surg Clin N Am* 2007;87: 157-184.

Miller MA, Levesky ME: Chest injury while wearing a bulletproof vest. *Am J Emerg Med* 2008;26:736.

Lanoix R: C-Spine injury associated with gunshot wounds to the head: A retrospective study and literature review. *J Trauma* 2000;49(5):860-863.

EXPLOSIONS AND BLASTS

Centers for Disease Control and Prevention: Blast Injuries: Fact Sheets for Professionals. http://emergency.cdc.gov/masscasualties/blastinjuryfacts.asp. Accessed September 24, 2009.

Columbia University Libraries: The Wall Street explosion: capitalism, terrorism, and the 1920 bombing of New York. http://app.cul.columbia.edu:8080/ac/handle/10022/AC:P:7431. Accessed September 24, 2009.

Cable News Network: Explosion damages Atlanta family planning clinic. http://cgi.cnn.com/US/9701/16/abortion/index.html. Accessed September 24, 2009.

Bureau of Alcohol, Tobacco, Firearms and Explosives: *Pararescue Medication and Procedure Handbook*, ed 2. 2001, p 56.

Bureau of Alcohol, Tobacco, Firearms and Explosives: *Special Operations Forces Medical Handbook*, ed 2. 2008, pp 7-25.

Bureau of Alcohol, Tobacco, Firearms and Explosives: *Fire Officers Handbook of Tactics*, ed 3. 2005, chapter 20.

LESS LETHAL MUNITIONS

Burgess L: Troops train to use nonlethal weapons to control crowds, reduce civilian deaths. *Stars and Stripes, Stripes Sunday Magazine*, December 22, 2002.

Godoy G: Police Oral Boards and the Use of Force Continuum. http:www.policetest.info. Accessed August 26, 2009.

National Tactical Officers Association: NTOA National Statistical Database. Less Lethal Database. Accessed September 11, 2009.

Olajos EJ, Stopford W: *Riot Control Agents: Issues in Toxicology, Safety, and Health*. Boca Raton, FL, CRC Press, 2004.

Defense Technology. Instructor Certification Program—Oleoresin Capsicum Aerosol Projectors. May 2009.

Wax PM, Becker CE, Curry SC: Unexpected "gas" casualties in Moscow: A medical toxicology perspective. *Ann Emerg Med* 2003;41:700-705.

Lavy T, Abu Asleh A: Ocular rubber bullet injuries. *Eye* 2003;17:821-824.

Mahajna A, Aboud N, Harbaji I, et al: Blunt and penetrating injuries caused by rubber bullets during the Israeli-Arab conflict in October 2000: A retrospective study. *Lancet* 2002;359:1795-1800.

Chute DJ, Smialek JE. Injury patterns in a plastic (AR-1) baton fatality. *Am J Forensic Med Pathol* 1998;19:226-229.

Gross M, Regev E, Hamdan K, et al: Penetrating rubber bullet into the ethmoid sinus: Should the bullet be removed? *Otolaryngology* 2005;133:814-816.

Steele JA, McBride SJ, Kelly J, et al: Plastic bullet injuries in Northern Ireland: Experiences during a week of civil disturbance. *J Trauma* 1999;46:711-714.

Roux FE, Mejdoubi M: Potential neurosurgical damage of rubber bullets. Analysis of 2 pediatric cases. *Neurochirurgie* 2001;47:576-579.

Defense Technology. Instructor Certification Program-Specialty Impact Munitions. May 2009.

Taser International. Law Enforcement Overview. www.taser.com. Accessed September 11, 2009.

Cronin JM, Ederheimer JA: Conducted Energy Devices: Development of Standards for Consistency and Guidance. US Department of Justice. Office of Community Oriented Policing Services and Police Executive Research Forum. Washington DC, 2006.

Amnesty International: List of deaths following use of stun weapons in US law enforcement. June 2001 to August 31 2008. *Amnesty International Publications* 2008.

National Institute of Justice: *Study of Deaths Following Electro Muscular Disruption: Interim Report*. US Department of Justice, Office of Justice Programs, 2008.

Rabinowitz CB: Use of Tasers by Law Enforcement Agencies (Resolution 401, A-08). American Medical Association. *Report of the Council on Science and Public Health. CSAPH Report* 6-A-09, 2009.

Anonymous: Conducted Energy Device (CED) Glossary of Terms. *Police Executive Research Forum*. PERF Center on Force and Accountability, 2005.

Stinger Systems: Stinger Systems Products. www.stingersystems.com. Accessed September 11, 2009.

Mehl LE: Electrical injury from tasering and miscarriage. *Acta Obstet Gynecol Scand* 1992;71:118-123.

US Army Medical Research Institute of Chemical Defense: *Medical Management of Chemical Casualties Handbook*, ed 3. 2000.

Lee RJ, Yolton RL, Yolton DP, et al: Personal defense sprays: Effects and management of exposure. *J Am Optometric Assoc* 1996;67:548-560.

Brown L, Takeuchi D, Challoner K: Corneal abrasions associated with pepper spray exposure. *Am J Emerg Med* 2000;18:271-272.

Granfield J, Onnen J, Petty CS: Pepper Spray and In-Custody Deaths. International Association of Chiefs of Police. *Executive Brief*. March 1994.

Fuller RW, Dixon CMS, Barnes PJ: Bronchoconstrictor response to inhaled capsaicin in humans. *J Appl Physiol* 1985;58:1080-1084.

Olivas T, Jones B, Canulla M: Abdominal wall penetration by a police "bean bag." *Am Surg* 2001;67:407-409.

Charles A, Asensio J, Forno W, et al: Penetrating bean bag injury: Intrathoracic complication of a nonlethal weapon. *J Trauma* 2002;53:997-1000.

Grange JT, Kozak R, Gonzalez J: Penetrating injury from a less-lethal bean bag gun. *J Trauma* 2002;52:576-578.

Suyama J, Panagos PD, Sztajnkrycer MD, et al: Injury patterns related to use of less-lethal weapons during a period of civil unrest. *J Emerg Med* 2003;25:219-227.

Kobayashi M, Mellen PF: Rubber bullet injury: Case report with autopsy observation and literature review. *Am J Forensic Med Pathol* 2009;30:262-267.

Geddes LA, Roeder RA: Evolution of our knowledge of sudden death due to commotio cordis. *Am J Emerg Med* 2005;23:67-75.

Balouris CA: Rubber and plastic bullet eye injuries in Palestine. *Lancet* 1990;335:415.

Laraque D, the Committee on Injury, Violence, and Poison Prevention: Injury risk of nonpowder guns. *Pediatrics* 2004;114:1357-1361.

Listman DA: Paintball injuries in children: More than meets the eye. *Pediatrics* 2004;113:e15-e18.

Fineman MS, Fischer DH, Jeffers JB, et al: Changing trends in paintball sport-related ocular injuries. *Arch Ophthalmol* 1990;22:416-418.

Hinchey PR, Subramaniam G: Pneumothorax as a complication after TASER activation. *Prehospital Emerg Care* 2009;13:532-535.

Ng W, Chehade M: Taser penetrating ocular injury. *Am J Ophthalmol* 2005;139:713-715.

Mangus BE, Shen LY, Helmer SD, et al: Taser and taser associated injuries: A case series. *Am Surg* 2008;74:862-865.

Jauchem JR, Sherry CJ, Fines DA, et al: Acidosis, lactate, electrolytes, muscle enzymes, and other factors in the blood of sus scrofa following repeated taser exposures. *Forensic Sci Int* 2006;161:20-30.

Jauchem JR, Cook MC, Beason CW: Blood factors of sus scrofa following a series of three TASER electronic control device exposures. *Forensic Sci Int* 2008;175:166-170.

Ho JD, Miner JR, Lakireddy DR, et al: Cardiovascular and physiological effects of conducted electrical weapon discharge in resting adults. *Acad Emerg Med* 2006;13: 589-595.

Vilke GM, Sloane CM, Bouton KD, et al: Physiological effects of a conducted electrical weapon on human subjects. *Ann Emerg Med* 2007;50:569-575.

Ho JD, Dawes DM, Bultman LL, et al: Respiratory effects of prolonged electrical weapon application on human volunteers. *Acad Emerg Med* 2007;14:197-2001.

Dawes DM, Ho JD, Johnson MA, et al: 15 second conducted electrical weapon exposure does not cause core temperature elevation in non-environmentally stressed resting adults. *Forensic Sci Int* 2008;176:253-257.

Ideker RE, Dosdall DJ: Can the direct cardiac effects of the electric pulses generated by the TASER X26 cause immediate or delayed sudden cardiac arrest in normal adults? *Am J Forensic Med Pathol* 2007;28:195-201.

Bozeman WP, Barnes DG Jr, Winslow JE III, et al: Immediate cardiovascular effects of the taser X26 conducted electrical weapon. *Emerg Med J* 2009;26:567-570.

McDaniel WC, Stratbucker RA, Nerheim M, et al: Cardiac safety of neuromuscular incapacitating defense devices. *PACE* 2005;28:S284-S287.

Lakkireddy D, Walliack D, Verma A, et al: Cardiac effects of electrical stun guns: Does position of barbs contact make a difference? *PACE* 2008;31:398-408.

Lakkireddy D, Khasis A, Anteacc A, et al. Do electrical stun guns (TASER X-26) affect the functional integrity of implantable pacemakers and defibrillators? *Europace* 2007;9:551-556.

Dennis AJ, Valentino DJ, Walter RJ, et al. Acute effects of taser X26 discharges in a swine model. *J Trauma* 2007;63: 581-590.

Valentino DJ, Walter RJ, Dennis AJ, et al: Taser X26 discharges in swine: Ventricular rhythm capture is dependent on discharge vector. *J Trauma* 2008;65:1478-1487.

Walter RJ, Dennis AJ, Valentino DJ, et al: Taser X26 discharges in swine produce potentially fatal ventricular arrhythmias. *Acad Emerg Med* 2008;15:66-73.

Ho JD, Dawes DM, Reardon RF, et al: Echocardiographic evaluation of a taser-X26 application in the ideal human cardiac axis. *Acad Emerg Med* 2008;15:838-844.

Vilke GM, Sloane C, Levine S, et al: Twelve-Lead electrocardiograph monitoring of subjects before and after voluntary exposure to the TASER X26. *Am J Emerg Med* 2008;26: 1-4.

Cao M, Shinbane JS, Gillberg JM, et al: Taser-Induced rapid ventricular myocardial capture demonstrated by pacemaker intracardiac electrograms. *J Cardiovasc Electrophysiol* 2007;18:876-879.

Haegeli LM, Sterns LD, Adams DC, et al: Effects of a taser shot to the chest of a patient with an implantable defibrillator. *Heart Rhythm* 2006;3:339-341.

Ho JD, Miner JR, Heegard WG, et al: Deaths in American police custody: A 12 month surveillance study. *Ann Emerg Med* 2005;46:S94.

Viala B, Blomet J, Mathieu L, et al: Prevention of CS "tear gas" eye and skin effects and active decontamination with Diphoterine: Preliminary studies in 5 French gendarmes. *J Emerg Med* 2005;29:5-8.

Horton DK, Burgess P, Rossiter S, et al: Secondary contamination of emergency department personnel from o-Chlorobenzylidene Malonitrile exposure. *Ann Emerg Med* 2005;45:655-658.

Jones JS, Rechtin C: Cardiac monitoring in adults after taser discharge. *Emerg Med J* 2009;26:666-667.

Wheary R, Szymasnki M: PA. Police Pepper Spray Exercise Goes Awry. PoliceOne.com News. 8/22/09. www.policeone.com. Accessed August 25, 2009.

Bui ET, Sourkes M, Wennberg R: Generalized tonic-clonic seizure after a taser shot to the head. *CMAJ* 2009;180: 625-626.

Anonymous: PERF Conducted Energy Device Policy and Training Guidelines for Consideration. PERF Center on Force and Accountability. *Police Executive Research Forum* October 2005.

Anonymous: Electro-Muscular Disruption Technology: A Nine-Step Strategy for Effective Deployment. Executive Brief. International Association of Chiefs of Police.

McBride DK, Tedder NB: Efficacy and Safety of Electrical Stun Devices. *Potomac Institute for Policy Studies Report* Number 05-04, Arlington, VA, March 2005.

Ordog GJ, Wasserberger J, Schlater T, Balasubramamium S: Electronic gun (taser) injuries. *Ann Emerg Med* 1987;16: 73-78.

Jenkinson E, Neeson C, Bleetman A: The relative risk of police use of force options: Evaluating the potential for deployment of electronic weaponry. *J Clin Forensic Med* 2006;13:229-241.

HEAD, NECK, AND SENSORY INJURIES

American College of Surgeons Committee on Trauma: *Advanced Trauma Life Support Student Course Manual*. Chicago, IL, American College of Surgeons, 2008.

Hammell CL, Henning JD: Prehospital management of severe traumatic brain injury. *BMJ*. 2009;338:b1683.

Kruger C, Lecky F: Best evidence topic reports: Is cervical spine protection always necessary following penetrating neck injury? *Emerg Med J*. 2009;26:883-887.

Kwan I, Bunn F, Roberts IG: Spinal Immobilisation for Trauma Patients. *Cochrane Database of Systematic Reviews* 2001, Issue 2. Art. No. CD002803. DOI: 10.1002/14651858.CD002803.

Marion DW, Pryzybylski G: Injury to the vertebrae and spinal cord, in Mattox KL, Feliciano DV, Moore EE (eds): *Trauma*. New York, NY, McGraw-Hill, 2000, pp 451-471.

McGuire RA, Neville S, Green BA, et al: Spine instability and the log-roll maneuver. *J Trauma*. 1987;27:525-531.

Michael DB, Guyot DR, Darmody WR: Coincidence of head and cervical spine injury. *J Neurotrauma*. 1989;6: 177-189.

Waninger KN: Management of the helmeted athlete with suspected cervical spine injury. *Am J Sports Med* 2004; 32:1331-1350.

PREGNANCY AND CHILDBIRTH

Gilbert ES: *Manual of High Risk Pregnancy and Delivery*, ed 4. St Louis, MO, Mosby Elsevier, 2007.

Gruenberg BU: *Essentials of Prehospital Delivery*. Upper Saddle River, NJ, Prentice Hall, 2006.

Maternal-Neonatal Nursing Made Incredibly Easy. Philadelphia, PA, Lipincott Williams & Wilkens, 2004.

INFANTS AND CHILDREN

Essentials of Paediatric Intensive Care. Differences between the child, the neonate and the adult. http://assets.cambridge.org/97818411/00531/sample/9781841100531ws.pdf. Accessed April 5, 2010.

Medline Plus. Medical Encyclopedia. http://www.nlm.nih.gov/medlineplus/encyclopedia.html. Accessed April 7, 2010.

National Highway Traffic Safety Administration: First Responder: National Standard Curriculum. US Department of Transportation. http://www.nhtsa.gov/people/injury/ems/pub/frnsc.pdf. Accessed April 5, 2010.

Nichols, DG, Helfaer, MA: *Rogers' Handbook of Pediatric Intensive Care*, ed 4. Philadelphia, PA, Lippincott Williams & Wilkins, 2008.

Pons, P, Cason D (eds): *Paramedic Field Care: A Complaint Based Approach*. St. Louis, MO, Mosby, 1997.

Sanders, MJ: *Mosby's Paramedic Textbook*, ed 3. St. Louis, MO, Elsevier, 2007.

INCARCERATION AND PRISONER CARE

Mapp v. Ohio, 367 U.S. 643 (1961).

Marx J, Hockberger W: *Rosen's Emergency Medicine: Concepts and Clinical Practice*, ed 5. St. Louis, MO, Mosby, Inc., 2002.

Industry Study by Hoover's Inc., a Dun & Bradstreet Company.

Grant BF, Dawson DA, Stinson, FS, Chou SP, Dufour, MC, Pickering RP: The 12-month prevalence and trends in DSM-IV alcohol abuse and dependence: United States, 1991–1992 and 2001–2002. *Drug Alcohol Depend* 2004;74(3): 2232-2234.

Greenfield L: *Alcohol and Crime, An Analysis on National Data on the Prevalence of Alcohol Involvement in Crime*. US Department of Justice, Office of Justice Programs, 1998.

Epilepsy Foundation of America: About Epilepsy. http://www.epilepsyfoundation.org/aboutepilepsy/index.cfm. Accessed February 27, 2012.

Merrill DB, Assistant Clinical Professor of Psychiatry, Department of Psychiatry, Columbia University Medical Center, New York, NY, February 2010.

Bender E: American Psychiatric Association. *Psychiatr News* 2006;41(13):29.

TRAVEL AND FOREIGN MISSIONS

Sleet DA, Ballesteros MF: *Centers for Disease Control and Prevention 2012 Yellow Book*. Chapter 2, Injuries and Safety. http://wwwnc.cdc.gov/travel/yellowbook/2012/chapter-2-the-pre-travel-consultation/injuries-and-safety.htm

Nicks BA, Kulkarni R: Medscape Travel Medicine and Vaccination. http://emedicine.medscape.com/article/811510-overview

Dupont HL: President's address: Travel medicine and principles of safe travel. *Transactions of the American Clinical and Climatological Association*. 2008;119:1-27.

Pipe AL: International travel and the elite athlete. *Clin J Sport Med* 2011;21(1):62-66.

Goodyear L, Gibbs J: Medical supplies for travelers to developing countries. *J Travel Med* 2004;11:208-212.

Zell SC: Environmental and recreational hazards associated with adventure travel. *J Travel Med* 1997;4:94-99.

Auerbach PS, Donner HJ, Weiss EA: *Field Guide to Wilderness Medicine*, ed 3. St. Louis, MO, Mosby, 2008.

Hamer DH, Connor BA: Travel health knowledge, attitudes and practices among United States travelers. *J Travel Med* 2004;11:23-26.

Leggat PA, Shaw MT: Travel health advice for backpackers. *J Travel Med* 2003;10:340-345.

Worley GH: Wilderness communications. *Wilderness and Environmental Medicine*. 2011, in press.

IN-FLIGHT EMERGENCIES

Aviation Medical Assistance Act of 1998. Washington, DC, National Archives and Records Administration, Office of the Federal Register, 1998.

Cummings RO, Schubach JA: Frequency and types of medical emergencies among commercial air travelers. *JAMA* 1989;261:1295-1299.

Gendreau MA, DeJohn C: Responding to medical events during commercial airline flights. *NEJM* 2002;346:1067.

Goodwin T: In-flight medical emergencies: An overview. *BMJ* 2000;321:1338-1341.

Medical Guidelines Task Force AMA: Medical guidelines for airline travel, ed 2. *Aviat Space Environ Med* 2003;74:A1. Available at www.asma.org

Newson-Smith MS: Passenger doctors in civil airliners-obligations, duties and standards of car. *Aviat Space Environ Med* 1997;68:1134.

Nordenberg T: Air Aid: Medical kits reach new heights. *FDA Consum* 1998;32.

Prout M, Pine J: Management of in-flight medical emergencies on commercial airlines. Available at http://utdol.com/online/content/topic.do?topicKey=ad_emer/4452&selectedTitle=1%7E150&source=search_result. Accessed October 1, 2009.

Speizer C, Rennie CJ, Breton H: Prevalence of in-flight medical emergencies on commercial airlines. *Ann Emerg Med* 1989;18:26.

MARITIME DEPLOYMENTS

The George Washington University Maritime Medical Access Program (Updated 2008). *Medical Emergencies at Sea, Course Curriculum & Outline*. Washington, DC.

McKay MP: *Maritime Health Emergencies*. Manuscript submitted for publication, 2006.

US Coast Guard: *The STCW Convention: A Handbook of Highlights*, 1999. http://www.uscg.mil/stcw/s-handbk10.htm. Accessed January 26, 2010.

US Department of Health and Human Services, Public Health Service: *The Ship's Medicine Chest and Medical Aid at Sea*, 2003. Government Publication no. (PHS) 03-2024. Washington, DC.

SPECIAL MISSIONS AND RESPONSES

National Tactical Officers Association: *NTOA SWAT Standards*. September 2008.

Hetzler MR, Ball JA: Thoughts on aid bags. *J Special Operations Med*. 2008;8(3).

Tang N: VIP protection and care, in Schwartz R, McManus J, Swienton R (eds): *Tactical Emergency Medicine*. Philadelphia, PA, Lippincott Williams & Wilkins, 2008.

Tang N, Gerold K, Carmona R: Tactical and protective medicine, in Bledsoe G, Manyak M, Townes D (eds): *Expedition Medicine*. New York, NY, Cambridge University Press, 2008.

Iselin B, Smith ER: Arlington County, Va., task force rethinks active shooter incident response. *J Emerg Med Serv*, December 2009.

Tang N, Kelen GD: The role of tactical EMS in support of public safety and the public health response to a hostile mass casualty incident. *Disast Med and Publ Health Prep* 2007;1(1):S55-56.

ANIMAL THREATS AND CONTROL

The Humane Society of the United States: Dog Aggression. http://www.humanesociety.org/animals/dogs/tips/aggression.html. Accessed February 27, 2012.

The Human Society of the United States: How to Avoid a Dog Bite. http://www.humanesociety.org/animals/dogs/tips/avoid_dog_bites.html. Accessed February 27, 2012.

ASPCA: Aggression in Dogs. http://www.aspcabehavior.org/articles/49/Aggression-in-Dogs.aspx. Accessed February 27, 2012.

ASPCA: Canine Body Language. http://www.aspcabehavior.org/articles/50/Canine-Body-Language.aspx. Accessed February 27, 2012.

AVMA: Dog Bite Prevention. http://www.avma.org/public_health/dogbite/default.asp. Accessed February 27, 2012.

Glossary

abandonment A type of negligence that arises when an emergency responder with a duty to provide care prematurely terminates the care and the termination of care results in harm.

abdomen The cavity that lies between the thorax and the pelvis and contains the digestive organs.

abdominal aortic aneurysm (AAA) A condition that results in a bulging of the aorta in the abdominal cavity. It is usually identified by the presence of a pulsating mass around the midabdomen and a sharp, stabbing pain that radiates directly to the lower back.

abdominal breathing Breathing using only the diaphragm, resulting in rising of the abdomen (not the chest) with each breath.

abrasions Injuries in which the outermost layer of skin, the epidermis, is scraped away. Commonly called road rash.

abruptio placentae An emergency in the second half of pregnancy that occurs when the entire placenta, or a portion of it, detaches from the wall of the uterus prior to childbirth.

absorption The introduction of a drug into the bloodstream.

acclimatization A mechanism triggered in an attempt by the body to limit the adverse effects on the body and to prepare the body to go to even higher altitudes.

action The therapeutic effect that a medication has on the body.

acute abdomen Not a specific diagnosis but rather a set of signs and symptoms, often very pronounced and dramatic, that can be caused by a variety of potentially serious underlying medical conditions.

acute mountain sickness (AMS) Range of illnesses affecting unacclimatized persons; these illnesses include a headache and one or more of the following symptoms: gastrointestinal complaint (nausea, vomiting, anorexia, or decreased appetite), insomnia, dizziness, light-headedness, or lassitude and fatigue.

adrenaline Hormone released by the adrenal gland that causes the blood vessels to constrict and the heart rate to increase.

advanced emergency medical technicians (AEMTs) Intermediate-level prehospital providers who possess the knowledge and skills set of the emergency medical responder (EMR) and emergency medical technician (EMT), as well as additional knowledge and skills.

advance directives Legal documents intended to provide guidance to family members, friends, and care providers on how to make medical choices on a patient's behalf in the event of decisional or communicating incapacity.

AEIOU TIPS A mnemonic for recalling the causes of altered mental status.

aggression A range of behaviors that may result in a sequence of increasing hostility or may occur at random with little or no warning.

airway The structures that allow the passage of air from the outside environment to the functional units of the lungs.

allergic reaction The body's immune system reaction to a foreign substance, which is usually localized. An allergic reaction can result from contact with the skin or mucous membranes, inhalation, ingestion, or penetration of the skin. Allergic reactions are generally less severe than anaphylaxis.

altered mental status (AMS) A change in a person's mental activity, state of mind, or responsiveness.

alveolar ventilation The exchange of oxygen and carbon dioxide that occurs in the alveoli.

alveoli The air sacs of the lungs where the exchange of oxygen and carbon dioxide takes place.

Alzheimer disease A chronic, progressive dementia that accounts for 60% of all cases of dementia in the United States.

amnestic syndrome A syndrome that involves a transient or a permanent memory loss.

amniotic sac A thin, membranous sac that protects the growing fetus. The fetus is cushioned in this sac with amniotic fluid.

amputation An injury in which a body part or limb is completely severed.

anaphylactic shock Shock caused by an allergic reaction so severe that patients experience dilated blood vessels and airway constriction, altering their perfusion.

anaphylaxis A more severe allergic reaction to a foreign substance that not only creates a localized effect but also creates the same reaction throughout the whole body. Anaphylactic reactions may be life threatening in some situations.

anatomic position The position used to study the body. The person is standing, facing forward, with palms turned forward.

anatomy The study of the parts of the body.

angina pectoris A type of cardiac disease resulting from coronary artery plaque buildup that causes chest pain when cardiac oxygen demand exceeds oxygen supply.

anterior The front of the body.

antihistamine A category of medications that work by reducing the release of histamine.

aorta The main artery that receives blood from the left ventricle of the heart and delivers it to all the other arteries that carry blood to the tissues of the body.

apneic Not breathing spontaneously.

apparent life-threatening event (ALTE) A sudden and unexplained occurrence of a breathing abnormality in an infant.

applied ethics The use of ethical values in real-life situations.

aqueous humor A clear fluid that fills the anterior chamber of the eye.

area of operation (AO) The location where a law enforcement mission or training detail is to occur. The boundaries of that area may be confined to a specific house address when serving a high-risk warrant or may be several city blocks where a demonstration is to occur.

arteries Blood vessels that carry blood away from the heart.

arteriosclerosis Hardening of the blood vessels, which makes the blood vessels stiff and unable to constrict or dilate as well when the body is stressed.

arthropods A class of animals characterized by their exoskeleton and jointed appendages. This class includes scorpions, spiders, centipedes, millipedes, lobsters, crabs, and shrimp.

asthma A condition caused by a sudden constriction of the airway, usually triggered by stress, exercise, cold air, or allergic reaction to something.

ataxia Lack of coordinated movement; unsteadiness with movement of the limbs.

atrial fibrillation A cardiac dysrhythmia common in the elderly that results in an irregular pulse.

atria The two upper chambers of the heart.

automated external defibrillators (AEDs) Devices that deliver an electrical shock to patients in cardiac arrest.

autonomic nervous system The part of the central nervous system that controls involuntary body functions.

autonomy The principle that a human being of adult years and sound mind has the right to determine what shall be done with his or her own body.

autoregulation The process in which the heart and blood vessel walls contract more or less to maintain an ideal and relatively constant mean arterial pressure.

avulsions Injuries in which a piece of skin is either torn completely loose from all of its attachments or is left hanging as a flap.

bag-mask device A device with a face mask attached to a ventilation bag containing a reservoir and connected to oxygen; delivers more than 90% supplemental oxygen.

bag of waters *See amniotic sac.*

ballistics The science of mechanics that deals with the flight, behavior, and effects of projectiles.

bandages Adhesive, roller gauze, cravats, or tape used to hold a clean, sterile dressing in place.

barotrauma Injury caused by increased pressure exerted on the body by deep water.

basal metabolic rate The rate at which humans use energy at complete rest.

baseline health assessment An annual physical examination by a health care provider that includes an electrocardiogram, blood pressure reading, chest X-ray, laboratory tests, and immunization updates.

Battle's sign Bruising behind one or both ears. Caused by a particular type of skull fracture.

behavior The manner in which people act or conduct themselves.

behavioral crisis A state of emotional turmoil in which a person has lost control of the balance between thoughts and emotions.

behavioral emergencies Situations in which a person acts in a way that is not acceptable or tolerable to those around them, often posing a danger to themselves or others.

beneficence An obligation to act in a helpful or therapeutic manner.

bilateral On both sides of the body.

bloat Twisting of the stomach that allows air to get in, but not out; also called gastric dilatation-volvulus.

bloodborne pathogens Microorganisms in the blood that are capable of causing disease.

blood The fluid contained in the blood vessels, consisting of plasma, formed elements (red blood cells, white blood cells, and platelets), dissolved gases, nutrients, and waste.

bone marrow The substance inside certain bones that is responsible for developing red blood cells, white blood cells, and platelets.

bones Complex living tissue that helps to make up the skeletal system.

brain The primary organ of the central nervous system, comprising millions of neurons separated into specialized functional units.

Braxton-Hicks contractions Irregular contractions, also called warm-up contractions, that produce no cervical change. They are not a sign of labor or imminent childbirth.

breathing The process of ventilation and respiration.

breech delivery Occurs when a baby enters the birth canal backwards and the buttocks emerge from the vagina first instead of the head.

bronchi The large tubes in the lower airway that connect to the trachea and channel air through the lungs.

bronchioles The smaller tubes in the lower airway that connect to the bronchi and channel air to the alveoli.

bronchitis A form of chronic obstructive pulmonary disease that is characterized by excessive mucus production in the larger airways and trachea.

bronchorrhea Excessive secretion production from the bronchioles; can result in copious amounts of sputum.

calcaneus The heel bone.

capillaries Blood vessels that are a single cell in thickness and allow for the exchange of gases, nutrients, and waste.

cardiac arrest See *sudden cardiac death*.

cardiac muscle The muscle that makes up the heart. Made of protein chains that give it a striated appearance, it functions involuntarily and is also called the myocardium.

cardiac output The amount of blood pushed out of the heart with each beat.

cardiac tamponade Caused by blood leaking into the sac that surrounds the heart. The bleeding will constrict the chambers of the heart and prevent the heart from pumping.

cardiogenic shock Shock resulting from inadequate functioning of the heart.

cardiopulmonary resuscitation (CPR) The process of manually circulating oxygenated blood in a patient whose heart is not beating.

cardiorespiratory failure A condition in which the heart and lungs stop functioning.

carpals The irregular bones in the wrist. These bones are relatively large and extend from the radius and ulna toward the metacarpals.

cartilage The dense, fibrous material used in the skeletal system to cover joints or create flexible structures.

cells The basic units of life; contain tiny structures called organelles that maintain the cell's regulation and function.

central nervous system Composed of the brain and spinal cord.

cerebrospinal fluid (CSF) A clear, watery, straw-colored fluid that fills the space between the brain and spinal cord and their protective coverings.

certification Verification of successfully completing a course or competencies and/or authorization to function at a given prehospital level within a state.

cervix The lower part of the uterus.

chain of command A rank structure, spanning the entry-level responder to the incident commander, to manage an incident.

chain of survival The five-link sequence for cardiac arrest care: early access, early CPR, early defibrillation, early advanced care, and post-arrest care.

chaplain A person who provides nondenominational spiritual guidance and support.

chemical chain reaction The exothermic (heat-releasing) process that results in maintaining a material at its ignition temperature in order to sustain combustion.

chemical name Technical formula used by scientists to identify a substance.

chronic obstructive pulmonary disease (COPD) A group of diseases, most commonly emphysema and chronic bronchitis, that affect the condition of the alveoli and lungs over a long period of time.

Cincinnati Stroke Scale A diagnostic test used to identify the signs of a stroke.

civil complaint A legal action that is filed when a person or group feels that they have not been treated in accordance with a statute.

clandestine drug laboratory A secret laboratory in which illicit drugs are manufactured.

clavicle The collarbone.

closed fractures Fractures in which the bone ends do not break the skin.

closed head injury Injury in which there is bleeding or swelling or both inside the skull.

cochlea The inner ear where sound is collected and processed, along with balance information.

combustion A rapid chemical process that results in the release of energy in the form of heat and (usually) light; also known as fire.

Committee for Tactical Emergency Casualty Care (C-TECC) The C-TECC was convened to expedite the appropriate transition of military medical lessons learned from the battlefield to civilian crisis response in order to reduce preventable causes of death in both our first responders and civilian population. The C-TECC is modeled after the Committee on Tactical Combat Casualty Care (CoTCCC) and is comprised of a broad range of interagency operational and academic leaders in the practice of high-threat medicine and fire/rescue from across the nation. http://c-tecc.org/

Committee on Tactical Combat Casualty Care (CoTCCC) The CoTCCC was established in 2001 to monitor new developments in prehospital trauma care and use this information to periodically update the TCCC guidelines. This committee is now part of the Defense Health board and is hosted by the Military Health System at the Department of Defense. http://www.health.mil/Education_And_Training/TCCC.aspx

communicable disease A disease that can be spread from one person or species to another.

compensated shock A stage of shock in which adrenaline keeps the patient operating and functioning at near normal levels.

concealment Visual shield from a threat, whether or not physically protected from the threat.

conducted energy device (CED) A device that delivers an electric current that causes uncontrollable muscle contractions and severe pain in order to incapacitate a subject.

congestive heart failure (CHF) A form of cardiac disease that results when one side of the heart fails to pump blood out at the same rate as the other side.

conjunctiva The thin outer covering of the eye.

continuous quality improvement A process involving multiple components that results in continual improvement within a given EMS system.

contraindications When a medication should not be given to a patient because of harmful effects.

CONUS Refers to an activity occurring within the continental United States.

Coordinated Universal Time (UTC) Also known as Greenwich Mean Time (GMT) or Zulu time; uses 24-hour military time notations and is based on the 0° longitude time meridian, which runs through Greenwich, England. Midnight is 0000 UTC; noon is noted as 1200 UTC.

cornea Clear tissue that sits in front of the iris and pupil and provides protection and structural support to these structures.

coronary arteries The arteries that take blood to the muscle of the heart.

corrosive A substance that destroys or damages other substances with which it comes in contact.

cover Physical protection from a threat.

crack cocaine A solid, smokable form of cocaine. It is a free-base form of cocaine that can be made using baking soda (sodium bicarbonate).

credentialing The process of acclimation and clearing to function within an EMS system.

cribbing Blocks of wood or other materials used to immobilize a vehicle.

criminal complaint A legal action that occurs when the statutes prescribe that error in application of the statute or defiance of the statute should result in the arrest of the alleged offending parties until an argument is made in front of a judiciary body.

critical incident stress An acute stress reaction that occurs following a significant or traumatic event.

Critical Incident Stress Management (CISM) A comprehensive, integrated, systematic, and multitactic approach designed to help the law enforcement officer cope with the stresses of the job and to rapidly return to the workplace.

crowning Appearance of the infant's head as it is pushed through the birth canal.

cumulative stress Stress accumulated over a period of time that results in symptoms of distress.

cyanosis Bluish coloration of the skin resulting from poor oxygenation of the circulating blood.

decompensated shock A stage of shock in which the effects of adrenaline are not able to keep up with the problem causing the shock (eg, blood loss, toxins).

decontamination The process of removing or neutralizing a hazard and properly disposing of materials such as clothing and personal protective equipment from patients and rescue personnel.

defendant The person or group against whom a complaint is lodged.

delayed neurocognitive sequelae Neurologic or psychiatric symptoms that occur 2 to 40 days after the initial insult. Symptoms may include mild memory loss, dementia, amnesia, and problems with peripheral nerves and movement.

delirium An acute change in mental status that can be caused by medications, physical or psychiatric illness, neurologic insults, trauma, or acute changes in an elderly person's environment.

dementia A progressive, irreversible decline in mental functioning marked by impairments in memory and reasoning.

dependent edema Fluid collection in the feet and legs of individuals with right-sided congestive heart failure.

depressant A classification of drug that depresses or decreases the activity of the central nervous system.

depression A psychiatric disorder marked by persistent feelings of sadness, hopelessness, and loss of interest in daily activities. At extremes, depression can lead to thoughts of suicide or attempts to harm one's self.

dermis The middle layer of skin, which contains nerve endings, blood vessels, hair follicles, sweat glands, and oil glands.

diabetes A medical condition in which the pancreas either fails to produce insulin or does not produce enough insulin. In some people, insulin is produced in the proper amount, but for some reason the cells cannot use the insulin.

diabetic coma See *hyperglycemia*.

dialysis See *hemodialysis*.

diaphragm A muscular dome that separates the chest from the abdominal cavity. Contraction of the diaphragm and the chest wall muscles brings air into the lungs; relaxation expels airs from the lungs.

diffusion The process in which a chemical moves from a higher concentration to a lower concentration until it is equally dispersed.

direct force injuries Injuries resulting from energy released directly to a part of the body, such as being hit in the head with a baseball bat.

dislocation A separation between two bones at a joint.

distal Away from the center of the body.

distribution The act of the body pushing the drug to the rest of the body after absorption.

distributive shock Form of shock in which a problem arises with the blood vessels and fluid cannot get to its intended destination.

diuretics Medications that produce greater urination and lower blood volumes.

dose The amount of a particular drug that the medical director has authorized you to give.

dressings Sterile gauze or clean cloth placed directly over a wound.

Drug Enforcement Agency (DEA) Organization established under the Department of Justice to become the lead federal law enforcement agency relative to drug law enforcement.

dry drowning Suffocation that occurs when a person is submerged and attempts to breathe, but laryngospasm occurs, closing the airway and preventing water from entering the lungs.

durable power of attorney Appoints another person to act as the patient's health care decision maker in the event of future incapacity.

duty to act When a medical responder becomes responsible to the public for rendering aid during a medical emergency.

dysphoria Restlessness, disquiet, depression.

dyspnea Shortness of breath.

ectopic pregnancy A pregnancy that occurs outside the uterus, usually in a fallopian tube.

elder abuse An action taken by a family member or caregiver that results in physical, emotional, or sexual harm to a person older than 65 years.

electronic control device (ECD) See *conducted electrical weapon*.

embryo The term for a developing baby during the first eight weeks after conception.

emergency contact form (ECF) A previously prepared, securely maintained document containing information and details pertaining to an officer who has been seriously injured or has died.

emergency medical responders (EMRs) The first responder level of prehospital provider offering basic life support care.

emergency medical technicians (EMTs) Basic life support prehospital providers with the skills and knowledge of an emergency medical responder (EMR) as well as additional knowledge such as performing additional patient care interventions, preparing a patient for transport, and providing transport to a medical treatment facility.

emphysema A form of chronic obstructive pulmonary disease that is characterized by the destruction and loss of elasticity of the alveoli of the lungs.

enzymes Chemicals that promote a reaction in the body; often used to break down other chemicals.

epidermis The outermost layer of skin.

epiglottis The flap that lies behind the tongue and covers the trachea when a person swallows.

epilepsy A disease manifested by seizures, caused by an abnormal focus of electrical activity in the brain.

epinephrine auto-injector A spring-loaded device, such as the EpiPen, that administers a preset dose of epinephrine to a patient experiencing an anaphylactic reaction.

erythrocytes Red blood cells.

esophagus The smooth muscular tube that takes food and fluid from the throat to the stomach.

ethics The standards that societies, organizations, and professions establish to define expectations for members of that group. They broadly define right from wrong and create expectations of appropriate behavior.

evisceration Open wound to the abdomen that exposes abdominal organs to the environment.

excited delirium A syndrome that presents with agitation, tachycardia (elevated heart rate), hyperthermia (elevated body temperature), and other symptoms and can result in sudden death.

excretion (The process of eliminating) a drug or its components from the body to the external environment. Excretion can occur through urination, defecation, sweating, breathing, and lactation.

executive protection The use of protective methodologies to reduce the opportunity for hostile forces to impair or eliminate a VIP or protectee.

exhalation The passive phase of breathing in which air is pushed out of the lungs.

expiration The movement of air out of the lungs.

expressed consent The act of the patient communicating to the responder verbally or nonverbally that he or she is willing to let the responder touch or care for him or her.

exsanguinating hemorrhage Major, ongoing, life-threatening bleeding.

extrication The disentanglement of the vehicle to free a trapped patient.

failed airway device A device that is used after an advanced life support provider has been unsuccessful in attempts to secure the airway through endotracheal intubation.

fallopian tubes Muscular tubes that connect the ovaries to the uterus. Eggs are fertilized in the fallopian tubes and travel down the tubes to the uterus.

fasciculations Muscular twitching involving the simultaneous contraction of contiguous groups of muscle fibers.

femur The large bone of the thigh.

feral pig A domestic swine that turns wild.

fetus A developing baby from the eighth week of pregnancy to delivery.

fibula The outer and smaller bone of the two bones of the lower leg.

fire tetrahedron The four factors necessary for a fire to occur: fuel, oxygen, heat, and a chemical chain reaction.

fixed wing aircraft An airplane.

flail chest A portion of ribs or sternum that has broken free from the rest of the chest. It moves in the opposite direction of the normal chest structures, creating inadequate respiration.

flat bones Broad and flat bones that are used for protection. Examples include the ribs, sternum, and the sides of the skull.

fontanelles Areas where the infant's skull has not fused together; usually disappear at approximately 18 months of age.

Food and Drug Administration (FDA) Organization developed to provide oversight and regulation to the drug industry.

forensics Belonging to, used in, or suitable to courts of judicature or to public discussion and debate; pertaining to the law.

fractures Broken bones.

frostbite Cooling of the body's tissue to the point at which injury occurs. The skin may initially become reddened, may blister, and then appears mottled and pale.

fuel Any material that is combustible.

full-thickness burns Burns involving all three layers of skin, possibly exposing muscle and bone beneath the charred area.

fundus The top part of the uterus.

Gamow bag A portable hyperbaric bag.

gastric insufflation A condition in which air fills the stomach as a result of high volume and pressure or airway obstruction during artificial ventilation.

gastrointestinal bleeding Bleeding that occurs along the digestive tract.

generalized seizure See *grand mal seizure*.

generic name Original name of a drug, which is not capitalized.

geriatric Older than 65 years.

glucose A simple sugar needed by cells. Glucose is derived either from food that has been digested by the body or from the breakdown of fat stored in the body.

Good Samaritan statutes Laws that shield persons without a legal duty to act from civil liability that may arise due to injuries resulting from the care provided.

grand mal seizure The most dramatic type of seizure, which presents with uncontrolled muscle contractions and loss of consciousness.

gross negligence A conscious, careless, and reckless disregard for the safety or lives of others.

gynecology The area of medicine that deals with women's reproductive health.

hazardous material Any material or substance that poses an unreasonable risk of damage or injury to persons, property, or the environment if not properly controlled during handling, storage, manufacture, processing, packaging, use and disposal, or transportation.

Health Insurance Portability and Accountability Act (HIPAA) A law that establishes standards to make the electronic transmission of health information easier and to create procedures to protect the privacy of patients' health information.

heart A two-stage pump that takes blood from the body, pushes it to the lungs for an exchange of gases, and then pushes the blood back out to the body.

heat Added or external energy that causes a rise in temperature in a potential fuel for a fire.

heat cramps Involuntary, spastic, and very painful contractions of isolated muscles occurring after physical activity in a warm environment.

heat exhaustion A heat illness brought on by dehydration and electrolyte losses. Patients appear with generalized exhaustion symptoms.

heatstroke An emergency characterized by an elevated temperature, hot skin with decreased sweating, a rapid pulse rate, and confusion, lethargy, seizures, or unconsciousness. Heat stroke is fatal if untreated.

hemodialysis A method of filtering toxins from the blood of patients with kidney (renal) failure by removing blood from the body, cleaning it, and returning it to the body.

hemoglobin A chemical made with iron that lies in the red blood cells. Oxygen attaches to this chemical, allowing it to be transported in the blood.

hemoptysis Coughing up blood.

hemostatic agents Chemical materials, usually in powder form or impregnated into a textile, that are designed to speed the natural clotting process.

hemothorax Bleeding inside the chest cavity, which may fill the pleural space.

high-altitude cerebral edema (HACE) Swelling of the brain as a result of altitude, with the hallmark symptoms of confusion and ataxia.

high-altitude headache (HAH) An initial symptom associated with developing cerebral edema without any other symptoms.

high-altitude pulmonary edema (HAPE) A disease involving the lungs and the blood vessels in the lungs that results in fluid filling up the air sacs, making it difficult to breathe and take up oxygen into the bloodstream.

high-risk warrant service A law enforcement operation in which an arrest warrant or search/seizure warrant is being served. Determination of "high risk" is made by the individual law enforcement agency.

histamine A protein released by the body during allergic and anaphylactic reactions that causes swelling, redness, and itching of the skin.

holistic wellness The balance needed in a person's life that includes physical, occupational, personal and emotional, family and social, and spiritual health.

homeostasis The process in nature by which an organism maintains equilibrium between the internal and external environment.

hormones Substances formed in specialized organs or glands and carried to another organ or group of cells in the same organism. They regulate many body functions, including metabolism, growth, and body temperature.

humerus The bone of the upper arm.

hydroponics A method of growing plants using mineral nutrient solutions, in water, without soil.

hyperadrenergic surge The body's release of adrenaline and the subsequent physiologic responses including tachycardia, hypertension, hyperthermia, and potentially agitation.

hyperglycemia A condition in which a high blood glucose level prevents normal cell function.

hypodermis The subcutaneous layer of skin, which is mostly fatty tissue.

hypoglycemia A condition in which a low blood glucose level prevents normal cell function.

hypothermia Condition in which the body can no longer maintain its core temperature, with a resultant fall in body temperature below 95°F (35°C). Blood vessels constrict to decrease heat loss through radiation and initiate shivering to produce more heat. The degree of heat loss eventually exceeds the capability of heat conservation or generation.

hypovolemic shock Loss of blood or fluid, which decreases the ability of the circulatory system to maintain adequate perfusion.

hypoxia A dangerous and potentially life-threatening condition in which the cells and tissues of the body do not have enough oxygen to survive.

hypoxic Experiencing a dangerous and potentially life-threatening condition in which the cells and tissues of the body do not have enough oxygen to survive.

ignition temperature The minimum temperature at which a substance will undergo combustion in a normal atmosphere without the additional application of external heat or source of ignition.

image armor The perceived image of oneself as the flawless responder—in the eyes of work peers, community, and family.

immune system The body's defense mechanism that responds to outside agents such as germs, foreign bodies, irritating substances, and chemicals.

impaled objects Objects, such as knives, tools, or shrapnel, that penetrate the body, become stuck in the tissue, and part may be visible outside the body.

implied consent Occurs when a responder initiates care and the patient fails to object or is unable to object.

incubation period The time between first exposure to a disease pathogen and the period when signs and symptoms appear.

indications The therapeutic uses for which a medication is prescribed and used.

indirect force injuries Injuries resulting from a secondary release of energy that is transferred or transmitted along a path to the site of the injury.

individual first aid kit (IFAK) A military approach to a self-care kit that meets the needs of the soldier on a battlefield, often packaged so the kit can be attached to load-bearing vests.

infectious disease A medical condition caused by the growth and spread of harmful organisms within the body.

inferior Lower than another point on the body (closer to the feet).

inferior vena cava The large vein that brings blood from the lower body to the heart.

informed consent Occurs when a patient is given enough information to make an informed choice regarding his or her treatment.

inhalation The active phase of breathing in which air is pulled into the lungs. As a medication route, medication is inhaled into the lungs either to work on the lungs or to be absorbed into the bloodstream quickly.

inspiration The movement of air into the lungs.

insulin A naturally occurring hormone secreted by the pancreas that is used by the body to break down large molecules of glucose.

insulin shock A life-threatening condition of severe low blood glucose levels that occurs in a diabetic patient who has taken too much insulin or has not eaten enough food.

intercostal muscles The muscles between the ribs that contract to expand the chest. In conjunction with the diaphragm, these muscles create a vacuum in the chest, allowing air to rush into the lungs.

intervertebral disk A cushion-like structure between each vertebrae body.

intramuscular (IM) injection Route of medication administration in which medication is injected into the muscle and absorbed quickly because of the vast blood supply to the muscles.

intraosseous (IO) injection Route of medication administration in which medication is injected into the bone, reaching the bloodstream through the bone marrow. Used when an intravenous route is needed and cannot be accessed.

intravenous (IV) injection Route of medication administration in which medication is injected directly into a vein. This is the fastest way to deliver a chemical substance.

iris The colored portion of the eye that contains structures that receive external information.

irregular bones Bones that do not fit into the other categories—for example, vertebrae.

irreversible shock The last stage of shock, in which organs are damaged and the body is near death.

joints The parts of the skeletal system where bones meet.

labor contractions Regular and progressive contractions that produce cervical change.

lacerations Jagged cuts or tears in the skin.

lacrimal gland The gland that creates tears and lubricates the space between the conjunctiva and the eyelid.

lacrimation Tearing.

laryngospasm A closing of the larynx preventing anything (air, water, etc) from entering the trachea.

larynx The opening into the trachea; it is made of cartilage and contains the vocal cords.

lassitude A condition characterized by weakness, exhaustion, or lethargy.

lateral Away from the midline.

laterally recumbent The patient is lying on his or her side. The recovery position is an example of a laterally recumbent position.

legal negligence Requires four elements be proved in court: (1) An injury or harm was suffered, (2) there was a duty to act by the health care provider, (3) the provider acted in a manner that falls below the standard of care, and (4) the actions of the provider were a substantial factor in causing the injury or harm.

leukocytes White blood cells.

license A privilege and authorization to function as a prehospital provider within a state.

ligaments Tough, fibrous cords of tissue that connect bones to bones across a joint.

limb presentation An emergency situation that occurs when a baby's arm or leg emerges from the birth canal first instead of the head. The mother cannot deliver vaginally and requires a cesarean section.

line of duty death (LODD) Any death of a law enforcement officer while on active duty.

lips The exposed covering of the oral cavity.

live load An energized vehicle that may be in gear and poses a significant threat to rescuers.

log-roll technique The means by which a patient with a suspected spinal injury is turned without twisting or bending the spine. This procedure involves at least three people.

long bones Bones that are used like levers by the body and are found in the thigh, leg, arm, and forearm.

malaria A bloodborne disease that is transmitted by certain species of mosquitoes.

mandible Lower jaw.

mastoid process Bony points behind the ear.

maxilla Upper jaw.

mechanism of injury (MOI) The way in which traumatic injuries occur; the forces that act on the body to cause damage.

meconium A dark green material in amniotic fluid that can indicate distress or disease in the newborn.

medial Closer to the middle of the body.

medical director The physician overseeing and responsible for the care provided by prehospital providers functioning in an EMS system.

medical negligence Occurs when a person is injured and becomes entitled to monetary compensation for the negligent actions of a health care provider.

medical protocols Standards to which EMS professionals must perform given particular emergency situations.

medical record Documentation of care provided to a patient that provides a historical record for other care providers to reference.

meninges Coverings inside the skull and spinal column that protect the brain and spinal cord.

mental status examination (MSE) A common tool used by physicians or counselors to assess a person with a mental illness or behavioral emergency.

metabolism The process of breaking down a substance so it can be released from the body. Starts as soon as the substance enters the body.

metacarpals The small bones in the hands that attach to the fingers.

metatarsals The small bones in the foot that attach to the toes.

midline An imaginary vertical line drawn from head to toe.

minute ventilation The amount of air pulled into the lungs and removed from the lungs in one minute.

morals A person's individual sense of right and wrong.

morbidity State of disease.

mortality State of death.

mottled A patchy skin discoloration caused by too little or too much circulation.

mucous membranes The tissue that lines body openings and contains specialized cells that create mucus.

mucus The opaque, sticky secretion of the mucous membranes that lubricates the body openings.

multi-system trauma Trauma that involves two or more organ systems.

muscles The tissue created out of protein that the body uses to perform work or motion.

myocardial infarction A form of cardiac disease that occurs when a lack of oxygen causes the death of heart muscle. Commonly called a heart attack.

Nadar bolt A pin or latch added to car doors to prevent them from opening during a crash. Ralph Nadar, a consumer activist, pushed for the addition of this mechanism in the United States.

nares The openings in the nose.

nasal bones The bony structures that make up and support the nasal cavity. Cartilage extends past the nasal bones to make the tip of the nose.

nasal cavity The large opening behind the nose, lined with mucous membranes.

nasopharyngeal airway (NPA) An airway adjunct that is inserted into the nostril of a patient who is not able to maintain a natural airway.

National Incident Management System (NIMS) The structure for managing an emergency incident, which may require a response of many different agencies; designed to provide efficient and effective management from initial response through recovery.

National Response Framework (NRF) A document that provides for the structure and mechanism for a national-level policy of incident response.

nature of illness (NOI) The general type of illness a patient is experiencing.

neuron The smallest functional unit of nervous tissue; neurons create impulses and transmit them to other nerves or muscles.

neurotransmitter The chemical that floods the space between nerves and activates specialized places on the receiving nerve or muscle.

new normal Creating, setting, and living life following the death of an officer, for family, friends, and peers.

nictitating membrane Located in the inside corner of each eye, this membrane is important in tear production and protection of the cornea. Also called the third eyelid.

nitroglycerin A medication that is taken by patients with angina pectoris for the purpose of dilating the coronary arteries and allowing more oxygen to reach the heart muscle.

nonmalfeasance An obligation to act in ways that do not cause harm.

nuchal cord When the umbilical cord is wrapped around the baby's neck.

obstetrics The area of medicine that deals with pregnancy, childbirth, and postpartum health.

occlusive dressings Dressings made of Vaseline-impregnated gauze, aluminum foil, or plastic that protects a wound from air and bacteria.

occupational health A person's interactions and view of the day-to-day routine in the workplace.

OCONUS Refers to any activity occurring in an area outside the continental United States.

open fractures Fractures in which the bone ends break the skin.

open head injury Injury in which a hole or crack in the skull allows blood or cerebrospinal fluid to leak out, relieving the pressure on the brain.

operational security (OPSEC) The approach and mechanism applied by a law enforcement agency or military force to ensure that vital mission information remains secure and unavailable to those who do not need the information.

optic nerve The nerve that takes the visual information from the eye to the brain for processing.

oral cavity The opening behind the lips, below the nasal cavity.

oral (PO) Route of medication administration in which medication is taken by mouth and enters the bloodstream through the digestive system.

orbit The bony socket in the skull where the eyes are located.

organelles The small structures in the cell that are used to maintain cellular function.

organism A living being supported by many different subparts.

organs Structures that provide a specific function within an organ system.

organ systems Groupings of organs that together perform a certain body function.

oropharyngeal airway (OPA) An airway adjunct that is inserted into the mouth to keep the tongue from blocking the upper airway.

osteopenia A bone condition characterized by reduced bone volume.

osteoporosis An abnormal brittleness of the bones caused by a loss of calcium. Affected bones are more susceptible to fractures.

ovaries Two small, almond-shaped organs that release eggs and female reproductive hormones.

oximetry Measuring the concentration of oxygen in arterial blood using a device called an oximeter.

oxygen A colorless, odorless gas that comprises approximately 21% of the volume of atmospheric air. It is the element present in air that supports combustion.

oxygenation The process of moving oxygen into an area. This occurs in the blood when air with a higher concentration of oxygen comes into contact with blood containing a lower concentration of oxygen. The higher concentration diffuses toward the lower concentration in an attempt to equalize concentrations.

pancreas An organ of the digestive and endocrine systems that releases several important hormones, including insulin and glucagon, in response to a person's intake of nourishment. These chemicals break down proteins, carbohydrates, and fats.

paramedics The highest level of civilian prehospital provider, who possess the knowledge and skills of the emergency medical responder (EMR), emergency medical technician (EMT), and advanced emergency medical technician (AEMT), as well as additional knowledge to provide advanced life support care.

parasitic infections Infectious diseases caused or transmitted by a parasite. Examples include yellow fever, malaria, and tapeworm.

parasympathetic nervous system The part of the autonomic nervous system that controls the vegetative functions of the body.

partial-thickness burns Burns involving the outer and middle layers of skin, resulting in extreme pain, redness, and blisters.

patella The kneecap.

patent airway An open and clear airway.

pathophysiology Abnormal function of the body.

patient care report (PCR) A report containing information regarding an emergency, including patient information, demographic information, patient care information, treatment, and transport and disposition information.

pediatric assessment triangle (PAT) A 15- to 30-second assessment tool used to assess the severity of the child's illness or injury.

pelvis Ring of bone at the bottom of the trunk; attachment point for legs and spinal column.

perfusion The process by which cells obtain oxygen and nutrients and use them to sustain life.

peripheral neuropathy Situation where the peripheral nerves are not working properly.

peristalsis Rhythmic muscular contraction of the intestines.

peritoneal dialysis A method of filtering out toxins from patients with kidney (renal) failure by infusing a concentrated solution into the abdomen.

personal and emotional health Who you are—your behavioral or mental health, your personality.

personal protective equipment (PPE) Devices such as gloves, eye protection, masks, and gowns, used as part of standard precautions to prevent the spread of transmittable diseases.

phalanges The fingers and toes.

pharmacology The study of the properties and effects of drugs and medications.

pharynx The cylinder-like tube that lies between the nasal cavity, oral cavity, and the larynx.

physical restraint Any method or device, physical or mechanical, that restricts movement or normal access to the patient.

physiology The study of how the body functions.

placenta A fleshy, vascular organ that transports nutrients and oxygen from the mother to the fetus, transports waste from the fetus to the mother, and serves as a blood barrier for harmful substances. The placenta is connected to the fetus by the umbilical cord.

placenta previa An emergency in the second half of pregnancy that occurs when the placenta attaches partially or completely over the opening of the cervix. Placenta previa is usually diagnosed through prenatal care.

plaintiff The person or group making a complaint.

plasma A fluid containing important proteins that circulate throughout the body.

platelets Small cells that fill holes in blood vessels, creating a clot; also called thrombocytes.

pleural space A space between the lining of the ribs and the lungs.

pneumomediastinum Air trapped in the portion of the chest that sets between the lungs and behind the sternum.

pneumopericardium Air trapped in the pericardial sac.

poison Chemical substance that has the potential to injure, harm, or kill in variable amounts and by various routes of exposure such as inhalation, ingestion, and skin contact.

polycythemia When bone marrow begins to produce more red blood cells after a prolonged altitude exposure.

positional asphyxia A condition in which the patient's own body weight impairs the ability to breathe and suffocates the patient.

positive pressure ventilation (PPV) The process of forcing air into the lungs using an external device.

posterior Toward the back.

postmenopausal The stage of life when a woman has stopped having her monthly menstrual cycle. It is marked by a decrease in estrogen, which can contribute to changes in a woman's health.

preterm birth Any newborn weighing less than 5 pounds or delivered before 36 weeks of pregnancy.

Privacy Rule Defines protected health information (PHI) as any health information that can identify an individual.

prolapsed cord An emergency situation that occurs when the umbilical cord emerges from the birth canal first instead of the baby's head. The mother cannot deliver vaginally and requires a cesarean section.

prone Lying on the front of the body.

prophylaxis Measure(s) taken to prevent a condition or disease.

protective medical support The plans and protocols that are set in place by a protective detail to respond to a broad range of medical emergencies.

proximal Closer to the center of the body.

psychogenic shock A temporary type of shock in which the blood vessels are dilated by an emotional stress response.

psychosis A loss of contact with reality, usually including false beliefs about what is taking place or who one is (delusions) and seeing or hearing things that are not real (hallucinations).

public safety access points (PSAPs) The access points for police, fire, and EMS services. Throughout most of the United States, PSAPs are accessed by dialing 911.

pulmonary edema The collection of fluid in the lungs of individuals with left-sided congestive heart failure.

pulmonary hypertension Increased blood pressure in the lungs.

puncture wounds Wounds caused by a sharp or pointed object.

pupil The dark open area inside the iris that controls the amount of light entering the eye.

pyrolysis The chemical decomposition of a condensed substance, such as a solid or liquid, that occurs at high temperatures and results in the release of combustible gases.

raccoon eyes Bruising around one or both eyes. This occurs as a result of a certain type of skull fracture.

radius The bone on the thumb side of the forearm.

rapid extrication Technique used to remove a patient from a vehicle when there is an immediate life threat and time is a significant factor for survival.

reasonable force The minimum strength needed to keep patients from hurting themselves or others, but no more.

receptors Specialized places on nerve or muscle cells that attach to a chemical messenger and send the message forward.

recovery position Placing the patient on his or her side, with an arm supporting the head and the legs positioned so the patient cannot roll onto his or her back or front. The intent of the recovery position is to allow the unconscious person to lie flat while allowing the airway an opportunity to drain secretions or vomit (see *lateral recumbent*).

rectal Route of medication administration in which medication is absorbed through the rectum in the form of a suppository.

red blood cells Specialized cells containing hemoglobin that move oxygen through the body; also called erythrocytes.

regulator A device applied to the neck of a gas cylinder that takes the cylinder pressure (2,000 psi) and reduces it to 40 to 70 psi.

respiration The exchange of gases in the alveoli or at the cellular level.

retina Located in the back of the eye, the structure that receives the visual cues from the lens, iris, and pupil. It collects the information for transfer to the brain.

rigid splints Splinting devices made of firm materials such as hard plastic, aluminum, or wood.

rotary-wing aircraft A helicopter.

rule of nines A way to calculate the amount of body surface burned; the body is divided into sections, each of which constitutes approximately 9% or 18% of the total body surface area.

SAFER-R model A tool used in crisis intervention to allow the LER to establish a conversation while gaining time, information, and trust with the patient.

scapula The shoulder blade.

sclera The white structural portion of the eye.

scope of practice The limits and boundaries of what skills and procedures prehospital providers can perform and the care they can provide given their certification or license level.

SEA-3 assessment tool A short, five-component mental status examination tool used to evaluate a patient's speech, emotion, appearance, alertness, and activity.

secondary drowning A postimmersion respiratory problem characterized by the decreased ability to deliver proper oxygen and gas exchange in the lungs.

seizures Disruptions of the normal electrical activity of the brain.

sensorium Mental awareness.

sepsis A condition of generalized infection that has spread throughout the body.

septic shock A type of shock created by the toxins from a severe infection, causing the blood vessels to dilate.

shepherd's crook An extendable pole with a blunt-end life hook large enough to encircle a victim safely.

shock A state of collapse of the cardiovascular system; the state of inadequate delivery of blood to the organs of the body.

short bones Bones that are found in the wrist and ankles.

side effects The undesirable actions, both predictable and unpredictable, of a drug. Side effects can occur even if the medication is taken or administered properly; not all drugs have side effects.

sign Something that you are able to observe or measure in a patient, such as blood pressure, bleeding, or deformity.

simple pneumothorax An accumulation of air in the pleural space, it may decrease the effectiveness of ventilatory efforts.

sinuses Hollow cavities in the skull, behind the nose and around the eyes.

skeletal muscles Tissues made of protein chains that are used to move bones. Skeletal muscle is under the voluntary control of the person.

skin The outer covering of the body, consisting of the epidermis, dermis, and subcutaneous layers.

sling and swathe Technique of using two cravats to secure the arm to the torso.

smooth muscle Short muscle fibers that are used to move, open, or close structures in the body. Smooth muscle movement is involuntary.

specialty impact munitions (SIMs) Munitions designed to incapacitate by direct force impact against the intended target.

spinal cord Specialized grouping of nervous tissue used to move messages to and from the body and the brain.

spinal shock Inadequate blood flow caused by damage to the brain or neck that prevents the central nervous system from controlling the size of the blood vessels.

spontaneous abortion Delivery of the fetus before it is mature enough to survive outside the womb. Also called miscarriage.

sprain A stretching injury that occurs to the supporting ligaments of a joint.

standard of care Defines the legal obligation of the duty to provide care within the limits of a practitioner's training, scope of practice, and equipment.

standard precautions Procedures for infection control that treat blood and certain body fluids as capable of transmitting diseases.

START system A system of casualty sorting using simple triage and rapid treatment.

status epilepticus A life-threatening condition that occurs when a patient experiences three or more seizures without regaining consciousness, or any seizure lasting more than 30 minutes.

statutory regulations The rules approved by a legislative body.

sternum The flat breastbone that sits in the center of the chest.

stimulant A classification of drug that increases the activity of the central nervous system.

strains Stretching or tearing injuries that occur to muscles or tendons.

stridor A high-pitched noise heard primarily on inspiration.

stroke A disruption in the supply of blood to any part of the brain. A stroke is a medical emergency that can cause disability or death.

subcutaneous (SC) injection Route of medication administration in which medication is injected into the tissue between the muscle and the skin. The absorption rate for this delivery method is slow because of the low blood supply in the area being injected.

sublingual Route of medication administration in which medication is absorbed through the oral mucous membranes under the tongue.

sudden cardiac death A form of sudden death that results from an interruption in the electrical activity of the heart. Also known as cardiac arrest.

sudden infant death syndrome (SIDS) The death of an infant during the first year of life, with no specific cause identified.

suicide The intentional taking of one's own life. Suicide is more commonly attempted and more commonly successful in elderly patients.

superficial burns Burns involving the outermost layer of skin, resulting in redness, pain, and swelling.

superior Closer to the head.

superior vena cava The large vein that brings blood to the heart from the upper body, head, and neck.

supine Lying on the back facing upward.

supine hypotensive syndrome Occurs when a pregnant woman is lying on her back and the weight of the fetus compresses the woman's large veins and aorta. The condition can reduce the amount of blood returning to the heart, causing harm to the fetus and possibly the mother.

supplemental restraint systems (SRSs) High-pressure curtains, bolsters, or bags that deploy when sensors detect a vehicle has been impacted at a certain speed. The devices are meant to protect the occupants of the vehicle, but can also cause certain injuries. These devices also are a potential threat to responders if they are not properly disconnected.

sympathetic nervous system Part of the autonomic nervous system that controls the stress response.

symptom Something subjective that a patient tells you, such as "My belly hurts" or "I feel like I'm going to throw up."

tactical combat casualty care (TCCC) Military medical paradigm that dictates care to be provided to a casualty based on the tactical scenario.

tactical emergency casualty care (TECC) Guidelines developed for high-threat civilian medical situations. Based on the concept of TCCC, takes into account differences in civilian populations and resources.

tactical emergency medical support (TEMS) Specially trained emergency medical technicians assigned to law enforcement special operations teams.

talus The bone at the ankle joint that connects the foot to the lower leg.

tarsals The irregular bones in the ankle and foot. These bones are relatively large bones extending from the ankle to the metatarsals.

technical negligence Occurs whenever a responder acts below the standard of care.

tendons Fibrous cords that are the terminal end of a skeletal muscle and attach the muscle to the bone.

tension pneumothorax A life-threatening collection of air within the pleural space from a hole in the chest or from damage to the lung due to a blunt or blast injury.

terminal ballistics The study of the behavior of a projectile when it hits its target.

thermoregulation The balance of heat production and heat loss.

thorax The cavity surrounded by the ribs and spinal column; contains organs from the cardiovascular and respiratory systems.

thrombocytes Platelets.

thrombosis Formation of a blood clot within the vascular system; of concern during travel because of prolonged immobility.

tibia The shin bone; the larger of the two bones of the lower leg.

tissue A group of like cells that come together for a specific purpose.

tongue The muscular structure in the oral cavity used for speech, taste, and movement of food.

topographic anatomy The superficial landmarks on the outer surface of the body that help in locating structures under the surface.

tort A civil complaint that results in personal injury.

tourniquets Constricting bands that reduce or stop blood flow to extremities.

toxidrome The specific signs and symptoms that a population exposed to a particular type of agent will display.

trachea The cartilaginous windpipe connecting the larynx to the bronchi.

traction splints Commercial splints used to apply consistent force on the femur, hence restoring alignment and stabilization of a suspected fracture.

trade name Brand name of a drug assigned by the manufacturer and marketed for sale.

transcutaneous Route of medication administration in which medication is absorbed through the skin, creating a slower, long-lasting effect.

traumatic asphyxia Crushing of the chest that pushes the chest contents up into the top of the thorax and neck.

traveler's diarrhea Increased frequency of unformed, watery stool during travel.

triage The sorting of patients into groups according to the severity of their injuries; used to determine priorities for treatment and transport.

22-hour rule The estimation that every 22 hours, a law enforcement officer ends his or her life by suicide.

twisting injuries Injuries resulting when a part of the body is forced beyond its normal limit due to a spiral or spinning-type motion. Injuries commonly seen in sports in which a part of the body is forced beyond its normal limits due to a spiral or spinning-type motion.

ulna The bone on the little-finger side of the forearm.

umbilical cord The fleshy, off-white cord that connects the placenta to the fetus, transports oxygen and other nutrients to the fetus, and removes waste from the fetus.

unilateral On one side.

unity of command A characteristic of the incident command system structure that has each individual reporting to a single supervisor and everyone reporting to the incident commander (IC) directly or through the chain of command.

unruptured amniotic sac Occurs when the amniotic sac does not rupture on its own before the baby crowns.

uremia A buildup of waste products in the blood caused by renal failure.

US Pharmacopoeia (USP) A comprehensive government publication that lists every drug and medication by its generic name.

uterus The vascular organ where the fetus grows, also called the womb.

vagina The vascular and muscular organ through which a baby passes when it is born, also called the birth canal.

vasalva maneuver A maneuver, conducted by advanced medical providers, in which the patient is instructed to force air out against a closed airway while forcibly contracting the abdominal muscles, bearing down in the abdomen and pelvis. This increases the pressure in the trunk and places pressure against the vagus nerve. The vagus nerve is the primary nerve of the parasympathetic nervous system. Employing this maneuver will promote a parasympathetic response in the body.

vasovagal episode A reflex of the involuntary nervous system that causes the heart to slow down, affecting the nerves to the blood vessels in the legs and permitting those vessels to dilate (widen). As a result, the heart puts out less blood, blood pressure drops, and what blood is circulating tends to go into the legs rather than to the head.

vector-borne disease A disease that is transmitted to humans or other animals.

veins Blood vessels that return blood from the capillaries to the heart.

ventilation The movement of air in and out of the lungs.

ventricles The two lower chambers of the heart.

vertebrae The irregular bones that loosely connect to make the spinal column. The vertebrae consist of the cervical, thoracic, lumbar, sacrum, and coccyx sections.

vitreous humor The clear, jelly-like fluid that fills the posterior chamber of the eye.

weapons of mass destruction (WMD) Weapons designed to bring about mass death, casualties, and massive damage to property or infrastructure using chemical, biological, radiological, nuclear, or explosive agents; also known as weapons of mass casualty (WMC).

wet drowning Suffocation that occurs when a person is submerged and attempts to breathe, drawing water into the lungs.

wheezing A high-pitched, continuous whistling sound produced when air is moved under pressure through the narrowed bronchi or bronchioles in the lower airways. The narrowing of these airways often occurs from asthma, an allergic reaction, inflammation, or deep airway burns.

white blood cells Specialized cells in the blood that identify and attack threats from invading chemicals or infections; also called leukocytes.

wildlife Animals that live on their own without domestic support.

work of breathing The amount of energy one has to expend in order to breathe.

xiphoid process The tip of the sternum that protrudes over the bottom of the thorax and over the abdomen.

Zero Hour Forward Defined as running from zero hour (the moment a line of duty death occurs), through the next critical minutes, and continuing through the 36 to 48 hours after the event.

Index

Note: *f* = figure; *sd* = skill drill; *t* = table

Photo Credits

Section 7 Opener © Kevin Higley/AP Photos.

Chapter 1

1-1 © Mike Meadows/AP Photos; **1-10** © Reuters/Gerald Reed Schumann/Landov; **1-12** © Crystal Kirk/ShutterStock, Inc.; **1-13** © Ron Heflin/AP Photos; **1-18** © Chris Bence/ShutterStock, Inc.

Chapter 2

2-5 Courtesy of the Center for Law Enforcement Medicine at Johns Hopkins University; **2-6** © Jane Mingay/AP Photos.

Chapter 3

3-2 Courtesy of USDA; **3-5** Courtesy of Kimberly Smith/CDC; **3-7** © Mark Winfrey/ShutterStock, Inc.; **3-8** © Mark C. Ide; **3-T1** Data from Twersky-Glasner, Aviva. Police Personality: What is it and why are they like that? Journal of Police & Criminal Psychology, 2005, Vol. 20 (1).

Chapter 4

Opener © Peter Casolino/Alamy Images; **4-2** © Mike Segar/Thomson Reuters; **4-4** © Elaine Thompson/AP Photos.

Chapter 5

Opener © Alan Kim/The Roanoke Times/AP Photos; **5-2** © ABC/AP Photos; **5-5** © Mark C. Ide; **5-6** Courtesy of FEMA

Chapter 6

6-2 Courtesy of Draeger Safety; **6-7** © Mark C. Ide; **6-8** Courtesy of the US Department of Transportation; **6-9** Courtesy of the US Department of Transportation; **6-10** © Archive Image/Alamy Images; **6-11** © Dean Musgrove/ZUMA Press/Corbis; **6-T4** Data from DEA Office of Diversion Control.

Chapter 7

7-2 © Dan Myers; **7-5A** © Zeljko Radojko/ShutterStock, Inc.; **7-9** © david hancock/Alamy Images; **7-10** © Antonio S./ShutterStock, Inc.; **7-11** © Karin Hildebrand Lau/ShutterStock, Inc.; **7-12** © Scott Sanders/ShutterStock, Inc.; **7-13** © Nir Levy/ShutterStock, Inc.; **7-14** © Christophe Rouziou/ShutterStock, Inc.

Chapter 9

Opener © Tom Carter/PhotoEdit, Inc.; **9-01** © Keith D. Cullom/www.fire-image.com.

Chapter 12

12-1 Courtesy of ED, Royal North Shore Hospital/NSW Institute of Trauma and Injury Management; **12-2** Courtesy of Kevin Reed; **12-4** © Photowitch/Dreamstime LLC; **12-8** Courtesy of Rhonda Beck.

Chapter 13

Opener © Marvin woodyatt/Alamy Images; **13-6** © Dr. P. Marazzi/Photo Researchers, Inc.; **13-8** © Chuck Stewart, MD.; **13-9A** Courtesy of Jeff E. Isaac; **13-10** © Dr. P. Marazzi/Photo Researchers, Inc.

Chapter 14

14-2 © Dallas Events Inc/ShutterStock, Inc.; **14-3** Courtesy of Meridian Medical Technologies, Inc. (A subsidiary of King Pharmaceuticals, Inc.); **14-4** © Philip Lewis/Alamy Images; **14-6A** © AbleStock; **14-6B** Courtesy of South Florida Water Management District; **14-6C** Courtesy of Ray Rauch/US Fish and Wildlife Services; **14-7** © Rolf Nussbaumer/age fotostock; **14-8A** © photobar/ShutterStock, Inc.; **14-8B** Courtesy of Kenneth Cramer, Monmouth College; **14-9** Courtesy of Department of Entomology, University of Nebraska; **14-10** © David Desoer/ShutterStock, Inc.

Chapter 15

Opener © Ed Troyer/Pierce County Sheriff's Dept./AP Photos; **15-1** © fcarucci/ShutterStock, Inc.; **15-3** © Steve Byland/ShutterStock, Inc.; **15-5** Courtesy of Neil Malcom Winkelmann; **15-6** © Photodisc.

Chapter 16

Opener © Thomas Winje/EPA/Landov; **16-3** Courtesy of Rhonda Beck.

Chapter 17

Opener Courtesy of Mass Communication Specialist 3rd Class Kelly E. Barnes/U.S. Navy; **17-1B** Courtesy of Staff

Sgt. Shawn Weismiller/U.S. Air Force/U.S. Department of Defense; **17-1C** Courtesy of Mass Communication Specialist 2nd Class Kenneth W. Robinson/U.S. Navy; **17-T2** Source: Data fromAmerican College of Surgeons-Consultation Verification Program. (ACS-COT), http://www.facs.org/trauma/vcprogram.html.

Chapter 18

Opener © Mike Meadows/AP Photos; **18-2** © Medical-on-Line/Alamy Images; **18-4** © Charlie Riedel/AP Photos; **18-5A** © John Jones/Alamy Images; **18-5B** Courtesy of Matthew Stajnkrycer; **18-5C** © prettyfoto/Alamy Images.

Chapter 19

Opener © Mark C. Ide; **19-3A** © E.M. Singletary, MD. Used with permission; **19-3B** © Chuck Stewart, MD.; **19-6** © English/Custom Medical Stock Photo; **19-8** © E.M. Singletary, MD. Used with permission; **19-10** © Amy Walters/ShutterStock, Inc.; **19-11** © E.M. Singletary, MD. Used with permission.

Chapter 20

Opener © Image Source/age footstock; **20-12** Courtesy of David J. Burchfield, MD.

Chapter 21

21-2 Used with permission of the American Academy of Pediatrics, Pediatric Education for Prehospital Professionals, © American Academy of Pediatrics, 2000; **21-6C** Courtesy of Ronald Dieckmann, MD.

Chapter 22

Opener © Mark C. Ide; **22-1** Data from the U.S. Census Bureau; **22-4** © E.M. Singletary, MD. Used with permission; **22-5** © dundanim/ShutterStock, Inc.; **22-6** Courtesy of Rhonda Beck.

Chapter 23

23-1 © Phartisan/Dreamstime.com; **23-3** © Craig Jackson/IntheDarkPhotography.com.

Chapter 25

Opener © Oscar Williams/Dreamstime.com; **25-1** Courtesy of the U.S. Customs and Border Patrol; **25-2** © Mikael Karlsson/Alamy Images; **25-3** © Mark C. Ide.

Chapter 26

26-1 © islandspics/Alamy Images; **26-2** © dundanim/ShutterStock, Inc.

Chapter 27

27-4 © Ed Andrieski/AP Photos; **27-5** © Marian Wilson/ShutterStock, Inc.; **27-7** © Laurie L. Snidow/ShutterStock, Inc.; **27-8A** © Photodisc; **27-8B** © Photodisc; **27-8C** © dotweb/ShutterStock, Inc.; **27-8D** © AbleStock.

Unless otherwise indicated, all photographs and illustrations are under copyright of Jones & Bartlett Learning, courtesy of Maryland Institute for Emergency Medical Services Systems, or have been provided by the author(s).